INSIDERS' GUIDE® SERIES

INSIDERS' GUIDE® TO
NORTH CAROLINA'S OUTER BANKS

TWENTY-SEVENTH EDITION

KAREN BACHMAN

INSIDERS' GUIDE®

GUILFORD, CONNECTICUT
AN IMPRINT OF THE GLOBE PEQUOT PRESS

The prices and rates in this guidebook were confirmed at press time. We recommend, however, that you call establishments before traveling to obtain current information.

To buy books in quantity for corporate use or incentives, call **(800) 962–0973, ext. 4551,** or e-mail **premiums@GlobePequot.com.**

INSIDERS' GUIDE ®

Text design by LeAnna Weller Smith
Maps by XNR Productions, Inc. © Morris Book Publishing, LLC

ISSN: 1082-9458
ISBN-13: 978-0-7627-4046-8
ISBN-10: 0-7627-4046-9

Manufactured in the United States of America
Twenty-seventh Edition/First Printing

An ultralight, carrying on the local tradition of innovative aircraft. KITTY HAWK KITES.

The Wright Brothers National Memorial, where the first powered airplane flew. OUTER BANKS VISITORS BUREAU

Roanoke Island's Elizabethan Gardens. ROANOKE ISLAND FESTIVAL PARK

Kiteboarding. KITTY HAWK KITES

Hang gliders often enjoy the warm, lofting air currents at Jockey's Ridge in Nags Head. KITTY HAWK KITES

The Outer Banks offers miles of coastline to explore by kayak. KITTY HAWK KITES

Many visitors choose kayaking to savor the natural beauty of the Outer Banks. KITTY HAWK KITES

Manteo is a picturesque waterfront community with a lighthouse and boardwalk. ROANOKE ISLAND FESTIVAL PARK

See local aquatic life at the North Carolina Aquarium on Roanoke Island. ROANOKE ISLAND FESTIVAL PARK

The Elizabeth II, *replica of a 16th-century ship.* ROANOKE ISLAND FESTIVAL PARK
An Outer Banks sunset. ROANOKE ISLAND FESTIVAL PARK

The Outer Banks is nationally renowned for being one of the country's best surf-fishing spots.
OUTER BANKS VISITORS BUREAU

Fog settles under the Kitty Hawk pier. D. NEIL SANDERS

Pier fishing in Rodanthe at sunrise. D. NEIL SANDERS

CONTENTS

CONTENTS

Directory of Maps

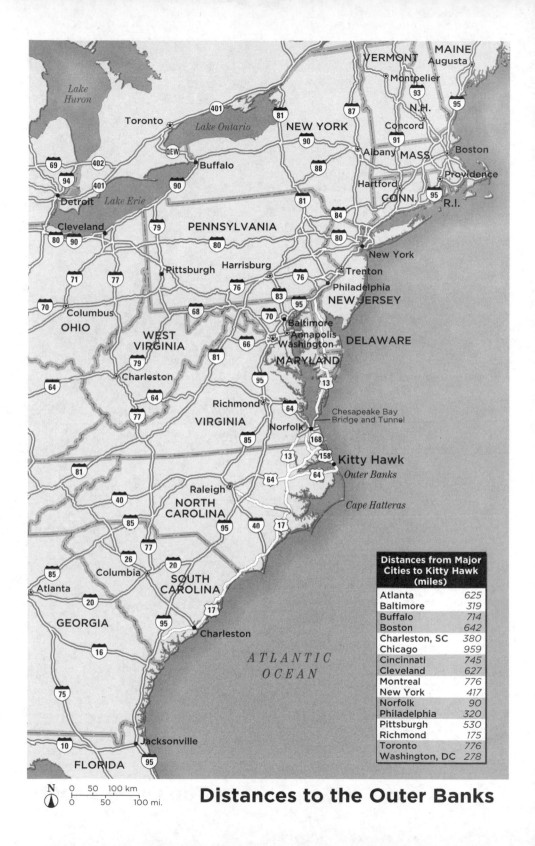

Distances from Major Cities to Kitty Hawk (miles)

Atlanta	625
Baltimore	319
Buffalo	714
Boston	642
Charleston, SC	380
Chicago	959
Cincinnati	745
Cleveland	627
Montreal	776
New York	417
Norfolk	90
Philadelphia	320
Pittsburgh	530
Richmond	175
Toronto	776
Washington, DC	278

N 0 50 100 km
0 50 100 mi.

Distances to the Outer Banks

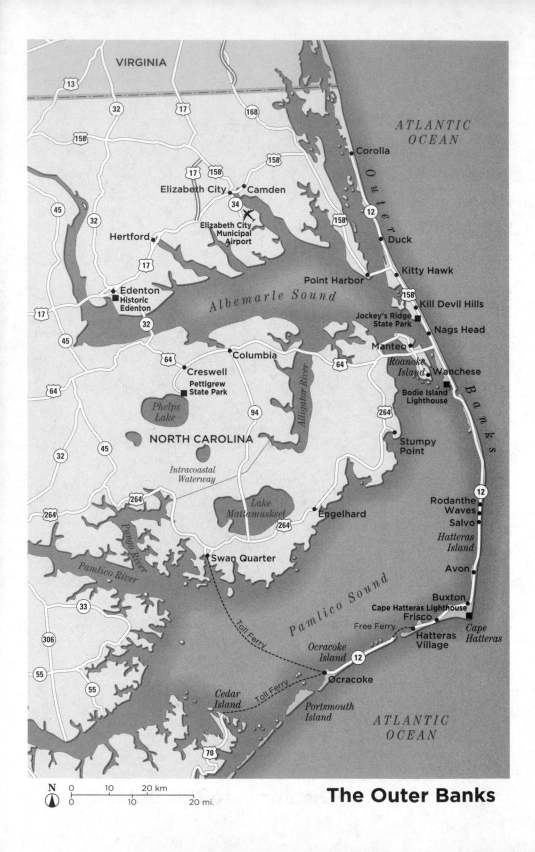

The Outer Banks

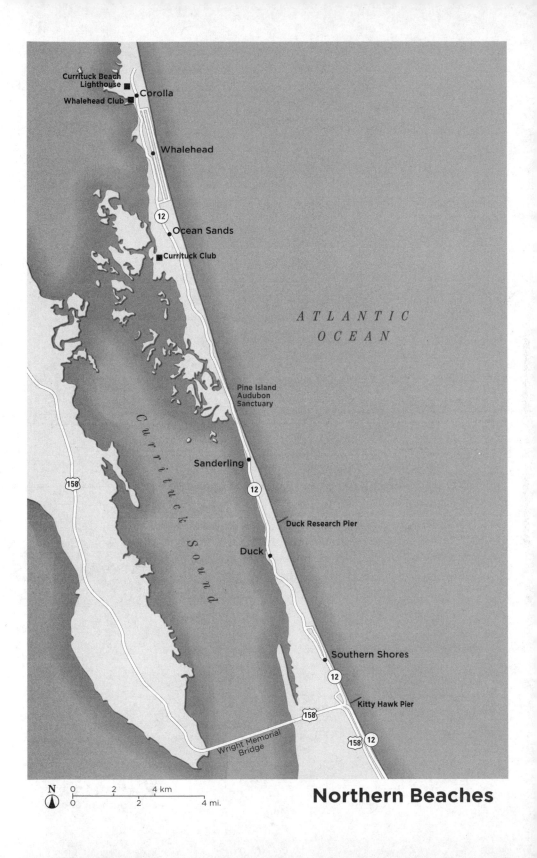

Currituck Beach Lighthouse

Whalehead Club

Corolla

Whalehead

12

Ocean Sands

Currituck Club

ATLANTIC OCEAN

Pine Island Audubon Sanctuary

Currituck Sound

Sanderling

12

158

Duck Research Pier

Duck

Southern Shores

12

Kitty Hawk Pier

158

158 12

Wright Memorial Bridge

N

0   2   4 km
0   2   4 mi.

Northern Beaches

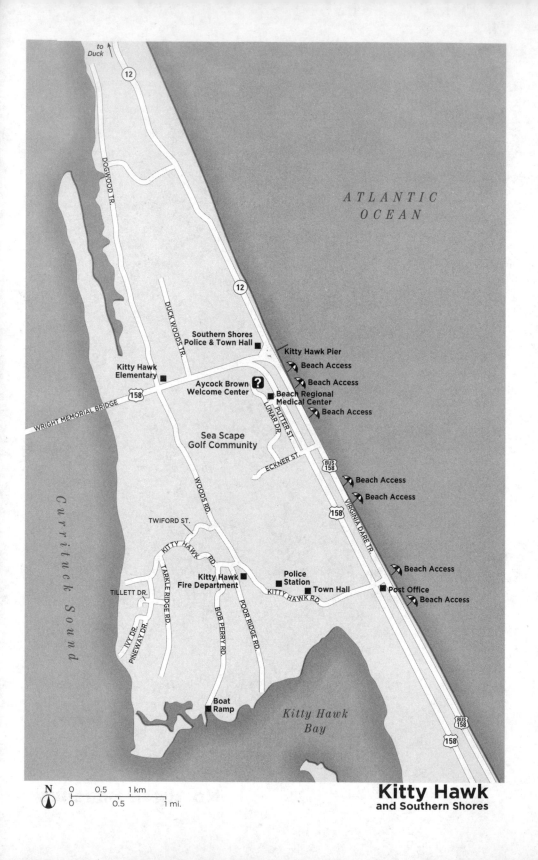

to
Duck

12

ATLANTIC
OCEAN

DOGWOOD TR.

12

DUCK WOODS TR.

Southern Shores
Police & Town Hall

Kitty Hawk Pier

Kitty Hawk
Elementary

Beach Access

Aycock Brown
Welcome Center

?

Beach Access

158

Beach Regional
Medical Center

Beach Access

WRIGHT MEMORIAL BRIDGE

PUTTER ST.

LUNAR DR.

Sea Scape
Golf Community

ECKNER ST.

BUS
158

Beach Access

Beach Access

158

WOODS RD.

VIRGINIA DARE TR.

Currituck Sound

TWIFORD ST.

KITTY HAWK RD.

Beach Access

TARKLE RIDGE RD.

Kitty Hawk
Fire Department

Police
Station

Town Hall

Post Office

TILLETT DR.

KITTY HAWK RD.

Beach Access

IVY DR.

PINEWAY DR.

BOB PERRY RD.

POOR RIDGE RD.

BUS
158

Boat
Ramp

Kitty Hawk
Bay

158

N

0   0.5   1 km
0   0.5   1 mi.

Kitty Hawk
and Southern Shores

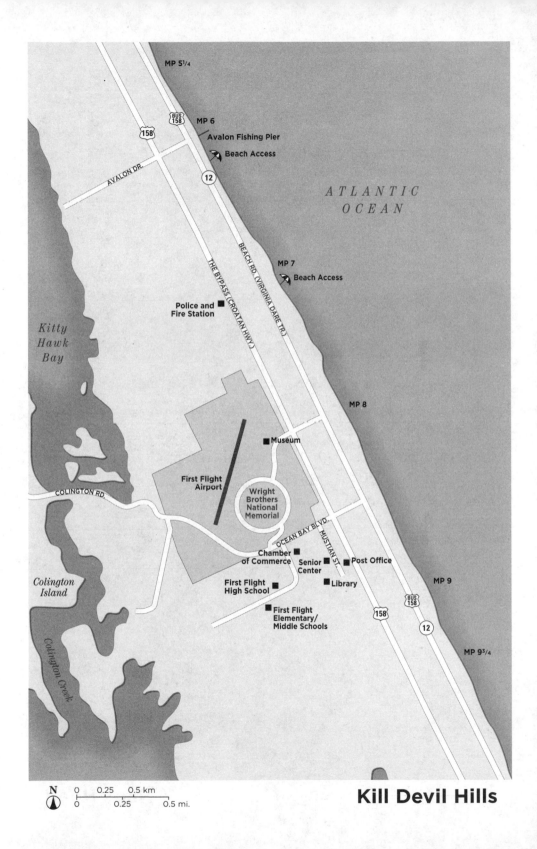

MP 5¼

BUS 158

158

MP 6

Avalon Fishing Pier

Beach Access

AVALON DR.

12

ATLANTIC OCEAN

THE BYPASS (CROATAN HWY.)

BEACH RD. (VIRGINIA DARE TR.)

MP 7

Beach Access

Police and Fire Station

MP 8

Kitty Hawk Bay

Museum

First Flight Airport

Wright Brothers National Memorial

COLINGTON RD.

Colington Island

OCEAN BAY BLVD.

MUSTIAN ST.

Chamber of Commerce

Senior Center

Post Office

First Flight High School

Library

MP 9

First Flight Elementary/ Middle Schools

BUS 158

158

12

MP 9¾

Colington Creek

N

0   0.25   0.5 km

0   0.25   0.5 mi.

Kill Devil Hills

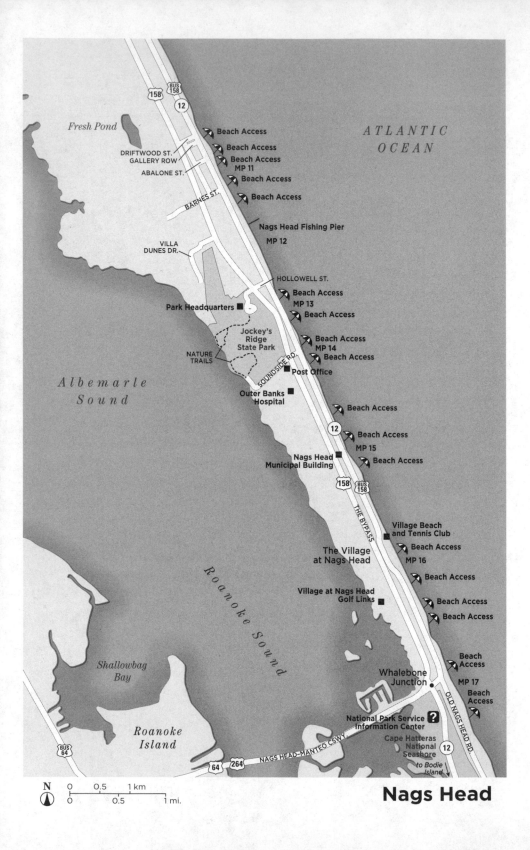

Nags Head

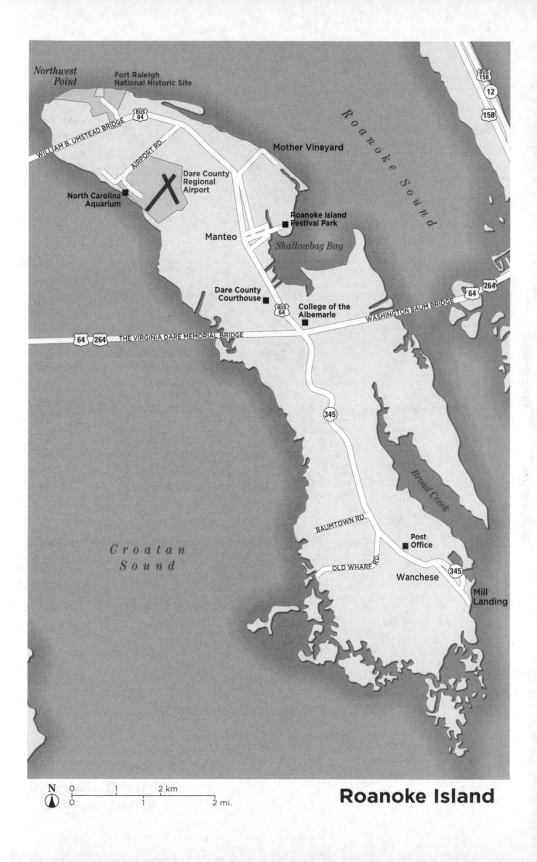

Northwest Point

Fort Raleigh National Historic Site

BUS 158

12

US 158

Roanoke Sound

BUS 64

WILLIAM B. UMSTEAD BRIDGE

AIRPORT RD.

Mother Vineyard

North Carolina Aquarium

Dare County Regional Airport

Roanoke Island Festival Park

Manteo

Shallowbag Bay

Dare County Courthouse

BUS 64

College of the Albemarle

WASHINGTON BAUM BRIDGE

64 264

64 264 THE VIRGINIA DARE MEMORIAL BRIDGE

345

Broad Creek

Croatan Sound

BAUMTOWN RD.

Post Office

OLD WHARF RD.

Wanchese

345

Mill Landing

N

0   1   2 km

0   1   2 mi.

Roanoke Island

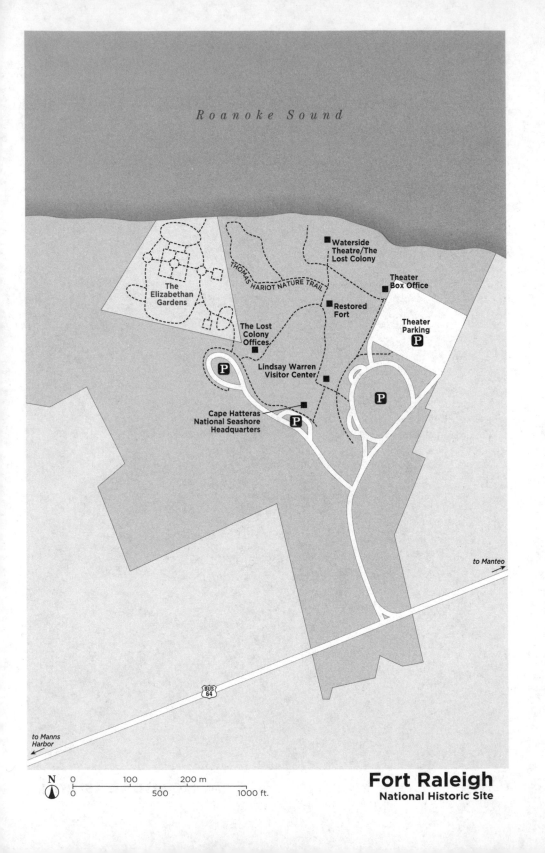

Roanoke Sound

Waterside Theatre/The Lost Colony

Theater Box Office

THOMAS HARIOT NATURE TRAIL

The Elizabethan Gardens

Restored Fort

Theater Parking
P

The Lost Colony Offices

P

Lindsay Warren Visitor Center

P

Cape Hatteras National Seashore Headquarters

P

to Manteo

BUS 64

to Manns Harbor

N
0   100   200 m
0   500   1000 ft.

Fort Raleigh
National Historic Site

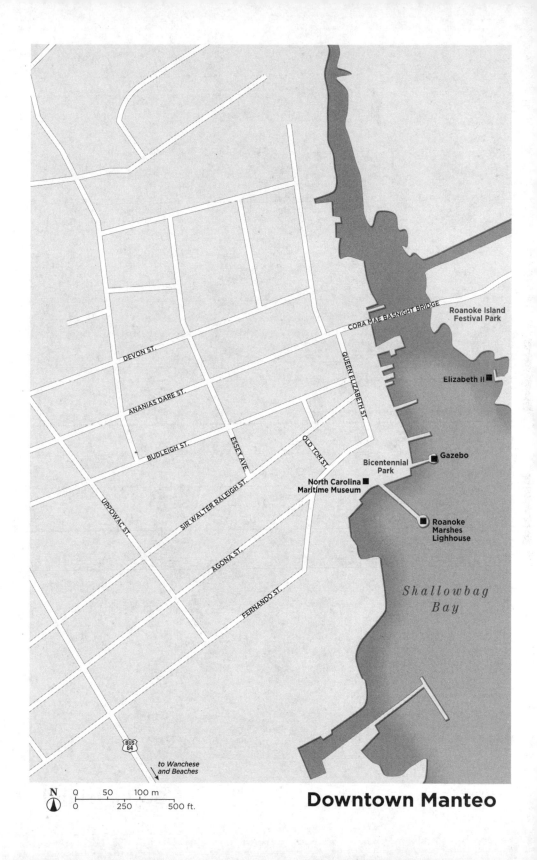

CORA MAE BASNIGHT BRIDGE

Roanoke Island
Festival Park

DEVON ST.

QUEEN ELIZABETH ST.

Elizabeth II

ANANIAS DARE ST.

BUDLEIGH ST.

ESSEX AVE.

OLD TOM ST.

Gazebo

Bicentennial
Park

North Carolina
Maritime Museum

UPPOWAC ST.

SIR WALTER RALEIGH ST.

Roanoke
Marshes
Lighhouse

AGONA ST.

*Shallowbag
Bay*

FERNANDO ST.

BUS
64

*to Wanchese
and Beaches*

N

| 0 | 50 | 100 m |
| 0 | 250 | 500 ft. |

Downtown Manteo

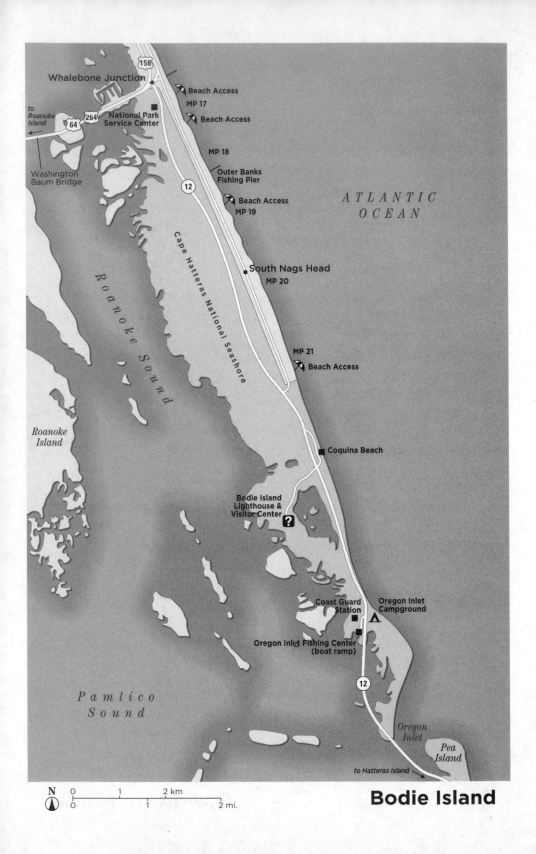

Whalebone Junction

158

to
Roanoke
Island

64   264

National Park
Service Center

Washington
Baum Bridge

12

Beach Access
MP 17

Beach Access

MP 18

Outer Banks
Fishing Pier

Beach Access
MP 19

*ATLANTIC
OCEAN*

South Nags Head
MP 20

Roanoke Sound

Cape Hatteras National Seashore

MP 21

Beach Access

*Roanoke
Island*

Coquina Beach

Bodie Island
Lighthouse &
Visitor Center

?

Coast Guard
Station

Oregon Inlet
Campground

Oregon Inlet Fishing Center
(boat ramp)

*Pamlico
Sound*

12

*Oregon
Inlet*

*Pea
Island*

to Hatteras Island

N

0   1   2 km
0   1   2 mi.

Bodie Island

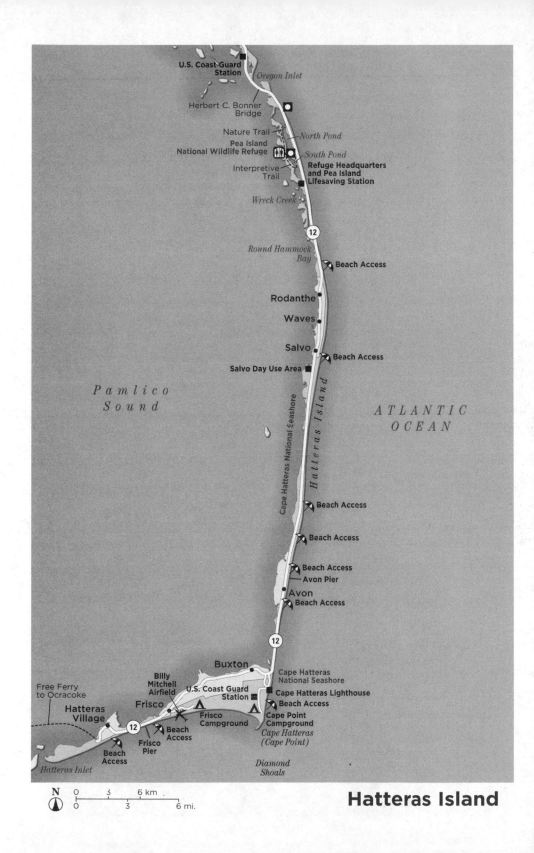

U.S. Coast Guard
Station

Oregon Inlet

Herbert C. Bonner
Bridge

Nature Trail — *North Pond*
Pea Island
National Wildlife Refuge
South Pond

Interpretive
Trail
Refuge Headquarters
and Pea Island
Lifesaving Station

Wreck Creek

12

*Round Hammock
Bay*
Beach Access

Rodanthe

Waves

Salvo
Beach Access

Salvo Day Use Area

*Pamlico
Sound*

Cape Hatteras National Seashore

Hatteras Island

ATLANTIC
OCEAN

Beach Access

Beach Access

Beach Access
Avon Pier

Avon
Beach Access

12

Buxton

Billy
Mitchell
Airfield
Cape Hatteras
National Seashore

Free Ferry
to Ocracoke
U.S. Coast Guard
Station
Cape Hatteras Lighthouse
Beach Access

Hatteras
Village
Frisco
Frisco
Campground
Cape Point
Campground

12
Beach
Access
*Cape Hatteras
(Cape Point)*

Beach
Access
Frisco
Pier

Hatteras Inlet
*Diamond
Shoals*

N
0   3   6 km
0   3   6 mi.

Hatteras Island

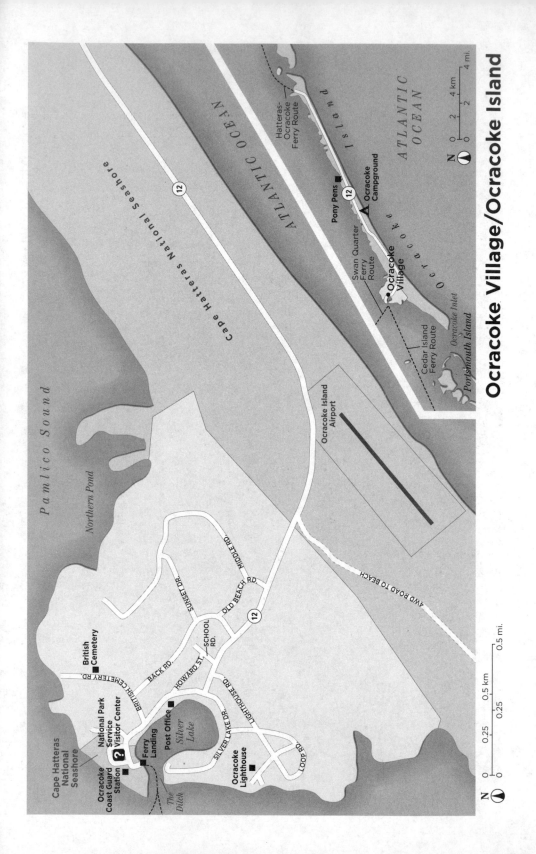

Ocracoke Village/Ocracoke Island

PREFACE

Part of the Outer Banks's charm is the remoteness of the area. Since it's accessible only by ferry or by driving over one of the bridges that connects it to the mainland, once you're here, you feel far removed from the rest of the world. It's really not that far. And in recent years, with an ever-growing tourism industry, goods and services have come to us. It's fascinating to hear locals tell of long drives to stores on the mainland to buy groceries or to receive medical care back in the old days. The "old days," however, were less than two decades ago. Those of us who live here year-round still make excursions to nearby cities for specific services, shopping, and cultural events, but we wouldn't trade island life for anything. Living here is a trade-off that is heavily weighted toward the good life; we're blessed, and we know it.

On NASA space maps, our strand of sand may look like the continent's afterthought, but our land was the welcome mat to the first English-speaking settlers in the country. The Outer Banks is stranded farther away from its main coast than any other barrier islands in the world. Although our shore has very slowly over the centuries crept west, it still tenaciously maintains its crooked hold miles out into the Atlantic. Pounded century after century by storms—many escorted in by the nearby mighty Gulf Stream—the geology of these narrow islands is unique in its adaptability. Its inhabitants have been no less resilient. When you step foot on these sandy shores, you join a legion of steely adventurers, renegade thinkers, and rugged individuals who have been captivated by the unbidden forces of nature.

Welcome to the land of beginnings! Feast your senses on wide beaches, whispering sea oats, and undulating dunes—a land where the pace of life is geared to the unceasing sand-sharpened breezes and wild winds. From the gifts and punishment of the glorious and untamed waters of these indomitable islands have sprung heroes, pioneers, pirates, and inventors. Tales of courage and creativity, bloody battles and savage shipwrecks, resourcefulness and compassion: All are part of the mystique of the Outer Banks.

Here, the first English colonists set up camp. Blackbeard and his band of buccaneers anchored sloops along the shallow sounds. Wilbur and Orville Wright also flew the world's first airplane, buoyed by stiff winds and brazen determination, and Billy Mitchell proved airpower to the world.

From remote national wildlife refuges, sheltered seashores, and protected maritime forests to upscale resort communities, these strips of shifting sand offer both peaceful retreat and awesome adventure. Kitesurf or JetSki. Surf fish or stroll the endless beaches. Charter a deep-sea fishing boat to fight an ocean giant. Grab the binoculars and watch birds. Soar from the East Coast's highest sand dune in a hang glider. Catch some waves and surf some of the best swells on the Atlantic Seaboard as breakers barrel toward the beach. It's all here for the choosing, and boredom is not an option.

Only in the last 20 years or so have these ribbons of sand confronted the rapid-fire development that other coastal areas experienced years earlier. One of only four states in the nation that forbids hard structures like seawalls, which can cause severe narrowing of beaches, North Carolina learned the tough lessons of coastal management by watching the mistakes of other ocean states. To a large extent, the Outer Banks owes its still healthy, wide beaches to the luck of its relatively late bloom. Isolated geographically by water, the barrier islands were accessible only by boat until the 1930s, when the first major bridges from the mainland were constructed. Once travel improved, word of the Outer Banks's lovely weather and beautiful beaches spread, and vacationers and transplants poured in a steady stream over the shallow sounds, fishing rods and bathing suits at the ready.

Life on the Outer Banks has changed dramatically since then, but much of the beauty and color remains unsullied. Some native families, many descendants of shipwreck survivors, still make their livings through commercial fishing. Much of the seafood for which we are so famous is caught locally by fifth-generation watermen. A visitor to Colington, Wanchese, Hatteras Island, or Ocracoke mingles among people who speak with the distinctive Outer Banks brogue, an accent carried over by English settlers and sustained by centuries of isolation.

Four lighthouses (Currituck's redbrick beacon, the mid-island light at Bodie Island, Cape Hatteras's famous candy-striped tower, and the squat, whitewashed watchdog on Ocracoke Island), once sentinels for sailors traversing the shipwreck-strewn Graveyard of the Atlantic, dot these storm-swept shores.

Wild horses roam the northernmost protected refuges and the Ocracoke beaches to the south, descendants, some believe, of Spanish mustangs that swam ashore from shipwrecks more than three centuries ago. Waterfowl abound throughout these islands, attracting bird-watchers, hunters, and long-lens photographers. The East Coast's best fishing also awaits anglers on the decks of offshore charter boats, atop numerous piers and bridges, and off miles of ocean and sound shores.

There are walking paths along flat roadways, and bikes can be rented for leisurely rides along the shore and on dirt roads through the island marshlands and woods.

Painters, sculptors, potters, and other artisans open their galleries to browsers in almost every village. Musicians, comedians, and poets provide evening entertainment in a variety of cafes and nightclubs. The entire family can gather under the stars at Roanoke Island's Waterside Theatre and watch the acclaimed historical production *The Lost Colony,* our nation's longest-running outdoor summer theater drama.

Despite its rise as a favorite resort destination, the Outer Banks continues to be a casual place. Shorts and sandals are accepted garb in even the finest establishments. Shrimp, crab, and dozens of species of fresh-caught fish (often hauled in that very day by Outer Banks fishermen) are available at nearly every one of the slew of restaurants that serve tourists and locals alike.

While you're trekking the dunes, frolicking in the pristine waters, or enjoying the Carolina blue skies and soothing sunsets, don't forget that these overgrown sandbars have provided the setting for some of the most dramatic moments in American history. Remember that you are walking the sands of some of the most dynamic barrier islands on Earth.

Some things have stayed the same since Sir Walter Raleigh's party first laid eyes on Roanoke Island more than 400 years ago. These barrier beaches still startle visitors as well as natives with their rugged beauty and capricious topography. The fragile landscape remains at the mercy of the sea, furious with storm one day, calm the next.

Summer isn't the only time to enjoy the Outer Banks, although the season from Memorial Day through Labor Day is by far the most packed with people and things to do. Fall offers fabulous fishing and windsurfing, spring brings bird-watching and bicycling, and winter is deliciously devoid of almost everyone.

Spend a little time here, and you'll understand why many of us came back to stay—or never left. We hope this book helps you find exactly what you want in your visit to our vibrant barrier beaches.

ACKNOWLEDGMENTS

This book is a compendium of the work of many authors, all of whom have left their mark in some way. While the changeable facts are updated every year, much of the text is still peppered with each author's voice, forming a melting pot of insights and perceptions. Special thanks to Molly Harrison, Diane Buccheri, and Billy Vaughn for their contributions in recent years.

HOW TO USE THIS BOOK ⟨?⟩

Continuing the 27-year tradition of the *Insiders' Guide to North Carolina's Outer Banks,* we've updated, revised, and added to our extensive collection of favorite restaurants, shops, attractions, events, getaways, activities, and much more.

Most information in our guide is arranged geographically from north to south. Besides introducing you to the area's fascinating history and hidden treasures, we provide practical information on medical services, camping, real estate, vacation rentals, ferry schedules, fishing sites, and other areas of interest. You'll also discover information on local media, children's activities, worship sites, and retirement, plus valuable tips—look for the ⓘ—that you could get only from an Insider. We've designed the *Insiders' Guide to North Carolina's Outer Banks* as a handy reference for all aspects of life here. Keep it in hand, and let us accompany and guide you along every step of your Outer Banks journey.

We begin with colorful overviews of each area along the barrier islands, from the sand-tail villages of Carova (at the Virginia–North Carolina border) to the windswept shores of Ocracoke Island; after that comes a chapter on the various ways to get to and around on the Outer Banks and a chapter on our history. Comprehensive chapters tailored to meet your personal needs follow. You'll find Accommodations, Real Estate, Arts and Culture, Annual Events, Kidstuff, Recreation, and more. If you're looking for a cozy dinner spot, browse through our Restaurants chapter. If you want to spend the afternoon in search of a special souvenir, turn to Shopping. If you've always wanted to try scuba diving, parasailing, or surfing, all the Information you'll need is in Water Sports.

We've arranged this book so you can read it bit by bit, opening to those particular pages that pique your interest while breezing by those that don't. But please go back and thumb through any parts you may have skipped at first. We bet you'll learn something interesting and maybe even discover some new favorite sports or pastimes along the way. To guide you along your adventure, a passel of excellent maps is tucked in at the book's beginning as well.

AREA OVERVIEW ⏁

The Outer Banks is a world unto itself, made of islands linked to the rest of civilization only by a few bridges and ferries. This fact lends a separatist character to the Outer Banks, with residents who are proud to have escaped the trappings of the mainland and vacationers who come here to put aside the city life. Days go by in the indescribable realm of "island time," becoming more surreal the farther south you go.

Cultural traditions and norms seem to fall by the wayside once one has crossed over onto one of the islands. Suddenly, it's perfectly acceptable to go barefoot all day, to wear your bathing suit to the grocery store, to get buried up to your neck in sand, to spend hours on the porch staring at the water, to stop to watch the sun set.

The area is a chain of several islands—Roanoke, Colington, Bodie, Hatteras, and Ocracoke—stretching more than 100 miles along eastern North Carolina. Bodie Island, the largest landmass of the Outer Banks, encompassing the land from the north side of Oregon Inlet through Carova, is technically no longer an island. Physically, it's connected to Virginia and is therefore a peninsula. However, since the state border is closed to land crossings, Bodie is, in many minds, an island.

Some people also consider the islands south of Ocracoke Island, from Cape Lookout and through Bogue Banks, part of the Outer Banks. But for the purposes of this book, the Outer Banks extend from the Virginia line through Ocracoke. If you'd like information on the beaches south of Ocracoke, the best spots in the area are revealed in *Insiders' Guide to North Carolina's Central Coast and New Bern* and *Insiders' Guide to North Carolina's Southern Coast and Wilmington*.

Bodie, Hatteras, and Ocracoke Islands are barrier islands, separated from the mainland by a system of wide, shallow sounds. The barrier islands are reefs of sand protecting the mainland from the ravages of the Atlantic Ocean. What keeps the barrier islands from washing away in the face of all that power is their ability to shift and move, to go with the flow of nature. On the other hand, vegetation plays a huge part in the stabilization of the islands, making them fit for human occupation.

The Albemarle-Pamlico Sounds system that separates the Outer Banks from the mainland is the second largest estuary in the United States, second only to the Chesapeake Bay. These sounds have 3,000 square miles of surface water and 30,000 square miles of watershed. The system consists of seven sounds—Albemarle, Pamlico, Currituck, Croatan, Roanoke, Bogue, and Core. These individual sounds are fed by inlets, cuts of water that slice through the skinny islands from the ocean, and by five major rivers. The Albemarle-Pamlico system is one of the most biologically productive estuaries in the United States, supporting a huge variety of wildlife, fish, shellfish, and plants.

Three North Carolina counties lay claim to these barrier islands—Currituck, Dare, and Hyde. Dare is the largest county, with 391 square miles of land, 509 square miles of water, and more than 32,500 residents. Dare County stretches from north of Duck to the tip of Hatteras Island, including Roanoke Island and a mass of mainland. Currituck County encompasses 255 square miles of land, most of it on the mainland and a small portion of barrier island from north of Duck to the Virginia border. Currituck County has a population of more than 19,000. Hyde County's Outer Banks portion is Ocracoke Island, a 9-square-mile island with around 760 residents.

The 34,000 or so year-round residents of the Outer Banks host more than seven million visitors a year. Due to bridges and air travel, the Outer Banks islands are now more easily accessible than ever. This has led to rapid development, along with a dramatic increase in the availability of goods and services. Residents have all the accoutrements needed for a comfortable way of life, including a thriving economy with low unemployment, affordable housing, retail stores offering almost everything, an abundance of restaurants, arts and entertainment, medical care, and recreational opportunities. With all this, however, no one will deny that the pulse of life on these barrier islands is still set by wind and water. The weather and the natural world play intimate and demanding roles in the lives of barrier island residents.

Much of what keeps the Outer Banks so special is the Cape Hatteras National Seashore, which encompasses more than 75 miles of rugged, undeveloped beaches, dunes, marshes, and flatlands. With commercial and residential development continually increasing on the barrier islands, the Cape Hatteras National Seashore—the first national seashore in the nation—is treasured and appreciated more than ever. Three national wildlife refuges further protect portions of the Outer Banks from development.

Whether it's the sunrise, the sunset, or what goes on between, the Outer Banks offers the most extraordinary of what island life has to offer. "The sunsets here are the prettiest I have ever seen," Orville Wright wrote to his sister in 1900. "The clouds light up with all colors, in the background, with deep clouds of various shapes fringed with gold before. The moon rises in much the same style, and lights up the pile of sand almost like day." We have more than just good looks and personality, though: We have history. We have drama. We have lots of good stories to tell.

In this chapter we offer overviews of the areas that make up the Outer Banks, taking you on a north-to-south tour of Corolla and Currituck beaches, Duck, Southern Shores, Kitty Hawk, Kill Devil Hills, Colington Island, Nags Head, Roanoke Island, Hatteras Island, and Ocracoke Island.

COROLLA AND CURRITUCK BEACHES

Not so long ago, Currituck County's Outer Banks beaches were the barrier islands' outback. Seeming to stretch infinitely from north of Duck to the Virginia border, wide windswept expanses of sandy terrain lay virtually untouched except by winds, blue herons, and wild horses (see our Close-up in the Attractions chapter). While other island communities on the Outer Banks became boomtowns in the late 1970s, the northern beaches remained virtually untouched. For many years, the area was blocked to vehicles on both ends—by the state of Virginia on the north end and by a private developer on the south end. In 1984 the state opened North Carolina Highway 12 into the tiny village of Corolla, and it wasn't long before developers and vacationers started setting their sights on the Currituck Outer Banks.

From these barren dunes harboring a few fishing shacks and a handful of private homes, thousands of upscale houses, including 7,000-square-foot mansions, have sprung up on miles of recently paved subdivision roads. A family-owned convenience store that once supplied the only local goods for fewer than 100 permanent residents has been overshadowed by a modern chain grocery store. A lighthouse completed in 1875 has become more important as a landmark for tourists than as a guide for sailors. Dozens of eateries offer a variety of cuisines, and three quality resort shopping plazas are available to serve the hundreds of thousands of visitors that flock to the northernmost Outer Banks each summer.

The tiny community where everyone knew everyone else has undergone enormous change with its transformation into a favorite travel destination, but development has been tasteful and aesthetically pleasing. (And everyone still knows almost everyone else.)

People now often refer to the whole of the Currituck Outer Banks as "Corolla."

Technically, Corolla is only the tiny, old village that sits on the west side of the island near the lighthouse. The Currituck Outer Banks has no incorporated towns and consists of several planned developments. From north to south, these are Ocean Hill, Corolla Light, Monteray Shores, Whalehead Beach, Buck Island, Crown Point, Ocean Sands, Ocean Sands South, and Pine Island.

From Fishing Village to Vacation Destination

The remoteness of Currituck's Outer Banks kept these spectacular sea oat–strewn dunes isolated long after the barrier islands' southern beaches started to be developed. The lack of a permanent population and accompanying services helped to check tourism and growth. In 1972 coastal officials called Currituck County's 23 miles of beaches "the longest undeveloped strip of coastal land on the Eastern Seaboard." One telephone, which allowed only outgoing calls, served the entire area. The spit island was not even connected to line-distributed electricity until the 1950s.

Winston-Salem developer Earl Slick saw possibilities in the vast stretches of untouched beach and soundfront, and in 1973 he changed the face of the northern Outer Banks. For $2 million, he and his Coastland Corporation purchased 636 acres just north of the Dare County line from Texas oil tycoon Walter B. Davis.

In 1975 Slick erected a wooden guardhouse at the southern tip of his property, barring all but residents or landowners from entering Currituck beaches. Impassioned protests, which at times came to blows, eventually put the matter in the hands of the North Carolina Supreme Court. Finally, on November 1, 1984, the state took over the road that stretched from the Dare County line north. As security guards watched, bulldozers toppled the guard post, opening free passage all the way to Corolla and clearing a path for widespread development.

Despite its relative isolation before Slick's arrival, the northern beaches have their own unique history and allure. After the Civil War, Currituck Beach was the largest community on the Outer Banks between Kitty Hawk and Virginia. Fishing families lived in small wooden houses near the sound. The area earned a reputation as a "Sportsmen's Paradise" at this time, when hunters discovered the plentiful waterfowl inhabiting the Currituck Sound.

In 1874, the U.S. Government put Currituck's beaches on the map by building the Currituck Beach Lifesaving Station and the Currituck Beach Lighthouse. The lifesaving station, one of the Outer Banks's original seven outposts, was first named Jones Hill, then Whaleshead, and finally, Currituck Beach. The 150-foot-tall, red-brick lighthouse was the last major lighthouse built on North Carolina's barrier islands.

The tiny fishing community was officially named Corolla the following year, when the federal government installed a modest post office down the road a bit from the lighthouse. Three names were rejected before a local teacher suggested that postal officials name the village after the inner petals of a flower, the corolla (pronounced "ka-RAH-la" by locals).

Throughout the early 1900s, Currituck County's barrier islands grew in popularity as a retreat for recreational hunters who flocked to the dense marshlands each fall for the annual waterfowl migration. You can still spot crudely built duck blinds along the swampy shores. Historic structures have been turned into resort community clubhouses, real estate offices, retail shops, restaurants, and county-owned tourist attractions. The Whalehead Club, the largest and most magnificent of all the Outer Banks hunting lodges, is being restored to its orginal beauty. This Currituck County facility is open for tours daily throughout the summer (see our Attractions chapter).

Putting aside its appeal as premier hunting and fishing grounds, Corolla was unsentimentally regarded as little more than a wasteland of sand. Into the 1970s, only about 15 people lived in the village.

Getting to Currituck County's Outer Banks

In the 1950s Virginia and North Carolina officials began talking about building a road from Sandbridge, in Virginia, to Corolla, traversing a long spit of sand and the state line. That route, however, was never started. Today, only longtime property owners with special permits can drive through the protected lands that lie between the Outer Banks's Carova Beach and Sandbridge. Fences and metal gates prevent access to anyone other than pass-holders. The rest of the populace must drive up NC 12 from the south to get to Currituck's beaches. Turn left onto NC 12 at its junction with U.S. Highway 158 in Kitty Hawk, 1.5 miles east of the Wright Memorial Bridge's eastern terminus, then travel through Southern Shores, Duck, and Sanderling to the county line. Although it's only about 10 miles from Kitty Hawk to the Currituck County border, and another 12 miles to the end of the paved road at Corolla, the trip can take an hour or more on weekends during the peak season.

Once you pass through Duck, you'll notice the roadside opens and the terrain looks sparser and wilder. Watch your speed limit, because police are on the lookout for speeders who forget themselves on the straight two-lane road when traffic is light.

Much debate has taken place over whether to construct a two-lane, 4.8-mile bridge spanning the Currituck Sound from the mainland to Corolla. The proposed project would cut about 40 miles off the trip from US 158 in Currituck County to NC 12 in Corolla.

Corolla Today

No other Outer Banks community has changed as much in the past decade as Corolla. Only 15 or so years ago, NC 12 took an abrupt right turn toward Whale-head Beach and continued on a circuitous route to Corolla Village. Now, Monteray Plaza—a huge shopping center housing a Food Lion grocery store, a movie theater, and a variety of restaurants and stores—stands where a sign on a vacant lot once welcomed visitors to Whalehead. Across the road, TimBuck II shopping center lures visitors to its specialty stores, eateries, and entertainment options. NC 12 doesn't veer off to the right anymore but continues northward past Monteray Shores, on through Corolla Light, Corolla Village, Ocean Hill, and the Villages at Ocean Hill.

The northern beaches are home to some of the most luxurious rental properties on the Outer Banks. Although the area still has no home mail delivery, you won't have any trouble finding upscale shopping and dining, medical services, amenities, and entertainment other than that provided by nature. And despite the fact that Corolla's popularity is continually rising, you still feel far away from the rest of the world while visiting this northernmost destination of the Outer Banks.

In the past few years, developers and individuals have built thousands of homes between the Dare County line and the Virginia border, and at least 100 businesses have opened their doors. One of the more recently developed areas of Currituck County is Pine Island, which has 3 miles of oceanfront land. Many of the Outer Banks's most spectacular homes are located here. Residents have access to an array of pools, playgrounds, athletic courts, and other amenities, and nature trails wind throughout this upscale community. Several well-known sports figures own homes on Pine Island (see our Real Estate chapter for more information).

Most visitors to Currituck's beaches rent the huge homes that straddle the undulating sand dunes. The average Corolla house sleeps 16 to 20 people, includes more than 4,200 square feet of living space, has a pool and hot tub, and is available for weekly rentals. Many of the contained communities also offer exercise facilities, racket or golf clubs, indoor and outdoor swimming pools, boardwalk beach access, and trolley services. The area's first chain hotel, a Hampton Inn, is located on the oceanfront in Pine Island, south of Corolla.

Retail stores scattered throughout this area sell items ranging from handmade hammocks to custom-designed jewelry. Restaurants appeal to all tastes, from raw or steamed seafood to elegant European dining. And water sports—kayaking, windsurfing, sailing, and more—are popular from early spring through fall (see our Shopping, Restaurants, and Water Sports chapters for details).

Although tourists flock to the northern beaches during the summer, the permanent population of Currituck County's' Outer Banks is still small, estimated at about 500 people. A county satellite office keeps them connected with Currituck's services.

Currituck National Wildlife Refuge

A few miles north of the Currituck Beach Lighthouse, the multistory mansions become sparser and the paved two-lane highway dead-ends at a sand hill. Here, a wildlife sanctuary provides a safe haven for endangered piping plover, wild boar, and other wildlife. A 4-foot-tall fence stretching a mile from sound to sea marks the southern barrier of this 1,800-acre sanctuary, where most of Corolla's wild horses still range (see the Close-up in our Attractions chapter). People can walk through the fence, however, and four-wheel-drive vehicles can cross over a cattle grate.

Once Corolla's most popular tourist attraction, the wild horses no longer roam freely in the populated village. The Corolla Wild Horse Fund is headquartered at county satellite offices, where membership information is available.

Isolated Outposts North of the Road's End

There is no paved route from Corolla to the Virginia border. Still, a few hundred homes line this expanse of sand. On summer afternoons, more than a thousand four-wheel-drive vehicles create their own paths on the beach as they drive into and around a community called Carova—where North Carolina meets Virginia. Note that Carova's name is a melding of both states.

In May 1998 an ordinance requiring permits to drive all-terrain vehicles (ATVs) to Carova went into effect. For more specific information, call the county satellite office at (252) 453–8555.

About 300 homes are located along these remote beaches, and new homes are built every year. Residents negotiate tides and the beach not only in off-road and four-wheel-drive vehicles but also in regular cars with big deflated tires. Bicyclists sometimes manage at dead low tide to scoot around the fence into Sandbridge, Virginia, as natives in pre-fence days did routinely.

Although relatively protected from civilization, the area is patrolled by county, state, and federal officers. A system of dirt roads behind the dune line allows residents access to their homes. Most residents and visitors to Swan Beach, Carova, North Swan Beach, and the Seagull subdivisions drive on the beach above the waterline or on well-tread tracks at the base of the dune line.

Without a four-wheel-drive vehicle, you should not drive on the beach. Local guides gladly show visitors around in off-road vehicles. Guided tours of the area are available (see our Recreation chapter). Watch out for tree stumps, though. An ancient forest that historians say grew along the sound more than 800 years ago still thrusts its sea-withered trunks through the waves at an area known as Wash Woods.

Whether you're staying in one of Currituck Beach's exclusive rental homes or camping somewhere on the southern Outer Banks, Corolla and the four-wheel-drive area are well worth exploring.

DUCK

What makes Duck unique is its village-like atmosphere and the incredible water views that run along the main street of town. In this upscale resort community, you'll find wonderful waterfront boutiques, art galleries, and a variety of fine restaurants and casual eateries within easy strolling distance of one another and within walking or biking distance of many of Duck's neighborhoods. In the busy season, Duck teems with visitors and traffic crawls along the two-lane highway that runs north to Corolla, but even if you're staying elsewhere, it's worth a special trip. The Travel Channel voted Duck one of the Top 10 Beaches in America in 2002.

Duck is the latest Dare County community to incorporate. In the November 2001 elections, the citizens of Duck voted in favor of incorporating into the town of Duck rather than adhere to the county rules as it had always done. Incorporation, which became official in 2002, allows the town to create its own zoning laws as well as receive a higher percentage of tax revenues. In 2005 Duck had about 500 year-round citizens.

Tourism was slow to find Duck. It began to catch hold in the early 1980s, but once it did, the town grew rapidly (too rapidly, according to many locals). Two decades ago, T-shirts that read "Stuck in Duck" seemed to speak for a lot of the young people who craved more excitement than could be found in this sleepy town. Today, it is affluent, busy, and thriving. In addition to the usual beach fare, you can find some real treasures, authentic and

one-of-a-kind items to bring home as souvenirs. Plan to enjoy at least one meal here: Duck boasts many outstanding restaurants, and some offer outdoor tables. Two bed-and-breakfast inns accommodate nightly guests, but don't expect to find strings of motels. Almost every visitor to Duck rents a vacation home.

Duck makes an excellent jumping-off point for the full range of water sports. You'll find places to rent kayaks, canoes, windsurfing equipment, sailboats, JetSkis, and Wave Runners, and you can launch very close to restaurants and shops. For extra exhilaration, try a few hours of kayaking followed by lunch or dinner at a soundside table.

The town grew up on one of the most slender strips of sand on the Outer Banks. The ocean and the sound are close enough here so that many cottages offer extraordinary views of both, and, when the weather turns nasty, NC 12 floods quickly in many sections around town. The neighborhoods in and around Duck are a pleasing mixture of graceful older cottages and luxurious new homes. The gently rolling terrain contrasts with the flatter areas of the Outer Banks. This is the place if you crave a shady, tree-lined escape or a hilltop retreat where you can watch the sun rise and set from two sides of the same home.

A Growing Economy

Like most barrier island communities, Duck started as a small fishing village. Families lived in rough-hewn wooden houses set atop 2-foot blocks that kept the floors above the level to which the sea or sound had been known to rise during storms. With more trees and thicker underbrush here than in other areas of the Outer Banks, many Duck residents farmed small garden plots to supplement their seafood and waterfowl diets. Hogs, cows, and chickens were raised in the woods while watermen worked from dawn until dark, netting fish from the beach with long-haul seines, taking dorries out in the sound to set pound nets, and trapping crabs with wooden crates. Crews of women, men, and children toiled together for days mending heavy cotton fishing nets, sometimes earning up to 25 cents an hour for their trouble. During the Great Depression children and sometimes grown-ups earned money by catching "peelers"—blue crabs that had shed their shells. The business of harvesting these soft-shell crabs, still a major fishing enterprise on the Outer Banks, began in Duck. Eel pots also were prevalent along the shallow shores and shoals. Made of thin wood and more rounded than the crab pots, these contraptions were used by local fishermen who packed the long, snakelike creatures in salt, stored them in barrels, and trucked them along the sand trails to Hampton Roads markets, where eel were once eaten in abundance.

In 1909 Duck's first post office opened when postmaster Lloyd Toler gave the community its charming moniker in honor of the area's abundant waterfowl. The facility was abandoned by 1950. Year-round residents today have to travel to Kitty Hawk for their mail, though residents and visitors can mail letters and postcards from the little postal station now located in the Barrier Island Shops.

Little changed in Duck until the late 1970s. Single-family homes were sparsely scattered throughout the thick shrubbery, and small wooden boats bobbed alongside tree trunks turned into pilings.

Tourism took over about 1980, when small shops began lining up along the two-lane road through town and larger houses were built upon the beach. Barrier

Island Station, among the biggest and most popular time-share resorts on the Outer Banks, now houses a restaurant and includes an indoor and outdoor pool, tennis courts, a communal hot tub, and live evening entertainment on a covered waterfront deck.

In 1990 you had your choice of five restaurants between Kitty Hawk and Corolla. Today more than 25 establishments offer breakfast, lunch, and dinner, including a coffeehouse, a pizza parlor, a deli with unusual homemade salads, bistros, sandwich shops, and a marvelous wine bar and cafe. Galleries, boutiques, and colorful shops offer offbeat wares, crafts created by local artisans, and quality sea-themed souvenirs (see our Restaurants and Shopping chapters for more details).

Recreational offerings abound here, too. You can learn to windsurf or rent a sailboat or a trimaran, speed across the sound on a JetSki, paddle around a marsh island in a canoe or kayak, or bounce about the waves on an inflatable banana boat.

No matter what your tastes in food, fashion, or fun, you will find something to enjoy in the now-bustling village of Duck.

Getting to Duck

If you're heading to Duck from the northern Outer Banks, turn left onto NC 12 at its junction with US 158 in Kitty Hawk, 1.5 miles after crossing the Wright Memorial Bridge. Travel past the flattop homes of Southern Shores, and wind around the dunes on the two-lane highway. On good days, Duck is a 10-minute drive from Kitty Hawk. In heavy summer traffic, bottlenecks form in the village, causing backups that stretch for miles and that sometimes last more than 30 minutes.

NC 12 curves through the center of Duck. All the commercial development is along this road, confined to the highway by zoning ordinances, landscaped with lovely local foliage. Drive slowly—even we locals are astounded by the fetching sights around every bend.

The Army Corps of Engineers Research Pier north of Duck is the only oceanographic research pier of its kind in the world. See our Attractions chapter for information on touring this facility.

The sea is quite close to Duck, as is the sound; many rental homes provide the rare opportunity for viewing both bodies of water from upstairs open-air decks. Wild beans, peas, and cattails cover the marshy yards, most of which are at least partially wooded, with the houses tucked among the trees.

True to its name, Duck is both home and passageway for a variety of nesting and migrating shorebirds and waterfowl. Streets are named after these feathered creatures, which often come to call. Loons, cormorants, gannet, and flocks of terns and gulls soak up the sun's warmth near the water's edge. You can sometimes see swans and mallards swimming in the sound at sunrise as well as otters playing in the sound.

On the northern edge of Duck, a U.S. Army Corps of Engineers research facility occupies the site of a former Navy bombing range. Military weapons recovery crews have dug up thousands of unexploded shells around here, and an 1,800-foot-long pier now provides scientists with an important opportunity to track subsurface currents, study the effects of jetties and beach nourishment projects, and chart the movements of the slender strips of sand (see our Attractions chapter for more information).

Beyond the pier, heading north toward Corolla, you'll find the Duck Volunteer Fire Department, the Dare County Sheriff's Office northern beach station, and the Duck Recycling Center.

About 5 miles north of Duck, through an open wilderness area, Sanderling is the northernmost community on Dare County's beaches—an isolated, exclusive enclave with 300 acres stretching from sound to sea.

The community itself was started in 1978, setting a precedent for excellence among vacation destinations. These neighborhoods, barely visible from the road, approach land planning sensitively, preserving as much natural vegetation as possible and always aiming for architec-

tural excellence. They are well worth searching out.

In 1985 the Sanderling Inn and Restaurant opened in the restored Caffey's Inlet Lifesaving Station, built in 1874. With cedar-shake siding, natural wood interiors, and English country antiques, it has the appearance of turn-of-the-20th-century Nags Head resorts and the ambience of a European escape. It's large and airy, with wide porches offering plenty of room for conversation, drinks, and soaking in the sunrise while rocking in wooden chairs (see our Accommodations and Restaurants chapters for details).

North of Sanderling, Palmer's Island Club is a 35-acre development with 15 oceanfront one-acre lots and at least eight estates ranging from 6,000 to 10,000 square feet each. The homes are engineered to withstand 120 mph winds. Signature architectural embellishments are scaled to match the grandeur of the natural environment.

SOUTHERN SHORES

Stretching from sound to sea, Southern Shores is heralded as one of the most beautiful, well-thought-out developments on the Outer Banks. Interwoven with canals, maritime hardwood forests, dunes, and private beaches, its scenic beauty is hard to match. Real estate agents call Southern Shores property one of the best Outer Banks values for long-term investment.

Southern Shores is south of Duck and north of Kitty Hawk. You can enter this community from the south via NC 12; by South Dogwood Trail, which runs alongside Kitty Hawk School; or by Juniper Trail, which runs perpendicular to The Marketplace shopping center.

Yesteryear and Today

Southern Shores was the first planned community on the northern Outer Banks and a pioneer for underground utilities. Frank Stick—developer, artist, outdoorsman, and self-trained ichthyologist—bought the land in 1947 for $30,000. Today it is worth more than $430 million.

Stick worked eight years developing Southern Shores, and his care is evident throughout the town today. A master illustrator who studied under the distinguished Howard Pyle, Stick later shared the task of developing the area with his son, David. Much like a watercolor from the era in which the senior Stick thrived, Southern Shores was developed to resemble a *Wind in the Willows* paradise.

Home to cardinals, finches, mockingbirds, Canadian grosbeaks, woodpeckers, quail, raccoons, deer, and squirrels, this idyllic place with seas of white dogwoods blooming in spring speaks of the Sticks' love and dedication for preserving the natural habitat. Perhaps nowhere else on the Outer Banks better illustrates the harmonious coexistence of human development and nature.

The small oceanside community consists of approximately 4 square miles and lies alongside NC 12 stretching through the northern Outer Banks. As you drive through the town along this winding, two-lane road, you'll see open skies, dunes with low scrub vegetation, vacation homes including old-style cottages with vintage flattops, intermittent with large, expensive beach homes. If you turn off the highway away from the ocean onto one of the side roads, the landscape changes dramatically. Here you'll find neighborhoods of year-round homes, green lawns, hardwood trees draped with Spanish moss, dogwoods, and a sprawling golf course.

A Haven of Solitude

Comprising mostly single-family homes, Southern Shores is predominantly a residential town uncluttered by the commercial aspects of other Outer Banks areas, making it the perfect place to seek solitude. Residents enjoy canoeing or kayaking in the canal system designed by David Stick, a local historian and published author. Though not the painter his father was, David's artistic talent was in full swing when he created these panoramic lagoons that connect interior properties to Jean Guite Bay and Currituck Sound.

The community includes two private marinas, soundside picnic and bathing areas, and ocean beach accesses situated every 600 feet. The accesses are available only to residents and vacationers staying in the area (make sure you display the proper permit), affording every beachgoer enough elbow room to comfortably spread a blanket or throw a Frisbee. A soundside wading beach on North Dogwood Trail is a favorite spot for families because the shallow sound water is a safer place for children to swim than the ocean. In the summer, the picnic area has toilet facilities. Paved and unpaved bike trails meander through the town. Anyone can use the facilities, but to park you must belong to the civic association or get a town sticker. In either case, you have to be a property owner or guest to park in Southern Shores.

The golf course at Duck Woods Country Club winds its way through a residential neighborhood of Southern Shores, offering outstanding play in a pristine setting among tall pines, dogwoods, and other foliage. The 18-hole course is the oldest on the Outer Banks and accepts public play year-round (see our Golf chapter).

The 40 original families who inhabited Southern Shores formed the town's first civic association. The Southern Shores Civic Association acts like a parks and recreation department. It owns, operates, and maintains the marinas, playgrounds, beach accesses, and crossovers for residents, property owners, and guests. Membership dues cover costs, but most of the physical upkeep is done by volunteers in the community.

Today the population has expanded to more than 2,600 year-round residents, swelling to 10,000 in the summer months. Until recently, most residents were retirees, but now Southern Shores has an equal number of young families living within its boundaries. The town hall sits on a small hill off US 158 on Skyline Road.

It's been more than half a century since Stick first purchased Southern Shores, but the slow pace of development means there still is real estate available. Raw land on the oceanfront or soundfront is hard to come by these days, but those wanting to purchase property can obtain homes or land in the beach zone, dunes, or woods. Due to careful planning, Southern Shores has land reserved for a future civic center and several plots to be developed for other town needs.

One of the town's two retail establishments, The Marketplace, includes a movie theater, a Food Lion, and a multitude of smaller shops (see our Shopping chapter). This complex sits at the edge of Southern Shores, just east of the base of the Wright Memorial Bridge. The new Southern Shores Crossing, situated behind Southern Shores Realty, offers more small shops, a day spa, and an upscale restaurant.

Southern Shores was incorporated in 1979 and growth has occurred in the development since Frank Stick's purchase, but the developers' spirit of conservation is felt with every bike ride, every sunset, and every tour of the waterways that weave together flora, fauna, and humankind. The town continues to be environmentally conscious and is the first Outer Banks community to offer curbside recycling.

KITTY HAWK

If you access the Outer Banks from North Carolina's Currituck County mainland, the first town you'll reach is Kitty Hawk. This beach municipality begins at the eastern end of the Wright Memorial Bridge over the Currituck Sound and stretches sound-to-sea for about 4 miles. Within its town limits are a maritime forest, a fishing pier, a golf course, condominiums, and a historic, secluded village where Wilbur and Orville

Wright stayed while conducting experiments with their famed flying machines.

Southern Shores forms the northern boundary of Kitty Hawk, and Kill Devil Hills is to the south. Milepost (MP) markers offer the best means of finding your destination. Most rental cottages, shops, restaurants, attractions, and resorts in this area can be located by green milepost markers along US 158 (Insiders call this the Bypass) and NC 12 (Insiders call this the Beach Road). The first milepost marker (MP 1) is in Kitty Hawk where the highway splits near the Aycock Brown Welcome Center.

With its name bonded to aviation history and its positioning as one of the gateways to the wide, undeveloped beaches of the Outer Banks, Kitty Hawk might not be what you expect—at least at first glance. Much of the 4 miles of beachfront here is narrower and appears more developed than any other place on the barrier islands. Even though Wilbur and Orville Wright certainly disembarked and stayed with the locals in the village of Kitty Hawk, they didn't fly here. Their experiments and successful flights were accomplished a few miles down the road in Kill Devil Hills.

Now that we've got that straight, enjoy Kitty Hawk for what it is: a vacation getaway offering lots of family-oriented activities, a fishing pier, some great eateries, convenient shopping, and all the fun you could want on a clean beach. Plus, tucked away within the borders of Kitty Hawk's 12 square miles are some of the loveliest and most exclusive communities in the central beach area.

Keep in mind that when you just feel like taking a ride, the Beach Road through Kitty Hawk is one of the few stretches on the entire Outer Banks where you can see the ocean from your vehicle. Cruising south along the beach, you'll notice some weather-beaten houses perched on the shoreline. At high tide and in stormy weather, waves crash under the house pilings and wash out truckloads of sand. The ocean plays chicken every year with these tired beach cottages, and just about every year a cottage cries uncle and collapses into the pounding surf. After every "big blow," local gossip (we love to talk weather here) inevitably comes around to an update on the Kitty Hawk cottages. You've likely gotten a good view of one of them on the Weather Channel, which, to the Tourist Bureau's chagrin, seems to delight in showing the wreckage of a Kitty Hawk beach house clinging pitifully to the sands during a storm. Once they're gone, they're gone, as federal coastal management law now forbids building closer than 60 feet from a coastline's first line of vegetation.

By one popular version, Kitty Hawk owes its colorful name to a derivation of local Indians' references to goose hunting season as "killy honker" or "killy honk." Eighteenth-century documents record this beach community as "Chickahauk," a name adopted by the prestigious southeastern section of Southern Shores. Other theories say the name evolved from "skeeter hawk," mosquito hawks that were prolific in the area, or from ospreys or similar raptors preying on the area's kitty wren.

The History of "A Hospitable People"

Primarily a fishing and farming community from the late 18th century through the early 1900s, Kitty Hawk Village matured along the wide bay that juts into the barrier islands along Albemarle Sound. By 1790 a builder, a merchant, a shoemaker, a minister, a planter, and a mariner all owned deeds to the sandy, sloping marshlands that now constitute Kitty Hawk. The community received additional goods from ships and ferries arriving from Elizabeth City, North Carolina, and Norfolk, Virginia.

In 1874 one of the Outer Banks's seven original lifesaving stations was built on the beach at Kitty Hawk. A U.S. Weather Bureau opened the following year and remained in service until 1904. This weather station provided the Wright brothers with information about local

wind patterns, which was the impetus for the Ohio bicycle shop owners to test their wings at Kill Devil Hill.

The first families of Kitty Hawk were named Twiford, Baum, Etheridge, Perry, and Hill. These hearty folk were quite self-sufficient, building their own boats and fishing, farming, and raising livestock on the open range. Many descendants of these early inhabitants still live on the west side of Kitty Hawk. A drive along winding Kitty Hawk Road, which begins just north of the 7-Eleven, leads to streets with such names as Elijah Baum Road, Herbert Perry Road, and Moore Shore Road. Along the latter is a monument that designates the spot where Orville and Wilbur Wright assembled their plane before successfully completing their historic flight a few miles away in 1903.

"I assure you, you will find a hospitable people when you come among us," Kitty Hawk Lifesaving Station Capt. Billy Tate wrote to Wilbur Wright in 1900. Tate described the local terrain as "nearly any type of ground you could wish . . . a stretch of sandy land 1 mile by 5 with a bare hill in the center 80 feet high, not a tree or a bush anywhere to break the wind current." The winds, he wrote, were "always steady, generally from 10 to 20 miles velocity per hour. If you decide to try your machine here and come, I will take pleasure in doing all I can for your convenience and success and pleasure."

Wilbur arrived at Kitty Hawk in September of that year. He traveled by rail from Dayton, Ohio, to Elizabeth City, where he boarded *The Curlicue* bound for the Outer Banks. (Before the Wright Memorial Bridge was built, visitors to the Outer Banks arrived by boat from Elizabeth City.) The boat trip took two days in hurricane winds. Wilbur stayed with the Tates until Orville arrived, then the two set up camp in Kitty Hawk Village.

Members of the Kitty Hawk Beach Lifesaving Station crew assisted the brothers with their early experiments. Even though many of the first flights were conducted near the town of Kill Devil Hills, the

Wrights' first Outer Banks visit—and their letters carrying a Kitty Hawk postmark—etched this town's name in the annals of history. Not surprisingly, many visitors think the Wright Brothers National Monument is in Kitty Hawk, instead of 3 miles south atop Kill Devil Hill, where the 100th celebration of flight was held in 2003.

The first post office in Kitty Hawk opened November 11, 1878. A second one was established in 1905 to serve the western section of the community. In 1993 the biggest post office facility on the Outer Banks was built on the eastern side of US 158 in Kitty Hawk.

Residents of this town floated their own $7,000 bond in 1924 to build a school. Housed in a single building, the combined grammar and high school served fewer than 100 students until a Dare County high school consolidated Outer Banks children at a single facility in Manteo. Today, Kitty Hawk still has its own elementary school. Older students travel by bus to Kill Devil Hills to attend First Flight Middle School or the new First Flight High School, which opened in the fall of 2004. Today more than 3,300 residents call Kitty Hawk home.

The Transition to Vacation Destination

Unlike Nags Head, which has been a thriving summer resort since before the Civil War, Kitty Hawk didn't become a vacation destination until about 70 years ago. A group of Elizabeth City businessmen bought 7 miles of beach north of Kitty Hawk Village in the late 1920s and formed the Wright Memorial Bridge Company. By 1930 they had built a 3-mile wooden span across the Currituck Sound from Point Harbor to the Outer Banks. Travelers could finally arrive at island beaches by car from the mainland. Kitty Hawk land became popular—and a lot more pricey. Summer visitors streamed across the new bridge, paying $1.00 per car for the privilege.

With the sudden boom in tourism, development shifted from the protected soundside hammocks to the open, windswept beaches. Small wooden cottages sprung from behind dunes on the oceanfront. As the beach eroded over the years, wind and water had its way with many of the beachfront homes. Houses were swept away during hurricanes and nor'easters, providing newfound ocean frontage for the neighbor cottage across the street. In 2003 Hurricane Isabel took an additional seven homes.

Even the original Kitty Hawk Lifesaving Station had to be jacked up and moved to a more protected site on the west side of the Beach Road to prevent tides from carrying it to a watery grave. The station is now a private residence, but travelers can still recognize the original Outer Banks gabled architecture of this historic structure.

In the western reaches of this community, the maritime forest of Kitty Hawk Woods winds for miles over tall ridges and blackwater swamps. Here, primarily year-round residents make their homes on private plots and in new subdivisions. Some lots are much larger than in other central beach communities. The twisting vines, dripping Spanish moss, and abundant tall trees offer seclusion and shelter from the storms not found in the expansive, open oceanfront areas. On summer days, locals often ride horses around the shady lanes of old Kitty Hawk Village, reminiscent of the days before bridges.

Although you'll find some businesses tucked back in the trees of Kitty Hawk Village at the western end of Kitty Hawk Road near the sound, most of this town's commercial outposts are along the Bypass and the Beach Road. The Outer Banks's only Wal-Mart is in Shoreside Center near the end of the Wright Memorial Bridge. Regional Medical Center at MP 1½ offers a full range of emergency and outpatient services.

If you're headed for the beach, you'll find a public bathhouse at MP 4½. The public is also welcome to use the Dare

County boat launch at the end of Bob Perry Road, where locals and visitors can set sail during a hot summer day and watch the dolphins frolic in Kitty Hawk Bay.

From waterskiing to fishing, Kitty Hawk presents exceptional recreational possibilities. With all the water fun rounded out with a fine selection of dining establishments, convenient shopping, and medical services, along with history and natural beauty, it's obvious why Kitty Hawk is a favorite beach retreat for families, retirees, and college students.

The Albemarle-Pamlico Sounds system is the second largest estuary in the United States, second only to the Chesapeake Bay. These sounds have 3,000 square miles of surface water and 30,000 square miles of watershed.

KILL DEVIL HILLS

Even among all the other romantic and striking names of Outer Banks communities, Kill Devil Hills swirls a little longer in the imagination. One legend has it that Kill Devil Hill, the sand dune where the Wright Brothers revolutionized transportation, was named after the wretched-tasting kill-devil rum that may have washed up in barrels from shipwrecks in early Colonial days. According to another tale these hills were named after a rogue called Devil Ike, who blamed the theft of shipwrecked cargo on the devil, whom he claimed to have chased to the hills and killed. Other local lore tells of a Banker who, atop one of the dunes, tried to kill the devil he had traded his soul to for a bag of gold.

The Outer Banks's first incorporated and most populous town, Kill Devil Hills is bookended by Kitty Hawk and Nags Head. Spanning the barrier island from sound to sea, this beach community is the geographic center of Dare County, with more

than 6,200 permanent residents. Hundreds of thousands of tourists visit this bustling beach town each summer. Indeed, the intersection of Ocean Bay Boulevard and Colington Road—where the Wright Memorial, a beach bathhouse, the post office, the town municipal center, the county chamber of commerce, the library, a school complex, and the entrance to the only road to Colington Island are grouped—is the busiest junction in the county and possibly the busiest secondary road in the state. Now that the new First Flight High School has opened, bottlenecks are common in the morning and mid-afternoon hours.

Despite the trend toward bigger and more exclusive resort homes and amenities elsewhere on the Outer Banks; Kill Devil Hills remains a family-oriented beach for visitors and a centrally located town of moderately priced housing for the permanent population. Kite flying, surfing, sea kayaking, windsurfing, sunbathing, air flight tours, shopping, restaurants, motels, churches, and schools combine to make this town a top choice for many, as it has been for more than a half-century.

Condominiums and franchise hotels dot the 5 miles of once-barren dunes. More than 41 miles of paved roads have replaced sandy pathways. Fast-food restaurants have sprung up along the five-lane US 158, forming the Outer Banks's commercial hub, known locally as French Fry Alley.

Building Bridges to the Tourist Trade

Kill Devil Hills's population did not really begin to grow until new bridges were constructed from the mainland across the sounds in the early 1930s. Kitty Hawk and Nags Head both had docks for steamer ships bringing passengers from Elizabeth City and Norfolk. Kill Devil Hills was seldom visited until cars could more easily reach the Outer Banks.

The federal government built a lifesaving station in Kill Devil Hills in 1879. At the time Wilbur and Orville Wright arrived from Ohio to test their famed flying machine at the turn of the 20th century, the few permanent residents living along the barren central beaches were mainly lifesavers, fishermen, and salvagers. Even on December 17, 1903, when the Wrights made their first historic flight on windswept flatland below Kill Devil Hill, only a handful of local people watched in awe as the airplane finally soared under its own power.

Schoolchildren and their parents going back and forth to First Flight Elementary, First Flight Middle School, and First Flight High School are treated to the sight of the Wright Brothers Memorial. Motorists spy it from the Bypass or Colington Road. A 2-mile bike path was constructed on the outskirts of the landmark, and now in-line skaters, bikers, and joggers exercise in range of the spell of history.

In the summer of 1952, U.S. Representative Lindsay C. Warren, D-N.C., was vacationing at the Croatan Inn on the Outer Banks. One night, historians say, Warren met Kill Devil Hills Coast Guard Capt. William Lewark on the hotel's sprawling deck. The men looked around them at the four dozen wooden "beach box" houses that had been built on the sand over the past 20 years. Warren warned of overexpansion. He told Lewark that his seaside village ought to be zoned. He told the captain to create a town. So Lewark drafted a petition, called on his neighbors, and convinced 90 of the area's 93 voters to support incorporation. On March 6, 1953, the General Assembly officially recognized Kill Devil Hills as the first town on Outer Banks beaches.

The new town almost died in infancy. On May 4, 1955, the day that Emily Long Mustian was scheduled to take office as the town's first elected mayor, the new town ceased to be a town. Fed up with taxes that had jumped to 30 cents from 10 cents per $100 of property value since incorporation, citizens passed a referendum repealing the town charter.

Kill Devil Hills won a reprieve on February 29, 1956, when the North Carolina Supreme Court ruled that the petition by which the referendum had been conducted was invalid and reversed the repeal vote.

Developers set out to sell prime properties in the newly incorporated town of Kill Devil Hills. Lots in Avalon, one of the Outer Banks's first subdivisions, were sold by developers who sat at card tables under beach umbrellas at the piers, hawking the plots for $250 each. Most of those early property purchasers had their permanent homes in Hampton Roads.

By the 1970s, business was booming in Kill Devil Hills—with summer cottage rentals, motel traffic, and year-round residents. The Outer Banks's first fast-food restaurant, McDonald's, opened in 1978. The next year, Pizza Hut set up shop on a nearby Bypass lot. The rest of what locals call French Fry Alley developed by the early 1980s. As developers began stacking condominiums on the beaches as fast as they could, county commissioners enacted a 35-foot building height moratorium to prevent spoiling the eye appeal of the barrier beaches.

In 1986 commissioners financed streetlights for the town's 5 miles of highway, giving their municipality a glow at night. The neighboring towns have yet to put up continuous streetlights. By the end of the 1980s, Kill Devil Hills town employees moved into a new complex on Veterans Drive, and the town got its first large-scale shopping center in 1989.

Only four years later when the town turned 40, about 98 percent of Kill Devil Hills's private property was already platted. Some residents began looking for ways to retain their small-town feeling while becoming increasingly citified. Others expressed amazement at the ways in which their community was developing: adding a new soccer field for children, creating adult recreation programs, and welcoming new retail shops each summer.

COLINGTON ISLAND

In 1633 Colington Island became the first land in Carolina to be deeded to an individual. Today this 2-mile-long, 2.5-mile-wide island, although developing rapidly, is one of the last of the Outer Banks communities to experience growth. In 2005 around 3,500 people made Colington their year-round home.

The east end of Colington Island lies a mile west of the Wright Brothers Memorial, linked by a bridge over Colington Creek, which separates the island from Kill Devil Hills and Dare County beaches. Colington's other borders are surrounded by open water. Kitty Hawk Bay is to the north and Buzzard Bay is to the south. The mouths of four sounds (Currituck, Albemarle, Croatan, and Roanoke) converge on the west side of this family community.

Colington, named after its first proprietor, Sir John Colleton, was originally tilled to grow grapes for a winery shortly after settlers in 1664 founded the first Outer Banks community. The grapes, along with crops of tobacco, fruits, and vegetables, failed after three successive hurricanes. But by the early 1800s, a thriving fishing community had grown on two halves of the island: Great Colenton and Little Colenton, cleaved in 1769 by the Dividing Creek. Fishing, crabbing, and hunting sustained islanders generation after generation. Eventually, years after the rest of the barrier islands, Colington natives got paved roads, telephones, and electric service.

Now, they have tourism as well. Just like the four- or five-generation families that live here, Colington Island has its own unique Outer Banks identity. High, uneven dunes meet dank, brackish swamplands. Thick groves of pine, dogwood, live oak, beech, and holly drip Spanish moss over expanses of sandy shoreline. Thin creeks widen to unexpected harbors and bays. In summer months, soft-shell crab holding pens illuminate strips of scrubby yard along the sounds at night, the naked light-bulbs glaring out of the darkness like a

Reno casino. Advertisements for waterfront property in pricey new subdivisions are posted not far from where trailers and campgrounds line the twisting road. Mansions are barely evident perched on their sandy shelves overlooking Colington Road, the most heavily traveled secondary road in Dare County.

Colington Harbour, the island's first subdivision, was built in 1965. Since then, numerous other subdivisions have been constructed along canals, marshlands, and soundfronts and in woodlands throughout Colington Island. After a year of weighing benefits and risks, newcomers and natives hammered out a reasonable zoning plan. Several restaurants, a storage garage, and a go-kart track mingling with crab shedders and fish houses along the road illustrate the conflict and challenges this sheltered community faced over dramatic change. With new development approved every year, residents have accepted the inevitability of growth. The future face of Colington will be determined by the strength of the zoning plan and the people who molded it.

NAGS HEAD

Home of the Outer Banks's first resort, the community of Nags Head is south of Kill Devil Hills and north of Oregon Inlet. It stretches from the Atlantic Ocean to the Roanoke Sound and has remained a popular vacation destination for more than 150 years. Many first-time vacationers mistakenly refer to the whole middle-Banks area as "Nags Head," lumping the town together with neighboring Kill Devil Hills and Kitty Hawk. Most likely this is historically based, due to the fact that at one time Nags Head was the only true destination on the middle Banks.

The booming summer scene was once anchored by cottages towering over the shallow sound, elaborate hotels facing the mainland, and calm-water canoeing, crabbing, and conversation. This relaxed style of soundside vacationing has long since been altered by shifting sands and changing values.

Nags Head History and the Story behind the Name

The primary resort destination on these barrier islands for more than a century, Nags Head has been the official name of the area since at least 1738, when it first appeared on maps. Historians say the beach town got its name from the horses that once roamed throughout the islands. The much more colorful legend we Insiders prefer is that Nags Head was derived from a custom locals used to lure ships to the shores. Securing a lantern from a Banker pony's neck, residents would drive the horse up and down the beach, the light swinging with the same motion as a sailboat. The unsuspecting offshore vessel would steer toward the light and proceed to get grounded on the shoals. The locals would then promptly ransack the hapless ship.

In the early 1830s, a Perquimans County planter explored the Outer Banks "with the view of finding a suitable place to build a summer residence where he and his family could escape the poisonous miasma vapors and the attendant fevers," wrote author and historian David Stick in *The Outer Banks of North Carolina*. "He explored the beach and the sound shore and picked his house site overlooking the latter, near the tallest of the sand hills." The planter paid $100 to an unknown Banker for the 200 acres and built the first summer house on the Outer Banks in Nags Head.

In 1838 the Outer Banks's first hotel was built in Nags Head midway between the sound and the sea. A two-story structure, the grand guesthouse had accommodations for 200 travelers, an elaborate ballroom, a bowling alley, covered porches, and a 5-foot-wide pier that extended from the hotel's front a half-mile into the sound.

The 1850 census showed that 576 people, including 30 slaves, lived year-round in Nags Head, but hundreds more came each summer. By that time the soundside community had become a well-known watering hole for the families of mainland farmers, bankers, and lawyers.

Elizabeth City doctor William Gaskins Pool was the first to build a home on the seaside in 1866, according to a 19th-century journal kept by Outer Banks resident Edward R. Outlaw Jr. On September 14, 1866, Pool purchased 50 acres "at or near Nags Head, bordering on the ocean, for $30" and constructed his one-story cottage 300 feet from the breakers. "But over there by themselves, his family was very lonely," Outlaw wrote in his book, *Old Nag's Head*.

Seeing that the Pools survived beside the sea, more people began building on the eastern edges of Nags Head. By the early 1900s, homeowners were erecting their cottages on logs so they could roll them back from encroaching tides. Some of the houses moved three or four times during residents' lifetimes. Oceanfront house moving is still a common practice in Nags Head today. The houses are jacked up, mounted onto a flatbed truck, and slowly inched away from the encroaching sea.

Nags Head became an incorporated town in 1961. This beach area continues to attract anglers and surfers, nature lovers and shoppers, families and fun-seeking adventurers. Charter boat captains Sam and Omie opened a restaurant at Whalebone Junction more than 50 years ago, serving breakfast to their fishing parties. The small wooden eatery still bears their names—and still serves some of the best she-crab soup around.

Nags Head Today

Today, Nags Head is home to almost 3,000 residents. Hotels, restaurants, piers, rambling residences, and luxurious vacation cottages line Nags Head's oceanfront, which remains predominantly vacation oriented. Local residents live in the middle and on the west side of the island, away from the harsh elements of the sea. The sound shores are filled with private cottages, except one portion of lower Nags Head that features watersports outfitters, go-kart tracks, and minigolf galore. South Nags Head, stretching from MP 17 to MP 21, is an exclusively residential area with no commercial development.

Jockey's Ridge State Park is Nags Head's most popular attraction aside from the beach. The best kite flying, hang gliding, and sunset views are found atop this natural phenomenon, which is the largest sand dune on the East Coast. Every summer day, the sprawling dune is dotted with hundreds of people who climb to the top for recreation and for the expansive views of sea and sound.

Another Nags Head natural attraction is the Nags Head Woods Preserve, actually in both Nags Head and Kill Devil Hills. Hikers, bird-watchers, and nature lovers delight in this wooded anomaly, where diverse flora and fauna can be enjoyed in stunning silence (see our Natural Wonders chapter).

Nags Head is well-known for its recreational opportunities. A paved bike path stretches almost the entire length of the town. A Scottish links–style golf course, The Village at Nags Head Golf Links, is one of the area's most beautiful and challenging courses. The village stretches along the Roanoke Sound, offering sound views and the opportunity to see a variety of waterbirds and wildlife. Dolphin tours, airboat rides, boat rentals, JetSki rentals, kiteboarding lessons, windsurfing, and sailing are all offered on the sound in lower Nags Head, around MP 16 and on the Nags Head–Manteo Causeway. Miniature golf and go-kart tracks also cluster in this area. Nags Head has the YMCA complex and the area's only bowling alley.

Shoppers flock to Nags Head's name-brand outlet stores and to its several strip malls and grocery stores. Nags Head is home to many art galleries, including an artists' enclave known as Gallery Row (see our Arts and Culture chapter). Restaurants and nightspots lure diners and revelers to Nags Head. Owens' Restaurant has been a Nags Head institution for more than 50 years; Kelly's Tavern is the most well-known nightspot on the Outer Banks.

Since it's centrally located on the Outer Banks, Nags Head is a favorite destination of people who want to take day trips to Hatteras Island and Corolla. If you don't want to get back in the car once you've arrived at your vacation destination, you can get everything you want within walking distance of most Nags Head hotels and cottages.

Whether you're looking to escape the bustle of the beach by taking a quiet hike through the Nature Conservancy's Nags Head Woods Ecological Preserve or dance the night away at a beachside tavern, this Outer Banks town remains one of the area's most popular resorts.

ROANOKE ISLAND

Nestled between the Outer Banks and the North Carolina mainland, Roanoke Island is one of the most historic places in America. People sometimes confuse our island's history with that of Jamestown, Virginia, where the first permanent English colony thrived in the early 17th century. The confusion between the two revolves around the word "permanent." Roanoke Island is the site of England's earliest attempts to plant a permanent colony in the New World. Beginning in 1584, Sir Walter Raleigh dispatched a series of voyages carrying courageous souls to settle in the New World. These journeys culminated in a colony of 117 men, women, and children, sent here in 1587, only to disappear mysteriously (see our History chapter); hence the lack of "permanence." The Lost Colony of Roanoke Island remains a puzzle. Theories concerning the colonists' fate abound, but until archaeologists dig up some real proof, we'll continue to wonder what really happened to these early settlers.

For those who appreciate concrete links to the past, relics have been retrieved from the waters surrounding Roanoke Island—artifacts that may provide clues to centuries-old puzzles. Numerous locals and archaeologists alike have combed the island for treasures from the Native American culture, earliest English settlements, and Civil War times (see our History chapter for more information on these Roanoke Island highlights). Old English coins, a powder horn, a vial of quicksilver, weapons, bottles, iron fragments, pottery, and arrowheads have been discovered here. In the winter of 1998-99, a strong nor'easter blew so much water out of the sound that some creek beds and sound bottoms were exposed for the first time in many decades. Locals harvested numerous arrowheads from the exposed muddy tracts. Some remnants can be seen at Fort Raleigh National Historic Site on the north end of the island (see our Attractions chapter), while others found their way into personal collections. Roanoke Island native Hubby Bliven opened The Roanoke Heritage Gallery and Museum on the island mostly with artifacts he's been collecting since his youth.

Roanoke Island tends to bring out the nature lover in all of us. In the spring, summer, and fall, early mornings and late afternoons find marsh rabbits nibbling roadside grasses. Red-winged black birds, looking much like holiday ornaments, adorn the bushes alongside the road. They really stand out in winter, when the leaves have left trees barren. Scan the creeks in the warm months, just before entering Roanoke Island from the west, and you can see turtles lined like soldiers on half-sunken logs and along the banks. Crossing the Washington Baum Bridge from the east, we regularly spot osprey flying overhead, clutching dangling snakes or fish in their claws. (Don't take your eyes off the road too long, and definitely do not stop on the bridge!) Of course, a wide variety of fish, such as spot, croaker, pig-fish, sea mullet, sheepshead, and stripers, inhabit the surrounding waters. Boats and recreational water vehicles of all sorts share the sounds and bays in fair weather.

By land, you can walk back into time at Roanoke Island Festival Park, formerly the *Elizabeth II* State Historic Site in Manteo. You can also examine history at Fort Raleigh. Make sure to explore the park's nature path, the Thomas Hariot Trail. Hariot, a 16th-century author, wrote the first book about the New World in Elizabethan English. His book is a study of the Native Americans and a survey of the area's natural resources. Only six copies of his literary treatise are said to exist.

Getting Here

Roanoke Island is west of Nags Head and due east of Williamston, North Carolina. It certainly is easier and quicker to get here now than it was centuries or even decades ago due to the construction of several bridges and new highways. While you won't have to forge a path through reeds, as our ancestors did, you still can reach the island by water. If a car is your mode of transportation, you can choose from at least four routes; all are scenic. Some wend through more remote regions than others. One two-lane road, U.S. Highway 64/264, has always carried all the local traffic plus vacationer traffic right down the spine of Roanoke Island, creating backups and bottlenecks. In 2002 a 5-mile bridge came into service. This bridge, the longest in the state, steers vacationer traffic and much of the local traffic away from the island. One end of the bridge is in Manns Harbor and the other is at the Manteo-Wanchese junction, which leads right to the beaches of the Outer Banks. If you wish to travel by air, the Dare County Regional Airport is on the north end of Roanoke Island. Private pilots fly into this airport daily and charter services are available. It's not unusual to see visitors riding in on bicycles. The Outer Banks's flat terrain makes for excellent bicycle touring.

For specific routes and directions see our Getting Here, Getting Around chapter.

Island Economy and Tourism

At the heart of Roanoke Island life is the inhabitants' desire to preserve a small-town feeling while finding ways to make a living. Islanders mostly work in tourist- and service-oriented businesses, at fishing-related jobs, as writers and artists, in local government, and in the public school system.

Roanoke Island has history to market. Our Attractions chapter describes the island's top sites: the Elizabethan Gardens, the North Carolina Aquarium, Fort Raleigh National Historic Site, the Outer Banks History Center, Roanoke Island Festival Park, the North Carolina Maritime Museum, and *The Lost Colony* outdoor drama.

The Outer Banks History Center, housed at Roanoke Island Festival Park (see our Arts and Culture chapter), is a font of Roanoke Island lore and has old photos and area maps on display.

The main branch of the Dare County Library on US 64, just across from Manteo Elementary School, is another good source for more island information. For overall Outer Banks information, such as maps, brochures, and other local data, stop in at the Outer Banks Visitors Bureau on US 64/264. The staff is friendly and helpful, and there's even a convenient drive-through window.

Talk with some of our old-timers for some really entertaining inside information. Conversation with lifelong locals is bound to reveal a colorful tale or two. Pick up a copy of *Memories of Manteo and Roanoke Island, N.C.,* by Suzanne Tate as told by the late Cora Mae Basnight, if you're unable to make a personal connection. This oral history, from the mouth of a much-loved native (and late mother of the current president pro tem of the North Carolina Senate, Marc Basnight), is a delightful book accented with interesting photographs. Ms. Basnight, according to Tate's book, held the record for playing the same role longer than any actress in American Theater, that of Agona, a Native American woman, in *The Lost Colony.* Many consider her the quintessential Agona. Another fantastic, more thorough history of the town and island is *Manteo, A Roanoke Island Town,* by Angel Ellis Khoury. It's filled with fascinating stories, anecdotes, and facts about this area.

Lots of exciting tales revolve around *The Lost Colony,* the historic outdoor drama that outlines the story of the first English settlement and its disappearance. Pulitzer Prize–winning playwright Paul Green wrote the drama, which debuted in 1937. It has played a major role in the lives of local folk ever since (see our Arts and Culture chapter). In 1997 the production observed its 60th anniversary, drawing former *Lost Colony* thespians and production members the world over to reminisce and celebrate the occasion. In 1998 a stunning $2 million renovation to the historic Waterside Theatre was completed.

Generations of families grew up acting in the annual play. From representing the infant Virginia Dare to playing the role of Gov. John White or Chief Manteo, many a Roanoke Island resident nurtured a love of history through the play and a love of theater as a result. Andy Griffith, who played Sir Walter Raleigh in his first acting stint, is a Roanoke Island resident.

William S. Powell's *Paradise Preserved* is the definitive source for the history of the Roanoke Island Historical Association, perpetuators of the historic play. Powell offers an exciting account of the creative endeavors of Mrs. Mabel Evans Jones, the author and producer of local pageants on

---

ℹ *In the Outer Banks economy, the largest percentages of people work in the service industries (21 percent), retail (19 percent), government (15 percent), and construction (8 percent).*

Roanoke Island that predate Green's play. Evans Jones, the former Superintendent of Schools in Dare County, ran a summer arts camp on the island in the early 1920s. As it is with an archaeologist, the more you dig, the more you're likely to uncover something concerning Roanoke Island's roots and tales of the people who called the island home.

Yesteryear and Today

Prior to the settling of Manteo in the 1860s, islanders had established two sparsely populated residential settlements on Roanoke Island called the Upper End and the Lower End. The Upper End referred to the north end of Roanoke Island, and the Lower End described the area that is now called Wanchese. A third settlement was formed by former slaves and has been referred to as California. Manteo and the village of Wanchese were named after two Native Americans who befriended the early English explorers.

In 1999 the town of Manteo celebrated its centennial. Manteo became Dare County's seat in 1870 and was incorporated as a town in 1899. Islanders soon erected the first courthouse and established a post office. The white-columned brick courthouse that stands in downtown Manteo today was built in 1904, replacing the original wooden structure. One of the earliest private homes built on the Upper End in the 1780s was the Etheridge home, also referred to as Drinkwater's Folley. It was moved in the 1930s from a wooded area between Heritage Point and the Elizabethan Gardens to its present location on US 64 at the Morrison Grove turnoff. Another private home that bears note is the 1872 Colonial-style dwelling built in Manteo that later became the Tranquil House, whose rooms entertained Thomas Edison and radio pioneer Reginald Fessenden. The Tranquil House also did a tour of duty as a barracks during World War II. The original Tranquil House is gone now, but the name lives on at a different loca-

tion. Today the Tranquil House Inn operates in downtown Manteo on The Waterfront. The Tranquil House is built in the style of 19th-century Outer Banks inns, but it has 21st-century conveniences, including an in-house, world-class restaurant, 1587.

In the late 1800s Roanoke Island served as a prominent port. Large boats from the Old Dominion Steamline of Norfolk, Virginia, made daily stops on the west end of the island at Skyco (between Manteo and Wanchese), while Manteo's Shallowbag Bay was a busy port for smaller boats. In 1906 Shallowbag Bay was dredged, allowing access to larger boats, such as the river steamer *Trenton*. For nearly 20 years, mail, freight, and passengers arrived daily on this vessel.

As new infrastructure tied the island to other areas, Roanoke Island became less remote. In 1928 the Washington Baum Bridge was completed, linking Roanoke Island to the Outer Banks beaches. Two years later the Wright Memorial Bridge was constructed to tie those beaches to Currituck from the north. New roads were built from Elizabeth City and Manteo, and as the automobile became more popular, boat usage declined somewhat. Today around 4,145 residents make their home on Roanoke Island

Fire ravaged the Manteo waterfront five times in the 20th century. The presence of oil storage tanks caused great problems when the town caught fire. All that was available to put out the early fires was an old-fashioned bucket brigade, with volunteers forming a line and handing buckets of water from one person to another. During the course of these five fires, various sections of town were destroyed, including the old Hotel Roanoke. The only mercantile building to survive all the fires is the little white building on Budleigh Street, where E. R. Midgett Insurance now operates. Adequate fire-fighting equipment, a modern water system, and brick construction were introduced to the town when rebuilding began in the 1930s.

Manteo continues to be the hub for Dare County's business. From 1983 through 1987, major renovations took place in the town as part of America's Quadricentennial. Fifteen hundred live oaks and flowering crape myrtle trees were planted on the island's main corridor along US 64. Buildings and streets were restored, bringing new glory to the town.

On July 13, 1984, Manteo entertained Princess Anne of England, North Carolina Gov. James B. Hunt Jr., and newsman Walter Cronkite as part of America's 400th Anniversary Celebration. A memorial stone on the waterfront commemorates the event.

Manteo today reflects its history. The downtown Manteo Waterfront complex featuring shops, restaurants, and private residences is built in old-style architecture. You can sit at outdoor picnic tables or benches along the docks or in one of the window-lined restaurants and view the *Elizabeth II* (see our Attractions chapter), which is berthed across the bay from the Manteo waterfront at Roanoke Island Festival Park. Reminders of Native American and English heritages are evident in many of the town's street names, including Ananias Dare, Wingina, Sir Walter Raleigh, Queen Elizabeth, Essex, and Uppowac. These streets of historic Manteo have a number of structures worth noting.

In Manteo proper on Budleigh Street, you'll find the English Tudor-style Pioneer Theatre, the oldest family-operated movie theater in the United States, which celebrated its 70th year in 2004 (see our Attractions chapter). Admission is only $5.00. The Theodore S. Meekins house on Sir Walter Raleigh Street that now operates as the White Doe Inn (see our Accommodations chapter) is one of Manteo's most elegant buildings. The basic structure of the house was built before 1900. Featuring long porches and bowed windows in its turrets, the white, three-storied inn is listed in the National Register of Historic Places. A reference for historic Manteo sites is *The Manteo Walking Tour,* available at the Manteo branch of the Dare County Library on US 64 or in local bookshops.

There are only about 1,050 residents in Manteo. The town continues to grow as it annexes outlying properties, and as far as new building, Manteo proper—the historic downtown area—is fairly well developed, with only a few select lots left. People are drawn to the charm, the quaintness, and the small-town atmosphere here. If there is any significant future growth to Manteo, which is currently home to five churches and four schools, expansion would be to the south, but that's very indefinite.

Wanchese

Wanchese, on the southern end of Roanoke Island, has a more isolated feel than Manteo. For years it has operated as a fishing port. Drive the streets and you'll see wooden houses, some built 80 to 100 years ago, that have been lovingly maintained. In many backyards you still find boats in various sizes and states of repair, linking their owners with the ever-important sea and sounds.

Many old seagoing vessels fill Wanchese Harbor, living out their last days in a place generations of fishermen have used as a regular point of departure. While time will always bring change in the fishing industry—change in species, seafood quantities, boat styles, and government regulations—in Wanchese today, you can track family occupations established long ago when mariners navigated solely by the stars. Still living are at least three or four generations of anglers—men and women alike—from families who have at one time or another called Wanchese home. The Tilletts, Baums, and Etheridges, names you'll notice a lot on the Outer Banks, are just a few. Some have crossed over from commercial fishing to become sport fishermen, and many work as boat builders.

Today, as many as 50 fishing trawlers from up and down the East Coast use Wanchese Harbor, as do hundreds of smaller commercial and sportfishing boats. From the village several seafood companies ship fish all over the country. Most seafood caught in Dare County goes through Wanchese and around 24 million pounds are landed in Wanchese annually. Boats fish North Carolina's offshore and inshore waters and depart Wanchese Harbor to fish off New England in the winter. On the east side of the harbor is the state-owned Wanchese Seafood Industrial Park, where seafood and marine-related industries are based (see our Attractions chapter). The park features boat-maintenance facilities, seafood plants, boatbuilders, and state fisheries operations.

Wanchese has an estimated population of 1,527 residents. An average of only three to four homes and/or buildable lots becomes available annually. There is plenty of undeveloped, buildable land in Wanchese, but it is privately owned.

Boatbuilding

A description of Roanoke Island would be incomplete without a nod to a very special livelihood shared by many native islanders. Boatbuilding was and continues to be a major part of life on Roanoke Island. From the small bateau put together in a backyard shed to the 72-foot yachts constructed at major boatbuilding operations, Manteo and Wanchese share in this rich heritage.

In 1998 the North Carolina Maritime Museum opened in the old George Washington Creef Boathouse on the Manteo waterfront as a tribute to the area's boatbuilding heritage. Here, you can watch old crafts being restored and view a variety of boat exhibits.

George and Benjamin Creef operated the facility as the Manteo Machine Shop and Railways in the 19th century. The shop was built in 1884. Boats were hauled out of the water and serviced there. At this location "Uncle Wash" Creef built the first shad boat, now documented as one of the most important fishing vessels of its time

because its design allowed it to effectively work nets and carry weight and still ride well in the water. Winters of the past found many fishermen holed up in shops crafting juniper vessels that took them farther from home than many had ever imagined. The Sharpie and the Shallowbag Shad Boat were designed and built in Manteo.

Boats are still built on Roanoke Island—huge, sleek vessels with their hulls buffed to a sun-splintering shine. Each spring these brand-new, 50-foot-plus boats emerge from private building barns and are tugged slowly down the highway to Wanchese to be put in the water for the first time. On board the boat, members of the construction crew carefully lift power lines as their vessel moves down the road, invariably delaying traffic. Smiles wreathe the faces of the crew: After six to eight months of hammering, sanding, and painting, they are ready to christen the fruit of their labor. It is a tense time, too, for no one really relaxes until everyone sees that the boat sits and moves "just right" in the water.

HATTERAS ISLAND

The sea is a strong tonic that humans often crave at the expense of security. Nowhere is this desire more obvious than on this little stretch of sand that juts precariously out into the Atlantic Ocean just off North Carolina's coast. Hatteras Island residents accept the stresses of living with a seasonal economy, storm damage, and cultural isolation as part of life in the shifting sand. The decision to live on the threshold of land and sea forges an intimate relationship with nature.

South of Nags Head and north of Ocracoke Island, Hatteras Island measures 60 miles from Oregon Inlet to Hatteras Inlet and consists of seven small towns with a total year-round population of about 4,000 residents. Running north to south they are Rodanthe, Waves, Salvo, Avon, Buxton, Frisco, and Hatteras Village. You can enter the island from the north by car via NC 12 after crossing the Herbert C. Bonner Bridge or from the south by ferry via Ocracoke Island. As with other townships and islands of the Outer Banks, you can also reach the area by air—setting down on a small airstrip in Frisco—or by boat. (See our Getting Here, Getting Around and Fishing chapters for airfield, marina, and ferry information.)

Island Living, Economy, and Tourism

Overall, Hatteras Island's residents live and work supported mostly by tourism, fishing, real estate, teaching, and government employment. Because of the seasonal economy, weather-related economic setbacks, and lack of corporations and industries that hire mass amounts of people, it's not unusual for residents to have more than one job. Cleaning rental cottages on the side provides extra money, and you may find that your waiter during the summer months is a professional from another trade altogether. Necessity also provokes creativity, and many locals sell their carvings or paintings in local shops and galleries.

Families thrive despite typical inconveniences to be expected in village living on a remote island. They pattern their living styles accordingly. You won't find a Kmart on the island, but mail-order companies get their share of business. A sense of community is evident in the packed stands at the Cape Hatteras High School basketball games (even folks with no kids attend).

It's only been during recent years that Hatteras residents have left the island in large numbers during county-mandated hurricane evacuations. More nonnatives who now live here are less likely to see out a storm. Storm danger and damage has increased due to development and tighter living quarters.

Weather plays a regular role in Hatteras life. When the island is evacuated during a hurricane warning, it's not

unusual for the locals to lose a week's worth of income. This creates great financial hardship for businesses since their annual income is made primarily during the 12 weeks of summer. Even smaller storms cause delays when the roads flood.

Despite the imposing hold nature can cast over the barrier island, visitors flock here annually to enjoy its beauty and seclusion. Today there are enough conveniences, restaurants, and diversions within reach to entertain even sophisticated vacationers. The Cape Hatteras School, with help from the local arts council, brings in cultural events for residents. There are also several noteworthy art galleries on the island (see our Arts and Culture chapter).

History tells us, though, that even without these modern additions, folks would still come to relax Hatteras-style, away from the busier pace of the towns farther up the barrier islands to do a little crabbing, clamming, fishing, beach walking, bird-watching, or chatting with the anglers who relax at the docks. Many a modern-day adult vacationer has been coming to the Outer Banks since childhood. In fact, generations of families can call Hatteras Island their summer home.

The island has two obvious drawing cards: the sea and unique landscape. Some of the best windsurfing and surfing in North America can be done in the waters along Hatteras Island (see our Attractions and Water Sports chapters). Surfers from all over the East Coast come to Hatteras Island to surf the breakers, especially during strong nor'easters. Surfers look forward to hurricane season from June through November, when big northern swells can push wave heights to 8 feet or more. National surfing championships are held in Buxton (see our Annual Events chapter).

Hatteras Island is famous as an East Coast fishing hot spot. About 40 miles offshore are the Gulf Stream, a shelf current, and the Deep Western Boundary Current, all of which cross near the continental shelf's edge. The influence of this convergence is both positive and negative. These crossing currents spawned Diamond Shoals, creating the groundwork for danger but also supplying a rich habitat for sport fish (see our Natural Wonders chapter). A wide variety of fish travel up the Gulf Stream, giving this area the reputation for being the "Billfish Capital of the World." World-record fish have been caught both offshore and in the surf at Cape Hatteras Point, where red drum and many other fish come to feed. Much of the tip of Hatteras is lined with marinas where recreational charter boats take visitors to inshore and offshore waters (see our Fishing chapter). Full-service tackle shops, staffed with knowledgeable Insiders, speckle the barrier island.

North of Rodanthe and just south of Oregon Inlet is Pea Island National Wildlife Refuge, where birding is popular and rewarding. A unique maritime forest lies farther south in Buxton, with a nature trail and informative signs (see our Attractions and Natural Wonders chapters for descriptions of both).

There are three National Park Service campgrounds on Hatteras Island (at Oregon Inlet, Frisco, and Cape Point) offering more laid-back and less expensive camping than the rest of the Outer Banks's camping facilities. Several private campgrounds also are established in the island communities (see our Camping chapter).

If nature hasn't sold you on Hatteras Island's wild, raw beauty, check out our Recreation chapter for those artificial amusements that can be enjoyed by the whole family.

Yesteryear and Today

Thousands of years ago, Native Americans settled on Hatteras Island and called it Croatan. Originally marked Cape S. John on 16th-century maps, the island has a history that is filled with diverse tales of Civil War battles, fabulous fishing, shipwrecks, and lifesaving efforts (see our History and Fishing chapters).

The residents of this barrier island, who could reach the outside world only by boat until the Bonner Bridge was built to span Oregon Inlet in 1963, were a people so isolated that their speech today still maintains the direct flavor of their ancestors. Need was the driving force behind livelihood choices. Everyone fished for food, and seafood was traded on the mainland for provisions and corn. Windmills provided the power to turn corn into flour. Commercial fishermen harvested whale oil, turtles, oysters, and even seaweed. And the island was once covered with roving livestock gobbling up protective vegetation.

The village of Kinnakeet, now Avon, was the heart of a thriving shipbuilding industry. Materials were gathered from the oak and cedar forests on the sound side of the island. The islanders built their homes there, in the woody hammocks, seeking safety from high waters and winds. Timbers also were used to fashion clipper ships. Kinnakeet was a base for a large fleet of small schooners, many of which were used to harvest oysters.

The Cape Hatteras Lighthouse in Buxton has towered over the island's low-lying terrain since 1870. Rising 208 feet, it is the tallest brick lighthouse in the nation (see our History and Attractions chapters). Within reach of the light cast by the tower are the treacherous and ever-changing Diamond Shoals, where hundreds of vessels met their demise. Lifesaving teams, at one time riding horse-drawn carts through the sand, saved thousands of seafarers' lives off these shores. Today, modern equipment

Cape Hatteras National Seashore was the first national seashore in the United States. Proposed in 1933 and authorized in 1937, it was not established until 1953 and was dedicated in 1958. The Seashore celebrated its 50th anniversary in 2003.

aids in navigation; but the Cape Hatteras Lighthouse still operates. The power of the sea, shuffling weather patterns, and changing inlets still cause captains to traverse the waters with care. The lighthouse, a pillar of security and hope for islanders, was moved from the water-torn edge of the shoreline slightly inland during 1999 to save it from toppling into the Atlantic.

Much of Hatteras Island is undeveloped National Park Service property. But scattered north to south along the coast are the seven villages, hugging what is loosely termed "Highway 12," a thin strip of blacktop often covered with sand and water. More often than not, it seems the children of Hatteras's old-timers stay or return to carry on family traditions in these villages. This may be why the flavor of the area has not changed too drastically over the years despite the influx of vacationers and outsiders looking for summer homes. Most of the people who move here are seeking just what the island presents: to live alongside the powerful sea within a small community where all of life bends to nature's will.

While 75 percent of Hatteras Island is National Park land, a limited number of lots and homes are available for purchase, and each village has a mix of low- to high-price choices. The addition of a reverse-osmosis water plant on the north end of the island breathed new life into the Rodanthe, Waves, and Salvo communities in the mid-1990s, allowing many additional parcels to be built upon. Residents formerly used electric-generated water pumps, but now they are able to maintain a steady water flow even when storms knock out the power. Avon, Buxton, Frisco, and Hatteras got their own reverse-osmosis water facility in 2000. Utility lines have been upgraded over the last few years, so power outages are not as frequent. Hatteras Island has some remaining real estate available, and its infrastructure is being expanded to accommodate new residents. An elementary school opened in Buxton Woods in August 2002.

Hatteras Island Communities

Rodanthe is Hatteras Island's northernmost village, situated about 12 miles from the northern tip of the island. Rodanthe blends seamlessly with Waves and Salvo to form what is sometimes referred to as the Tri-Village area. The three towns were once one, called Chicamacomico, but by the early 1900s they had separated into three individual villages. Of the three, Rodanthe has the most commercial offerings, including restaurants, an amusement park, gas stations, a shopping center, and tackle shops, but it is primarily a residential and vacation village. Rodanthe is home to the restored 1874 Chicamacomico Lifesaving Station, a historic tourist attraction that offers many activities. It also has a popular fishing pier.

Waves is a sleepy little·village of mostly vacation homes. It's hard to know when you are actually in Waves because there are no signs welcoming you. Surfers stole those so many times that the villagers finally gave up installing them. This village was known as South Rodanthe until 1939, when it got its own post office and a new name.

Salvo also has nebulous village boundaries. The locals know them, though, and that's all that matters. Salvo is vacation-oriented, although there aren't many commercial enterprises. Originally called Clark, this village was reportedly named for a salvo (simultaneous firing of cannon) it was given by Union soldiers during the Civil War. At the south end of the village is a National Park Service day-use area that's great for soundside picnicking, swimming, windsurfing, and kiteboarding.

Avon is about 10 miles south of Salvo, separated from the northern villages by a long, beautiful stretch of undeveloped National Park Service property. Avon was originally called Kinnakeet, a name that is still used by many old-timers. The name changed when the village got a post office in 1883. Avon has a wealth of vacation rental homes, hotels, and commercial businesses, including the island's only large chain grocery store and movie theater. It has many shops, restaurants, watersports rentals, and a fishing pier. A medical facility opened in 2001. One of the most well-known windsurfing spots in the world, Canadian Hole, is on the south end of Avon. Old Avon Village, on the west side of the island, offers a chance to see local life. Turn toward the sound at the stoplight to see the old cottages, fishing gear, boats, and villagers.

Buxton is at the widest part of the island, on a point of land that juts into the sea and is known as Cape Point. Buxton is the hub of Hatteras Island. Hotels, restaurants, shops, and small-town grocery stores line the highway. Tackle shops are abundant here because fishing at Cape Point is rightly famous, as is surfing. The black-and-white candy-striped Cape Hatteras Lighthouse is, of course, the most popular attraction here. Buxton Woods, a rare maritime forest, provides protection for the village. When Buxton got its post office in 1873, it was called simply The Cape. The name changed in 1882.

Frisco, the next town heading south, is the perfect place to get away from it all, with many vacation rental homes, a couple of art galleries, a pier, some shops and restaurants, and a Native American museum. But mostly it is the fishing, uncrowded beaches, and solitude that attract people to Frisco.

Hatteras Village, at the southernmost end of the island, is a picture-book fishing village and the ferry embarkation point for Ocracoke Island. When people say they're going to Hatteras, they mean the village, not the lighthouse, the cape, or the inlet. With its proximity to the Gulf Stream, Hatteras is a world-famous fishing locale, especially renowned for its bluefin tuna fishery in winter. Several marinas and charter fishing vessels call Hatteras Village home. The village has always had a quaint, homespun appeal,

with independently run restaurants and shops, small motels geared to anglers, and simple homes. Lately, however, Hatteras Village has seen the addition of upscale oceanfront homes, a fancy shopping complex, and the first chain hotel on the island, a Holiday Inn. The Graveyard of the Atlantic Museum, at the southernmost point of the village, opened in the spring of 2003.

OCRACOKE ISLAND

Insiders generally see Ocracoke as a tourist attraction during the warm months and romantic hideaway during the off-season, but this is a wonderful place to visit any time of the year. There's just no place like this quaint island with its pristine beaches and homey atmosphere. Nearly all development on the island surrounds Silver Lake in Ocracoke Village. The island is but a slender strip of sand, geographically much like the other Outer Banks islands. At its widest, the 16-mile-long island is only about 2 miles across, narrowing in some sections to a half-mile, where sound and sea are both visible from the two-lane road.

Getting Here

Access to Ocracoke Island is limited to sea and air. A free 45-minute ferry ride across the waters of Pamlico Sound transports islanders and visitors to the north end of Ocracoke from Hatteras Island. From the ferry terminal at the north end of the island, it's a 12-mile drive past undeveloped marshlands and dunes to Ocracoke Village. Two toll ferries connect the island with the mainland. The Cedar Island and Swan Quarter ferries, each a two-and-a-half-hour ride, cost $15 per car and arrive and depart from the heart of Ocracoke Village on the southern end of the island. A small airfield allows private planes to land just outside of the village (see our Getting Here, Getting Around chapter).

Island Economy and Tourism

Vacationers flock to Ocracoke during the warm months. Once a simple fishing village where islanders primarily lived off the sea, Ocracoke now operates as a vacation resort nine months out of the year. Tourism and traffic have changed the pace of this traditional fishing village, but the influx of visitors is necessary to maintain a healthy economy.

While many Ocracokers work at tourist-related businesses, year-round residents also are employed by the National Park Service, in the local school, in the building industry, or as commercial and recreational fishermen. The island's natural beauty and easy pace act as a magnet for artists, craftspeople, and writers.

Ocracoke Island offers a variety of sightseeing options that radiate from a core village atmosphere. You can ride bikes all over the island; it's best to explore the village by foot. You can park your vehicle after arriving on the island and not use it again until you leave. Make sure to stroll through the village, which surrounds Silver Lake. Wander the back roads: Specialty shops, galleries, and old island cottages are waiting to be discovered. Casually elegant restaurants and come-as-you-are eateries offer several meal choices, and friendly islanders will make recommendations, pointing you in the right direction (we outline more than a dozen spots in our Restaurants chapter).

Sailboats moor in the protected cove of Silver Lake, and charter and commercial fishing boats fill the downtown docks. You can book half- and full-day fishing excursions year-round. All accommodations—bed-and-breakfast inns, hotels, rental cottages, and private campgrounds—are close to the island's activity (see our Shopping, Fishing, and Accommodations chapters for details).

On the oceanside about halfway to the village from the Hatteras ferry dock, tents and camping trailers dot the secondary dunes. This popular National Park Service campground is open from late spring to early fall and requires advance reservations (see our Camping chapter). Our Attractions chapter describes the island's historic sites in detail. Make sure you take in the British Cemetery and the stately Ocracoke Inlet Lighthouse. Come January, the flow of visitors subsides, and islanders take a break from long, seven-day workweeks. Off-season tourists still can find accommodations.

Yesteryear and Today

As the story goes, when the first English explorers arrived at Ocracoke, the island was attached to Hatteras Island and jointly they bore the name of Croatan. Old maps indicate that Ocracoke may once have been connected to its southern neighbor, Portsmouth Island, and together the islands were called Wokokon.

Names are great history trackers, and while there are many stories as to how Ocracoke was named, two theories hold most popular. One is that the name descended from Wokokon, not a far stretch from the island's current moniker. The Wokokons, a tribe of Native Americans, journeyed to Ocracoke to feast on seafood, historians say. A survey map from 1657 showed the island as Wococock. A more fanciful story surrounds the legend of Blackbeard, the pirate. It is said that on the morning of Blackbeard's demise, his assassin impatiently awaited the dawn and the coming of his enemy, looking ashore to the island and yelling, "O Crow Cock Crow! O Crow Cock!" The legendary Blackbeard, aka Edward Teach, is only a small part of Ocracoke history. And while there are several shops and a museum dedicated to his legend, some Ocracokers today don't care to place importance on the 18th-century villain. His fleet included four boats and 400 crewmen, and by the mid-1700s he'd plundered at least 25 ships.

During Blackbeard's era the need to improve trade and navigation along the coast became clear to the colonists of North Carolina. The Colonial assembly passed an act in 1715 to establish Ocracoke Island as a port and to maintain pilots and their assistants who helped guide ships safely from sea to shore at "Ocacock Inlett."

It was not until 1730 that the pilots actually came. Their numbers increased over the years, and 33 years later these "squatters" were given 20 acres of land for themselves and their families. By November 1779 the Ocracoke Militia Company was established to protect the inlet (see our History chapter).

In the colonial era, Ocracoke initially was owned by several inhabitants. Three successions of absentee owners followed. The fourth owner, William Howard, bought the island in 1759 and at his death deeded all his land to his son, Wallace Howard. Land was sold by both Howards to various families on the island. Descendants of the Howards reside on the island today. A family graveyard is near Village Craftsmen on Howard Street, a craft and gift shop run by Philip Howard. Walking down Howard Street is a step back in time, with its stately live oaks, the Howard Cemetery, the oldest homes on Ocracoke Island, right down to the oyster shells embedded in the narrow and rutted dirt road.

Ocracoke history is filled with stories of shipwrecks and lost lives. The islanders worked to rescue stranded sea travelers and ships, housing and feeding survivors. Crabs and a wide variety of seafood kept their bellies full. While the island inhabitants were forced to witness the ocean's wrath as it smashed ships and stole human life, as if in repayment the sea also provided for them, though sometimes in the most unlikely way. Wrecked ships tossed up goods, including lumber, shoes, clothing, and bananas. But these island luxuries were small in contrast to the toll the sea took as the churning waters swallowed not only sailors but also women and children.

In response, the Ocracoke Inlet Lighthouse was constructed in 1823. The white-brick structure has stood in Ocracoke Village for 182 years, guiding sailors to safety and housing residents during hurricanes (see our Attractions chapter). Also, several lifesaving stations were built on the island in the late 1800s and early 1900s. In 1940 a Coast Guard station was erected. Coast Guardsmen continue to watch over Ocracoke waters today, but the island lost eight Coast Guard families within the last few years when federal budget cuts forced a closing of the island's Coast Guard building. Service is still provided around the clock by a rotating group of 10 men, but the families were relocated to Hatteras Island. Modern technology has helped diminish the number of wrecks these days. When accidents do occur, they usually involve offshore fishing vessels caught by foul weather.

The dredging of Cockle Creek and creation of Silver Lake Harbor in 1931 played a role in Ocracoke's development as host to a sizable fishing industry. Access to the village was improved, and fairly large boats could safely enter and dock at the village. In 1953 most of the island became part of the Cape Hatteras National Seashore, with the exception of the village. The first hard-surfaced road was constructed four years later, connecting the village to a spot near Hatteras Inlet. These changes came during a decline in the fishing industry.

Though tourism replaced fishing as Ocracoke's main source of income, islanders continue to ply the sea for food, fun, and livelihoods. Two fish houses operate throughout the year, and a variety of species including Spanish and king mackerel, bluefish, red drum, cobia, amberjack, tuna, and billfish are caught in sound, inlet, and ocean waters.

Gas and water shortages in the 1970s and 1980s caused a decline in Ocracoke's boating traffic. Gas shortages were, of course, widespread, but water shortages were specific to Ocracoke Island. At that time, the only freshwater sources were individual wells and cisterns. With increased tourism and more demand placed upon wells, so much water was drawn that saltwater intrusion resulted. The ensuing severe water restrictions limited personal use to specific times of the day and forbade any outside use. Therefore, no water was available at the boat docks.

The water district has since constructed a water desalination plant, and now the island has enough fresh water for locals, tourists, and boaters. As on any island, electrical outages are not uncommon. Many local businesses operate their own electrical generators, and a municipal generator provides power in the event of extended outages due to storms. The generator is used in the event that an outage lasts more than four hours.

The year-round population of Ocracoke has not changed dramatically since 1850. Today about 750 people call Ocracoke Island home. Children in grades K–12 attend classes at the Ocracoke School. Community concerns are aired at the Ocracoke Community Center, where the Ocracoke Civic and Business Association meets. Welcome progress to the barrier island includes the addition of several vegetable stands, and the once totally isolated community supports two grocery stores and a hardware store.

Ocracoke Island's real estate market is busy. Even though a recent revaluation brought about tax increases of 200 to 300 percent for some property owners, the limited amount of property available is in high demand. The few available lots are mostly inland; it's rare to find a waterfront lot for sale. Only one to two canalfront lots sell per year. The island's beauty and isolation will always be a major drawing card. Situated on the eastern flyway of migrating land and waterbirds, Ocracoke is a birder's paradise, with brown pelicans flying in formation over the waves, sandpipers leaving thin footprints in the sand, herons gracing the salt marsh, and warblers, grosbeaks, and cardinals adorning the trees. Live oaks lend majesty and a sense of strength to the fragile isle.

Famous for its legendary wild ponies, Ocracoke has 180 fenced-in acres set aside for the small herd to roam, and visitors to the island can see a group of them at a special lookout midway down NC 12. The National Park Service rotates four ponies at a time from the range to a pen to let admirers get a close-up view (see our Attractions chapter).

GETTING HERE, GETTING AROUND

In the not-so-distant past, travel to the Outer Banks was an ordeal. Before the bridges were built, many visitors reached these barrier islands by ferry from Elizabeth City, and some people with four-wheel drive vehicles drove down the beach from Virginia. Thankfully, we now have two bridge access points, one in Kitty Hawk, used most by travelers from the north, and one from Roanoke Island to Nags Head, used most by visitors from the south and west. North Carolina's Department of Transportation has spent considerable time and money improving state routes, making it increasingly easier to get to the bridges.

Another way to get to the Outer Banks is via long ferry rides from the North Carolina mainland to Ocracoke Island. In fact, ferry travel is still the only way to reach Ocracoke Island—outside of private motorboat or private plane—and no change is foreseeable.

But other than the state-run ferries to Ocracoke, there is no public transportation to the Outer Banks. The nearest Amtrak station is in Newport News, Virginia, and the nearest bus stations are in Elizabeth City, North Carolina, and Norfolk, Virginia. The nearest commercial airport is in Norfolk. Once you arrive by bus, train, or plane, however, you must either rent a car and drive to the Outer Banks or hire a private plane or shuttle service.

This chapter outlines the best routes for getting here by land, sea, and sky. Once you arrive, however, know that you will need some form of transportation—a motorcycle, a car, a bicycle, a scooter, or at least enough money for a cab—if you plan to venture around a bit. Don't even think of complaining about the lack of public bus transportation. Instead, while you're still unwinding from your trip, venture on down to the beach. Remove your shoes, take off your socks, and walk in the tideline. Now, are you really concerned about bus transportation? If so, you haven't walked far enough.

GETTING HERE
By Land

You can't get to any islands without spanning water, and thankfully we have several bridges. In a state of emergency, such as a hurricane evacuation, our bridges are the only ways off the island. During such mass exits, local officials sometimes close the bridges to incoming traffic and use all the lanes to expedite evacuation. In peak travel times (summer weekends), the bridges, especially the Wright Memorial Bridge, bottleneck, so drive cautiously.

ARRIVING FROM THE NORTH: TO THE WRIGHT MEMORIAL BRIDGE

Since so many of our visitors are from Pennsylvania, New York, New Jersey, Connecticut, and Washington, D.C., we begin this section with directions from Richmond, Virginia, which from the north can be reached on Interstate 95 South. If you're coming from north of the Outer Banks but south of Richmond, read through the directions and select the route nearest your location.

From Richmond, follow Interstate 64 East to Interstate 664 East at Hampton/Newport News and take the Monitor-Merrimac Bridge/Tunnel across the James River to I-64. The Virginia Highway 168 Bypass allows you to skirt the traffic lights and congestion on Battlefield Boulevard in Chesapeake, thus easing your drive to and from the Outer Banks. From I-64, take exit 291B to VA 168 South. VA 168 becomes U.S. Highway 158 in North Carolina; don't worry, both names refer to the same road.

You now have two options for traveling on VA 168, but both get you to the same place. The new VA 168, linking I-64 in Chesapeake with US 158 to the Outer Banks, is known as the Chesapeake Expressway and is a faster, four-lane option, although there is a toll of $1.00 per axle to use it. The second choice is to take Battlefield Boulevard. Past Chesapeake on VA 168, it's a straight shot to the Wright Memorial Bridge, which crosses the Currituck Sound to Kitty Hawk on the Outer Banks. The drive from the Virginia/North Carolina border takes about an hour, though you may wish to stop at the many antiques shops, thrift stores, and produce stands. You'll pass Mel's Diner, a 1950s-style diner in Grandy that thrives on tourism and has a loyal local following as well. If you just can't wait for some Carolina barbecue, stop at Dixie Bar-B-Q Pit in Powells Point or Saul's Cafe in Harbinger. For good ol' Southern cookin' and great value, Pot's On 'N' Kitchen, about 1.5 miles north of the Wright Memorial Bridge, is an excellent choice.

Another option coming from the north is to take U.S. Highway 17 South from I-64 in Virginia. This span of highway flanks the Intracoastal Waterway through the aptly named Great Dismal Swamp. Follow US 17 South to South Mills, where you take North Carolina Highway 343 to Camden, following signs to US 158 and the Outer Banks.

ARRIVING FROM THE WEST: TO THE WASHINGTON BAUM BRIDGE

From I-95 in North Carolina, take U.S. Highway 64 East toward Rocky Mount, passing through Williamston, Jamesville, Plymouth, Creswell, Columbia, over the Alligator River, and through East Lake and Manns Harbor to Roanoke Island.

The bridge over the Alligator River, part of the Intracoastal Waterway, is an old-fashioned drawbridge, opened as needed by an on-site bridge tender. If you're lucky enough to get caught by a bridge opening, get out of the car and enjoy the unique vantage of peering over the railings into the water.

It is a sparse area with few stops between Plymouth and the Outer Banks, so fuel up before you leave either Williamston (approximately 1 hour and 45 minutes from Manteo) or Plymouth, especially if you're traveling at night. If you have to pull off the road, do so carefully and choose a wide shoulder if possible. In areas where canals alternate sides of the road, pull off on the side without a canal. The State Department of Transportation installed guardrails alongside the canals to make travel on this road safer.

Along this route watch for deer, black bears, red wolves, and a wide variety of birds. You'll spot an occasional blue heron wading in the roadside creeks. The state adorns the byways with an abundance of colorful poppies and other wildflowers. It's tempting to pick the lush beauties, but it's illegal.

Continuing east on US 64, you'll cross the William B. Umstead Bridge, or as locals call it, the Manns Harbor Bridge, to Roanoke Island. The Roanoke Island Visitor Center at Fort Raleigh is the first information center from this direction. (See the section on visitor centers later in this chapter.) Momentarily, you'll pass through

The bridge spanning Croatan Sound is officially named the Virginia Dare Memorial Bridge, but it's also known as the Croatan Sound Bridge. Insiders call it "The New Bridge." All three names are recognized, but not by everyone. You may have to ask for it by three different names before you get a response.

the quaint town of Manteo, which cele-brated its centennial in 1999.

In the summer of 2002, a bridge to the mainland opened. The Virginia Dare Memorial Bridge (known as "The New Bridge" to locals) stretches from the mainland at Manns Harbor to the Manteo-Nags Head Causeway, completely bypass-ing Roanoke Island. This 5.2-mile bridge, the longest in the state, shaves 20 min-utes or so from the trip to the beaches because it avoids the two-lane bottleneck through Manteo. An Outer Banks Visitors Bureau welcome center and rest area at the bridge's eastern terminus opened in the summer of 2002. However, the old Manns Harbor Bridge remains open and should be used if you want to visit the attractions, restaurants, and shops of Roanoke Island and Manteo.

Once through Manteo, if you wish to go to the fishing village of Wanchese, turn right at the junction of US 64 and North Carolina Highway 345 (referred to by locals as Midway). For Outer Banks beaches, Cape Hatteras, Nags Head, and points north, veer left after passing through Man-teo, remaining on US 64. Overhead signs make getting lost unlikely, but if you find yourself off your intended route, blame it on the scenery and turn back. You can't get too lost here on these Islands and peninsu-las! US 64 will take you across the Manteo-Nags Head Causeway and the Washington Baum Bridge.

ARRIVING FROM THE WEST: TO THE WRIGHT MEMORIAL BRIDGE

Backtrack to Williamston for an alternate route to the Outer Banks. Instead of trav-eling on US 64 along the southern route, you can choose to take US 17 to Elizabeth City. Both routes take about the same traveling time. From Elizabeth City, follow signs on US 158 to Nags Head and Man-teo, and arrive on the island from the north, crossing the Wright Memorial Bridge. US 17 seems to be the route pre-ferred by most visiting Virginians.

ARRIVING FROM THE SOUTH: TO THE OCRACOKE FERRIES

From points south, take I-95 North to Rocky Mount, North Carolina, then US 64 East to Williamston, following the direc-tions given earlier for arriving from the west. For an alternate southern route, fol-low the coastline north to Morehead City and Cedar Island, where you board a toll ferry to Ocracoke Island. Another option is to take US 17 North from Wilmington, North Carolina, through Jacksonville and New Bern to Washington. From Washing-ton, take U.S. Highway 264 East to Swan Quarter and follow signs to the Swan Quarter toll ferry, which brings you to Ocracoke Island. The route goes through the Swan Quarter National Wildlife Refuge, with gracious old cedars lining the way. From Ocracoke, follow North Car-olina Highway 12 to the Ocracoke-Hatteras ferry for passage to Hatteras Island and points north. For ferry schedules and fur-ther information, see the Ferries section of this chapter.

CROSSING THE WRIGHT MEMORIAL BRIDGE

No matter which route you choose, the destination is well worth the journey. Because the Wright Memorial Bridge is the main thoroughfare to and from the Outer Banks, bear in mind that summer season peak travel time (going to the island) is from noon to 6:00 P.M. on Saturday and Sunday. This is rush-hour traffic, Outer Banks style. Peak travel time leaving the island is from about 8:00 A.M. to noon on the same days. Delays are possible from

The Bypass (US 158) and the Beach Road (NC 12) are marked by mileposts that originate at the Wright Memorial Bridge in Kitty Hawk and continue through MP 21 in South Nags Head. An address that reads "MP 7, Beach Road, Kill Devil Hills" is located 7 miles south of the Wright Memorial Bridge on NC 12.

i **Cell phone service is nonexistent or sporadic in certain areas of the Outer Banks. If you must get in touch with someone (or vice versa), be sure that you have a land-line phone number.**

Memorial Day to Labor Day; for your convenience, travel advisories are posted on a flashing sign at the bridge.

Once you cross the bridge into Kitty Hawk, you can't miss the bigger-than-life signs that lead you to your destinations. To get to Southern Shores, Duck, Sanderling, Corolla, or Carova, turn left on NC 12 and head north. For destinations south of Kitty Hawk, continue on US 158 to Kill Devil Hills and Nags Head. Just past 16 miles south of the bridge, the road veers right toward Roanoke Island and Manteo and branches left toward Oregon Inlet and the Cape Hatteras National Seashore. Follow NC 12 on Hatteras Island to the communities of Rodanthe, Waves, Salvo, Avon, Buxton, Frisco, and Hatteras. In Hatteras Village, a ferry provides free transport to Ocracoke Island.

At the junction of US 158 and NC 12 in Kitty Hawk is the Aycock Brown Welcome Center, which offers a wealth of information to visitors. Another great information stop is the Outer Banks Chamber of Commerce, located on Ocean Bay Boulevard about 1 block west of US 158 in Kill Devil Hills.

CROSSING THE WASHINGTON BAUM BRIDGE

The Washington Baum Bridge from Roanoke Island leads to South Nags Head, where you can choose to travel north toward Nags Head, Kill Devil Hills, Kitty Hawk, Duck, and Corolla, or south to Hatteras Island and Ocracoke Island. The Cape Hatteras turnoff is on the right, about a mile from the bridge's eastern terminus. At this intersection—referred to as Whalebone Junction—you bear left onto US 158 in Nags Head or go straight to connect with the Beach Road (NC 12),

either of which takes you north from Nags Head through Kitty Hawk. (Note that South Nags Head is accessed in this area via Old Nags Head Road.) A right turn at Whalebone Junction puts you on NC 12 toward Bodie Island, the Oregon Inlet Fishing Center, and points south. If you continue on NC 12 across the Herbert C. Bonner Bridge onto Hatteras Island, the road goes through Rodanthe, Waves, Salvo, Avon, Buxton, Frisco, and Hatteras Village. A ferry in Hatteras Village goes to Ocracoke Island.

By Air

AIRPORTS AND AIRSTRIPS

Note to pilots: Several Outer Banks airstrips are unattended, as explained in this section. Call the State Division of Aviation at (919) 571-4904 for information not covered in the following entries.

Dare County Regional Airport
Airport Road, Roanoke Island
(252) 473-2600
If you'd like to fly your own plane to the Outer Banks, this is the airport to call. Dare County Regional Airport's two runways measure 3,300 feet and 4,300 feet, and both are lighted. Jet-A and 100 LL fuels are available, as is unleaded auto fuel. Operating hours are 8:00 A.M. to 7:00 P.M. daily. This airport has a terminal VOR, DME, and NDB, plus automated weather updates through AWOS, which you can access at radio frequency 128.275 or by calling (252) 473-2826.

Flightline Aviation (800-916-3226) and Outer Banks Airways (252-441-7677) are local carriers offering charter service to and from Dare County Regional Airport. Car rentals are available at the airport; call in advance.

First Flight Airstrip
Wright Brothers National Memorial
US 158, MP 8, Kill Devil Hills
(252) 473-2111

Every pilot visiting the Outer Banks should sign in at least once at this historic location. At First Flight your stay is limited to 24 hours. This unattended 3,000-foot strip is maintained by the National Park Service. Since there are no lights, takeoffs and landings are permitted during daylight hours only. Reservations are not necessary, and a sign-up book is on premises. No fuel is available. Bring your own tie-downs.

Billy Mitchell Airstrip
NC 12, Frisco
(252) 995-3735

Also known as Hatteras Mitchell Field, this Hatteras Island airport is on National Park Service land. The airport is unattended; call the telephone number listed above for an automated weather observation report. Billy Mitchell Airstrip's unlighted runway is approximately 3,000 feet long, and fuel is not available. There is a parking lot. A shelter on the premises has a phone and toilets.

Ocracoke Island Airstrip
NC 12, Ocracoke Island
(252) 928-9901

Another airstrip maintained by the National Park Service, this unattended facility has a 3,000-foot-long runway and no lights. There is a parking lot and a pay telephone. The runway has brush and 25-foot sand dunes at either end. Listen to the weather radio or call for weather updates.

Norfolk International Airport
2200 Norview Avenue, Norfolk, VA
(757) 857-3351
www.norfolkairport.com

Open 24 hours a day, Norfolk International Airport offers air service on American, Continental, Delta, Northwest, United, USAirways, and Southwest Airlines. Major rental car companies have offices at the airport. For main passenger information, call the airport. For private charter information, see the following entries.

AIR SERVICE

Burris Flying Service
Hatteras Village
(252) 986-2679

Burris Flying Service, operating from the Billy Mitchell Airport, offers air tours and aerial photography for the Outer Banks.

Flight Line Aviation
(252) 338-5347, (800) 916-3226
www.flightlineair.com

You can get charter service to the Outer Banks or eastern North Carolina from almost anywhere with Flight Line Aviation. Flight Line operates to Manteo, First Flight, Pine Island, Hatteras, Ocracoke, or any local airport.

Outer Banks Airways
1714 Bay Drive, Kill Devil Hills
(252) 441-7677

Outer Banks Airways offers charter service from just about anywhere you want to fly. Most of its passengers choose to land at Dare County Regional Airport, First Flight Airstrip in Kill Devil Hills, or the private Pine Island airstrip between Duck and Corolla.

Outer Banks Airways is affiliated with Kitty Hawk Aero Tours, which offers sightseeing flights (see our Attractions chapter for information on advance reservations).

Pelican Airways
Ocracoke Island
(252) 928-1661

Pelican Airways offers flights to and from Ocracoke as well as services all along the East Coast. It also offers sightseeing air tours and instrument flight lessons.

By Water

The best way to beat the traffic—and to see some incredible scenery while you're at it—is to arrive at the Outer Banks by boat. Only very experienced boaters should attempt to navigate these tricky waters, and only with proper equipment in the best weather. Discuss your trip with a local sailor or captain while making your plans, and be sure to pick up a copy of the Mid-Atlantic Waterway Guide; it provides the most detailed information available about the area's waterways. Current chart numbers from the Intracoastal Waterway (ICW) to Manteo on Roanoke Island are 12204 and 12205. Chart 12204 is a large map of the North River, and chart 12205 is a strip map that includes both the Alligator and North Rivers. Both charts cover the inlet, although 12205 provides more detail.

FROM THE NORTH

If you're boating from points north, you can enter the ICW in Norfolk, Virginia. The trip from Norfolk to Manteo is about 80 nautical miles. In fair weather and with a fast boat, you can make it to the Outer Banks in five to six hours; if you're sailing, you may wish to spend your first night at the Coinjock Marina. Be prepared for wind, chop, and shallow waters in the Albemarle Sound. As long as you remain within the ICW markers, you won't have to worry about depth.

Any of the following three routes lead you to the Outer Banks. One takes you from Norfolk, Virginia, across the Currituck Sound to Coinjock, North Carolina, the North River, and the Albemarle Sound. From the ICW mid-sound marker, head east and look for day markers leading to the waterfront town of Manteo on Roanoke Island.

An alternate route from Norfolk leads to Deep Creek, Virginia, through the Great Dismal Swamp to Lake Drummond, North Carolina. From there, travel through South Mills to the Pasquotank River, where the ICW—locally known as The Ditch—joins the Albemarle Sound. Refer to your charts for navigating across the Albemarle Sound to the Alligator River, and then travel either the Croatan Sound or the Roanoke Sound to Manteo.

The third—and probably the easiest— route takes you from the end of the North River into the Albemarle Sound. Look for marker number 173, then bear left and follow the day markers leading behind Powell's Point. The first marker you'll come to is number 4; from there look for number 2 and then MG (the middle-ground marker). From MG head nearly due south. Look for another number 2 day marker, which takes you from the north end of East Lake toward Manns Harbor Channel, where day markers lead to the Roanoke Island Channel. (All of these markers are noted on the charts.)

FROM THE SOUTH

If you are boating to the Outer Banks from the south, pick up the ICW between Beaufort and Morehead City, North Carolina, and follow it to the Neuse River. Take the ICW north from the Neuse River across the Pamlico River to Belhaven on the Pungo River. You may want to stop in Belhaven at the River Forest Manor, a country inn, restaurant, marina, and shipyard, where you can fuel up while touring the century-old Southern plantation mansion or getting a bite to eat in its historic restaurant. Sunday brunch alone is worth the trip. An alternative stop is the new Dowry Creek Marina, with slips and fuel. After you leave Belhaven, continue north on the ICW to the Alligator River, then travel east until you spot the Roanoke Sound day markers, which lead to Manteo on Roanoke Island.

If seas aren't rough, the fastest route from the south is to go through the Pamlico Sound from either the Pamlico or Neuse River. After you pass under the Manns Harbor Bridge, look for the Roanoke Sound day markers leading to Manteo.

ROANOKE ISLAND MARINAS

Manteo has several docks within walking distance to restaurants and attractions. Locations and amenities are as follows. Also see the Boating section of our Water Sports chapter.

Waterfront Marina
Manteo Historic District
(252) 473-3320
The Waterfront Marina provides public
docking facilities with water and power at
each slip. Charges are on a per-foot basis
for semiannual, annual, and transient
boaters. Call ahead or radio the dockmaster on your approach to the marina.
Laundry and shower facilities are available.
The marina's boardwalk extends along the
waterfront and is within walking distance
of shops, restaurants, and other diversions. In Manteo you'll find friendly merchants and interesting sights, and several
lovely inns offer a respite from your berth.
A brief stroll across the bridge takes you
to Roanoke Island Festival Park (see our
Attractions chapter for more information).

Pirate's Cove Marina
Roanoke Sound, between Manteo
and Nags Head
(252) 473-3906
www.fishpiratescove.com
Open year-round, Pirate's Cove can accommodate boats from 25 to 110 feet in 179
slips. Transients are welcome, and many
slips are rented year-round. Daily rates are
$1.80 per foot. Monthly rates are $24 per
foot. Call for off-season and annual rates,
as prices vary. Slip rental includes water
and electricity, showers, cable TV hookup,
and laundry facilities. Pirate's Cove offers
one courtesy car that boaters can use on a
limited basis to fetch supplies or other
necessities. Boaters can use the tennis
courts, pool, and other on-site facilities.

The on-site ship's store and restaurant
are open to the public, as is the fuel dock.
On the top deck of Hurricane Mo's Restaurant & Raw Bar, you can have a cold
drink and some steamed shrimp while
getting a bird's eye view of one of the
area's most beautiful sportfishing fleets.

Salty Dawg Marina
US 64/264, Manteo
(252) 473-3405
www.saltydawgmarina.com
This facility sports 55 slips, all with power

and water, plus a modern, air-conditioned
bathhouse. On-site is a ship's store, dry
dock, and repair facilities. You can fuel up
with either diesel or plus. Salty Dawg has
a lift to accommodate larger boats. If you
get into trouble out on the water, radio in
for Salty Dawg's commercial towing service. Salty Dawg monitors Channel 16, the
hailing and distress frequency on marine
radios. The marina is just minutes from
downtown Manteo and is within walking
distance of a laundromat, drugstore, grocery store, and several excellent restaurants. A courtesy car is available. The
marina is open every day year-round,
except Christmas week. Call ahead for
reservations on holidays.

Ferries

Landlubbers also can enjoy an Outer Banks
arrival by boat thanks to the North Carolina
Ferry System. One picturesque route is to
follow U.S. Highway 70 East from New Bern
to Havelock. Pick up North Carolina Highway 101, follow to North Carolina Highway
306, and then take the ferry to Bayview
near historic Bath. Follow North Carolina
Highway 99 to Belhaven, picking up US
264 to Swan Quarter. From here, you can
take North Carolina Highway 94 across
Lake Mattamuskeet, then US 64 to Manteo—or ride another ferry from Swan Quarter to Ocracoke Island. It sounds
complicated, but signs will guide you.

An alternate route is to take US 70
through Havelock to Beaufort. US 70 continues from Beaufort to Harkers Island, following the Core Sound to NC 12, where
the Cedar Island Ferry takes you to Ocracoke Island. The voyage across the Pamlico Sound is well worth the time it takes
to arrive in Ocracoke. Cross Ocracoke
Island from south to north via NC 12, and
pick up the Hatteras Island Ferry to the
upper Outer Banks.

Ferry passage is a good way to
reduce your driving time if you're heading
to the southern portion of the Outer
Banks. It also gives you a chance to

stretch and move around while still making progress. Unless you have your own boat or plane, ferry service is the only way to reach picturesque Ocracoke Island. The ferries transport cars to the island, although we suggest that you park your car after arriving on Ocracoke and get around on foot or by bike.

Following is information on the Outer Banks ferry services. Although it is rare to have a time change, you may wish to call ahead and verify departure times. You can get more information by writing to Director, Ferry Division, Morehead City, NC 28557, or by calling (800) BY FERRY. Truckers: For information about weight and size limitations, call the specific ferry location. The toll-free number is operable east of the Mississippi River only.

Hatteras Inlet (Ocracoke) Ferry

This free, state-run service links the islands of Hatteras and Ocracoke, across the Pamlico Sound. The ferries accommodate 30 vehicles—including cars and large camping/recreational vehicles—and run frequently during the summer to avoid excessive delays. The Hatteras ferry does not require reservations and the trip takes about 40 minutes. Public restrooms are at the Hatteras dock, and heads are on board. For more information, call (800) 368-8949 or (252) 986-2353.

Summer Schedule
May 2–October 30, 2006

Leave Hatteras	Leave Ocracoke
5:00 A.M.	5:00 A.M.
6:00 A.M.	6:00 A.M.
7:00 A.M.	7:00 A.M.
7:30 A.M.	8:00 A.M.
Then every 30 minutes until . . .	
7:00 P.M.	7:30 P.M.
8:00 P.M.	8:00 P.M.
9:00 P.M.	9:00 P.M.
10:00 P.M.	10:00 P.M.
11:00 P.M.	11:00 P.M.
Midnight	Midnight

Winter Schedule
January 3–May 1, 2006 and October 31, 2006–April 30, 2007

Ferries leave Hatteras and Ocracoke every hour on the hour from 5:00 A.M. to midnight. Additional departures may be scheduled as needed.

Swan Quarter and Cedar Island

Make a reservation to avoid possible delays in boarding the Ocracoke–Cedar Island toll ferry and the Ocracoke–Swan Quarter toll ferry. You can reserve space in person at the departure terminal or call the ferry location from which you're departing. For reservations from Ocracoke, call (800) 345-1665 or (252) 928-3841; from Cedar Island, call (800) 856-0343 or (252) 225-3551; and from Swan Quarter, call (800) 773-1094 or (252) 926-1111. Office hours are usually 6:00 A.M. to 6:00 P.M., but the offices stay open later during the summer.

Reservations may be made up to one year in advance of departure date and are not transferable. You must claim your reservation at least 30 minutes prior to departure time. Information on tolls and vehicle weight limits follows the schedules.

Ocracoke–Swan Quarter Toll Ferry

This 28-car ferry connects Swan Quarter in Hyde County on the mainland with Ocracoke Island, crossing Pamlico Sound in two and a half hours. The scenic trip provides a wonderfully relaxing break from driving. See Arriving from the South for directions to Swan Quarter.

Summer Schedule
May 23–September 4, 2006

Leave Ocracoke	Leave Swan Quarter
6:30 A.M.	7:00 A.M.
12:30 P.M.	9:30 A.M.
4:00 P.M.	4:00 P.M.

Winter Schedule
January 1–May 22, 2006 and
September 5, 2006–May 21, 2007

Leave Ocracoke	Leave Swan Quarter
6:30 A.M.	9:30 A.M.
12:30 P.M.	4:00 P.M.

One-way fares and rates are listed at the end of this section.

OCRACOKE–CEDAR ISLAND TOLL FERRY
This ferry is a popular link between Cedar Island and Ocracoke Island. It accommodates 50 cars and crosses in two hours and 15 minutes. Take along a good book, a snack, and enjoy the view. See Arriving from the South for directions to Cedar Island.

Summer Schedule
May 23–September 25, 2006

Leave Cedar Island	Leave Ocracoke
7:00 A.M.	7:00 A.M.
8:15 A.M.	
9:30 A.M.	9:30 A.M.
10:00 A.M.	10:45 A.M.
Noon	Noon
1:00 P.M.	—
1:45 P.M.	—
3:00 P.M.	3:00 P.M.
—	4:30 P.M.
6:00 P.M.	6:00 P.M.
8:30 P.M.	8:30 P.M.

Spring and Fall Schedules
April 11–May 22, 2006 and
September 26–November 6, 2006

Leave Cedar Island	Leave Ocracoke
7:00 A.M.	7:00 A.M.
9:30 A.M.	9:30 A.M.
Noon	Noon
3:00 P.M.	3:00 P.M.
6:00 P.M.	6:00 P.M.
8:30 P.M.	8:30 P.M.

Winter Schedule
January 1–April 10, 2006 and
November 7, 2006–April 2, 2007

Leave Cedar Island	Leave Ocracoke
7:00 A.M.	7:00 A.M.
10:00 A.M.	10:00 A.M.
1:00 P.M.	1:00 P.M.
4:00 P.M.	4:00 P.M.

Toll Ferry One-Way Fares
• Pedestrians, $1.00
• Bicycles and riders, $3.00
• Single vehicles or combinations 20 feet or less in length, $15.00
• Vehicles or combinations from 20 to 40 feet in length, $30.00
• All vehicles or combinations 40 to 65 feet in length, $45.00
• Motorcycles, $10.00

GETTING AROUND
By Auto

We've gotten you here; now we'll get you around.

Let's get the traffic report out of the way first. The number of travelers on our roads increases dramatically during the summer. Traffic more than triples from Memorial Day through Labor Day. We realize that visitors enrich our economy, and we welcome you—cars, trucks, SUVs, and all. If you're used to big-city driving, you'll find the summer traffic tolerable. Naturally, roads get very congested during hurricane evacuations, despite the advance warnings county authorities give (see the Waves and Weather: How to Stay Safe chapter for more). If you bear in mind the following tips, your drive should be a smooth one.

The northern route up NC 12 through Duck and Corolla can get bogged down on summer weekends and during weekday lunch and dinner hours. If the weather's bad, many more people shop rather than go to the beach, so expect heavier traffic when skies are gray. Allow an extra half-hour or so when traveling to the northern Outer Banks on summer weekends. You may want to call the various municipalities or radio stations to see when traffic is heaviest during holidays. And if you must travel during peak traffic hours, try not to lose your cool. Relax—you're at the beach! There are plenty of places to stop for food, drinks, and shopping, though you may also want to pack some snacks, especially if you have young children.

While we do have congested areas to deal with from time to time, we have a simple road layout that makes getting lost almost impossible. These barrier islands, including Roanoke Island to the west, have only three major roadways. US 158 crosses the Wright Memorial Bridge into Kitty Hawk and winds through the center of the island to Whalebone Junction in Nags Head. This five-lane highway (the center lane is for turning vehicles only) is also called the Bypass, Croatan Highway, or the Big Road. In this book, we will refer to it as the Bypass or US 158.

NC 12 runs along the beach, parallel to US 158. A two-lane road, it stretches from the southern border of the Currituck National Wildlife Refuge at the Villages at Ocean Hill development in Corolla to the ferry docks at Hatteras Island's southernmost tip. NC 12 picks up again on Ocracoke, spanning the length of the tiny island, ending in picturesque Ocracoke Village. NC 12 is also called Ocean Trail in Corolla, Duck Road in Duck and Southern Shores, Ocean Boulevard in part of Southern Shores, and either Virginia Dare Trail or the Beach Road from Kitty Hawk through Nags Head. In this book, we refer to it as NC 12 (or occasionally as the Beach Road, when talking about that stretch from Kitty Hawk through Nags Head).

On Roanoke Island, US 64/264 is also called US 64 or Main Highway. This stoplight-filled road begins at the Nags Head–Manteo Causeway and runs across the Washington Baum Bridge through Manteo, across the William B. Umstead Bridge, and through Manns Harbor on the mainland. School traffic clogs US 64/264 on weekday mornings and afternoons. On rainy days in summer, this road is extremely congested with visitors

When biking any of the paths in the area, be sure to wear proper safety gear. Sand blown along the pavement can cause your wheels to catch or skid suddenly and unexpectedly.

headed to Roanoke Island's attractions and shops. Some congestion has been alleviated by the Virginia Dare Memorial Bridge.

US 158 and NC 12 run mainly north and south. Smaller connector streets link seaside rental cottages to year-round neighborhoods west of the Bypass.

If you truly want to relax and spend your vacation days island-style, kick off your shoes and travel on foot. You can walk for miles down the beaches, collecting shells and wading. Plenty of restaurants and fishing piers run the length of the Outer Banks, so you're usually not far from food and drink. Most spots welcome casual diners. When walking the Beach Road, watch out for vehicles with projecting mirrors—the road is narrow. It is not the best choice for biking, except in Nags Head, where there is a bike path. You can easily explore Manteo on foot, and biking is a safe alternative in that town.

By Bike

The Outer Banks boasts several paved bike paths. Running the length of Roanoke Island is a 7-mile asphalt path, which has awakened the athlete in many locals, young and old, who are now regularly seen walking, riding bikes, and skating on the route. It's a wide, safe path that we are grateful to have.

An 11-mile bike path runs along NC 12 almost the entire length of the town of Nags Head. In South Nags Head, the path is concrete, and in the rest of the town it is asphalt. The town of Kill Devil Hills sports a scenic asphalt route along Colington Road, running down the National Park Service property past the Wright Brothers National Memorial. Kitty Hawk's bike path meanders through the maritime forest along Woods Road, off US 158 between the Wright Memorial Bridge and the Kitty Hawk Wal-Mart Shopping Center.

A great place to ride is through Southern Shores and Duck. A bike path extends the entire length of NC 12 in Southern Shores and Duck. Duck's path extends through town to just north of Sanderling. Call each township for specific rules on using the bike paths.

While pedaling these paths or biking anywhere else on the Outer Banks, please wear a helmet. You can rent bikes at several rental services, and many accommodations offer bikes and helmets as a courtesy (see our Recreation and Accommodations chapters). Watch out—the sand that blows on the road can get in your eyes as you pass the dunes and can be slippery when you brake. Follow the normal rules of the road that apply to cars, stopping at lights and stop signs and yielding to pedestrians. There is a lot of activity near the beach, so whether you're on a bike or in a car, watch out for that rolling beach ball—it is usually followed by a child.

Transportation for Hire

Even though you won't find any public transportation here, you do have a number of alternatives. Since demand for taxicabs and limousines can be great at times, make sure to call in advance.

Bayside Cab
(252) 480-1300, (252) 441-5488
On US 158 at MP 6, Bayside offers point-to-point service 24 hours a day.

Beach Cab
(252) 441-2500
The vans of Beach Cab offer 24-hour service and Norfolk International Airport pickups.

Coastal Cab Company
(252) 449-8787
Coastal Cab offers radio-dispatched 24-hour service on the Outer Banks. Service to airports in Norfolk and Raleigh is available with advance reservations. Credit cards are accepted for out-of-town trips.

The Connection
(252) 449-2777
www.calltheconnection.com
This shuttle service operates daily between Norfolk and the Outer Banks with door-to-door shared-ride and private service to Norfolk International Airport (other airports upon request) as well as Norfolk's bus and train stations. Full-size, air-conditioned passenger vans can accommodate groups,

families, bicycles, surfboards, sailboards, etc. Drivers are fully licensed and insured. Private towncars are also available. Reservations are recommended.

Historically Speaking's Outer Banks Tours for Motor Coaches
(252) 473-5783

Historically Speaking offers year-round step-on tour guiding and receptive tour services (lodging, meals, attractions) for bus groups, conferences, and conventions, featuring entertaining commentary on the natural and cultural history of Roanoke Island and the Outer Banks. Call for a tour consultation. Private evening programs offer traditional Outer Banks music and sea song sing-alongs as well as costumed living-history performances of Elizabethan music and culture from the time of Sir Walter Raleigh's Roanoke colonies (see our Attractions chapter).

Island Hopper Shuttle
(252) 995-6771

Island Hopper Shuttle serves Hatteras Island with transportation to and from Norfolk International Airport, plus courier service on weekdays to Nags Head and Manteo.

Island Limo
(252) 441-LIMO, (800) 828-LIMO

If it's a stretch limo you want, Island Limo's selection suits your every need. Island Limo provides transportation to and from Norfolk International Airport via private sedan and limousine year-round.

Outer Banks Suburban
(252) 305-5466

You'll spot Outer Banks Suburban on the Outer Banks in a 12-passenger super-stretch Suburban limo. Also offering a vintage Rolls Royce sedan, Outer Banks Suburban will pick you up anywhere on the Outer Banks from Corolla to Ocracoke. Call for reservations.

Car Rentals

Whether you need something to get around town in or something more substantial, like a four-wheel-drive vehicle, to really explore the island, you have a number of rental options.

Cars Only
- Dare County Regional Airport, on Roanoke Island, off Airport Road, (252) 473-2600
- B&R Rent-a-Car at R. D. Sawyer Motor Company, US 64 in Manteo, (252) 473-2141
- Enterprise Rent-a-Car in Kill Devil Hills and Manteo, (252) 480-1838, (800) 736-8222

Cars and Four-Wheel-Drive Vehicles
- Outer Banks Chrysler, Plymouth, Dodge, Jeep, Eagle, US 158 at MP 5 in Kill Devil Hills, (252) 441-1146
- U-SAVE Auto Rental, US 158, 1 mile north of the Wright Memorial Bridge in Point Harbor, (252) 491-8500, (800) 685-9938
- Cape Point Exxon in Buxton, (252) 995-5695

Beach Driving

Off-road access is possible on the Outer Banks but only in designated areas and at certain times of the year. Use of a four-wheel-drive (4WD) vehicle is mandatory. Check with each township for specific rules; some places even require a permit.

Generally, 4WDs are allowed on the beach in Kill Devil Hills and Nags Head from October 1 through April 30. However, permits are required in Nags Head. Southern Shores and Kitty Hawk prohibit driving on the beach at all times. As far north as Corolla and Carova in Currituck County, there are specified areas where you can drive on the beach. Hatteras Island operates under the guidance of the National Park Service (252-473-2111); call with any questions you have concerning off-road driving.

On Hatteras Island, driving is not allowed on the beach at Pea Island National Wildlife Refuge (the area from Rodanthe Pier north to Oregon Inlet), but farther south, there are access areas marked by a sign featuring a symbol for off-road vehicles where you can travel on the beach. Obviously beach driving is not allowed at access areas that have signs with an X through the symbol. It's a good idea to stop at one of the National Park Service visitor centers or campgrounds to chat with a ranger before taking to the beach on wheels. Rangers supply up-to-date information on unusual conditions, such as eroded beach areas, that could prove hazardous to you and your vehicle.

Some areas of Hatteras Island are open year-round for beach driving:

- From ramp 23 to ramp 34, the area that stretches from the south end of Salvo to the north side of Avon.
- The beach around Cape Point, which continues all the way to a Frisco Campground access. You can also enter the beach at Cape Point Campground and head north to the Point or south to Frisco.
- Hatteras Ferry dock to Hatteras Inlet.
- The north end of Hatteras Inlet, depending on how much beach front is available due to surge conditions.
- The south end of Ocracoke Island toward the village to the beach behind the airport.

These Hatteras Island areas are open to vehicular traffic on a seasonal basis:

- Ramp 20 to ramp 23, from Rodanthe to Salvo, closed from the end of May until the second week in September.
- Ramp 34 to ramp 38, the area in front of the village of Avon, closed from the end of May until the second week in September.

DRIVING RULES AND SAFETY TIPS

The maximum speed for beach driving is 25 mph, but even that can be too fast on a crowded day. The speed limit is strictly enforced by park rangers and local law officials. Where the sand is soft, you may have to drive slower than 25 mph.

Beach drivers follow the same rules that apply when driving on asphalt: Keep to the right, pass on the left, etc. All vehicles must be street-legal with valid plates, insurance, and inspection stickers, and driven by a licensed individual. Seat belts must be worn by anyone in the front seat. Standing is not allowed in any vehicle. If you are riding in the back of a pickup truck, you must sit on the bed, not on the side rail or wheel well. Jeep passengers must be seated and may not stand and hold onto the roll bar. No open containers of alcohol are allowed in vehicles.

Pedestrians have the right-of-way at all times on the beach, regardless of where they are in relation to your vehicle. Look out for children, pets, sunbathers, and anglers. Expect the unexpected. Often, the wind hampers hearing, so use caution when approaching pedestrians. If the wind is blowing away from them and toward you, they may not hear your approach.

When driving back to the road, please keep your eye on pedestrian traffic. The edge of the Beach Road grabs the wheels a bit and can pull you to one side or another abruptly. Maintain a wide berth for anyone walking near you.

And a caution to pedestrians: Wear light clothing at night if you intend to walk near car traffic. While most drivers respect driving safety rules, some really let their hair down at the beach. Pedestrians need to be as conscientious as drivers on both sand and roadways.

VEHICLE PREPARATION

Many, many drivers get stuck because they don't let air out of their tires before

Avoid parking on the pedestrian walkways that thread through the beach. A ticket will cost around $125, and you'll have to return to the Outer Banks if you want to challenge it.

driving on the beaches. The National Park Service says its rangers generally drive with 20 pounds of pressure in their tires. This applies to vehicles of any size, from large trucks to smaller sedans. Lowering the pressure also helps prevent the engine from overheating when traveling through soft sand. Rangers advise reinflating tires when returning to the paved roads.

Please don't block the beach ramps when you lock hubs or deflate tires. We suggest pulling well off to the side of the ramp or using the parking areas found at most vehicle accesses.

DRIVING ON SAND

Once on the beach, try to drive on the firm, wet sand below the high-tide line and if there are previously made tracks, follow them. Areas with no tracks may be avoided for good reason. Watch out for areas of the beach with shell-laden, reddish sand and depressions with a bit of standing water. These can be very soft.

RESTRICTED AREAS

You are prohibited from driving on, over, or in between the dunes for any reason at any time. The dunes and their fragile vegetation create our protective barrier and are extremely vital to the delicate ecology of animal and plant life.

Please obey all the area designations on the beaches. Many portions of the beach are roped off, allowing shorebirds and turtles to nest. These areas change throughout the seasons, so areas that were open in April could be closed in August. Through traffic can be curtailed by these closings, especially at high tide. Stay alert for changes, and respect the limitations. Violations can bring substantial fines.

When driving by the waterline, always drive behind surf anglers. You don't want to snap their nearly invisible monofilament fishing line or upset their fishing activity.

WELCOME AND VISITOR CENTERS

**Aycock Brown Welcome Center
at Kitty Hawk
US 158, MP 1½, Kitty Hawk
(252) 261-4644
www.outerbanks.org**
Constructed in the style of an old lifesaving station, this center is called "Outer Banks at a Glance" and includes several continuously state-of-the-art displays, a continuously rinning film, and a brochure gazebo. By combining computers, photography, video graphics, period music, and sound effects, the displays offer an entertaining overview of the Outer Banks, and well-informed local staff members are ready to answer questions. Named for a 1950s photographer who has since become a local legend, this building sits a mile east of the Wright Memorial Bridge at the juncture of US 158 and NC 12. The Outer Banks Visitors Bureau operates three such welcome centers.

Resources include area maps, tide charts, ferry schedules, and brochures. Free community newspapers such as The *Coast,* published by The *Virginian-Pilot,* and the locally published *North Beach Sun* offer features that highlight the area.

The center is open daily from 9:00 A.M. to 6:00 P.M. from Memorial Day through August and 9:00 A.M. to 5:30 P.M. daily from September through April. It is closed Thanksgiving Day, Christmas Day, and New Year's Day. The building and public restrooms are wheelchair accessible, and the picnic area is a welcome outdoor respite for those who have been riding a long time. Contact the Outer Banks Visitors Bureau at (877) 298-4373 for more information.

**Outer Banks Chamber of Commerce
101 Town Hall Drive, Kill Devil Hills
(252) 441-8144
www.outerbankschamber.com**
On the south side of Colington Road, near the corner of US 158 at MP 8, a wooden building with a covered porch houses the chamber of commerce in Kill Devil Hills.

This center offers free information that's helpful to both visitors and permanent residents. It's a clearinghouse for written and telephone inquiries, and the friendly staff give information on activities, accommodations, and annual events.

Mail inquiries to P.O. Box 1757, Kill Devil Hills, NC 27948. The center is open year-round Monday through Friday from 9:00 A.M. to 5:00 P.M.

Outer Banks Visitors Bureau
704 US 64/264, Manteo
(252) 473-2138, (800) 446-6262
www.outerbanks.org

The Outer Banks Visitors Bureau relocated in the summer of 2002 to a 10,000-square-foot facility near the eastern terminus of the new Croatan Sound Bridge. This visitors bureau houses both the Outer Banks Welcome Center and the bureau's administrative offices. The visitors bureau provides almost any Outer Banks information requested by visitors and residents, including a huge collection of brochures, maps, and promotional materials about area offerings. Staffers also can supply information on demographics and business opportunities on the Outer Banks. The center features a rest area, toilets, and an RV dump station.

The Outer Banks Visitors Bureau is open year-round, 9:00 A.M. to 5:30 P.M. every day.

Nags Head Visitor Center at Whalebone
Whalebone Junction, Nags Head
(252) 441-6644

Operated by the Outer Banks Visitors Bureau, this welcome center is just south of the Whalebone Junction intersection on NC 12. It's open daily from 9:00 A.M. to 5:30 P.M. Memorial Day through Thanksgiving. It closes during January and February and reopens around March. The staff can answer all kinds of questions about southern destinations along the Outer Banks. Restrooms here are some of the few you'll find on this remote stretch of NC 12. The wooden structure also serves as a hunter contact station.

Pea Island Visitor Center
NC 12, Pea Island
(252) 987-2394

The Pea Island Visitor Center offers information, free public restrooms, and paved parking. This facility also houses wildlife exhibits and plenty of nature-related gifts, including an excellent assortment of wildlife books for all ages. In summer the center is open daily from 9:00 A.M. to 4:00 P.M. Off-season you can visit Thursday through Sunday from 9:00 A.M. to 4:00 P.M. It's closed Christmas Day. The center is staffed by volunteers, so the hours are occasionally modified. This area is an exciting stop for birders. A nature trail winds through the refuge, which is a haven for a wide variety of seasonal and year-round species. Pick up a free nature trail map at the center. Pea Island trails and beaches are open year-round during daylight hours.

Hatteras Island Visitor Center
Off NC 12, Buxton
(252) 995-4474

About 300 yards south of Old Lighthouse Road, past the Texaco station and Cape Sandwich Co., a large wooden sign welcomes visitors to the Cape Hatteras National Seashore and Cape Hatteras Lighthouse Historic District. Turn left toward the white painted fence from the north and follow the winding road past turtle ponds and marshes.

At the four-way intersection, turn left to get to the original lighthouse location, marked by a circle of granite stones etched with the names of 83 former lighthouse keepers. Or, at the four-way intersection, turn right and park the car in the parking area while exploring the lighthouse in its new location. The visitor center, called the Museum of the Sea, and the bookstore, both housed in the historic former keepers' quarters, were moved to this location before the lighthouse was moved. Restrooms are located here as well. If you continue past the parking area, you'll pass the picnic area, the Buxton Woods Nature Trail, the Cape Point Campground, and

When on Ocracoke Island, do yourself a favor and abandon your vehicle. Explore on foot and on bicycle to experience the true flavor of the island.

off-road vehicle ramps. The beach here is great for wading, sunbathing, surfing, and fishing. Four-wheel-drive vehicles are permitted along many sections of the beach year-round. Park rangers and volunteers are willing to answer questions in the visitor center and on the historic district grounds. Visitor center and bookstore hours are 9:00 A.M. to 6:00 P.M. Memorial Day through labor Day, and 9:00 A.M. to 5:00 P.M. the remainder of the year.

Ocracoke Island Visitor Center
Near the Cedar Island and Swan Quarter Ferry Docks, Ocracoke Island
(252) 928-4531
This visitor center at the southern end of NC 12 is full of information about Ocra-coke Island. It's located across from Silver Lake and operated by the National Park Service. If you arrive on the island from the Hatteras ferry, stay on the main road until you reach the T intersection at Silver Lake. Veer right and continue around the lake, counterclockwise, until you see the low brown building to the right. Parking is available at the visitor center.

Inside you'll find an information desk, ready staff, a small bookshop, and exhibits about Ocracoke. You can pick up maps of the winding back roads that make great bicycle paths and arrange to use the Park Service's docks.

The visitor center is open daily from 9:00 A.M. to 5:00 P.M. year-round. Rangers offer a variety of free summer programs through the center, including beach and sound hikes, pirate plays, bird-watching, night hikes, and history lectures. Check at the front desk for weekly schedules. Restrooms are available during peak season.

HISTORY 🏛

The narrow strand of barrier islands known as North Carolina's Outer Banks strings for more than 90 miles along the coast from Virginia's border south through Ocracoke and Portsmouth Islands. Bordered by bodies of brackish water on the west (known as "sounds") and by the Atlantic Ocean on the east, these fragile islands are accessible by plane, boat, or by driving over one of several bridges that provide links to the mainland. At the narrowest points, the islands are less than a half-mile wide, and in some areas, they extend out more than 20 miles east of the North Carolina mainland. Despite the apparent inaccessibility, the Outer Banks has been populated for thousands of years. Although today's year-round population barely tops 50,000 people, the area draws nearly seven million visitors each year. Many consider the banks a vacation paradise, owing to its wide sandy beaches, unspoiled natural terrain, abundant clean water, and relatively mild temperatures. Aside from the allure of the untamed beach, recreational activities include all water sports, great East Coast surfing, world-class sportfishing, and world-class golf. Since the towns of Kitty Hawk and Kill Devil Hills are home to the world's first powered flight, the area is a magnet for aviators and hang gliders. It's a place where adventure is still possible, where romance thrives, and where tide charts, seagulls, and wild ponies take precedence over convention and pretense.

IN THE BEGINNING

About 18,000 years ago, when continental glaciers held much of the world's ocean water, sea levels were almost 400 feet lower than they are today. North Carolina's coastline was 50 to 75 miles east of its present location. At that time, the region's principal rivers—the Neuse, Tar, Currituck, and Chowan—flowed across the continental shelf and emptied into the Atlantic Ocean.

When the sinking sea reached its lowest level and winds began carrying sediment from the west, a high ridge of sand dunes formed on the easternmost edge of the mainland. As glaciers began to melt, causing the sea level to rise, the land's vast forests and marshes slowly retreated from the rising waters. In their wake, they left huge river deltas pooled into sounds, and ultimately the Outer Banks was sculpted.

Sea levels continued rising over the next few thousand years, but the barrier islands that paralleled Carolina's coast remained above the tides. An unusual combination of winds, waves, and weather enabled the Outer Banks to maintain its elevation and to remain intact.

Today, the islands' eastern edges still move backward, responding to rising waters. The land builds up on the western side and creeps farther west, slowly narrowing the sound waters separating the barrier islands from the mainland.

Ocean levels rise about 1 foot every 100 years. The shoreline moves west about 50 to 200 feet per century along most of North Carolina's coast. Although these figures aren't startling, in areas of Hatteras Island the Atlantic reclaims about 14 feet of beach every year.

Geologists refer to the Outer Banks and similar land forms as "barrier islands" because they block high-energy ocean waves and storm surges, thus protecting the coastal mainland. Barrier islands are common to many parts of the world, and many share similar characteristics, yet no two systems are alike. Winds, weather, and waves form individual structures. Ever-shifting inlets from the sounds to sea can open new channels to the ocean one century, or close off primary passageways the next.

If you travel from one area of the Outer Banks to another, you'll soon realize that even along this small stretch of sand there is a vast variety of topography, flora, and temperatures (see our Natural Wonders chapter). Sixteenth-century paintings, drawings, and maps created by explorer Gov. John White reveal this same diversity. Even more important, they provide valuable documentation suggesting what the land was like, and when compared with today's geological maps, they illustrate the transformations that have occurred since the first English explorers arrived here.

EARLY EXPLORERS

Jutting far into the ocean near the warm, circulating waters of the Gulf Stream, the Outer Banks was the first North American land reached by English explorers. A group of colonists dispatched by Sir Walter Raleigh set up the first English settlement on North American soil in 1587. But Native Americans inhabited these barrier islands long before white men and women arrived.

Historians believe humans have been living in the area that now encompasses North Carolina for more than 10,000 years. Three thousand years ago, people came to the Outer Banks to hunt, fish, and live off the land. The Carolina Algonkian culture, a confederation of 75,000 people divided into distinct tribes, spread across 6,000 square miles of northeastern North Carolina.

Archaeologists believe that as many as 5,000 Native Americans may have inhabited the southern end of Hatteras Island from 1000 to 1700. These Native Americans, known as the Croatan, formed the only island kingdom of the Algonkians. Isolation provided protection and the exclusive use of the island's seemingly limitless resources. For more than 800 years, the Croatan lived comfortably in what is now known as Buxton Woods Maritime Forest at Cape Hatteras. Contact with Europeans proved fateful, however. Disease, famine, and cultural demise eliminated all traces of the Croatan by the 1770s.

Early ventures to America's Atlantic Seaboard proved dangerous and difficult for European explorers because of the high winds, seething surf, and shifting sandbars. In 1524 Giovanni da Verrazano, an Italian in the service of France, plied the waters off the Outer Banks in an unsuccessful search for the Northwest Passage. To Verrazano, the barrier islands looked like an isthmus and the sounds behind them an endless sea. According to historian David Stick, the explorer reported to the French king that these silvery salt waters must certainly be the "Oriental sea . . . the one without doubt which goes about the extremity of India, China, and Cathay." This misconception—that the Atlantic and Pacific Oceans were separated by only the skinny strip of sand we now call the Outer Banks—was held by some Europeans for more than 150 years.

About 60 years after Verrazano's visit, two English boats arrived along the Outer Banks, searching for a navigable inlet and a place to anchor away from the ocean. The captains, Philip Amadas and Arthur Barlowe, had been dispatched by Sir Walter Raleigh to explore the New World's coast. They were hoping to find a suitable site for an English settlement.

The explorers finally found an entrance through the islands, well north of Cape Hatteras, probably at the present-day Ginguite Creek in northern Kitty Hawk. Traversing the inlet, they sailed south through the sounds to Roanoke Island. There, they disembarked, met the natives, and marveled at the abundant wildlife and cedar trees. Of their successful expedition they told Raleigh about the riches they discovered and the kindness with which the Native Americans had received them.

During the next three years, at least 40 English ships visited the Outer Banks, more than 100 English soldiers spent almost a year on Roanoke Island, and Great Britain began to gain a foothold on the continent, much to the dismay of Spanish sailors and fortune-seekers.

LOST COLONISTS

In May of 1587 three English ships commanded by naturalist John White set sail for the Outer Banks with Sir Walter Raleigh's (thus Queen Elizabeth's) backing. Earlier explorers had dubbed the land "Virginia," in honor of the virgin queen Elizabeth. This first expedition to include women and children arrived at Roanoke Island on July 22. Colonists worked quickly to repair the cottages and military quarters left by the earlier English inhabitants. They rebuilt a fort the soldiers had abandoned on the north end of the island and made plans for a permanent settlement. Less than a month later, the first English child was born on American soil. Virginia Dare, granddaughter of Gov. John White, was born on August 18, a date still celebrated with feasts and festivities at Fort Raleigh.

One week after his granddaughter was baptized, John White left her and 110 other colonists on the Outer Banks while he returned to England for food, supplies, and additional recruits for the Roanoke Island colony. A war with Spain, meanwhile, broke out. When White was again ready to set sail for the Outer Banks the following spring, Queen Elizabeth refused to let any large ships leave England, except to engage in battles. White did not return to the American settlement until three years later, in 1590. By then, the settlement had disappeared.

The houses were destroyed or deserted. White's own sea chests had been dug from their shallow hiding places in the sand, broken open, and their contents raided. His daughter, granddaughter, and all the other English colonists had vanished—leaving no trace except for two cryptic carvings in the bark of Roanoke Island trees. "CRO" was scratched into the trunk of one tree near the bank of the Roanoke Sound. "CROATOAN" was etched into another, near the deteriorating fort. White thought these mysterious messages meant the settlers had fled south to live with the friendly Croatan Indians on Hatteras Island.

If you're interested in learning more about the history of the area, read *The Outer Banks of North Carolina* by David Stick (University of North Carolina Press, 1958).

The abandoned settlement site showed no signs of a struggle, no blood or human remains. Some believe that the colonists were killed by natives or carried away in a skirmish. Others think they were lost at sea, trying to sail home to England. Still others believe they skirted west across the sounds and began exploring the Carolina mainland. Or perhaps they headed to other areas of the Outer Banks, their footprints erased in the blowing sands.

Historians have debated the "Lost Colony's" fate for more than 400 years. Archaeologists continue to scour Roanoke Island's eastern edges, scouting for clues to "history's greatest mystery." Scholars from across the country gather to discuss the strange disappearance and still speculate where the colony may have traveled.

Erosion from Hurricane Emily in 1993 unearthed remnants of a Croatan Indian civilization in Buxton. Phelps's team uncovered artifacts that could prove that some members of Sir Walter Raleigh's "Lost Colony" migrated south to Hatteras Island from the Fort Raleigh area. The discovery of lead bullets, fragments of European pottery and brass, and copper coins indicate a mingling of the Croatan and English cultures.

Each summer, for more than 60 years, actors have re-created the unsolved mystery in America's longest-running outdoor drama, *The Lost Colony,* held at the settlement site in Waterside Theatre (see our Attractions chapter for more information about the play).

SHIPPING AND SETTLEMENT INTO THE 1700S

A century passed before English explorers again attempted to establish settlements along the Outer Banks. Throughout this time, however, European ships continued to explore the Atlantic Seaboard, searching for gold and conquerable land. Scores of these sailing vessels wrecked in storms and on dangerous shoals east of the barrier islands. Spanish mustangs, some say, swam ashore from sinking ships; descendants of these wild horses roam in the Currituck National Wildlife Refuge. Others are corralled in a National Park Service pen on Ocracoke Island.

Although the Outer Banks beaches had few permanent European settlers until the early 1700s, small colonies sprouted up across the Virginia coast and what is now the Carolina coast in the late 1600s. The barrier islands' inlets, with their ever-shifting sands, blocked deep-draft ships from sailing into safe harbors, but smaller vessels, fit for navigating the shallow sounds, transported goods from the Outer Banks to the mainland. People passed through these strips of sand long before settling here.

Ocracoke Inlet, between Ocracoke and Portsmouth Islands, was the busiest North Carolina waterway during much of the colonial period. The inlet was a vital yet delicate link in the trade network, and it was deeper than most other area egresses. Navigational improvements to the inlet began as early as 1715, when the British government made it an official port of entry. Pilothouses were established at Ocracoke to dock the small transport boats and to temporarily house goods headed inland. Commercial traffic increased along this Outer Banks waterway for many years.

Countless inlets from sea to sound have opened and closed since the barrier islands first formed, many due to hurricanes and nor'easters. More than two dozen inlets appear in the historical record and on maps dating from 1585, but only six inlets currently are open between Morehead City and the Virginia border. Studies of geographic formations and soil deposits indicate that almost 50 percent of the Outer Banks has been covered by inlets at some point. Attempts to control the inlets have proven costly and, for the most part, have failed. In the late spring of 2003, the long battle over constructing jetties in an attempt to stabilize Oregon Inlet ended when the U.S. Army Corps of Engineers and the Departments of the Interior and Commerce announced they would not proceed with construction. This news was met with much dismay by the sportfishing and commercial fishing industries that travel the unstable Oregon Inlet. Many lives have been lost along the most dangerous passageway to the sea on the East Coast, and many of the fleet felt the jetties were the only way to protect their livelihood. The inlet is the only access to the sea between Hampton Roads and Hatteras, a 200-mile distance.

The first land grant made by the British government in North Carolina was what is now Colington Island, a small spit of land surrounded by the Currituck, Albemarle, and Roanoke Sounds between Kill Devil Hills and the mainland. Sir John Colleton, for whom the island is named, set up a plantation on the island's sloping sand hills in 1664. His agents planted corn, built barns and houses, and carried cattle across by boat to graze on the scrubby marsh grasses. According to historians, Colleton's plantation was the beginning of the barrier islands' first permanent English settlement.

Over the next several decades, stockmen and farmers set up small grazing stocks and gardens on the sheltered sound side of the Outer Banks. Runaways, outlaws, and entrepreneurs also arrived in small numbers, stealing away in the isolated forests, living off the fresh fish and abundant waterfowl, and running high-priced hunting parties through the intricate bogs and creeks. Inhabitants also engaged in salvaging: When a shipwrecked vessel floated onto shore, local residents quickly appropriated the wood off the boat, loosened sails from the masts, and scavenged anything of value that was left on board. If victims were still struggling ashore, the locals helped them, even setting up makeshift hospitals in their humble homes.

The inaccessibility of the barrier islands and the wealth of goods that passed through the ports made the Outer Banks a prime target for plundering pirates. The most infamous of all high seas henchmen was Edward Teach, better known as Blackbeard, whose raucous crew set up shop on the south end of Ocracoke Island. After waylaying ships and stealing valuable cargo for more than two years, Blackbeard was captured and beheaded by a British naval captain in 1718, in a slough off Ocracoke.

Settlement and sparse development continued through the early 1700s, and by 1722 almost all of the Outer Banks was secured by private ownership. Large tracts of land, often in parcels with 2,000 acres or more, were deeded to noblemen, investors, and cattle ranchers. Some New England whalers also relocated to the barrier islands after British noblemen encouraged such industry. The whaling industry supplied blubber, oil, and bones to overseas markets. The huge marine mammals were harpooned offshore from boats or merely harvested on the sand after dying and drifting into the shallow surf.

Although small settlements and scores of fish camps were scattered from Hatteras Village almost to the Virginia line, Ocracoke and the next island south, Portsmouth, remained the most bustling areas of the Outer Banks through the middle of the 18th century. British officials enlisted government-paid pilots to operate transfer stations at Ocracoke Inlet and carry goods across the sounds to the mainland. A small town of sorts sprang up, as inhabitants finally established some steady occupation and were assured of regular wages.

In 1757 the barrier islands' first tavern opened amidst a sparse string of wooden warehouses and cottages on Portsmouth Island. About 11 years later, a minister made the first recorded religious visit to the Outer Banks when he baptized 27 children in the sea just south of the tavern. Today, a Methodist church and a few National Park Service-supervised cottages are all that remain on Portsmouth Island (see our Day Trips chapter).

WAR AND STATEHOOD

As much of a hindrance as the string of barrier islands and their surrounding shoals and sounds had been to shipping, the Outer Banks proved equally invaluable as a strategic outpost during the Revolutionary War.

Only local pilots in small sailing sloops could successfully navigate the shifting sands of the often unruly inlets that provided the sole passageways between the Atlantic Ocean and the North Carolina mainland. Consequently, big British warships could not anchor close enough to sabotage most North Carolina ports. Colonial crafts, instead, ferried much-needed supplies through Ocracoke Inlet and up inland rivers and small waterways to New England.

By the spring of 1776, British troops began threatening the pilots at Ocracoke, even boarding some of their small sloops and demanding to be taken inland, where they could better wage war. Colonial leaders then hired independent armed companies to defend the inlets, but they abandoned these small forces by autumn of the following year. British boats continued to beleaguer the Outer Banks. Ships crept close to the islands, enabling sailors to steal cattle and sheep. The redcoats anchored off Nags Head, going inland for freshwater and whatever supplies they could pilfer. They raided fishing villages, plundered small sailboats, and came ashore beneath the cloak of darkness. Ocracoke Inlet, especially, suffered under their persistent attacks.

In November 1779, North Carolina legislators formed an Ocracoke Militia Company and hired 25 local men as soldiers to defend their island. This newly armed force was issued regular pay and rations. Its members successfully protected the inlet and American supplies until fighting finally stopped in 1783, six years after America declared its independence.

About 1,000 permanent residents made their homes on the Outer Banks by the time North Carolina became a sovereign state in 1789. Most of these people sailed south from the Tidewater area of Virginia or west from the Carolina mainland. These settlers lived primarily in two-story wooden structures with an outdoor kitchen and privy. They dug gardens in the maritime forests, built crude fish camps on the ocean, and erected rough-hewn hunting blinds along the waterfowl-rich marshlands. After frequent storms crashed along their coasts, the residents continued to profit from the shipwrecks strewn along nearby shoals and shores.

LIGHTHOUSES ALONG THE OUTER BANKS

More than a dozen ships a day carried cargo and crew along Outer Banks waterways by the dawn of the 19th century. Schooners, sloops, sailboats, and new steamers all journeyed around the sounds and across the oceans, often dangerously close to the coast, in search of the ever-shifting and shoaling inlets.

At that time, waterways were the country's primary highways, and North Carolina's barrier islands were part of most eastern routes.

Hurricanes and nor'easters took many boats by surprise, ending their voyages and hundreds of lives. Alexander Hamilton dubbed the ocean off the barrier islands "the Graveyard of the Atlantic" because its shoals became the burying grounds for so many ships. In an attempt to help seamen navigate the treacherous shoals, the federal government authorized the Banks's first lighthouses in 1794: one at Cape Hatteras in the fishing village of Buxton and the other in Ocracoke's harbor, on a half-mile-long, 60-mile-wide pile of oyster shells dubbed Shell Castle Island. Shell Castle Lighthouse first illuminated the Atlantic in 1798. The Cape Hatteras beacon was finally erected in 1802. Two subsequent structures have sat on the same

Buxton spot, but the Shell Castle beacon has long since succumbed to the sea.

Ship captains complained that the early lighthouses were unreliable and too dim. Vessels continued to smash into the shoals. So in 1823 the federal government financed a 65-foot-high lighthouse on Ocracoke Island. Whitewashed with a glass tower set slightly askew on its top, it is the oldest lighthouse still standing in North Carolina.

Officials raised the Cape Hatteras tower to 150 feet in 1854. Five years later, two new Outer Banks beacons were built, at Cape Lookout and on Bodie Island, both of which were improved and rebuilt in later years.

On December 16, 1870, the third lighthouse at Cape Hatteras was illuminated. Standing 208 feet tall and using a multi-faceted lens to refract its beam across miles of sea, this spiral-striped structure is the tallest brick lighthouse in the world (see our and Attractions chapter for more information on the Hatteras Lighthouse).

Currituck Beach's redbrick beacon was the last major lighthouse to be built on the barrier island beaches. The 150-foot tower was completed in 1875. It watches over the Whalehead Club, near the western shores of Corolla. It is the only unpainted lighthouse on the Outer Banks.

In September 2004, a reproduction of the original Roanoke Marshes light was completed. It sits at the southern end of Queen Elizabeth Street in Manteo at the end of a 600-foot pier. The original light sat in Shallowbag Bay and was one of more than a dozen screw-pile lighthouses in North Carolina. These lights were designed like a common house, not a tower. The screw-pile lights were so named because screws were dug into the sand at the bottom of pilings supporting the home. A lighthouse keeper and his family lived in the house overlooking the water. The original Roanoke Marshes light (constructed in 1857) was lost when a barge moving the light capsized. None of the original North Carolina screw-pile lighthouses exist in their original locations.

SUMMER SETTLEMENTS

In the early 1800s malaria was a common affliction among mainland farmers and wealthy families along Carolina's coast. This feverous condition was thought to be caused by poisonous vapors escaping from the swamps on hot, humid afternoons. Physicians recommended escaping to the seaside for brisk breezes and salt air.

Nags Head was established as a resort destination when a Perquimans County planter bought 200 acres of ocean-to-sound land for 50 cents an acre in the early 1830s. Eight years later the Outer Banks's first hotel was built near what is now Jockey's Ridge State Park. Guests arrived at the 200-room Nags Head Hotel from across the sounds on steamships and spent weeks enjoying the beaches and the hotel's formal dining room, ballroom, tavern, bowling alleys, and casino.

In 1851 workers enlarged the hotel and added a mile-long track of rails so mule-pulled carts could ease vacationers' journeys to the ocean. The hotel burned down and was rebuilt; later, it was buried by sand. Jockey's Ridge, the East Coast's tallest dune, swallowed the two-story structure bit by bit. Hotel clerks offered discounts during the final years for those who didn't mind digging their way into their rooms.

Wealthier visitors who wanted to stay the whole summer built their own vacation cottages on the barrier islands' central plains and eventually on oceanfront property. Some farmers carried their entire households—cows, pigs, sheep, and all—across the sounds on small sailing sloops to summer at Nags Head. By 1849 a local visitor remarked that between 500 and 600 visitors bathed daily at the barrier island beach.

Meanwhile, locals lived in small wooden houses within the woods, selling fresh fish and vegetables to the new tourists, thereby earning extra income each summer.

CIVIL WAR SKIRMISHES

Outer Banks inlets again proved important military targets during the Civil War. Union and Confederate troops stationed armed ships at Hatteras and Ocracoke Inlets and set up early encampments. North Carolina crews captured Union boats filled with fruit, mahogany, salt, molasses, and coffee along the enigmatic inlets. Forts, too, were built along the barrier islands, although erosion and storms have long since erased all traces of such structures. Fort Oregon was constructed on the south side of Oregon Inlet; Fort Ocracoke on Beacon Island, inside Ocracoke Inlet. Fort Hatteras and Fort Clark were across from each other at Hatteras Inlet, by then the primary passageway between the ocean and sounds.

By the fall of 1861, however, Union forces overtook Hatteras Inlet and controlled most of the Outer Banks and lower sounds. Confederate troops still ruled Roanoke Island and the upper sounds. They built three small fortresses on the north end of their stronghold, reinforcing their position and to block all access through Croatan Sound.

Union troops also were massing. In January 1862 Gen. Ambrose Burnside led an 80-boat flotilla from Newport News to the Outer Banks. Water was so scarce on this trip that some soldiers resorted to drinking vinegar out of sheer thirst. Others died of typhoid before the battle even began. Nevertheless, on February 7 more than 11,500 members of the federal army amassed for a Roanoke Island attack (an overlook at Northwest Point on the northern end of the island commemorates this site today). At least 7,500 men raided the shores at Ashby's Harbor that night, near Roanoke Island's present-day Skyco. About 1,050 Confederate soldiers fought to maintain their foothold.

After hours of battle around what is now the Nags Head–Manteo Causeway, Confederate troops finally were forced to surrender. Union troops captured an estimated 2,675 of these Southerners. Federal forces held Roanoke Island, and most of the Outer Banks, for the rest of the Civil War.

A SETTLEMENT FOR FREED SLAVES

After Roanoke Island fell to the Union, Union leaders had to decide what to do with the slaves from the former Confederate camp. Gen. Benjamin F. Butler at Fortress Monroe set a precedent by declaring slaves as contraband. Word spread of this action, and black women and children began flocking to Union camps where they were allowed to settle peacefully. Once word reached the underground network of servants, abolitionists, and free blacks, the number of freedom-seeking individuals migrating to Dare and Currituck Counties increased. At the outbreak of the Civil War, only a few hundred slaves lived along the Outer Banks. But two months after falling to Union troops, Roanoke Island was filled with more than 1,000 runaway and recently freed slaves. Inhabitants of the colony worked as porters for Union officers and soldiers, and as cooks, teamsters, and woodcutters. The federal government offered men $8.00 per month plus rations and clothing to build a fort, Fort Burnside, on Roanoke Island's north end. Women and children, who made up three-fourths of the population of blacks on the island at that time, collected $4.00 a month, including clothing and ration benefits.

By June 1863, officials had established an official Freedmen's Colony on Roanoke Island, west of where the Elizabethan Inn now stands. The government granted all unclaimed lands to the former slaves and outfitted them with a steam mill, sawmill, gristmill, circular saws, and other necessary tools. About 3,000 freed slaves lived here in a village with more than 600 houses, a school, store, small church, and hospital.

Union forces began accepting black troops soon after they established the settlement. By the end of July, more than 100 members of the Freedmen's Colony had formed the nation's first African-American army regiment. The new colony would have survived were it not for the government's decision to return all lands to the original landowners after the war was over. When the Freedmen's Colony was abandoned in 1866, federal officials quickly transported many of the former slaves off the Outer Banks. Others remained on Roanoke Island to work the waters and the land.

LIFESAVING STATIONS

After the war, commerce began again along the ocean, increasing quickly with steamers now outnumbering sailboats and onetime warships joining private shipping companies. Storms, too, continued to wrack the shores and seamen, even sinking iron battleships into oblivion along this rough coast.

Seven U.S. lifesaving stations were established on the Outer Banks in 1874 in an attempt to help save sailors' lives, if not salvage some of the ships. The stations were located at Jones Hill near the Currituck Beach Lighthouse; Caffey's Inlet north of Duck; Kitty Hawk Beach south of the present pier; Nags Head within current town boundaries; Bodie Island south of Oregon Inlet; Chicamacomico, which is still open to visitors in Rodanthe and conducts simulated rescue drills each summer; and Little Kinnakeet, on the west side of North Carolina Highway 12 in Avon.

The stations were operated mostly by native Outer Bankers. Good swimmers and sea captains who knew the wild waters, these men risked their lives (and many perished) trying to pull others from the ocean. In March of 1876 the entire Jones Hill station crew was lost during an attempt to rescue seven sailors aboard the Italian ship *Nuova Ottavia*.

Many complained that the lifesaving service had two major flaws: They were only open for four months of the year, and the seven stations were too far apart, up to 15 miles in some cases, for the surfmen to adequately patrol the beaches on foot. In 1877 and 1878, two major shipwrecks that resulted in the loss of 188 lives provoked the government to build more stations. The wreck of the USS *Huron* in Nags Head occurred in November 1877 when the Nags Head station was closed for the season. The wreck of the *Metropolis* in January 1878, 4.5 miles south of the Jones Hill station, was a fiasco of a rescue operation, with 85 lives lost because it took more than five hours for the lifesaving station to respond. By 1879, 11 new stations were in operation on the Outer Banks at Deal's Island (later Wash Woods), Old Currituck Inlet (later Penny's Hill), Poyners Hill, Paul Gamiels Hill, Kill Devil Hills, Tommy's Hummock (north of Oregon Inlet and later named Bodie Island), Pea Island, Cedar Hummock, Big Kinnakeet, Creeds Hill, and Hatteras (later named Durants). The schedule was switched to eight months of the year at that time and later became year-round. The Pea Island station was the only all-black lifesaving station in the nation.

Rescue techniques advanced with new equipment and the surfmen's experience in ocean survival. Before motorized rescue craft were available, lifesaving teams had to row deep-hulled wooden boats, often through overhead waves. If they made it through raging seas to shipwrecks, they sometimes couldn't carry all of the sailors back to shore in one trip. As a result, they devised a pulley system to haul men off the sinking vessels. Dubbed a britches buoy, the device consisted of a pair of short pants sewn around a life preserver ring and hung on a thick rope by wide suspenders; the rope was wound around a handle crank mounted to a wooden cart on shore. Shipwreck victims struggled into the britches, usually with the assistance of surfmen in the rescue boat, and gave an "all-clear" tug on the rope. With the buoy sewn into the seams around their waists, these sailors didn't sink. Even in the highest seas, they could keep their heads

above water while lifesaving crews back on shore reeled them safely onto the sand.

Surfmen at Outer Banks lifesaving stations saved thousands of lives during hurricanes and hellacious northeast blows. In 1915 the Lifesaving Service became part of the U.S. Coast Guard. Coast Guardsmen continue to aid barrier-island boaters with a variety of state-of-the-art rescue craft stationed at modern Oregon Inlet and Hatteras Island stations. The old lifesaving stations are still scattered around the Outer Banks today. Some were moved and transformed into private homes. The Wash Woods station is a rental house north of Corolla. A store in Corolla, Outer Banks Style, occupies the old Kill Devil Hills Lifesaving Station, which was moved north. To see a restored lifesaving station and learn about the history of the service and the surfmen, visit Chicamacomico Lifesaving Station in Rodanthe (see our Attractions chapter).

HISTORIC HAPPENINGS

The government provided increasing numbers of jobs for lifesavers, lighthouse keepers, and postmasters at the dawn of the 20th century. Other locals continued to profit from summer tourists. But most Outer Bankers remained poor fishermen, farmers, stockmen, store clerks, hunters, and hunting guides. Currituck Sound was known as the premier hunting spot on the East Coast, and many hunt clubs were established along the northern Outer Banks. Market hunting was a huge business for the locals on the northern Outer Banks in the late 1800s and early 1900s. During this time it was legal for hunters to kill as many ducks and waterfowl as they could and sell them on the market, to be shipped through the mainland to Norfolk and on to bigger cities.

Locals also made a living as hunting guides. According to the record book of the Pine Island Club, from 1888 to 1910 its members killed a total of 72,124 waterfowl, including geese, swans, snipes, black ducks, mallards, widgeon, gadwall geese, and Canada geese. The record kill for a day's hunt, according to David Stick in *The Outer Banks of North Carolina,* was 892 ruddy ducks by Russell and Van Griggs. This reckless killing decimated the numbers of waterfowl on the Currituck Sound, and market hunting was outlawed in 1918 by an act that made the selling of migratory waterfowl illegal. Much later, in the 1930s, game laws were passed shortening the season and lowering the bag limit. Sport hunting continues along the Outer Banks today, but on a much smaller scale.

In 1902 the barrier islands recorded another first when Thomas Edison's former chief chemist began experimenting with wireless telegraphy. Radio pioneer Reginald Fessenden transmitted the first musical notes received by signal from near Buxton on Hatteras Island to Roanoke Island. He wrote to his patent attorney that the resulting sounds were "very loud and plain, i.e., as loud as in an ordinary telephone."

In 1900 Ohio bicycle shop owners Wilbur and Orville Wright arrived by boat at Kitty Hawk, drawn by accounts of prevailing winds, isolation, and soft landing spots. They spent some time in Kitty Hawk and received mail there, but the Wright Brothers camped and flew their glider on Kill Devil Hill. They brought with them a 17-foot glider, but when they flew it the wings generated less lift than they expected. Wilbur kept it aloft for only 10 seconds. In 1901 they returned with another glider, which also failed to fly as

they had hoped. In 1902 the persistent Wright brothers tried another machine that flew more than 1,000 glides. In 1903 the Wrights returned to Kill Devil Hills with a new 40-foot, 605-pound Flyer. When they tested it on December 14, 1903, the Flyer was damaged and required repair. On December 17, 1903, the Wrights made a second attempt despite the 27 mph wind. Orville positioned himself in the flyer and at 10:35 A.M. left the ground, keeping the Flyer aloft for 120 feet, with Wilbur running alongside. The brothers took turns flying three more times that day, increasing their flight distance each time. The fourth and last flight of the day, Wilbur's second, was the best: 852 feet in 59 seconds. The site is now marked with a stone monument in a National Park set along the original runway. Replicas of the historic airplane, hangar, and brothers' shack are on display at the Wright Brothers National Memorial (see our Attractions chapter).

MODERN INFLUENCES

In the 1930s, bridges linking the Outer Banks to the mainland brought thousands more tourists forever changing the islands. Visitors could drive to popular summer resorts at Nags Head rather than rely on steamships. Hotels, rental cottages, and restaurants appeared to accommodate the influx.

During the Great Depression, the Civilian Conservation Corps (CCC) set up six camps along the barrier islands. Throughout the 1930s, CCC workers performed millions of dollars' worth of dune construction and shoreline stabilization. The dunes you see along the east side of NC 12 did not develop naturally. CCC workers planted much of the grass and shrubbery to help stave off erosion along the ocean.

Although it was mostly waged on other continents, World War II did come to the Outer Banks's doorstep. German U-boats lurked in near-shore shipping lanes, exacting heavy damage on Allied vessels.

ℹ *World War II came closer to home than many Americans know. German U-boats prowled the Atlantic coast off the Outer Banks. The first U-boat sunk by Americans lies in a shallow grave off the coast of Bodie Island. Residents of these islands witnessed many attacks at sea and faced the debris brought in by the tide.*

At least 60 boats fell victim to the submarines, though the Germans experienced losses of their own: The first U-boat sunk by Americans lies in an Atlantic grave off the coast of Bodie Island. Outer Banks residents of that era recount having to pull their shades and extinguish all lights each night during the war so ships and submarines could not easily discern the shoreline.

Talk of the country's first national seashore began in the 1930s. By 1953, when the Cape Hatteras National Seashore finally was established under the auspices of the National Park Service, it stretched from Nags Head through Ocracoke Island.

Today, the Outer Banks is home to some of the most popular yet pristine beach resorts on the Atlantic coast. About 34,000 people make the barrier islands their permanent home. Please see our Area Overview chapter for a modern portrait of the Outer Banks communities.

RESTAURANTS

When you visit the Outer Banks, be sure to bring your appetite. In this seemingly remote area of the world, we have the basic ingredients from which world-class cuisine is created. We have bounty from the mainland, the sounds, and the ocean. We have innovative, educated, experienced chefs and restaurateurs. And we have an atmosphere that lends itself to an eclectic variety of hip, funky, chic, laid-back, comfortable, rustic, family-style places. In short, we have cutting-edge cuisine and we know how to serve it.

Just across the Wright Memorial Bridge on the Currituck mainland grow the vegetables found on many Outer Banks menus: Silver Queen sweet corn, red bliss potatoes, sugar snap peas, luscious tomatoes, brightly colored bell peppers, slender green beans. And we can't forget about the fields of strawberries and melons or the orchards of trees laden with succulent peaches and figs. The source of smoke-cured country hams and the largest peanuts you've ever eaten lies farther inland. Wanchese Produce on Roanoke Island plays a starring role on a daily basis supplying restaurants with herbs. Organic lettuce, mesclun mix, and bunches of fresh basil, thyme, rosemary, lemongrass, dill, and edible flowers are just a few of the fragrant wonders delivered to the back doors of kitchens all along this sandy bar.

And then there's the seafood. So much tuna is caught in the warm waters of the Gulf Stream that the tiny fishing village of Wanchese exports literally thousands of tons each year. In addition to tuna, local menus sport mahimahi, wahoo, and mako shark from the Gulf Stream. From inshore ocean waters and our sound waters come fresh flounder, Spanish and king mackerel, bluefish, black grouper, drum, striped bass (locally known as rockfish), speckled trout, gray trout, oysters, clams, mussels, shrimp, and crabs. Along Colington Road and the streets of Kitty Hawk Village, you can easily spot the long wooden shedder beds, brightly lighted all night long, where soft-shell crabs are gathered as soon as they molt.

Big-city purveyors supplement our local seafood and produce; while the grocery stores carry mainly the basics, our restaurants pride themselves on offering daring ingredients.

Wine has become one of our restaurants' biggest drawing cards. Wine dinners abound during the off-season, and many are attended by the vintners themselves. Wine-loving restaurateurs are happy to accommodate a variety of tastes, as evidenced by the increasing number of wines by the glass that we see cropping up on lists. Lists of bottled wines lengthen each season, and restaurants along the northern beaches sometimes offer 100 or more varieties of the world's finest wines. A surprising number of Outer Banks restaurants have received coveted awards of excellence from *Wine Spectator* for their wine selections and for their pairing of wine with food.

Many area restaurants serve alcoholic beverages, at least for dinner; however, those in Southern Shores and those on Colington, Roanoke, Hatteras, and Ocracoke Islands are forbidden to offer mixed drinks and serve only beer or wine. Some establishments allow brown bagging, which means you can bring in your own liquor.

Restaurants are opening earlier in the spring and staying open longer into the fall each year. The shoulder seasons have become popular times to dine out. Most eateries open by March and don't close their kitchens until after Thanksgiving. Some open briefly for the holidays. A few stay busy enough to stay open year-round.

Dinner isn't the only meal to eat out, of course. A variety of bakeries, diners, and even seafood restaurants serve big breakfasts, lunches, and weekend brunches. A few welcome bathing suit-clad customers just off the beach. The majority of restaurants, however, require you to wear shirts and shoes. Many cooks will package meals to go and some eateries deliver, with menus offering much more than just pizza.

If you're eating an evening meal out, feel free to dress as comfortably as you desire. Even most of the expensive, elite establishments welcome sundresses, sandals, and shorts. Restaurant managers say everything from evening gowns and suits to jeans and T-shirts is acceptable at their tables.

Reservations aren't taken at many restaurants. Others, however, suggest or even require them. The Blue Point, The Left Bank, and Elizabeth's Cafe in Duck; Carolina Blue in Southern Shores; Ocean Boulevard in Kitty Hawk; Colington Cafe on Colington Island; and 1587 in Manteo all get so booked up during summer that it's best to call at least three days ahead to secure a table. The fare at these fabulous places, however, is well worth the advance planning.

If sticking to a budget is a concern, you can have homestyle meals from tuna steaks to North Carolina barbecue for less than $8.00 in many Outer Banks family-style restaurants. Sure, you'll find a few of the nationally popular fast-food chains, complete with drive-through windows, uniformed employees, and a known commodity, but if you want something ranging from a little bit different to extraordinary, read on. With our diversity of restaurants, you're bound to find something to suit any appetite.

Restaurants in this chapter are arranged from north to south from Corolla through Ocracoke. Seasons and days of the week each place is open are included with every profile. Unless otherwise noted, these eateries accept MasterCard and Visa, and many accept other major credit cards as well.

We've included some primarily carry-out and outdoor dining establishments that offer quick, cheap eats, cool ice-cream concoctions, and perfect items to pack for a picnic or offshore fishing excursion.

PRICE CODE

For your convenience, we've included a pricing guide with each restaurant listing to give you a general idea of what to expect when the tab comes. The costs are based on main courses for two people and do not include appetizers, dessert, and alcoholic beverages. Many area eateries also have senior-citizen discounts and children's menus to help families cut costs. Most entrees include at least one vegetable or salad and some type of bread. Here's our breakdown:

$	Less than $25
$$	$25 to $45
$$$	$46 to $75
$$$$	More than $75

Prices do not include North Carolina's 8 percent sales tax or the gratuity, which should be 15 to 20 percent, depending on the quality of service. Some restaurants offer early evening dining discounts to encourage patrons to avoid peak dining hours. Most have at least two or three daily specials that change according to the availability of food and the whims of the chef.

COROLLA

Corolla Pizza & Deli $
Austin Complex, NC 12, Corolla
(252) 453-8592
This takeout-only deli serves hot and cold subs and sandwiches, Philly cheese steaks, and pizza by the pie or slice for lunch and dinner. Each pizza is made to order on hand-tossed dough. Regular red sauce and gourmet white pizzas, including the ever-popular chicken pesto pizza, are available. During the summer season, Corolla Pizza offers free delivery. You can

walk in or call ahead to have your order waiting. Corolla Pizza is open seven days a week in summer. Call for off-season hours.

Nicoletta's Italian Cafe $$$
Corolla Light Town Center
NC 12, Corolla
(252) 453-4004

Nicoletta's Italian Cafe is a cornerstone of fine dining on the northern Outer Banks. White linen tablecloths and a view of the Currituck Beach Lighthouse please the eye as sounds of classical jazz mix with Sinatra and friends to set the mood in the dining room.

Nicoletta's menu features fresh seafood, pork, and a wide selection of gourmet pasta combinations, all prepared in the Italian tradition with a creative touch. An extensive wine list with more than 30 selections complements the fare, and sinful desserts end the meal satisfactorily. Nicoletta's has been a frequent winner of the *Wine Spectator* award. Children can create their own pasta dish by selecting from three pastas, three sauces, and meatballs.

Nicoletta's is open for dinner year-round. In season, it is open seven days a week; call for off-season hours. Dress is casual, and reservations are requested. Catering and private parties are available.

The Wild Horse Cafe $$
Corolla Light Town Center
NC 12, Corolla
(252) 453-8463

The Wild Horse Cafe brings Southwestern cuisine to the northern Outer Banks. Here you'll find homemade crab cakes seasoned lightly with chili powder for that Tex-Mex flair. Vegetarian chili also is a standout. There's also plenty of good seafood, steaks, chicken, and barbecue on the menu. All the desserts are homemade, from key lime pie to sopapillas drizzled with honey.

The decor fits the theme. Bull horns, wool rugs, cacti, and horseshoes adorn the walls. A Mexican-tile bar offers a cool place to sit and sip one of 25 beers served. The wine list is extensive, too.

The Wild Horse Cafe serves breakfast, lunch, and dinner seven days a week in summer and is open Easter through October. Sandwiches are available for a light supper along with the full entree offerings. A children's menu offers smaller portions and prices, and the waitstaff provides crayons to keep your tykes occupied. Large parties can be accommodated.

Smokey's Restaurant $
Monteray Plaza, NC 12, Corolla
(252) 453-4050
www.Smokeysrestaurant.com

This down-home, family-style restaurant opened in 1991 and is a Corolla original. Its specialties include house-prepared barbecue true to the original North Carolina recipe, delicious baby back ribs, half-pound burgers, Southern fried chicken, fresh yellowfin tuna steaks, homemade Currituck crab cakes, fried and steamed shrimp, and fried clams accompanied by all the trimmings, from coleslaw and baked beans to hush puppies, sweet potato sticks, and onion rings. Many appetizers are available, including cheddar cheese–stuffed jalapeño peppers, buffalo wings, hush puppies, and the "Corolla Burst," a super-colossal onion cut in the shape of a flower and deep fried. Salads are available throughout the day.

Smokey's offers a children's menu and will package most of its items for takeout. Desserts, wine, and beer are also available. Open for lunch and dinner, March through December, Smokey's serves seven days a week in season. Call for off-season hours.

Bacchus Wine & Cheese $
Monteray Plaza, NC 12, Corolla
(252) 453-4333
(252) 453-2429 to fax orders
www.bacchuswineandcheese.com

Bacchus Wine & Cheese carries more than 4,000 bottles of domestic and imported wines and beer plus some fantastic deli sandwiches, subs, and tortilla wraps. You can eat in the shop, at an outside table, or get anything to go. While your food is prepared, you can browse through the wine racks or select a cold drink from the refrigerator cases. Cappuccino and espresso are available, too. The owners use Boar's Head meats and domestic and imported cheeses in their enormous sandwiches. There's a nice selection of gourmet foods and gifts. Ask about the popular wine tastings during the summer. You can also order special party platters and gift baskets. Bacchus is open for lunch and dinner daily in season; call for off-season hours.

Corolla Brew Pub $$
Monteray Plaza, NC 12, Corolla
(252) 453-6638
If you want a light meal and a mug of beer, check out this little pub at the northern end of the Outer Banks. Serving locally brewed Weeping Radish beers along with more traditional ales, this pub offers burgers and sandwiches. Dinner entrees include fresh seafood and several German selections. It's open until 9:00 P.M. in the summer; call for off-season hours.

Sundogs Sports Bar and Grill $-$$
Monteray Plaza, NC 12, Corolla
(252) 453-4263
Sundogs is the top sports-viewing facility in Corolla. It has the traditional decor of a sports bar and the features you would expect—a long bar, a pool table, video games, and TVs. If there's a game on, customers like to sidle up to the bar, drink a few beers, and chow down on jumbo buffalo wings served with ranch or blue cheese dressing, beer-battered onion rings, mile-high nachos with tri-colored tortillas, or personal flat-bread pizzas. A steam bar offers shrimp, crab legs, and more. For meals try hearty sandwiches like the black Angus burger or the Carolina crab cake sandwich. Fish and chips are available along with a 12-inch Coney Island hot dog. There is a children's menu, a late-night menu, and a full bar. Sundogs is open year-round. In season Sundogs has live entertainment sevens nights a week.

Does a gourmet meal cooked in your rental cottage sound like a winning option? Call At Your Service to arrange in-house personal chef service at (252) 261-5286 or (800) 259-0229.

Stripers Bar & Grille $$
Monteray Shores Plaza
NC 12, Corolla
(252) 453-4345
www.stripersbarandgrille.com
This dining spot is a sister restaurant to the popular Chilli Peppers in Kill Devil Hills and Stripers in Shallowbag Bay, Manteo. The Corolla restaurant has unique decor that includes Norman Rockwell reproductions adorning the walls.

If you enjoy Outer Banks cuisine, then Stripers makes a great choice for lunch or dinner. The crab dip with toasted bread is a palette-pleasing way to begin a meal. Regular entrees include crab Norfolk and a mouthwatering grilled prime rib served with red-skin mashed potatoes and seasonal vegetables. Soups, salads, sandwiches, pasta, and other steak and seafood dishes round out the menu. You can also order an appetizer or meal from the Bearded Clam steam bar. Stripers has a full bar and wine list and is open April through October; call for hours of operation.

North Banks Restaurant & Raw Bar $$
TimBuck II Shopping Village
NC 12, Corolla
(252) 453-3344
This 50-seat restaurant and raw bar serves lunch and dinner all year. Lobster, shrimp, oysters, clams, and mussels are available as well as filet mignon, fresh locally caught fish, grilled beef, chicken, and sandwiches. Diners enjoy the waterside view from this upscale but casual restaurant that boasts 28-foot vaulted ceilings. If you have to wait for a table, you can wear a "patron pager" and stroll through TimBuck II Shopping Village until you're beeped. North Banks also offers desserts and appetizers as well as

imported and domestic beers, wine, and Black and Tans (that hearty, layered combination of Guinness and Bass Ale) to complement the fresh local seafood. Next door, North Banks Wine Shop offers an interesting array of wines.

Grill Room $$
TimBuck II Shopping Village
NC 12, Corolla
(252) 453-4336
www.grillroomobx.com

Mike Dianna's Grill Room prides itself on being family owned and operated. Steaks, veal, lamb, ribs, chicken, and seafood are all cooked over a mesquite grill, bringing you aromatic wood cooking at its best. The homemade French bread that accompanies the meals is excellent. Four or five different fish specials are offered each night. The Grill Room is also known for its fine selection of wines. The restaurant serves dinner nightly during the summer; call for off-season hours. A kid's menu is available. Live music is scheduled most nights in season.

Steamer's Shellfish To Go $
TimBuck II Shopping Village
NC 12, Corolla
(252) 453-3305
www.steamersshellfishtogo.com

Steamer's Shellfish To Go is Corolla's version of the popular New England–style clam bake. This gourmet seafood market offers full takeout of the best the Outer Banks has to offer presented in a refreshingly different fashion. Steamer's offers high-quality gourmet lunch and dinner entrees (grilled fish, chicken, baby back ribs, and vegetarian lasagna, to name a few), fantastic homemade soups, salads, and desserts. Steamer Pots To Go are made to order and layered with seafood, red bliss potatoes, yellow onion, and corn on the cob with cocktail sauce, butter, lemon, and claw crackers. Choose from live Maine lobster, littleneck clams, mussels, Alaskan snow crab legs, and jumbo king crab legs. Take home your Steamer Pot To Go, place it on the stove, add a cup of

water, and in 30 to 45 minutes, you'll have a seafood feast like no other! Steamer's also offers a full menu of steamed ready-to-eat seafood for carryout. The steamed spiced shrimp is a house specialty not to be missed! Shellfish To Go is open in season for lunch and dinner, April 1 through Columbus Day weekend. There's a waterfront deck for outdoor dining.

Grouper's Grille & Wine Bar $$$
TimBuck II Shopping Village
NC 12, Corolla
(252) 453-4077

Tucked between handmade hammocks and quaint gift shops at this upscale shopping village, Grouper's opened in 1996 and visitors have been singing its praises ever since. This restaurant provides an array of enticing offerings in an atmosphere of understated elegance.

Angus beef, free-range chicken, fresh local seafood, and vegetarian entrees are made all the more mouthwatering with unusual spices and sauces. The menu changes seasonally, so that only the freshest available ingredients are used. Local seafood is served with an international twist. Pasta, chicken, lean-generation pork, and beef are all prepared with flair.

Each meal begins with freshly baked bread. Huge appetizers include such temptations as grilled romaine salad, seared tuna loin sashimi, and blackened jumbo sea scallops with fresh mango papaya relish. Organic salad greens are mixed with an assortment of delicious in-house dressings. Grouper's extensive wine list boasts more than 100 varieties by the bottle and a large by-the-glass selection. A generous number of domestic, imported, and microbrewed beers round out the drink choices. Desserts are made on the premises, and the selections are beyond sinful.

The atmosphere here is as delightful as the dinners, with open post-and-beam wooden ceilings, butter-colored tablecloths set with flickering candles, and large windows surrounding the dining room. Upscale but casual, the eatery makes diners comfortable in suit and tie or in blue jeans. Grouper's is open for dinner from March through October. Reservations are recommended.

Route 12 Steak & Seafood Co.　$$
TimBuck II Shopping Village
NC 12, Corolla
(252) 453-4644

Route 12 pleases diners with one of the best kid's menus in Corolla, tempting nightly dinner specials, an outstanding wine list, and a fully stocked bar. The owner recommends the grilled sashimi-grade ahi yellowfin tuna encrusted with black peppercorns, served over sautéed baby spinach and garlic mashed potatoes with a demiglaze of brandy and pepper corns. Open seven days a week in season. Lunch is served in season from 11:30 A.M. to 3:00 P.M. and dinner from 5:00 to 9:00 P.M. Call for off-season hours.

Blue Water Seafood　$
Ocean Club Centre, NC 12, Corolla
(252) 453-9921

Blue Water Seafood is located at the south end of the Currituck Club. The restaurant prides itself on serving the finest fresh local seafood available. Shrimp, tuna, swordfish, scallops, mahimahi, and sea bass make up just a portion of the selection. Imported from Maine, live lobsters and lobster tails are ready to go. Blue crabs are a popular delicacy sold here. For a fun evening meal, try the steamer pot: You choose the seafood and vegetable ingredients; if you want something a little different, try adding andouille or Cajun smoked sausage to the pot. Delicious. Blue Water is open seven days a week in season from 11:00 A.M. to 7:00 P.M. Call for off-season hours.

DUCK

The Lifesaving Station
at the Sanderling　$$$
NC 12, Sanderling
(800) 701-4111, ext. 133
www.thesanderling.com

A great time to eat out on the Outer Banks is Sunday night. Many folks have just checked into their cottage and don't go out for dinner. Often, you can get seated more quickly and have a wider choice of where to eat on Sunday evening.

The Lifesaving Station, part of the Sanderling Resort north of Duck, is one of the Outer Banks's loveliest restaurants, housed in a restored 1899 lifesaving station that is a National Historic Landmark. The dining rooms reflect turn-of-the-20th-century coastal architecture and are enhanced with rich woods and brass, nautical antiques, and original artifacts of the lifesaving station. Contemporary American cuisine emphasizing local seafood is the specialty of executive chef Christine Zambito. The restaurant serves breakfast, lunch, and dinner every day to everyone, not only guests of the resort.

The restaurant's breakfasts are more formal than your standard Outer Banks morning meals. A smoked salmon platter, waffles, and eggs are specialties. For lunch, expect fancy salads, crab cakes, seafood, and sandwiches. Dinner is a special affair. Local fish, fowl, beef, and vegetarian dishes are finely crafted with fresh ingredients. A favorite appetizer is the Sanderling Signature Seafood Chowder with corn, crab, and shrimp. Desserts are out of this world.

The restaurant has an award-winning wine list and a full bar. The upstairs Swan Bar and Lounge are good places to relax before or after your meal. A children's menu is available. Dinner reservations are highly recommended. All three meals are served seven days a week year-round. T-shirts and jeans are not allowed at dinner, and tasteful attire is requested at breakfast and lunch.

The Left Bank　$$$
NC 12, Sanderling
(252) 261-8419, (252) 449-6654
www.thesanderling.com

Part of the Sanderling resort complex, The

Left Bank is a French-inspired restaurant that features delicious simplicity. The Left Bank offers panoramic vistas of Currituck Sound and marsh grasses through a half-moon-shaped window wall. The interior is sublimely chic, like nothing else on the Outer Banks, with leather banquettes, mohair chairs, a bar top of blonde onyx lit from underneath, and a museum-quality collection of porcelain Doughty birds—all backgrounded by the spectacular view. A display kitchen affords diners a peek at the behind-the-scenes magic. The emphasis is on the freshest regional foods available. Signature touches of Chef George Robinson include predinner *amusé granité* and palate cleansers between courses. The wine list is a careful selection of boutique wines. A martini list is also available. Dinner is served Tuesday through Saturday. Reservations are recommended. Blazers are required dress for men (spares are available should you need one). Long pants and covered footwear are also required.

Cravings Coffee Shoppe $
Duck Common Shopping Center
NC 12, Duck
(252) 261-0655
This delightful eatery is the perfect place to pop by for a quick breakfast before hitting the beach or to indulge yourself in a delectable dessert and coffee after dinner. You can eat inside, on an open-air deck, or take the tasty treats with you. Table service is not available; you order and pick up your food from the counter.

Order a fresh New York–style bagel with one of six flavored cream cheeses.

It's not vacation if you spend the whole time in the kitchen. If you've got a houseful of people, consider hiring a personal chef. You can choose a chef who cooks all three meals in your house or one who just drops off dinner every evening. Ask your rental company for suggestions.

Pastries and muffins also are baked each day. Cravings also makes its own ice cream. Out-of-town newspapers are available each morning.

For lunch, Cravings has a light-fare menu. Every type of coffee drink you can concoct is available, from several types of brewed coffee that change daily to espresso, cappuccino, mocha drinks, and other fancy combinations. Chai tea is served either iced or hot, and you can choose from a variety of iced blended coffee drinks and blended smoothies. Cravings is open year-round. In summer the eatery serves into the afternoon; off-season it's open weekends.

Fishbones Sunset Grille and Raw Bar $$
NC 12, Duck
(252) 261-3901
Opened in 2001 by the owners of the popular Fishbones Raw Bar & Restaurant, Fishbones Sunset Grille and Raw Bar is quickly becoming another favorite Duck dining spot. The restaurant sits by the Currituck Sound and is the village 's prime sunset-watching spot. It is patterned after the older Fishbones, with Caribbean-influenced entrees and appetizers, moderately priced food, a fun atmosphere, and good service for locals and visitors alike.

Fishbones Sunset is known for its extensive drink menu. Specialty drinks are served in novelty vessels, like a tiki god, a monkey, or a pineapple. The full bar list is available upstairs at a stunning horseshoe-shaped bar covered with coral tiles, downstairs at another bar and raw bar, and outside at a tiki bar. Meals are served upstairs or down or outside on the deck. Dinners focus mostly on seafood, and the blackened fish and conch fritters are standouts. The raw bar serves all the freshest Outer Banks favorites. For lunch, seafood, sandwiches, and burgers are served. Lunch and dinner are served every day year-round.

Fishbones Sunset also offers breakfast, daily in season and on weekends in the off-season. Breakfast choices include omelets, skillet dishes, smoked salmon bagels, and a wonderful cinnamon French toast served with a guava-banana syrup. It is a popular nighttime hangout, with live music four or five nights a week in the summer and one or two nights in the off-season (see our Nightlife chapter). Fishbones Sunset offers catering and site rental for weddings and large parties.

Elizabeth's Cafe & Winery $$$
Scarborough Faire, NC 12, Duck
(252) 261-6145

Well-known across the nation for its wine and wonderful cuisine—and perfectly matched combinations thereof—Elizabeth's is a perennial *Wine Spectator* award winner. In 1999 the International Restaurant and Hospitality Rating Bureau awarded Elizabeth's its International Award of Excellence. In 2000 executive chef Brad Price was recognized as one of America's Top 100 Chefs by the same organization. In 2003 Elizabeth's was the grand winner of Sante's "Best Fine Dining Wine Restaurant in the United States." In 2004 Elizabeth's was inducted into the Sante Hall of Fame as one of only two restaurants chosen. Also in 2004 the restaurant won the "Award of Ultimate Distinction," the highest award offered by *Wine Enthusiast Magazine*. Elizabeth's was one of only 16 restaurants in North America to receive that award. DiRONA (Distinguished Restaurants of North America) gave Elizabeth's the "Award of Excellence" in 2004. Year after year, Elizabeth's sweeps the fine dining awards.

Elizabeth's is warm and casual inside, with a fireplace that's usually lit on chilly evenings. Service is always excellent. If you have trouble selecting a wine from the extensive wine list, owner Leonard Logan is more than happy to help you choose a bottle to complement any meal. Leonard loves a celebration and is always ready to pop open a bottle of champagne.

Besides the regular menu offerings, which include country French and California eclectic, two prix fixe dinners (six- or seven-course meals and accompanying wines) are available every night. All the dishes are made with fresh ingredients, from seafood and steak to unusual pastas. A pastry chef creates different desserts daily.

This cafe is very popular—and small, seating only about 40 diners. Reservations are highly recommended. In addition to some of the finest wines available, the restaurant has a full bar. Patrons with disabilities can be accommodated. This is a nonsmoking establishment. Dinner is served seven nights a week in season; call for winter hours.

Elizabeth's Wine Gallery is an area of the restaurant where shoppers can choose from more than 1,650 selections. Tastings of reasonably priced, featured wines are offered before you make your purchase. The wine bar is open in the afternoons, and if you choose to savor a glass, you may do so inside the gallery, outside on the porch, or in the adjacent garden.

Fishbones Raw Bar & Restaurant $$
Scarborough Lane Shoppes
NC 12, Duck
(252) 261-6991

Specializing in locally caught seafood, this raw bar and grill opened in the summer of 1995 and won the Outer Banks chowder cook-off with an original recipe during its first year in business.

Lunch items include sandwiches, crab cakes, fried seafood, and creamy soups such as tomato conch and, of course, chowder. Dinner entrees feature such Caribbean cuisine favorites as calypso eggplant and coconut shrimp, as well as pastas with fresh clam sauce, lobster tails, crab legs, and more than a dozen raw bar selections. The hot crab dip, barbecue shrimp, and conch fritters are outstanding appetizers. This is a casual place with a full bar, five types of beer on tap, 50 bottled beers from all over the world, a wine list, and several microbrews.

Fishbones serves lunch and dinner seven days a week year-round, and specials change daily for both meals. Takeout is available for all menu items. Reservations are not accepted.

The Blue Point Bar & Grill $$$
The Waterfront Shops, NC 12, Duck
(252) 261–8090

This beautifully renovated and expanded bistro is one of our favorite places to dine on the Outer Banks. It's been open for dinner since 1989 and consistently receives rave reviews from magazines such as *Southern Living, Gourmet,* and even *Outside*. Here, regional Southern cooking takes on a cosmopolitan flair. A 1950s-style interior with black-and-white checkered floors, red upholstery, and lots of chrome provides an upbeat, bustling atmosphere. An enclosed pórch not only overlooks the sound, it actually overhangs it. From the small bar facing the aromatic kitchen, you can watch your appetizers being prepared while you sip a cocktail and wait for a table.

The Blue Point's menu is contemporary Southern cuisine and changes seasonally. Starters range from Hatteras tuna to fresh tomato-mozzarella stacks, each artistically arranged and flavored with a fresh combination of seasonings. Entrees include jumbo lump crab cakes served with Currituck corn on the cob, homemade soups, unusual seafood dishes, steaks, salads, and perfect pastas. Desserts, like warm Kentucky bourbon pecan tart with caramel ice cream or key lime pie, are divine.

If you're into creative cooking that's sure to tantalize every taste bud—and awaken some you might not realize you have—this restaurant is a must-stop on the Outer Banks. It's open for dinner, and reservations are highly recommended; in summer, dinner reservations are required. The Blue Point is open for lunch Tuesday to Sunday from 11:30 A.M. to 2:30 P.M. and for dinner seven days a week in season; call for off-season hours.

Roadside Raw Bar & Grill $$
NC 12, Duck
(252) 261–5729

Occupying a renovated 1932 cottage, this restaurant is warm and homey, with hardwood floors inside and a patio with umbrella-shaded tables out front. In season, live jazz is performed here two nights a week (see our Nightlife chapter).

A casual, fine-dining establishment, Roadside offers half-pound Angus burgers, fresh fish sandwiches, meat loaf, and a variety of salads and sandwiches for lunch. The Roadside clam chowder is chock-full of shellfish, and you can choose from steamed and seasoned shrimp by the pound or half-pound and steamed clams by the dozen. In addition to mixed green and Caesar salads is our favorite: a warm salad of bay scallops, black beans, corn, and red bell peppers, with sesame-soy dressing. Weather permitting, enjoy your meal on the patio while watching the summertime foot traffic in downtown Duck.

For dinner you can choose from a variety of starters, including Roadside's own shrimp—served over cheese grits with red-eye gravy. Dinners highlight fresh seafood, although you can choose from chicken, beef, and vegetarian pasta options as well.

In season, there's an oven-roasted half lobster, stuffed with crabmeat and served with wild rice and corn on the cob, or pan-seared, cornmeal-encrusted black grouper with black sticky rice and mango-strawberry salsa. Beef lovers will appreciate the 10-ounce Angus filet mignon served with gorgonzola cheese and sour cream, with green onion and bacon mashed potatoes. Yes, the desserts are just as enticing. There's a full bar with a satisfying selection of microbrewed beers. The restaurant serves lunch and dinner year-round; call for off-season hours. Reservations are not accepted.

Duck Deli $$
NC 12, Duck
(252) 261–3354

This casual deli on the east side of the highway opened in 1987 primarily to serve lunch. Since then, Duck Deli has expanded to offer breakfast, lunch, and dinner seven days a week, year-round.

Barbecued pork, beef, chicken, and ribs are the specialties here. Sandwiches,

Philly cheese steaks, and subs are served all day, as are side salads, garden burgers, and coleslaw. A full breakfast menu includes eggs, pancakes, and omelets. For dessert, you can get sweet on cherry and peach cobblers, homemade brownies, or a frozen yogurt bar with plenty of toppings. Everything is available to eat in or take out. The Marketplace in Southern Shores is home to a second location of Duck Deli.

Herron's Deli and Restaurant $
NC 12, Duck
(252) 261-3224

With a full menu available for takeout or to eat in, this casual deli serves breakfast and lunch seven days a week all year and adds dinner hours in the summer. Booths and tables are available indoors, and picnic tables allow you to enjoy outdoor dining. Hot and cold Italian subs, cheese steaks, cheeseburgers, and crab cakes are among the most popular items in the afternoon and evening. We recommend the soups, from chili specials to she-crab bisque and Hatteras-style chowder.

A big breakfast menu features French toast, sausage gravy, omelets, eggs, and homemade biscuits. Desserts range from cakes and brownies to homemade strawberry pie. Beer and wine are also available.

Tommy's Gourmet Market and Wine Emporium $$$
NC 12, Duck
(252) 261-8990, (800) 692-2168
www.tommysmarket.com

Tommy's is famous for its Angus steaks, aged for 21 days and cut to order. The market also offers fresh-baked goods and a deli that features roasted ham and chicken, shrimp, sandwiches, fresh salads, and daily luncheon specials. Tommy's also will prepare dinner for you. Preset menus or items a la carte can be carried out ready to eat. In addition to providing a full range of groceries, Tommy's has an extensive wine selection and carries imported beer. The market is open March through New Year's.

Herron's Waterfront Restaurant $$
NC 12, Duck
(252) 255-0500

Herron's Waterfront Restaurant, formerly Swan Cove, is located on one of the most picturesque spots in Duck. The spectacular view from the soundfront dining room makes a meal here truly special. A separate lounge upstairs has a full bar with an extensive wine list. Herron's has a variety of dishes from the land and from the sea. For a delicious seafood meal, try the waterfront seafood platter. It's a combination of flounder, shrimp, scallops, and oysters—lightly fried and served with cocktail or tarter sauce. Landlubbers will enjoy the veal marsala. Veal medallions are dusted with seasoned flour and sautéed with garlic and mushrooms in marsala wine. There are also two vegetarian choices on the menu.

The restaurant is open seven days a week in season. Call for off-season hours. Dinner is served from 5:00 P.M. until 9:00 P.M. A children's menu is available.

SOUTHERN SHORES

Meridian 42 $$
Southern Shores Crossing
Ocean Boulevard, Southern Shores
(252) 261-0420
www.meridian42.com

Meridian 42, which opened in the fall of 2002, offers patrons outstanding coastal Mediterranean cuisine, along with an eclectic wine list, daily-made breads, pastas, and desserts, an open kitchen, and an ocean view. The name, Meridian 42, is derived from the latitude line that runs from Barcelona, Spain, to Rome, Italy, and the cuisine is inspired by the flavors and ingredients of that area. The owners are Chuck Arnold, previously the chef at The Blue Point Bar & Grill and Ocean Boulevard, and Bryan Ellis, formerly with Ocean Boulevard and Miriam's.

Meridian 42 is open for lunch and dinner. For lunch, one offering not to be missed is the chef's favorite summer pastry pizza with tomato, Serrano ham, caramelized onion, paprika goat cheese, Gruyère cheese, and fresh basil. The entire dinner menu offers many tempting entrees, including the pan-seared local shrimp with a red chili glaze, baby greens, sliced mango, crispy risotto cake, pickled cucumbers, and a cucumber-mango coulis. The menus change seasonally in accordance with the freshest ingredients available.

Meridian 42 is open year-round, and reservations are recommended for dinner. Lunch may be served at times during the off-season. Call for confirmation. Meridian 42 is a smoke-free restaurant. Catering is available both on and off the premises.

KITTY HAWK

Rundown Cafe   **$$**
NC 12, MP 1, Kitty Hawk
(252) 255–0026
Open since 1993, this Caribbean-style cafe has been a big hit with locals, offering spicy, unusual alternatives to traditional Outer Banks seafood. Named for a Jamaican stew, Rundown serves island entrees flavored with African and Indian accents.

Specials change daily, and you'll find the enormous lunches the best deal on the beach. Try a huge platter of fish taco fixings, a big salad of mixed greens and vegetables with grilled beef, fresh fish, or the best fried conch sandwiches anywhere. Some say that Rundown's fries are the best on the beach, too. There's a steam bar for shellfish of all sorts and vegetables. Dinner items include grilled chicken breasts with garlic-peppercorn cream sauce or Jamaican pork—dry jerk-marinated pork loin, grilled and served with a red pepper glaze and apple chutney.

There's a full bar, and the bartenders can come up with some pretty potent concoctions. Guinness Stout, Bass, Pyramid, and Harp beers are on tap. The upstairs bar is a great place to soak in the sunset, catch a few rays, or linger over a

cool cocktail after a hot day in the sun. Lunch and dinner are served seven days a week. A kid's menu is available, and take-out orders are welcome. Rundown is closed in December and January.

Southern Bean   **$**
Dunes Shops, US 158, Kitty Hawk
(252) 261–JAVA
This gourmet coffee shop caters to folk looking for healthful light meals with a great cup of java. Southern Bean serves breakfast and lunch year-round. Three types of just-brewed coffee always simmer, filling the air with tantalizing aromas.

This comfortable place serves every type of specialty coffee drink imaginable, from espresso and cappuccino to iced lattes—even in decaf varieties. More than 30 flavors of freshly roasted coffee beans are sold by the pound here. You can eat inside at Southern Bean, sip a warm blend at an outdoor table, or order your drinks and your food to go. All menu items are either vegetarian or seafood, and sandwiches range from hummus to tuna salad to peanut butter and honey; try the Bean bagel topped with sun-dried tomatoes, pesto, red onion slices, cream cheese, and sprouts. Southern Bean's coffee goes well with its muffins, croissants, cinnamon rolls, and other bakery items, too. No sandwich costs more than $5.00. Southern Bean is also one of the few places on the Outer Banks where you can get freshly squeezed juices and a wide variety of fruit smoothies.

Southern Bean is open daily year-round from 7:00 A.M. to 8:00 P.M. in the summer, and from 7:00 A.M. to 6:00 P.M. in the off-season.

Ocean Boulevard   **$$$**
NC 12, MP 2, Kitty Hawk
(252) 261–2546
www.ocean-boulevard.com
This cozy, upscale eatery gives you a great feeling from the second you walk into the gold-walled dining room until you leave full and relaxed after a fabulous meal. It opened in September 1995 and quickly became one of the most popular

places on the Outer Banks. Manteo residents drive 30 miles each way to treat themselves to a midweek dinner here. No wonder—it's owned by the same culinary masters who brought us the inimitable 1587 Restaurant in Manteo (see listing under Roanoke Island).

This restaurant occupies the former 1949 Virginia Dare Hardware store, and you won't believe what the builders and decorators did with the place. It's accented with warm woods, burgundy fabrics, and forest-green chairs. Cobalt blue glasses grace every tabletop. There's even an open kitchen where you can watch the chefs work.

Selections are all prepared with locally grown herbs, produce, and just-caught seafood. Influences and ideas from around the world give the food a flavor all its own, and the menu changes according to the season. For an appetizer try the goat cheese and butternut squash skillet with grilled apples, roasted garlic, house-made sausage, fig preserve, and toasted bread or the crispy duck confit made with sweet corn flan, mushroom duxelle, onion, frisco salad, and roasted pear demiglaze. The "big plates" are all delicious and usually include chicken, beef, pork, seafood, and vegan dishes.

Ocean Boulevard's wine list, which has won the *Wine Spectator* Award of Excellence, contains more than 100 selections. Microbrewed beer is available, and the bar specializes in martinis.

Dessert offerings include a white chocolate crème brûlée and a macadamia nut torte with caramel ice cream. A full line of coffee drinks and herbal teas tops off your dining experience.

This elegant eatery will please even the most discriminating diners. It's open year-round for dinner only. During summer, doors are open seven days a week. Call for off-season hours. Reservations are highly recommended.

Art's Place $
NC 12, MP 2½, Kitty Hawk
(252) 261-3233

Serving good, basic meals for more than 20 years, this tiny eatery across from the ocean is a Kitty Hawk standby well-known among locals. The food here isn't fancy, but it's inexpensive, filling, and all-American. Sausage gravy is the most popular breakfast entree, although Art's also serves eggs, pancakes, and biscuits. The same entrees are available for lunch and dinner, along with daily specials such as fish, steaks, fried chicken, shrimp, clam strips, and cheeseburgers—all served with french fries, coleslaw, and a cucumber and onion salad. Jalapeño poppers are a hot bet for an appetizer, and calamari is available most of the time. Art's is open seven days a week year-round. Reservations are accepted but not necessary.

Jimmy's Seafood Buffet $$
US 158, MP 4, Kitty Hawk
(252) 261-4973

Jimmy's Seafood Buffet specializes in food and fun. Some say that the only thing more exciting than the food is the atmosphere. Start your evening off on the open-air thatched-roof porch, where the bar offers eight frozen drinks with a souvenir glass. "Kiddie cocktails" are available for the younger set.

Inside this tropical paradise you'll find all of your favorite seafood and all you'll want of it! Choose from crab, shrimp, oysters, clams, and lobster. Landlubbers can opt for barbecued ribs, chicken, and prime rib, among more than 100 selections. There's also a soft-serve ice-cream bar. All shellfish is available to go in one of Jimmy's soon-to-be-famous buffet buckets. Pick and choose what you want, and Jimmy's will pack it up in a bucket to go. It's a great way to enjoy seafood at

Very few restaurants on the Outer Banks serve dinner past 8:30 or 9:00 P.M. However, during the lively summer season you may be able to get a late dinner from one of the carry-out restaurants on the islands.

home, on the beach, or at a backyard party.

Jimmy's is open nightly for dinner starting at 3:30 P.M. in season; call for off-season hours and for info on the early-bird special.

Keeper's Galley $$
US 158, MP 4, Kitty Hawk
(252) 261-4000

Keeper's Galley is run by Rufus Pritchard Jr., the same fellow who owns The Dunes Restaurant in Nags Head (see listing under Nags Head). The menu is slightly different here, and Keeper's Galley serves breakfast, lunch, and dinner seven days a week in season.

Breakfast, which is available until noon, features waffles, eggs, pancakes, country ham, grits, toast, biscuits, vegetarian breakfast sandwiches, and fish roe stirred into eggs. A breakfast buffet is also available in season. For lunch, order a cold plate, shrimp or tuna sandwich, homemade seafood gumbo, or a big bowl of clam chowder. Dinner entrees change daily but regularly offer prime rib, crab cakes, seafood fettuccine, chicken, and a surf-and-turf platter. All desserts, including cheesecakes, are made from scratch. Keeper's Galley has a large children's menu and a full bar. Call for reservations. Keeper's Galley is closed November through February or March. Call for off-season hours.

Capt'n Frank's $
US 158, MP 4, Kitty Hawk
(252) 261-9923

Capt'n Frank's is an institution on the Outer Banks, serving three sizes of all-beef Oscar Mayer hot dogs with a variety of accompaniments. First of all, decide among the regular dog, a quarter-pounder, or a foot-long. Then, choose from at least a half-dozen specialty creations. The Chicago Dog tops the popularity list, with chili, mustard, onions, and slaw. Runner-up is the eight-item Junk-yard Dog, topped with chili, cheese, sauer-kraut, onions, mustard, ketchup, slaw, and

relish. We're partial to the Mad Dog, served with chili and hot peppers.

If "going to the dogs" doesn't appeal to you, Capt'n Frank's also offers barbecue sandwiches and addictive nacho fries—french fries with chili, cheese, hot peppers, and sour cream. Steamed shrimp is served nightly in season. Wash down the tasty morsels with a cold beer. Capt'n Frank's serves lunch and dinner daily Memorial Day through Labor Day. Off-season, the restaurant is open every day for lunch except Sunday.

Black Pelican Oceanfront Cafe $$
NC 12, MP 4, Kitty Hawk
(252) 261-3171
www.blackpelican.com

This casual restaurant is in an old Coast Guard station and features an enclosed deck overlooking the Atlantic. It's roomy and wide, with three separate levels and a huge bar with several TVs (see our Nightlife chapter). Hardwood floors, tongue-and-groove appointments, light gray accents, burgundy carpeting, and black bentwood chairs all add to the comfortable ambience of this moderately priced eatery.

Here, gourmet pizzas are cooked in a wood-hearth oven. Try the steamed shell-fish fresh from the sea. An extensive selection of appetizers is made from scratch. Dinner offerings include pasta and seafood specials, grilled or blackened to suit your taste. A children's menu is also available. Black Pelican serves lunch and dinner seven days a week year-round.

Sunburn Sports Bar & Grill $$
US 158, MP 4, Kitty Hawk
(252) 261-7833

Sunburn is the newest sports bar on the Outer Banks. Try your hand at a game of darts or pool, or root for your favorite team on one of the many televisions situated around the restaurant. Entrees include traditional Outer Banks fish, great crab cakes, and shrimp jambalaya. Specials change daily. A children's menu is available at this kid-friendly restaurant, and little ones receive crayons and a placemat to color while waiting for their meals. Dinner is served seven days a week. Open year-round; call for off-season hours.

John's Drive-In $
NC 12, MP 4³/₄, Kitty Hawk
(252) 261-6227
Home of the planet's best milk shakes, John's has been an Outer Banks institution for years. Folks have been known to drive two hours from Norfolk just to sip one of the fruit and ice-cream concoctions, which are often so thick they won't even flow through the straw. Our favorite is the chocolate, peanut butter, and banana variety, but you'll have to sample a few first and create some of your own combinations before making that call for yourself.

You can't eat inside here, but plenty of picnic tables are scattered around the old concrete building across from the ocean. Everything is served in paper bags to go. While you're waiting for your food, check out the faded photographs of happy customers lining this diner's salt-sprayed windows. You may even recognize a few local friends.

Besides the milk shakes and ice-cream-sundae treats, John's serves delicious mahimahi, trout, and tuna sandwiches or boats with the fish crispy-fried alongside crinkle fries. Dogs love this drive-in, too. If your pooch waits patiently in the car, the worker behind the window probably will provide him or her with a free "puppy cup" of soft-serve vanilla ice cream. We can't think of a better doggie treat on a hot summer afternoon.

John's Drive-In is open from May through September or October for lunch and early dinner. It's closed Wednesday, unfortunately (we could eat there seven days a week). No credit cards are accepted.

La Fogata Mexican Restaurant $
US 158, MP 4¹/₂, Kitty Hawk
(252) 255-0934

A traditional Mexican restaurant, La Fogata gets its name from the Spanish word for "campfire." For the price, La Fogata serves the best ethnic food on the beach. People wait in line to eat here on weekend nights. You'll see a lot of locals in this colorful spot year-round.

Airy, bright, and decorated with Mexican art and photographs, the interior of this ultra-casual eatery usually hums with Latin tunes. The waiters bring baskets of crispy tortillas and bowls of homemade salsa as soon as they distribute the menus. All entree portions are generous, so save room for the main course. Recommended appetizers include the hot queso (cheese) dip and stuffed jalapeño peppers.

Specialties here are fajitas, beef and chicken tacos, enchiladas, and chiles rellenos. The cooks make the dishes hot or mild, depending on your desire. Selections come in every possible combination, vegetarian varieties, and a la carte if you want to try one of everything. (Actually, that's impossible here. The menu has more than 36 dinner selections, many starting at $6.50.) A full bar offers a wide selection of Mexican, American, and imported beer. Mixed-drink and margarita prices are among the lowest on the beach. La Fogata is open for lunch and dinner year-round, seven days a week.

KILL DEVIL HILLS

Coastal Cactus $
Seagate North Shopping Center
US 158, MP 5, Kill Devil Hills
(252) 441-6600
www.coastalcactus.com
For more than 12 years, Jim and Deby Curcio have been serving the best the Southwest has to offer to the Outer Banks. Visitors from Arizona, Texas, New Mexico, and California have raved about the authentic regional flavor of the menu offerings at this affordable, casual eatery decorated in a Southwest style. The menu has more than 60 choices of entrees, combination plates, and a la carte items

prepared from scratch daily using fresh vegetables and meats and hot-off-the-grill tortillas. Start your meal with nachos piled high and covered with cheese, jalapeños, onions, tomatoes, and your choice of beef, chicken, or beans. It's all smothered in Coastal Cactus's own fresh homemade salsa, which is bottled for purchase if you want to take some home.

For an entree, the signature dish is sizzlin' fajitas served still smoking in a cast-iron skillet. You can choose from shrimp, steak, tuna, chicken, pasta, ribs, lobster, or vegetarian combinations. Other selections include tacos, enchiladas, burritos, chiles rellenos, tamales, and tequila-lime shrimp. The tempting desserts reflect the Tex-Mex theme. Fried ice cream, banana chimichangas, apple enchiladas a la mode, and coconut caramel flan are just some of the yummy offerings.

From the bar, the golden margaritas are marvelous and made from scratch, as are several other fresh-fruit varieties. Wine, beer, and other mixed drinks also are available. A children's menu is available, and separate smoking and nonsmoking dining rooms are provided. A general store on the premises has Navajo pottery, Hopi jewelry, hot sauces, and other unusual gift items for sale. The Coastal Cactus is open seven days a week for dinner in season. Call for off-season hours.

Chilli Peppers $$
US 158, MP 5, Kill Devil Hills
(252) 441-8081
www.chilli-peppers.com

World fusion with a Southwestern twist describes the cooking at this fun, bustling restaurant. Owner Jim Douglas has worked in Outer Banks eateries for years and has brought some of the most creative cooking around to Chilli Peppers. Adventuresome diners are wowed by the chefs' wild concoctions. Most dishes have some type of chile in them. If you prefer a milder meal, they can do that too and still tickle some untapped taste buds. The menu here changes frequently, with daily lunch and dinner specials sometimes stun-

ning even the regulars. Weekly Tapas Nights, which feature little plates of dishes from a chosen cuisine, are held on Thursday nights in fall, winter, and spring. One week you might taste samples of German food, the next Italian, the next Moroccan, and so on. This is a big hit with the locals. Sushi nights also are popular.

A full bar separate from the cozy dining room offers fresh-fruit margaritas, a nice wine selection, and more than a dozen varieties of bottled beer. Nonalcoholic fruit smoothies are a treat in the early afternoon. Happy hour is held from 3:00 to 5:00 P.M. every day in the summer. Steamed seafood and veggies are served at the bar until closing (see our Nightlife chapter). Chilli Peppers serves lunch and dinner seven days a week year-round. Sunday brunches, with a make-your-own Bloody Mary bar, are worth getting out of bed for. Also, you can take home a bottle of Chilli's award-winning original hot sauce, barbecue sauce, or hot salt. Chilli Peppers is open 11:00 A.M. to 2:00 A.M. A children's menu is available.

Front Porch Cafe $
US 158, MP 6, Kill Devil Hills
(252) 449-6616
www.frontporchcafe.net

The Front Porch Cafe sources top-quality coffee beans from all over the world, then roasts each batch by hand in their store. Owners Paul Manning and Susannah Sakal enjoy chatting with customers in their friendly, relaxed community coffeehouse. Freshly baked cinnamon rolls, scones, and muffins are available every day. Customers can also select from the wonderful varieties of teas on hand.

Awful Arthur's Oyster Bar
& Restaurant $$
NC 12, MP 6, Kill Devil Hills
(252) 441-5955
www.awfularthursnc.com

Located across from Avalon Pier, this authentic raw bar and restaurant is usually crowded throughout the year. Wooden tables are laid out along the oblong room, and a bar stretches the entire length of the downstairs eatery. Upstairs, a separate lounge offers an ocean view. A live lobster tank and huge saltwater reef tank give you something to watch as you dine.

Awful Arthur's is a comfortably casual place where you won't mind peeling seasoned shrimp or picking the meat from succulent crab legs with messy fingers. Seafood is the specialty here. You'll find scallops, oysters, clams, mussels, homemade crab cakes, and daily entree specials. The bartenders are some of the fastest shuckers in town. Bass Ale and several other varieties of beer are on tap, or order from a full line of liquor and specialty drinks. For landlubbers, several non-seafood sandwiches are served.

At night, Awful Arthur's is usually packed. A late-night menu is available. Awful Arthur's T-shirts are seen all over the world and are local favorites. This popular eatery is open seven days a week year-round for lunch and dinner.

Carolina Seafood $$$
NC 12, MP 6¼, Kill Devil Hills
(252) 441-6851

For an elaborate, all-you-can-eat seafood buffet where "fried has died," try Carolina Seafood. Here, you can enjoy 36 items for less than $25 a person: salad, soups, hush puppies, garlic crabs, crab legs, scallops, stuffed shrimp, and several types of fish served baked, broiled, blackened, steamed, or sautéed. Roast beef is cut to order, and a variety of desserts are included in the price. If you're not feeling hungry enough to tackle the buffet, Carolina Seafood serves crabs, scallops, shrimp, and other seafood by the basket, too. A children's menu also is available. This restaurant is open at 4:30 P.M. seven nights a week from May through September. Call for off-season hours.

Jolly Roger Restaurant $$
NC 12, MP 6, Kill Devil Hills
(252) 441-6530

Serving some of the locals' favorite breakfasts, this lively restaurant is open for three meals a day 365 days a year. Besides the usual eggs, pancakes, sausage, bacon, and toast, Jolly Roger's bakery cooks up some of the biggest muffins and sticky buns you've ever seen. For lunch, choose from sandwiches, local seafood, or daily specials. Dinner entrees include homestyle Italian dishes, steaks, broiled and fried fish, and a popular $10.95 prime rib special each Friday. All the desserts are homemade, and special orders are accepted for items to go. The food isn't fancy, but the portions are enormous. You'll have no excuse if you leave here hungry. Jolly Roger also steams spiced shrimp in the separate bar area each afternoon and is the karaoke headquarters of the Outer Banks seven nights a week.

Mako Mike's $$
US 158, MP 7, Kill Devil Hills
(252) 480-1919

This is the most outrageously decorated dining establishment on the Outer Banks. The fluorescent shark fins outside, decorated with swirls, stripes, and polka dots, don't give even a glimpse into what you'll see once you step inside. Some patrons compare it to an underwater experience. We think it's almost like visiting an octopus's garden complete with three separate levels of dining, fish mobiles dangling overhead, painted chairs, bright colors exploding everywhere, and murals along the deep blue walls.

The menu is impressive and varied. Appetizers include hot crab dip and calamari. Dinner offerings are seasoned with Mediterranean, Cajun, Asian, and other exotic spices and include nine varieties of

If you're heading out for a day on the sand, Stop 'N' Shop Convenience and Deli on the Beach Road in Kill Devil Hills is a great place to stock up. It has one of the best delis on the beach, an excellent selection of wine and beer, everything you'll need for a successful day's fishing, and all the latest water toys, too.

ℹ️ *The soft-sculpture ceiling at Goombays Grille & Raw Bar is an amazing work of art. While sitting in the dining room, you can look up and imagine you're seeing what a fish sees when it glances up toward the ocean's surface.*

fresh pasta, seven wood-fired pizzas, several varieties of fresh blue-water fish, beef, pork, vegetarian stir-fries, mixed grills, scallops, shrimp, and dozens of other options.

This huge restaurant caters to couples, families, and large groups. A small meeting room is available for private parties. A separate bar serves frozen drink specials in addition to dozens of bottles of beer and wine. A children's menu is provided. Dinner is served seven days a week year-round. Call for winter hours. Mako Mike's owner, Mike Kelly, also operates Kelly's Restaurant and Tavern and is part owner of Penguin Isle, both in Nags Head.

Goombays Grille & Raw Bar $$
NC 12, MP 7, Kill Devil Hills
(252) 441–6001
www.goombays.com

This island-style eatery is light and bright inside with lots of artwork, an outrageous fish tank, and a wall-size tropical mural in the dining room. The ambience is upbeat and casual, with wooden tables and chairs and a bare tile floor. The horseshoe-shaped bar, which is separate from the eating area, is a great place to try some of the delicious appetizers or drink specials that Goombays makes. We especially recommend the spicy crab balls and sweet coconut shrimp. Some of the drink offerings, both alcoholic and children's cocktails, come with zany toys to take home.

For lunch or dinner, try a fresh pasta entree, including everybody's favorite Rasta Pasta, locally caught seafood, a juicy burger topped as you wish, the Southwestern sampling, or one of the half-dozen daily specials, such as pork, barbecued shrimp, and steak stir-fry. Everything here

is reasonably priced and flavorful. A raw bar is open until 1:00 A.M., serving steamed shrimp, oysters, vegetables, and other favorites. Key lime pie is always a smart choice for dessert. In season, Goombays has live music every Wednesday. Goombays is open for lunch and dinner seven days a week in summer. Call for off-season hours. Goombays closes for December and January.

The Good Life Gourmet $$
The Dare Center, US 158, MP 7½
Kill Devil Hills
(252) 480–2855
www.goodlifegourmet.com

Aptly named, The Good Life offers house-made breads and pastries, sandwiches, soups, salads, and some incredibly decadent desserts. One great sandwich is the warm Cubana torta, a potato brioche roll filled with roast pork, country ham, jalapeño jack cheese, guacamole, and black beans. Vegetarian options include a black bean and three-cheese burrito with grilled vegetables, tomato salsa, and sour cream, or the brie salad sandwich, with sliced apples and grape vinaigrette on whole wheat. Another great sandwich is the hot roast beef with bacon barbecue on potato brioche. Salads include a mixed green salad with granny smith apple slices and Brie cheese served with raspberry vinaigrette dressing, green salads and pasta salads.

For dinner, try the Italian sausage meatballs with cheese tortellini and fresh marinara or the Good Life Gourmet famous meat loaf.

Not only can you get a good cup of coffee, you can opt for espresso or cappuccino, as well as beer or wine. Wine is available by the glass, and there's a nice selection of retail bottled wine, too. While you're in the shop, tear yourself away from the pastry and dessert display and check out the selection of artisan cheeses, olives, and sauces. Gift baskets are available here, too. Menu items are available for dining in or for takeout. The Good Life opens at 8:00 A.M. each morning.

Port O' Call Restaurant
& Gaslight Saloon $$$
NC 12, MP 8½, Kill Devil Hills
(252) 441-7484

This antiques-adorned restaurant offers fresh seafood cuisine with entrees including an array of seafood, veal, chicken, pasta, and beef. Blackboard specials change nightly. Each dinner comes with fresh-baked bread, starch of the day, and salad. The soups and chowders are hot and succulent, and all the desserts are luscious. A children's menu is also offered.

Frank Gajar opened the restaurant in 1974, decorating it with a collection of Victorian furnishings. The dining room is warm and romantic, with flickering gaslights and brass accents. Special early bird dinners are served from 4:30 to 6:00 P.M. Live entertainment is offered in a large, separate saloon (see our Nightlife chapter). A full bar is available, and the gift shop/art gallery carries unusual, eclectic items. Port O' Call is open from mid-March through December. A children's menu is available.

The Thai Room $$
Oceanside Plaza
NC 12, MP 8½, Kill Devil Hills
(252) 441-1180

The Thai Room has been an Insiders' favorite for years. Jimmy, the fast-talking, fast-moving owner, lets his patrons choose their own level of spice—from mild to gasping hot. When he asks, "Very hot?"—think twice before you say yes. He means it.

Besides the daily specials, an in-season buffet dinner allows you to sample several of the wonderful choices. Try the deep-fried soft-shell crabs when they're in season; they're perfectly crunchy and beyond description. To complete your meal, choose from more than a dozen American-style desserts. As for decor, the Thai Room is unlike any other eatery on North Carolina's barrier islands: paper lanterns, Asian portraits, and red-tasseled lamps adorn the dining room. Family members prepare and serve each delectable meal—and they'll be happy to make suggestions if you're overwhelmed by all the options.

The Thai Room is open for lunch and dinner March through December. All items are available for takeout. The restaurant also has a full bar where you can indulge in exotic drinks and Thai beer while you wait for a table or take-out order.

Outer Banks Brewing Station $$
US 158, MP 8½, Kill Devil Hills
(252) 449-BREW
www.obbrewing.com

Everything about the Outer Banks Brewing Station is first class. Fine hand-crafted brews, inspired cuisine, and noble yet subtle decor all work together to provide a sublime culinary experience. The Brewing Station opened in 2001 to rave reviews. Customers who expected standard brewhouse pub fare were pleasantly surprised to find contemporary, cutting-edge cuisine prepared by schooled chefs. The signature beers have gone over well. Olsch is always on tap, and five other brews change according to the season, the brewer's whim, or the alignment of the stars.

The owners say they believe that fine brewing deserves to be paired with revolutionary cuisine, and they certainly have the goods to prove it. The food is outstanding. Start with ahipoké, sashimi with mixed greens, tossed with soy vinaigrette and wasabi cream, or the chardonnay mussels. The specials are always appealing, but the jerk-basted wahoo over jasmine rice with pineapple beurre blanc is astounding. Desserts are extremely tempting; so is a glass of tawny port. The restaurant also has an excellent wine list.

The Outer Banks Brewing Station occupies a unique, church/barnlike building built especially for this use. Two silos anchor the building, prompting the owners to advertise their location as "between the silos in Kill Devil Hills." Inside, cathedral ceilings lined with tin are more than 20 feet high, with windows that reach to the ceiling along the front of the building. Rustic cement and brick floors, honey-toned walls adorned with Middle Eastern rugs, and warm woods create a comforting atmosphere. The serpentine bar stretches into the back of the restaurant, where a crowd gathers for drinks until the wee hours (see our Nightlife chapter). The Brewing Station is a year-round restaurant. Lunch and dinner are served daily, and a kid's menu is available.

JK's   **$$$**
US 158, MP 9, Kill Devil Hills
(252) 441-9555
www.jksfoods.com
Fine-dining Insiders love JK's selection of mesquite-grilled meats. JK's serves Western beef shipped directly from Nebraska, lamb and veal from Summerfield Farms in Virginia, and ribs from the Midwest. A seasoned, professional staff fits right in with the classy, comfortable dining room and bar. Three to four varieties of fresh fish are offered nightly. The menu varies, according to the best meats available, but generally has a prime rib chop, porterhouse steak, New York strip, Kansas City strip, top sirloin, veal rib chop, and lamb loin chops. Ribs and chicken are dry-marinated with JK's special seasoning and are then mesquite-grilled. JK's has a full bar and an excellent wine list with some really good values. Dinner is served from 5:00 P.M. year-round; takeout is available.

Bob's Grill   **$**
US 158, MP 9, Kill Devil Hills
(252) 441-0707
Bob serves big, cheap breakfasts all year seven days a week, until 2:30 P.M.—and that's hard to find around here. The blueberry pancakes are big enough to cover the entire plate. Eggs are made any way you want, and the hash browns flavored with onions and peppers are some of the best around.

For lunch, a hamburger, tuna steak, or one of several traditional hot and cold sandwiches will fill you. Owner Bob McCoy cooks much of the food himself. A hot lunch special is available every day. You can't leave town without trying Bob's No. 1 seller—Philly steak and cheese. Dinners feature the biggest cuts of prime rib on the Outer Banks, Cajun beer

batter-dipped shrimp, and fresh mahimahi caught just offshore. The salads are also good. Save room for the hot fudge brownie dessert.

Bob's casual atmosphere has a regular-folk appeal that makes everyone comfortable. Even McCoy's well-known gruff motto, "Eat and get the hell out," has obviously not offended any locals, since the parking lot is packed with loyal customers more days than not. Service is fast and friendly, beer and wine are available, and everything can be ordered for takeout. Bob's is closed from 2:30 to 5:00 P.M. daily, but it's open for three meals a day every day all year.

The Pit Surf Shop, Bar and Grill   **$**
US 158, MP 9, Kill Devil Hills
(252) 480-3128
www.pitsurf.com
The Pit is the favorite counterculture hangout of the beach. It's the prime après-surf spot, where the food is good and cheap, the staff has personality, and board-sport videos are always shown. The hallmarks of Pit dining are economy and portion size; the West Coast-style wraps are big and filling. Beans, meats, cheese, veggies, and even mashed potatoes are blended into a variety of creative wraps. The Pit makes a mean quesadilla, hot sandwiches, salads in a fresh tortilla bowl, appetizers, fries, rings, wings, and more. Nothing costs more than $8.00. Drinks run the gamut from alcohol to up-to-the-minute So-Be flavors and everything in between. Food is served continuously from 11:30 A.M. until 9:00 P.M., and delivery is offered on weekdays in the off-season. People always hang around The Pit, killing time and meeting friends. See our Nightlife and Water Sports chapters for more about The Pit.

Dirty Dicks Crab House   **$$**
US 158, MP 9, Kill Devil Hills
(252) 480-3425
www.dirtydickscrabs.com
The litany of crab choices at Dirty Dicks

Crab House reminds us of Bubba's roster of shrimp in *Forrest Gump*. There are snow crab legs, soft-shell crab sandwiches, spiced crabs, crab cakes, and steamed crabs, plus steamed shrimp, clams, clam chowder, gumbo, jambalaya, and Cajun creole. The popular Dick Burger is a crab and shrimp patty with Cajun sauce. There are sandwich platter specials and offerings for the kids. You can purchase Dicks special spice and famous Dirty Dicks T-shirts. Crustaceans are cooked to order for takeout. This location of Dirty Dicks is a sit-down restaurant. A Dirty Dicks on the Beach Road offers takeout only. Dirty Dicks has a third Outer Banks location—a sit-down crab house restaurant—on North Carolina Highway 12 in Avon, by the Avon Pier. All locations are open seasonally; call for hours.

Dare Devil's Authentic Pizzeria $
NC 12, MP 9, Kill Devil Hills
(252) 441-6330, (252) 441-2353

This pizza parlor has been in business for more than a decade and is known for its superb stromboli and hand-tossed pizzas. Chicken wings, mozzarella sticks, nachos, Greek salads, and pizza bread also are available here, as are subs and salads. Dare Devil's has four types of beer on tap served in frosty glass mugs. The interior is low-key, with laminated tables and a long bar where you can eat. A big-screen TV in the corner usually is tuned to whatever hot sporting event happens to be going on. You can also order any item for takeout. Dare Devil's is open seven days a week for lunch and dinner from March through November.

Mama Kwan's Grill and Tiki Bar $$
US 158, MP 9½, Kill Devil Hills
(252) 441-7889
www.mamakwans.com

Mama Kwan's is a favorite surf-style hangout in Kill Devil Hills, a haven of good food sandwiched between McDonald's and Pizza Hut on French Fry Alley in the cedar-shake building. The atmosphere is laid-back and fun, with classic and current surf videos and occasional Elvis movies playing on TVs. Children are welcomed with a special menu and toys to keep them entertained.

Mama's features local seafood, land food, and veggies with touches from some of the world's best surf spots. There's blackened Hawaiian chicken seasoned with Jamaican and Hawaiian spices in a rum butter sauce with pineapple mango salsa, pad Thai and rice noodles, California-style fish tacos, and Outer Banks crab cakes. Mama recommends the Special Occasion Pasta: penne with red peppers, shiitake mushrooms, snow peas, and scallions in a soy cream sauce with or without tuna. The full bar serves beer, wine, and specialty frozen drinks in novelty glassware. Lunch and dinner are served daily. This is a popular nighttime hangout, and a late-night menu is served every night in season and on weekends in the off-season (see our Nightlife chapter).

Peppercorns $$
Ramada Plaza, NC 12, MP 9½
Kill Devil Hills
(252) 441-2151

With a wide, open dining room overlooking the Atlantic Ocean, Peppercorns has a traditional family menu with something for everyone.

Chef Greg Sniegowski prepares many Outer Banks favorites, including locally caught shrimp and crab cakes. The soup du jour is always filling and delicious. Entrees include chicken stuffed with crab meat, andouille sausage, and smoked gouda cheese and jerk mahimahi served with a mouthwatering pineapple sweet-and-sour sauce. Vegetarian entrees are always provided. There's a full bar and a children's menu. Peppercorns provides take-out food and room service for Ramada guests. This restaurant is open daily year-round for breakfast, lunch, and dinner. There's nightly entertainment in season on the outdoor tiki deck and in the lounge. Peppercorns is a popular spot for banquets and wedding receptions.

Pigman's Bar-B-Que $
US 158, MP 9½, Kill Devil Hills
(252) 441–6803
www.pigman.com
Bill and Jen Ulmer are the owners of Pigman's, known for its delectable food. Daisy Q, their potbellied pig, likes the kids to visit her at the Pigman's on sunny days. At this counter-service eatery, you can get beef, pork, chicken, and barbecue. Try the low-fat creations: catfish, turkey, and tuna barbecue. Each dinner comes with coleslaw, hush puppies, and baked beans and is served on disposable plates with plastic utensils. The sweet potato fries here are spectacular. You can purchase all four Pigman barbecue sauces and Pigman meat rub at the restaurant. Catering is available. Pigman's is open for lunch and dinner seven days a week, year-round. Piggy Lou's Little Squealers is a special menu for those younger than age 10 or older than age 65. A second location in Duck (by Carolina Outdoors) is open for carry out only.

Flying Fish Cafe $$
US 158, MP 10, Kill Devil Hills
(252) 441–6894
www.flyingfishcafe.net
This delightful restaurant serves an array of American and Mediterranean dishes. The interior is spruce green and adobe white with purple accents, and color photographs grace the walls. Brightly colored tablecloths adorn each table, illuminated by sconce wall lights crafted from wine boxes and by candles set in the center of each table or booth.

Chefs at Flying Fish make their own pasta daily and offer an assortment of seafood, vegetarian entrees, and a variety of unusual grains and starches. Gourmet pot pies, eggplant parmesan, at least four types of fresh fish, and exceptional beef dishes are always on the menu. All entrees come with a starch of the day, vegetables, and just-baked bread, including focaccia. Appetizers include baked spinach parmesan pie with wild mushrooms and bacon, topped with golden fried oysters, and Thai coconut shrimp bisque. At dessert time, can you resist the Grecian Urn, a waffle filled with ice cream and topped with glazed fresh fruit and whipped cream? Chocoholics will love the Chocolate Hurricane, a flourless chocolate brownie with mousse and a liquid chocolate center, wrapped in a white and dark chocolate shell topped with ganache and completed with a white chocolate flying fish jumping out of the top.

The Flying Fish Cafe has won several *Wine Spectator* Awards of Excellence. More than 40 types of wine are served either by the bottle or by the glass. A children's menu also is available. Early-bird dinner specials are served from 5:00 to 6:00 P.M. The Flying Fish is open for dinner every day year-round. Reservations are recommended.

COLINGTON ISLAND

Colington Cafe $$
Colington Road, 1 mile west of US 158
Kill Devil Hills
(252) 480–1123
www.colingtoncafe.com
Step back in time at this cozy Victorian cafe, nestled among live oaks on Colington Road. This popular restaurant is only a mile off the Bypass but once you've arrived, you'll feel worlds away from the busy beach. This restored old home set high on a hill is tranquil and absolutely lovely. This is one of our favorite places to come for an intimate dinner, and the chefs prepare some of the most marvelous meals around for extremely reasonable prices. Three small dining rooms are adorned in tasteful decor.

Hot crab dip slathered on buttery crackers and bowls of homemade she-crab bisque make outstanding appetizers. Nightly specials may include wonderful pasta dishes, a mixed grill with hollandaise, game fish, and tender filet mignon. Seafood entrees depend upon what's just been caught. Only fresh herbs and vegetables are used in cooking and as side dishes. Salads are served a la carte.

Owner Carlen Pearl's French heritage permeates her restaurant's delicious cream sauces, and she makes most of the irresistible desserts herself—from blackberry cobbler to chocolate tortes and crème brûlée. Restaurants in Colington may serve only beer or wine by law, but you'll have plenty of choices at Colington Cafe. Check out the reserve wines and be sure to save room for a glass of port with dessert. Colington Cafe is open for dinner seven days a week, April through November, and for the Christmas holidays. Call for off-season hours. Reservations are highly recommended.

NAGS HEAD

Mrs. T's Deli $
US 158, MP 10, Nags Head
(252) 441-1220
This homey deli is a great bet for quick, satisfying lunches and some of the friendliest chatter in town. Most of Mrs. T's three-dozen-plus sandwiches are named after friends and family members. We like the Stacy sub, with four cheeses. The three varieties of veggie burgers get rave reviews. Club sandwiches are stacked so high they barely fit in your mouth. The Outer Banks curly fries, lightly seasoned and made to order, are wonderful. Cakes, pastries, and gourmet jelly beans are available for dessert, and kosher food, including matzos, is available all year. Mrs. T's serves lunch and dinner seven days a week from mid-March through early February. Everything can be packaged to go.

Red Drum Grille and Taphouse $$
NC 12, MP 10, Nags Head
(252) 480-1095
Since opening in 1998, the Red Drum Grille and Taphouse has been carving out its niche on the Outer Banks. The handsome redbrick exterior presents an apt introduction to the tasteful decor: Glossy, deep rust-colored tables and cozy oak booths give the room a warm, inviting feel. A gleaming redwood bar stretches along the length of the back wall and lures you in for one of 18 beers on tap. In the back room—away from the dining room—are a pool table and a foosball table for those who want to stay and play after dinner.

The menu has something for everyone. For starters, try the Hatteras-style clam chowder, the calamari, or the shrimp con queso dip. The homemade stuffed jalapeños are just hot enough and full of flavor. Lunch fare from the steamer menu includes crab legs, shrimp, vegetables, clams, and oysters. Large burgers, a chicken sandwich with Smithfield ham and havarti cheese, fish and chips, and a fish burrito are some of the locals' favorites.

At dinner, Red Drum offers simple country fare. It's reminiscent of the Outer Banks of old or of Mom's cooking taken a step further and served with diligence and a smile. You'll find apple-glazed pork chops, ribs, steaks, a mixed grill of the day, and lots of fresh seafood, including seafood pasta with large shrimp and scallops and a mixed seafood platter. Entrees are served with mashed potatoes or wild rice. (Insiders' tip: The potatoes will knock your socks off.) Grilled or fried fresh fish, pasta, and vegetarian dishes are also available.

The Red Drum Grille and Taphouse serves lunch and dinner from February through November and has a kid's menu.

Kelly's Outer Banks
Restaurant & Tavern $$$
US 158, MP 10½, Nags Head
(252) 441-4116
www.kellysrestaurant.com
Kelly's is an Outer Banks tradition and one of the most popular restaurants. Owner Mike Kelly gives his personal attention to every detail, so the service and selections are consistently first-rate. This is a large, upscale eatery and a busy place. The decor reflects the area's rich maritime heritage, with abundant examples of fish,

birds, and other wildlife. The tavern is hopping seven nights a week (see our Nightlife chapter).

Dinner is the only meal served here, and it's offered in several rooms upstairs and downstairs. Kelly's menu offers fresh seafood dishes, chicken, beef, pastas, and a raw bar for those who enjoy feasting on oysters and other steamed shellfish. An assortment of delicious homemade breads accompanies each meal. Kelly's sweet potato biscuits are succulent—we usually ask for a second basket. Desserts are flavorful and filling. A separate children's menu is available, complete with crayons and special place mats for coloring. Kelly's also caters private parties, weddings, and any style event imaginable. The restaurant and lounge are open year-round.

**Slammin' Sammy's Offshore
Grille & Stillery**   **$$**
US 158, MP 10½, Nags Head
(252) 449-2255
www.slamminsammys.com
Slammin' Sammy's is the place to go for a frolicsome atmosphere of food, fun, and fuel. With 43 TVs plus four giant screens, you can get an eyeful of sporting events. There's also a pool and tabletop shuffleboard. Sammy's is open for lunch and dinner, serving sandwiches, salads, "hot spot" jumbo baked potatoes loaded with plenty of extras, appetizers, prime rib, and pizza. Sandwiches include the Hogs Breath shrimp po'boy, the Incredible Edible crab-

cake sandwich, a Clubwater Club, and grilled game fish. Slammin' Sammy's has daily chef's specials, a children's menu, and a full bar. Lunch and dinner are served daily year-round.

Mulligan's Oceanfront Grille   **$$**
NC 12, MP 10½, Nags Head
(252) 480-2000
Mulligan's can lay claim to serving some of the best burgers on the beach. The burgers are big, juicy, and tasty and come with a variety of toppings. Mulligan's also serves steak, seafood, and an array of pasta entrees for lunch and dinner. Occupying the old Miller's Pharmacy building, the eatery is divided in half lengthwise by wooden and glass partitions. The south end is flanked by a long, low bar. Scores of old Outer Banks photographs, painted mirrors, and other memorabilia decorate this comfortable, inviting full-service bar, where appetizers and light dinners are available.

The north half of Mulligan's is the restaurant, where steamed seafood, sandwiches, pasta, and steak are available. Live entertainment and karaoke fill the atmosphere year-round (see our Nightlife chapter). Mulligan's is open seven days a week all year long. A children's menu is available.

Prime Only   **$$$**
MP 10¾, Nags Head
(252) 480-0047

Prime Only is a new yet familiar restaurant in Nags Head. It was a popular Outer Banks restaurant in the mid-1990s but had to relocate upon losing its lease. Now back and better than ever, Prime Only offers fine food at a moderate price. Its specialty is Midwestern corn-fed aged beef, hand cut and broiled to perfection.

Freshly caught seafood, chicken, pork, and fresh pasta are among the other offerings in this casually elegant restaurant. Vegetarian dishes are available as well. This Insider recommends the Caesar salad, prepared by your table from scratch along with the signature filet mignon, served so tender that it can be cut with a butter knife. Desserts are all prepared in house, and the delicious, flaming Bananas Foster is prepared tableside. A menu for tykes is available.

Prime Only has a sister restaurant in Raleigh that offers an identical wine list, and that location won a 2003 and 2004 *Wine Spectator* award. There is a full bar at the Nags Head location. Smoking is allowed upstairs, while the downstairs remains smoke-free. Reservations are recommended. Open daily year-round for dinner only. Call for off-season hours.

Tortuga's Lie Shellfish Bar and Grille $
NC 12, MP 11, Nags Head
(252) 441-RAWW
www.tortugaslie.com

A locals' favorite on the Outer Banks, this small, upbeat eatery is housed in a turquoise cottage across from the ocean near a great surf break. Tortuga's features an enclosed porch furnished with hand-made wooden booths, table seating, and an expanded bar that seats more than two dozen people. There's a sand volley-ball court out back where pickup games are played—and watched from the outdoor picnic tables. The bartenders and waitstaff are some of the friendliest folk we know. The creatively concocted food is good and the atmosphere inside is fun and casual, with turtle-themed batiks hanging from the white walls and more than 100 license plates, some with unusual

personal messages, from across the country tacked to the low ceiling beams.

The menu here offers quick-fried fish bites, supersize fish and black bean burritos, sandwiches, seafood flavored with outrageous spices, and a full raw bar. The french fries are among the best on the Banks. Dinner entrees include pork medallions, steak stir-fries, just-off-the-boat tuna steaks, succulent shrimp, and pasta plates. Most meals come with rice and beans, but the cooks will substitute fries if you ask. The daily specials are tempting; sushi is served on Wednesday night, and the place usually is packed with locals. Desserts are delicious and change daily.

The full bar offers loads of specialty drinks such as Black and Tans, a combination of Bass Ale and Guinness Stout. This hip, laid-back eatery is open seven days a week for lunch and dinner from February through December. Call for winter hours. (See also our Nightlife chapter.)

Pier House Restaurant $
Nags Head Fishing Pier
NC 12, MP 12, Nags Head
(252) 441-5141

With an amazing ocean view on the beach, this family-style restaurant allows patrons to sit right above the ocean. You can feel the salt spray if you dine on the screened porch, and inside the air-conditioned building, waves sometimes crash beneath the wooden floor's slats. This is a great, easy-going place to enjoy a big breakfast before a day of fishing or to take a break from angling on a hot afternoon.

The staff at Pier House is friendly, and all three meals of the day are traditionally prepared. The Em Special is an Insiders' favorite for breakfast. Lunch includes sandwiches, soups, and seafood specials. Dinner entrees include local fresh seafood, steaks, and chicken. All-you-can-eat din-

Clean the fish you catch, and the Pier House Restaurant in Nags Head will broil or fry it right up for you.

ners are popular picks, accompanied by coleslaw, hush puppies, and french fries. You can have your fish grilled, broiled, or fried. Appetizers and desserts also are available. Free sightseeing passes come with supper so you can stroll along the long pier after your meal and watch the anglers and surfers. Pier House Restaurant is open seven days a week from March through November. Breakfast, lunch, and dinner are served until mid-October, and the restaurant has all liquor permits.

Don Gatos $-$$
NC 12, MP 11½, Nags Head
(252) 441-9330

This restaurant is fast becoming a local favorite. Chef Amando brings his inspirations from Oaxaca, Mexico. He offers vegetarian dishes, chicken, beef, and fresh Outer Banks seafood dishes in an authentic Mexican atmosphere. The interior of the restaurant is beautifully decorated and evokes the feeling of an upscale cantina.

Daily specials like the delicious smoked tuna tostada are available. Lunch begins at 11:30 A.M., and dinner is served until 10:00 P.M. The food is fresh, healthy, and filling. A favorite menu item is the Camarones al Mojo de Ajo, jumbo shrimp sautéed with onion and cilantro in a hearty garlic sauce. The ceviche and guacamole are stellar. You may want to sip a Mexican beer or a made-to-order margarita with your meal. A children's menu is available.

Don Gatos is open year-round. Look for the bright orange building with the surfer on the roof.

Austin Fish Company
US 158, MP 12½, Nags Head
(252) 441-7412
www.austinfishcompany.com

A visit to Nags Head isn't complete without visiting Austin Fish Company, across from Jockey's Ridge. The store stocks an extensive seafood collection—including crabmeat, steamed crabs, shrimp, oysters, clams, fish, scallops, and tuna—for customers to take home and cook. Even selective locals drive out of their way to purchase Austin's fresh seafood. If you've enjoyed a good day fishing, Austin's will vacuum pack your catch and ship it home for you.

Jockey's Ribs $$
NC 12, MP 13, Nags Head
(252) 441-1141

For dining in or for takeout, Jockey's Ribs has been serving finger-licking barbecue for more than 15 years now. Entrees include lean and meaty slabs of pork ribs, hot and spicy barbecued chicken wings, roasted chicken, steaks, chops, chicken and rib combos, and seafood. A variety of warm breads is served with each entree, along with hash browns or a baked potato. The seafood gumbo is always a favorite. If you're looking for a light dinner, sandwiches are served each evening, along with such appetizers as crab-stuffed mushroom caps and French onion soup. A children's menu is available. Dinner is served nightly from 5:00 to 10:00 P.M. in season. Call for off-season hours.

Country Deli $
Surfside Plaza, NC 12, MP 13, Nags Head
(252) 441-5684

Strictly a take-out place, Country Deli offers breakfast breads plus some of the biggest sandwiches on the beach. Our favorite is the "Killer," with turkey breast, ham, Muenster and Havarti cheeses, lettuce, tomato, and hot peppers on a sub roll. You can create your own sandwiches as well. Side salads of macaroni, pasta, potato, and vegetables also are served. Pick from several types of chips; sour pickles come free with every option. Brownies and cheesecake are tempting dessert selections.

Don't leave without checking out the philosophical ponderings employees leave on the blackboard behind the cash register—they could change the way you think about the world while you're trying to decide what to order. Country Deli is open for lunch and dinner seven days a week during the summer and offers free delivery to Nags Head and parts of Kill Devil

Hills. This eatery is open for lunch only during the off-season (call for hours and days). No credit cards accepted.

Bad Barracuda's Raw Bar & Grille $$
US 158, MP 13, Nags Head
(252) 449-0223
www.badbarracudasnc.com

Brought to us by the same folks who own Awful Arthur's, Bad Barracuda's Raw Bar & Grille serves up a broad assortment of just about any type of seafood you might be craving, plus clam chowder, seafood gumbo, lobster bisque, salads, pastas, and a variety of hearty dinner entrees. If you're looking for bar food and sandwiches, you won't be disappointed: The menu has a nice selection of appetizers and sand-wiches, as well as a number of burger options. How about the Backfin Burger, topped with your choice of cheese and backfin crabmeat? Or, there's the Big "B" Burger ("the burger that Bad Barracuda eats"), made with a half-pound of freshly ground beef. The restaurant offers lunch and dinner specials daily and specializes in large parties. Bad Barracuda's has a full bar plus specialty drinks (try the Awesome Barracuda), a nice wine selection, a chil-dren's menu, and soon-to-be-famous T-shirts. The restaurant is wheelchair accessible. Insiders recommend that you save room for the double-cooked key lime pie. The pie alone will lure you back.

Bad Barracuda's is open year round, serving dinner nightly and lunch on the weekends.

Grits Grill $
US 158, MP 14, Nags Head
(252) 449-2888

Just north of the Outer Banks Mall is Grits Grill, which has a strong local following. The restaurant offers a standard-fare breakfast and lunch menu plus fresh bakery items and fresh Krispy Kreme donuts. If you can't live without your Krispy Kremes, make sure you get to Grits early in the morning, because they sell out quickly. Grits special-izes in take-out orders and is open all year from 6:00 A.M. to 4:00 P.M.

La Fogata Mexican Restaurant $
US 158, MP 14, Nags Head
(252) 441-4179

Across from the Outer Banks Mall, La Fogata joins its original Kitty Hawk sister restaurant with the same name and some delicious Mexican food at affordable prices. These restaurants boast a strong Outer Banks following. The mall location has the same menu and similar decor as the Kitty Hawk restaurant (see the listing under Kitty Hawk for more information).

Bacu Grill $$
US 158, MP 14, Nags Head
(252) 480-1892

Located across from Seamark at the Outer Banks Mall, the Bacu Grill serves authentic flavors from the East Coast to Cuba and beyond. The restaurant's name comes from the Cuban-American term for a taste or sight that reminds one of home. At Bacu Grill, you'll experience a homey atmosphere with a metropolitan feel.

You can get three different types of burgers for lunch: American, blackened, or with jerk seasonings. Sandwiches include soft-shell crab, blackened tuna, pit beef, and a Cuban mix. Side orders include Cuban beans and rice, chips and salsa, fries, and corn on the cob. The raw bar serves stone crab, crab legs, clams, oysters, mussels, and spiced shrimp; fish, steak, seafood, and pasta dishes make up the dinner entrees. The popular porter-house steak is 20 to 22 ounces and is cooked Tuscan style—seared in olive oil and finished with garlic butter and cracked black pepper. For appetizers, try some West Indies coconut shrimp, cracked conch, hurricane wings, or baked Brie.

Bacu Grill has a world-class wine list, a full bar, nonsmoking dining, and a smoking lounge. Cigars and wines are sold in Bacu's retail shop. The restaurant is open year-round for lunch and dinner.

Taiko Japanese Restaurant
and Sushi Bar $$
Outer Banks Mall, US 158, MP 14
Nags Head
(252) 449-8895

This Outer Banks restaurant serves sushi all day, for lunch and dinner. Taiko's sushi is top-notch, rolled tightly and cut into perfect, bite-size pieces. Our favorite is the spicy tuna roll, with fresh raw tuna, a kick of spices, and a hint of crunch. We also like the spider roll special—fried soft-shell crab—and the dragon roll with tuna, crab, and cucumber wrapped in masago, avocado, and eel. The miso and clear soups are refreshing, as are the udon and soba noodle dishes and the seaweed salad. Japanese-style entrees include steak teriyaki, shrimp tempura, and chicken sukiyaki. Lunch boxes combine sushi or sashimi with seaweed, rice, and a shrimp dumpling.

The dining room is peaceful and serene, with soft music and tasteful, understated Asian decor. You can eat at the bar and watch the chefs prepare your meal or sit at a table. Japanese beer, sake, plum wine, green tea, and many other beverages are served. Everything at Taiko is available for takeout. Taiko is open year-round, serving lunch and dinner daily in season. Call for off-season hours.

Outer Banks Steak House $$
US 158, MP 14½, Nags Head
(252) 449-4448

If you're craving a big juicy piece of meat, you might as well come to the place that devoted itself primarily to steak. Outer Banks Steak House serves certified Angus beef; center-cut sirloin, prime rib, rib eye, filet mignon, New York strip, porterhouse, and ribs are favorites here. To combine the best of both worlds, try the sirloin topped with fried oysters, the prime rib with broiled shrimp, or the half-rack of baby back ribs with stuffed shrimp. Seafood entrees, like crab cakes, fish, and a seafood platter, are available as is pasta. Side dishes range from fried oysters to sautéed onions to steak fries. The Steak

House has a full bar along with beer and wine, and is open for lunch and dinner every day in season. A children's menu is available.

Penguin Isle Soundside Grille $$$
US 158, MP 16, Nags Head
(252) 441-2637
www.penguinisle.com

Penguin Isle is truly a peaceful place to enjoy a special, intimate meal. The decor is tasteful and creative, with displays of local art, hand-carved decoys, authentic ship models, and light wood accents around the airy dining room. Linen tablecloths cover every table, and the lights and jazz music are soft and low.

Not only a premier place to dine, Penguin Isle is also a wine destination. The staff is very knowledgeable, and the much-heralded *Wine Spectator*'s Award of Excellence has identified this restaurant's wine list as "one of the best in the world" for more than a decade. Seasonal wine dinners are offered in the off-season.

A separate window-walled lounge with full bar, an abbreviated menu, and small tables overlooks the sound. Patrons can have a cocktail before dinner on the outdoor deck, and a lobby with comfortable couches affords an alternative place to await your table. Owner Mike Kelly, general manager Tom Sloate, and head chef Lee Miller combine their talents here to create a truly distinctive restaurant. Miller's reputation is well-known on the Outer Banks, and the staff members are friendly and professional.

Penguin Isle serves fresh local seafood, handmade pasta, certified Black Angus beef, chicken, duck, fresh-baked breads, and many other appetizing offerings. Creative food pairings are the chef's specialty. Penguin Isle's portions are generous, especially for such an upscale restaurant. All of the desserts are delectable. The menu changes seasonally to make use of the freshest ingredients.

Only dinner is served from March through December. Penguin Isle caters private parties, wedding receptions, and almost any occasion on-site. A children's menu is available, and early dining specials are offered from 5:00 until 6:00 P.M.; reservations are recommended.

Bushwackers $
NC 12, MP 16, Nags Head
(252) 480-1993

Bushwackers Restaurant is a family-friendly spot to dine whether you're having lunch or dinner. Delights from the sound and sea are featured at the raw and steamer bar: Choose from shrimp, crab legs, mussels, oysters, clams, spiced crabs, and more. Lots of appetizers tempt your palate, including the salads; try the marinated chicken salad with fruit and walnuts or the Caesar salad. Barbecue ribs, several wrap choices, quesadillas, and hot and cold sandwiches round out the menu. Low and no-carb dinners are available. A full bar is offered, and entertainment in the summer season keeps Bushwackers hoppin' into the night. Open March through December. Lunch and dinner served daily in season; call for off-season hours. A children's menu is available.

Windmill Point $$$
US 158, MP 16½, Nags Head
(252) 441-1535
www.windmillpointrestaurant.com

From Windmill Point's wide windows, you'll catch magnificent views of the sound at sunset, punctuated by the bright sails of windsurfers. Famous for its memorabilia from the elegant ocean liner SS *United States,* this restaurant's excellent cuisine matches the outdoor sights. The two dining areas are tastefully furnished down to the tablecloths, linen napkins, and comfortable chairs that hug rather than support you. Service is fast and unobtrusive. The upstairs lounge, styled with the authentic kidney-shaped bar from the ship—complete with plaques from famous 1950s statesmen and actresses who sipped cocktails there—is a pleasant place to await your call to dinner.

Menu favorites include a seafood trio, poached or grilled with flavorful sauces,

and a seafood pasta entree of lightly seasoned scallops. The chefs also prepare roasted prime rib, sautéed duck, fettuccine primavera, and capelli con scampi. Cooked with fresh herbs and creative sauces, the entrees get better each season. Windmill Point's menu offers heart-healthy selections. A little mate menu for kids is available. Dinner is served seven nights a week. Windmill Point is open year-round; reservations are accepted. On-premise and off-premise catering is available.

The Dunes $
US 158, MP 16½, Nags Head
(252) 441-1600
www.thedunesrestaurant.com

When a large crowd or big family is gathering for a meal, this restaurant accommodates all in its three huge dining rooms. Breakfast at The Dunes is a Nags Head tradition—you can tell by the packed parking lot—where every early morning entree in every imaginable combination is offered. A popular breakfast bar is set up during weekends in the off-season and daily in the summer. Lunches include great burgers and homemade crab cakes served with fries and coleslaw. The rib-eye steak sandwich is also a good choice.

Dinners feature local, well-prepared seafood moderately priced and a huge salad bar. All-you-can-eat specials are popular. There are also plenty of desserts to choose from if you're not already too full. The Dunes serves beer and wine and offers a children's menu. The service is fast and friendly at this nonsmoking establishment. The Dunes serves breakfast and lunch every day except in late December and most of January. Dinner is served mid-February though November.

Owens' Restaurant $$$
NC 12, MP 16½, Nags Head
(252) 441-7309
www.owensrestaurant.com

The oldest Outer Banks restaurant owned and operated continuously by the same family, Owens' is a local legend. This eatery celebrates 60 years in 2006.

Clara and Bob Owens first owned a small hot dog stand in Manteo. In 1946 they opened a 50-seat cafe in Nags Head on the deserted strip of sand that's now filled with hotels, rental cottages, and thousands of vacationers who arrive each summer. The Owenses reared their two children, Bobby and Clara Mae, in the restaurant, serving breakfast, lunch, and dinner during those early days. Today, Clara Mae and her husband, Lionel, run the family restaurant. R. V., Clara Mae's nephew, runs his own eatery on the Nags Head–Manteo Causeway. Together, this food-loving family serves some of the best traditional Outer Banks–style seafood in the area.

Owens' Restaurant now seats more than 200 people and offers only evening meals. More than 90,000 dinners are served from this Beach Road eatery each season. The atmosphere is still homey, yet upscale; the food is still fresh and made from scratch; the large lobby overflows with memorabilia of the barrier islands and Owens family heritage. Even the building's architecture is reminiscent of the Outer Banks's past, patterned after an old Nags Head lifesaving station. The menu, however, combines modern tastes with traditional recipes. Owens' renowned Southern Thanksgiving buffet is worth experiencing just to sample the range of delights this restaurant is capable of creating.

Locally caught seafood, often fresh off the boat, is broiled, fried, sautéed, or grilled each evening. Coconut shrimp, "Miss O" crab cakes, and pasta are among the most popular entrees. There's a mixed grill for patrons who prefer prime rib with their fish. Live Maine lobsters, plucked from the tank, are steamed just before serving. Owens' soups, including Hatteras-style clam chowder and lobster bisque, are delicious. All of the homemade desserts are well worth saving room for.

A full bar upstairs in the Station Keepers' Lounge serves beer, wine, mixed drinks, and special coffee concoctions.

Light fare is also available upstairs. Owens' is open from mid-March through New Year's Eve. Dinner is served seven days a week. Reservations are not accepted.

Sam & Omie's $$
NC 12, MP 16½, Nags Head
(252) 441-7366
www.sam-n-omies.com

Begun as a place for early morning anglers to indulge in a big breakfast before the Oregon Inlet charter fishing fleet took off, Sam & Omie's is one of the oldest family restaurants on the barrier islands. In fact, the famed *Lost Colony* production and Sam & Omie's will both celebrate their 70th anniversary in 2007. Omie Tillett recently retired his boat, *The Sportsman,* and he long ago sold this little wooden building at Whalebone Junction. The restaurant, however, retains its old beach charm and continues to produce hearty, home-style food based on traditional local recipes for breakfast, lunch, and dinner.

This is a very casual place with wooden booths and tables and a full-service bar. Local fishermen congregate to contemplate the day's catch, and families flock to enjoy the low-priced, filling meals. Photographs of famous Gulf Stream catches line the walls, and the TV usually is tuned in to some exciting sporting event. For breakfast, omelets are a favorite. We like to make a meal of the rich she-crab soup and red chile poppers for lunch. Salads, sandwiches, hamburgers, fish fillets, turkey clubs, and daily specials also are served. A steamer has been added for healthy vegetables and fish. For dinner, try a soft-shell crab sandwich in season or a prime rib entree on Thursday. Sam & Omie's is open from early March through November, at least. Call for winter hours.

RV's Restaurant $$
Nags Head–Manteo Causeway
Nags Head
(252) 441-4963

Opened in 1982, RV's is one of the most popular places on the beach for lunch and dinner. Owner R. V. Owens is likely to stop by your table to greet you, offering his warm smile, a firm handshake, and maybe an opinion or two as an appetizer to an abundant meal. Eat at the full-service bar in this casual restaurant or sit at a table in one of the soundfront dining rooms. The seafood stew is extremely tasty and overflowing with shrimp and scallops. Marinated tuna is a must for fish lovers. A gazebo raw bar on an attached deck overlooking the water takes on a life of its own in the evening. Prices are reasonable, and the atmosphere is lively and fun. RV's is open from March through Thanksgiving seven days a week.

Tale of the Whale $$
Nags Head–Manteo Causeway
Nags Head
(252) 441-7332
www.taleofthewhalenagshead.com
Family-operated and -owned for more than two decades, Tale of the Whale is situated on Roanoke Sound. You can enjoy the delightful views either looking through the expansive windows inside while savoring dinner or on the 75-foot deck and gazebo while sipping a refreshing cocktail. This roomy establishment is bright and airy, with big wooden booths lining the walls. Tables fill out the center of the two dining rooms, and a 40-foot bar is on the north side where diners can watch sunsets and birdlife on the water.

Tale of the Whale serves a variety of the freshest available food in generous portions. Seafood, lots of pasta, steaks, chicken, and prime rib are menu staples. Specials are offered daily, and early bird specials are available from 4:00 to 5:00 P.M. in season. Combination platters are prepared fried or broiled. Desserts are made on the premises. Tale of the Whale is open daily for dinner from April through November. A children's menu is available and seniors receive a 10 percent discount on their entree.

Basnight's Lone Cedar Cafe $$
Nags Head–Manteo Causeway
Nags Head
(252) 441-5405
www.lonecedarcafe.com
The Basnight family of Manteo operates this casual, upscale eatery where diners wearing everything from shorts to suits are welcome. In fact, it's not unusual to see the president pro tem of the state senate himself, Marc Basnight, talking with guests and removing dinner plates. Checkered green-and-white tablecloths cover every table. You'll notice the hunting motif with duck decoys and fishing memorabilia in honor of the former barrier island hunt club for which the eatery is named.

Appetizers are plentiful, ranging from onion straws to clam chowder, seafood bisque, clam and oyster fritters, hot crab balls, and hot crab dip plus soups and other specials of the day. Lunch entrees start at $6.95 and include sandwiches and fresh local seafood. For dinner try Black Angus beef, homemade pasta, sliced duck breast, fried or broiled seafood, or order any of the evening specials. Choose a beverage from the full bar and an extensive wine list. Desserts, home-baked daily, include pumpkin and pecan praline cheesecakes; pecan, peanut butter, lemon, or key lime pie; banana fritters; and 16-layer chocolate cake.

This cafe offers a view of the water from every table and is open for lunch and dinner daily year-round. Vegetarian and children's offerings are available. Reservations are not accepted.

ROANOKE ISLAND
Manteo

Hurricane Mo's Restaurant & Raw Bar $$
Pirate's Cove Marina, Manteo–Nags Head Causeway, Manteo
(252) 473-2266
This restaurant sits high atop Pirate's Cove Marina overlooking Roanoke Sound. Own-

Celebrate Oktoberfest on the Outer Banks at the Weeping Radish Brewery & Bavarian Restaurant in Manteo each September. There's a German oompah band and other bands, traditional dancing, beer, food, and activities for the whole family.

ers Jeff and Maureen Ashworth, who have been in the restaurant business for more than 20 years, wanted a toned-down, classic feel with an authentic Outer Banks focus. Dine in a the cozy dining room or relax on the screened-in porch. The restaurant serves traditional fresh seafood, steaks, pasta, and some Cajun selections. Vegetarians have their choices from their own menu as do children. Seafood lovers enjoy the steamed and raw shellfish bar. This eatery has a full bar including wine and beer.

Inside the restaurant is a collection of mounted game fish. From the covered outdoor porch, watch the fishing boats return daily with their Gulf Stream catch, then enjoy dinner before heading to *The Lost Colony* drama or the sights in Manteo. Hurricane Mo's serves lunch and dinner in the summer. Call for off-season hours. Prices of all dinner entrees served before 5:30 P.M. are reduced by 10 percent.

Stripers Bar & Grille $$
Shallowbag Bay, Manteo
(252) 473-3222
www.stripersbarandgrille.com
This dining spot is a sister restaurant to the popular Chilli Peppers in Kill Devil Hills and Stripers in Corolla. Seafood enthusiasts will love the three-level Manteo Stripers. The first floor contains a full steamer bar and a raw bar, the second floor contains a continental dining room, and the third floor offers another steamer bar and an intimate atmosphere. The menu includes everything from soups, salads, sandwiches, and pasta to steak and (of course) seafood. Popular entrees include the delicious homemade crab cake sandwich and grilled prime rib

served with red-skin mashed potatoes and seasonal vegetables.

Stripers is open from 11:00 A.M. to 9:00 P.M. every day (until 10:00 P.M. in the summer), and it serves beer and wine. On Sunday brunch is served from 10:00 A.M. to 3:00 P.M. Bananas Foster French toast, eggs Benedict, crab Benedict, and steak Benedict are just a few of the tempting items on the brunch menu.

The Weeping Radish Brewery & Bavarian Restaurant $$
US 64, Manteo
(252) 473-1157
www.weepingradish.com
Next to The Christmas Shop on the main highway in Manteo, this large restaurant includes an outdoor beer garden, separate pub, children's playground, and dining room. A European flavor prevails throughout. Traditional German meals include veal, sauerbraten, and a variety of sausages. Homemade spaetzle noodles and cooked red cabbage are side dishes offering tastes you won't find elsewhere on the Outer Banks. Also featured are free-range hormone-free North Carolina beef and pork fresh from their farm to you.

The restaurant's name comes from the radish served in Bavaria as an accompaniment to beer. Cut in a spiral, it's sprinkled with salt and packed back together. The salt draws out the moisture and gives the radish the appearance of weeping. Beer isn't served with radishes here (except by special request), but the brews are certainly the best part about this place. A microbrewery opened at The Weeping Radish in 1986, offering pure, handcrafted German-style beer without chemical additives or preservatives. You can watch this "nectar of the gods" being brewed on-site on a tour. Take home an extra pint to enjoy later. The Weeping Radish is open for lunch and dinner April through December, seven days a week. The pub is open into the evening. Call for off-season hours. Visit their Jarvisburg brewery in Currituk to take home fresh beer and meats.

Garden Deli & Pizzeria $
US 64, Manteo
(252) 473-6888

Shaded by pine trees, this tiny restaurant has a breezy outdoor deck perfect for summer dining. The cheerful, hometown crew has watched this Garden grow into one of the most popular lunch spots for the working crowd in Manteo. Here, New York–style stone-oven pizzas are cooked to order and packaged to go, if you wish. White pizza, one of our favorites, is topped with ricotta, mozzarella, parmesan, and romano cheeses, broccoli, and minced garlic. Traditional red sauce pizzas and specialty pizzas are also offered. The Philly cheese steaks, burgers, gyros, and a wide assortment of deli sandwiches, homemade salads, and antipasto salads are wonderful. Fresh tuna and chicken salad plates are just right for a light lunch or dinner.

Garden Pizzeria delivers free of charge to Roanoke Island and Pirate's Cove. The restaurant is open for lunch and dinner Monday through Saturday year-round. Call about delivered boxed lunches for charter boat trips. Garden Deli specializes in party-boat catering.

Big Al's Soda Fountain & Grill $
US 64/264, Manteo
(252) 473-5570
www.themefifty.com

You can't miss Big Al's, across from The Christmas Shop in downtown Manteo. Owners Diana Croswait and Vanessa and Allan Foreman originally planned to open a little ice-cream parlor, but the concept expanded into a full-blown soda fountain and family restaurant. It's definitely a place to take the kids. With '50s decor and memorabilia, Big Al's is a great place to kick back and enjoy some good ol' American food and fountain treats. Plus, you can get fish so fresh, it's literally off-the-boat, says Vanessa Foreman. She knows because Allan catches most of it.

Children's meals are available for $4.99. Kids can have fun in the game room, with a pinball machine, video games, and a jukebox. There's even a dance floor. Big Al's serves lunch and dinner daily.

Darrell's Restaurant $$
US 64, Manteo
(252) 473-5366

This down-home restaurant started as an ice-cream stand more than 30 years ago and has been a favorite family-style eatery for the past two decades. It's common knowledge that the fried oysters at Darrell's are among the best in town. Menu items such as popcorn shrimp, crab cakes, grilled marinated tuna, and fried scallops are served with french fries, coleslaw, and hush puppies to provide more than enough to fuel you through the day. Soups such as Dare County–style clam chowder and oyster stew are hard to resist. Salads, sandwiches, and steamed and raw seafood are additional options for the hungry diner. Meat-eaters will be satiated by Delmonico steak, barbecued minced pork, and grilled marinated chicken. Daily seafood specials are served for dinner; a children's menu is available. The hot fudge cake is a must for dessert. Beer and wine are served. Darrell's is open for lunch and dinner year-round but is closed Sunday.

Duncan's Bar-B-Q and Family Buffet $
US 64, Manteo
(252) 473-6464

The atmosphere is casual, and the food is spicy at this family-style restaurant known for its North Carolina–style hand-picked barbecue. The all-you-can-eat lunch and dinner buffets include fried chicken, coleslaw, and other vegetables—besides the barbecue, of course. Rose Bay oysters are available in season, and the fried and steamed shrimp on the dinner buffet are great. The ambience is family friendly. Eat in or call for takeout. Duncan's also caters off-site pig-pickin' parties and family barbecues. It's open Tuesday through Saturday for lunch and dinner in season. Call for winter hours.

Waterfront Trellis $$-$$$
The Waterfront Shops, Manteo
(252) 473-1723

Overlooking Shallowbag Bay and the state ship *Elizabeth II*, this is a favorite Manteo eatery for watching boats on the water or a romantic summer moon. It's a casual, relaxing restaurant with good service and equally admirable food. The dinner menu at Waterfront Trellis has delicious hot soups, seasonal salads, and a selection of specials. The extensive menu offers over-stuffed sandwiches, a steam bar, pasta dishes, and fresh local seafood. Sushi is served on Tuesday nights and a sizable pasta station is offered on Thursday evening.

Locals and visitors reserve Waterfront Trellis for wedding receptions, family par-ties, or reunions. Since this restaurant is less than a 10-minute drive from *The Lost Colony,* it's a good place to take in an early meal before the outdoor drama begins. Beer, wine, and champagne are available, and brown bagging of other alcoholic drinks is allowed. A children's menu is provided. Lunch and dinner are served seven days a week from March through December.

Full Moon Cafe $$
Creef's Corner
Queen Elizabeth Avenue, Manteo
(252) 473-MOON

This eclectic eatery opened in late 1995 and consistently overflows with local and visiting patrons. A Manteo favorite for lunch and dinner, this cozy cafe occupies a building on the corner of Queen Eliza-beth Avenue and Sir Walter Raleigh Street. This location allows diners a view of the local streetscape, great for people-watchers and those who like being part of the waterfront scene. The innovative cui-sine has a nouveau American flair. Most of the entrees and specials (which usually involve creative takes on pasta and seafood) are so unusual we haven't seen them anywhere else on the Outer Banks.

Hummus spread, baked Brie, and mushroom caps stuffed with shrimp are succulent appetizers. Lunch specials include gourmet sandwiches to satisfy everyone's tastes, vegetarian offerings, seafood, chicken, and homemade soups, such as Hungarian mushroom, curried spinach, and spicy tomato. Each entree is served with corn chips and Full Moon's own salsa. The dinner menu features enticing seafood dishes, stuffed chicken breasts, roasted eggplant with other veg-etables in marinara sauce and provolone cheese, and a beef dish with portobello mushrooms and a Gorgonzola cheese sauce. Daily pasta specials are also avail-able as a half-serving with a side salad. All the desserts are delightful. Beer (including some microbrews) and a good selection of wine are available. You can eat inside the dining room or dine outdoors in the courtyard if you take any meal to go. Reservations are accepted for parties of six or more.

Full Moon is open for lunch and dinner seven days a week in summer. Hours are reduced off-season, so call for specific schedules.

Poor Richard's Sandwich Shop $
The Waterfront, Manteo
(252) 473-3333

With half the workforce in Manteo making a beeline to Poor Richard's every day, this casual eatery is a local gathering spot for reasonably priced food with fast counter service and interesting offerings. Try the cucumber sandwich with cream cheese—a cool meal that surprises your palate. Cold and grilled sandwiches are made to order, and specials are offered daily. Homemade soups, meatless chili, hot dogs, salad plates, cookies, and ice cream are also available. Breakfast includes scrambled egg and bacon sandwiches, bagels and cream cheese, and fresh fruit. Steamed shrimp is available for lunch and dinner.

Whatever your mode of transporta-tion—boat, bike, car, or legs—Poor Rich-ard's is a worthy filling station. You can eat inside at a roomy booth or take your meal out on the back porch and enjoy the waterfront view—there always seems to be enough room for everybody. Poor Richard's is open daily in the summer for breakfast, lunch, and dinner. Occasionally, the restaurant hosts live music in the evenings. Though it's open year-round, call for off-season hours.

1587 $$$
Tranquil House Inn
Queen Elizabeth Street, Manteo
(252) 473-1587
www.1587.com

The owner of this critically acclaimed restaurant can make your mouth water just by reading his menu aloud. The offerings are unusual, upscale, cosmopolitan, and some of the most ambitious on the Outer Banks. Ambience is elegant and romantic: The soft glow of intimate lighting, a gleaming copper-topped bar in a separate lounge area, and polished wood and mirrors reflect the lights sparkling off boats anchored in Shallowbag Bay. Executive Chef Donny King creates a constantly changing menu that's always as fresh and fabulous as the food.

Soups prepared each day might include Mediterranean mussels and crayfish with spring vegetables and feta cheese in a light tomato broth. For appetizers, select sesame-encrusted colossal scallops with spicy vegetable slaw and soy-wasabi cream, or duck confit with sweet potato cornbread and cherry-citrus compote and herb jus. Salads, served a la carte, offer mixed greens with caramelized onion puff pastry tart, marinated sun-dried tomatoes and goat cheese, finished with spiced port drizzle.

Dinner entrees range from crispy cornmeal orange roughy accompanied by roasted vegetable risotto and whole-grain mustard cream, finished with white-wine-sautéed shrimp and vegetables, to Asiago risotto with sea scallops, shrimp, and vegetables surrounded by crawfish gumbo. Another excellent choice is chargrilled filet mignon served with garlic mashed potatoes and seasonal vegetables.

A children's menu offers simpler dishes for younger tastes. Vegetarian

If you're going to watch the entertainment under the stars at Illuminations Summer Arts Series at Roanoke Island Festival Park, Manteo restaurants and caterers will provide boxed picnics to take with you. Call Festival Park at (252) 475-1500 for information.

requests are welcome. The exquisite dessert creations are delicious and are so beautiful that you may want to take a snapshot before digging in!

Named for the first year English colonists attempted to settle on Roanoke Island, 1587 serves a wide selection of wine and beer and permits brown bagging. This outstanding restaurant is open for dinner daily in the summer. Call for off-season hours. Reservations are requested.

Magnolia Grille $
Magnolia Market
408 Queen Elizabeth Street, Manteo
(252) 475-9877

Magnolia Grille serves a variety of good eats. Breakfast, lunch, and dinner are offered. Hot dogs, burgers, deli sandwiches, several vegetarian options, quesadillas, and daily specials are prepared as ordered. Appetizers include chili cheese fries, onion rings, and soups. The salads, with grilled chicken if you like, are fresh. Kids can get grilled cheese and other favorites. If you're headed to Roanoke Island Festival Park for Summer Scenes concerts, this is a great place to pick up a picnic on the way.

The Green Dolphin Restaurant and Pub $
Sir Walter Raleigh Street, Manteo
(252) 473-5911

This downtown Manteo eatery has been a popular pub for more than 20 years. It's casual and comfortable inside, with wooden booths and tables fashioned from the hatch covers taken off old ships. Old nautical memorabilia lines the walls, and a long bar stretches along the back of the restaurant.

Food here is simple, satisfying, and a good value. Charbroiled hamburgers, she-crab soup (some say it's the best on the Outer Banks), crab cakes, lasagna, manicotti, Italian sausage, and french fries are just a few of the offerings served for lunch and dinner. Appetizers and desserts also are available, and the pub serves pizzas and small-fry portions for the kids. The Green Dolphin is open year-round Tuesday through Sunday. Live entertainment is usually offered on Friday nights (see our Nightlife chapter).

The Coffeehouse on Roanoke Island $
106-A Sir Walter Raleigh Street, Manteo
(252) 475-1295

Here is the perfect coffeehouse atmosphere: sofas, newspapers, local chatter, tables inside or on the deck, and a friendly owner who handles the busiest of morning rushes with aplomb. The coffee is just right, not overly strong, and the espresso and cappuccino drinks are expertly prepared. A selection of loose teas is available. Iced coffees are good for summer days, and the chai milk shake beats everything. Milk shakes and smoothies are large, and the staff will give you the leftovers if they make one that's too big for your cup. The Coffeehouse serves heavenly cinnamon oat and blueberry scones, muffins, bagels, cinnamon bread, pastries, biscotti, granola, and fruit. You can have your granola with soy milk or yogurt, if you'd like. The Coffeehouse is open every day for breakfast, light lunches, and snacks.

Wanchese

Queen Anne's Revenge $$
Old Wharf Road, Wanchese
(252) 473-5466

Named after one of Blackbeard's famous pirate ships that plied the waters off North Carolina's coast during the early 1700s, Queen Anne's Revenge is snuggled in a grove of trees in the scenic fishing village of Wanchese. The restaurant is well off the beaten path at the end of a winding lane.

Wayne and Nancy Gray have operated this outstanding restaurant since 1978, serving seafood fresh from the Wanchese docks. They use only quality ingredients, and their attention to detail really shows.

The restaurant has three dining rooms, one with a fireplace that provides a cozy ambience during cold winter months. A large selection of starters is offered, including bouillabaisse (full of fresh seafood) and black bean and she-crab soups. All the seafood here is excellent, from Blackbeard's Raving to the locally landed shellfish and fish served with the Wanchese platter. There's chateaubriand for two, carved at your table. Queen Anne's chefs make their own pasta; in fact, their fettuccine is a staple around Wanchese. All the desserts are homemade and served in generous portions. This lovely restaurant offers a children's menu and a nice selection of beer and wine. The dining room serves dinner seven days a week during the summer months. Enjoy the Sunday lunch buffet from January through May. Queen Anne's is open all year but closes Tuesday during the off-season.

HATTERAS ISLAND
Rodanthe, Waves, and Salvo

Austin's South Island Seafood & Produce
NC 12, Rodanthe
(252) 987-1352

Austin's South Island Seafood & Produce has everything you need for a classic Hatteras Island cookout. Austin's will send you on your way with shrimp, clams, scallops, oysters, and blue crabs, all steamed to perfection. The specialty, the Hatt'ras Island steamer pots, feed two or more. They come with a variety of seafood (you can choose what you'd like in addition to shrimp, scallops, corn, potatoes, and more); just be sure to call at least two hours in advance.

Fresh-cut steaks and chops are available at Austin's for the landlubbers in your crowd. Lots of fresh produce and a wide variety of sauces and marinades are in house, too. A bonus: After a day of fishing, bring your catch to Austin's and they will vacuum pack it for you. Austin's is open seven days a week from April through October.

Lisa's Pizza $
NC 12, Rodanthe
(252) 987-2525

Specialty pizzas, deli sandwiches, subs, calzones, chicken parmagiana, and salads are among the most popular items at this restaurant. Lisa's also serves breadsticks, hot wings, and garlic and cheese bread. Beer and wine are available, and there's a separate children's menu. Lisa's serves lunch and dinner seven days a week beginning at 11:00 A.M. from early April through November. All items can be eaten inside the restaurant, carried out, or delivered. Call for off-season hours.

Tiki Grill $$
NC 12, Salvo
(252) 987-1088

A former owner of the Down Under Restaurant opened the smaller Tiki Grill a few years ago. Caribbean decor gives an atmosphere of quiet celebration and ease. Simple, delicious food is served—burgers, salads, seafood, and vegetables. Most likely a surfer, possibly with traces of salt and sand from the day's romp in the waves, will serve you. It's all fun and good. Entertainment is held in season. Call for hours and times of operation, but they are usually closed on Sundays.

Leonardo's Pizza $
NC 12, Rodanthe
(252) 987-6522

Located beside the Reef, Leonardo's Pizza has delicious pizza, calzones, and subs. Pizzas are prepared in the traditional thin-crust Sicilian style. Sauces and dough are homemade daily, and only the freshest ingredients are used. Salads and antipasto and a wide variety of nonalcoholic drinks round out Leonardo's offerings. Delivery is free within Rodanthe, Waves, and Salvo villages. At lunch, pizza by the slice is available, along with subs and calzones. Leonardo's is open in season every day from 11:30 A.M. until 9:00 P.M. and from 11:30 A.M. until 9:00 P.M. Tuesday through Saturday in the off-season.

Top Dog Cafe $
NC 12, Waves
(252) 987-1272

Specializing in burgers that weigh up to one-and-a-half pounds, Top Dog Cafe also serves steamed seafood, Philly-style steak subs, shrimp and oyster baskets, all-beef hot dogs, salads, and appetizers. The restaurant has a casual atmosphere, and you can choose to eat on the shady screened porch or on the sundeck. This establishment has a kid's menu and sometimes live music. Beer and wine are served. Open for lunch and dinner; call for hours and days.

Down Under Restaurant & Lounge $$
NC 12, Rodanthe
(252) 987-2277

This Australian-style restaurant is family friendly and offers wonderful views of the sound. Decorated with authentic Australian art and memorabilia, Down Under is one-of-a-kind on the Outer Banks. Lunch specialties include the Great Australian bite, similar to an Aussie burger, made with hamburger, a fried egg, grilled onions, cheese, and bacon. Spicy fish burgers, Vegemite sandwiches, and marinated chicken sandwiches are good authentic options, too. Kangaroo, a delicious meat that is very popular at Down Under, is imported from Australia for 'roo stew, 'roo burgers, and kangaroo curry. Try the stuffed jalapeños served with Down Under's famous sweet chile sauce.

Dinner selections include Down Under shrimp stuffed with jalapeño peppers and cream cheese wrapped in bacon. Enjoy a side order of the foot-high onion rings and a Foster's lager or Cooper's Stout. Parents will appreciate the children's menu, and kids will appreciate the extraordinary decor. Everyone will enjoy the view. Down Under is open seven days a week for lunch and dinner from April through early September. The restaurant is wheelchair accessible. Large parties are welcome.

Avon

Dirty Dicks Crab House $-$$
NC 12, Avon
(252) 995-3708
www.dirtydickscrabs.com
Adjacent to the Avon Pier, Dirty Dicks serves an incomparable selection of crabs, including snow crab legs, soft-shell crabs, spiced crabs, crab dip, crab cakes, and steamed crabs. The steamed, spiced crabs are superb, and Dicks sells its special spice. The menu also includes steamed shrimp, clams, clam chowder, gumbo, jambalaya, and Cajun and Creole dishes. Sandwich platter specials and other offerings satisfy the kids. The tasty Dick Burger is a crab and shrimp patty with Cajun sauce. Dirty Dicks T-shirts are popular for their suggestiveness, and you can buy them here. Order any of the menu items and steamed crabs for takeout. Dirty Dicks has two other locations in Kill Devil Hills, one a sit-down place like this one and the other for takeout only. Dirty Dicks is open for lunch and dinner in season and closes for a couple of months in the winter. Call for off-season hours.

Hodad's $-$$
NC 12, Avon
(252) 995-7866
This casual restaurant with surfboards, surfer pics, and a Dewey Webber board out front is the perfect place to have a good, filling meal without having to change out of your beachwear. Hodad's is a great place to hang around the bar and shoot the breeze or to sit at a table with a group of friends. The list of appetizers is extensive. Fried pickles with horseradish sauce, anyone? If that's not your style, try the oven-baked Brie, shrimp roll-ups, conch fritters, hummus, rumaki, jalapeño poppers, or the Mondo Combo with a little taste of several things, including the pickles. Burgers, veggie burgers, crab cake sandwiches, fish sandwiches, and a portobello mushroom sandwich are favorites here, but there's also a lighter side of offerings, including Hatteras clam chowder, a Caesar salad, a spinach salad, and a warm garlic shrimp salad. After 5:00 P.M. dinner-style entrees are offered. Try the flash-fried oysters, catch of the day, prime rib, or creative pasta dishes. Vegetarians will appreciate the Buddha Delight, stir-fried veggies and tofu over rice. If you've worked up a killer appetite on the waves, you might be able to tackle the Duke Seafood Combo, with shrimp, scallops, crab cake, catch of the day, oysters, and calamari. Beer and wine are served. Hodad's makes lunch and dinner every day from St. Patrick's Day through Thanksgiving. A menu just for the kids is available.

Chinatown $$
NC 12, Hatteras Island Plaza, Avon
(252) 995-0118
Chinatown provides a welcome alternative to Hatteras Island's typical cuisine. The restaurant features family-value meals, special lunches, combination dinners, and Szechuan, Cantonese, and Hunan specialties with hot and spicy alterations available. Open late morning and serving the latest dinner on the island, the restaurant offers eat-in or take-out options. Chinatown is open seven days a week year-round.

Bubba's Too $$
NC 12, Avon
(252) 995-4385
For lip-smackin', finger-lickin' barbecue, Bubba's is the place on Hatteras Island. Meeting undeniable success, Bubba opened his second location next to the Food Lion many years ago. Bubba's fame

has survived him, as have his eateries. Customers relish the ribs, sandwiches, Bubba's original barbecue sauces, and mouthwatering desserts. Eat at the restaurant or take the food out. Either way, have plenty of napkins and a big appetite ready. Bubba's is open for lunch and dinner April through October.

Buxton

Diamond Shoals Restaurant $$
NC 12, Buxton
(252) 995-5217
The parking lot at this eatery, which is within walking distance of several Buxton motels, always seems to be crowded around breakfast time. Here you'll find one of the best breakfasts on Hatteras Island, featuring all your early-morning favorites. Diamond Shoals is also open for lunch and dinner, with plenty of local seafood choices, a salad bar, and some good nightly specials. Steaks and other landlubber specials are also available.

A remarkable 200-gallon saltwater aquarium is stocked with tropical and Gulf Stream sea life. Diners can get an up-close-and-personal look at corals, anemones, and a variety of fascinating marine creatures. Diamond Shoals is open from March through December.

Tides Restaurant $$
NC 12, Buxton
(252) 995-5988
The driveway for this family-style restaurant is just south of the entrance to the Cape Hatteras Lighthouse, on the sound side. Dinner selections include a fresh catch of the day, steaks, chicken, and ham. Try the chef's special shrimp gumbo. One menu favorite is the Tides' Way, broiled fresh fish topped with onions, green peppers, tomatoes, and cheese. All the portions are large, and the service is attentive. Beer and wine are available; brown bagging is allowed. This restaurant is open daily from Easter through Thanksgiving. Dinner is served from 5:00 to 9:00 P.M.

Orange Blossom Cafe and Bakery $$
NC 12, Buxton
(252) 995-4109
The Orange Blossom starts the day with a delicious array of baked goods for breakfast. The famous Apple Uglies—huge apple fritter–style pastries piled high with fruit—are favorite early-morning treats. This restaurant is open year-round, except for a spell during the winter, for takeout or eat in. The bakery opens at 7:00 A.M. Monday through Saturday and closes at 11:30 A.M. No credit cards accepted.

Fish House Restaurant $$
NC 12, Buxton
(252) 995-5151
Can you tell this always-bustling eatery occupies a former fish house? If the simple wooden architecture and wharf-front location didn't give it away, you might notice something fishy when you glimpse down and see the slanted concrete floors sloped for easy washing so the fish scales flow back into the sound. The Fish House is now a comfortable restaurant where everything is casual and easygoing. Overlooking Buxton Harbor, it serves some of the best Outer Banks seafood prepared with traditional, local recipes. The tilefish is a popular choice, as are the homemade crab cakes. Each entree comes with your choice of vegetables and hush puppies. Sushi is on the menu each Wednesday night. Everything is served on disposable plates with plastic utensils. Beer and wine are served. Fish House is open for lunch and dinner daily from March through Thanksgiving. A kid's menu is available.

The Pilot House $$$
NC 12, Buxton
(252) 995-5664
Set well off the road to capture spectacular, panoramic views of the sky, water, and setting sun, The Pilot House offers soundside dining amid a decor that's unobtrusively nautical. The Captain's Lounge serves beer and wine, and if you bring

your own liquor, they'll provide the setups. The Pilot House is a popular place, so you may have to wait for a table. But you won't mind waiting when you see the view and the enormous outdoor porches where you can plop down in an Adirondack chair with a cool beverage. With the view and the freshest seafood, this is the kind of dining experience you'd expect on Hatteras Island. The Pilot House serves fresh local seafood, steaks and beef entrees, pastas, and vegetarian dishes. Nightly specials are offered. Don't pass up the opportunity to try the seafood bisque or one of the delectable desserts. The Pilot House serves dinner seven days a week, from mid-April through late fall. Call for hours.

Frisco

Quarterdeck Restaurant $$
NC 12, Frisco
(252) 986-2425
Fresh local seafood served broiled or fried, crab cakes packed with jumbo lump meat, and Hatteras or New England clam chowder are among the most popular offerings here. Crab puffs and stuffed flounder are house specialties. The Quarterdeck has an 18-item salad bar. For dessert, the coconut cream, lemon meringue, and key lime pies are delicious. Beer and wine are available, as is a children's menu. This low-key spot occupies a 70-year-old building that housed Hatteras Island's original bar. For more than 25 years, the same family has owned and operated the Quarterdeck, which is open for lunch and dinner daily (except on Saturday, when it is not open for lunch) from mid-March through late November.

Gingerbread House Bakery $
NC 12, Frisco
(252) 995-5204
From this tiny cottage flanked by gingerbread-style fencing, breakfast and dinner are served Tuesday through Sunday in season. To start the day, sample egg biscuits, French toast, omelets, or waffles. If you'd rather indulge yourself in delicious baked goods, try a frosted doughnut, cookie, or freshly made bagel. By early evening, you can order a gourmet pizza made on the bakery's own dough. Crusts range in thickness from hand-tossed to pan depth and are offered in white and whole-wheat varieties with 30 toppings to choose from. Ice cream, brownies, and sweet breads all are great dessert options. You can eat inside or get your pizza and sweets to go. During the summer, the Gingerbread House also delivers from Buxton to Hatteras Village, and its bakers make super specialty cakes on a day's notice for any occasion. Call for off-season hours. No credit cards accepted.

Bubba's Bar-B-Q $$
NC 12, Frisco
(252) 995-5421
If you're in the mood for some genuine Carolina barbecue, just follow your nose to this acclaimed roadside joint. The hickory fires start early so the pork, chicken, beef, ribs, and turkey can cook slowly over an open pit. The late Larry "Bubba" Schauer and his wife, Julie, brought their secret recipe from West Virginia to Hatteras Island more than 20 years ago—and the food has been drawing locals and tourists to their eatery ever since. Homemade coleslaw, baked beans, french fries, and corn bread round out the meal.

The sweet potato and coconut custard pies, cobblers, and other desserts are delectable. Mrs. Bubba's Double Devil Chocolate Cake is astounding. Bubba's has a children's menu and a nice selection of beer and soft drinks. All items are available for eating in or taking out. Bubba's Sauce is a hot commodity with barbecue fans and is sold at retail and specialty shops across the Outer Banks. Bubba's is open daily for lunch and dinner from 11:00 A.M. to 9:00 P.M. during the summer; call for winter hours. You'll find a second Bubba's, Bubba's Too, farther north on NC 12 in Avon, next to the Food Lion.

Hatteras Village

The Channel Bass $$
NC 12, Hatteras Village
(252) 986–2250

Owned by the Harrison family, which is well-known for its fishing heritage, this canalside restaurant has been a Hatteras Village institution for more than 30 years. You'll notice all of Mrs. Shelby Harrison's fishing trophies in the foyer. The Channel Bass has one of the largest menus on the beach, loaded with seafood platters, crab imperial, crab cakes, veal, and charbroiled steaks that the chefs cut on-site. The seafood is deep-sea and sound-caught. An old family recipe is used for the hush puppies, and all the salad dressings are made from scratch. Try the key lime pie for dessert. A private dining room is available, and large groups are welcome. The Channel Bass has early-bird discounts and different dinner specials every night. Beer and wine are served; brown bagging is allowed. A children's menu is available. The Channel Bass serves dinner six days a week (Monday through Saturday) from Easter through Thanksgiving.

Breakwater Island Restaurant $$
NC 12 at Oden's Dock, Hatteras Village
(252) 986–2733

If dining in a comfortable atmosphere with a stunning view of Pamlico Sound or relaxing with some live music on a deck at sunset sounds good, then this restaurant is the place for you. Here, a second-story dining room, deck, and bar overlook a small harbor and stone breakwater, providing a unique feel to this locally loved outpost.

The dinner menu features fresh, innovative seafood dishes, prime rib, veal, and pasta, all served in generous portions. Entrees are accompanied by a selection of vegetables, salad, and fresh-baked breads. Live entertainment is performed atop the deck on select evenings in summer. Dinner is served every day but Tuesday during the season. A good selection of beer and wine is available, and brown bagging is allowed. Children's items are also offered. Check for winter hours.

Fish Tales $
NC 12, Hatteras Village
(252) 986–6516

Fish Tales offers breakfast, lunch, and dinner daily in a friendly family-style atmosphere. Breakfasts are killer, with omelets, eggs, meats, Spanish home fries covered with cheese and salsa, and French toast. The pancake flavors will astound you: bacon, banana, blueberry, coconut, Carolina pecan, corn, chocolate chip, strawberry, and apple. There are even silver-dollar–size pancakes.

For lunch, Fish Tales serves appetizers, chili, salads, seafood salad, burgers, chicken and seafood sandwiches, subs, and more pancakes. For dinner, there are more appetizers, soups, salads, seafood platters, and landlubber dishes like steak, pork, chicken, and spaghetti. All entrees are served with hot rolls and butter and your choice of two vegetables. Kids have their own menu and seniors save $2.00 on entrees. Fish Tales's food is well prepared, and the owners pay careful attention to customer satisfaction. Call for hours.

Austin Creek Grill $$
NC 12, Hatteras Landing
(252) 986–1511
www.hatteraslanding.com

Austin Creek Grill brings something unexpected to southern Hatteras Island: contemporary, artful Southern cuisine. This waterfront bistro is located at Hatteras Landing, right on the docks, with an awesome view of the fleet and the harbor. Executive chef Ed Daggers is a graduate of the Culinary Institute of America and has won numerous awards for his accomplished cooking. Before coming to Hatteras he was executive chef at some of the finest resorts, hotels, and clubs on the Eastern Seaboard, including Sheraton Norfolk Waterside Hotel and Kingsmill in Williamsburg.

Daggers uses the bounty of the sea and region to create incomparable, unforgettable dishes. For an appetizer, try a baby spinach, apple, and poached pear salad with caramelized pecans, red onion, Maytag blue cheese, and warm bacon dressing. Or how about starting with ginger crab and sweet corn soup? Entrees include such combinations as panko jumbo fried shrimp with citrus cocktail sauce and hot basil slaw or pomegranate-glazed duck breast with macadamia sweet potatoes and apple basil salad. Austin Creek will even cook your freshly caught fish for a fee if you bring it in. Dessert selections include white chocolate praline cheesecake with vanilla and caramel sauces, and pecan apple cake with maple whipped cream and cinnamon anglaise. All dishes are a work of art. The wine list has been carefully selected to accompany the meals, and beer is available as well.

Austin Creek Grill's atmosphere synchronizes well with the fare—it's lively and contemporary in a coastal way. Windows open up to spectacular water views, and nostalgic wall treatments, interior windows, blond woods, and sea blues give the feeling of dining in a well-heeled Martha's Vineyard cottage. Austin Creek Grill prepares lunches for charter boats if you call a day ahead. Austin Creek has a separate bakery that offers surprising pastries, pizzas, grains, and beans served tastefully. The restaurant is open for dinner every day. Call for off-season hours. Smoking is permitted only at the bar.

OCRACOKE ISLAND

Jason's Restaurant $
NC 12, Ocracoke Village
(252) 928-3434
On the north end of the village, Jason's has a casual, come-as-you-are atmosphere that welcomes islanders and vacationers alike. You can sit outside on the spacious screened porch or hang at the bar and watch the chefs at work. Standouts on the menu are pizzas and Italian specialties, including lasagna and vegetarian lasagna, spaghetti with meatballs,

chicken parmagiana, and fettuccine Alfredo. Salads, sandwiches, and subs, plus dinner entrees such as New York strip steak, Jamaican jerk chicken, and seafood add to the list of goods. If you just want a few munchies to get you by, try an appetizer. We liked the spinach and artichoke dip and shrimp quesadillas. To wash it down, choose from a wide variety of beers, including several on tap, and wines. Carryout is available for all menu items. Lunch and dinner are served daily year-round 11:30 A.M. until 10:00 P.M.

sMacNally's Raw Bar and Grill $-$$
On Silver Lake, NC 12, Ocracoke Village
(252) 928-9999
sMacNally's is smack in the middle of the village action, at the Anchorage Inn Marina and is a popular gathering spot on the island. It's an outdoor establishment, on the docks, with the smell of salt and fresh-caught fish coming off the water and charter boats tied up practically to the bar. Fishermen walk off the boats and have a beer in their hand before they can say "Budwei . . . ." sMacNally's claims to serve the coldest beer on the island. Patrons hang around the raw bar and at tables on the dock. The raw bar serves fresh local seafood, including oysters, clams, and shrimp. A grill cooks burgers and the like. Lunch and dinner are served daily in the warm season, through November. The bar stays open until midnight. It's closed in the colder months. Steamed seafood buckets and boxed lunches are sold to go.

Sargasso Grill $$
NC 12, Ocracoke Village
(252) 928-2874
Sargasso is becoming a favorite spot to dine in Ocracoke. For an appetizer, try the tequila shrimp or something from the steamer menu. Entrees include veal, rack of lamb, and locally caught fresh seafood; all are served with fresh bread and a salad. Several delicious vegetarian entrees are also on the menu. Indulge in Sargasso's outstanding desserts, including pecan pie and tiramisu. Sargasso offers more than 40

wines and a large selection of beer. A children's menu is available. Sargasso is open nightly from 5:00 to 10:00 P.M. in season. Call for off-season hours.

Pony Island Restaurant $$
NC 12, Ocracoke Village
(252) 928-5701

A casual, homey place that people have come back to time and again since 1960, this restaurant features big breakfasts of biscuits, hotcakes, omelets, and the famous Pony Potatoes—hash browns covered with cheese, sour cream, and salsa. Dinner entrees include a variety of interesting fresh local seafood creations, pastas, steaks, and salads. The kitchen will even cook your own catch of the day for you, as long as you've cleaned the fish first. Beer and wine are served, and homemade desserts finish the tasty meal. The Pony Island Restaurant is adjacent to the Pony Island Motel. Breakfast is served from 7:00 to 11:00 A.M. The restaurant closes during lunchtime and reopens nightly for dinner from late March through November. Take-out orders are welcomed.

Flying Melon $$
NC 12, Ocracoke Village
(252) 928-2533

Ocracoke's newest restaurant has a unique decor and yummy food to tempt any palate. Brunch is served from 9:00 A.M. to 2:00 P.M. and includes fresh fruit, biscuits, and New Orleans–style French toast. On its lunch menu, the Melon has a portobello sandwich, a Philly cheesesteak, hamburgers, and more. The dinner entrees are often Louisiana-inspired dishes. For an appetizer, try the sea scallops over baby greens or the lamb satay. Main courses include the popular shrimp Creole, crawfish cakes, a 16-ounce double-cut pork chop, and the curry-of-the-day dish. The Flying Melon offers imported beer and a full wine list, and there is a menu for the wee ones in your party. Reservations are not necessary. Smoking is allowed on the porch but not within the building. Open year-round, serving Tuesday through Sunday in season and Wednesday through Sunday in the off-season.

The Back Porch Restaurant $$$
1324 Country Road, Ocracoke Village
(252) 928-6401

Whether you dine on the wide screened-in porch or eat in the small nooks or open dining room of this well-respected restaurant, you'll find that dinners at The Back Porch are some of the most pleasant experiences on the Outer Banks. This older building was renovated and refurbished to blend with the many trees on the property. It's off the main road, surrounded by waist-high cacti, and is a quiet place to enjoy appealing entrees and comfortable conversation. Overall, it's one of our favorite restaurants on the 120-mile stretch of barrier islands and well worth the two-hour trip from Nags Head.

Advertising "original dishes with a personal touch," the menu is loaded with fresh vegetables and local seafood and changes seasonally to offer the freshest ingredients. All sauces, dressings, breads, and desserts are made in the restaurant's huge kitchen and each piece of meat is hand-cut. The chefs come up with some pretty outrageous taste combinations, and all of them seem to blend perfectly. The crab cakes with red pepper sauce are outstanding. And you won't want to miss the jumbo shrimp rolls with sweet soy sauce or crab beignet appetizers. Non-seafood dishes are a tasty option as well. The Cuban black bean and Monterey jack cheese casserole is a perennial favorite.

Reduced prices and smaller portions are available. All the desserts are divine. Freshly ground coffee is served here, and the wine selections and imported beer are as ambitious as the menu. If you get hooked—like we are—you can try your hand at some of the restaurant's recipes at home by buying a copy of *Back Porch Cookbook*. After reading the recipes you'll be even more impressed with the upscale culinary concoctions served in this laid-back island eatery. Dinner is offered nightly in season. Call for off-season hours.

The Back Porch Lunchbox, next to the Pony Island Motel, offers homemade bag lunches or picnics for the beach or ferry. Sandwiches, cold steamed shrimp, baked goods, drinks, and fruit are available. Call (252) 928-3651.

Thai Moon $
Spencer's Market, NC 12
Ocracoke Village
(252) 928-5100
Here's something different on Ocracoke Island: ethnic food, which is a refreshing change of pace on the Outer Banks. Thai Moon offers authentic Thai specialties for takeout only. Whet your appetite with Tom Yum Goong, a hot and sour shrimp soup with lemongrass, straw mushrooms, Thai chili, lime juice, onions, and cilantro. Other appetizers include moon egg rolls, spring rolls with an addictive peanut sauce, and satay. If you love seafood, you'll love it even more prepared with Thai flair: fish fillet crispy fried with mushrooms, carrots, onions, and cashews; crabmeat fried rice with onion and basil; or Thai lo mein with shrimp, cabbage, and scallions. Chicken, pork, beef, and vegetarian options are also available. Pad Thai and fried rice with shrimp, chicken, or bean curd are specialties. Thai Moon is open for lunch and dinner Tuesday through Saturday and for dinner only on Sunday and Monday. Call for off-season hours.

Capt. Ben's $$
NC 12, Ocracoke Village
(252) 928-4741
Serving Ocracoke locals and guests since 1970, Capt. Ben's is a casual restaurant. Owner and chef Ben Mugford combines Southern tradition with gourmet foods. Ben is especially revered for his crabmeat, prime rib, and seafood entrees. He also serves a mean Caesar salad and comes up with some good pasta and chicken creations. Sandwiches, crab cakes, and shrimp salad are good for lunch; each comes with chips or fries. Dinners come with soup, baked potato, and salad. And all the desserts are delicious. A large vari-

ety of domestic and imported beer is available, and the wine list complements the menu. The decor in this family eatery is nautical and friendly. The lounge and sundeck are comfortable places to relax if you have to wait for a table. Lunch and dinner are served daily from April through mid-November. Call for off-season hours. Children have their own menu at Capt. Ben's.

Howard's Pub & Raw Bar
Restaurant $-$$
NC 12, Ocracoke Village
(252) 928-4441
www.howardspub.com
Always a fun, friendly place to go for a meal, Howard's Pub has continued to expand its floor space, seating capacity, and menu diversity. Don't be misled by the selection of more than 200 imported, domestic, and microbrewed beers. The crew at Howard's Pub has established its "little corner of paradise" as the choice hangout for families, couples, and individuals alike. The restaurant's various areas—including the long wraparound bar, the main floor and game area, the large screened porch, and the ocean-to-sound-view deck—provide plenty of room for your group.

Howard's Pub & Raw Bar Restaurant is the only Outer Banks place we know that can boast that it has opened every day since 1991—including Thanksgiving, Christmas, Easter, and hurricane evacuations! This place has become a must-stop for everyone visiting Ocracoke, with great local flavor and guaranteed good times. (See our Nightlife chapter for more on Howard's Pub.)

The restaurant boasts the only year-round raw bar on the island and is home to the spicy Ocracoke Oyster Shooter. We love these raw oyster, hot sauce, pepper, and draught combinations, especially when washed down with an unusual or hard-to-find imported beer. Appetizers range from soups, salads, and snow crab legs to hot wings, Southwestern black bean eggrolls, and Howard's famous peel-

and-eat steamed shrimp. Entrees include steaks, barbecued ribs, live Maine lobster, and various catch-of-the-day recipes, including blackened tuna, wahoo with tropical salsa, and mahimahi. Wine is available by the bottle.

The upstairs deck with observation tower affords breathtaking views of the ocean, sound, salt marshes, and sand dunes. On a clear day, you can even see Portsmouth Island! There are big-screen TVs and many smaller ones for viewing any number of events from just about anywhere in the restaurant. Board games, darts, a pool table in the off-season, and coloring books for the wee ones, plus live music and a 17-speaker sound system, guarantee that you can party to your heart's content. The full menu and drinks are served every day from 11:00 A.M. to 2:00 A.M.

Cafe Atlantic $$
NC 12, Ocracoke Village
(252) 928-4861

Proprietors Bob and Ruth Toth operate Cafe Atlantic in this traditional beach-style building. There's not much that's traditional about their innovative, fantastic food, however. Views from the dining room look out across marsh grass and dunes. The gallery-like effect of the restaurant is created with hand-colored photographs by local writer and artist Ann Ehringhaus and watercolors and oils by Debbie Wells.

Dinner is served at this upscale yet casual eatery seven days a week in season. The Sunday brunches are among the best on the Outer Banks. Brunch menus change weekly, but champagne and mimosas are always served. We're partial to the blueberry pecan pancakes, chicken and broccoli crepes, and huevos rancheros served over black beans in a crisp tortilla shell. Hash browns come with almost every entree.

The Toths make all their soups, dressings, sauces, and desserts from scratch. Dinner entrees include fresh Atlantic seafood, beef, pastas, and vegetarian entrees. Each meal is served with salad, rice or potato, and steaming rolls just out of the oven. You've got to leave room for dessert here—or take one of their outrageously ornate cakes, pies, or cobblers home. A children's menu is available, and the restaurant has a nice selection of wine and beer. Cafe Atlantic is open from early March through October. Lunch openings may vary off-season, so call for hours. This nonsmoking cafe, though isolated on tiny Ocracoke, is certainly among the best dining experiences the Outer Banks has to offer.

Ocracoke Coffee $
Back Road, Ocracoke Village
(252) 928-7473

The neatest place on the island to take care of caffeine and sugar cravings, Ocracoke Coffee has enjoyed tremendous success since opening in 1995. The aromatic eatery offers bagels, pastries, desserts, brewed coffee drinks, espresso, shakes, whole bean and ground coffees, and loose tea. The shop is nestled under tall pines on Back Road, within an easy walk of almost anything in the village. We know you'll find your way here in the morning (everyone does), but why not walk in after dinner for something sweet as well? The shop's feel is way hip, but it's also cozy and inviting, and the folks frothing your concoctions are friendly as can be. Look for more than 10 varieties of smoothies for a cool respite from the summer heat. Ocracoke Coffee is open daily from 7:00 A.M. to 9:30 P.M., and live music plays during summer evenings on the deck. The shop closes December through March.

Island Inn Restaurant $$
Lighthouse Road, Ocracoke Village
(252) 928-4351

This family-owned and -operated restaurant at the Island Inn is one of the oldest establishments on Ocracoke. Its main dining room and airy porch are furnished in a traditional country style, with blue and white china to dine on and bright, nautical touches throughout. Owners Bob and Cee Touhey welcome everyone; you don't have to be a guest at the inn. Standard breakfast fare, such as pancakes, eggs, and hash browns, is available. The cook also comes up with some unusual creations, such as oyster omelets with spinach and bacon and shrimp omelets loaded with melted jack cheese, green chiles, and salsa. For dinner, locally landed seafood and shellfish entrees are grilled, fried, or broiled to your liking. Beef, pork, lamb, pasta, and stir-fry dishes also are available, as are vegetarian offerings. All the breads and soups are made daily at this restaurant, and homemade pies are perfectly delicious. Beer and a selection of wines are served here, and a children's menu is available. Reservations are needed for large groups; the owners are happy to accommodate private party requests. The Island Inn Restaurant is open for breakfast and dinner daily except in the dead of winter. Call for off-season hours.

Creek Side Cafe $
NC 12, Ocracoke Village
(252) 928-3606

Overlooking Silver Lake Harbor from a second-story vantage point, this restaurant offers wonderful views. A covered porch that wraps around two sides of the wooden building has ceiling fans and breezes to cool afternoon diners. Inside, the eatery is casual and friendly, serving brunch items daily and lunch and dinner from a single menu from April to early November. Soups, salads, seafood, and pasta dishes are the afternoon and evening fare here. The blackened chicken sandwiches are so popular that the owners decided to package and sell the spices. French dips, fresh fish sandwiches, oyster baskets, crab cakes, and Greek-style linguine with feta cheese and black olives all are great choices. For brunch, we recommend the Tex-Mex: scrambled eggs, onions, peppers, tomatoes, and salsa served in a tortilla shell with a dollop of guacamole. Desserts include parfaits, cheesecakes, key lime pie, tollhouse pie, and pecan pie—all homemade. Beer and wine are available, and four champagne drinks offer unusual alcoholic creations.

Jolly Roger Pub & Marina $$
NC 12, Ocracoke Village
(252) 928-3703

Jolly Roger is the perfect place to kick back and relax on Ocracoke Island. Although a roof, canopy, and umbrellas cover many of the dining tables, the entire restaurant is open, with tables on large decks overlooking the harbor. This is one of our favorite places for a casual meal in Ocracoke. There's nothing fancy here—

wooden tables, paper plates, and plastic cutlery—but the service is good, the beer is cold, and the food is wonderful. The menu features homemade soups, sand-wiches, salad plates, local seafood, and daily specials. Stop in for live entertain-ment at sunset; you'll hear the music waft-ing down the street as you stroll through the village. Beer and wine are served, and there's a good-size bar on premises. Jolly Roger serves lunch and dinner daily in season.

The Pelican Restaurant $$
NC 12, Ocracoke Village
(252) 928-7431

In an old home tucked under a grove of trees in the heart of the village, the Peli-can serves breakfast, lunch, and dinner. There's a great patio where you can enjoy beer and 15-cent shrimp from 3:00 to 5:00 P.M. and live entertainment five nights a week in summer from 6:00 to 10:00 P.M. Outside is lively, inside is romantic and softly lit. Meals include seafood entrees, hand-cut prime steaks, and a wonderful seafood pasta swimming in a light lemon-butter broth. A good wine list is available. Sushi is served here one night a week. The Pelican Restaurant is open daily from 7:00 A.M. to 10:00 P.M. in season; call for off-season hours.

NIGHTLIFE ♗

For many of us who live here—and for many visitors as well—the best evening entertainment is watching the sun set over the sound waters. Sound-front decks, piers, gazebos, and public beaches are perfect spots to toast your friends and the setting sun. It's not uncommon for us to rush home in the evening, call our friends, and arrange for a rendezvous spot at which to watch the sunset. Many locals sail or motor their boats out into the sound in anticipation of our favorite entertainment, provided free each day. Moonrise over the ocean is pretty spectacular too, and under a Carolina moon, just about anything is possible.

The Outer Banks after hours isn't like other resort areas. So many families—and early-rising anglers—come here that many people bed down for the evening early. We don't have the huge strips of late-night entertainment joints that you find in many other vacation destinations, but a number of bars and dance floors are scattered across the barrier islands. If you are a night owl, or at least like to stretch your wings a bit in the dark, you will find fun and frolic in dozens of establishments from Corolla all the way to Ocracoke.

Families enjoy a variety of early evening entertainment options here. Miniature golf, go-kart tracks, movie theaters, bumper boats, even a small amusement park and a bowling alley are listed in our Recreation chapter. And don't forget *The Lost Colony* outdoor drama; that's detailed in our Attractions chapter.

There are plenty of places to shoot pool, catch sporting events on big-screen TVs, play interactive trivia, throw darts, listen to some quiet music, or boogie the night away to a live band.

Outer Banks musicians play everything from blues to jazz to rock to alternative and country tunes. Both local and out-of-town bands take the stage often during the summer season. Several area nightclubs assess nominal cover charges at the door, usually ranging from $1.00 for dueling acoustic guitar duos to $10.00 or more for the national acts that grace these sands between mid-May and Labor Day. Many acoustic acts, however, are heard for free.

If live music is what you're listening for, the *Virginian-Pilot*'s weekly *Coast* supplement—available free at area grocery and convenience stores and motels—has up-to-date listings in its "Club Hoppin'" section plus music scene information in the "After Dark" column (see our Media chapter for more on the *Coast*). Local stations WVOD 99.1 FM and WOBR 95.3 FM give daily concert updates on evening radio broadcasts. (See our Annual Events and Arts and Culture chapters for more nighttime possibilities.)

Alcoholic beverages are available at most Outer Banks lounges until around 2:00 A.M. Beer and wine are offered throughout the barrier islands. In Southern Shores, and on Colington, Roanoke, Hatteras, and Ocracoke Islands, it is illegal to serve mixed drinks. However, with the exception of Colington Island, state-run ("ABC") stores sell liquor in each of these areas. Most nightclubs in areas that serve only wine and beer allow brown bagging, which means customers may bring in their own alcohol for the evening. Call ahead to make sure that brown bagging is allowed where you're going.

Several restaurants on the Outer Banks offer late-night menus or at least raw and steamed bar food until closing. Every nightclub operator will be glad to call a cab to take you home or to your hotel or rental cottage after an evening of imbibing. **Beware:** The legal drinking age in North Carolina is 21, and the blood-alcohol content level for a drunken-driving arrest is only .08. Law enforcement is strict. So even if you have only a couple of cocktails, play it safe and take a taxi. Besides, we want your experience here to be memorable in a good way! .

Although several area restaurants offer happy-hour specials and most have bars within their establishments, we've only included those eateries that are open until at least midnight in this chapter. Check our Restaurants chapter for sunset entertainment options. Several spots also feature outdoor acoustic music until dark—but this section is for those who like to stay out late.

COROLLA

Sundogs Sports Bar and Grill
Monteray Plaza, NC 12, Corolla
(252) 453-4263

Sundogs is a sports bar, so expect a lot of people hanging out watching *Monday Night Football* and the like. But it's also a gathering spot, where people linger at the bar until the late hours. A pool table and video games provide other entertainment.

DUCK

Fishbones Sunset Grille and Raw Bar
NC 12, Duck
(252) 261-3901

Situated right on Currituck Sound across from the entrance to Barrier Island Station, Fishbones Sunset Grille and Raw Bar is the only place in Duck to see live bands. During the summer, Fishbones has live music every night except Sunday and Monday. In the off-season, there's live music at least twice a week. The house band is Jah Seed, which plays at least once a week. Other bands, including blues, rock, and a Jimmy Buffett–style act, play here as well. In season, the raw bar and sushi bar are open until 10:00 P.M. or later, so you can get a bite before the bands really kick in.

Fishbones Raw Bar & Restaurant
Scarborough Lane Shoppes
Duck Road (NC 12), Duck
(252) 261-6991

This raw bar and restaurant is one of Duck's most popular evening hangouts. Open daily, it features a full bar with five beers on tap, 50 international bottled beers, various microbrews, and a wine list. During summer, deck parties are held outdoors when the weather is good.

Roadside Raw Bar & Grill
Duck Road (NC 12), Duck
(252) 261-5729

Low-key, casual, and serving great food, Roadside is a favorite early evening hangout for locals and tourists alike. This 1932 restored cottage with hardwood floors exudes a cozy, homey feeling. On the outdoor patio you can hear live jazz on Tuesday and Thursday evenings in summer months. Appetizers and cocktails are served outside during the music. Roadside is open year-round, but call for off-season hours.

KITTY HAWK

Sunburn Sports Bar & Grill
US 158, MP 4, Kitty Hawk
(252) 261-7833

A popular nightspot for locals year-round, this restaurant features a large, three-sided bar and beautiful terrariums and aquariums throughout the dining area. It's open seven days a week and has karaoke on Friday and Saturday nights year-round. Sunburn is popular all year with the 30-plus crowd. It's open until 2:00 A.M. in season and has a late-night munchies menu.

For up-to-date nightlife listings, the Coast, *a free tabloid published by the* Virginian-Pilot, *is the most comprehensive place to look. You'll find it in racks everywhere.*

Black Pelican Oceanfront Cafe
NC 12, MP 4, Kitty Hawk
(252) 261-3171

With 12 TVs and an enclosed porch overlooking the ocean, this Kitty Hawk hangout is a fun place to catch up on sporting events or relax at the bar. It's in a former Coast Guard station and still features hardwood floors, tongue-and-groove appointments, and light gray accents reminiscent of days gone by. In the evenings its upbeat atmosphere is anything but antique. Interactive TV trivia is available for the contemporary crowd. Gourmet pizzas are a great treat for late-night munchies. Takeout is available, too. The Black Pelican is open year-round.

KILL DEVIL HILLS

Chilli Peppers
US 158, MP 5, Kill Devil Hills
(252) 441-8081
www.chilli-peppers.com

This restaurant's bar area always teems with partying people who often come here to eat and stay late, especially on sushi nights (Wednesday and Friday year-round) and tapas nights (Thursday in the off-season). Chilli's has live bands or acoustic acts every Tuesday all year. Seven nights a week, you can enjoy fresh fruit margaritas, a nice wine selection, and dozens of domestic and imported beers from the full bar. Bartenders also serve nonalcoholic beers and fruit smoothies. The outdoor patio invites you to sip your drinks under the stars. Steamed seafood and vegetables are served until closing.

A good source for entertainment schedules on the Outer Banks and in nearby cities is 99.1 The Sound radio station, which airs daily updates on who's performing where and when. This information is also on the Web at www.wvod.com.

Jolly Roger Restaurant
NC 12, MP 6, Kill Devil Hills
(252) 441-6530

Adorned with hanging plants and colorful lights, the lounge at this restaurant is separate from the dining area at this mainstay restaurant. The bar is open seven nights a week. Every night Jolly Roger hosts karaoke or offers interactive TV with games covering sports, movie trivia, and more. Both draw a regular audience, and prizes are even awarded to some of the big winners. Locals love this place. People from their early 20s to late 60s enjoy relaxing and dancing in this lounge.

Goombays Grille & Raw Bar
NC 12, MP 7, Kill Devil Hills
(252) 441-6001
www.goombays.com

This popular nightspot is packed with tourists and locals and is open seven nights a week. It's fun and colorful with a tropical island flair and flavor. Goombays is Caribbean and casual, where you feel right at home even if you've never visited the Outer Banks.

On Wednesday live bands play for "Locals Night" year-round. Wednesday night shows begin at 10:30 P.M. A horseshoe-shaped bar is set to the side of the dining area, so you can lounge on a stool or high-backed chair in the bar area or have a seat at a nearby table after the dining room closes at 10:00 P.M. Goombays serves imported and domestic beer, wine, and mixed drinks until 2:00 A.M. Try some of the special rum, vodka, and tequila combos that come with toys to take home. Steamed shrimp and veggies are served until 1:00 A.M.

Port O' Call Restaurant
& Gaslight Saloon
NC 12, MP 8½, Kill Devil Hills
(252) 441-7484

One of the area's most unusual places to hang out—and one of the few local nightclubs that attract national bands in the summer—the Gaslight Saloon is decorated in an ornate Victorian style complete with overstuffed armchairs, antique wooden tables, and a long mahogany bar. The dance floor is a good one and an upstairs lounge (with separate bar) overlooks the stage.

Port O' Call hosts live entertainment seven nights a week in season and every weekend while the restaurant is open from mid-March through December. There's usually a cover charge here. Cover may be waived for diners. In recent years, Port O' Call has hosted such national acts as Southern Culture on the Skids, Leon Russell, Fishbone, Molly Hatchet, and an array of first-rate reggae artists. Beer, wine, and liquor are served until 2:00 A.M.

Shucker's Pub and Billiards
Oceanside Plaza, NC 12, MP 8
Kill Devil Hills
(252) 480-1010

This pub and billiards room serves more than 50 types of beer and has the only 9-foot pool tables on the Outer Banks. Eleven billiard tables offer people the chance to play by the game or by the hour. Darts, foosball, and pinball are popular pastimes, and the many TVs keep sports fans entertained. Would-be pool sharks who get beached by too much cigarette smoke will be happy to know that Shucker's operates heavy-duty electronic "smoke-eaters" in every room. It's open year-round, seven nights a week until 2:00 A.M. Wine is available, and Shucker's serves pizza, fries and onion rings until closing. You must be 21 or older to play in this pub after 9:00 P.M.

Outer Banks Brewing Station
US 158, MP 8½, Kill Devil Hills
(252) 449-BREW
www.obbrewing.com

Outer Banks Brewing Station is one of the hottest restaurants and nightspots on the beach. Outside, it looks like a big white barn with silos at either end (the silos are for making beer). Inside, it's absolutely inviting and city-chic, with a stretch-

The Outer Banks has a rich music scene that showcases entertainers from around the country as well as local talent. You can hear rock, bluegrass, country, heavy metal, classical, Creole, and reggae played at concerts, pubs, and restaurants, or around bonfires at the beach. Check out the **Outer Banks Sentinel** *for listings.*

length bar, high ceilings, warm wood tones, an open kitchen, innovative house-made beer, well-chosen wines, and sublime food. The brew is a big draw, with selections like a Hefewiezen wheat beer, Mutiny Pale Ale, and Kolsch summer brew. After dinner hours, the Brewing Station stays open late, treating a crowd of lingerers to "righteous music"; blues, jazz, and funk bands and sometimes acoustic acts play all year. Both regional bands and national acts are booked here, and the Sunday open-mike and sushi night is very popular. You can watch the band from a table in front of the stage, from the bar area, or get a bird's-eye view from the upstairs loft. Expect large crowds on band nights. Live entertainment is held Friday and Saturday in season. You can also expect music every night in the summer. The Brewing Station is open until 2:00 A.M. seven nights a week. Call or check the Web site for entertainment schedules.

The Pit Surf Shop, Bar and Grill
US 158, MP 9, Kill Devil Hills
(252) 480-3128
www.pitsurf.com

The Pit is a conglomerate surf shop, hangout, restaurant, cybercafe, bar, band venue, and teen scene. It's a popular, casual hangout spot all day and all night and was named one of the best bars in the world for 2003 in *Men's Journal* magazine. Every summer night, and most off-season nights, something fun happens at The Pit. Thursday night is Mug Night with a DJ, when you pay $5.00, bring your own mug, and drink beers for as little as a buck. Bands play every Tuesday and Sunday, and The Pit consistently gets the biggest names in talent. Burning Spear, The Wailers, 2 Skinnee J's, The Connells, All Mighty Senators, and Everything are just a few of the bands that play here. The sound and lighting production are state of the art. Band covers range from $5.00 to $20.00. The Pit serves food until 9:00 P.M. and has pool tables, foosball, videos, Internet access, and boardsport videos to keep you otherwise entertained.

The Pit is one of the only places on the beach welcoming the under-21 crowd. Underage revelers have three summer nights of their own—Monday, Wednesday, and Friday—(once in a while in the off-season) with no alcohol served. These nights feature DJs or occasionally a band. Cover charges vary.

Peppercorns
Ramada Plaza, NC 12, MP 9½
Kill Devil Hills
(252) 441-2151
Enjoy a breathtaking ocean view from the plate-glass window wall while visiting with friends and listening to acoustic soloists or duos in the Ramada Inn's intimate lounge area. Live music is performed daily throughout summer and often starts earlier here than elsewhere on the Outer Banks—sometimes they get started at 8:00 P.M. This is an open, laid-back place with booths, tables, and a full bar. The music is never too loud to talk over. But if you'd rather listen, some of the best guitar talent on the beach shows up here in season.

Mama Kwan's Grill and Tiki Bar
US 158, MP 9½, Kill Devil Hills
(252) 441-7889
www.mamakwans.com
This retro-Hawaiian restaurant and bar is always packed late with young partiers. It's often the place local restaurant workers go when they get off work. In summer, on Tuesday and Thursday nights either a band or a DJ plays. Mama's keeps things

going in the off-season too, usually with a band on Thursday night. Tiki lights create an island atmosphere. The bar's specialty is frozen drinks served with surprises. It's open every night until 2:00 A.M.

NAGS HEAD

Red Drum Grille and Taphouse
NC 12, MP 10, Nags Head
(252) 480-1095
Red Drum pours 18 beers on tap, including hard-to-find brews like Sierra Nevada, J.W. Dundee's Honey Brown, Woodpecker Cider, Black Radish, and Pyramid-Hefeweizen. You can get wine by the glass or the bottle. Red Drum also serves liquor from its beautiful long, redwood-colored bar.

Mulligan's Oceanfront Grille
NC 12, MP 10½, Nags Head
(252) 480-2000
Mulligan's is heralded as a popular evening hot spot and maintains its image as the Outer Banks's own version of TV's *Cheers*. A wooden partition separates the long, three-sided wooden bar from the dining room, and loads of local memorabilia adorn the walls. Mulligan's serves micro-brewed beer on tap or in iced-down bottles. Wine and liquor are available. Acoustic music plays on weekends in the off-season and on Wednesday, Friday, and Saturday in summer.

Kelly's Outer Banks Restaurant & Tavern
US 158, MP 10½, Nags Head
(252) 441-4116
www.kellysrestaurant.com
Probably the most consistently crowded tavern on the Outer Banks, Kelly's offers live bands five nights a week in season and an open-mike fest with a lip-synch contest and cash prizes on Tuesday. During fall and winter, rockin' bands take the stage, and fun people always fill this place.

A full bar serves suds, shots, and everything in between. Folks often line up around its three long sides two or three people deep. The big dance floor is usually shaking after 10:00 P.M. If you're in the mood just to listen and watch, secluded booths surround the dance floor a few steps above the rest of the lounge, and tables are scattered throughout the tavern. A dartboard and fireplace adorn the back area. Featuring a tasty variety of foods served late into the night, a lounge menu offers appetizers and steamed shellfish. An old-fashioned popcorn popper provides free munchies served in wicker baskets throughout the evening. Singles seem to really enjoy this tavern.

Slammin' Sammy's Offshore Grille & Stillery
US 158, MP 10½, Nags Head
(252) 449-2255
www.slamminsammys.com
Slammin' Sammy's is the area's only dedicated sports bar, with 43 TVs tuned to the sports du jour. Sammy has even put TVs in the bathroom. If you'd rather play than watch, there are pool tables and darts. It's right across the street from Kelly's Tavern, so people often hop back and forth between the two bars. Be careful crossing the highway at night! Slammin' Sammy's has a full bar, offers a late-night menu, and is open until 2:00 A.M. every night.

Tortuga's Lie Shellfish Bar and Grille
NC 12, MP 11, Nags Head
(252) 441-7299
www.tortugaslie.com
Our favorite place to meet friends for a laid-back evening—or to hang out with long-lost local pals—Tortuga's offers probably the most comfortable atmosphere you'll find on the Outer Banks most of the year. The bar winds around a corner to allow at least a half-dozen more stools to slide under the refurbished countertop. Old license plates are perched on the low, wooden ceiling beams, and the sand volleyball court remains ready for pickup games out back all summer. Bartenders serve Black and Tans in pint glasses—that's right, Tortuga's has Guinness and Bass Ale on tap. Beer is served by the

Parents looking for some alone time without the children should ask their vacation rental company about babysitting services and children's programs in the area. These types of services are quickly growing in popularity on the Outer Banks.

longneck bottle or by the iced-down bucket. Shooters, mixed drinks, and tropical frozen concoctions are sure to please any palate.

The steamer is open until closing, so you can satisfy late-night appetites with shellfish or fresh vegetables. Whether you're visiting or here to stay, Tortuga's is one place you won't want to miss. Most nights, it remains open until 2:00 A.M. Tortuga's closes for a brief spell in December and January.

Bacu Grill
Outer Banks Mall, US 158, MP 14
Nags Head
(252) 480-1892
This Cuban-inspired restaurant and bar is about the only late-night place in lower Nags Head. Blues and jazz bands play several nights a week in the summer and occasionally in the off-season. You may be charged a small cover for the bands. This is the favorite end-of-the-workweek gathering spot for Nags Head locals, so Friday nights are often packed. Bacu has a worldly wine list and a European beer engine that pours a perfect draft beer, such as Harp, Guinness, or Sierra Nevada. Appetizers and other food are served late.

ROANOKE ISLAND

The Green Dolphin Restaurant and Pub
Sir Walter Raleigh Street, Manteo
(252) 473-5911
If you're looking for late-night fun in Manteo, this is the only place to find it. Acoustic guitarists perform here on Friday nights year-round, playing jazz, rock, folk,

and blues. A bar serves a variety of beer, and there's never a cover charge for live music.

This pub is warm and comfortable. Upon wooden floors and booths sit tables made from old ship-hatch covers and Singer sewing machine stands. The staff is friendly, and locals like to hang out here. It's a fun place with a pool table and pockmarked dartboards set in a separate room. The restaurant serves appetizers and sandwiches late into the night. Call for seasonal schedules of entertainment. The Green Dolphin is open Tuesday through Saturday until 1:00 A.M.

HATTERAS ISLAND

Froggy Dog Restaurant & Bar
NC 12, Avon
(252) 995-5550
Late-night acoustic music plus bands and karaoke singers take the stage at this casual Hatteras Island nightspot. The Froggy Dog is open nightly in season, serving beer and wine and entertainment on most Sundays; call for schedule.

OCRACOKE ISLAND

Howard's Pub & Raw Bar Restaurant
NC 12, Ocracoke Village
(252) 928-4441
www.howardspub.com
This is our absolute favorite place to hear live bands. Featuring the friendliest crowd of locals and visitors around, Howard's Pub has an atmosphere and feeling all its own. Once you've visited, you'll plan to stop at this upbeat yet casual place at least once during every visit to Ocracoke. Howard's is open every day of the year until 2:00 A.M.—the only place on the Outer Banks that can make that claim— and has done so for more than 10 years.

The pub serves more types of beer than any place we know—more than 200 varieties are available. There's a second-floor outdoor deck with breath-taking, ocean-to-sound views, perfect for catching sunsets or falling stars. A huge, screened porch—complete with Adiron-dack rocking chairs for relaxing in the evening breezes—borders an entire side of the spacious wooden building. The dance floor has more than doubled in

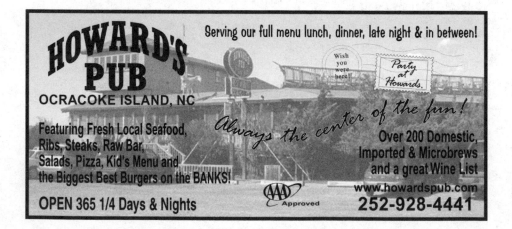

recent years. Two big-screen TVs and numerous smaller ones offer sports fans constant entertainment. Howard's has a dartboard, a pool table in the off-season, board games, and card games available free for playful patrons. The full menu, including pizza, sandwiches, and raw bar items, is offered until closing time.

Bands play most nights during summer season and several times a week during winter. Music covers rhythm and blues, bluegrass, jazz, rock, and originals. The occasional open-mike and karaoke nights are favorites for locals and visitors alike. Howard's Pub never charges a cover, and even when electricity fails the rest of the island, this place is equipped with a generator so the crew keeps cooking—and the beer stays cold.

Jolly Roger Pub & Marina
NC 12, Ocracoke Village
(252) 928-3703
A waterfront eatery with an open bar overlooking Silver Lake, this pub has a huge outdoor deck that's covered in case of thunderstorms. Local acoustic guitarists perform Caribbean and country music with no cover charge Thursday and Friday nights. Jolly Roger serves beer, wine, and great food throughout the warm summer months.

WEEKLY AND LONG-TERM COTTAGE RENTALS

If your idea of the perfect vacation is to settle down with all the comforts of a home away from home, the Outer Banks is a perfect choice. By far the most popular accommodations here are private beach cottages. More than 13,500 rental cottages are available in Dare County, and that's not including the thousands of cottages available in Corolla in Currituck County or on Ocracoke Island in Hyde County. From the unique off-road beaches of Carova just south of the Virginia line to the removed island of Ocracoke, accessible only by plane, boat, or ferry, you'll find a tremendous variety in price, location, and character. Although most vacationers stay for a week, longer- and shorter-term rentals are available throughout the year.

Most beach cottages are owned by individuals and are represented by a property management firm. Usually, these cottages reflect the individual tastes and preferences of their owners. Although property management firms or rental companies will set their own minimum standards for the homes they represent, beach homes vary widely in design, decor, and the amenities they offer. You can rent anything from a palatial nine-bedroom oceanfront mansion with a private pool, home office, and media room to a cozy little saltbox on the sound side.

Rental companies compete rigorously to secure the greatest possible number of bookings for their owners, and the trend is to add more amenities, thus encouraging guests to return again and again. In recent years, many companies have encouraged their cottage owners to add greater value to a week's vacation by including, as standard, amenities that used to be luxuries. Whirlpool baths, hot tubs, appealing interior decorating, book and video libraries, fireplaces, baby cribs, and playpens are becoming increasingly common, particularly in the newer properties. Veteran visitors to the Outer Banks are accustomed to bringing their own linens and towels, but more cottages now supply linens. Only a few property management firms require their owners to provide linens.

Of course, you'll pay more for these luxuries. Rental prices are based primarily on the season, the cottage's proximity to the ocean, the number of occupants it "sleeps," and the amenities it offers. The peak, most expensive, season runs from mid-June through the end of August. Substantial discounts are offered in the fall and spring, considered "mid-season" by most companies, and, of course, the best bargains are from late November to late March. More vacationers are discovering the joys of the Outer Banks during seasons other than summer: With its temperate climate, the Outer Banks offers a great variety of outdoor activities to enjoy, even if the weather is too cold for ocean swimming or lounging on the beach.

LOCATION, LOCATION, LOCATION!

An "oceanfront" cottage is one that sits directly on the beach with no cottages or lots to the east facing the ocean. Some, but not all, have private walkways to the ocean, an especially convenient and important feature if the cottage sits behind a dune. (Dunes are fragile and need protection. It's against the law to climb them.) If your cottage doesn't have a private walkway, you'll have to use the community or public access; check on this when you make your reservation. Also, although most oceanfront cottages offer spectacular vistas, some have tall dunes obstructing the view from one or more levels. Oceanfront cottages without views are more the exception than the rule, but you won't encounter any disappointing surprises if you double-check at the time of rental.

There's no underestimating the convenience of an oceanfront cottage. You don't have to schlep the beach equipment very far, and when the little ones get cranky, you can sun yourself on your deck or patio and listen to the pounding surf while they nap inside.

The next best thing to oceanfront is "semi-oceanfront," which usually means one lot back from oceanfront. The distance to the ocean varies, but many semi-oceanfronts still offer good views of the water and reasonable beach-going convenience. In some areas, especially Kitty Hawk, Kill Devil Hills, and Nags Head, you'll have to cross the Beach Road (North Carolina Highway 12) to get to the surf.

When a cottage is described as "between the highways," it is located between the Beach Road and U.S. Highway 158. Actual distances from the beach vary, but you can expect a 5- to 15-minute walk. Cottages identified as "westside" are located west of US 158 in Kitty Hawk, Kill Devil Hills, and Nags Head. Those west of NC 12 in Corolla, Duck, and Southern Shores are referred to as "soundside." Of course, "soundfront" cottages are those with no houses or lots between them and the sound.

Westside or soundside cottages tend to be among the last to book and can offer a very affordable and pleasant alternative to costlier oceanside cottages. Many communities offer pools, tennis courts, hiking trails, and other amenities on the soundside to enhance rentals. Some vacationers have come to prefer the soundside areas for their tranquillity and the convenience of certain water sports, such as windsurfing and canoeing. Finally, many soundfront cottages offer views as spectacular as those

on the ocean. It's the place to be if you prefer the sunset to the sunrise. (See our Real Estate chapter for more information on individual communities.)

Most rental companies identify, either in terms of number of lots from the beach or distance measured in feet, how close (or far) cottages are to the ocean, so you should get an idea when you make your reservation how long a trek you can expect.

"Cottage" is the traditional beach name for a vacation rental house on the Outer Banks. A "cottage" may be a tiny salt-box, of which there are only a few, or a mansion with numerous bedrooms, bathrooms, and Jacuzzis or hot tubs. Take your pick! Either way, it's a "cottage" to Insiders.

WHEN AND HOW TO RESERVE YOUR COTTAGE

As you might imagine, properties closest to the ocean are snatched up quickly. Many rental companies offer returning guests the opportunity to make advance reservations for the next year as they check out, so cottages in prime locations will often have several weeks reserved even before the New Year. Expect to make your reservation in January or February if you have your heart set on a particular cottage on the ocean. Otherwise, you'll still have a good variety from which to choose if you reserve by the end of March. Don't despair, however, if you can't make a decision until later. You might have to call around, but you can usually find something to rent, possibly even at the last minute. (One caveat: The pickings will be slim for spur-of-the-moment trips in summer months.)

Nearly all rental companies publish a color brochure or catalog describing their properties; the new editions typically are available after Thanksgiving. You'll find photos and property descriptions not only in a company's brochure but on its Web site as well. Online availability and reservation booking capabilities are increasingly used.

The rental company's catalog or Web site will almost certainly cover the essential elements of the lease. Make sure you read these thoroughly before making your reservation, and form a list of questions you want to ask the reservationist. You'd be surprised at how familiar many reservationists are with the properties they rent. This is also the right time to discuss any special needs anyone in your party may have. You'll typically be asked to secure your cottage with a deposit— usually 50 percent, with the balance due 30 days in advance of your visit.

AMENITIES

Rental companies list the amenities offered at each cottage in their catalogs; some include this information on their Web sites. In addition, most companies require their owners to supply certain amenities as standard. Typical standard items include air-conditioning, a telephone, television, VCR, washer and dryer, barbecue, microwave—most appliances and items you'd expect to find in the typical home. Still, don't take anything for granted. Read the descriptions and your lease thoroughly to avoid misunderstanding.

Unless the lease stipulates that your rental is equipped with linens and towels, bring your own. The cottage listing will tell you the sizes and number of beds in the home. You'll also need to supply your own toiletries, paper products, and cleaning

Before making your cottage reservation, check online to see if the homes you're interested in offer a virtual tour. If so, you'll be able to view several rooms within each home before making your choice.

supplies such as laundry and dishwashing detergents, sponges, and paper towels. It's a good idea to arrive with enough of the basics to get you through a half-day so you won't need to visit the grocery store immediately.

If you don't feel like hauling a lot of extra stuff to the beach, you can rent just about anything you need, including linens, towels, beach equipment, bicycles, outdoor furniture, and recreational equipment. At the end of this chapter is a list of companies you can call in advance; many will deliver the items you request right to your cottage.

MINIMUM STAYS

During the mid- and off-seasons, you'll of course have more options than in peak season, when occupancy runs at close to 100 percent. During the summer it's very difficult to find a cottage to rent for less than a week. Most rent from Saturday to Saturday or Sunday to Sunday. Some families enjoy renting for two or even more consecutive weeks, but don't expect a price break.

You'll have better luck finding a shorter-term rental during slower seasons. Most companies offer what they call "partial" rentals from September through May or June. Some charge a flat fee for a three- or four-day period; others charge a nightly fee. Make sure you understand how the fee is determined. In the off-seasons, many rental companies get creative to increase bookings. That's the time to look for special getaway packages. As you might expect, the mid- and off-seasons offer some excellent bargains and are especially popular with vacationers who don't have school-age children in tow. If you have the option of enjoying the Outer Banks during the slower seasons, you'll be delighted with the meandering pace and quiet. Most restaurants and shops now stay open at least through Thanksgiving, and more and more are extending their operating times well beyond that. Visiting the Outer Banks during off-season holidays is becoming increasingly popular.

ADVANCE RENTS

Expect to pay an advance rent, typically 50 percent of the full lease amount, soon after you make your reservation. It's usually due within 10 days. Personal checks are commonly accepted if the reservation is made in plenty of time for the check to clear. Some companies allow credit-card transactions, but be aware that some will charge an additional fee to cover the extra costs charged by the bank that handles the card. In most cases, the balance of the lease amount is due 30 days prior to arrival. If payment is accepted at check-in, it's usually required in the form of a certified check or cash. Most rental companies will not accept a personal check upon arrival.

SECURITY DEPOSITS

Besides advance rents, most rental companies also require their guests to pay a security deposit. This, of course, is for the owner's protection. The amounts required vary depending upon the company's policies. Cottages are typically inspected between check-ins to make sure everything is in order. If you notice any damage in a cottage just after arriving, inform your rental company immediately. A little extra caution on your part will help prevent any misunderstanding about who caused the damage. Remember that rental companies are anxious to please you, but they also answer to their owners.

If anything is damaged during your stay or is determined missing after you leave, expect to have an amount deducted from your security deposit. Cottages that allow pets usually require an extra deposit for possible pet damage and a standard fee for flea extermination after you and your pet depart.

HURRICANE EVACUATION REFUNDS

Most rental companies now offer insurance with each reservation made. In accordance with North Carolina's Vacation Rental Act, if a guest buys vacation insurance, or if a guest is offered insurance but declines the offer, the real estate company is not required to reimburse that guest for any rental days that he or she loses as a result of hurricane evacuation. Each rental company sets its own policy governing refunds in the event of a hurricane. The few remaining companies that do not offer insurance generally will issue a partial or full refund in the event of a mandatory evacuation. Each area's local government officials are ultimately responsible for issuing evacuation orders. The County of Currituck has jurisdiction over Corolla and the four-wheel-drive beach areas, Hyde County has jurisdiction over Ocracoke, and Dare County governs every place in between.

The island of Ocracoke is usually evacuated before all other areas because access and egress is only by ferry or boat, and the rough waters stirred up by a hurricane even hundreds of miles away will make passage difficult or impossible as the storm approaches. Hatteras Island also tends to evacuate early because sections of NC 12 quickly flood when waters rise. If a mandatory evacuation of your area is ordered, comply.

Most rental companies will not issue refunds for days you don't occupy the property once reentry is permitted. Most Ocracoke property managers make exceptions for refunds in case the ferries aren't operating. These policies do vary from business to business, so make inquiries along with your reservation.

Consider buying travel insurance, which will protect your vacation investment in a variety of unexpected scenarios.

HANDLING AND INSPECTION FEES AND TAXES

Some rental companies charge a handling fee for processing information and an inspection fee for cottage inspection following your checkout. This is a nonrefundable fee assessed in addition to other charges.

In Dare County, a combined 12 percent tax is tacked on to all rents and fees. The taxes in Currituck County total 11 percent.

PET RULES AND COSTS

Some cottage owners allow guests to bring pets, within certain limits, but you'll be assessed extra fees for the privilege. You can usually count on an extra cleaning and extermination fee and a higher security deposit. Rental companies will often restrict the size of the pets accepted (for example, dogs up to 75 pounds), but if your pet does not conform to the restrictions, ask the rental manager if it's possible to make an exception. Many companies will contact the cottage owner in an attempt to accommodate a reasonable request. Be aware, too, that some cottages will allow dogs but not cats and vice versa. Whatever you do, don't bring a pet "illegally"—this is almost always grounds for eviction without a refund.

CHECK-IN AND CHECKOUT TIMES

Of course you're anxious to begin your vacation, but you'll save yourself (and others) aggravation if you respect check-in and checkout times. Rental companies need this time to clean and inspect cottages and perform minor maintenance.

Checkout is usually by 10:00 A.M.; check-in is usually at 4:00 P.M., give or take an hour. (These standard times account for the heavy traffic on Saturday and Sunday mornings and afternoons.) Most companies allow you to occupy your cottage earlier if it has been serviced properly, but don't arrive expecting this. If you want to travel during off-peak hours in the summer and plan to arrive several hours before check-in, head for one of the beach access areas that has showers and changing facilities, and just plan to spend the time relaxing. If you plan to check in after the rental company's office closes, most will make arrangements to leave your keys and cottage information in an outside box for pickup.

Be prompt when you check out. This is a courtesy to the rental company and the next guest. You might be assessed an extra fee if you overstay your welcome!

OCCUPANCY

The number of people your cottage can accommodate is listed in the description of the property in the rental brochure. This is determined by the number and type of beds and the septic and water capacity. Do not exceed the maximum occupancy or you could risk eviction. Most rental companies rent to family groups only and will not rent to minors. Any violation of this policy could result in a ruined vacation—and no refund.

MAIL, TELEPHONE, AND FAX SERVICES

When you make a reservation, you can request the cottage's phone number to leave with those back home who may need to reach you. Often the cottage's physical address and telephone number are printed on your lease, which you'll receive after making your initial payment. Almost all cottages have telephones these days, although a few of the older ones do not (and with the proliferation of cell phones, this may not be a problem for you). At any rate, the caveat once again is to know exactly what you're renting. Of course, you'll be required to pay for long-distance calls, and many homeowners have a block on their lines to prevent direct-dialed long-distance calls. Either bring along a calling card or buy a pre-paid phone card, but don't make calls from your cottage that will be charged to the homeowner.

If you expect to receive mail while on vacation, ask the reservationist for the proper mailing address and make sure you tell your correspondents to mark the envelope clearly with your name and cottage identification. The same common sense applies if you expect to receive faxes while you're on vacation. Most rental companies either have a fax machine set aside for guest use or will let you use theirs, but a fee is almost always charged. If you're expecting something important, it's a good idea to instruct the sender to call you when the fax has been sent to be sure it arrives. Rental companies are exceptionally busy during summer and peak holiday times, so your fax might be one of a few dozen that come in over the course of a day.

TRASH PICKUP AND RECYCLING

Rental companies usually supply information on designated trash pick-up days in the check-in packet. When you check out, bag your refuse securely and make sure the receptacle sits beside the road, ready for pickup.

Recycling is with few exceptions the renter's responsibility. Some communities provide recycling service and the proper bins, but in most areas you'll need to carry your recyclables to one of the collection points. Ask your rental company for the location nearest your cottage and for sorting instructions.

Many beach access areas now have recycling bins in addition to trash cans to keep the beach litter-free.

EQUIPMENT RENTALS AND RELATED SERVICES

If you'd rather not take everything with you to the beach, Outer Banks equipment rental companies from north to south can provide almost anything you need or want, including baby furniture, beach chairs, umbrellas, bicycles, linens, fishing gear, grills, and more. You can also rent recreational equipment such as personal watercraft, boogie boards, surfboards, and kayaks. Check the Water Sports chapter for companies that specialize in these. The following listings cover companies that supply the widest variety of equipment and services.

At Your Service
(252) 261-5286
www.atyourserviceobx.com
With more than 15 years of experience on the Outer Banks, At Your Service takes on such tiresome chores as running errands and buying groceries by acting as your personal concierge. The service has babysitters (it's the oldest babysitting and eldercare service on the Outer Banks). It can also help in stocking your vacation cottage with groceries and other necessities before you arrive, providing linens and cleaning service, arranging in-house personal chef service, and seeing to details to make a vacation run smoothly. Barbara Hall is the energetic owner of At Your Service, and she has a well-trained and competent staff. For more information, see our Education and Child Care chapter.

Ocean Atlantic Rentals
(800) 635-9559

Corolla Light Town Center, Corolla
(252) 453-2440

Duck Road, Soundfront, Duck
(252) 261-4346

NC 12, MP 10, Nags Head
(252) 441-7823

NC 12, Avon
(252) 995-5868
www.oceanatlanticrentals.com
Ocean Atlantic combines quality equip-

ment with reasonable rates and full service to give you the best values in rental ware on the beach. All baby items meet federal safety standards, and Ocean Atlantic uses well-known brand-name equipment. Beach umbrellas and chairs, bikes, cribs, TVs, VCRs, DVD players, kayaks, linens, grills, the latest videos and DVDs, and watersports equipment are among the items Ocean Atlantic offers.

Surfing lessons for all skill levels are taught out of their four locations. Ocean Atlantic also has a wedding service rental package.

Moneysworth Beach Home Equipment Rentals
947 West Kitty Hawk Road, Kitty Hawk
(252) 261-6999, (800) 833-5233
www.mworth.com
With an advance minimum rental order of $20, all items are delivered to your vacation home on your check-in day and picked up after you check out. This company is the only one that services the real estate companies directly. It has a wide assortment of beach and sports equipment, TVs, VCRs, grills, baby items, and bicycles. And the best part is you do not have to be present for delivery or pickup service. They'll deliver whatever you need from Ocean Hill to Hatteras Village.

Lifesaver Rent Alls
Lifesaver Shops, NC 12, MP 9
Kill Devil Hills
(252) 441-6048, (800) 635-2764
www.outer-banks.com/lifesaver
Delivery is available, or you can stop in the store to browse through numerous items. Beach equipment, bikes, baby supplies, linens, fishing supplies, and beach wheelchairs are among the items this company leases. Retail items like fishing tackle and floats are also available.

Metro Rentals
US 158 and Colington Road, MP 8
Kill Devil Hills
(252) 480-3535
www.metrorentalobx.com
This company specializes in wedding and catering needs, party supplies and tents, construction equipment, and beachcombing devices such as metal detectors.

Beach Outfitters
NC 12, Ocracoke
(252) 928-6261
www.ocracokeislandrealty.com
Beach Outfitters, at Ocracoke Island Realty, is open all year and accepts reservations. Free delivery and pickup are available on Ocracoke Island with an order of more than $100. Available rental items include beach chairs and umbrellas, towels and linens,

bikes, rollaway beds, baby equipment, TVs, VCRs, steamer pots, and kitchen appliances.

COTTAGE RENTAL COMPANIES

In this section, we've listed rental companies according to the physical location of their headquarters office. Many have more than one office, so check the listing to see which areas they serve. Listings proceed from north to south.

A company's inventory of cottages can change from year to year, but almost all companies offer some accommodations that allow pets, a few wheelchair-accessible cottages, and partial-week rentals in the mid- and off-seasons. In the following listings, we concentrate on which areas companies cover and approximately how many cottages they represent. We recommend that you contact companies directly for comprehensive information. Nearly all will supply you with a free brochure or catalog of their rental properties.

Corolla

Twiddy & Company Realtors
1127A Schoolhouse Lane, Corolla
(252) 457-1100, (800) 489-4339
www.twiddy.com
Twiddy & Company offers exceptional Outer Banks vacation rentals from Carova to Southern Shores. Special event and wheelchair-friendly homes are available, as are homes from the oceanfront to the sound. Weddings, corporate retreats, and other functions can be accommodated. Many of Twiddy's choice homes include private pools and spas; pets are allowed at some accommodations.

Corolla Classic Vacations
1196 Ocean Trail, Corolla
(866) 453-9660
www.corollaclassicvacations.com
Corolla Classic Vacations manages vacation homes in the Corolla area, including

Pine Island, Ocean Sands, Ocean Lake, Crown Point, Ocean Hill, and Corolla Village. Many of their homes are equipped with elevators and are wheelchair friendly. Properties with access to golf, tennis, private pools, and hot tubs are available, and some units allow pets. Beds are made and bath towels are ready upon your arrival.

Élan Vacations
Hunt Club Drive, Currituck Club Center, Corolla
(866) 760-ELAN
www.elanvacations.com
Élan Vacations is a full-service travel company representing luxurious vacation homes along the Outer Banks. Élan Vacations likes to provide a relaxing and fun-filled experience with highly personalized service to guests and owners. A concierge is available who can reserve anything from maid service to hang-gliding lessons to dinner reservations at your favorite restaurant. Élan guests are greeted with an assortment of gifts, including select North Carolina wine, coffee, and other Élan products.

ResortQuest Outer Banks
(800) 688-2813
www.resortquestouterbanks.com
ResortQuest Outer Banks, part of Resort-Quest International, is fairly new to the Outer Banks. The company bought several of the best northern Outer Banks property management companies and rolled them into one. ResortQuest manages properties from Corolla to Southern Shores. Oceanfront, soundfront, and in-between properties are available. Four check-in offices are available: one in Corolla at 1023 Ocean Trail, two in Duck at 1316 Duck Road and 1184 Duck Road, and one in Nags Head at milepost 14½. Concierge services are available in the summer months. Leaseholders receive a complimentary beach souvenir.

Karichele Realty
TimBuck II Shopping Village
66 Sunset Boulevard, Corolla
(252) 453-4400, (800) 453-2377
www.karichele.com

Karichele Realty manages properties in Corolla and the four-wheel-drive area. During the off-season, weekend packages are available. Pets are accepted in some units. Wheelchair-accessible cottages also are available.

Stan White Realty & Construction Inc.
812 Ocean Trail, Corolla
(252) 453-9619, (800) 338-3233
www.outerbanksrentals.com
This is the northern beaches location for Stan White Realty, renting properties from Whalehead to Nags Head. This location serves as the check-in office for rentals in and around Corolla.

Village Realty
501B Hunt Club Drive, Corolla
(252) 453-9650, (877) 546-5362
www.villagerealtyobx.com

The northern beaches' location of Village Realty represents oceanfront, soundfront, and in-between homes in Pine Island, Ocean Sands Whalehead, Corolla Light, and the Currituck Club, the only golf community on the Currituck Outer Banks. Rentals at the Currituck Club include use of the pool, fitness center, and other amenities. Ask about golf packages.

Duck

Carolina Designs Realty
Village Square, 1197 NC 12, Duck
(252) 261-3934, (800) 368-3825
www.carolinadesigns.com
Carolina Designs manages weekly rentals ranging from one-bedroom condos to eight-bedroom estates, with linens included. Properties are primarily from

Corolla to Southern Shores and Nags Head. Many of the homes have pools and allow pets and most offer wireless Internet.

Duck's Real Estate
A Stan White Company
1232 NC 12, Duck
(252) 261-4614, (800) 992-2976
www.outerbanksrentals.com
Duck's Real Estate manages weekly rentals from Corolla to Southern Shores. Three-day golf packages also are available. Pets are accepted in some units. Some cottages are equipped for disabled guests.

Twiddy & Company Realtors
1181 NC 12, Duck
(252) 457-1100, (800) 489-4339
www.twiddy.com
Twiddy & Company manages rental properties from Carova to Southern Shores and offers several specialty properties that accommodate weddings, corporate retreats, and other special functions. A special-events coordinator can be recommended. All of the company's cottages include linen and towel service as a standard amenity. A number of cottages allow pets. Many include private pools and spas.

Southern Shores

Southern Shores Realty
5 Ocean Boulevard, Southern Shores
NC 12, Kitty Hawk
(252) 261-2111, (800) 334-1000
www.southernshores.com
Southern Shores Realty manages year-round and weekly rentals throughout the Outer Banks. Weekend packages also are available year-round. Dogs are accepted in some units. Ramps and elevators are offered in some cottages.

Kitty Hawk

Atlantic Realty
US 158, MP 2½, Kitty Hawk
(252) 261-2154, (800) 334-8401
(252) 453-4110, (800) 669-9245 in Corolla
www.atlanticrealty-nc.com
This company manages rental homes and condominiums from Corolla to South Nags Head for year-round and seasonal rental. Pets are accepted in some units.

Kitty Dunes Realty
US 158, Kitty Hawk
(252) 261-2326, (800) 334-DUNE
www.kittydunes.com

Kitty Dunes manages rental properties from Corolla to South Nags Head. Most properties rent by the week, but long-term rentals are offered in Colington Harbour. Three-night weekend packages are often available, even during the summer. Pets are accepted in many units, and a few cottages are wheelchair-friendly. Some properties include private pools and spas.

Joe Lamb Jr. & Associates
US 158, MP 2, Kitty Hawk
(252) 261–4444, (800) 552-6257
www.joelambjr.com
This company manages properties ranging from 2-bedroom cottages to 13-bedroom homes and year-round rentals from Corolla to South Nags Head. Three-night packages are offered during the off-season. Pets are accepted in some cottages. Wheelchair-accessible rentals are also available. Units in some developments include pool access. Many have private pools.

Seaside Vactions
1070D Ocean Trail
Corolla
5727 South Croatan Highway
MP 13.8, Nags Head
(252) 255–5500, (888) 685-9581
www.outerbanksvacations.com
Seaside Vacations offers the best service possible for every guest. The company represents a select group of vacation rental accommodations. Properties range from Corolla to South Nags Head and include condominiums, cottages, and palatial oceanfront estates. Staff members have personally visited every property and can make the best recommendations for a property based on a guest's needs.

Prudential Resort Realty
3608 North Croatan Highway
Kitty Hawk
(252) 261-8282

791-A Sunset Boulevard, TimBuck II
Shopping Village, Corolla
(252) 453-8700

1248 Duck Road, Duck
(252) 261-8888

5129 South Croatan Highway
Nags Head
(252) 441-5000, (800) 458-3830
www.resortrealty.com
Prudential Resort Realty manages weekly
rental properties from Corolla to South
Nags Head. Some three-night packages
are available with a maximum of five days'
notice. Some cottages allow pets. Renters
leasing a special resort club home can
check in as early as 11:00 A.M.

*If you're traveling in Kitty Hawk, Kill
Devil Hills, or Nags Head and the bypass
is congested, try driving along NC 12.
Although the speed limit is 35 mph, it
can actually get you to your destination
more quickly on some days.*

Wright Property Management (WPM)
US 158, MP 4$3/4$
3719 North Croatan Highway
Kitty Hawk
(252) 261-2186, (800) 276-7478
www.wpmobx.com
Wright Property Management offers cottages and condominiums for weekly,
partial-week, or year-round rentals from
Duck to South Nags Head. Some WPM
units offer swimming pools, tennis facilities, hot tubs, and private pools; many units

will accept pets. Rentals can be booked tentatively on the Web site or from 9:00 A.M. to 5:00 P.M. by telephone. Wright Property Management specializes in affordable cottage rentals for Outer Banks vacationers.

Kill Devil Hills

Kitty Hawk Rentals/
Beach Realty & Construction
US 158, MP 6, Kill Devil Hills
(252) 441-7166, (800) 635-1559
(252) 261-6605 in Duck
(252) 453-4141 in Corolla
www.beachrealtync.com
This company manages properties from Ocean Hill to South Nags Head. Some are available for year-round rental, but most rent by the week. Several of the properties are wheelchair accessible, and pets are accepted in some other units.

Sun Realty
US 158, MP 9, Kill Devil Hills
(252) 441-7033, (800) 334-4745
www.sunrealtync.com
Satellite offices are at Corolla, Duck, Kitty Hawk, Salvo, and Avon. Sun Realty offers the largest inventory of rental properties on the Outer Banks from Corolla through Hatteras Island. Weekly, monthly, and year-round rentals are available. A special program for disabled guests is offered. Pets are accepted in some units. Check out Sun Realty's Guest Advantage rewards program.

Nags Head

Bodie Island Realty
NC 12, MP 17, Nags Head
(252) 441-9443, (800) 862-1785
www.bodieislandrealty.com
This office manages time-shares and two wholly owned units in the Bodie Island Resort for weekly rental year-round. Three-night rentals are offered during the off-season. An elevator is located in one building.

Conner Resorts
US 158, MP 10½, Nags Head
(252) 261-8861, (800) 624-7432
www.connerresorts.com
Conner Resorts manages weekly rental properties from Sanderling to South Nags Head. Properties are small to medium sized and are in unique locations. Advance reservations are available in the off-season for weekend packages. Some cottages allow pets, and some units are equipped with elevators. Ask about specials when looking to book reservations.

Gateway Realty
2808 North Croatan Highway
Nags Head
(252) 480-0093, (800) 633-4491
www.gatewayobx.com
Gateway specializes in sales, long-term rentals, and property management from North Currituck beaches to South Nags Head.

Outer Banks Resort Rentals
Croatan Centre, MP 13½ Nags Head
(252) 441-2134
www.outerbanksresorts.com
Ronda Williams manages the sales and rentals of time-shares from Duck to South Nags as well as a few in Hatteras. Sixteen time-share resorts are represented.

Cove Realty
Between NC 12 and US 158
MP 13½, Nags Head
(252) 441-6391, (800) 635-7007
www.coverealty.com
Cove Realty manages properties in Old Nags Head Cove and South Nags Head for year-round, weekly, and student rental. Pets are accepted in some units. Weekend packages are available during the off-season. Guests have access, for a small fee, to a swimming pool as well as to tennis courts in Old Nags Head Cove.

Nags Head Realty
US 158, MP 10½, Nags Head
(252) 441-4315, (800) 222-1531
www.nagsheadrealty.com

Nags Head Realty manages weekly rentals from the Crown Point development in the northern beaches to South Nags Head. Three-day rentals are offered during the off-season. Some units accept pets.

Rentals on the Ocean
US 158, MP 16½, Nags Head
(252) 441-5005
www.rentalsontheocean.com
Do you want to reserve your spot on the beach and bring Fido, too? Rentals on the Ocean may have just what you're looking for. They offer cottages for families of all sizes from 2 to 26, and all their cottages accept pets. Every cottage is either oceanfront or oceanside. Rentals on the Ocean offers cottages year-round.

Stan White Realty & Construction Inc.
US 158, MP 10½, Nags Head
(252) 480-2224, (800) 548-9688
www.outerbanksrentals.com
Stan White Realty likes to find the perfect rental home for families, renting from Whalehead to Nags Head. Weekly and year-round rentals are available. Pets are allowed in some of the weekly rentals. Wheelchair-accessible units are available. Two other Stan White offices are on the northern beaches, one in Corolla and one in Duck, called Duck's Real Estate.

Village Realty
US 158, MP 14½, Nags Head
(252) 480-2224, (800) 548-9688
www.villagerealtyobx.com
Village Realty manages vacation rental properties in the development of the Village at Nags Head. Special weekend and golf packages are available. Some units include access to a beach club with an outdoor swimming pool, tennis courts, a game room, and family activities. Golf and tennis lessons are available. A golf course, private oceanfront access, and two private soundside piers also are on the premises. Some cottages allow pets. Some have elevators and can accommodate disabled vacationers. Village Realty has a second office at The Currituck Club in Corolla.

Roanoke Island

Pirate's Cove Realty
Manteo-Nags Head Causeway, Manteo
(252) 473-6800, (800) 537-7245
www.piratescoverentals.com
Pirate's Cove Realty manages properties in the Pirate's Cove Resort for weekly rentals. Two-night weekends also are offered during the off-season. Some cottages accept pets. All units include access to an outdoor swimming pool, tennis courts, playground, and free boat slips. Pirate's Cove Realty also manages properties at the Shallowbag Bay Club, a nearby development on the water closer to downtown Manteo. These one- to three-bedroom luxury waterfront condominiums are in an upscale marina. Several secluded waterfront properties are also offered in downtown Manteo.

20/20 Realty Ltd.
516 South Main Highway, Manteo
(252) 473-2020, (877) 520-2044
www.2020realtyinc.com
This company manages year-round rentals from Kitty Hawk to Manns Harbor. With a modern logo design and an old-fashioned company office, this realty maintains real estate on historic Roanoke Island and other fine properties on the Outer Banks.

Hatteras Island

Avon Cottages
NC 12, Avon
(252) 995-4123
www.avoncottages.com
Each of Avon Cottages' rental homes has a magnificent view of the Atlantic Ocean. Eight are oceanfront, seven are semi-oceanfront, and 11 are oceanside, ranging from one to five bedrooms. All cottages have a large combination living room/dining room/kitchen, plus central heat and air, a microwave oven, and remote color TV with HBO. Fully equipped kitchens include plates and utensils; you may bring your own sheets and towels or

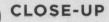

Old Nags Head: Authentic Outer Banks Architecture

For much of the 19th century, Nags Head was a getaway for the wealthy; a place to relax and recuperate; a safe haven from disease and so-called toxic vapors that doctors believed promoted illness. Summer after summer, growing families and networks of friends made this then-isolated beach one of the East Coast's most popular resort communities.

The Nags Head of yesteryear is still evident in a mile-long row of cottages that line the oceanfront east of Jockey's Ridge. Weathered and stately, about a dozen homes built between 1860 and 1940 best characterize the unique Nags Head–style architecture that has become one of the Outer Banks's signatures. State historians say the Nags Head Beach Cottage Row Historic District is one of the few turn-of-the-20th-century resort areas remaining on the Eastern Seaboard that has maintained its original character.

For the last few Septembers, Preservation North Carolina, a private non-profit historic preservation group, has opened up many of the Nags Head cottages, with the owners' cooperation, for public tours. Scores of people eagerly took the group up on the offer, strolling from house to house and meeting the owners, some of whom spent almost every summer of their lives in the family's Nags Head oceanside retreat.

The beach cottages were designed to be functional and practical. Most notable for large porches lined with windproof built-in benches that wrap around three, even four, sides, the houses feature unpainted wooden siding, weathered by salt air to a deep brown, and angled porches and roofs. Shuttered windows offer ready shelter from sun and wind, but they are easily propped open with an attached stick. Pilings boost the floors away from encroaching waves. And if the ocean came a little too close for comfort, the houses were made to be moved easily. Some already have been moved away from the surf four times.

Most of the homes are one- or two-storied and have three or four bedrooms. Stairwells to upper floors are narrow and the steps are creaky and often uneven. In some places on the first floor, you can see through cracks to the scrubby plants and sand beneath the house. All houses now have flush toilets, rather than employ the former outhouses, but many still depend only on the original outdoor shower installed away from the living quarters. Former servants' quarters have been changed into spare bedrooms, offices, or storage areas. Most cottages now have new kitchens in former breezeways, which separated the original kitchens from living space for heat and safety reasons.

What hasn't changed is the remarkable airiness and light that the rooms are effused in—and the way the steady heaving and sighing of ocean waves dominate the background sounds. The homes were all designed to foster air circulation; many cottage owners find no need for air-conditioning. Sea breezes flip and billow curtains away from bedroom windows, opening to spectacular oceanfront vistas.

Although there was already a thriving resort community near what is now Soundside Road in Nags Head, no one dared build near the Atlantic until 1866, when Dr. William Gaskins Pool erected the first beachfront house on the Outer Banks. According to historical documents, Pool paid $30 for 50 acres of land along the Atlantic. In the interest of securing companionship, he gave 130-foot-wide lots away to friends, who built their own homes. Eventually, others followed, and one of the oldest beachfront settlements in the state took hold. The 13 original Nags Head cottages were built between the end of the Civil War and World War II's onset.

Some cottages that have been part of the Preservation North Carolina tours include:

The Windemere

Erected by well-known builder S. J. Twine, who constructed many of the cottages in the historic district. This one-story house was completed in the 1930s.

Fred Wood Cottage

This two-story house, also constructed by Twine, has two gable-end chimneys and a covered porch surrounding all four sides.

Whedbee Cottage

One of the few Civil War–era homes, this two-story frame home was finished in 1866.

Badham-Kittrell Cottage

Another house built by Twine, this 1928 home is one story with an L-shaped wing extending from the back of the house. The second level perches over the main living area.

Miss Mattie Midgett's Store

Moved from the soundside in 1933, this 1914 store supplied vacationers and locals with groceries, mail, and the area's only telephone. It still houses the booty from years of beachcombing by Miss Mattie's daughter, Nellie Myrtle.

Martha Wood Cottage

This two-story house was likely built in 1870 or earlier. Possibly the oldest of the historic district's remaining cottages, it is distinguished by two projecting dormers on the beach side and a small, L-shaped addition in the rear.

The Silver Cottage

Built in 1883, this home's original owner paid $6.06 in annual taxes. The cottage was moved farther back from the ocean after the 1997–98 nor'easters.

For more information about future tours, please call Preservation North Carolina at (252) 832-1651 in Raleigh or (252) 482-7455 in Edenton.

rent them on-site. Laundry facilities, outside showers, and fish-cleaning tables are provided. Parking is also available.

Colony Realty Corp.
NC 12, Avon
(252) 995–5891, (800) 962–5256
www.hatterasvacations.com
Colony handles affordable weekly units and long-term rentals in Avon, Buxton, Frisco, and Hatteras. Most of the units, which are single-family cottages or condos, will accept pets. Three-day minimum stays can be arranged in the off-season. Several wheelchair-accessible units are available. Colony Realty specializes in reasonably priced Cape Hatteras family vacations.

Dolphin Realty
NC 12, Hatteras Village
(252) 986–2562, (800) 338–4775
www.dolphin-realty.com
This company manages properties, including homes and one-room efficiencies, throughout Hatteras Island. Some are available for year-round rental. Pets are accepted in some units.

Hatteras Realty
NC 12, Avon
(252) 995–5466, (800) HATTERAS
www.hatterasrealty.com
Hatteras Realty manages properties on Hatteras Island for weekly rental only. Units may be rented by partial weeks during the off-season. Pets are accepted in some units. Wheelchair-accessible cottages are available. More than half of this company's units are furnished with hot tubs. Every guest has free access to the pool and tennis courts at Club Hatteras. Vacationers have depended on Hatteras Realty for their accommodations since 1983. A fee-based kid's program for ages 4 to 12 both entertains and educates the little ones.

Midgett Realty
NC 12, Hatteras Village
(252) 986–2841, (800) 527–2903
www.midgettrealty.com
Midgett Realty manages properties from Rodanthe to Hatteras Village for weekly rentals. Three-night rentals are available during the off-season, and some units accept pets. Several wheelchair-accessible units are offered. Serving Hatteras Island has been a family tradition for more than 100 years. Nightly rentals are sometimes available.

Outer Beaches Realty
NC 12, Avon
(252) 995–4477, (252) 995–6137,
(800) 627–3150 in Avon
(252) 987–2771, (888) 627–3750 in Waves
(252) 986–2900, (888) 627–3650 in
Hatteras Village
www.outerbeaches.com
Outer Beaches Realty manages a large
selection of rental cottages from Rodanthe to Hatteras Village. Weekly and
three-day rentals are available. A few
allow pets. Some wheelchair-accessible
properties also are offered. Dedicated
exclusively to Hatteras Island, Outer
Beaches Realty offers the island's largest
selection of vacation rental cottages.
Upon check-in, you'll find a welcome bag
inside your cottage. Concierge services
are available.

Surf or Sound Realty
NC 12, Avon
(252) 995–5801, (800) 237–1138
www.surforsound.com
Surf or Sound Realty offers more than
300 cottages on Hatteras Island. Pets are
accepted in some units. Wheelchair-
accessible rentals also are available. You
can make reservations on the Web site.

Ocracoke Island

Ocracoke Island Realty Inc.
NC 12, Ocracoke Village
(252) 928–6261
www.ocracokeislandrealty.com
Ocracoke Island Realty manages weekly
rental properties on Ocracoke. Three-night
packages are available during the off-
season. A few of these cottages allow
pets.

Sandy Shores Realty
NC 12, Ocracoke Village
(252) 928–5711, (252) 928–1691
www.sandyshoresocracoke.com
Sandy Shores manages Ocracoke Island
properties, one of which is wheelchair

accessible. Only weekly rentals are available during the peak season. In the off-
season, three-day minimums are available.
Pets are accepted in some units.

YEAR-ROUND RENTALS

It can be quite a challenge to find a suitable
property for long-term residential rental.
However, it's not terribly difficult to find
what most people on the Outer Banks call
a "winter rental," a time period that usually
refers to late fall through early spring, when
the cottage is not usually booked for
weekly rentals. If you're looking for year-
round residential or seasonal accommodations during summer, you'll need to begin
your search as soon as possible.

Some rental companies deal lightly in
long-term rentals, but few make it a specialty. It's worth some phone calls to the
companies that specialize in the areas in
which you're interested, but a better bet is
probably to check the classifieds in the
local newspapers. If you plan to spend the
summer working on the Outer Banks, ask
your employer for suggestions. Some smart
businesspeople are beginning to help their
seasonal workers by offering housing.

Good places to look for long-term
rentals are in Colington Harbour, on
Roanoke Island, and between the highways in Nags Head, Kill Devil Hills, and
Kitty Hawk. Southern Shores has a large
year-round community. Currituck County,
just north of the Wright Memorial Bridge,
also offers some affordable options.

The following companies manage
year-round rentals. After the name of the
company and phone number, we list the
areas in which they have year-round
options. Most of these companies are
listed in greater detail either above or in
our Real Estate chapter.

Atlantic Realty
(252) 261-2154, (800) 334-8401
**Colington, Kill Devil Hills,
and Kitty Hawk**

Colony Realty Corporation
(252) 995-5891, (800) 962-5256
Avon, Frisco, and Hatteras

Cove Realty
(252) 441-6391, (800) 635-7007
Old Nags Head Cove
and South Nags Head

Dolphin Realty
(252) 986-2241, (800) 338-4775
Hatteras Island

Gateway Realty
(252) 480-0093, (800) 633-4491
North Currituck beaches to
South Nags Head

Jim Perry & Company
(252) 441-3051, (800) 222-6135
Duck to South Nags Head

Joe Lamb Jr. & Associates
(252) 261-4444, (800) 552-6257
Kitty Hawk to Nags Head

Kitty Dunes Realty
(252) 261-2326, (800) 334-DUNE
Colington Harbour, Kill Devil Hills,
and Kitty Hawk

Kitty Hawk Rentals/Beach Realty &
Construction
(252) 441-7166, (800) 635-1559
Duck, west of US 158, and between
the highways in the central areas
of the beach

Resort Central Inc.
(252) 261-8861, (800) 334-4749
Kitty Hawk to Manteo

Seaside Vacations
(252) 261-5500
Kitty Hawk to Nags Head

Southern Shores Realty
(252) 261-2111, (800) 334-1000
Duck to Kitty Hawk

Stan White Realty & Construction
(252) 480-2224, (800) 548-9688
Kitty Hawk to Nags Head

Sun Realty
(252) 441-7033, (800) 334-4745
Corolla through Hatteras Island

20/20 Realty Ltd.
(252) 473-2020, (877) 520-2044
Kitty Hawk through Roanoke Island

Wright Property Management
(252) 261-2186, (800) 276-7478
Ocean Sands to South Nags Head

What's the weather like? During summer, of course, expect hot days and balmy nights. In spring and fall, temperatures can range from the 80s to the 40s. Winter weather fluctuates from warm (70s) and sunny to starkly cold (30s and 40s), with averages in the 50s. Bring a variety of clothing for maximum comfort.

ACCOMMODATIONS 🛏

When it comes to accommodations, just like every other thing on the Outer Banks, you can have it as small and peaceful or big and busy as you choose. Visitors looking to stay a night, several days, or a week can choose from a range of family-owned seaside motels to multiple-story franchises of national lodging chains. The farther south you go, the fewer chain-owned accommodations you'll find; in fact, they almost disappear. And north of Kitty Hawk, you'll find only two hotels and two bed-and-breakfasts. In recent years, elegant inns and a variety of bed-and-breakfast establishments have opened their doors—offering a little more luxury and personal attention than the traditional barrier island hotels.

A few of these motels and hotels require two-night minimums on the weekends, and many require at least three-day stays for Memorial Day weekend, July Fourth weekend, and Labor Day weekend, since those are, by far, the busiest times on these barrier islands. A lot of Outer Banks hotels also have suites, efficiency apartments, and cottage units that rent by the day or week. Of course, you can stay in any room in any of these accommodations for a week or longer if you wish.

More and more, however, the Outer Banks is a vacation rental destination, where an increasing number of private homes rent by the week rather than hotel rooms renting by the night. In Dare County alone (excluding the Currituck beaches and Ocracoke) there are approximately 13,500 rental cottages compared with 3,000 or so rooms or apartment-style rooms in hotels, bed-and-breakfast inns, and cottage courts. Modest cottages that offer comfort and convenience line the ocean from Kitty Hawk through Hatteras Village. Many families and groups of friends choose to rent these cottages for a week's vacation or longer. Companies that lease these properties are included in our Weekly and Long-Term Cottage Rentals chapter.

If you're planning a summer stay on the Outer Banks, call early for reservations. Most accommodations are filled to capacity from early June through the first week of September. Sometimes, you can obtain walk-in rooms during the week; however, if you know the exact week or weekend that you're planning to visit, your best bet is to book a room immediately.

Locations are indicated by milepost and town. Most of the hotels, motels, and inns are along North Carolina Highway 12. A few line U.S. Highway 158, which is also called the Bypass. Roanoke and Ocracoke Islands have several tucked beneath the trees off the beaten paths. Bed-and-breakfast inns are becoming more popular on the Outer Banks, with the largest numbers on Roanoke and Ocracoke Islands. There are now more than 180 bed-and-breakfast rooms on the Outer Banks.

Rates vary dramatically from one area of the Outer Banks to another, from oceanfront rooms to those across the highway, between in- and off-season times, and especially depending on the amenities offered with each unit. In general, fall, winter, and early spring prices are at least one-third lower than midsummer rates—sometimes as little as $30 per night. The most expensive season, of course, is from mid-June to mid-August, when rates in general range from $50 a night for two people with two double beds to nearly $380 per night in some of the fancier establishments.

Many hotels and motels honor AARP and other discounts and often allow children to stay free with paying adults.

More and more accommodations providers keep their doors open all year, catering to fall fishing parties, spring visitors, and people who like the Outer Banks best in winter when few others are around. If you prefer isolation at the beach and don't mind wind and temperatures in the 40s and 50s, November through February is a wonderful time to visit. September and October, however, are our favorite months. The ocean is still warm enough to swim in, the daytime temperature seldom drops below the mid-60s, most restaurants, attractions, and retail shops remain open, yet the prices are much lower and most of the bustle is gone once school starts up again.

PRICE CODE

For your ease in checking our price ranges, we've created a dollar-sign key showing a range of the average cost for a double-occupancy one-night stay in a room with two double beds during peak summer season. Extra charges may apply for holiday weekends, additional people in the room, efficiency apartments, or pets. These prices do not include local and state taxes. Unless otherwise indicated in the listing, all accommodations accept major credit cards.

$	Less than $60
$$	$60 to $80
$$$	$81 to $125
$$$$	More than $125

DEPOSITS AND CHECK-IN TIMES

Most motels and hotels require deposits to hold advance summer registration. Policies vary, but the average deposit is 25 percent to 35 percent of the total reservation cost or one night's rate. Ask about specific provisions when reserving your room, and call to confirm reservations before leaving for the Outer Banks.

Many proprietors require the balance of your bill to be paid on arrival. Be prepared with cash, traveler's checks, or a credit card. Personal checks often are not accepted for this final payment. Again, ask

when booking your room. Automated teller machines (ATMs) are available at most local banks.

Before making reservations, be sure to check on the cancellation or refund policies. If you are concerned a hurricane might brew during your visit, ask about refund policies in case of evacuation.

Check-in times vary; most places won't allow you into your room before 2:00 P.M. but will hold a room for you until 10:00 or 11:00 P.M. if necessary. If you know you'll arrive earlier, ask about early check-in provisions or spend the first few hours on the beach. Public showers are provided at some beach accesses, so you can clean off before getting into your hotel room. Several motels, inns, and bed-and-breakfast establishments also offer outdoor showers for their guests. Checkout times in general are between 10:00 A.M. and noon. Occasionally, later checkouts can be accommodated. Ask for a late checkout if you know you'll want to linger the last day.

LOCATIONS AND AMENITIES

In this chapter, "oceanfront" means that the property has at least some rooms facing the ocean right on the beach. Most of these units have balconies and picture windows. Rooms on the ground level or behind sand dunes, however, may not have views of the Atlantic, even if they're oceanfront. Ask about what's available, and clarify which type of location you'd prefer. Remember, you'll almost always pay more to watch the waves from your room.

Conveniences and luxuries included in rooms at motels, hotels, inns, efficiencies, and bed-and-breakfasts usually vary, even in the same structure. Some include kitchenettes, king-size beds, whirlpool baths, and fireplaces. Others may have double beds and an extra sleeper sofa for the kids. All, however, have air-conditioning, and places that remain open in the fall and winter provide heat.

Many motels and hotels, especially the older beachfront structures and newer high-rise units, have meeting facilities, conference rooms, and large common areas to accommodate family reunions, business workshops, and tour groups. Although most newer accommodations are wheelchair accessible, many of the older motels and hotels are partially accessible or not at all. When making your reservation check that your particular needs can be met. If you are a pet owner and want your furry friend to vacation with you, your pickings are going to be much slimmer. Most motels and inns do not allow pets, so assume that pets are not permitted unless otherwise noted. Many companies that rent cottages, however, welcome pets in specified homes. See our Weekly and Long-Term Cottage Rentals chapter.

Amenities run the gamut from the most basic (bed and shower only) to places that provide microwaves, refrigerators, televisions with free movie channels or videocassette recorders, telephones, fluffy bathrobes, fancy soaps, free coffee, cocktails and afternoon tea, gourmet breakfasts, bicycles, and golf clubs. A few hotels offer "big-city" advantages such as room service, assistance with luggage, and wake-up calls—but most don't, so read the descriptions carefully if you require such services, and call ahead with other specific questions.

All Outer Banks accommodations provide free parking for at least one vehicle per unit. Keep valuables with you rather than leaving them locked in the car. Some hotels offer safes in the main office for their guests to stow valued items.

Many motel, hotel, and inn managers provide recreation packages with your room, especially during the off-season. For the most part, golf courses, tennis facilities, and health clubs are open year-round. Call about these special combinations, or ask the proprietor about discounts available to guests. Daily or weekly memberships are offered at most private facilities. Some accommodations also include volleyball courts, horseshoe

pits, picnic tables, gas grills, and small putting greens on-site for their guests.

AREA PROFILES

Accommodations in the northern beaches are much more sophisticated than on the rest of the Outer Banks. Corolla has only two hotels that rent rooms by the night— the Inn at Corolla Light and Hampton Inn. Duck boasts two by-the-night establishments, both of them bed-and-breakfast inns, and the Sanderling Inn Resort, between Duck and Corolla, offers hotel rooms in a classic resort atmosphere. Nearly all accommodations in the northern beaches area lie along the main artery, NC 12, which is known as Ocean Trail in Corolla and Duck Road in Duck.

Kitty Hawk was one of the first Outer Banks beach towns to develop a tourist trade, and some of its hotels and motels are reminiscent of the early cottage courts. These primarily family-run businesses are small, clean, and often cheaper than nationally known hotels. There's also a Holiday Inn Express on US 158 and a couple of bed-and-breakfast inns west of the highway.

Kill Devil Hills is the most central—and most populated—place on the barrier islands. Many of its accommodations are within walking distance of restaurants, shopping, and recreational attractions. Quaint motels with fewer than two dozen rooms are common here, as are big chain establishments with oceanfront conference centers. Public beach and sound accesses abound in this town.

The Outer Banks's first resort destination was Nags Head, so here you'll find everything—a 1930s-era inn and the tallest hotel on the Outer Banks. Some accommodations retain the old-timey feel of cedar-shake cottages, while others have gone for the ultramodern, multiple-floor look complete with elevators and room service from the in-house restaurant. Like Kill Devil Hills, but a lot more spread out and slightly less populated, Nags Head has plenty of restaurants, retail shops, and recreation.

Roanoke Island's accommodations range from modest motels to fine, fabulous inns. All are just a bike ride away from the historic waterfront, and many are perfect for a romantic weekend getaway or cloistered honeymoon stay. Rental cottages aren't prevalent here because the large majority of the population, even in the summer, is made up of permanent residents; however, if you want to get away from the bustle of the beach and still be close to the sound, wetlands, and wonderful historic attractions this island has to offer, you won't have difficulty finding a room to suit your tastes.

Motels and hotels on Hatteras Island are, in general, more relaxed and simple than on other parts of the barrier islands. There are now two national chains on the island (one in Buxton and one in Hatteras), but family-owned and -operated places still dominate the accommodations. Many of these units are no-frills without phones in the rooms or fancy furnishings, but if you are looking for an affordable place to stay along the quieter stretches of beach, don't overlook Hatteras Island's short-term room, inn, and efficiency accommodation options.

Ocracoke Island's lodgings are, in general, the most personal on the Outer Banks. Here, you'll find old inns, newer motels, upscale bed-and-breakfast inns, efficiency apartments, and a few folks who will rent you a room in their house, sometimes right next to their own.

COROLLA

The Inn at Corolla Light   **$$$$**
1066 Ocean Trail, Corolla
(252) 453-3340, (800) 215-0772
www.corolla-inn.com
Located within walking distance of the

Currituck Beach Lighthouse, The Inn at Corolla Light is a luxurious place where guests can plan their days around an incredible array of recreational activities available nearly at their doorstep—or they may wish simply to relax in full view of the sparkling waters of Currituck Sound and bask in the serenity of this beautifully appointed facility.

The year-round inn opened in 1995 in the ocean-to-sound resort community of Corolla Light. This upscale development offers wooded walking, biking trails, and every leisure amenity a vacationer could dream of: an indoor sports center with an Olympic-size pool, hot tub, saunas, clay tennis courts, racquetball courts, and fitness equipment; an oceanfront complex that boasts two outdoor pools, a video game room, a restaurant, and exclusive access to the beach; soundfront pools; play areas for basketball, shuffleboard, tennis, horseshoes, and more; and terrific shops and restaurants nearby (see our Shopping and Restaurants chapters). Guests of the inn have unlimited access to all of the resort's facilities. There is a nominal fee for use of the indoor tennis courts, but all other courts are free.

Guests may also use the inn's own waterfront swimming pool, hot tub, and private 400-foot pier on Currituck Sound. The inn furnishes bicycles to guests for leisurely tours of the resort's landscaped grounds. Guests are also invited to use the complimentary video library inside.

In season, parasailing, kayaking, eco-touring, and personal watercraft (JetSkis, Wave Runners, and others) are available at a watersports-rental site on the resort. A championship golf course is nearby. A must-do is to take the proprietor's wild horse tour by a four-wheel-drive Suburban into the off-road and largely undeveloped area north of Corolla. Although sparsely inhabited, the northern beaches are rich in history, local lore, and of course, wild horses (and plenty of other wild sights).

Some of the inn's 43 spacious guest rooms include kitchenettes, cable TVs,

radios, VCRs, and private baths. Many have fireplaces and whirlpool tubs. The rooms are designed for single or double occupancy, and some are equipped with sleeper sofas, too. Guests can enjoy a free continental breakfast daily.

The Inn at Corolla Light has two- and three-night minimum stays on weekends and charges $15 per night for each additional person. Special rate packages are offered throughout the year.

Hampton Inn and Suites Outer Banks Corolla $$$$
NC 12, Pine Island (north of Duck)
(252) 453-6565, (800) HAMPTON
www.hamptoninn.com

Those looking for short-term lodgings on the northern Outer Banks have never had many options, but the oceanfront Hampton Inn helps fill the void. Opened in May 2002, the inn has 123 sleeper rooms, a mix of guest rooms, and studio suites. Room decor has a coastal theme with ceiling fans and private balconies. Each room has a television, microwave, refrigerator, hair dryer, ironing equipment, coffeemaker, pay Nintendo, pay-per-view movies, and two two-line phones. Most rooms feature a pull-out sofa, and some have whirlpool tubs. Studio suites also feature a wet bar. The majority of rooms have an ocean view. Public areas include a heated indoor pool and whirlpool spa, an exercise room, a game room, four meeting rooms, coin-operated laundry facilities, and the Suite Shop with sundries, beach supplies, sodas, and snacks. Outdoors is a pool, kiddie pool, and a lazy river. Direct beach access is provided. Continental breakfast is served to guests each morning.

DUCK

Sanderling Inn Resort $$$$
1461 NC 12, Duck
(252) 261-4111, (800) 701-4111
www.sanderlinginn.com

The Sanderling Inn Resort is situated on 12 acres of oceanside wilderness about 5 miles north of the town of Duck. The Sanderling was built in the style of the old Nags Head beach homes with wood siding, cedar-shake accents, dormer windows, and porches on each side. Rocking chairs line the wide porches, providing a relaxing way to pass sultry afternoons while overlooking the ocean or sound.

All 87 rooms at the Sanderling are comfortable, lush, and accommodating. The inn provides guests with lounging robes, luxury soaps, toiletries, and a welcome gift featuring North Carolina products. A continental breakfast and afternoon tea also come with each room.

The main lobby and gallery of the Sanderling are decorated in an English country theme, adorned with contemporary finishes, and accented by polished wood floors and wainscoting. The inn's main building has 29 rooms, all with kitchenettes. Audubon prints and artwork line the walls. Another 32 rooms in Sanderling Inn North are filled with wicker furniture and are equipped with kitchenettes. The 26 rooms in the newest South Wing each have a king-size bed, wet bar, and kitchenette. Six of the units in the South Wing are deluxe suites that feature two televisions with VCRs (one in the bedroom and one in the living area), a double sleeper sofa, a stereo with compact disc player, and one-and-a-half baths. Some suites also have hot tubs. All Sanderling rooms have telephones and televisions and VCRs with remote control and cable.

Sanderling Inn is designed for the comfort and privacy of two guests per room, but sleeper sofas and cribs are available for an additional charge.

A separate building at the Sanderling houses conference and meeting facilities as well as the Presidential Suite, complete with whirlpool bath, steam shower, and two decks—one overlooks the ocean and the other overlooks the sound. For an additional charge, the inn's housekeeping staff provides laundry service with a 48-hour turnaround. Room service is provided by the Sanderling Restaurant (see our Restaurants chapter).

This is a complete resort with private beaches, a full-service spa, and state-of-the-art fitness center. The amenities continue with an indoor pool, a separate whirlpool room, locker rooms, steam rooms, an outdoor pool, tennis courts, and a natural walking or jogging trail. The Audubon Wildlife Sanctuary and the Pine Island Tennis and Racquet Club are nearby. An eco-center offers kayaks for visitors to use. A seasonal outdoor pavilion and four three- and four-bedroom villas have been added to Sanderling's already extraordinary offerings. The villas are perfect for families.

The new spa houses six treatment rooms and offers extended services, including manicures, pedicures, facials, massages, and more.

Full package deals are available for New Year's Eve, Valentine's Day, honeymoons, and winter escapes. Packages generally include one or more meals at the Sanderling Restaurant, full use of the fitness center and indoor pool, welcoming gifts, and other extras. Some seasonal discounts are available. Weekend guests must stay both Friday and Saturday nights during the summer, and a three-day minimum stay is required for in-season holidays. Wheelchair access is provided for all buildings on the property, and wheelchair-accessible rooms are available. The Sanderling Inn is open year-round.

Advice 5¢ $$$$
111 Scarborough Lane, Duck
(252) 255-1050, (800) 238-4235
www.advice5.com

Advice 5¢ exudes an air of casual simplicity. Here, Nancy Caviness and Donna Black provide their guests with private baths, rocking chairs, and decks. The suite also includes cable TV, a stereo, and whirlpool bath. Hardwood floors and juniper appointments, comfy Lexington cottage furniture, ceiling fans, quilts, colorful bath towels, linens, and greenery galore lend this idyllic beach getaway a crisp, unaffected atmosphere. Just 0.3 mile from the ocean, this sunny, spacious bed-and-breakfast has beautiful views of both sea and sound.

A common area with a fireplace for chilly off-season evenings is a popular gathering place for guests. A continental breakfast buffet of fresh fruit salad and just-baked breads and muffins is served daily in the common room. Afternoon tea tempts guests with more homemade delights as well as hot and cold beverages.

Two outdoor showers allow beachgoers to wash off after a long day in the sun. A locking storage shed also provides protected shelter out of the elements for storing bicycles, boogie boards, golf clubs, and other gear. An in-ground pool across the street and tennis courts are available for guests.

All rooms at this establishment are nonsmoking. It is not accessible to the disabled, and young children cannot be accommodated here. Advice 5¢ closes in mid-November and reopens in March.

The Duck Inn Bed and Breakfast $$$$
1158 Duck Road, NC 12, Duck
(252) 261-2300
www.mayslandingduck.com
Nestled within the town of Duck is a true Insiders' find. Charlie and Donna of The Duck Inn Bed and Breakfast offer guests a perfect coastal getaway to relax and enjoy this picturesque inn.

A short walk or easy bicycle ride gets you to plenty of shopping, gourmet restaurants, and watersport activities. Bicycles and kayaks are available for guest use. If you're in a more reflective mood, observe the birds on the sound. The Duck Inn Bed and Breakfast is located on the Atlantic flyway—wild geese and ducks abound as they travel their centuries old migration pathways. With beautiful Currituck Sound located yards from the back

deck of the Duck Inn, guests enjoy breathtaking sunsets from the decks and gazebo.

The Duck Inn offers three rooms, each with a private bath. A full breakfast buffet is served each day with fresh fruit and an array of juices, cereals, and pastries. Hot entrees such as omelets, quiches, souffles, pancakes, and waffles accompanied with bacon, sausage, or ham are served. Tea and coffee are brewed. At the end of a busy beach day, snacks and beverages are ready in the family room.

The Duck Inn is open May 1 through October 31. The inn is pet-free as well as smoke-free. Children over 12 are welcome, and the Duck Inn is wheelchair accessible.

KITTY HAWK

Hilton Garden Inn $$$$
NC 12, MP 1, Kitty Hawk
(252) 441-2151, (877) 629-4586
Brand new for 2006, the Hilton Garden Inn is conveniently located on the oceanfront across from the former Kitty Hawk Pier. The inn will offer a choice of suites and rooms with whirlpool baths. All will be equipped with a microwave, refrigerator, and coffeemaker. Indoor and outdoor pools and a fitness area will be available. A guest laundry facility, business center, and restaurant will be on-site. At the time of printing, the inn is scheduled to open in late spring of 2006.

3 Seasons Bed & Breakfast $$$
Sea Scape Drive, MP 2, Kitty Hawk
(252) 261-4791, (800) 847-3373
www.threeseasonsouterbanks.com
This bed-and-breakfast inn is tucked away from the ocean and highways at Seascape Golf Course on the west side of the Bypass. Golf enthusiasts find the location ideal: The putting green is in front of the property, and the ninth hole is behind it.

Less than 3 blocks from the ocean, 3 Seasons sits on a high sandhill, so guests can enjoy views of the Atlantic. Susie and

Tommy Gardner have been operating the bed-and-breakfast since 1992. It's a five-bedroom house, and four of the rooms are available for double occupancy. Each guest room has a private bath and TV. The decor feels like home—comfortable and "beachy." Guests can gather around a fireplace in the common area or take in the ocean breezes off the canopied deck. The hot tub on the deck creates a big splash.

Complimentary cocktails are served afternoons on the enclosed patio. Guests also enjoy a full breakfast cooked to order daily between 8:00 and 10:00 A.M. Bicycles are available for a ride to the beach or along trails nearby. The entire establishment is nonsmoking, although smoking on the outdoor deck is fine. Note that 3 Seasons is not equipped to accommodate children younger than age 18 or the disabled. Two-night stays are required on summer weekends, and a three-day minimum is requested for holiday weekends. This inn is open April through November.

Sea Kove Motel $$$
NC 12, MP 3, Kitty Hawk
(252) 261–4722

This family-owned and -operated establishment rents 10 one-bedroom efficiency units, 10 two-bedroom units, and two cottages by the week only from April through November. It's across from the ocean and includes full-size kitchens and televisions in each apartment. A playground and outdoor pool also are available. No credit cards accepted.

The Baldview
Bed & Breakfast $$$-$$$$
3807 Elijah Baum Drive, Kitty Hawk
(252) 255–2829
www.baldview.com

You can view glorious sunrises and sunsets from The Baldview Bed & Breakfast on Kitty Hawk Bay. The inn, with more than 1,000 feet of property on the sound, houses four exclusive rooms with private baths; 11 acres of maritime forest with nature walks surround the properties, yet the main house is located only five minutes from the ocean.

The Baldview offers a quiet getaway for adults who enjoy tranquil, natural surroundings, and houses an authentic carriage house for the ultimate romantic experience. Smoking is restricted to a separate designated house on the property. A light breakfast is served each morning, and there's a weekly wine and cheese night. This is a perfect venue for larger party rentals, weddings, and corporate retreats. The Baldview is open year-round.

Beach Haven Motel $$$
NC 12, MP 4, Kitty Hawk
(252) 261–4785, (888) 559–0506
www.beachhavenmotel.com

This small motel sits across the road from its own private beach and has two buildings with a total of six efficiency units. Owner Joe Verscharen makes sure his motel provides guests all they need for a peaceful and relaxing stay. A practical, homey atmosphere prevails at this motel, where each room has a refrigerator, microwave, hair dryer, cable TV, telephone, and porch chairs. Coffee can be brewed in each room at this uniquely groomed establishment, which Verscharen boasts has earned a Grade A cleanliness rating year after year from the Dare County Health Department. Beach Haven has also received AAA's three-diamond rating.

Beach Haven is in uncrowded surroundings with natural beach landscaping that will remind visitors of a lovely oasis. Guests can loll on the elevated deck and enjoy the scenery. A grass-carpeted picnic area with tables and a gas grill is on the premises. Bike rentals are available, as are many beach accessories. You can practice your classic stroke on a putting green situated on the cashmere lawn, where you might also show off your talents in a game of croquet.

Economy rooms sleep two people, and deluxe rooms can accommodate up to four guests. Cribs are provided for infants. The decor throughout reflects a contemporary beach look with rattan and wicker furniture. Joe lives at the motel and promises to make your stay as pleasant as possible. Beach Haven is open mid-March through mid-November.

Holiday Inn Express $$$
US 158, MP 4¼, Kitty Hawk
(252) 261–4888, (800) 836–2753
www.hiexpress.com
Situated on the east side of US 158, Holiday Inn Express has an outdoor swimming pool and is a short walk to lifeguarded Kitty Hawk Beach, where guests can use the motel's private access and oceanfront deck. The motel's 98 rooms are spacious and have cable TV, telephones, and refrigerators. Some also have couches, and all have microwaves. Most offer two double beds and some rooms have queen-size beds. All are attractively furnished in soft beach decor.

The inn provides a complimentary continental breakfast bar for guests each morning in the lobby. Nonsmoking and wheelchair-accessible rooms are available. Children age 17 and younger stay free if accompanied by an adult. Year-round group rates are available. This motel is within walking distance of shopping and several restaurants and is open all year.

Cypress Moon Bed and Breakfast $$$$
1206 Harbor Court, Kitty Hawk
(252) 261–5060, (800) 905–5060
www.cypressmooninn.com
You'll find Cypress Moon Bed and Breakfast nestled in the maritime forest with the sound just behind. Owners Linda and Greg Hamby have furnished their home with antiques throughout the residence.

Three soundfront rooms are available at the Cypress Moon Bed and Breakfast. All rooms have a queen-size bed, entertainment centers, and refrigerators. Brunch is served daily. You can choose to be served in the dining room, in your bedroom, or on your porch. Brunch includes crab cakes or shrimp, along with a breakfast meat, fresh bread, fruit, Cypress Moon specially blended coffee, and fresh-squeezed orange juice.

If you choose to spend a day away from the beach, guests are welcome to

use the kayaks or sailboards provided. A nice walkway leads to the water, and outdoor showers are available. The inn welcomes people age 18 and older and is smoke-free. Cypress Moon is closed for the month of December.

Buccaneer Motel
and Beach Suites $$$
NC 12, MP 5½, Kitty Hawk
(252) 261–2030, (800) 442–4412
www.buccaneermotelouterbanks.com
Repeat business is the name of the game at the Buccaneer, where folks who stayed here as teenagers now bring their grandkids for visits. Owners Sandy and Dave Briggman foster the authentic Outer Banks charm that's made the Buccaneer a place vacationers return to year after year. Travelers have their choice of one- and two-bedroom units, and efficiency apartments with one to three bedrooms are available for those wishing to stay longer. Each unit has a refrigerator, coffeepot, cable TV, and microwave.

While the Buccaneer is across the highway from the beach, there are no buildings between it and the ocean, and guests only have to cross a small sand dune to reach the surf. A dune-top deck and private beach access make enjoying the Atlantic from this establishment almost as easy as if the motel were right on the ocean. Other amenities include a large, outdoor swimming pool with adjoining deck, a children's playground, a basketball court, charcoal grills, and a fish-cleaning station. The Buccaneer is open year-round.

KILL DEVIL HILLS

Days Inn Mariner Motel $$$$
NC 12, MP 7½, Kill Devil Hills
(252) 441–2021, (800) 325–2525
www.outer-banks.com/days-mariner
A total of 70 units—58 of which are oceanfront—comprise the accommodations here, with 33 rooms offering two double beds, and 37 one- and two-bedroom apartments complete with

kitchens. Each room and apartment includes a telephone, refrigerator, and cable TV. All the rooms have a fresh, contemporary beach look.

There's easy access to the Atlantic, and the units are spacious enough to offer flexible living arrangements for families or groups. A recreation area has facilities for volleyball, and an outdoor swimming pool and showers are just off the ocean. Nonsmoking and wheelchair-accessible rooms are available. All Days Inn programs are honored, and AARP discounts are available. The Mariner is open year-round, except Christmas week, with rates discounted in the off-season.

Sea Ranch Hotel $$$$
NC 12, MP 7, Kill Devil Hills
(252) 441-7126, (800) 334-4737
www.searanchhotel.com

Stay at the Sea Ranch for a classic Outer Banks vacation. It is locally owned and operated, with a five-story oceanfront tower and a two-story building that contains 50 motel-style rooms. Each unit has cable TV and free HBO, a refrigerator, microwave, coffeemaker, and telephone. About half of the hotel rooms have oceanfront views. Nonsmoking rooms are available, and the hotel is wheelchair accessible. It has a heated indoor pool. The Sea Ranch is open year-round.

Travelodge Nags Head
Beach Hotel $$$
NC 12, MP 8, Kill Devil Hills
(252) 441-0411, (800) 338-7761
www.nagsheadbeachhotel.com

This 97-room, four-story hotel is across the highway from the ocean, so some guest rooms have views of the Atlantic, while others afford glimpses of the Wright Brothers National Memorial. Twelve of the first-floor guest rooms open directly onto the outdoor courtyard and pool.

Each room has a microwave, refrigerator, color TV (with remote control, cable, and free HBO), telephone, and private balcony or patio, with nonsmoking and wheelchair-accessible rooms available. A

complimentary continental breakfast featuring cereals, pastries, juices, coffee, tea, and fresh fruits is served daily in the lobby from 7:00 A.M. until 9:00 A.M. Discounts are available to AARP members. Children age 18 and younger stay free in their parents' room, and pets are welcome for a $20 per day additional charge. During summer holidays, three-night minimum stays are required. The Nags Head Beach Hotel is open all year.

Comfort Inn North $$$$
NC 12, MP 8, Kill Devil Hills
(252) 480-2600, (800) 854-5286

This three-story property includes 119 rooms that open along exterior corridors. They're filled with natural light and decorated tastefully. The building is T-shaped, so not all rooms have views of the Atlantic; however, oceanfront units have private balconies.

All rooms at this Comfort Inn have refrigerators, microwaves, full baths, cable TV and HBO, telephones, and coffeemakers. Nonsmoking and wheelchair-accessible rooms are available. Amenities include an oceanfront pool and coin-operated laundry facilities. A complimentary breakfast is provided. Children age 18 and younger stay free with an adult. A two-night minimum stay is required on summer holiday weekends. Managers honor AARP discounts. The Comfort Inn is open all year.

Cypress House Bed and Breakfast $$$$
NC 12, MP 8, Kill Devil Hills
(252) 441-6127, (800) 554-2764
www.cypresshouseinn.com

This historic bed-and-breakfast inn was originally built as a private hunting and fishing lodge in the 1940s. Located 150 yards from the Atlantic Ocean, the inn, with its original tongue-and-groove cypress-paneled walls and ceilings, exudes a cozy, casual charm. Six guest rooms with queen-size beds and private shower baths are equipped with ceiling fans, cable TV, and central air. The wraparound porch is ideal for enjoying the ocean breezes. In cold weather relax with a good book in front of a blazing fire in the common room. Early risers awake to self-serve coffee and tea on the baker's rack outside the rooms; a full gourmet breakfast is served each morning. Afternoon refreshments are also served.

Bikes, beach towels, and chairs, along with an outdoor shower, enhance your enjoyment. Cypress House is smoke-free. Children age 14 and older are welcome, and pets are not allowed.

Cavalier Motel $$$
NC 12, MP 8½, Kill Devil Hills
(252) 441-5585
www.thecavaliermotel.com
The Cavalier has 54 rooms with double and single beds and six one-room efficiency units with two double beds and kitchenettes right on the beach. Some rooms have full baths, while others have shower stalls. All are equipped with telephones, refrigerators, microwaves, cable TV, and free HBO. Three one-story wings surround the adult swimming pool, the kiddie swimming pool, a volleyball court, a children's play area, and shuffleboard courts.

The motel also has 13 cottages that rent by the week. Pets are allowed in the cottages only. There is some wheelchair access here, and ramps are on the premises.

Parking is available outside each room, and the covered porch with outdoor furniture is just right for relaxing with a free cup of coffee while watching the sunrise. An observation deck sits atop the oceanfront section. Children age five and younger stay for free in their parents' rooms. The Cavalier Motel is open year-round.

Days Inn Oceanfront $$$-$$$$
NC 12, MP 8½, Kill Devil Hills
(252) 441-7211, (800) 325-2525
www.outer-banks.com/days-oceanfront
An oceanfront property on a wide stretch of beach, this facility opened as an Outer Banks motel in 1948. It was built to resemble an old mountain lodge and offers an inviting lobby, decorated in the nostalgia of Old Nags Head, where guests can read the newspaper and sip a cup of free cof-

fee. The room is further enhanced by Oriental rugs on polished hardwood floors and a fireplace large enough to take away the chill on cold beach evenings during the off-season.

Guests enjoy balconies with old-fashioned furniture and nice views. The 52 rooms include singles, doubles, kings, king suites, and efficiency units that sleep six and include a living room, adjoining bedroom, and complete kitchen. All rooms have telephones, cable TV, and refrigerators. Oceanfront rooms also have microwaves. Nonsmoking and wheelchair-accessible rooms are available.

A complimentary continental breakfast is available throughout the year. Hot apple cider and popcorn are served around the fireplace during the winter, and lemonade and cookies are served in the summer. Leisure amenities include a large outdoor pool, sundeck, volleyball court, barbecue pit, and a boardwalk to the beach.

Children age 12 and younger stay for free, and AARP discounts are honored. There's a two-night minimum stay for summer holiday weekends, and Saturday check-ins are allowed only for weekly rentals. Daily and weeklong rentals are available throughout the year.

Best Western Ocean Reef Suites $$$$
NC 12, MP 8½, Kill Devil Hills
(252) 441-1611, (800) 528-1234
www.bestwestern.com/oceanreefsuites
All 71 one-bedroom suites in this newer oceanfront hotel are decorated and arranged like luxury apartments with a contemporary beach decor. The views are great, and you'll find everything you need for a truly luxurious beach vacation. Each room has a telephone, cable TV, free coffee, and a fully equipped galley-style kitchen. The bath area has a double vanity.

Nonsmoking and wheelchair-accessible rooms are available. Upper-floor rooms have private balconies overlooking the ocean. Some first-floor units open onto the oceanfront pool and courtyard, while others offer a private patio. The Ocean Reef is one of the few facilities on the beach to have a penthouse suite; this one boasts a private Jacuzzi and rooftop deck.

A heated, seasonal outdoor pool and a whirlpool are available to guests in the courtyard, and the exercise room features a sauna. Other amenities include a laundry facility on the premises and year-round bar and food service. Children age 13 and younger stay free with adults. A two-day minimum stay is required on summer weekends. Ocean Reef is open all year.

Colony IV Motel $$$
NC 12, MP 8½, Kill Devil Hills
(252) 441-5581, (800) 848-3728
www.thecolonyivmotel.com
This modern family-owned and -operated oceanfront motel is well-maintained and offers lots of amenities, including an outdoor heated pool with a whirlpool and patio, an indoor heated pool, a dune-top gazebo, and a private beach with life-guard. A complimentary continental breakfast is served every morning. Laundry facilities are available on the premises.

The motel has 80 units, 8 of which are efficiencies. Most offer two double beds, but rooms with king-size beds are also available. Telephones, refrigerators, microwaves, TV with remote control and cable, and clock radios are provided in the units. Some rooms have direct access to the beach, while others have a small balcony overlooking the ocean. The efficiencies have an eating area and, when combined with adjoining rooms, create a good arrangement for family vacationers. Nonsmoking units are available.

Children age 12 and younger stay for free. Discounts of 10 percent are provided for AARP and AAA members. The motel is also wheelchair accessible. A two-night minimum stay is required on summer weekends. The Colony IV Motel is open February through October.

Budget Host Inn $$$
US 158, MP 9, Kill Devil Hills
(252) 441-2503, (800) BUD-HOST
www.budgethost.com
This motel is on the Bypass, about 2 blocks from the ocean. All 40 rooms are tastefully furnished and well maintained, with either king-size beds or extra-length double beds. Each unit has a telephone, cable TV, and tub/shower combination. Refrigerators and microwaves are available upon request. The lobby also has a guest refrigerator, microwave, and a coin-operated laundry room.

The entire second floor of the inn has been made into a nonsmoking floor. Wheelchair-accessible rooms are available. The motel offers two family rooms that sleep six to eight people comfortably. Free coffee and tea are available in the lobby each day. Cribs are provided free of charge, and children age 16 and younger stay free with an adult. The Budget Host Inn is open year-round.

If you like your accommodations and want to stay in the same place again next year, make your reservation now.

First Flight Inn   **$$$**
NC 12, MP 9, Kill Devil Hills
(252) 441-5007
www.netnc.com/firstflight
Of the 55 units at this oceanfront inn, 15 are efficiency apartments and one is a separate cottage. Most rooms have two double beds, and five have just one double bed. Rooms are equipped with small refrigerators, microwaves, and telephones. The inn has 256 feet of private beach, and an outdoor pool and deck. A fish-cleaning station and outdoor showers are available. Children age 12 and younger stay free with their parents. On summer holiday weekends, a three-day minimum stay is required. Two fishing piers and several shops and restaurants are nearby. First Flight Inn is open from April through October.

See Sea Motel   **$$-$$$**
NC 12, MP 9, Kill Devil Hills
(252) 441-7321
A small, family-run motel across the street from the ocean, See Sea offers 21 rental units, including 11 motel rooms, 6 efficiencies, 3 two-bedroom apartments, and 1 three-bedroom cottage. The motel rooms and efficiencies rent by the day (the apartments and cottage require a one-week minimum stay in season). All units have a refrigerator, microwave, telephone, and cable TV. There's a pay phone on the premises. Laundry is on-site, and free coffee is provided.

Amenities include an outdoor swimming pool and a picnic area. Nonsmoking rooms are offered. See Sea Motel is open year-round.

The Clarion Oceanfront Hotel   **$$$$**
NC 12, MP 9½, Kill Devil Hills
(252) 441-6333, (800) 424-6423
www.clarionhotel.com/hotel/nc416
This oceanfront hotel has 105 rooms, many with spectacular ocean views. Banquet and conference facilities accommodate 10 to 200 people. Amenities include an on-site restaurant and lounge, a coin-operated laundry, an outdoor pool, and a whirlpool.

Keep in mind that if you stay in an inn or a motel or hotel, usual household chores are taken care of by staff. If you stay in a rental cottage, household chores are your responsibility. When you leave, you are required to clean the home.

All rooms include telephone, cable TV with remote, free high-speed Internet access, microwave, and refrigerator. The Clarion has two nonsmoking floors and wheelchair-accessible rooms. Children age 18 and younger stay free, and AARP members receive a 10 percent discount. Weekends require minimum stays during summer. The Clarion is open all year.

Ramada Plaza Resort and
Conference Center   **$$$$**
NC 12, MP 9½, Kill Devil Hills
(252) 441-2151, (800) 635-1824
www.ramadainnnagshead.com
This five-story, 171-room oceanfront hotel was built in 1985. It's popular with tour groups and hosts many meetings throughout the year. All rooms have a balcony or patio, cable TV with pay-per-view movies, small refrigerator, and microwave. Bellhop and room service are available here. Nonsmoking, wheelchair-accessible, and pet rooms are offered, along with guest laundry facilities and an exercise room. Meeting facilities are on the fourth floor overlooking the ocean. Several suites are available to fit a variety of conference and workshop needs.

An indoor swimming pool and Jacuzzi are off the second floor atop the dunes surrounded by a large sundeck. A flight of steps takes you onto the beach where volleyball is a popular pastime. Seasonal food and beverage services are available at the oceanfront bar adjacent to the pool. Peppercorns, the hotel's fine oceanview restaurant, serves breakfast and dinner year-round and offers lunch on the deck during the summer (see our Restaurants chapter). The Ramada Plaza Resort is open all year.

Ocean House Motel   **$$$**
NC 12, MP 9½, Kill Devil Hills
(252) 441-2900, (800) 699-1963
www.oceanhousemotel.com

This seaside motel is an Outer Banks legend offering unique, individually designed accommodations the owners call Carolina Collection Rooms. Legend has it that original owner Tanya Young and a designer friend decided to do a theme room at the motel. Their ideas got a little out of hand, and they ended up selecting separate themes for each of the 43 rooms. There's the Carolina Party Room, Jonathan Seagull's Nest, and dozens more. No two rooms at this motel are alike.

All units have refrigerators and cable TV with HBO. Oceanfront rooms offer microwaves. Telephones are not provided.

Guests enjoy a 40-foot outdoor pool surrounded by umbrella-shaded picnic tables. Free coffee is provided throughout the day. A two-night minimum stay is required on summer weekends. The seventh night is free if you stay a week. Children younger than age 13 stay free, and AARP discounts are honored. Ocean House is open April through mid-October.

Miller's Outer Banks Motor Lodge   **$$$**
NC 12, MP 9½, Kill Devil Hills
(252) 441-7404, (877) 625-6343
www.obxmotorlodge.com

An oceanfront motel with 30 efficiency units and 8 regular rooms, Miller's rents some units only by the week during the peak season. Other units, however, are available by the day. Each room has cable TV, a refrigerator, and a microwave. Wheelchair-accessible units are available. Amenities include an on-site washer and dryer, a playground, an outdoor swimming pool, and a restaurant. Children age nine and younger stay free here. Miller's is open from February through November.

Quality Inn John Yancey   **$$$$**
NC 12, MP 10, Kill Devil Hills
(252) 441-7141, (800) 367-5941

This family hotel is on a wide beach that's lifeguarded during the summer. Shuffle-board courts, an outdoor heated pool, and a playground are on the premises.

The hotel has 107 rooms, most of them doubles, housed in three buildings. The oceanfront units each have a balcony or patio so you can see and hear the waves from your room. Cable TV with optional in-room movies, a small refrigerator, and a telephone are in each room. Ten units also offer a microwave, five have a fully equipped kitchen, and three include a hot tub. Coffeemakers and coffee are provided in all rooms. About half of the rooms are nonsmoking, and this inn offers wheelchair-accessible units.

Other amenities include a coin-operated laundry, VCRs, movies, and free coffee in the lobby. This Quality Inn has 24-hour front desk and maintenance service. Children age 18 and younger stay free, and rollaway beds are available for an extra fee to accommodate additional kids. A two-night minimum stay is required on summer weekends. AARP and other discounts are honored. The Quality Inn John Yancey is open all year.

The Ebb Tide   **$$**
NC 12, MP 10½, Kill Devil Hills
(252) 441-4913

The ocean is just across the road from this family-run motel, which has 41 rooms with refrigerators, microwaves, and cable TV. Three seaside apartments across the street are right on the beach. Wheelchair-accessible rooms are available. Guests have full use of the outdoor pool, picnic table, and restaurant on the premises. Children younger than age 13 stay free. The Ebb Tide is open from mid-March until the end of September.

NAGS HEAD

Beacon Motor Lodge   **$$$**
NC 12, MP 10¾, Nags Head
(252) 441-5501, (800) 441-4804
www.beaconmotorlodge.com

Visitors will find lots of options for seasonal and off-season stays at this family-oriented, comfortable oceanfront lodge. The James family has owned the 48-room Beacon Motor Lodge since 1970, offering one-, two-, and three-room combinations, including motel-type rooms and efficiencies, plus two cottages. Nonsmoking rooms are available. Attractively finished in mauve, turquoise, and peach, the rooms are equipped with small refrigerators, phones, and cable TV with remote control. All units also have microwaves.

Guests gather on the oceanfront patio, a grand place for enjoying the beach scene from a comfy lounge chair. Oceanfront rooms open onto a large, walled terrace, affording wonderful views of the ocean. Amenities include two children's pools, a large outdoor pool with tables and umbrellas, a playground, patios with grills, an electronic game room, and laundry facilities. Some provisions have been made for disabled guests, including a ramp for beach access.

Inquire about discounts and weekly rentals (credit cards are not accepted for some discounts). The Beacon Motor Lodge is open late March through late October.

Colonial Inn Motel $$$-$$$$
NC 12, MP 11½, Nags Head
(252) 441-7308
www.colonialinnmotel.com

At the Colonial Inn Motel you can stay in an oceanfront room, standard room, efficiency unit, or apartment—some of which accommodate as many as 10 guests. All of the apartments and efficiencies have kitchens and are equipped with basic kitchenware. Some efficiencies have queen-size beds; all rooms feature double beds. Every unit has cable TV, air-conditioning, and carpet. All are wheelchair accessible. Enjoy the beach, swim in the pool, or fish off the adjacent Nags Head Fishing Pier. Colonial Inn Motel is open for business from March to December. For a preview, visit the Web site and take a virtual tour of the inn, both inside and outside.

Nags Head Inn $$$-$$$$
NC 12, MP 14, Nags Head
(252) 441-0454, (800) 327-8881
www.nagsheadinn.com

This white stucco building with blue accents and plush lawns is a tasteful contrast to the older Nags Head–style cottages nearby. Designed for family enjoyment, the oceanfront inn features a sunny lobby where greenery thrives.

Guest rooms begin on the second floor of this five-story building, and all oceanside rooms afford panoramic ocean views from private balconies. Rooms on the street side do not have balconies, but the view of Roanoke Sound from the fifth-floor rooms is notable. All rooms have small refrigerators, cable TV with HBO, phones, and full baths. Nonsmoking rooms are available, and each floor has wheelchair-accessible rooms. A heated indoor pool and spa are available. The Nags Head Inn also features one suite with an adjoining sitting room, wet bar, and hot tub—a perfect honeymoon setting.

A small conference room with adjoining kitchen/sitting area accommodates about 30 people comfortably. Tour groups are welcome. The inn is closed from the Sunday after Thanksgiving until December 26.

Oceanside Court $$$
NC 12, MP 15½, Nags Head
(252) 441-6167
www.oceansidecourt.com

There's nothing like an oceanside stay on the Outer Banks, and that's what you'll get here. This small establishment offers four efficiencies (with cable TV and full kitchens) and seven cottages. Phones are not available in any of the units. The Court is open from March 1 to December 1. Pets are not allowed.

Sandspur Motel and
Cottage Court $$-$$$
NC 12, MP 15¾, Nags Head
(252) 441-6993, (800) 522-8486
www.sandspur.net

At the Sandspur you can choose from a room, efficiency, or cottage. All rooms feature two double beds, cable TV, ceiling fans, refrigerators, and microwaves. The efficiencies also have stoves. The rooms have no phones, but a pay phone is on the premises. The motel has a coin-operated washer and dryer. The Sandspur closes in December and reopens March 1.

Surf Side Hotel $$$$
NC 12, MP 16, Nags Head
(252) 441-2105, (800) 552-7873
www.surfsideobx.com
This attractive five-story hotel is situated on the oceanfront, rooms facing north, south, and east for ocean views. Some rooms have views of Roanoke Sound as well. All rooms have private balconies and are decorated attractively in muted beach tones. Refrigerators, cable TV, hair dryers, coffeemakers, microwaves, irons and iron-ing boards, and phones are standard in all rooms. The honeymoon suites feature king-size beds and private Jacuzzis. An elevator provides easy access, and wheelchair-accessible rooms are available; so are nonsmoking rooms. An adjacent three-story building offers rooms and efficiencies with either ocean or sound views.

A continental breakfast is provided each morning, and the staff hosts an after-noon wine and snacks social hour for guests. You can choose between an indoor pool and hot tub that are open all year and an outdoor pool for swimming in warm weather. The Surf Side is open all year.

First Colony Inn $$$$
US 158, MP 16, Nags Head
(252) 441-2343, (800) 368-9390
www.firstcolonyinn.com
Back in 1932, this gracious old structure was known as Leroy's Seaside Inn. The

146

landmark hotel was moved and refurbished, but it's still a favorite for those who like the ambience of a quiet inn. The old Nags Head–style architecture, resplendent under an overhanging roof and wide porches, has been preserved and is listed in the National Register of Historic Places. The First Colony received a historic preservation award from the Historic Preservation Foundation of North Carolina.

The Lawrence family, with deep roots in the area, rescued the hotel from demolition in 1988. The building was sawed into three sections for the move from its oceanfront location to the present site. The interior was completely renovated and now contains 26 rooms, all with traditional furnishings and modern comforts.

In the sunny breakfast room, you can enjoy a complimentary continental breakfast and afternoon tea. Upstairs, an elegant but cozy library with books, games, and an old pump organ is a favorite place to read the paper or meet other guests. A great selection of jazz as well as classical music wafts throughout the reception area.

Each room is appointed in English antique furniture. Special touches, such as tiled baths, heated towel bars, English toiletries, telephones, TVs, iron with ironing board, individual climate control, and refrigerators, are standard. Some rooms have a wet bar, kitchenette, Jacuzzi, VCR, and private balcony; some rooms include an additional trundle bed or day bed for an extra person. The first floor is wheelchair accessible, and one room is designed for disabled guests. Smoking is not permitted in the inn.

Guests are invited to relax at the 55-foot swimming pool and sundeck behind the inn or to follow the private boardwalk across the street to the oceanfront gazebo. This magnificent year-round inn provides easy access to the ocean and is close to many shops and restaurants. The inn has a policy of Thursday night free for stays of five weeknights or longer (must include consecutive Sunday, Monday, Tuesday, Wednesday, and Thursday stays).

Islander Motel $$$$
NC 12, MP 16, Nags Head
(252) 441-6229
www.islandermotel.com
The Islander is a small, popular oceanfront property featuring an attractive landscape and well-maintained rooms. Most rooms have an ocean view, and all have either a balcony or patio, although some of the first-floor units tucked behind dunes do not offer ocean views. The motel has 24 rooms and two efficiency apartments. The rooms are large and frequently refurbished and have either double or queen-size beds. One king is available. All have sitting areas, coffeemakers, and refrigerators. Some first-floor units offer kitchenettes.

Guests enjoy the pool and private dune walk to the ocean. This property is convenient to Nags Head restaurants, shops, recreational outlets, and attractions. The Islander is open April through October.

Blue Heron Motel $$$
NC 12, MP 16, Nags Head
(252) 441-7447
The Blue Heron Motel is considered one of the Outer Banks's best-kept secrets among the small motels in the area. The family-owned facility provides a year-round indoor swimming pool, a spa, and outdoor pools. The Gladden family lives on the premises and pays careful attention to the management of the property. It's in the midst of fine Nags Head restaurants and offers plenty of beach for those who come to relax.

Nineteen rooms offer double or king-size beds, and 11 efficiencies sleep up to four people and provide full kitchens. All units have refrigerators, microwaves, coffeepots, cable TV, phones, and shower/tub combinations. A wheelchair-accessible room is available. Second- and third-floor rooms offer private balconies. The Blue Heron Motel is open all year and offers weekly rates.

Owens' Motel $$$
NC 12, MP 16, Nags Head
(252) 441-6361
www.owensmotel.com

The Owens family has owned and operated this attractive motel, one of the first on the beach, for 50 years. Adjacent to the family's famous restaurant (see our Restaurants chapter), this property across the highway from the ocean is well maintained.

This three-story oceanfront property includes efficiencies with large, private balconies. Each efficiency has two double beds, a tile bath and shower, cable TV, and a kitchen. Regular rooms have two double beds, one queen-size bed, or one double bed with one single bed.

The motel swimming pool on the west side of the property provides an alternative to the ocean. Easy access to Jennette's Pier and a comfortable oceanfront pavilion with rocking chairs is enticing. Owens' Motel is open April through October.

Sea Foam Motel $$$
NC 12, MP 16½, Nags Head
(252) 441-7320
www.seafoam.com

This attractive oceanfront motel is made up of 29 rooms, 18 efficiencies, and 3 cottages. Efficiencies accommodate two to four people, and cottages sleep up to six comfortably. The efficiencies and cottages rent weekly. Rooms are decorated in mauve and green, and some have washed-oak furniture. All rooms have cable TV with HBO, refrigerators, microwaves, and phones. Some have king-size beds, and each has a balcony or porch. Some units in the one- and two-story buildings have ocean and poolside views.

Children are welcome, and they will enjoy the playground. Other features include a large outdoor pool, children's pool, sundeck, shuffleboard area, and a gazebo on the beach for guests' pleasure. Sea Foam Motel is within walking distance of several restaurants. Free coffee is provided until 11:00 A.M., and a special family plan allows children younger than age 12 to stay free with parents. Sea Foam Motel is open March through mid-December. Pets are not allowed.

Quality Inn Sea Oatel $$$$
NC 12, MP 16½, Nags Head
(252) 441-7191, (800) 440-4386
www.qualityinnnagshead.com

This year-round Quality Inn has an excellent location near restaurants, recreation, shops, and Nags Head attractions. Each of the 47 rooms is tastefully furnished, and nonsmoking rooms are available; all are just across the street from the beach.

Pets are allowed free of charge from Labor Day to Memorial Day. The front desk is open 24 hours a day, and all rooms conform to Quality Inn's high standards. Each room has a coffeemaker, microwave, refrigerator, telephone, and cable TV with HBO. You'll also find a large outdoor pool, a children's pool, a coin-operated laundry, snacks, and ice. The inn is open all year.

Dolphin Oceanfront Motel $$$
NC 12, MP 16½, Nags Head
(252) 441-7488, (800) 699-1962
www.dolphinmotel.net

The Dolphin Motel has 45 rooms with 11 efficiencies. Some rooms have an ocean view. The breezeway to the beach and an outdoor pool add special touches. All rooms and efficiencies have cable TV. Nonsmoking rooms are available. The Dolphin opens the last Friday in March and closes the last Saturday in October. Pets are allowed.

Comfort Inn Oceanfront South $$$$
NC 12, MP 17, Nags Head
(252) 441-6315, (800) 334-3302

The Comfort Inn South, a seven-story oceanfront hotel, is the tallest building on the Outer Banks. The light peach-and-teal exterior gives this hotel a clean, contemporary beach look. The 105-room hotel has deluxe oceanfront rooms with magnificent views from private balconies; oceanside and streetside rooms are available too.

Each room has a cable TV, phone, refrigerator, and microwave. Nonsmoking rooms are available. A honeymoon suite with a hot tub is popular, as are rooms with king-size beds. One wheelchair-accessible room is available. Corporate meeting rooms accommodate groups of 350 people.

The oceanfront pool and deck are favorite places. Other amenities include a game room and a playground. A complimentary continental breakfast is offered in the lobby. The Comfort Inn South is open all year.

Whalebone Motel $$$$
NC 12, MP 17, Nags Head
(252) 441-7423, (888) 685-9581
www.whalebonemotel.com

The Whalebone Motel is open all year and has standard motel rooms and efficiencies in its three buildings. One efficiency has a king, a double, and two single beds. Three have king-size beds, and others feature one double and two single beds. Some units have two double beds. All rooms have stoves, refrigerators, and cable TV with HBO. Pets are welcome at $5.00 extra per day.

Fin 'N Feather Waterside Inn $$-$$$
Nags Head–Manteo Causeway
Nags Head
(252) 441-5353, (888) 441-5353
www.finnfeather.com

A small motel along the water's edge, the Fin 'N Feather is popular with anglers and hunters. If you're planning to come in the fall or spring, call well in advance for reservations. This motel's proximity to Pirate's Cove Yacht Club is convenient for anyone headed out for a day on the open seas. The motel also has its own boat ramp.

Housekeeping units are available year-round at Fin 'N Feather and feature double-bed efficiencies. Each efficiency has a stove, refrigerator, and cooking utensils. Renters take care of their own needs. The rooms are clean and comfortable with blue and white decor. Large windows open onto the water from either side and offer stunning views of the sound. All rooms are nonsmoking, and dogs are welcome.

ROANOKE ISLAND
Manteo

Island Motel & Guesthouse $$$
US 64, Manteo
(252) 473-2434
www.theislandmotel.com

In the heart of Manteo, convenience is a hallmark at this neat little motel. Most of the 14 rooms have their own microwave or full kitchen, cable TV, air-conditioning, and two double beds. Foldaway beds are available for children. Daily, weekly, and monthly rates are offered. Amenities include courtesy bikes, fishing poles, other sports equipment, and surfing lessons. Nonsmoking rooms are available, and smoking is not allowed in the main house. Dogs are allowed for a nominal fee. This motel is open all year.

The Island Motel also operates four adorable theme cottages located 1 block away. In-season rates start at $200. These cottages are nonsmoking and do not allow pets.

The Elizabethan Inn $$$
US 64, Manteo
(252) 473-2101, (800) 346-2466
www.elizabethaninn.com

The Elizabethan Inn is a year-round resort facility with spacious shaded grounds, country manor charm, and Tudor architecture reflecting the area's heritage. The hotel consists of three buildings providing more than 80 rooms, efficiencies, and apartments, plus conference facilities, a spa, and a gift shop. Nonsmoking and wheelchair-accessible rooms are available. All rooms have cable TV with HBO, refrigerators, and direct-dial phones. Rooms are available with a king-size bed or two queen-size or double beds, and two rooms have whirlpool baths. All have coffeemakers.

The inn's Nautics Hall Fitness Center is available for guests (see our Recreation chapter). Guests may also use the outdoor pool and a heated, competition-size indoor pool.

Roanoke Island Inn $$$$
305 Fernando Street, Manteo
(252) 473-5511, (877) 473-5511
www.roanokeislandinn.com

With the sparkling Roanoke Sound and quaint Manteo waterfront just a stroll away, you'll find yourself easing into the relaxed village pace the moment you step up to this attractive inn. The distinctive white clapboard building with dark green shutters distinguishes a gracious, restored residence with the comforts of a small, well-designed bed-and-breakfast. The furnishings are handsome, reflecting the meticulous care of the owner, designer-architect John Wilson IV.

Each of the inn's eight rooms features a private entrance, private bath, TV, and phone. Guests may choose to stay in the bungalow behind the inn, which is complete with an antique tub and furnishings, wet bar, and refrigerator. Browse through a collection of Outer Banks–related books and artwork in the lobby. A light breakfast is offered in the butler's pantry. The private grounds are landscaped with gardenia, fig bushes, and native plants. Relax by the picturesque pond complete with koi and sweet-smelling lotus plants. Dip nets are provided so guests can net crabs along the bay's edge. Bicycles are furnished for touring the town and nearby historic attractions, including the Elizabeth II and the Outer Banks History Center. For a more adventuresome vacation, guests may rent a house on their own private island in the sound. Guests must provide their own boat to make the 10-minute journey to the home, available May through September. Guests must provide their own cell phone. Reed Hill is another choice rental located on the oceanfront in historic Nags Head. The home can be rented by the week through Roanoke Island Inn.

Roanoke Island Inn is open from April through October.

The White Doe Inn $$$$
Sir Walter Raleigh Street, Manteo
(252) 473-9851, (800) 473-6091
www.whitedoeinn.com

In a restored 1898 home, The White Doe Inn retains its turn-of-the-century charm and offers guests an elegant escape in its rooms and hideaways. It is one of only two Dare County houses listed on the National Register of Historic Places. The inn offers eight guest rooms, each with a private bath and fireplace. Honeymoon suites are available. Lounge on the large, wraparound porches; guests also have full use of the library, formal parlor, foyer, and dining room of this stately old home. Afternoon tea, coffee, and desserts are served, as is evening sherry.

The inn serves a full Southern-style, four-course breakfast every morning, a time for guests to read the newspapers, enjoy the fine food, and prepare for a day of exploring historic Manteo and Roanoke Island. This is a nonsmoking establishment, but smoking is allowed on the porch.

Special events for up to 50 people, including weddings, reunions, or retreats, can be accommodated. Check the Web site for special-interest weekend packages. The inn is open all year, and off-season rates are available.

The Cameron House Inn $$$$
300 Budleigh Street, Manteo
(252) 473-6596, (800) 279-8178
www.cameronhouseinn.com

Comfort and elegance are the hallmarks at this well-appointed inn. Some rooms feature fireplaces, soaker tubs, or down-stuffed sofas, and all have luxurious tiled bathrooms. All rooms are nonsmoking and all have Internet access. A big breakfast is set out each morning, usually offering homemade muffins and breads, quiches, fresh fruit, granola, juices, coffee, and tea. Afternoon treats perk you up after a long day on the beach or visiting attractions, especially if you also take a moment to relax on the antique front porch swing or in the comfy wicker chairs. The inn is in historic downtown Manteo where restaurants, attractions, and shopping are all just a few minutes' walk away.

The Cameron House Inn also offers some of the best advice on what to see and do while you are on the Outer Banks—advice not easily matched, considering that the owners of this inn masterminded and developed the Insiders' Guide series. The Cameron House is frequently the site for conferences, retreats, and business meetings.

Scarborough Inn $$$
524 US 64, Manteo
(252) 473–3979
www.scarborough-inn.com
Across from the Christmas Shop, this small inn is a delightful and friendly place to stay. The two-story structure was modeled after a turn-of-the-20th-century inn. Each of the guest rooms is filled with authentic Victorian and pre-Victorian

antiques and other interesting furnishings, mostly family heirlooms.

The inn's main rooms are set away from the street and offer king-size or double beds, cable TV, phone, microwave, private bath, small refrigerator, and coffeemaker. A light continental breakfast is delivered the night before, an especially nice treat for early risers.

Rooms in the two-story inn have exterior entrances and open onto a covered porch. The annex has four units: two suites with queen bedrooms and sitting rooms and two regular queen rooms. The barn has two king rooms. All six units in the annex and barn are equipped with wet bars and small storage spaces for kitchen utensils and miscellaneous items. Pets are not allowed.

Complimentary bicycles are available for guests age 18 and older. Scarborough Inn is open year-round.

Nothing feels better on your skin than the Atlantic Ocean at the Outer Banks, but beware! Sharks are everywhere. Stay behind the breakers in shallow water where you can see through the water to the sandy bottom. Flat beaches far from fishing piers and surf fishermen are the safest.

Tranquil House Inn $$$$
405 Queen Elizabeth Avenue
on the Waterfront, Manteo
(252) 473-1404, (800) 458-7069
www.tranquilinn.com

This lovely 25-room country inn on Shallowbag Bay was modeled after an old hotel that stood on this site. Although the inn looks authentically aged, it is enhanced by up-to-date conveniences: TVs, telephones, and private baths. Two of the 25 rooms are one-bedroom suites that feature a queen-size bed and a separate sitting room with sofa and two TVs.

Large rooms on the third floor have high ceilings. Nonsmoking rooms are available, and the inn has one room equipped for disabled guests. A ramp to the first floor makes rooms on that level accessible to all.

The spacious second-floor deck faces east toward the bay. The *Elizabeth II,* the flagship attraction of Roanoke Island Festival Park, is docked across the water. Shops along the waterfront are a few steps away, and the marina behind the inn is convenient for those arriving by boat.

The inn's restaurant, 1587, specializes in gourmet cuisine and offers an extensive selection of wines (see our Restaurants chapter). Guests have free use of bicycles. The inn is open all year.

Scarborough House Bed and Breakfast $$$
Fernando and Uppowac Streets, Manteo
(252) 473-3849
www.scarbourghhouseinn.com

The Scarborough House, owned by Phil and Sally Scarborough, opened in 1995. Each of the four guest rooms has its own refrigerator, microwave, and private bath. Nonsmoking rooms are available. A romantic loft room has a king-size bed and a whirlpool bath. This inn is appointed with period antiques and other fine furnishings. A continental breakfast is served daily. Everything about these accommodations reflects the owners' care and personal touch. The Scarborough House is open year-round.

Duke of Dare Motor Lodge $$
US 64, Manteo
(252) 473-2175

On the main street and only a few blocks from the Manteo waterfront, this 57-room family motel provides the basics in accommodations: clean rooms with full baths, cable TV, and phones. All rooms have queen-size beds. Wheelchair-accessible rooms are available. The lodge also has an outdoor pool.

The Creef family has owned and managed the motel for more than a quarter-century. The Duke of Dare is close to shopping, restaurants, and attractions. It is open all year.

Dare Haven Motel $$
US 64/264, Manteo
(252) 473-2322
www.darehaven.com

The Dare Haven, a family-run motel suited to the cost-conscious vacationer, is toward the north end of Roanoke Island and is a favorite place for families and fishing enthusiasts—there's enough room here to park your own boat and trailer. Visitors planning to attend *The Lost Colony* or visit any of the other Roanoke Island attractions and historic sites of Fort Raleigh find this location convenient.

The 27 motel-style rooms are basic, clean, and comfortable, and have cable TV and telephones. Most are decorated in traditional Outer Banks style, with paneled walls and wraparound porches. All are ground level.

Call for special rates for groups and extended stays. The motel is open all year and is pet friendly. A large dog run has been added recently.

Wanchese

Island House of Wanchese
Bed and Breakfast $$$-$$$$
104 Old Wharf Road, Wanchese
(252) 473-5619
www.islandhouse-bb.com
This old home, built in 1902, was converted into a bed-and-breakfast several years ago. Furnished in period antiques with Oriental rugs and cabana fans, the small but cozy establishment offers many comforts, including private baths, cable TV, radios in every room, beach towels and chairs, and a hot tub for guests. Each of the four rooms and one suite has a double bed.

Island House offers a breakfast buffet often including casseroles, grits, fresh fruit, sweets, and juice. Evening tea is served with snacks. A guest pantry is open 24 hours a day. This is a nonsmoking establishment, but smoking is allowed on the porch. This is an adults-only inn. Island House is open year-round.

HATTERAS ISLAND

Rodanthe

Sea Sound Motel $$
Sea Sound Road, Rodanthe
(252) 987-2224
http://seasound.home.mindspring.com
Sea Sound is between NC 12 and the ocean and offers 11 efficiencies and regular motel-style rooms. The efficiencies have fully equipped kitchens including microwaves. Motel rooms feature either one double or two queen-size beds. All accommodations have heat and air-conditioning, color TV, and phones, and most have coffeemakers. An outdoor pool is available. Sea Sound also features an

outdoor grill, picnic area with table, and small basketball court. It's open March through mid-December. Pets are welcome for an additional fee.

Avon

Avon Motel $$-$$$
NC 12, Avon
(252) 995-5774
www.avonmotel.com
This 45-unit establishment has been in business for more than 50 years and offers oceanside motel rooms and a handful of efficiency apartments. Motel rooms come with either two double beds or one queen-size or one king-size bed, and each has a microwave, compact refrigerator, and coffeemaker. The efficiencies have either two or three rooms with a variety of bed setups along with fully equipped kitchens. All rooms and efficiencies have air-conditioning, cable TV with free HBO, and in-room phones (local calls are free). For the anglers in the group, there is a lighted fish-cleaning station at the motel, and a guest laundry.

The motel is located near tackle shops, a fishing pier, four-wheel-drive beach accesses, windsurfing and beach shops, restaurants, and gift stores. The Cape Hatteras Lighthouse is 6 miles away. The Avon Motel is open March through December.

Buxton

Cape Hatteras Motel $$$$
NC 12, Buxton
(252) 995-5611, (800) 995-0711
www.capehatterasmotel.com
Cape Hatteras Motel's 30 efficiency units and 11 motel rooms are popular with anglers, surfers, and folks who enjoy Hatteras Island's beaches. Windsurfers especially like this facility because it is near Canadian Hole, one of the best windsurfing spots on the East Coast (see our Attractions chapter).

Efficiencies sleep up to six comfortably, offer double beds as well as queen-size and king-size beds, and have full kitchens. The newer, more modern town houses and apartments have a great view of the beach. The motel has an outdoor swimming pool and spa, and its position at the north end of Buxton is convenient not only to pristine, uncrowded beaches but also to restaurants and services. Cape Hatteras Motel has no nonsmoking rooms but does offer a ZonTech clean air machine.

Efficiencies rent weekly, but nightly rentals also may be available. Cape Hatteras Motel is open year-round.

Outer Banks Motel $$$
NC 12, Buxton
(252) 995–5601, (800) 995–1233
www.outerbanksmotel.com
Situated next to the Cape Hatteras Motel, this establishment offers 3 motel-style rooms, an efficiency unit, and 11 two- and three-bedroom cottages. Units accommodate up to eight people comfortably, and some of the units provide an ocean view. Rooms and the efficiency offer enclosed porches with sliding windows and screens

for a relaxing evening listening to the ocean. The pine-paneled rooms have tiled baths, microwaves, toasters, and small refrigerators. All units have cable TV and telephones.

The owners also have additional cottages in Buxton Village, a mile from the ocean, near Connor's Market. Because these units are not oceanfront, rental rates are lower. If you rent one of these cottages, you are welcome to use the motel pool and beach facilities. The cottages are clean, simply furnished, and provide the basics for family vacationers, including cable TV. The motel has a coin-operated laundry, a fish-cleaning station, and a guest freezer to store your big catch. If you enjoy crabbing or you just want to paddle around on Pamlico Sound, the motel has several rowboats that guests may use free of charge. This motel is open year-round.

Lighthouse View Motel $$$$
NC 12, Buxton
(252) 995–5680, (800) 225–7651
www.lighthouseview.com
Lighthouse View is easy to find on the big curve in Buxton, where the Hooper family has been serving vacationers for almost

60 years. Located within a mile of the Hatteras Lighthouse, the motel has 78 units including motel rooms, efficiencies, duplexes, villa units, and cottages. Most units are oceanfront, and all are oceanside. The complex has an outdoor pool and hot tub. Surfers, windsurfers, and anglers enjoy the proximity to ocean and sound.

Rooms have cable TV, phones, full baths, and daily maid service. Efficiencies accommodate two to six people and are equipped with complete kitchens. The oceanfront villas offer balconies on both the oceanside and soundside, so you can enjoy sunrises and sunsets. The six duplexes offer two decks and sleep up to six people each. Efficiencies and villas usually rent on a weekly basis, and there is a three-night minimum stay, but they can be rented nightly when available. Note that there is no daily maid service for the villas, efficiencies, and duplexes, but linens can be exchanged. Cottages are rented by the week only. Efficiencies, duplexes, villas, and cottages are fully furnished. Wheelchair-accessible, one-room efficiencies are also available. Lighthouse View is open year-round.

Falcon Motel $$$
46854 NC 12, Buxton
(252) 995-5968, (800) 635-6911
www.falconmotel.com

Falcon's traditional Outer Banks–style rooms appeal to family-oriented guests who appreciate moderate prices, accommodations with character, and the peaceful environment of Hatteras Island. Owners Tracy and Chris Latta are known for their attention to detail, which is apparent in the clean, well-maintained rooms and grounds.

This motel includes 35 units with 30 rooms, three two-bedroom, fully equipped apartments, and three one-room efficiencies, all at ground level. All rooms and apartments have daily maid service. Non-smoking rooms are available. The rooms include cable TV with HBO, and many have a refrigerator and microwave. All rooms have wooden deck chairs on a wide, covered porch. Complimentary breakfast is served daily during the summer season. Falcon offers six pet-friendly rooms in which one or two pets may stay for an extra $20 per night, plus tax. Call ahead for reservations.

Guests have use of the swimming pool and complimentary bikes. You'll also find a shaded picnic area with barbecue grills amid mature oak trees, away from the road. The landscaping includes martin and bluebird houses, palm trees, and planted shrubs and flowers that attract the local bird population.

The Falcon Motel is within an easy walk of several shops and restaurants, including

Diamond Shoals Restaurant (see our Restaurants chapter) across the street. Apartments rent mostly on a weekly basis.

Comfort Inn of Hatteras $$$$
NC 12, Buxton
(252) 995-6100, (800) 432-1441
www.outerbankscomfortinn.com

The Comfort Inn is in the heart of Buxton, close to the beach and shops. The 60 units and one suite with exterior access are standard motel-style rooms with king-size or double beds. Rooms are decorated in attractive, soft beach colors; all have cable TV with HBO, refrigerators, direct-dial phones, and microwaves. Nonsmoking and wheelchair-accessible rooms are available.

Free ice and guest laundry are available. A complimentary continental breakfast is served in the lobby. Guests have use of the outdoor swimming pool, gazebo, and three-story watch tower, the latter two providing panoramic views of the ocean, the sound, and nearby Cape Hatteras Lighthouse (see our Attractions chapter). AARP and AAA discounts are honored.

Comfort Inn of Hatteras Island has ample parking for boats and campers and is open year-round.

Cape Hatteras
Bed and Breakfast $$-$$$
46223 Old Lighthouse Road, Buxton
(252) 995-3002, (800) 252-3316
www.surforsound.com

A short walk to the beach makes this bed-and-breakfast inn popular with wind-surfers as well as beach lovers, lighthouse enthusiasts, honeymooners, surfers, and couples who just want to get away. The two-story inn offers several styles of accommodations. All nine units are non-smoking, and six are on the first floor. Each has its own entrance opening onto a covered porch running the length of the building. Two of the rooms offer two dou-ble beds, and the rest have king- or queen-size beds. The inn has two effi-ciency units. A two-room unit features a bedroom with a queen-size bed, a living room with a queen sleeper sofa, and a full kitchen. The one-room unit has a queen-size bed and kitchenette. All units have cable TV and private baths. A large sun-deck with comfortable chairs, a gas grill, and a table are available for guests' use.

Amenities include a common dining and living area upstairs (where a compli-mentary full gourmet breakfast is served), color cable TV, VCR, and hot and cold out-door showers. Beach gear, coolers, bicycles, and beach toys are available along with lockable storage for surf- and sailboards. Daily maid service is provided. Weekly rentals are available, with special accom-modations available for honeymooners. The inn is open April through mid-December.

Tower Circle Motel $$
Old Lighthouse Road, Buxton
(252) 995-5353
www.towercirclemotel.com

This small motel, just off NC 12 oceanside, is one of the friendliest spots on the Outer Banks. The Gray family, which has owned Tower Circle for some 40 years, treats guests like old friends, and many of them are.

The 15 units, including 8 duplexes, 4 two-room suites, and 3 efficiency apart-ments, open onto the porch. All have cable TV and sleep from two to six people comfortably in twin to king-size beds. Suites and apartments have complete kitchens. A pay phone is on-site. All linens are provided as well as daily maid service. A washer and dryer are provided, as well as a fish-cleaning station and a freezer to store your catch. A children's play area is available.

It's just a short walk to the beach, restaurants, and stores. Tower Circle is open April through mid-December. No credit cards accepted.

Cape Pines Motel $$$
NC 12, Buxton
(252) 995-5666
www.capepinesmotel.com

Cape Pines Motel, a mile south of the Cape Hatteras Lighthouse, is a one-story facility with private exterior entry to each room. Each of the 26 rooms offers cable TV and a full bath. Furnishings have a contemporary beach look. Some rooms have queen-size beds, and nonsmoking rooms are available. Cape Pines Motel has three apartments, each offering separate bedrooms, a living room, and a full kitchen. In the summer season, the apartments rent on a weekly basis only. Deluxe rooms are available with microwaves, coffeemakers, and refrigerators.

Stretch out and relax around the pool and the lawn, which has picnic tables and charcoal grills. Fish-cleaning tables and a pay phone are on the premises. High-speed Internet hookup is available in the office from 9:00 A.M. to 9:00 P.M. daily. Cape Pines is close enough to walk or bike to shopping or attractions. The motel is open year-round.

Hatteras Village

Breakwater Inn $$$-$$$$
NC 12, Hatteras Village
(252) 986-2565
www.harbormotel.com

This beautiful new inn is in the heart of Hatteras Village. Convenient to restaurants, shops, and services, it's adjacent to the Hatteras charter boat fleet. Visitors park their cars and walk or bike to most places in this community.

Breakwater Inn has 21 new rooms with 2 queen-size beds and a kitchenette and 2 oversized king suites with living area, full kitchen, a king-size bed, and a whirlpool tub. These rooms have a spectacular view of the Hatteras harbor. The 12 rooms in the Fisherman's Quarters are standard hotel rooms, and one large efficiency is located there also. All rooms have cable TV, microwaves, refrigerators, and telephones. Daily maid service and fresh linens are provided. Guests enjoy the in-ground pool and kiddie wading pool and the long, shaded porches.

Pets are allowed in some rooms for a $30 fee per night.

Hatteras Marlin Motel $$$
NC 12, Hatteras Village
(252) 986-2141, (866) 986-2141
www.hatterasmarlin.com

The recently renovated Hatteras Marlin Hotel is in sight of the harbor fishing fleet, restaurants, and shops. The 39 units are divided among three buildings and consist of standard motel rooms with king- or double-size beds and one-bedroom efficiencies. A newer building near the back of the property away from the road offers a pair of two-bedroom suites with combined living, kitchen, and dining areas.

All rooms have cable TV, microwaves, refrigerators, coffeemakers, and telephones. Accommodations sleep one to six people comfortably and rent weekly or nightly depending upon availability. The motel has an in-ground swimming pool and sundeck. Hatteras Marlin Motel is open all year, except for Christmas.

OCRACOKE ISLAND

The Anchorage Inn & Marina $$$-$$$$
NC 12, Ocracoke
(252) 928-1101
www.theanchorageinn.com

The Anchorage Inn overlooks Silver Lake and the village. Besides 35 motel-style rooms, the inn has a marina and fishing center, recreational amenities, an outdoor cafe, and gift shops nearby. The attractive five-story redbrick building with white trim has elevator access to each floor.

Accommodations offer some of the best bird's-eye views available of the harbor and Ocracoke Village, especially from upper-floor rooms. Most of the rooms have some view of Silver Lake Harbor. Each of the rooms has a king- or queen-size bed or two double beds, full bath, direct-dial phone, and cable TV with Showtime and Cinemax. The fourth-floor units are nonsmoking rooms and have king-size beds. Wheelchair-accessible rooms are available. Pets are allowed in some rooms for a $20 fee. This is also the only hotel in Ocracoke with an elevator.

The Anchorage Inn offers its guests a complimentary continental breakfast, a private pool with a sundeck situated on the harbor, and an on-premises boat dock and ramp. The gazebo at Silver Lake is a perfect place to watch an early evening sunset. Guests can walk to restaurants, shops, and the historical sites on Ocracoke Island. Bike rentals are available. Fishing charters, which depart from the dock across the street, can be booked with the marina's dockmaster. The inn is open year-round.

Blackbeard's Lodge $$$$
Back Road, Ocracoke
(252) 928-3421, (800) 892-5314
www.blackbeardslodge.com

Ocracoke's oldest hotel, Blackbeard's Lodge, was built in 1936 by local entrepreneur, developer, and visionary Stanley Wahab. The building's first floor originally housed Ocracoke's only movie theater on one side and skating rink on the other. "Rooms for hire" occupied the second floor and often accommodated visiting dignitaries, movie stars, and well-heeled types who flew their planes to the island, landed on the barren sand flats, and taxied right up to the front door. A subsequent owner added some rooms to the gabled third floor and stretched the building out with additional rooms in the wing now called the annex.

In 1999 Ann and Buffy Warner (owners of Ocracoke's popular Howard's Pub) purchased the 37-unit lodge and undertook a complete renovation.

This is a family-oriented property during the vacation season that changes focus to accommodate "outdoors and sporting types" and those wanting to quietly get away from it all during the fall, winter, and spring. Blackbeard's units range from a room with one double bed to a room that sleeps eight with a full kitchen and dining area. All rooms have television. Some rooms feature whirlpool baths, while others may include a kitchenette, king-size bed, refrigerator, or wet bar. Several pet-friendly rooms are available; call ahead to reserve.

A game room complete with pool table, foosball, and electronic games is available for inclement days or for nights when friendly competition is in order. A fleet of bicycles are for rent. The lodge has a heated swimming pool with sundeck, wrap-around porch with rockers, fish-cleaning table, and free water access for rinsing the salt and sand off your vehicle if surf fishing or beach driving is your passion. Blackbeard's Lodge is open all year long. In the off-season, a complimentary hot breakfast is served from 8:00 to 10:00 A.M.

The Captain's Landing $$$$
324 NC 12, Ocracoke
(252) 928-1999
www.thecaptainslanding.com

Breathe in the fresh sea air and feel the soft ocean breeze while you stay at The Captain's Landing on scenic Silver Lake in Ocracoke. Luxury suites and a penthouse apartment provide panoramic views of the lighthouse, the village, and harbor life. The first and second floors offer suites with queen-size beds, one and a half baths, a sleeper sofa in the living area, a fully equipped kitchen, and a spacious private deck. The penthouse has a queen-size bed in the master suite and a guest room with two double beds. A sleeper sofa is located in the office. The penthouse has two full baths, a laundry room, expansive dining and living areas, and a well-stocked gourmet kitchen. Enjoy spectacular sunsets from the decks, which are accessible from most rooms.

The Castle Bed & Breakfast on Silver Lake $$$$
155 Silver Lake Road, Ocracoke
(252) 928-3505, (800) 471-8848
www.thecastlebb.com

Among the finest accommodations on Ocracoke Island, the Castle has been part of the local scenery and part of the island's rich history for more than 50 years. Each of the 11 bedrooms, which have been extensively renovated and redecorated, are furnished with antiques and offer a private bath, television, small refrigerator, and

phone. The house has a large living room with a surround-sound entertainment system, central air-conditioning, and a custom 9-foot pool table. A full country breakfast is served from 8:30 to 9:30 A.M. (Breakfast is for bed-and-breakfast guests only.) Children age 12 and older are welcome.

The top of the Castle has a cupola, private to the Lighthouse Suite, that overlooks the Silver Lake with panoramic views from the sound to the ocean. There is also a large deck extending from the cupola that may be used for sunning, relaxing, or watching the sunset. The pier on Silver Lake offers large and small boat dockage in slips up to 50 feet. Hookups are 50 and 30 amp, with telephone and cable service. Dockage is available on a complimentary first-come basis for all guests.

In addition to The Castle Bed & Breakfast, Courtyard and Villa suites are available. One-, two-, and three-bedrooms are available, each with large whirlpool tubs, full kitchens, and spacious, comfortable living areas. Studio bedrooms are also available with kitchenettes.

Everyone who stays at any of the Castle properties may use the heated pool, steam showers, sauna, bicycles, and the conference room equipped with an Internet-access computer.

Located within the pool house is the Deep Blue Day Spa. Amy Borland Hilton, a certified massage therapist and yoga instructor, operates the spa.

The Cove Bed and Breakfast $$$–$$$$
21 Loop Road, Ocracoke
(252) 928–4192
www.thecovebb.com

The Cove is a beautiful beach home located within walking distance of Ocracoke's many shops and restaurants. This bed-and-breakfast is a large place—more than 5,000 square feet—and is within view of the sound and Ocracoke's lighthouse. Rooms come equipped with cable TVs and hair dryers. Each room has its own balcony and bath. Full breakfasts are served each day in the large common area. A large screened porch beckons you to sit awhile and absorb the wonderful, clean Ocracoke air at the end of a beach day.

Two suites are available with queen-size four-poster beds and large jetted tub/shower combinations. Two rooms are available, each with a queen-size bed and one single bed.

The inn is a nonsmoking establishment; children age 15 and older are welcome, but pets are not. A public boat dock for launching a kayak or small craft is nearby.

Complimentary bicycles are available for touring around town. Transportation is provided to and from the airstrip.

Crews Inn Bed and Breakfast $
Back Road, Ocracoke
(252) 928-7011

The Crews Inn is a place to get away from it all. No phones or TVs will disturb your privacy here. Three rooms have private baths, and two share a bath. All have double beds. The wraparound porch is an especially nice spot for guests to gather, for the building is surrounded by large live oaks and is far enough away from traffic for easy chatting. This is a nonsmoking establishment, but smoking is allowed on the porch. The inn serves mostly a continental but occasionally a full breakfast. Crews Inn is open year-round. No credit cards accepted.

Edwards of Ocracoke $$
Pony Island Road, Ocracoke
(252) 928-4801, (800) 254-1359
www.edwardsofocracoke.com

This refurbished motel, away from the center of Ocracoke and off the main route near The Back Porch Restaurant, consists of eight motel rooms, three efficiencies, six apartments, and two cottages. Most of the units have screened porches and phones. Some open onto a veranda. All have cable TV. Cottages rent weekly during the summer, and efficiencies require a three-day minimum stay. Some have refrigerators. The rate guideline above pertains to nightly rentals of the motel rooms only.

The motel offers inexpensive accommodations in a family setting with a carefully landscaped green lawn, flower beds, and pine trees. The motel is open mid-March through Thanksgiving and for New Year's eve.

Harborside Motel $$$
Across from Silver Lake Harbor
Ocracoke
(252) 928-3111

This charming motel offers 18 rooms and 4 efficiencies, all well kept and comfortable with cable TV, phones, and refrigerators. Most rooms offer two double beds; one has three double beds, and two have one double bed. Guests can use the waterfront sundeck, docks, and boat ramp across the street. Nonsmoking rooms are available.

Harborside has its own gift shop offering a wide selection of clothing, books, gourmet foods, and small gifts. Other shops and restaurants of Ocracoke Village are within walking distance. The Swan Quarter and Cedar Island ferry docks are nearby. The same family has owned this property since 1965, and their hospitality and service are firmly established.

A complimentary breakfast of homemade muffins, coffee, juice, and tea is provided. The motel is open Easter through mid-November. AAA members receive a discount.

The Island Inn $-$$$
NC 12, Ocracoke
(252) 928-4351, (877) 456-3466
www.ocracokeislandinn.com

The Island Inn, owned by Cee and Bob Touhey, provides a variety of accommodations suitable for single adults, couples, and families with children. Originally built as an Odd Fellows Lodge in 1901, the main building has served as a school, a private residence, and naval officers' quarters. It was restored by former owners and has been recognized in *Country Inns of the Old South, Southern Living, Cuisine,* and *The Saturday Evening Post*.

The owners had their first date on Ocracoke Island and vacationed here for many years; they returned to live and work. The main building is a nonsmoking establishment. Many of the 28 rooms reflect the inherently romantic style of this country inn. The main building houses individual rooms and suites, all uniquely furnished with antiques and quilts. The adults-only rooms and suites accommodate a wide range of needs. If you're looking for a contemporary feel, ask for the Crow's Nest, which offers spectacular views of the postcard-pretty village.

Across the street, a much newer three-story structure includes two rooms with king-size beds. Families with children find these casual accommodations a welcome retreat. The third floor has one- and two-bedroom luxury villas overlooking the heated pool. Each beautifully furnished villa has a kitchen, living and dining area, washer and dryer, plenty of windows, and a whirlpool tub. The inn also rents a number of cottages, some of which accommodate pets with no fee attached, and has a heated swimming pool that is kept open as long as weather permits. Cable TV with free Showtime is available in every room. The inn has an on-site restaurant (see our Restaurants chapter), a large lobby for lounging, and a covered porch with rocking chairs. Island Inn closes for a few weeks in January but otherwise is open year-round.

Joyce's of Ocracoke Waterfront Motel and Dockage $$$$
Silver Lake, Ocracoke Village
(252) 928-6461
www.joycesofocracoke.com
Joyce's offers water views of Silver Lake from a large deck. Four of the smaller efficiencies are larger than standard motel rooms. Each is set up with a queen-size bed and queen-size sofa bed. The two larger efficiencies have two queen-size beds and a queen-size sofa bed plus a full-size refrigerator, range, microwave, coffeemaker, toaster, and kitchen utensils. Daily housekeeping is offered; linens are furnished. Room amenities include phones, cable TV with HBO, air-conditioning, and heat. Nonsmoking rooms are available. Boaters love the location—you can pull your boat up at the establishment's 10-slip boat dock. Joyce's is open year-round.

The Ocracoke Harbor Inn $$$
On Silver Lake Harbor, across from the Coast Guard Station, Ocracoke
(252) 928-5731, (888) 456-1998
www.ocracokeharborinn.com
This lovely 16-room, 7-suite inn overlooks picturesque Silver Lake Harbor. The inn's private decks with Adirondack chairs are a great place to kick back, relax, and enjoy the view.

Each room features either two queen-size beds or one king-size bed and includes a mini-fridge, cable TV, coffeepot, hair dryer, and climate control. The suites have two-person whirlpool tubs and kitchenettes. Suites are studio style or one bedroom. Three three-bedroom island homes and a two-bedroom apartment are also offered. All rooms are nonsmoking, and wheelchair-accessible rooms are available.

A complimentary continental breakfast is served each morning. Also available are complimentary boat docking, outdoor showers, barbecue grills, bicycle rentals, and lots of outdoor decks. The Ocracoke Harbor Inn is open year-round. Pets are not allowed.

Oscar's House $$
One block from Silver Lake Harbor
Ocracoke
(252) 928-1311
Oscar's House was built in 1940 by the keeper of the Ocracoke Lighthouse and was first occupied by the World War II commander of the Ocracoke Naval Base. Stories abound about Oscar, who lived and worked on the island for many years as a fisherman and hunting guide. This guesthouse has operated as a bed-and-breakfast since 1984. It is managed by Ann Ehringhaus, a massage therapist, local fine-art photographer, and the author of *Ocracoke Portrait*.

The house retains the original beaded-board walls, and all four guest rooms are delightfully furnished. One upstairs bedroom has a loft creating a comfortable setting. Two baths, one upstairs and one down, accommodate guests, as does an outdoor shower (with dressing room). The house has central heating and central air-conditioning and is comfortable and welcoming. The large kitchen with a big table is available to guests; however, the stove is off-limits. Ann serves a complimentary full breakfast to all guests and will gladly adhere to special preferences for vegetar-

ian or macrobiotic meals. Smoking is allowed on the back deck only. You can treat yourself to one of Ann's therapeutic massages. In spring and fall, Ann offers workshops in photography and therapeutic bodywork. Call for details.

Oscar's House has a deck area complete with barbecue grills. Meals are eaten inside or outdoors. Oscar's House is within walking distance of all village shops and restaurants, and bicycles are free for guests. Ann also gladly transports guests to and from the Ocracoke Airport, which is open to single- and twin-engine planes. This bed-and-breakfast is open from April to October.

Pelican Lodges $$$
Across from fire station, Ocracoke
(252) 928-1661
Built as a lodge, Pelican features a full sit-

down breakfast. The four rooms, one with two double beds and the others with one double bed, are spacious and carpeted, with private baths. Nonsmoking rooms are available. Amenities include cable TV, a small pool, and free use of bicycles. The lodge is open year-round.

Pony Island Motel $$$
NC 12, Ocracoke
(252) 928-4411
www.ponyislandmotel.com
At the edge of Ocracoke Village, a short distance from Silver Lake Harbor, Pony Island Motel offers 54 rooms, efficiencies, and suites. The grounds are spacious and inviting. Family-owned for more than 25 years, the inn hosts families and couples in search of peace and solitude on Ocracoke Island.

Most of the units have either single or double occupancy, but the motel offers some rooms that accommodate up to five people. Each room has a telephone, refrigerator, and color cable TV with Showtime, and the efficiencies have fully equipped kitchens. Rooms are refurbished regularly but maintain a traditional decor. Nonsmoking rooms and one wheelchair-accessible room are available.

A newer 23-unit, three-story addition overlooks the pool. Rooms have a kitchenette. Suites have a full kitchen and whirlpool tubs.

The motel is within walking distance of the Ocracoke Lighthouse and other island attractions. Bike rentals and boat docking are available. The pool and spacious lawn with picnic tables and grills offer plenty of room for family activities. The Pony Island Restaurant, a local favorite, is next door (see our Restaurants chapter). Pony Island Motel is open year-round.

Sand Dollar Motel $$
Sand Dollar Lane, Ocracoke
(252) 928–5571, (866) 928–5571
www.ocracokeisland.com
This establishment is in the heart of Ocracoke Village behind The Back Porch Restaurant (there are no street signs). Fresh flowers welcome guests to the lobby. You're likely to be greeted by Roger Garrish, the property's personable owner and an Ocracoke native, who is a great

source of island information. The Sand Dollar has 11 rooms and a two-bedroom cottage. Two of the rooms are efficiencies with small microwaves and coffeemakers; all rooms have refrigerators and cable TV. Bedding options include queen- and double-size beds. One special room is connected to the pool and has a private deck and a king-size bed. Nonsmoking rooms are available. Guests enjoy a continental breakfast and a dip in the pool. Repeat visits are common at this neat little place, so book your stay early. The inn is open from April 1 to mid-November.

Thurston House Inn $$$
NC 12, Ocracoke
(252) 928–6037
www.thurstonhouseinn.com
The Thurston House Inn was built in the 1920s. The former home of Capt. Tony Thurston Gaskill is now on the Register of Historic Places in North Carolina. It was renovated in 1996 by the captain's granddaughter, Marlene Mathews, and her husband, Randal. An addition was completed next to the inn in 1999. The inn offers six rooms, each with a private bath. A phone is available in the hallway, and each room has cable TV. All rooms are heated and air-conditioned and have private decks and porches with either king- or queen-size beds.

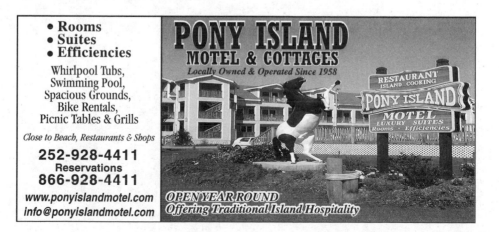

Guests enjoy relaxing on the covered porches and deck, which connects the inn's two buildings. A continental breakfast is part of the package. Children older than age 12 are welcome. This is a nonsmoking establishment, but smoking is allowed on the porches. The inn is within walking distance of Silver Lake, Ocracoke Lighthouse, and various stores, restaurants, and historic sites. Local airport pickup is available. Reservations are recommended. The inn is open March 1 through November.

CAMPING

Imagine drifting off to sleep on a bed of soft sand with the murmur of waves gently kissing the sandy shoreline. A whispering breeze ruffles your tent, ushering in the sounds of nocturnal creatures and the salt-laden air. Now imagine waking up to a spectacular sunrise over the ocean as gulls begin to wheel and turn above the waves looking for breakfast and dolphins play just off the beach. Welcome to an experience you won't soon forget—camping on the Outer Banks. From spring through autumn, lovers of the outdoors make their way to the numerous campgrounds that line these barrier islands to experience nature. Whether choosing to bed down with nothing more than a tent and a sleeping bag or deciding to "camp" in a recreational vehicle, opportunities abound.

When word first got out that the Outer Banks was a desirable location for a little rest and relaxation, campgrounds were popular—and sometimes the only choice—for accommodations. Many of the visitors to the Outer Banks were hunters and anglers, people who relished the natural world and took pleasure in sleeping under the Carolina moon. For other tourists, camping was an alternative because motels and rental cottages were few and far between. Many of the older campgrounds have given way as development continues to encroach on former open areas, but today you can choose from many campgrounds on Colington, Roanoke, Bodie, Hatteras, and Ocracoke Islands. Whether you desire a location right next to the ocean or protected in a wooded site, you have numerous spots to explore.

Most people think summer is the best time to camp on the Outer Banks because of the warm temperatures, but arm yourself with bug repellent. Many of the campgrounds listed are near the sound or in wooded areas where mosquitoes are always hungry for a juicy camper. Don't forget that the summer months are also a ripe time for thunderstorms and hurricanes. Read the chapter on Waves and Weather for additional information on how to stay safe while vacationing on the Outer Banks.

Some campers, many of them locals, prefer to get away from it all by camping during the off-season, or "shoulder seasons," as we call them. This includes spring and fall, when the temperatures are warm enough to enjoy all the outdoor activities. In the fall, the humidity lessens, along with some of the crowds, and evenings are crisp and clear, perfect for stargazing.

More than 100,000 people frequent the National Park Service campgrounds for their home away from home each year, while thousands of other nature lovers set up camp at privately owned campgrounds. Some private campgrounds only open during the summer season, offering few creature comforts besides cold showers, but others are year-round establishments providing electric and water hookups, sewage disposal, laundry facilities, swimming pools, game rooms, bathhouses, and cable television. Some campgrounds rent furnished RVs. All have well-maintained roads and drive-up sites that accommodate any type of vehicle. Note that taxes are not included in any of the prices quoted.

National Park Service campgrounds operate under the same rules and regulations and charge the same fees. Park Service campgrounds do not take reservations (except the Ocracoke Campground between Memorial Day and Labor Day) and accept payment in cash or credit cards upon arrival. Sites operate on a first-come, first-served basis. The National Park Service provides lifeguards at Coquina Beach, Cape Hatteras Lighthouse, south of the Frisco Pier at Sandy Bay, and on

Keep your dog leashed on the beach. The National Park Service and most towns have leash laws for several good reasons. Free-roaming dogs can cause irreparable damage in bird- and turtle-nesting areas by scattering or destroying eggs, killing newborns, or separating young ones from their parents, leaving them vulnerable to harm. Also, migrating shorebirds need to feed and rest in order to complete their journeys, so don't allow your dog to chase them up and down the beach.

Ocracoke Island. For more information on any of the local National Park Service campgrounds, call (252) 473-2111, and check the Park Service's Web site for the most up-to-date information on the opening and closing dates of each campground: www.nps.gov/caha.

Camping on the beach is prohibited, as is wilderness camping in open areas, including Nags Head Woods, Kitty Hawk Woods, and Buxton Woods. But there is one spot where wilderness camping is allowed—Portsmouth Island. This now-uninhabited island is accessible only by boat. So if you really want to get away from it all, check out our Day Trips chapter for information on Portsmouth Island.

Remember, these islands are home to a variety of wildlife, locals included. Please respect their homes by not littering or disturbing the environment in any way. We want to keep it just the way it is so you can come back and enjoy camping again next year.

NORTH OF OREGON INLET

Joe & Kay's Campground
Colington Road, Little Colington Island
(252) 441-5468
About a mile west on Colington Road, before you get to the first bridge, Joe & Kay's Campground has 70 full hookup sites rented on a yearly basis. An addi-

tional 15 tent sites are also available from April through November. Rates in 2005 were $20.00 a night for two people, with a $5.00 per night charge for each additional person. Reservations aren't accepted, so sites are secured on a first-come, first-served basis. Credit cards and personal checks are not accepted.

Oregon Inlet Campground (NPS)
NC 12, Bodie Island
(252) 473-2111
http://reservations.nps.gov
The northernmost National Park Service campground on the Outer Banks, this facility offers 120 sites along the windswept dunes just north of Oregon Inlet. If you're arriving from the north, look for the campground entrance on the east side of North Carolina Highway 12 just before crossing the Bonner Bridge. It is located on the ocean almost directly across from the Oregon Inlet Fishing Center.

Water, cold showers, modern toilets, picnic tables, and charcoal grills are available here. There aren't any utility connections, but dumping stations are nearby.

Most of these sites are in sunny, exposed areas on the sand. Park rangers suggest that campers bring awnings, umbrellas, or other sources of shade. You may need mosquito netting and long tent stakes.

Oregon Inlet Campground is open April through October. Campers are limited to a two-week stay. Reservations are not accepted, and sites are assigned on a first-come, first-served basis. Fees begin at $20 per night. Golden Age Passport holders receive a 50 percent discount. This campground accepts cash, credit cards, and personal checks with Social Security numbers printed on them.

HATTERAS ISLAND

Cape Hatteras KOA
NC 12, Rodanthe
(252) 987-2307, (800) 562-5268
www.koa.com
A large campground approximately 14

miles south of the Bonner Bridge across Oregon Inlet, Cape Hatteras KOA has about 300 sites, including one- and two-room "Kamping Kabins." These units feature locking doors, ceiling fans, electricity, and picnic tables, and each has a porch. Ask about wheelchair-accessible units. Friendly, attentive staff greet campers as they arrive at this well-equipped campground. The campground is open March 1 through November and accepts reservations.

Besides hot showers, drinking water, and bathhouses, Cape Hatteras KOA offers campers a dump station, laundry facilities, two pools, a hot tub, a playground, a game room, a restaurant, and a well-stocked general store. Campers can even take in a round or two of miniature golf or a whirl on the campground's "Fun Bike"—a low-slung three-wheeler ridden inside the park. The ocean is just beyond the dunes for fishing and swimming, and a 200-foot soundside pier is the perfect place to fish, crab, or watch spectacular sunsets. The campground's recreation program offers varied activities in the summer. In 2005, rates for tent sites were $45 in summer and $40 in the off-season. Rates for RV sites ranged from $59 to $69, depending on the number of amenities and the site location; they are discounted in the off-season. Rates for Kamping Kabins were $76 in season and $66 off-season. Prices do not include tax.

**Rodanthe Watersports
and Shoreline Campground
NC 12, Rodanthe
(252) 987-1431
www.watersportsandcampground.com**
This soundfront campground is open year-round for recreational vehicles and tents. Windsurfers and kiteboarders especially enjoy this campground because they can sail right to some of the campsites. Other campers enjoy swimming, boating, and fishing in the sound. The watersports business next door rents kayaks, sailboats, Wave Runners, surfboards, and bicycles (see our Water Sports chapter). But what really keeps campers coming back are the spectacular, unobstructed sunset views.

In season, sites with electricity and water hookups start at $25 per night. Tent sites include water and start at $19.25 a night. Hot showers, picnic tables, and a few grills are on-site. If you'd rather not cook, you can grab a pizza from Lisa's Pizza right next door (see our Restaurants chapter). Pets are allowed. Reservations are recommended. Personal checks and credit cards are accepted.

**North Beach Campground
NC 12, Rodanthe
(252) 987-2378**
In the village of Rodanthe, North Beach Campground sits alongside the ocean south of the Chicamacomico Lifesaving Station. Here, 110 sites, all with water and electric hookups, offer campers both tent and RV accommodations and a wide range of amenities. Bathhouse, hot showers, picnic tables, a laundry facility, an outdoor swimming pool, and a pump-out station are available. There aren't any grills here, and open fires aren't allowed, so bring your own grill or camp stove if you want to cook.

North Beach Campground's grocery store sells fuel and convenience-store items. Pets are allowed on leashes. Reservations are accepted.

The campground is open from March through November. 2005 rates began at $18 a night for tents. Full hookups start at $24 a night.

**Camp Hatteras
NC 12, Rodanthe
(252) 987-2777
www.camphatteras.com**
A 50-acre campground, Camp Hatteras is a complete facility open year-round, offering many amenities. The site includes 1,000 feet of ocean and sound frontage. Nightly and monthly reservations are accepted.

All of Camp Hatteras's 400-plus sites have full hookups, concrete pads, and paved roads. Tent sites are also available. Laundry facilities, hot showers, full bathhouses, and picnic tables are available.

Camp Hatteras has expanded soundside with 92 paved full hookups.

For recreation, this campground provides three swimming pools, a clubhouse, a pavilion, a marina, fishing, two tennis courts, a nine-hole miniature golf course, volleyball, basketball, kayaks, windsurfers, and shuffleboard. A free boat ramp for campers is available. Sports and camping areas are separate, so sleeping outdoors is still a quiet experience—even if you nap midday.

2005 rates for tent sites ranged from $25 to $46, and rates for full hookup sites ranged from $30 to $63. Call for details and ask about discounts. Personal checks and credit cards are accepted. Pets are allowed on leashes for an additional fee. Wireless Internet available.

Ocean Waves Campground
NC 12, Waves
(252) 987–2556

Open March 15 through November 15, Ocean Waves Campground is a seaside resort with sites for RVs and tents. Of 68 spaces, 64 offer full hookups and concrete pads. Each has its own picnic table. Three bathhouses, hot showers, and laundry facilities are available. Campers enjoy the game room and outdoor pool. Asphalt roadways are well maintained.

Rates begin at $20 for a tent site, or $29 for a full hookup. Cable TV is an additional $2.00.

Sands of Time Campground
North End Road, Avon
(252) 995–5596

This year-round Avon campground has 51 full hookup sites and 15 tent sites, some with full shade. Hot showers, flush toilets, laundry facilities, a dump site, picnic tables, and a pay telephone are offered to all Sands campers.

Visitors enjoy swimming, fishing, and sunbathing at the nearby beach. Grills aren't provided, and open fires are not allowed. Bring your camp stove to cook.

Pets are allowed on leashes. Reservations are accepted and recommended for summer and fall. Rates for tent sites in 2005 were $20 a night in season and $18 a night off-season. Rates for full hookups were $30 a night in season and $28 a night off-season. Credit cards are not accepted.

Cape Woods Campground
Buxton Back Road, Buxton
(252) 995–5850
www.capewoods.com

Clean, quiet, and green best describe this campground. Scattered throughout the pine, live oak, and ash trees are 125 sites, some for tents, some with water and electricity, and some with full hookups. Cape Woods is open year-round and gladly accepts reservations. This full-service campground provides fire pits, grills, and picnic tables, as well as hot showers in two bathhouses, one of which is wheelchair accessible and one of which is heated for winter campers. An outdoor swimming pool, a playground, a small game room, a volleyball court, and a horseshoe pit are also available. Children and grown-ups freshwater fish in the canals surrounding the campground. Laundry facilities are available, and ice and propane gas are for sale.

Depending upon the season, a family of four, including two children age 15 or younger, stays for $20 to $40 a night with no hookups, or $40 for a site with full hookups and cable TV. One- and two-room cabins are available for $30 to $70. Discounts are honored, and credit cards are accepted. Open March through December.

Cape Point Campground (NPS)
Off NC 12, Buxton
(252) 473–2111
http://www.nps.gov/caha

The largest National Park Service campground on the Outer Banks, Cape Point is about 2 miles south of the Cape Hatteras Lighthouse, across the dunes from the Atlantic. This campground has 202 sites—none with utility connections. It's open from Memorial Day through September but does not accept reservations.

Flush toilets, cold showers, drinking water, charcoal grills, and picnic tables are provided. Each site has paved access. A wheelchair-accessible area is available, and a dumping station is nearby.

The campground is a short walk from the ocean. Most of these sites sit in the open, exposed to the sun and wind. Bring some shade, long tent stakes, lots of bug spray, and batteries. Cost is $20 a night; pets are allowed on leashes. Payment may be made with cash, credit cards, or personal checks with Social Security numbers printed on them.

Frisco Woods Campground
Frisco Woods, off NC 12, Frisco
(252) 995-5208, (800) 948-3942
www.outer-banks.com/friscowoods
This 30-acre soundside campground boasts abundant forest and marshland beauty and at least 150 sites in a wooded wonderland.

Electricity and water are available at 122 campsites. Full hookups are offered at 35 other sites, and there are 100 tent sites.

Amenities include an in-ground swimming pool, picnic tables, hot showers, a small country store, propane gas, and public phones. Windsurfers like this campground because they can sail directly from the sites onto Pamlico Sound. Crabbing, fishing, kayaking, and wandering through the woods are also readily available to campers staying at Frisco Woods.

2005 in-season rates for two people began at $32 a night for tent sites, $35 a night with electricity and water. Each additional adult is charged $6.00 per night. RV sites began at $40 per day in-season. Camping Cabins are also available. The one-room cabins sleep up to four people, and rates started at $65 per night. The two-room cabins sleep up to six people; rates started at $75 a night.

Frisco Woods is open March 1 through December 1, and reservations are accepted. Pets are allowed on leashes. Weekly, monthly, and seasonal rates are available on request, and special event and group rates also are offered.

Take it from those of us who know . . . if you leave your shoes and other useful items on the beach when you take a shoreline stroll, look for a landmark and make sure that your stuff is well above the surf line. You'd be surprised how easy it is to forget where you started, especially at Cape Hatteras National Seashore, where there are no buildings to use as landmarks.

Frisco Campground (NPS)
NC 12, Frisco
(252) 473-2111
http://reservations.nps.gov
Frisco Campground is operated by the National Park Service and sits about 4 miles southwest of Buxton. Just off the beach, next to ramp 49, this is the area's most isolated and elevated campground. Its undulating roads twist over dunes and around small hills, providing privacy at almost every site. Some tent areas are so secluded in stands of scrubby trees that you can't see them from where you park your car.

Frisco Campground has 127 no-frills sites, each with a charcoal grill and picnic table. Flush toilets, cold-water showers in bathhouses, and drinking water are available. There aren't any hookups here, but RVs are welcome. A wooden boardwalk crosses from the campground to the ocean.

Reservations aren't accepted; payment may be made with cash or credit cards (or personal checks with Social Security numbers printed on them). Cost is $20 per night. Pets are allowed on leashes. Frisco Campground is open April through October. Golden Age discounts are honored.

OCRACOKE ISLAND

Teeter's Campground
British Cemetery Road, Ocracoke Village
(252) 928-3135, (800) 705-5341
Near the heart of Ocracoke Village, tucked in a shady grove of trees, Teeter's Camp-

ground offers 2 full-hookup sites, 12 sites with electricity and water, and 10 tent sites. Rates for two people begin at $20 a night for tents, $25 a night for electricity and water, and $30 a night for full hookups.

Hot showers are available. Six charcoal grills are installed at tent sites, and each site has a picnic table. There aren't any public laundry facilities on Ocracoke, so don't plan to machine wash any of your clothes while camping here.

Teeter's Campground is open March 1 through November. Reservations are recommended on holiday weekends. Credit cards are not accepted.

Beachcomber Campground and Ocracoke Station
NC 12, Ocracoke Village
(252) 928-4031

Less than a mile from Silver Lake and the nearest beach access, Beachcomber Campground has 29 sites with electricity and water and 7 tent sites. Rates for two people begin at $25 a night for tents. There's a $5.00 charge per person for more than six people. RV hookups are also available for $30 to $35 a night. Different rates apply for holidays.

Hot showers and fully equipped bathrooms are available, as are picnic tables and grills. A deli on the premises offers

Even though it looks like an inviting spot, camping on the beach is not permitted. Local officers and National Park Service personnel patrol the areas regularly and will ask you to leave.

fresh sandwiches. Gourmet groceries and a large wine selection are available, as well as beach supplies, souvenirs, and T-shirts.

Leashed pets are allowed at Beachcomber for a one-time fee of $5.00. The campground is open year-round. Reservations are recommended for summer camping.

Ocracoke Campground (NPS)
NC 12, Ocracoke Island
(800) 365-CAMP (reservations)
http://reservations.nps.gov

An oceanfront campground 3 miles east of Ocracoke Village just behind the dunes, this National Park Service campground maintains 136 campsites. No utility hookups or laundry facilities are available, but there are cold showers, a dumping station, drinking water, charcoal grills, and flush toilets. As at all Park Service campgrounds, stays are limited to 14 days. The facility is open May through September.

Since most of these sites sit directly in the sun, bring some sort of shade. Long tent stakes help to hold down tents against the often fierce winds that whip through this campground. The breeze, however, is a welcome relief from summer heat. Bug spray is a must in the summer.

Ocracoke is the only campground on the island operated by the National Park Reservation Service. Call or visit the Web site from mid-May through mid-September to make reservations. Major credit cards are accepted.

Sites are assigned on a first-come, first-served basis. All sites cost $20 per night.

SHOPPING

Shopping on the Outer Banks is a unique pursuit—and a busy one on rainy days when attention shifts from the beach to the stores. Still, rain or shine, there's so much to explore and to be found on side streets in quiet villages or between the Beach Road (North Carolina Highway 12) and the Bypass (U.S. Highway 158), not necessarily visible from the road. So take your time. Consider it a treasure hunt.

Outer Banks retailers make the vast majority of their income during the peak season, but as tourism during the quieter seasons increases, more shops remain open throughout more of the year. The holiday season is particularly strong in Manteo. If you haven't visited Roanoke Island lately, you'll be amazed at the interesting new shops you'll find there.

The growth isn't just occurring on Roanoke Island, however; every year brings a sprinkling of new shops among the established favorites. You'll find usual souvenirs, such as seashells, inexpensive T-shirts, and lighthouses in every form imaginable, but a great many boutiques offer one-of-a-kind gifts, fine arts, and crafts. Young kids love the big stores filled aisle after aisle with colorful souvenirs, and the ubiquitous stores where nothing costs more (or less) than a dollar. Bring the little ones to one of these places to pick out a special memento (or several).

If your tastes are more sophisticated, you'll find plenty of places to indulge your material desires. Corolla and Duck shopping is higher-end and contemporary, catering to urban-dwelling tourists. Shop owners in these towns cater to big spenders. Kitty Hawk, Kill Devil Hills, and Nags Head shopping is more modest, geared toward casual shoppers and vacation browsers. Manteo shopping has gone full circle in recent years, and now it's a wonderful blend of antiques shops, art and craft galleries, and high-end shops. Many people cross the bridge to Manteo just to shop. Hatteras Island shopping is the most sporadic of all. Mostly, its little shops and galleries are spread out. Hatteras Island vacationers aren't usually die-hard shoppers—they're mostly outdoor types who are in or on the water. Ocracoke Village shopping is quaintly wonderful, with shops all over the village. People stroll or bike around and stop in the shops casually. The shops are not upscale or stuffy and the goods are unique and affordable.

If your shopping pursuits are more for nourishment than indulgence, you'll find a variety of food stores. We have an abundance of seafood stores carrying fresh fish such as tuna, dolphin, wahoo, king mackerel, bluefish, snapper, croaker, and flounder, along with crabs, shrimp, mussels, clams, and oysters in season. The seafood at Seamark Foods—one is next to Wal-Mart in Kitty Hawk, another at the Outer Banks Mall in Nags Head—is reasonably priced, fresh, and diverse. The Food Lion grocery chain has stores spaced along the Outer Banks, so there's no need to carry perishables from home if you're coming for an extended stay. Many visitors, though, relish a change in pace and shop at the smaller stores.

Many shops have seasonal hours, and most close from December to March. During the height of the summer season, the majority are open seven days a week (some with extended evening hours). A good many shops in Southern Shores, Kitty Hawk, Kill Devil Hills, and Nags Head are open year-round, though not every day. Corolla and Hatteras shopping tends to be more seasonal, but some keep their doors open through the fall and winter.

Here is a list of some of our favorite shopping spots on the Outer Banks, organized by community beginning at the northern reaches of Corolla and Duck running south through Ocracoke Island. Outer Banks retailers offer service, goods, variety, and a hometown greeting that's second to none. And just to show how much Bankers appreciate your business, we'll share an Insiders' secret: There are unbeatable sales on the Outer Banks during our shoulder seasons.

COROLLA

Corolla, about 10 miles north of Duck, offers convenient and novel shopping along NC 12. We begin at the northernmost point. Most Corolla shops close in the off-season.

Austin Building
NC 12, Corolla
Winks of Corolla is the anchor of this shopping center near Historic Corolla Village. Winks is the oldest store in the area; it's been around since before NC 12 was opened to the public. Winks sells gas, sundries, groceries, snacks, drinks, toiletries, and any other convenience items you'll need. Next door is the **Corolla Post Office, Corolla Pizza,** and an ice-cream store. Nearby, across and down the street at the satellite building, is the ABC store, the only place you can buy packaged liquor.

Historic Corolla Village
This off-the-beaten-path section of town, which is really Corolla proper, was the original town center in the days of old Corolla. Today, you see remnants of old Corolla by walking down the dirt roads north of the lighthouse. New stores have

The MacArthur Center is an enormous mega-mall in nearby Norfolk, Virginia, and its big-name stores (Nordstrom, Dillards, Restoration Hardware, and the like) lure shoppers from all over North Carolina and Virginia. If you're a serious shopper, this is the place for you, only an hour and 15 minutes from the Outer Banks.

been built here as well, but in an old style that gives visitors the feeling of how things looked in old Corolla. Shop owners are proud to bring vitality back to this historic area and share the histories of their buildings with visitors. A walking-tour map also gives historic information. You can easily walk from The Whalehead Club to the lighthouse to the shops in Historic Corolla Village.

Outer Banks Style
NC 12, Corolla
(252) 453-4388
Outer Banks Style is housed in the old Kill Devil Hills lifesaving station, built in 1878. The Wright brothers walked on these floors, and some lifesavers from this station witnessed the world's first powered aircraft flight. Local lore also has it that a friendly ghost resides here.

Outer Banks Style offers a distinctive collection of fine art, decorative art, and handpainted furniture. Each item in this inviting shop is unique and handmade. You'll find the whimsical renderings and musings of Brian Andreas, whose art is known as StoryPeople. You'll be tempted by rugs, photography, artwork, furnishings, linens, and gifts.

Lighthouse Garden
Corolla Village Road and
Schoolhouse Road, Corolla
(252) 453-0171
Lighthouse Garden is located in the former Helen Parker House (c. 1920). The home has been restored to its original charm. The Lighthouse Garden brings the spirit of outdoor living with decor for porches, gardens, and homes. Silk flowers and topiaries, concrete statuary, botanical prints, locally crafted iron works, birdbaths, mosaic furniture, and candles are among the great finds.

Old Corolla Trading Company
Corolla Village Road, Corolla
(252) 453-9942
Just north of Lighthouse Garden, this store occupies a new cedar-sided building made

to look old. The shop has a nautical theme, with antiques, prints, pillows, lanterns, telescopes, and more. It's not just nautical though. It sells frames, weather vanes, vintage posters, gifts, and Bauer International Furniture, featuring refined leather, monhogany, and wicker items.

Spry Creek Dry Goods
Corolla Village Road, Corolla
(252) 453-0199

Spry Creek is a fun and funky shop. One step inside, and you may think you're in Tuscany or the Mediterranean. Bright yellow walls are a perfect backdrop for the Spanish, Mexican, and Portuguese pottery and ceramics on sale. Shoppers will delight in the jewelry, artwork, and decoys produced by local artisans. Mouth-blown glassware from Mexico, pampering soaps and linen sprays, and vivid stained-glass pieces round out the eclectic offerings.

The Island Bookstore
1130 Corolla Village Road, Corolla
(252) 453-2292

This shop is built on the site of Callie Parker's old general store. John Wilson IV (who has designed many of Manteo's historical reproductions) designed this new

building, reminiscent of a mercantile in the 1930s. Bill and Ursula, the owners of Island Bookstore, bring more than 35 years of bookselling experience to Corolla. Best sellers are discounted here, and books are available on just about any subject matter imaginable. Southern and regional books are well represented in this atmospheric bookshop.

Lightkeeper's Wife
Corolla Village Road, Corolla
(252) 453-4190

This adorable building is the restored outbuilding of the Lewark/Gray home housing The Cottage Collection. This boutique is a wonderful find, with dresses, sportswear, and hip clothing by Juicy Couture, Free People, and Seven Jeans. Jewelry, hats, bags and purses, and scarves round out the merchandise.

Corolla Light Town Center
NC 12, Corolla

The shops of Corolla Light Town Center are clustered outside the entrance to the Corolla Light development. Dining, shopping, and convenience items are found within. These are mostly seasonal shops, open from Easter through October.

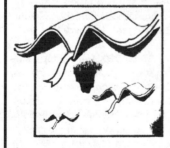

If you're looking for all things surfing, Gary can hook you up at the **Corolla Surf Shop.** This store and the one at TimBuck II carry a great selection of surfboards, plus clothing, shades, and shoes. Rentals and lessons are available. **Ocean Threads** specializes in swimwear for the entire family and features maternity, mastectomy, and long-torso suits. This shop is packed with lots of sportswear for men and women, including name brands such as Billabong, Airwalk, Rusty, Arnette, Oakley, Emeric, Janco, Roxy, Quicksilver, Rusty Girl, and more. The shop also carries hats, stickers, and incense.

Ocean Atlantic Rentals offers bikes, strollers, cribs, bedding, beach chairs, umbrellas, watersports gear—you name it. For anglers, **Corolla Bait and Tackle** has it all, including rods and reels, live bait, tackle and lures, advice, charter booking, and a friendly dog sitting by the door.

Surf Source
NC 12, Corolla
(252) 453-0222

This surf shop, in the same building as the gas station across from Monteray Plaza, offers lessons, rentals, gear, and clothing for men and women.

The Farmer's Daughter
NC 12, Corolla
(252) 453-9116

In the same building as Stan White Real Estate, The Farmer's Daughter adds country charm to your home. Choose from home accessories, crafts, decoys, collectibles (such as Department 56, Boyds Bears, and Byers' Choice babies), and a variety of gift items such as T-shirts, lighthouses, statues, and Christmas decorations. Local artisans' work is for sale, as is the world's first and only supply of saltwater fudge. This location is open year-round.

Monteray Shores Shopping Plaza
NC 12, Corolla

The plaza is anchored by **Food Lion** and speckled with several locations to buy ice cream or other goodies to taste between stops on your shopping excursion. The plaza has public restrooms and plenty of parking. This shopping center is the home of RC Theatres' Corolla location (see our Recreation chapter).

Gray's Department Store is an Outer Banks clothing tradition for men and women. Celebrating more than 50 years of business, Gray's offers name-brand swimwear and sportswear, a wide variety of top-quality T-shirts, sweatshirts, and everyday shoes. **Ocean Annie's** sells handcrafted functional and decorative pottery, jewelry, wind chimes, fine gifts, and gourmet coffee. **Outer Banks Outdoors** is an outfitter for hiking and climbing clothing and offers a variety of T-shirts, ladies' wear, and children's clothing, plus jewelry and souvenirs. This sporting goods business is operated by Kitty Hawk Kites and features an outdoor climbing wall in the courtyard. Kayak tours and hang-gliding lessons are available.

Serendipity is a gift shop that sells fun cards, frames, wind chimes, and unique items. **Top Nails of Corolla** will help you keep a smooth polished look while visiting the Outer Banks. T-shirts, swimwear, and beach equipment are all available at **Just for the Beach. Donna Designs** sells handpainted clothing adorned with crabs, fish, turtles, flowers, frogs, and many other motifs. The baby clothes are adorable. The store also sells gift items, jewelry, and painted furniture. **Sound Feet Shoes,** with several Outer Banks locations, is the most trusted name in shoes on the Outer Banks, offering name-brand shoes including Birkenstock, Naot, Dansko, Nike, Adidas, Reebok, Saucony, and more.

Birthday Suits/OBX Gear is a beachwear boutique carrying casual sportswear and accessories for the entire family. The store is packed with an extensive line of swimwear for men, women, and children. Check out the selection of sunglasses, shoes, accessories, and swim goggles. **Bacchus Wine & Cheese** carries one of the most extensive selections of domestic and imported wines on the Outer Banks as well as wine accessories and delicious deli sandwiches. **Dockside North Seafood Market,** on the other end of the plaza from Bacchus, sells fresh fish, scallops, shrimp, clams, crabmeat, and oysters in season.

In front of Monteray Plaza is a shopping strip that includes many more dining options; see our Restaurants chapter. In this same center, **Outer Banks Video** stocks a large selection of movies and allows vacationers to rent.

Old Stony's Beer and Wine
NC 12, Pine Island
(252) 457-1050

Right across from the Pine Island beach access, Old Stony's specializes in adult libations: imports, domestics, microbrews, kegs, and wines of all kinds. If you're destined to the beach, you'll find coolers, ice, soda, mixers, boogie boards, chairs, and anything else you'll need.

TimBuck II Shopping Village
785 Sunset Boulevard, NC 12, Corolla
(252) 453-9888
www.timbuckii.com

TimBuck II is a shopping, dining, and entertainment village with more than 60 shops and restaurants. The entire family could spend a day here, with everyone happily entertained. Shops are geared to all interests, restaurants abound, and the entertainment factor is high. We can't list every single store at TimBuck II. But we'll give you a sampling of what's available and let you discover the rest on your own. While you shop, you can drop the kids off at the **Corolla Raceway** for go-karting and bumper boating, or the **Golf Links** for miniature golf. **Kitty Hawk Kites** offers kite-flying lessons, and **Kitty Hawk Sports** offers parasailing, kayaking, JetSkiing, and more. Everyone can meet for a meal at one of many restaurants.

Ground-level parking, covered decks, public restrooms, a recreation area, and playground are features. The shopping center is open daily from Memorial Day to Labor Day from 10:00 A.M. to 9:00 P.M. During the rest of the year, individual shop

Bargain hunter's alert: The best time to shop on the Outer Banks is during the off-season. You'll find deals on many things from swimsuits to sunglasses to surfboards. Retailers offer their greatest deals around Thanksgiving and Christmas, right before they close their doors for the winter.

schedules may vary, and only some shop-keepers stay open year-round. Operating hours in the shoulder seasons vary from store to store.

Joan's is a staple at TimBuck II. Owner Joan Estes offers complete interior design and furnishing services. Her boutique has home furnishings and accents, including upholstery, dressers, nightstands, silk flower arrangements, lamps, pictures, and wall hangings. We found exquisite glass decanters, mango soap, lotus flower candles, and hydrangea flower arrangements that took our breath away. Joan tries to keep her shop open all year. **Tar Heel Trading Company** carries American hand-crafted decorator items, accessories, and serving pieces, puzzle boxes, pottery, wind chimes, and designer jewelry. This popular business has several locations. At the Corolla shop look for contemporary cottage decor, including art for the walls and exquisite blown glassware.

Looking for Beanie Babies? **Corolla Book 'n Card** has those popular little critters as well as beautiful gifts and items for the entire family—posters, candles, Corolla souvenirs, greeting cards, florals, Jelly Bellies, jewelry, and local T-shirts and hats. A large children's department sells hats, shirts, toys, books, and games. And the store offers a wide selection of local books and best-sellers in hardcover and paperback. It's open from Easter through Thanksgiving.

Island Tobacco houses a selection of cigars, tobacco, pipes, and related items, plus fine art and prints. **Carolina Moon** is one of our favorite places on the Outer Banks to shop for gifts, ornaments, jewelry, cards, and New Age notions. **Michael's Gems and Glass** is a fun shop for kids of all ages. It offers rocks and minerals, fossils, marbles, and other toys plus sterling silver jewelry.

Cotton Gin offers quality clothing and gifts, including Department 56 collectibles and Tom Clark gnomes, decoys, and carvings. The store's primary location is a sprawling barn-red building on US 158 on the Currituck mainland. The Corolla shop features gifts, unique bedding, and bath and kitchen supplies.

Gourmet Kitchen Emporium and Confectionery features a full line of specialty foods including pasta, jams, jellies, and hot spicy stuff. You can also find unique culinary gadgets, kitchen accessories and appliances, gift baskets, linens, and cookbooks.

Try My Nuts Nut Company sells gourmet nuts and candies, Try My Nuts apparel, and Wall of Fire sauces and nuts, which are so hot the owners say they'll hurt your feelings. Don't believe it? Free samples are offered daily. **The Glass Shop** sells bright handpainted glassware and accessories by local designer Renee Hilimire, who can custom design everything from stemware to furniture to floorcloths. If you're worried about getting the glass home in one piece, they'll ship it to you.

Gray's Department store is huge, selling the largest selection of Tommy Bahama and Fresh Produce sportswear on the Outer Banks. Gray's sells T-shirts, sweats, hats, sportswear, and swimwear for the whole family. **. . . get the picture?** is a one-hour photo store selling cameras, film, batteries, frames, photographs, and gift items. A northern location of **Nags Head Hammocks** sells handcrafted rope hammocks and swings.

Casual Creations offers golf accessories and unique outfits. Great jewelry, gifts, and swimwear can also be found here. **Corolla Candles** is a candle lover's dream come true. Hundreds of fragrances, colors, and styles of candles are available. **DogNutz** features items for more than 350 breeds; check out the OBK9 line.

Spend some time in **Miss Kitty's Old Time Photo** studio. Choose from 3,000 costumes and several settings to produce old-time photos. Once you select your costumes, whether a Civil War hero, a 1920s flapper, or a cowgirl, it only takes three minutes to see the results. Antique-style frames are available.

Surfside Casuals sells swimwear, surfwear, sportswear, dresses, sandals, jewelry, sunglasses, and everything you want to wear at the beach. **Mystic Jewel** brightens and calms your mind, body, and spirit with their eclectic offerings. Unique candles, semiprecious jewelry, and home accents help make up their incredible selection. **Ocean Threads** sells swimwear for the entire family, plus name-brand sportswear for men and women. You'll also find stickers, sunglasses, sandals, and more. Labels include Roxy, Hurley, Volcom, Billabong, Quicksilver and Rusty. **Mustang Sally's** offers clothing, jewelry accessories, and gifts for creative people. **Sarandebity** carries hot trendy items for the home and garden. Decor, fashion accessories, and collectible items are generally bright and funky.

If you're hungry after all that shopping, you're at the right place. TimBuck II has more than 10 places to eat at, including ice-cream shops, a pizza parlor, a deli, a Subway, a fudge shop, and sit-down restaurants. See our Restaurants chapter for some of the options.

DUCK

Duck is a shopper's best friend—and a budget's nemesis. People from all over the Banks come here for spending sprees. This small village is packed with shopping centers tucked into small nooks on the waterfront or in the trees.

Duck is walkable; in fact walking is preferable to maneuvering a vehicle around all the SUV-filled parking lots and on the crowded two-lane road. A paved bike path runs the length of the village, making it safe to walk from place to place.

Parking is at a premium in Duck, so once you find a space, hold on to it. Remember, the sound of rain is every shopper's battle cry, so if you want to avoid crowds, don't go on a rainy day.

Barrier Island Office Plaza
NC 12, Duck

This shopping center is on the north end of the village, across from Sunset Grill and Raw Bar. In it you'll find **The Duck-Duck Shop,** which houses the post office. **The Duck-Duck Shop** also sells North Carolina decoys and duck-themed gifts, greeting cards and post cards, and prints. It is open year-round. **Eden Spa and Salon** is a full-service salon and day spa where you can pamper yourself with massage therapy, manicures, pedicures, salt rubs, facials, and more.

Duck Waterfront Shops
NC 12, Duck

These shops provide all kinds of shopping opportunities. **Sunset Ice Cream** is just the spot to sip or slurp a refreshment. Entertainment is provided by dozens of mallards and other web-footed friends paddling around in the Currituck Sound shallows just below the railings. It's open Easter through Thanksgiving. At **Duck's General Store** you'll find a wide variety of gifts. Some of the most popular items include finely crafted sterling silver jewelry; a wide selection of T-shirts, sweatshirts, and hats; postcards and humorous greeting cards; and books on North Carolina and the Outer Banks. It's open year-round.

Islands By Amity offers stylish clothing from such lines as Juicy Couture, Three Dot, and Seven Jeans. Islands has a large aromatherapy section with lotions, soaps, and candles. You'll also see lots of artistic gifts and jewelry, including sterling silver baby gifts and music, picture frames, and stuffed animals. It's open year-round. **Barr-ee Station and Catalogue Outlet** features low prices on name-brand men's and women's clothing, shoes, and accessories—priced up to 50 percent off the regular retail price. And **Barr-ee**

Station Swimwear Outlet, inside the same shop, sells discounted name-brand swimwear at up to 50 percent off.

For one-of-a-kind clothing for women and children, visit **Donna Designs,** a shop featuring handpainted artwork—crabs, fish, turtles, flowers, and frogs, to name a few subjects—on cotton T-shirts including crop-top tees for adults and children, sweatshirts, sundresses, and French terry. A line of gifts and home decor items called "Out Of The Blue" was introduced recently, featuring lampshades and lamps, glassware, toy chests, and children's tables and chairs all handpainted in Donna's inimitable style. **North Beach Outfitters** sells outdoor clothing for men and women and adventure gear, including kayaks. High-end sunglasses, such as Oakley, Revo, and Costa del Mar, and rack sunglasses are available. Names include Patagonia, The North Face, Royal Robbins, Horny Toad, Columbia, Naot, Teva, Reef, Ocean Kayak, and Necky. **Candy and Corks** offers a nice variety of wines and yummy sweets. Fudge, taffy, chocolate, and some classic candies are all available.

In a newer section of this building are several exciting shops. **Dazzles** is a magical shop with mobiles, hanging glass lanterns, whimsical plant stakes, chimes, jewelry, unique cards, frames, doormats, candles, and many more items. **Gray's** sells clothing for men, women, and children, including a large selection of Tommy Bahama and Fresh Produce. **The Kid's Store** has kites, toys, games—something for all ages. **Sea Dragon Gallery** offers exquisite American-made crafts, with local, North Carolina, and national artists represented. **Cynthia's Lingerie and Home Decor** is a sensual shop, right on the waterfront. Inside this heavenly smelling store, you'll find sexy or sensible nightgowns and pajamas, stuffed animals, baskets, soaps, candles, photos, and items for the home. **Life's a Beach, A Lily Pulitzer Shop** stocks fun, colorful dresses and clothing for women and girls plus shoes and accessories. Lily fans were happy to see this shop come to Duck. Be sure to stop in **Duck's Cottage** in the Waterfront Shops parking lot. Inside this inviting building, you'll find best-selling books and a great choice of more eclectic reads. Tempting pastries, coffees, and teas round out their offerings.

Tommy's Gourmet Market and Wine Emporium
NC 12, Duck
(252) 261–8990
www.tommysmarket.com
At Tommy's, pick up delicious, fresh-baked goods such as pastries, turnovers, breads, bagels, and doughnuts. The deli features roasted ham and chicken, ready-to-eat spiced shrimp, sandwiches, fresh salads, fresh-baked pies, and daily luncheon specials. Tommy's is famous for its Angus steaks, aged for 21 days and cut to order. Tommy's maintains an extensive wine selection and carries imported beers in addition to a full range of groceries. It's open March through New Year's.

Wee Winks Square & Vicinity
NC 12, Duck
Wee Winks, across the street from Wee Winks Square, is a practical stop for a wide variety of needs. Wee Winks is the place for last-minute food and gas purchases or for a newspaper. An ABC package store is in the vicinity.

We dare you to make it through the **Lucky Duck** without buying at least one remembrance of your visit. Every nook and cranny is filled with unique home accessories, local arts and crafts, pictures, shells, woven throws, bath items, books, and even fudge. This store is open from March through December. **Artisan's Boutique,** inside the Lucky Duck, offers an eclectic combination of ladies' apparel, T-shirts, women's hats, shoes, jewelry, and gift items, all of which bring to mind an artistic touch.

Stop by **Beach Essentials,** open March through October, for boogie boards, lotions, rafts, and lots more. Children are fascinated by the shop's hermit crabs. At

Lady Victorian you'll find contemporary styles for today's woman. Outfits and suits are the emphasis here, in cotton, silk, and linen plus quality dresses, evening wear, intimate apparel, travel accessories, and personal items such as bath products, soaps, and powders. Lady Victorian is open year-round.

All kids big and little should make a stop at **Kitty Hawk Kites.** They stock a remarkable selection of toys for all ages. Shoppers can choose from a full range of kites, wind chimes, pirate treasures, water toys, and even t-shirts and sweatshirts. Across the street at **Carolina Outdoors,** outdoorsy types find stylish travel wear. Nearby at **Kitty Hawk Sports,** all types of beach-lifestyle clothes are available. Swimsuits, sandals, pants, dresses, and jackets are just some of the trendy items they carry.

Nags Head Hammocks
NC 12, Duck
(252) 261–1062
www.nagshead.com
Tucked into the trees on the waterfront, this shop is huge, with plenty of display space for the hammocks, footstools, and porch swings made by this company. These are quality, handmade hammocks durable enough to last for years. Nags Head Hammocks has numerous Outer Banks locations.

Loblolly Pines Shopping Center
NC 12, Duck
Loblolly Pines is a complex of shops and eateries where you can purchase anything from decals to precious gems. Whet your appetite with an ice-cream cone or sweet treat as well. **Yesterday's Jewels** carries an interesting collection of old and new jewelry, including gold and sterling silver. **Just for the Beach** sells everything you need for a good day at the beach, including towels, chairs, coolers, sunglasses, buckets, and accessories. It also rents chairs, umbrellas, boogie boards, and more. If it's T-shirts you're looking for, **T-Shirt World** has thousands with all sorts of decals and sayings

and Outer Banks motifs. **Outer Banks Running Company** sells running shoes in trusted brands, and the staff is very helpful with fittings. The shop also sells running wear and workout clothes and has information on local races.

Osprey Landing
NC 12, Duck

Osprey Landing is a smaller shopping area overlooking the sound. **Outer Barks** is a must-stop for dog and cat lovers. Check out the terrific selection of jewelry, ceramics, art, clothing, and pet accessories. This shop even offers life preservers for your beloved pooch. Bring Fido along and he'll get his picture mounted on Outer Barks's wall of fame. Once a week in the afternoon, your best friend can enjoy complimentary doggie daquiris at Yappy Hour. Arf-d'hoeuvres are served, and pooches can create a paw painting. Call Outer Barks, (252) 261-6279, for the Yappy Hour schedule. Outer Barks is open March through the end of December.

Tarheel Fine Jewelry specializes in jewelry sales, service, and repair. Tarheel's collection includes nautical jewelry, crystal gift items, and Seiko watches.

Just north of Osprey Landing are two other spots. **Sound Feet Shoes** sells the biggest selection of shoes on the Outer Banks, including Birkenstock, Naot, Dansko, Nike, Reebok, and more. A branch of **Ocean Atlantic Rentals** is also here; it rents any items you might have left behind, such as linens, towels, cribs, baby items, bikes, and watersports gear.

Scarborough Lane Shoppes
NC 12, Duck

Scarborough Lane features amenities you won't find elsewhere in Duck Village, including covered parking, sheltered walkways, and public restrooms. Most of these shops are open part of the week March through December; in summer, they tend to stay open late, seven days a week.

Look to the **Island Trader** for sterling silver jewelry and a variety of gifts, plus home and garden accessories. Here you'll find baskets and candles, kitchen linens, and North Carolina food products with a flair—hot sauces, chutneys, and barbecue sauces. **Exotic Cargo** "brings the world to you," featuring handcrafted home accents, furniture, sterling silver jewelry, sundresses, sarongs, incense, and much more from India, Indonesia, Thailand, Mexico, and Guatemala. This shop has five other locations on the Outer Banks.

At **Tar Heel Trading Co.,** you'll see silver and gold jewelry and a wide variety of elegant items handcrafted in America by local and nationally known artists. Tar Heel is known for its collection of wooden puzzle boxes and museum-quality wildlife art. Different items are available at the store's other two locations, in Sea Holly Square in Kill Devil Hills and TimBuck II in Corolla. **Confetti Clothing Company** has casual sportswear for the whole family. It stocks clothing made by small design firms. The shop carries novelty items and home accessories. Check out the home furnishings, and also look for silver and ceramic gifts. This eclectic shop is open year-round. **Toy-rific** features top-of-the-line playthings for infants, toddlers, and school-age kids, including stuffed animals, puzzles, beach toys, and kites. **The Wooden Feather** offers something really different in Duck for decorators, decoy collectors, and wildlife enthusiasts. Even if you don't think you are one of those people, you should stop by this gallery. Handmade decoys, wildlife sculptures, art furnishings, prints, fish carvings, birdhouses, and collectibles with a natural theme fill this charming shop. Some of the bird carvings are made by the owner's father, and these are fascinating, amazingly detailed works of art. Bird-watchers find supplies here.

Birthday Suits is a favorite local store specializing in bathing suits for adults and children; it also has hip clothes for men and women, sandals, jewelry, hats, and more. Many visitors return to this shop every year for a new suit. Be sure to check out the annual sale in January.

Diane Strehan, owner of **Diane's Lavish Linens,** will help you add just the right touch to your beach cottage or help you pick out a special gift, maybe for yourself. The shop has embroidered towels, face cloths, lace tablecloths, curtains, and body luxuries, like specialty soaps and lotions. Vera Bradley products are available, as are window coverings and gifts for little ones.

Carolina Moon Gallery has been a favorite store among locals for more than 20 years. This stellar store has fun jewelry, pottery, and clever home furnishings. Vintage clothing and puzzles and games for the kids are also available. Christmas lovers will delight in a trip to the **Christmas Mouse.** Stunning ornaments and holiday decor abound here. The mind, body, and spiritual powers of gemstones are celebrated at the **Mystic Jewel.** Shoppers will find jewelry to love year-round. The **Nags Head Shop** takes care of shoppers from head to toe with sunglasses, hats, shoes and sandals, coffee, smoothies, and bagels.

Outer Banks Bear Factory is a fun stop for the kids. Choose a bear, pig, or elephant and watch it be sewn up. Then dress your new friend in an outfit chosen at this store. Vintage collectables like tin signs, furniture, linens, and other home features are featured at the **Rusty Hinge. Sand Castle Arts** specializes in arts that are both fine and functional. Dinnerware, lamps, clocks, tiles, and photography are some of the items stocked here. For some great snacks to take home for gifts, stop in **Try My Nuts.** Sauces, chocolates, and other treats are sold here, too.

Scarborough Faire
NC 12, Duck

Scarborough Faire features a series of boutiques and businesses in a garden setting. The facade is reminiscent of the architecture of old-time lifesaving stations. The buildings are set into a grove of trees, and the shops are connected by a walkway through the woods, creating one of the shadiest spots in Duck in midsummer.

Rainbow Harvest is an eclectic gift boutique featuring American-made crafts. This colorful and fun-filled shop has delighted its customers with the creative and the unusual. Rainbow Harvest is known for its fabulous collection of hand-crafted jewelry, including exclusive Outer Banks representations of world-renowned designer Ed Levin. If you're looking for a keepsake of your visit to the Outer Banks, Rainbow Harvest carries a wide range of Christmas ornaments that can be especially personalized just for you. Its enchanting collection of clocks and other home furnishings is simply delightful. Also check out its toy collection.

The Island Bookstore sells established works of fiction, discount hardcover best sellers, a wide variety of nonfiction, children's books, and specialty selections. The collection of works by Southern authors is extensive, and you also can find audio books and jazz and blues on compact disc. Visit the new upstairs addition, which features expanded offerings in many subjects, including travel, art, war, sports, and cooking. It's a book-lover's dream. Special orders are welcome. The shop is open year-round.

Solitary Swan Antiques features cherry, pine, and walnut furniture and accessories such as porcelains, glassware, and pewter, plus traditional crafts and outdoor garden pieces, decoys, and folk art. The shop is open all year. **Ocean Annie's,** another Outer Banks store chain with a location in just about every town, is tucked under the trees at the back of this center. Ocean Annie's sells handmade pottery by a variety of artists. Some of it is functional, some decorative, and it's all beautiful. Gift items include wooden boxes, chimes, clocks, jewelry, and frames. The gourmet coffee beans smell so good you'll want a cup, but you'll have to get the beans to go and make yourself a cup at home. **The Culinary Duck** has everything for the kitchen—cookbooks, utensils, pots and pans, sauces, and more. A visit to **Rub A Dub Duck Bath Shop** will set you up with everything you need to pamper yourself, including soaps, bath oils, aromatherapy products, and more.

Sticking with OBX

Chances are if you've looked into any aspect of the Outer Banks, you've run into its alter-ego designation: OBX. This seemingly official shorthand has made its way into print and Web sites everywhere, and most people seem to understand what it means . . . but it wasn't always that way. In fact, sales of the first euro-style OBX stickers were usually preceded by an explanation of what OBX meant.

The oval euro-decal phenomenon itself had its beginnings in 1969 with none other than the United Nations. Most license plates at the time looked the same regardless of the country of origin, so the UN developed codes for the oval stickers, and they were issued in addition to license plates. The stickers eventually made their way into the U.S. pop culture first as status symbols for imported cars and later as a way to identify preferred vacation spots, like MV for Martha's Vineyard.

In 1994, Outer Banks local Jim Douglas, owner of Chilli Peppers restaurant, was sitting at a cafe on Nantucket Island and noticed people buying oval stickers with the letters ACK. He thought the Outer Banks ought to have something similar. Jim's plan was to sell a few thousand oval stickers with OB for a small profit, but when the X was added, the little stickers caught on. Not only did the X act to make OB plural, it subliminally borrowed from everything X in our culture, from the X generation to the X games and all things X-treme. And what started as a small venture for Jim gradually mushroomed into a true phenomenon.

The first stickers were sold at the Stop-N-Shop in Kill Devil Hills in 1994, and partners Jill and Greg Bennett started selling OBX clothing items at their swimsuit shop, Birthday Suits, in 1996. With any good idea will come imitators, so Jim and company formed OBX Stock Inc, and after a four year battle, successfully registered OBX as a legal trademark. OBX Gear is the headquarters for all things OBX, and only authorized dealers may sell the trademarked merchandise. As the OBX designation has taken on a life of its own, the entrepreneurs have lent the three letters to everything from surf contests and hang-gliding competitions to charity fund-raisers and art shows.

Since the euro-decal phenomenon has matured, the multiletter designations can be for anything from "anytown USA" to political statements. Some oval stickers have become as arcane as personalized license plates, with casual observers trying to puzzle out just what the letters might mean. If parody is a complement, the OBX oval sticker gets high marks. A recent spoof has the letters OBX in a black rectangle with small letters below stating: THINK OUTSIDE THE OVAL.

The refreshing **Urban Cottage** offers home furnishings and gifts that you won't find anywhere else. It's a home decor boutique with everything from sofas and beds to candles and glasses. Fabulous furniture pieces are handmade and can be custom ordered to suit your needs. You'll swoon over the Sandra Drennen bedding and pillows, which are handcrafted from antique and European linens and dish towels. Housewares, lamps, rugs, mirrors, wall art, candles, unique gifts, and handpainted peppermills and glassware are just some of the other things you'll find here. If you need help putting it all together, the friendly, talented ladies at this shop offer interior design services.

For unique jewelry and gifts from Scotland, Ireland, and England, visit **Cara Magnus Celtic.** Within the walls of **Mango's Boutique** are fine women's fashions and great shoes, along with jewelry and accessories. **Smash Hit Tennis & Golf** has clothing for men, women, and children and leading brands of equipment.

Lilly's Closet stocks cool clothing for boys and girls. Adorable shoes and accessories are sold here as well. **Gray's Department Store** outfits shoppers with shoes, clothing, hats, and more. Tommy Bahama, Fresh Produce, and OBX apparel can be found at this popular Outer Banks store.

Duck Village Outfitters
NC 12, Duck
(252) 261-7222
This funky shop looks like it should be on a Caribbean island, but here it is in the heart of Duck, next to the Burger King and gas station. DVO sells surfwear for all four seasons as well as surfboards, wetsuits, kayaks and kayaking gear, bikes and bike-related stuff, skateboards and the accompanying hard goods, shoes, and sunglasses. You can rent sports gear and bikes, too.

Duck Soundside Shoppes
NC 12, Duck
For fine women's apparel, unique jewelry, and accessories, stop in at **La Rive Boutique.** The focus is on handpainted cloth-

ing featuring motifs such as fish, flowers, fruit, cats, and dogs rendered in bold colors. Many of the clothing lines come from California, so the fabric used is wearable year-round. The shop is open year-round.

To add country charm to your home, visit **The Farmer's Daughter,** which sells home accessories, crafts, decoys, collectibles (such as Department 56, Boyds Bearstones, and Byers' Choice babies), and a variety of gift items such as lighthouses, statues, T-shirts, and Christmas decorations. This shop is open year-round.

A location of **Surfside Casuals** offers thousands of swimsuits by names such as Roxy, Raisins, Jantzen, Quicksilver, Billabong, Rusty, Roxanne, and others. There are eight locations of this store on the Outer Banks. **Bob's Bait and Tackle** is Duck's only tackle shop. Come here for live bait, lures, tackle, rods and reels, charter information, and advice.

Greenleaf Gallery
NC 12, Duck
(252) 261-2009
On the southern end of the village, Greenleaf Gallery is considered the classiest gallery on the Outer Banks. You'll find the work of several accomplished local artists, including painter Rick Tupper, who owns the gallery with his wife, Didi. Didi sets a high mark for inclusion in her gallery, so everything here is finely crafted and one of a kind. Glass, wood, oil, watercolor, fiber, pottery, and sculpture are among the mediums featured. See our Arts and Culture chapter for more information.

SOUTHERN SHORES

The Marketplace
US 158, MP 1, Southern Shores
The Marketplace in Southern Shores is the large shopping center on the north side of US 158 at MP 1. A **Food Lion** grocery store and a CVS pharmacy are its anchor stores. The following are the specialty shops that fill out The Marketplace selection.

Island Opticians is a good place for emergency eyeglass repair or replacement. The shop also has a selection of sunglasses—both prescription and non-prescription. **Robin's Fine Jewelry** has a loyal local following. A stunning array of rings, bracelets, necklaces, and other jewelry items will catch your eyes. The shop also offers stone replacement, remounting, and ring-sizing services.

Cap't Party has a huge selection of necessities for your party or wedding, including decorations, balloons, invitations, imprinted napkins, and catering supplies. In addition, the store carries birthday and anniversary supplies, Beanie Babies, candy, and every imaginable sort of party favor. The store is open year-round. **Total Communications** is an Outer Banks source for pagers, cellular phones, and two-way radios. Weekly rentals are available along with Internet access.

Miss Lizzie carries clothes for women in size 4 to extra large, from formal wear to jeans to jackets, in stylish cuts and fabrics. Jewelry, purses, belts, and more are also available. The **Wellness Center of the Outer Banks** is the chiropractic office of Dan Goldberg, and vacationers are welcome if they need an adjustment or wellness care. **Dollar General** competes with **Dollar Tree** across the highway with a broad selection of inexpensive items. **Movie Gallery** always hops—in the winter, it's where the locals catch up on island happenings. The shop rents and sells films on VCR and DVD and has video games. **Women's Total Fitness** is an exclusive workout club for women.

The U.P.S. Store provides 26 business communication and postal services all under one roof, including packaging, shipping, copying, faxing, and mailbox rental. If you've bought too much on vacation to easily cart home, owner Bart Smith will ship it for you.

Sea Breeze Florist specializes in fresh flowers and arrangements by designers on staff. Dried arrangements incorporate shells and flowers resulting in tasteful beach mementos. Nautical baskets are very popular, and Sea Breeze delivers balloons, plants, and flowers for all occasions. Weddings are a specialty. Sea Breeze offers worldwide FTD and Teleflora services. The florist is open throughout the year. A realty company, a pizza parlor, a bagel shop, a dry cleaner, and a Chinese restaurant add to the offerings at The Marketplace.

Southern Shores Crossing
1 Ocean Boulevard, Southern Shores
This fun shopping spot is tucked behind Southern Shores Realty, just past the traffic light on Ocean Boulevard. The upscale dining spot **Meridian 42** (see our Restaurants chapter) is located here along with a number of tempting shops.

Diva Day Spa is a full-service day spa offering massages, facials, and nail care in a friendly, upscale environment. You can find catalog clothing at the **Barr-ee Station** outlet. **Knitting Addiction** fills all your knitting needs with the latest yarns and accessories. Astonish someone special with a gift from **Millennium Jewelers,** which features a selection of keepsake pieces.

KITTY HAWK

Central Garden Center & Nursery
US 158, MP ¼, Kitty Hawk
(252) 261–7195
This family-owned and -operated business has been serving the area for more than 40 years. The garden center sells indoor plants, shrubs, and trees plus annuals and perennials. Landscape services are also available, and you'll find Christmas trees and wreaths here at the holidays. It's open year-round.

Islander Flags
US 158, MP ¼, Kitty Hawk
(252) 261–6266
www.flagfinder.com
Islander Flags specializes in custom flags. The professionals here can help you design a flag to suit your needs, or they

can turn a logo or artwork into a flag. This is a big store, and you'll be surprised at all the flags in stock—decorative flags, military flags, national and state flags, marine flags, and more. This shop is next to Coastal Auto Mart and is open all year.

The Shoreside Center
US 158, MP 1, Kitty Hawk

This center features national chains including **Wal-Mart, Radio Shack, Subway, Dollar Tree, Cato's,** and **McDonald's.** The shops are open year-round. **Natural Creations Fine Jewelry** is a locally owned shop selling a variety of contemporary and traditional jewelry. **Seamark Foods** is a large grocery store with a terrific bakery, deli, and salad bar. Seamark has an extensive selection of cheeses and wines as well as other gourmet foods not always available in other supermarkets on the Outer Banks. Seamark carries a large selection of fresh fish, shellfish (including live lobsters), and everything else you need to fix a seafood feast. There's another location in Nags Head at the Outer Banks Mall. Both stores are open year-round.

Carawan Seafood
US 158, MP 1, Kitty Hawk
(252) 261–2120

Situated on the lot in front of The Shoreside Center, locally owned Carawan Seafood sells fresh local fish and shellfish in season plus flown-in fish, seafood, and live lobsters. We know quite a few Insiders who frequent this shop several times a week. The store also carries a growing selection of wine and beer, gourmet food items, seashells, lures, and tackle. An

In summer months, food stores are exceptionally busy during late afternoon and just before dinnertime, particularly on weekends. Early morning and late evening are the least crowded hours to purchase groceries.

expanded area next to the seafood shop sells Southwestern crafts, including rugs, pottery, dolls, jewelry, and gift items. Carawan is open year-round.

Ocean Centre
NC 12, MP 1½, Kitty Hawk

This inviting band of shops is located across the road and south of Kitty Hawk Pier. **Surfside Casuals** has an amazing amount of name-brand swimsuits and beachwear. **Books N Things** has best sellers and books for the beach, plus gifts and souvenirs. **Haircanes Category 2** is a full-service salon offering the latest hair styles. **Island Art Supply** stocks anything your inner artist desires.

Ambrose Furniture
US 158, MP 2, Kitty Hawk
(252) 261–4836

Ambrose Furniture is a family-owned and -operated furniture showroom that has conducted business in the area for more than 50 years. The store has a free design service and a qualified staff to assist you with your selection of furniture, blinds, and housewares. Check out the Corolla location at Monteray Shores Plaza. Both locations are open year-round.

Winks Grocery
NC 12, MP 2, Kitty Hawk
(252) 261–2555

Winks is what shopping is supposed to be like at a beach store—a sometimes-sandy floor, beach music filling the air, and an easy feeling. Winks has a deli, lots of edibles, beach supplies, beer, wine, and deli sandwiches, plus sweatshirts and T-shirts, toys, and gag gifts. The shop is open all year.

Old Firehouse Gourmet Foods & Winery
NC 12, MP 2, Kitty Hawk
(252) 261–5115

Inside this red building you'll find gourmet foods, spices, cheese, chocolate, cooking utensils, and so much more. Along with the great wine selection, wine tastings happen daily. Gift baskets are a specialty of this store. The proprietor is helpful and friendly and will help you make a decision.

Wave Riding Vehicles
US 158, MP 2½, Kitty Hawk
(252) 261-7952
www.waveridingvehicles.com
Wave Riding Vehicles is the largest surf shop on the Outer Banks. WRV stocks beach fashions, swimsuits, and gobs of T-shirts in the popular brands (see our Water Sports chapter for surfing equipment information). It also offers snowboarding equipment and apparel. It's open year-round.

Hotline Pink
US 158, MP 3½, Kitty Hawk
(252) 261-8164
In the hot-pink building next to Ace Hardware, this community thrift shop functions to benefit the local women's shelter. You'll see books, furniture, clothes, and household items. Remember this place when you're spring cleaning—donations are needed.

Your Office by the Sea
US 158, MP 4, Kitty Hawk
(252) 261-2400
Your Office by the Sea is a complete office supply store featuring computer supplies, stationary, and other accessories. You can rent typewriters, and a fax service is available. It's open year-round.

Kitty Hawk Plaza
US 158, MP 4, Kitty Hawk
(252) 261-8200
Daniel's Homeport is the largest store in this complex. Daniel's specializes in housewares and accessories such as candle holders, dried flowers, picture frames, wine racks, rugs, bedding, lamps, wicker and outdoor furniture, and much more. A full window-treatment department supplies curtains and shades, blinds, and shutters (some on order). In the same shopping center you'll find **Red's Army Navy,** a military surplus supply store, **Soundfeet Shoes** outlet shop, **Wild Birds**

Unlimited, and the **Children's Hospital of the King's Daughters Thrift Store,** where frugal folks find all sorts of used goods.

Buccaneer's Walk
US 158, MP 4, Kitty Hawk
Right next to Capt'n Frank's hot dog restaurant is Buccaneer's Walk, an attractive shopping complex fashioned after 19th-century fishing and whaling villages and coastal places the owners have visited. **Capt'n Frank's Peanut Shop** sells, of course, peanuts, in addition to candy, Carolina stuff, candles, linens, and gifts.

Coastal Attitude offers a variety of home accessories, and decorating items. **The Toy Boat** toy store offers diversionary wares for kids of all ages. There are puzzles, games, dolls, baby toys, toddler toys, books, and more, all of it educational. **Elizabeth Lord** has handmade soaps and luxury bath items in stock. **Tar Heel Trading Company** stocks fine American handicrafts, artwork, and gift items.

Craft kits for all ages make a rainy day fun. **Ambrose Art** has a great selection. **Island Nautical** supplies you with a bounty of sea-inspired gifts, artifacts, and books. If you're worn out from all that shopping, let **Java Sweets** revive you with coffee drinks and ice cream.

Ocean Plaza
US 158, MP 4, Kitty Hawk
This is one of the newer shopping strips on the Outer Banks. **Plum Crazy** brings hip, cool ladies' clothing, handbags, and accessories to the beach. Funky gift and home items will delight shoppers. Clothing by XOXO, Seven Jeans, and Luon St. Pierre furniture make a stop here worth the trip. **Cybercade USA** is a computer and gaming center where you can rent computer time at reasonable prices. You can set up a vacation Internet account or ongoing account if you don't have your own computer. At **Havana Cigar, Wine & Sandwich Co.** you can indulge two favorite vices and have lunch. The wine selection is good, with unusual items plus hard-to-find dessert wines and port. The

cigars are stored in a humidor for preservation purposes. The deli makes a mean sandwich. Luxurious red velvet furniture awaits you if you need to sit down. **Cigarette City** sells discount cigarettes, beer, and cigars.

KILL DEVIL HILLS

Shore Fit Sunwear
US 158 and East Helga Street
MP 5½, Kill Devil Hills
(252) 441–4560
www.yoursuit.com
You're sure to find a suit to fit at Shore Fit, where the mission is to find a suit for the hard-to-fit woman. This swimwear boutique stocks swimsuits in sizes from 8 to 28, many that will enhance or flatten your curves. The store carries maternity suits, suits for women who've had mastectomies, athletic suits, cover-ups, sarongs, swim dresses, and more. The staff is very helpful, and you can order suits from the Web site. The boutique closes in the off-season.

Seagate North Shopping Center
US 158, MP 5½, Kill Devil Hills
At the north end of Kill Devil Hills, Seagate North offers a variety of shopping experiences. **TJ's Hobbies and Computer Rx** carries hobby and craft materials, model cars, airplanes, boats, rockets, and kites plus radio-control supplies for models and railroading equipment. The shop, open year-round, has metal detectors and computer sales, service, and consultations.

Black Tie Affair offers wedding services, formal-wear rentals, gifts, and more. **Z-1 Gold-N-Gifts** has gold, silver, diamond, and gemstone jewelry for sale; baby gifts and John Perry figurines are also in stock. **Sun Shack** is a tanning and clothing salon. **Movies, Movies** rents videos and provides all the services you would expect; it's open year-round.

The **Coastal Cactus Southwest Restaurant** is much more than a tantalizing restaurant. Inside, a unique Southwest gift shop sells collectibles like Peggy Karr

Glass and Robert Shields Designs, wind chimes, nightlights, stuffed kokopellis and lizards, cooking apparel, salsas, and the largest selection of hot sauces available on the Outer Banks. There are numerous home accessories with Southwest designs and jewelry for kids and adults.

Cyber Dog is a holistic pet food and supply store. The **Outer Banks Center for Alternative Medicine** offers a variety of health items and natural remedies and occasionally hosts speakers.

Norm Martinus at **Nostalgia Gallery** specializes in antiques, vintage paper, antique advertisements, and custom matting and framing. If you're looking for picture-framing perfection, this is the place to go, and it's open all year. Martinus is the coauthor of *Warman's Paper,* an encyclopedia of antiques and collectibles. He's a real Insider on the subject and a local favorite. Stop and chat with him—he holds a warehouse of knowledge and is very personable.

Corner Stitch and Frame sells the area's largest selection of needlepoint and cross-stitching supplies, and **A Penny Saved Consignments** has a variety of used goods for sale.

In the parking lot of Seagate North is one of our favorite produce stands, **Tarheel Too.** You'll find a variety of fruits and vegetables, locally grown when possible, as well as some of the best mesclun mix around. Homemade baked goods and jellies are delicious.

Cooke's Corner
US 158, MP 6, Kill Devil Hills
(252) 480–0519
Cooke's Corner features a surf shop, children's clothing store, women's apparel shop, health food store, and NASCAR sports paraphernalia shop. Anchoring Cooke's Corner is **Colington Speedway Sport Shop,** offering NASCAR hats, shirts, cars, mugs, and sunglasses year-round.

Lit Records and Snowboards sells just that. **Gaea Gifts for the Soul** stocks jewelry, hand-blown glass, pottery, and windchimes. **Glazin' Go Nuts** is a paint-your-own pottery studio that everybody loves, especially on a rainy day (see our Kidstuff chapter). Glazin' Go Nuts shares a space with **Front Porch Cafe,** a coffee shop that makes heavenly coffee drinks and baked goods and roasts its own coffee.

Awful Arthur's Beach Shop
NC 12, MP 6, Kill Devil Hills
(252) 449-2220

This shop is a haven for Awful Arthur's paraphernalia inspired by the popular oyster bar next door. You'll find T-shirts, sweatshirts, golf shirts, hats, beach towels, and glassware bearing the eatery's infamous logo. Shop for beach needs, including beer and groceries, beach chairs and umbrellas, fireworks, seashells, tackle, coolers, and hermit crabs. Bad Barracuda's merchandise is available here, too. Awful Arthur's Beach Shop is open year-round.

The Dare Centre
US 158, MP 7, Kill Devil Hills

This center is anchored by **Belk's** department store, which stocks clothing and shoes for men, women, children, and babies. There are also large shoe, accessory, jewelry, makeup, perfume, lingerie, and home decor departments. **Food Lion,** a national chain grocery store, is also here. Other stores include **Atlantic Dance and Boutique,** an Outer Banks dance studio. The boutique sells dancewear for adults and children. Next door is a thrift store, and next to that is **Hairoics,** one of the best hair salons on the Outer Banks. **Fashion Bug** offers discount fashions, and **Dollar Tree** has everything under the sun for $1.00. Kids love this store, but there are also good deals on toiletries and household items. **Pilpel** has everything you need for the beach—sunglasses, chairs, towels, clothing, and more. The **Outer Banks Sports Locker** specializes in sporting goods, sportswear, and fitness apparel and equipment. **Good Vibes Video** is a rental shop that offers box-office hits and esoteric art films. This location is open all year. **The Blue Dolphin Full**

Body Dimensions is a wellness center that offers massage therapy, nutrition counseling, and, surprisingly, tanning beds.

You'll find plenty to eat at this shopping center. **The Good Life Catering Co.** is open for breakfast, lunch, and dinner and has great coffee and some of the best homemade breads and desserts on the beach (see our Restaurants chapter). **New York Bagels** has fresh, yummy bagels every day for breakfast and lunch. **Little Caesar's Pizza** is here, as are **Subway** for sandwiches and **China King** for take-out Chinese.

North Carolina Books
US 158, MP 7½, Kill Devil Hills
(252) 441-2141

In the Times Printing building, North Carolina Books is chock-full of secondhand paperbacks and reduced-price hardcover books. Bring in your old paperbacks and use them as credit toward the purchase of other secondhand books from the store. The store also has new books and tapes and is open year-round.

Stop 'N' Shop Convenience and Deli
NC 12, MP 8½, Kill Devil Hills
(252) 441-6105

Insiders consider this little treasure trove a hidden gem. More than your average gas and goodies store, the Stop 'N' Shop offers an upscale convenience alternative. The 7,000-square-foot store is jam-packed with tempting items. The deli (which starts serving fresh bagels, hot coffee, and breakfast sandwiches at 6:30 A.M. year-round) uses Boar's Head meats, and the store boasts a wide variety of gourmet food products and one of the best selections of wine and microbrewed beer on the beach. There are large selections of beach and fishing equipment; the store sells boogie boards, sand chairs, and umbrellas, and it sells and rents rods and tackle. The variety of daily newspapers is impressive. During the summer season, the store is open until midnight, 11:00 P.M. in the off-season.

The Trading Post
NC 12, MP 8½, Kill Devil Hills
(252) 441-8205
Here's a good general store to buy things for the beach. It carries T-shirts, souvenirs, swimwear, and convenience grocery items. A branch post office functions here. It's closed from late November through early March.

Kill Devil Hills Cooperative Gallery
US 158, MP 8½, Kill Devil Hills
(252) 441-9888
This gallery, a cooperative of numerous local artists, provides an eclectic mix of artworks that creates an interesting shopping experience. Upstairs, several artists work in their studios. See our Arts and Culture chapter for more information.

The Bird Store
US 158, MP 9, Kill Devil Hills
(252) 480-2951
The Bird Store carries a complete line of antique and new decoys produced by local carvers. Antique fishing gear, fish prints, and original art are also on display. It's open Easter through Christmas.

The Pit Surf Shop, Bar and Grill
US 158, MP 9, Kill Devil Hills
(252) 480-3128
The Pit's surf shop is huge and stocks a selection of surf and skate wear and gear, plus sunglasses, shoes, women's clothing, and more. See our Water Sports chapter for more information.

Davis Everything to Wear
US 158, MP 9, Kill Devil Hills
(252) 441-2604
Davis is a long-standing Outer Banks clothing store, carrying clothes for men and women. Davis stocks wedding dresses, bridesmaid dresses, and wedding accessories.

Charlotte's Web Pets and Supplies
US 158, MP 9, Kill Devil Hills
(252) 480-1799
Charlotte's pet shop sells fish, commercial and residential fish tank maintenance, birds, reptiles, small animals, pet food, and supplies. It's open year-round.

Compass Rose
US 158, MP 8¾, Kill Devil Hills
(252) 441-9449
Compass Rose sells a unique blend of gift items imported from Thailand, Vietnam, and Indonesia from their bright pink building. You'll find candles, ornately carved furniture, fine paper, frames, jewelry, chimes, and much more. Be sure to check out the pots out front. Some great deals can be found.

Lifesaver Shops
NC 12, MP 9, Kill Devil Hills
Lifesaver Shops features practical shops. **Lifesaver Rent Alls** fills rental needs and offers thrifty bargains—these folks rent it all! Look for beach umbrellas, chairs, TVs, VCRs, baby equipment, cottage supplies, portable radios, microwaves, charcoal grills, and blenders. Linen service complete with sheets, pillowcases, and bath towels is offered. Sports items abound, too—look for surfboards, ocean kayaks, boogie boards, snorkel and fishing equipment, and bikes galore. It's open March through November.

Nags Head Hammocks
US 158, MP 9½, Kill Devil Hills
(252) 441-6115, (800) 344-6433
www.nagshead.com
You can't miss the setting, with its palm trees and lush landscaping. At the shop you'll find the famous, durable, high-quality handmade hammocks; single- and double-rope rockers, footstools, and bar stools; single and double porch swings; "slingshot" swings; captain's chairs; and double recliners. You can also purchase items via mail order all year.

T-Tops Racing
US 158, MP 9½, Kill Devil Hills
(252) 441-8867
For everything NASCAR under the sun, make a pit stop at T-Tops. This is a licensed NASCAR store with merchandise covering all NASCAR drivers. The main selling items

here are die-cast cars, but there are also NASCAR-inspired jackets, sweatshirts, T-shirts, hats, clocks, wallets, jewelry, and more in this 4,000-square-foot store. It's one of the largest NASCAR stores in the nation and is open year-round.

The Bike Barn
Wrightsville Avenue, MP 9½
Kill Devil Hills
(252) 441-3786

The Bike Barn, located behind Taco Bell between the Beach Road and the Bypass, sells a wide variety of bikes, parts, and accessories. Skilled mechanics are on staff to service all types of bikes. The shop rents 18-speeds and 21-speed hybrids, gear bikes, and beach cruisers and is open year-round.

Island Dyes
NC 12, MP 9½, Kill Devil Hills
(252) 480-0076

Island Dyes offers T-shirts and a full line of women's clothing, reggae and Grateful Dead T-shirts, and tobacco accessories. Adventurers get hairwraps and henna tattoos here, too. Call for store hours or more information.

Beach Barn Shops
US 158, MP 10, Kill Devil Hills

On the west side of the Bypass, the Beach Barn Shops is the place to stop. It houses **Birthday Suits/OBX Gear,** a popular swimsuit and sportswear shop. *Southern Living* magazine wrote, "Everybody goes to Birthday Suits for a new bathing suit." For women, there's an unbelievable selection of cute suits in all styles, including mix-and-match separates, bra-size tops, and maternity, mastectomy, athletic, and long-torso suits. Women also love the contemporary sportswear, a fine selection of dressy dresses (including some by Betsey Johnson), and accessories—purses, shoes, hats, luggage, and pajamas. Men find trunks and briefs and a whole selection of sportswear and Hawaiian surf shirts. Kids' and babies' suits are adorable. **Carolina Moon** is a great place for finding unusual gifts, scents, pottery, stationery, and greet-

ing cards. The shop has an outstanding line of jewelry of all kinds—you'll find pieces you've never seen before. The delightful Christmas ornaments add a whimsical touch. The shop has a New Age ambience and a fine collection of esoteric gifts. The Kill Devil Hills store is open year-round.

Roanoke Press and Croatoan Bookery
US 158, MP 10, Kill Devil Hills
(252) 480-1890

This shop is owned by the same folks who publish the *Coastland Times* newspaper and operate Burnside Books in Manteo. Here you'll discover secondhand and new books; both bookstores carry an extensive line of books about North Carolina and the Outer Banks. This one is open all year.

Wright Place Gourmet Market and Catering
US 158, MP 10, Kill Devil Hills
(252) 441-1497

If you don't feel like cooking, head to the Wright Place. This gourmet market and deli sells a variety of deli items and sandwiches plus family dinners to go. Try shrimp with bacon, eggplant parmesan, shepherd's pie, sausages, or macaroni and cheese with any of a number of sides. Salads, cheeses, sweets, and tapenade are also available. Choose from a modest wine selection and plenty of gourmet items. **Fat Cat Ice Cream** is right next door.

NAGS HEAD

Nags Head is a shopper's mecca with its boutiques along the Beach Road, US 158, and the Nags Head–Manteo Causeway, and larger shopping destinations such as the Outer Banks Mall and the Tanger Outlet Stores on US 158.

Ben Franklin
US 158, MP 10, Nags Head
(252) 441-7571

Across the street from the Food Lion Plaza, Ben Franklin carries clothing for all ages and everything you need for the beach. There are some great buys on ladies' dresses here. It is open Easter through mid-November.

Something Fishy
NC 12, MP 10½, Nags Head
(252) 441-9666
Here's a fun shop swimming with fish. You'll delight in the fish-print clothing made by owner Sherrie Lemnois, who has been creating these masterpieces for years. Clothing, jewelry, toys, home decor, and gifts are available with a fishy theme. Also in the shop are Asian-inspired items, prompting the owner to say she sells everything from "fish to Feng Shui." Lucky Bamboo home decor products are best-sellers here.

Gallery Row
Gallery Row and Driftwood Street
Nags Head
Around MP 10 are numerous art galleries that are collectively referred to as "Gallery Row." If you're shopping in Nags Head, you'll want to see these wonderful art galleries situated between the highways. See our Arts and Culture chapter for a complete listing.

The Christmas Mouse
US 158, MP 10½, Nags Head
(252) 441-8111
This holiday-oriented shop brims with Christmas collectibles, Cairn Gnomes, papier-mâché Santas, Snow Babies, porcelain dolls, unique ornaments, and nautical- and Midwestern-themed trees. Sixty decorated trees get you in the spirit. It is open year-round.

Gulf Stream Gifts
NC 12, MP 10½, Nags Head
(252) 441-0433
Gulf Stream features contemporary nautical gifts, jewelry, and lighthouse and dolphin memorabilia. The store is open from Easter until Thanksgiving.

The Barefoot Gourmet
US 158, MP 11, Nags Head
(252) 449-8716
This specialty grocery and wine market

offers gourmet treats, hard-to-find ingredients, and a wide selection of wine, beer, and cheese. Hand-dipped ice cream is available from the window. A variety of cookbooks, cookware, and cutlery round out the stock. Open 10:00 A.M. to 7:00 P.M. with extended hours in season.

Central Square
US 158, MP 11, Nags Head
This weathered cottage-style complex of shops has come to house a conglomeration of antiques shops. **Edith Deltgen's Gallery** is owned by local artist Edith Deltgen, and some of her unique sculptures and creations are housed here. She also offers antiques, including furniture, estate jewelry, and household items. **Mystic Antiques** sells a variety of true antiques, including furniture, dressers, and beds. These shops make for great browsing.

Meme's Attic features home decor, gifts, and antiques. **N Style** sells brand-name clothing and audio equipment. **Shooters at the Beach** is a full-service photography studio.

Pirate's Quay
US 158, MP 11½, Nags Head
Boutiques, stores, offices, and eateries carry tobacco, jewelry, crafts, and clothing in this shopping center.

Cloud Nine is an adventure in clothing, accessories, and other discoveries from around the world. Owner Ginny Flowers has beads and lots of them. Other finds include recycled sea glass, Grateful Dead merchandise, T-shirts made by locals and visitors, beautiful batiks, and treasures from Africa and Nepal. Cloud Nine also carries gold and silver jewelry. Bring in your sea glass and have a custom necklace made. It's open Easter through Thanksgiving.

The **Quaker Connection** offers both antique and new decoys as well as hand-painted furniture. **Nags Head Skate** offers a variety of skateboards, skimboards, and accessories. **Lou's Deli** sells yummy sandwiches and take-out items prepared in-house.

Austin Fish Company
US 158, MP 12½, Nags Head
(252) 441-7412

Austin is a Nags Head fixture near Jockey's Ridge. It's a full-service seafood store that also serves as a gas station with some of the lowest prices on the beach. The store stocks crabmeat, steamed crabs, shrimp, oysters, clams, fish, scallops, live lobsters, and more. If you would like your catch shipped home, the staff will vacuum-pack and freeze it for you. Austin's is open May through November.

Jockey's Ridge Crossing
US 158, MP 13½, Nags Head

At this complex, **Kitty Hawk Kites/ Carolina Outdoors** sells kites, windsocks, and banners, as well as quality men's and women's sportswear and outerwear, sandals, T-shirts, and sweatshirts. This year-round shop also offers a large selection of toys. (See our Water Sports chapter for exciting sporting opportunities offered by these folks.)

Also open year-round, **Kitty Hawk Sports** carries popular name-brand clothing, boogie boards, accessories, and sunglasses plus windsurfing and kayaking gear. It offers all sorts of sporting opportunities (see our Water Sports chapter).

How Sweet It Is is the place to stop for homemade ice-cream, tasty deli sandwiches, and delicious ice cream cakes. To satisfy a yearning for fudge, stop by **The Fudgery.** A stop in **Miss Kitty's Old Time Photos** will send you on your way with a memorable picture of your group.

Surfside Plaza
US 158, MP 13, Nags Head

This is a great mix of shops where you'll find everything from comic books to contemporary clothing and crafts.

Surfside Casuals has more swimsuits than just about any other store on the beach. This shop also carries an extensive line of casual wear for men and women. All of Surfside's many Outer Banks shops are open Easter through Thanksgiving. **Beach Peddler,** open Easter through

October, sells what you need at the beach and also has jewelry, shells, postcards, souvenirs, gifts, hats, hermit crabs, and T-shirts.

Donna Designs, which also has locations in Duck and Corolla, sells the wonderful fish-print clothing created by the owner. It's not just fish, though; it's also crabs, turtles, flowers, frogs, and more, all printed on cotton T-shirts, sweatshirts, dresses, baby clothes, onesies, and other items.

Adults and kids alike will love **Outer Banks Cards and Comics,** a collectors' paradise that features sport and nonsport cards and a massive collection of comic books, both foreign and domestic. It also sells action figures and T-shirts and holds Magic card tournaments during winter. It's open all year. Art lovers enjoy **We're Art** year-round for posters, prints, local artwork, and custom framing or ready-made frames. If you're hungry, **The Country Deli** has delicious, huge, and inexpensive sandwiches for lunch.

Find outlet-priced T-shirts, sunglasses, jeans, and more at the **Nags Head Harley-Davidson** shop. **The Lady from New York Cards & Gifts** stocks doll collections, candles, seashell gifts, and cards.

Croatan Centre
US 158, MP 14, Nags Head

This is a fun group of shops featuring gifts from around the world, fine jewelry, CDs, and shoes. **Halloran & Co.** offers sterling silver jewelry, 14-karat gold and gemstones, and sterling silver watches. **Sound Feet Shoes,** open year-round, offers a wide variety of men's, women's, and children's casual and fancy shoes and sandals, including popular sports shoes by Reebok and Nike.

If you're looking for new and used CDs, look no further than **Surf Sound Records,** which offers a wide variety of music for all tastes. It also sells music videos, T-shirts, posters, and accessories. If they don't have something in stock, ask them to special order it for you; they can usually turn such requests around in a couple of days at no extra charge. The store is open all year.

Bosko Wood sells solid finished and unfinished wood furniture.

Island Tobacco offers cigars, tobacco products, and smoking implements. **Rock-A-Bye Baby** sells gently used goods such as clothes, cribs, toys, and high chairs.

Outer Banks Mall
US 158, MP 15, Nags Head

The Outer Banks Mall is open year-round. **Seamark Foods** (see The Shoreside Center listing in our Kitty Hawk section) anchors the center of the complex, which is home to a mix of shopping, service, entertainment, and dining businesses. The north wing of Outer Banks Mall is predominantly food oriented, but there are a few stores, including **GNC,** which stocks vitamins, herbs, health and beauty products (including the popular Burt's Bees line), and sports and nutritional supplements. **Video Andy** stocks a good selection of videos, including an entire foreign film section, new releases, a cult classics section, a kids section, and a classics section, among others. Video Andy rents videos and players. **Outer Banks Cleaners** is also here.

On the south wing of Outer Banks Mall, **West Marine** offers boating hardware, gear, cleaning and repair supplies, Mercury engines, life jackets and safety equipment, marine electronics, and more. West Marine also sells fishing equipment, including gear, coolers, rods, reels, tackle, and lures. **Outer Banks Furniture** is a huge home-furnishings store with sofas, chairs, beds, dining tables, rugs, home accessories, and much more.

Mule Shed features ladies' apparel and lovely purses, gifts, and wedding, household, and outdoor garden items such as statuary and a sweet little brass bunny doorbell. At **T-Tops Trading Company,** you can choose from T-shirts, shorts, hats, mugs, and souvenirs. The **Cottage Shop** sells items that will give your home or cottage a relaxing, warm feeling. Everything from trendy welcome mats to functional backyard grills is stocked here.

Habitat Earth carries groovy knit dresses, wild pants, couch throws with dancing bears, jewelry, CDs, and more. **Lil' Grass Shack/Bikini Hut** offers bathing suits for women in sizes 3 to 28 as well as swimwear for girls and sportswear for adults. You'll also find **Ocean Threads,** specializing in swimwear. **Peggy's Hallmark** has a world of cards, wrapping paper, stuffed animals, and gifts, and **Outer Banks Books** is a huge warehouse-style bookstore with some great bargains.

Dare Jewelers offers sea life and nautical jewelry along with traditional fine jewelry. Locally created stained-glass items are also showcased.

Forbes Candy & Gift Shop
US 158, MP 15½, Nags Head
(252) 441-7293

You can't come to the beach without picking up a box of saltwater taffy. Forbes, an Outer Banks tradition, has it here. Stop in for a box or three of the company's famous homemade gooey goodies. The shop, which is open year-round, also features a gift and souvenir selection.

The Chalet Gift Shop
NC 12, MP 15½, Nags Head
(252) 441-6402

The Chalet is one of the nicest stores on the beach. The gifts, collectibles, and souvenirs are exquisite. Collectors love the selection of Harbour Lights, Lilliput Lane, Collectible Dolls, Legends, Left on Lighthouses, and Madam Alexander dolls. The large collection of sterling silver jewelry is gorgeous, and the unique designer pieces are tempting. The shop also carries fine home accessories and beach items. It's open March through December; mail orders are welcome.

Cahoon's
NC 12, MP 16½, Nags Head
(252) 441-5358

Cahoon's is a large, family-owned grocery and variety store operating for more than four decades. It's a nice change of pace from chain supermarkets. Dorothy and

Ray Cahoon bought the store shortly before the Ash Wednesday storm of 1962 and, despite what must have been a rather wild start, continue to stock everything you'll need for your visit to the beach, including good meats that butcher Robert Heroux cuts to perfection. The store is open March through Thanksgiving.

Tanger Outlet Center
US 158, MP 16½, Nags Head
(252) 441-5634

Tanger is a discount-outlet shopping center brimming with great buys in all sorts of merchandise, from clothes to dishes to shoes. Once you park, you'll wander for hours here. Bring plenty of cash! And when you get hungry, take a break at **Stone Oven Pizza.**

All shops in the Tanger complex are open year-round. **Pfaltzgraff** has dishes, glasses, and knickknacks. **London Fog** is very popular with locals and visitors alike who stop here for their yearly coat purchases. Check out the great buys on a vast selection of outerwear, including casual jackets and rainwear. At **Rack Room Shoes** you can outfit the entire family with quality discounted tennis shoes and casual and dressy year-round footwear. **Cabin Creek Gifts** offers stylish home accessories. **Michael's Gems & Glass** sells jewelry, rocks, minerals, and glass of all kinds.

The **Corning/Revere Store** is a kitchen supply shop. Of course you'll find traditional Corningware with pretty designs, but the shop's also chock-full of gadgets that make your kitchen experiences easier. We've found fashionable short leather boots at **Nine West** that really last, plus lots of dressy and casual shoe selections for women only. **The Dress Barn** has sweaters (dressy, sporty, and casual dressy) for women and some super tops for all occasions.

Claire's Accessories overflows with hair accessories, jewelry, fashionable clear plastic purses for kids, sunglasses, fuzzy cloth key chain books, and hats. Kids love this shop. The prices are extraordinary. For a few dollars, the little ones feel they've had a big shopping spree.

In the front parking lot of Seagate North is an Insiders' favorite—the Tarheel Too produce stand. You'll find a variety of fruits and veggies, locally grown when possible. Prices are great, and the homemade baked goods and jellies are delicious.

No visit to Tanger Outlet Center is complete without a stop at **Gap Outlet,** where bargains are abundant. Locals stop in every week to pick up fun fashions at great prices.

Other store names you'll recognize include **Polo/Ralph Lauren, Nautica, Izod, Kitchen Collection, Publishers Warehouse, Wilson Leather Outlet, Vitamin World, Van Heusen, Geoffrey Beene, Bass, Big Dogs, Coach, L'eggs Hanes Bali,** and **Sunglass Hut.**

Whalebone Seafood Market
US 158, MP 16½, Nags Head
(252) 441-8808

Whalebone is run by the Daniels family, known locally for their commercial-fishing roots. The full-service seafood market sells whatever's in season. It's open Easter through October.

Shipwreck
Nags Head-Manteo Causeway
Nags Head
(252) 441-5739

Shipwreck is another gift store with a nautical twist. Local crafts, driftwood, nets, shells, and other sea treasures are piled everywhere. It's open March through Thanksgiving.

ROANOKE ISLAND

The Town of Manteo is undergoing something of a renaissance. New retail shops have opened, and much more is in the planning stage. There is so much to see, do, and buy now in Manteo that parking can be a challenge, but that just means you'll need to park on a side street and walk a few blocks. Or you can park in the Roanoke Island Festival Park lot, where you'll find space almost any time of year, and take a pleasant stroll over the Cora Mae Basnight Bridge to shop and eat.

We start with the shops along U.S. Highway 64, where you can find bargains as well as unusual gifts. Then we move on to downtown Manteo.

Manteo

Pirate's Cove Ship's Store
Pirate's Cove Yacht Club
Nags Head–Manteo Causeway, Manteo
(252) 473-3906
This marina store has a selection of active sportswear, including Kahalas, a Hawaiian line of beautifully hand-screened and batiked clothing. The shop also carries gifts, picture frames, windup crabs, marina supplies, and groceries as well as a line of 14-karat gold jewelry with a fishy flair. It's open year-round.

Silver Bonsai Gallery
905 US 64/264, Manteo
(252) 475-1413
In a restored home on the main highway, Silver Bonsai is a gallery owned by local artists Ben Stewart and Kathryn Holton-Stewart. The Stewarts are silver- and goldsmiths and bonsai artists. Their work fills the gallery along with the work of many local artists. One of the artists is often at work in the studio. The artwork and gifts in Silver Bonsai are distinctive. You'll find paintings, sculpture, candles, soaps, exquisite jewelry, copper items, quilts, furniture, Japanese pottery and local pottery, and more. See our Arts and Culture chapter for more information. This store is worth a stop just to admire the incredible etch-a-sketch drawings.

Island Produce
US 64/264, Manteo
(252) 473-1303
Island Produce offers fresh seasonal vegetables and fruits as well as flowering plants for the garden and home, including beautiful lilies, pumpkins, and Christmas trees in season. Statuary and fountains to adorn your garden are here, too. It's open April until Christmas.

Jeanine's Cat House
US 64/264, Manteo
(252) 473-1499
Cat lovers revel in this shop filled with delightful gifts and necessities ranging from "purr-ty" cat earrings to beds and carrying cases for the furry felines. Cat-motif sculptures, wall art, clothing, collectibles, cards, and stationery fill this pussycat palace. Jeanine's is next to the Christmas Shop and is open daily year-round.

Chesley Mall
US 64/264, Manteo
Food-A-Rama and **CVS** pharmacy hold down the fort at this year-round shopping venue. **Island Pharmacy** is an old-fashioned store where you can buy prescription and over-the-counter medicines, sundries, film, and gifts, and use the UPS and Airborne Express services in the back of the store. Island Pharmacy also sells gift items, including glass and china knickknacks and some stuffed animals. One of the best selections of gift cards on the beach can be found here, too.

The Video Store has an array of first-rate drama, comedy, adventure, martial arts, horror, and children's movies. It also rents VCRs, Super Nintendo, Nintendo, and Sega Genesis games. **Susan's Hallmark** carries a wide variety of party supplies, religious products, candy (try the spicy jelly beans), cards, stationery, and photo albums. **Subway** and **Top China** offer options for quick meals.

Burnside Books
US 64/264, Manteo
(252) 473-3311
Burnside carries office and art supplies and a selection of historical and children's books. Upstairs you'll find used hardback and paperback books and a North Carolina book section. It's open all year.

Hotline Thrift Shop
US 64/264, Manteo
(252) 473-3127
West of the Dare County Public Library, Hotline Thrift is a fund-raising shop for Outer Banks Hotline, a crisis intervention service that also operates a shelter for battered women and their children. Hotline may be the most popular secondhand store on the Outer Banks. The bargain-priced inventory includes furniture, toys, books, knickknacks, and clothing for men, women, and children. It's open year-round.

The Cloth Barn
Etheridge Road, Manteo
(252) 473-2795
Returning to US 64, head north toward Manns Harbor and turn left onto Etheridge Road. Drive a short distance, and you'll be at a store packed nearly floor to ceiling with fabrics, notions, and patterns. The selection of woven tapestry cloth is unbelievably beautiful. The Cloth Barn closes mid-December through mid-January.

Downtown Manteo

Wanchese Pottery
107 Fernando Street, Manteo
(252) 473-2099
This artistic shop is a small business near The Waterfront on Fernando Street, where customers watch local potters Bonnie and Bob Morrill at work (see our Arts and Culture chapter). The shop is known locally for its beautiful, useful art, and it also features handmade baskets and fresh cooking herbs. It's open year-round, but call for winter hours.

Manteo Furniture
209 Sir Walter Raleigh Street, Manteo
(252) 473-2131
Manteo Furniture stocks a large selection of home and cottage furnishings ranging from traditional to contemporary. The store, which has been in operation more than 50 years, offers down-home friendly service. Allow yourself plenty of time to browse through the many rooms of furnishings in this 48,000-square-foot showroom/warehouse. The company sells a full line of General Electric appliances and offers financing and free delivery. It's open year-round.

Outer Banks Quilts and Antiques
108 Sir Walter Raleigh Street, Manteo
(252) 473-4183
This large store carries the goods of more than 12 antiques and collectibles dealers. It's also the Outer Banks's only official quilt shop, with handmade quilts and quilting supplies.

Manteo Booksellers
105 Sir Walter Raleigh Street, Manteo
(252) 473-1221
Housed in charming quarters dotted with wing chairs, cozy corners, and quaint antiques, Manteo Booksellers is a must-browse for every reader. Three rooms are packed with books ranging from literary classics to delightful children's stories. The Outer Banks and Latin American sections (they also have books in Spanish) are excellent, as are the historical, self-help, Civil War, and North Carolina fiction areas. The cookbook selection is extensive.

The bookstore has a busy calendar filled with book signings and free readings by authors, poets, and storytellers. Manteo Booksellers is open year-round.

My Secret Garden
101 Sir Walter Raleigh Street, Manteo
(252) 473-6880
Next door to Manteo Booksellers, My Secret Garden features Tiffany-style lamps, custom wreaths and swags, unique garden accessories and statuary, handmade birdhouses, and mermaid items. This shop offers handpainted furniture, including mirrors, lamps, dressers and servers, plus indoor fountains, Muffy Vanderbears and Beanie Babies, and pottery. This is a charming shop with lots of gift ideas. It's open year-round.

Old Creef's Corner
Corner of Queen Elizabeth and
Sir Walter Raleigh Streets, Manteo

In a slightly askew building on the corner, this former gas station houses **Water Street Station,** a women's apparel store. This shop offers casual island wear for women and girls. Colorful dresses, linen clothing, fine accessories, luggage, handbags, hats, and babies' apparel are available. **Waterfront Salon & Day Spa** offers relaxing day-spa services and the latest in great hairstyles. Next door, **Full Moon Cafe** serves delicious and affordable food. It also sells T-shirts, inexpensive toys and candy for the kids, and small gift items.

Centennial Square
Sir Walter Raleigh, Queen Elizabeth, and Fernando Streets, Manteo

This beautiful square of buildings offers interesting shops on the first level with apartments above. On the Sir Walter Raleigh Street side, you'll find the Dare County Arts Council's **Sea and Sounds Gallery** (see our Arts and Culture chapter). Around the corner on the Fernando Street side is **Muzzie's Antiques,** which offers an assortment of antiques and treasures. Estate and heirloom jewelry, Shabby Chic and April Cornell linens, antique and rag dolls, vintage accessories, and wedding gowns are just a few of the items. There are also furnishings, mosaic tables, painted furniture, lamps, trinket boxes, pillows galore, cards, and bath products. Carry home some tropical style at the **Beach'n Life.** Imported goods from the Caribbean are featured in this shop that brings Key West to Manteo. Everything from music to handpainted furniture to palm trees is stocked in this fun shop.

The Waterfront Shops
Queen Elizabeth Street, Manteo

Along the Manteo Waterfront sits this four-story complex with businesses, restaurants, residential space, and covered parking.

Charlotte's is a quality women's boutique that features traditional and contemporary fine and casual clothing, accessories, gifts, and a beautiful sweater collection, including ones by designers Lisa Nichols and Michael Simon. The store is open year-round.

Sleeping In sells comforts for the bed and bath. Everything is luxurious: lingerie, gowns, robes, bath items, body care products, candles, bedding, and home decor.

Ken Kelley and Eileen Alexanian are the owners of **Diamonds and Dunes,** a full-service jewelry shop. The "designing couple" produces fine handcrafted work, drawing on more than two decades of experience in the jewelry business. Services include setting stones, sizing rings, and creating one-of-a-kind keepsakes. They showcase their very own lighthouse bracelet, which features reproductions of the five Outer Banks lighthouses. They also offer Belgian diamonds and gold, silver, or gem-studded ear pins to give you the three-earring look without all the holes. The store is open year-round.

Andrus Gallery and Studio showcases the masterworks of painter Steve Andrus. The artist works within the gallery and enjoys discussing his work. If you're looking for locally produced items, stop in at **Roanoke Marshes Trading Company.** They offer such items by Outer Banks artists as shell candles, hand painted glassware, and nautical wall decor. For a good summer read or a yummy frozen treat, visit **Mother's Money.** Along with books and desserts, Outer Banks gift items and lots of wine and wine accessories are stocked here. **Island Accent Gifts** features glass sea life sculptures, metal art jewelry, and more.

Magnolia Market Square
Queen Elizabeth Street, Manteo

This group of shops opened in 1999 across from The Tranquil House Inn. Here you will find **Magnolia Grill,** where you can purchase drinks, snacks, sundries, and gourmet foods or eat lunch or dinner. The hamburgers here are fabulous. The **Blacksmith's Store** offers live demonstrations of 19th-century blacksmithing. Ornamental ironwork is for sale here.

Endless Possibilities
105 Budleigh Street, Manteo
(252) 475-1575

This shop recycles, gives back to the community, and offers stylish accessories for sale all at once. Clothing specially selected from Hotline, a community thrift store, is shredded into strips. The fabric is then hand-woven on looms into colorful boas, pocketbooks, rugs, and hats. Volunteers do the weaving, and proceeds benefit the Outer Banks Crisis Intervention and Prevention Center. Every item is custom made and one of a kind. You can pay a fee and weave your own item, if you are feeling creative. Open Monday through Saturday from 10:00 A.M. to 5:00 P.M.

Outer Banks Yoga and Pilates
105 Budleigh Street, Manteo
(252) 480-3214
www.outerbanksyoga.com

Outer Banks Yoga and Pilates operates above Endless Possibilities. A selection of yoga items, such as T-shirts, films, and CDs are sold here. Drop-in classes are offered in yoga and Pilates. The Web site offers class times.

Phoenix Shops
Between Budleigh and
Ananias Dare Streets, Manteo

This strip of shops faces an inner courtyard instead of the street. **Something Special** is just that. Brimming with items from the world over, you'll find unique gifts sure to please. **Outer Banks Posters** sells posters, offers custom framing, and sells lighthouse figurines, clocks, and other items. **Inspired by the Sea** sells hand-painted furniture and decor pieces. Lighthouses and seascapes are often painted on their work. Prada and Gucci purses, along with fine women's clothing are offered at **Sugar & Spice and Everything Nice.** Beachwear items are also sold here.

Finally Mine
Across from Magnolia Market, Manteo
(252) 473-1387
www.finallymine.com

For unique gifts for yourself or someone special, Finally Mine is the place to stop. There's quite a bit of sterling silver jewelry and earrings, including many pieces fashioned with glass. Home accessories, including old English stained-glass windows, blown glass, frames, pottery, and lamps, are one of a kind. You'll also find Martha Johnson framed collages, bath and body treats, garden accessories, mirrors, and more.

Nancyware Pottery
402 Queen Elizabeth Street, Manteo
(252) 473-9400

In a building across from The Tranquil House Inn, this is the pottery studio of artist Nancy Hase. The potter's wheel is on display, and you can see her work from time to time. She also offers classes on the wheel. In this year-round shop you'll find Nancy's pottery, jewelry, and tile work. The pottery is high-fire functional stoneware that is dishwasher, microwave, and oven safe. There's a great variety of kitchen items, including deep-dish fluted pie plates, colanders, three-piece child dining sets that can be personalized, vases, dishes, and spoon rests.

400 Budleigh Antique Mall
Budleigh Street, Manteo
(252) 473-9339

This mall features more than 25 rooms filled with antiques, furniture, and more. Vintage Christmas decorations and collectible kitchenware are among the popular items for sale. Open Monday through Saturday from 10:00 A.M. to 5:00 P.M.

The Museum Shop
Roanoke Island Festival Park, Manteo
(252) 475-1500

This Museum Shop at Roanoke Island Festival Park goes beyond what you'd expect at a museum store. This store is huge, packed with historically themed gifts and items for the home. Inspired by Roanoke Island life and history, sections include Elizabethan, Civil War, nautical, and Native American themes. In the book section, books about the Outer Banks are extensive, and there are handsome leather-bound blank journals and a wide range of music. In the Elizabethan section, you'll find teapots, tea, biscuits, and other English items. The nautical section has books, telescopes, tide clocks, old maps, models, and more. The toys include hats, swords, and capes for playing dress-up. Jewelry, candy, food, games, gifts, and home decor items are all here.

Clemons on Budleigh
406 Budleigh Street, Manteo
(252) 473-9870
Clemons is a cute antiques shop housed in a little white cottage a couple of blocks from the waterfront. The shop stocks antiques and newer items for the home and garden. Three rooms are filled with china, furniture, linens, clothing, mirrors, frames, hats—you name it. Garden statuary and yard ornaments sit on the porch. Open May through October 10:00 A.M. until 5:00 P.M.

Wanchese

After you cross Roanoke Sound westbound on the Nags Head–Manteo Causeway and pass Pirate's Cove, turn left at the next intersection onto North Carolina Highway 345 and head toward Wanchese. Turning to the right onto Old Wharf Road (less than a mile from the intersection with US 64/264), you'll find **Nick-E Stained Glass,** a studio and gallery, which is a veritable stained-glass wonderland featuring the original creations of Ellinor and Robert Nick (see our Arts and Culture chapter).

DARE COUNTY MAINLAND

Nature's Harmony
Shipyard Road, Manns Harbor
(252) 473-3556
Nature's Harmony is a full-scale nursery with three greenhouses, specializing in herbs, perennials, and wildflowers. It offers a plant-maintenance service for

your office or home. This store sells pottery and garden-related accessories plus fertilizers and mulches. Landscaping services are available. It's a lovely, peaceful spot that's open from February through Christmas.

HATTERAS ISLAND

Rodanthe

Rodanthe has several general stores where you can find groceries, camping and fishing supplies, bait, and seafood—the vacation necessities—and arty shopping experiences.

Pamlico Station Shops
NC 12, Rodanthe
(252) 987-1080
This two-story shopping center is located on the east side of NC 12 in Rodanthe. **Moon Over Hatteras Gift Shoppes** has a great selection of gift items. **Village Video** offers a wide selection of rental movies as well as VCR and Nintendo system rentals. **Hatteras T-Shirts** stocks a wide selection of T-shirts, hats, and accessories, plus hermit crabs. **Exotic Cargo** carries interesting and unique imported gift items not easily found elsewhere. Bathing suits fill the **Surfside Casuals** shop, located on the first level. This store offers a great selection of clothing to make your shopping quest on Hatteras Island a success.

The Island Convenience Store
NC 12, Rodanthe
(252) 987-2239
This is a one-stop shopping place for groceries, rod and reel rentals, bait and tackle, propane gas, gasoline, and deli items, including breakfast biscuits, sandwiches, hand-dipped ice-cream cones, and fried chicken. You can take your food with you or eat at the tables. The store also carries souvenirs, gifts, and beach supplies and offers 24-hour wrecker service and auto repair. It's open year-round.

Rodanthe Surf Shop
NC 12, Rodanthe
(252) 987–2412
Rodanthe Surf Shop has been the place to get your custom surfboard or really happening clothing for men, women, and kids for 15 years.

Reef
NC 12, Rodanthe
(252) 987–2821
All your beach needs can be found in one stop at Reef. Stocking sunglasses, toys, towels, chairs, rash guards, and more, you'll be fully outfitted for the beach by the time you leave the store.

Ocean Gourmet and Gifts
NC 12, Rodanthe
(252) 987–1166
Just north of Camp Hatteras, this is the place to come for fresh fudge, ice cream, and candy. Other vacation necessities are available, too, such as hermit crabs, fireworks, bathing suits, beachwear, and nautical gifts and lighthouses.

Waves

Waves is home to only a few businesses, including Hatteras Island Surf Shop (see our Water Sports chapter) and Michael Halminski's Photography Gallery (see our Arts and Culture chapter for details). St. Waves Plaza is a new shopping complex. **Kitty Hawk Kites** is a traditional stop when visiting the Outer Banks. Find kites, toys for all ages, and outdoor wear for the adventure minded. **Ocean Annie's** stocks some of the most beautiful pottery you'll find anywhere. Wind chimes, jewelry, and gourmet coffee are also sold here. **Just for the Beach** rents bicycles, kayaks, beach gear, and baby needs.

Salvo

Salvo is a sleepy little village, so don't expect much in the way of shopping.

The Blue Whale
NC 12, Salvo
(252) 987–2335
The Blue Whale offers a mix of the usual beach items (T-shirts, groceries, beach supplies) and the unusual (gourmet coffees and hot sauces). The Blue Whale imports beer and wine and specializes in jams, jellies, and salad dressings. Crafts created by Jeanette and Laura are sold here.

Fishin' Hole
NC 12, Salvo
(252) 987–2351
The Fishin' Hole is best known as a general tackle shop, but the shop, open April through mid-December, also sells beach supplies and groceries. If the little white poodle doesn't greet you at the door, it will meet you at the cash register.

Avon

Island Shoppes
NC 12, Avon
This small shopping center houses two of the Outer Banks's most popular stores— **Ocean Annie's** and **Kitty Hawk Kites/ Carolina Outdoors.** Ocean Annie's is a craft gallery that sells pottery, wind chimes, prints, artwork, wooden boxes, coffee, and the like. Kitty Hawk Kites/Carolina Outdoors is a sports store selling kites and offering kayak ecotours, kiteboarding lessons, and parasailing. It's also an outfitter, selling sporty outdoor clothes and gear for all your adventures.

The Fisherman's Daughter
NC 12, Avon
(252) 995–6148
The Fisherman's Daughter offers clothing and swimwear from Vix, Vera Bradley, and other popular name brands, along with Brighton accessories. It also carries OBX and HI products, Yankee Candles, and Cat's Meow. Check out the souvenir and gift area upstairs.

Mill Creek Gifts
NC 12, Avon
(252) 995-3188

This true Hatteras Island shop, owned by a real local, is filled with delightful gifts. Boyds Bears, porcelain dolls and angels, lighthouse collectibles and candles, sea shells, and souvenirs wait on the shelves. Wind chimes catch the constant breeze, while fish mobiles and stained glass twinkle in the sun. Sun-Com digital phones are now sold here, too.

Island Spice and Wine
NC 12, Avon
(252) 995-7750

Island Spice and Wine is a little bit of wine heaven. Specializing in California, Italian, and French wines, it has some tasty accompaniments, including gourmet coffees, foods, and cheeses. How about a gourmet gift basket? You can sneak in some neat kitchen gadgets or cute cookie cutters. There's also wine racks, serving ware, barbecue tools, Gourmet Kitchen cooking supplies, and cookbooks. A selection of specialty beer and Asian food products includes sushi-making supplies. An expanded gift section carries North Carolina food products, such as delicious sauces and preserves and organic North Carolina cooking wine flavored with basil, tarragon, and rosemary. Check out the line of collectibles, huge mug selection, angel items, and whimsical salt and pepper shakers. The store is open year-round.

Nags Head Hammocks
NC 12, Avon
(252) 995-3744
www.nagshead.com

Here's another branch of the Outer Banks's legendary hammock shop. Nags Head Hammocks are known for their sturdiness. Select from traditional hammocks, hammock porch chairs, hammock tables, hammock swings, or hammock stools. Fitted pillows make them even more comfortable.

Dairy Queen Shopping Center
NC 12, Avon

Take a break from the sun and while away an afternoon in the **Dairy Queen Shopping Center. The Glass Bead** has all the supplies for jewelry making, including a fabulous selection of beads. Crystal beads, handmade beads, and semiprecious stones make up just a part of their selection. The painting and photography of artist Zofia Lategano is featured in **Zofia's Art Gallery.** Art classes for kids are offered here, too. If shopping for windsurfing gear is on your list, stop in at **Sailworld.** They offer a complete range of windsurfing and kiteboarding accessories.

Country Elegance
Harbor Road, Avon
(252) 995-6269

As you head south, if you turn right on Harbor Road at the only stoplight south of Whalebone Junction, you'll come across this store in Old Avon Village. This shop features birdhouses, aromatherapy oils, lighthouses, handpainted shirts, antique quilted heirlooms, whimsical art, designer dolls, and baskets. There are also wood crafts, cake candles, and lots and lots of lace. This shop is open Easter through mid-November.

Home Port Gifts
NC 12, Avon
(252) 995-4334

Home Port Gifts is one of the loveliest upscale gift shops on the Outer Banks. Original artwork, crafts, and exquisite jewelry in fine silver and 14-karat gold (much of it with a nautical theme) will tempt you. You'll also find quality accessories for the home and nautical antiques, including Tiffany-style stained-glass pieces, nautical sculptures, handcarved decoys, terra-cotta sculptures, and sea candles by Sally Knuckles. The work of about 120 artists is on display.

Village Grocery
NC 12, Avon
(252) 995-4402

The Village Grocery is a one-stop shop

that carries everything a regular grocery store does while catering to your specialty needs. Boar's Head deli meats, Certified Angus Beef, organic foods, and gourmet cheeses are just some of the finer items they carry. A convenient salad bar and delicious Boar's Head sandwiches, wraps, and paninis are available for a quick lunch or dinner. Open year-round. Located next to Kinnakeet Corner.

Hatteras Island Boardsports
NC 12, Avon
(252) 995-6160

The island-style decor in this shop invites you to enter and browse clothing and equipment or get serious about surfing, windsurfing, and kitesurfing. Buy or rent equipment, have a lesson, and see Hatteras Island from a different perspective on a kayak tour in Pamlico Sound.

Hatteras Plaza
NC 12, Avon

This Avon plaza is anchored by **Food Lion** and an **Ace Hardware** store. **Exotic Cargo** features beautiful, handcrafted home accents brought to you from the world over. **Ocean Threads** and **Surfside Casuals,** right next door to each other, have similar offerings—surfwear by Billabong, Roxy, and others plus bathing suits, T-shirts, sandals, sunglasses, and stickers. On the other end of the plaza is **Island Cycle,** which rents, repairs, and sells bicycles. **Beach Pharmacy** is here and sells an assortment of arts-and-crafts supplies besides the usual drugstore items. **Sea Treasures** sells fudge, beachwear, and knickknacks. **Try My Nuts** has yummy treats of all types, including, of course, nuts. Chocolates, candy, popcorn, and even T-shirts are sold here. **Sew Many Things** has beach souvenirs, jewelry, stained glass, and more.

If you'd like to keep the rest of the family entertained while you shop, drop them off at **RC Theaters.** The theater has four showings daily of first-run films during summer. Call for off-season schedule.

Buxton

A 5-mile drive south of Avon through Cape Hatteras National Seashore brings you to the village of Buxton, where your discoveries will range from a general store and bait and tackle shop to specialty boutiques. Buxton's market, **Conner's,** offers groceries and basic supplies year-round.

Daydreams
NC 12, Buxton
(252) 995-5548

Daydreams has earned a reputation for having stylish clothing and a selection of top name brands such as Patagonia, Dansko, and Birkenstock. The shop, open March through Christmas, carries clothing for men, women, and children, plus accessories and jewelry.

Dillon's Corner
NC 12, Buxton
(252) 995-5083

This bait and tackle shop carries fishing rods, including custom-built ones. It is also jammed with gifts, Yankee Candles, jewelry, pottery, lighthouse replicas, T-shirts, and a bevy of Beanie Babies. Gas is available as well. It's open year-round.

The Cottage Shop
NC 12, Buxton
(252) 995-3960

A bright yellow building serves as a beacon for those interested in functional and imaginative décor. Inside the Cottage Shop, shoppers find items for the kitchen, bedroom, porch, and garden and pretty much the rest of the home. Rental-cottage packages are offered to outfit your entire home.

The Old Gray House
Light Plant Road, Buxton
(252) 995-6098

This shop is located within a historic Hatteras home and is filled to the brim with birdhouses, dolls, garden statuary, and handcrafted gifts.

Hatteras Island Toy Store
Geo. Gaskins Lane, Buxton
(252) 995-7171
Toys for kids of all ages are stocked at the Hatteras Island Toy Store. Popular toys like Groovy Girls can be found here, as well as educational toys and musical instruments.

Natural Art Surf Shop
NC 12, Buxton
(252) 995-5682
Natural Art is owned by Scott and Carol Busbey, serious surfers who love the sport and the lifestyle. During the 25-plus years the shop has been in business, it has gained a reputation for being "the surfer's surf shop," specializing in surfing only. Scott, who has his own line of boards called In The Eye, manufactures custom boards and does repairs. Carol makes clothing (her hand-sewn women's and men's tops and children's shirts and dresses are unique and colorful). The shop rents surfboards, boogie boards, swim fins, wet suits, and surf videos and sells surfing gear, clothing, T-shirts, and sweatshirts. It's open March through December. (See our Water Sports chapter for more information.)

Osprey Shopping Center
NC 12, Buxton
Osprey is behind Natural Art Surf Shop and Buoy's Restaurant and has an ABC package store. **Ocean Notions Gift Shop** has a selection of gifts, including candles, bath products, and nautical trinkets as well as women's and men's clothing and a small selection of children's apparel. Look no further for beach supplies and a selection of gold and silver jewelry. It's open March through mid-December.

Buxton Village Books
NC 12, Buxton
(252) 995-4240
Comfortably nestled in what was once the summer kitchen of an island house, Buxton Village Books has been a village landmark since 1984. This charming space is packed with lots of good reads, including all the current best-sellers, sea stories, hard-to-

find Southern fiction, kids' books, and saltwater fly-fishing titles. In a room overlooking Pamlico Sound, you can browse over a delightful selection of notecards and stationery. The owner, Gee Gee, is an avid reader and willing to discuss literature. The shop has a public fax machine; ask about the shop's mail-order catalog. It's open year-round.

Frisco

Indian Town Gallery and Gifts
NC 12, Frisco
Nestled in the woods, Indian Town represents artists from the local villages. Many of the paintings have an Outer Banks offshore-fishing theme. The gallery also features pottery, chimes, cards, gifts, lighthouses, and jewelry. Artist Wayne Fulcher is often at work right in the store.

Red Drum Pottery
NC 12, Frisco
(252) 995-5757
Accomplished potters Rhonda Bates and Wes Lassiter moved their studio from Edenton, North Carolina, to Frisco in the summer of 2001. Watch them as they turn their wonderful creations at the wheel. These are well-crafted, artistic pieces, whether intended for functional or decorative use. It's definitely worth a stop to see their bowls, pitchers, vases, vessels, platters, teakettles, miniatures, and fabulous fish- and crab-imprinted hanging wall tiles. Late afternoons, these hospitable potters invite customers to paint a piece of pottery and fire it raku style. The gallery is open seven days a week year-round.

Islander Gifts
NC 12, Frisco
(252) 995-5427
An incredible selection of gifts and souvenirs awaits you at Islander Gifts. Shoppers can purchase anything from a seashell to Christmas ornaments. You'll also find home decor pieces, pirate toys, and bird carvings.

Scotch Bonnet Candies and Gifts
NC 12, Frisco
(252) 995-4242
www.scotchbonnetcandies.com
The sweetest spot on Hatteras Island has homemade fudge (more than 20 varieties, including sugar-free), ice cream, bulk taffy, Jelly Belly jelly beans, and other sweet treats. Scotch Bonnet also carries T-shirts, sweatshirts, jewelry, gifts, hermit crabs, and accessories. Don't miss the hermit crab races every Friday during the summer.

Browning Artworks
NC 12, Frisco
(252) 995-5538
In addition to clay, wood, fiber, metal, and glass pieces made by North Carolina's craftspeople, Browning Artworks offers an exclusive selection of original works by well-known Outer Banks watercolorist Russell Yerkes and photographers Michael Halminski and Ray Matthews. The ambience, both inside and out, makes shopping—or browsing—at Browning's a real pleasure. The shady deck invites you to sit for a while and enjoy the fountain pool and the beautifully landscaped grounds. Visiting artists, from wood turners and jewelry designers to potters and painters, provide demonstrations for parents and kids during summer. Use Browning's convenient shipping service to get your purchases home, and if you're planning a wedding, Browning's bridal registry can accommodate both the resident and the visiting bride. Call ahead for hours of operation, which vary with the season.

All Decked Out
NC 12, Frisco
(252) 995-4319, (800) 321-2392
Owner Dale Cashman and his crew hand-craft outdoor furniture such as picnic tables, Adirondack chairs, benches, wooden recliners, and hammocks, and they ship anywhere in the United States. Stop by and try a seat. It's open year-round with the exception of two weeks at Christmas. Call for a free catalog.

This Little Cottage
Southside Center
NC 12, Frisco
(252) 995-3320
This Little Cottage is a little bit hip, a little bit elegant, and lots of fun! It's all here for your fabulous lifestyle, from the latest names in home decor such as Maine Cottage, Shabby Chic, and Pine Cone Hill, to the hippest names in jeans and tees. You can also find great gifts, bath and body items and baby and toddler clothing. Open March through November.

The Frisco Market
NC 12, Frisco
The Frisco Market is directly across from the entrance road to Ramp 49 and Billy Mitchell Air Field. The market stocks groceries, beer, wine, reading material, gas, and beach supplies. **Frisco Rod & Gun** specializes in fishing and hunting equipment, including offshore, inshore, and surf-fishing equipment, as well as fly-fishing equipment, guns, ice, bait, tackle, and one of the best selections of knives we've seen anywhere. The local owners carry camping supplies, name-brand outdoor apparel, Sperry Topsiders, and T-shirts and offer free air for your tires. They are open year-round.

Hatteras Village

Hatteras Village offers a mixture of services, including a pharmacy, grocery store, and other shops. The ferry terminal's Ship's Store, located in the lobby, offers a selection of T-shirts, coffee mugs, coloring books, and souvenirs.

Sandy Bay Gallery
NC 12, Hatteras Village
(252) 986-1338
At the north end of Hatteras Village, this gallery showcases Outer Banks artists. Sandy Bay is filled with original watercolor and acrylic paintings and local photography. Potters, jewelers, glass artisans, and paper, wood, stained glass, and fiber artists

have wares on display. Glass boxes with silver trim by Mary Anne feature a geometric collage of colored and clear glass—they are exquisite. If you're having a hard time making a decision in this shop, head out to the large porch and plop into an Adirondack chair for a spell. Gift registry and shipping are available. The gallery is open March through Christmas Eve.

Izabella's Closet
NC 12, Hatteras Village
(252) 986-6575

This is a special women's clothing boutique, one you wouldn't really expect to find on southern Hatteras Island. The Flax line of clothing is featured, though there are many other brands as well, including Kiko, Click, and April Cornell. Most of the clothing is flowing and casual, with a lot of linen and a few dressier dresses. Separates include pants, skirts, tanks, sweaters, and light jackets. Upstairs are sundresses, workout wear, T-shirts, and swimsuits. Hats, jewelry, and bags round out the offerings.

Burrus' Red & White Supermarket
NC 12, Hatteras Village
(252) 986-2333

A Hatteras Village tradition, Burrus' Red & White has been serving locals and visitors since 1866. It carries seafood and freshly cut meat and has a full-service deli and salad bar. You'll also find gourmet and Eight O'Clock coffee, fresh produce, frozen foods, dairy products, and health and beauty aids. This market, a locals' favorite and a welcome respite from chain grocery stores, is open year-round.

Hatteras Harbor Marina Store
Hatteras Marina, NC 12, Hatteras Village
(252) 986-2166

The marina store has jewelry, name-brand sportswear, fishing supplies, unique gifts, deck shoes, and other items. Geared to please visitors, it's open year-round and caters to charter-boat fishermen and their families.

Lee Robinson General Store
NC 12, Hatteras Village
(252) 986-2381
www.obag.com

The original Lee's opened in 1948 but was replaced by a replica several years ago. We're glad it kept the old look, including the wide front porch and the wooden floors. Owners Belinda and Virgil Willis carry items you need for a vacation at the beach, plus something you wouldn't necessarily expect to find at a beach general store: a great selection of fine wine. The store also carries groceries (including gourmet items), chocolates, fudge, books and magazines, T-shirts, sweatshirts, jewelry and gifts, plus sundries such as film, lotions, boogie boards, and hats. Don't miss the upstairs gift gallery. You can rent bicycles here, too. It's a good place to buy a Coke in a glass bottle and something to snack on for the ferry ride to Ocracoke. It's open year-round.

Hatteras Landing
NC 12, Hatteras Village
(252) 986-2205

Right next to the Hatteras-Ocracoke ferry docks at the southern end of Hatteras Village, this spiffy shopping center means you'll never again have a boring wait for the ferry. The only problem is that people get carried away with shopping and are late for boarding.

Hatteras Landing Provision Company stocks a large selection of sweatshirts, T-shirts, and other clothing with Outer Banks themes, along with jackets, windbreakers, hats, and other clothing. **Graveyard Deli and Market** opens into the Provision Company and offers deli sandwiches, snacks, candy bars, chips, gum, drinks, beer, wine, and many sundries that you'll need for a day on the boat.

Birthday Suits is an Outer Banks favorite, carrying fashionable swimwear for the whole family. For hard-to-fit women, there are bra-sized tops that can be mixed with separate bottoms, plus long-torso suits and maternity suits. Men's sizes range from 28 to 4XL and include competition briefs and volleyball and surf trunks. Kids' swimwear ranges from size 2 to preteen, as well as swim diapers. Birthday Suits has a huge selection of OBX gear and contemporary sportswear for women, men, and children.

Surfside Casuals is a surfwear store selling swimsuits for men, women, and children, plus casual beach clothing, sandals, sunglasses, and T-shirts. Women love the fact that they can buy separates here, mixing and matching bottoms and tops. **Farmer's Daughter** brings a country-casual look to your home. Gifts and collectibles are the hallmarks of this store, which is an Outer Banks favorite. There are also original artworks by Outer Banks artisans, and the world's first and only supply of saltwater fudge.

Lightkeeper Gallery features exclusive artwork by local artists. Photographs by Scott Geib are stunning, and there are numerous paintings with Outer Banks themes and beautiful cards. Gift items are also available, including T-shirts, coffee mugs, coasters, and prints. **Kitty Hawk Kites/Carolina Outdoors** is an outdoor store selling kites, toys, outdoor apparel, sunglasses, sportswear, and more. This location has a rock-climbing wall right in the middle of the shopping center.

OCRACOKE ISLAND

Shopping in Ocracoke is casual, interesting, and easily managed on foot. Small shops are scattered throughout the village and along the main street, on sandy lanes, and in private homes. You'll also discover that some dockside stores have the feel of a general store. Ocracoke Village shops offer a variety of local crafts, artwork, quality accessories for the home, antiques, beachwear, books, music, and magazines as well as the ubiquitous T-shirts and even a few souvenir mugs. An ABC package store is adjacent to the Ocracoke Variety Store.

Ocracoke Variety Store
NC 12, Ocracoke
(252) 928-4911
Ocracoke Variety is on NC 12 before you enter the village from the north. Shop for groceries and fresh meat, beer, wine, T-shirts, beachwear and accessories, ice, gifts, books, magazines, camping and fishing supplies, household items, health and beauty aids, and even a few art supplies. True Value Hardware is conveniently located next door. There's a bulletin board posted at the front entrance featuring menus of the local restaurants and community information. It's open all year.

Pirate's Chest Gifts and T-shirts
NC 12, Ocracoke
(252) 928-4992
Peruse the variety of merchandise sold here: T-shirts, souvenirs, jewelry, local shells, books, scrimshaw, coral, lighthouse prints, 14-karat gold jewelry, Joan Perry sculptures, and more. Look for the shell-filled boat in the parking lot. The store is open March through November.

Island Ragpicker
NC 12, Ocracoke
(252) 928-7571
Island Ragpicker will catch your eye with an attractive mixture of bells, baskets, and hand-woven rugs displayed on the porch and everywhere inside. Owners Mickey Baker and Carmie Prete offer fine quality crafts (some by local craftspeople), handmade brooms, cards, decoys, pottery, dishes, jewelry, and casual cotton apparel. Look for local and nature books, short story collections, and self-help books along with an amazing assortment of easy-listening music. The Ragpicker has great cards. The shop is open March 1 through January 4.

Spencer's Market
School Road and NC 12, Ocracoke
This shopping complex houses **Sally Newell Interiors,** with furniture, home-decor accessories, window treatments, and more for the home. Newell is a mem-

ber of the American Society of Interior Designers and has designed many residential and commercial interiors. **Eleven Eleven Shades and Movies** offers just that—high-end sunglasses and video rentals. **Ocracoke Restoration Co.** is stocked with English stained glass, old and new furniture, architectural ornaments, old doorknobs and drawer pulls, and interesting salvaged materials.

Deepwater Pottery & Books to Be Red
School Road and NC 12, Ocracoke
(252) 928-7472 (Deepwater Pottery)
(252) 928-3936 (Books to Be Red)
On the corner of School Road and NC 12, a lovely historic home under a canopy of trees houses these two wonderful shops. Deepwater Pottery is a working pottery studio and gift shop, carrying handmade stoneware, candles, and glass; surprising home and garden accents; and a special bath section, which is filled with soaps and other great-smelling bath luxuries. The bath section carries Burt's Bees products as well. Books to Be Red has a wonderful selection of books by local authors, new-age journals, magazines, cards, and a paperback section of fiction, nonfiction, and children's books. There's a section of gently used books also. The shop is open March 1 through Christmas.

Natural Selections
School Road, Ocracoke
(252) 928-HEMP
Natural Selections, The Ocracoke Island Hemp Shop, offers a great selection of products made from hemp and other natural fibers. Natural Selections is a socially and environmentally conscious shop, committed to the belief that the use of hemp will save the planet from herbicides, pesticides, fertilizers, and deforestation. Once you feel the natural fibers, you'll want to wear the pants, dresses, shirts, jackets, and hats sold here. Natural Selections also sells bags, hemp home accessories, natural cosmetics, jewelry, and gifts.

Captain's Landing
NC 12 on Silver Lake, Ocracoke
Just past the Jolly Roger Pub and Marina is this little conglomeration of shops, not really connected but clustered around the post office. **Downpoint Decoys,** a small rustic shop under an old oak tree, sells decoys both old and new and the local carver/proprietor is available to talk to. He also sells lures, painted oars, and wildlife art.

Mermaid's Folly
NC 12, Ocracoke
(252) 928-RAGS
At this shop you'll find finely crafted works of art. The clothing, T-shirts, hats, bags, and jewelry are imaginative and casual, making this store a fun place to shop. It also has furniture, trunks, lamps, and home accessories.

Island T-Shirts Shop
NC 12, Ocracoke
(252) 928-6781
In an old island home built in 1910, this shop offers stacks of T-shirts in every size and color. Look for children's wear, beach shoes, bathing suits, shorts, sweatshirts, and gift items, including frames, wind chimes, books, jewelry, and beach toys. A whole roomful of Christmas ornaments and decorations crafted by locals awaits.

The Community Store
Ocracoke Waterfront, Ocracoke
(252) 928-3321
Operating since 1918, The Community Store is the place to shop for essential items in the heart of Ocracoke Village. It seems incongruous that you can rent videos here, for walking through the door is like stepping back in time. There's a cooler full of ice cream and frosty-cold sodas and beer.

Joyce's of Ocracoke Gifts & Clothing
Ocracoke Waterfront, Ocracoke
(252) 928-6461
On the waterfront, Joyce's occupies the first-floor space of Joyce's of Ocracoke

Motel and Dockage. Owner Joyce L. Barnette offers well-made, comfortable men's and women's apparel, including a collection of classic, sophisticated clothing for women in sportswear and dressier island styles. Joyce also offers an intimate apparel section. The shop carries lovely accessories for the home, such as collectors' items with frogs, cows, rabbits, fish, shells, and teddy bears. Other great finds are handcrafted fashion jewelry in all price ranges, mobiles, gifts, cards, stationery, wrapping paper, and T-shirts with unique designs. It's open March through Thanksgiving.

Harborside Gift Shop
NC 12, Ocracoke
(252) 928-3111

Harborside is one of the many pleasant surprises for visitors to Ocracoke. Quality sportswear for the family, a gourmet food section, gift basket service (some ready-mades are available), teas, cooking items, pottery, books, and magazines share the shop with an interesting collection of T-shirts and—look up!—a model train that chugs along overhead throughout most of the store. You'll also find domestic and imported wine and beer. It's open Easter through Thanksgiving.

Village Craftsmen
Howard Street, Ocracoke
(252) 928-5541, (800) 648-9743

Village Craftsmen is an Ocracoke landmark—it's been in business more than 30 years—but it isn't as easy to find as, say, the lighthouse. The shop is on the narrow dirt lane known as Howard Street, a bit of a walk from the main street. Here you'll discover an abundance of North Carolina crafts, pottery, rugs, books, locally made soaps, candles, and jewelry. You can buy stoneware, tie-dyed dresses, and T-shirts, too.

Owner Philip Howard, a seventh-generation Ocracoke Island resident, sells his pen-and-ink and watercolor prints in his shop. A fine selection of cassettes and CDs features Celtic, blues, jazz, and blue-

Walk in any direction in the heart of Ocracoke, and soon you'll notice little signs that point down narrow lanes to marvelous galleries and shops. Some are tucked into the woods; others are in garages or little buildings behind artists' houses. Each one is a treasure in itself.

grass music. Musical instruments, such as catpaws and strumsticks, help set a creative mood at this out-of-the-way place. The instruments are lightweight and simple to play. You can pick up a mail-order catalog at the shop or have one mailed to you. Village Craftsmen closes for the month of January.

Over the Moon
British Cemetery Road, Ocracoke
(252) 928-3555

Over the Moon is a wonderful shop filled with handmade contemporary crafts. More than 100 artists and craftspeople provide work such as jewelry, porcelain, and Brian Andreas's StoryPeople—books, prints, and sculptures with insights written on the work. There are also pins and magnet cards, Metamorphicards, and hammock chairs. Pace yourself; this is a place to linger. It is open Easter through Thanksgiving.

Island Artworks
British Cemetery Road, Ocracoke
(252) 928-3892

A brightly colored little shop across from Over the Moon, Island Artworks is a fun place to browse. It's a contemporary craft gallery, with colorful jewelry by local artist Kathleen O'Neal; fused glass and mosaics by Libby Hicks; photography, watercolors, pottery, woodworking, sculpture, mosaics, birdbaths, garden stakes, and more.

Ocracoke Island Hammocks Co.
British Cemetery Road, Ocracoke
(252) 928-4387

These folks weave their own hammocks on the premises, and you are welcome to watch the process. The shop offers island mementos, lighthouse afghans, jewelry, and unique candles. You'll find a wide variety of bath and body and aromatherapy products and gourmet foods. In addition to the gift shop, **Candyland** guarantees to satisfy any sweet tooth. It's open Easter through Christmas.

Teach's Hole Pirate Gifts
Back Road, Ocracoke
(252) 928-1718
www.teachshole.com

Come listen to the tales of the notorious Edward Teach—better known as Blackbeard the Pirate—at Teach's Hole. The "piratical pirate-phernalia," as George and Mickey Roberson call their collection, includes a gift shop and exhibit. More than 1,000 pirate items, including a life-size recreation of Blackbeard in full battle dress and artifacts from the 17th and 18th centuries, form the exhibit. One exhibit features "Blackbeard's Doom" on an eight-minute video viewed for a fee. Items in the gift shop include pirate toys, music boxes, movies, and more than 100 pirate book titles, plus maps, flags, hats, T-shirts, costumes, ship models, and treasure coins. For more information, see our Kidstuff chapter. Teach's Hole open Easter though Thanksgiving from 10:00 A.M. to 6:00 P.M., Monday through Saturday.

Ocracoke Coffee Co.
Back Road, Ocracoke
(252) 928-7473
www.ocracokecoffee.com

This aromatic shop is filled with bagels, baked goods, brewed coffee drinks, espresso, smoothies, shakes, more than 30 flavors of ground and whole bean coffee, and loose teas. You'll also find a selection of gift items, such as beautiful, hefty coffee mugs. Ocracoke Coffee is open daily from 7:00 A.M. until 9:30 P.M., and live music plays during summer evenings on the deck.

Heart's Desire
Back Road, Ocracoke
(252) 928-4104

Artist Mary Bassell combines her own creations of custom stained-glass windows, beach glass jewelry, papier-mâché, and folk art with fine crafts by other artists. Heart's Desire also carries a nice selection of antique English stained glass and antique collectibles. The studio/gallery is open April through December.

Ocracoke Restoration Co.
NC 12, Ocracoke
(252) 928-2669
www.ocracokerestoration.com

Formerly known as Roadhouse Stained Glass Co. of Ocracoke, Ocracoke Restoration carries antique English stained glass, wrought-iron gates, and other decorative items. Most of their glass decorates windows and doors, though smaller stained-glass pieces, many originally from porch lanterns, can be found here. You can find such imports as lamps and garden pieces, plus an occasional armoire or table. The store is open from March through January. Shipping is available anywhere.

Ride the Wind Surf & Kayak
NC 12 and Silver Lake, Ocracoke
(252) 928-6311

Open April through Christmas, Ride the Wind Surf & Kayak offers complete surfing equipment and gear, swimsuits, ladies' and men's clothing, shoes, sandals, handbags, suntan lotions, sunglasses, watches, and jewelry. See our Water Sports chapter for surf and boogie board rentals as well as kayak tour information.

Ocracoke Island Trading Company
NC 12, Ocracoke
(252) 928-7233

This Aussie outfitter sells casual clothing. T-shirts range from size small to XXXL, adorned with "Ocracoke" or funny sayings. The store also stocks sportswear, hats, dresses, fish-print clothing, shorts, and more. If you're looking for gift items and souvenirs, look here.

Bella Fiore Pottery
109 Lighthouse Road, Ocracoke
(252) 928-2826
Talented artist Sarah Fiore creates colorful handmade pottery in this working artist studio and gallery. She also features natural body products, lampworked hair picks, and other art pieces.

Village Diva
NC 12, Ocracoke
(252) 928-2828
Step into Village Diva and marvel at the incredible selection of women's clothing that Village Diva carries. Lines like CP Shades and Flax are sold here. Village Diva also sells home accessories and garden accents.

Blue Door
Lighthouse Road, Ocracoke
(252) 928-7216
This fun shop is in an old house surrounded by a picket fence. A big spinning wheel and several antiques rest on the porch. Inside you'll find more antiques, unique gifts, art supplies, art, and the weaving studio of the owner. So you don't miss this shop, look for the sign made from—what else?—a blue door.

Silver Lake Trading Co.
Back Road near British Cemetery Road Ocracoke
(252) 928-3086
Silver Lake Trading Co. is one of the best gift shops on Ocracoke Island, with goods that are eccentric, fun, and fashionable. You'll find things for your home and garden, including Christopher Radko ornaments, Asian-inspired pottery, locally made pottery and wooden bowls, picture frames, funky lamps, Sandra Drennen linens, pillows, candles and soaps, garden statues, and even plants. Other goods include off-the-wall refrigerator magnets and poetry kits, lunch boxes, unique toys, naughty but hilarious cards and cocktail napkins, and Dirty Girl soap and bubble bath.

ATTRACTIONS

The Outer Banks's biggest attraction is, of course, the water. Nine hundred square miles of water surround these islands, providing a huge, liquid playground for swimmers, boaters, sailors, surfers, anglers, waders, and divers. For those who don't want to get wet, just being on these narrow islands with 175 miles of Atlantic Ocean beaches and views of sparkling blue from every angle is enough.

Nature is so stark and apparent on the Outer Banks that no man-made attraction could ever compare with its glory. But we also have an abundance of stellar man-made attractions, many the sole reason people travel to the Outer Banks. These attractions satisfy many—history buffs, nature lovers, arts aficionados, and thrill seekers.

Some of the Outer Banks attractions were created by men and women out of pride for the significant historic events that took place here, such as the Wright brothers' first flight and the first attempted English settlement in the New World. Others, like *The Lost Colony* outdoor drama, are themselves as much a part of history as the events they portray.

If you're accustomed to metropolitan-area prices, you're in for a real treat. Local attractions are affordable, with most costing less than $10 and many open for free. The priciest attractions are worth every penny and still affordable compared with city prices. Most places offer special family, child, or senior discounts. While some of the attractions stay open year-round, many close in the winter months or strictly curtail their hours. Call ahead.

The Outer Banks is not just the home of two of the most significant events in the nation's history—the first English-speaking colony and the first powered flight—it's also gifted with an extraordinary coastline. Between lighthouses, lifesaving stations, wild horses, and shipwrecks, visitors can get lost in our long, lively history.

Wide-open wildlife refuges spread across the islands, and fluorescent-lighted fish tanks glow at the state aquarium. You can dive into history by boarding a reproduction of a 16th-century sailing ship or scuba dive into the Atlantic to explore a Civil War shipwreck. There's never enough time to see everything the Outer Banks has to offer.

In this chapter, we highlight our favorite attractions. Many others are there to be discovered; Insiders often share their own secret spots. Many of these places have free admission or request nominal donations. We begin with the northernmost communities and work southward. Each area has its own section, so pick your pleasure.

Also, read our Recreation, Shopping, Arts and Culture, Water Sports, Fishing, Kidstuff, Natural Wonders, and Nightlife chapters for more exciting, educational, and unusual things to do and places to play on the Outer Banks.

COROLLA

Historic Corolla Village
Schoolhouse and Corolla Village Lanes
Corolla Village
(252) 453-3341

Though everyone refers to the whole Currituck Outer Banks as "Corolla," technically Corolla is the small village center on the unpaved road behind the lighthouse. Few people realize that Corolla was a thriving community that began to grow in 1875 after the lighthouse was built. In 1890, at the peak of the area's waterfowl-hunting market, 200 residents lived in the village. The village population declined during World War II and the following years. Only a few residents lived in Corolla well into the 1980s, when a paved public road was opened to the area and development of the Currituck Outer Banks began. The faces of the Currituck Outer Banks and Corolla Village have changed dramatically, but you can still get a sense of the old village by walking on the dirt road on the west side of North Carolina Highway 12 behind the lighthouse. In the shade of the oaks and pines, it is easy to imagine the life of the early residents.

A few of the historic buildings from the old village remain and have been restored to look as they did when they were built. A walking-tour map is available at many of the shops in the area or at Twiddy & Company Realtors, whose owners took charge of restoring the buildings. The restored Corolla Schoolhouse is on the tour, though you can't go inside. The charming schoolhouse, on the corner of Schoolhouse Lane and Corolla Village Lane, was built in the mid- to late 1890s and finally closed in 1958. Also on the tour are several restored historic homes that have been converted into shops, so you can go inside, including the Lewark and Parker residences. A new building was built to look like Callie Parker's store. The walking tour will also take you past the 1878 U.S. Lifesaving Station that was moved to the village, the Currituck Beach Lighthouse and Lightkeeper's Residence, and the historic Whalehead Club.

Kill Devil Hills Lifesaving Station
Off NC 12, Corolla
Built in 1878, the Kill Devil Hills Lifesaving Station is now the setting for Outer Banks Style, a specialty shop in Corolla (see our Shopping chapter). The interior doesn't look anything like the old outpost, but the exterior appearance, a peaked roof and crossed timber frame, remains relatively unchanged.

The U.S. Lifesaving Service was established in the late 19th century, and stations were built every 7 miles along the Outer Banks. Crews lived in the wooden structures throughout winter months, patrolling the beaches for shipwrecks and survivors.

This station, which was moved almost 30 miles north of its original location, is especially significant because it was frequented by the Wright brothers during their several sojourns to the barrier islands. The Kill Devil Hills Lifesaving Station crew assisted Orville and Wilbur with their early experiments in flight, and some crew members witnessed the world's first powered airplane soar over the sand dunes.

This lifesaving station was brought from Kill Devil Hills to Corolla in 1986, where it was restored and renovated. History buffs are welcome to visit Outer Banks Style and the lobby of Twiddy & Company Realtors (behind the station), where a collection of memorabilia used by the lifesaving service and the Wrights is on display. This unique, hand-wrought structure is at the foot of the Currituck Lighthouse on the west side of NC 12 in historic Corolla Village.

The Whalehead Club
Currituck Heritage Park, NC 12, Corolla
(252) 453-9040
www.whaleheadclub.com
Overlooking the windswept wetlands of Currituck Sound, this grand dame of days gone by was once the Outer Banks's biggest, most modern structure. Today, the Whalehead Club is one of the area's most magnificent attractions and affords a romantic trip back in time to an era of lavish accommodations and elaborate ornamentation.

The house was built as a private residence between 1922 and 1925, when the Currituck Outer Banks was in its heyday as a waterfowl-hunting paradise. The owners, a wealthy northerner named Edward Collins Knight and his wife, Marie Louise LeBel Knight, originally called their home Corolla Island because the house was situated on an islandlike mound that was created when a circular canal was dug around the lot. The Knights spent their winters and hunted at Corolla Island from 1925 to 1934.

The 21,000-square-foot house has seen many uses since then. It sat empty for years, as relatives of the Knights were not interested in the remote location. In 1969 the house was sold to Ray Adams of Washington, D.C., for a reported $25,000. It was Adams who named the home the Whalehead Club. This grand and beautiful home sat empty for nearly 25 years, suffering significant vandalism.

The house, on the National Register of Historic Places, is now owned by Currituck County and has been restored to the way it looked in 1925. The multimillion-dollar restoration project began in 1999 with the replacement of the copper roof. The exterior was painted its original canary yellow. The interior has been completely restored, down to the paint, cork floors, Tiffany glass, and Art Nouveau details. A team of researchers and restoration specialists has tracked down as much information as possible to make the restoration as accurate as possible.

Visitors are welcome and can take a guided tour of the house. Tours begin on the half hour and include a self-guided exhibition on display in the basement gallery. A special "behind the scenes" tour is offered daily (by reservation only). Guides are very knowledgable about the home as well as the history of the area. The museum shop stocks an interesting array of tasteful merchandise that is unique to the Whalehead Club, including hand-crafted jewelry, picture frames, ornaments, and birdhouses made from the original copper roof shingles. The Whalehead Club is situated on 39 acres, known as Currituck Heritage Park. It offers an ideal location for picnics, leisurely walks, fishing, or enjoying a beautiful Outer Banks sunset.

The Whalehead Club is open from May 1 through October 31 and during the weeks of the Easter, Thanksgiving, and Christmas holidays (not on the actual holidays themselves). House tours take place daily from 10:00 A.M. until 5:00 P.M. The tours last 45 minutes. Cost is $6.00 for adults and free for children age eight and younger. A children's tour and treasure hunt and ghost tours are also held Monday through Friday in season and require advance reservations.

Currituck Beach Lighthouse
Off NC 12, Corolla
(252) 453-4939
www.currituckbeachlight.com
Visitors can climb the 214 steps to the top of the lighthouse, coming eye-to-eye with the 50,000 candlepower lamp that still flashes every 20 seconds and can be seen for 18 nautical miles. The climb up the narrow, winding staircase is not for the faint of heart, but a panoramic view of the Currituck Outer Banks is your reward.

Inside, at the base and on the first two landings, are lighthouse exhibit panels installed in 2001. They cover the broad history of coastal lighthouses, including all of the North Carolina lighthouses, and give an in-depth history of the Currituck Beach Lighthouse and its buildings. The Fresnel lens is explained, and there is a special exhibit on the former Currituck Beach Lighthouse keepers.

The Lightkeepers' Residence, a beautiful Victorian dwelling, was constructed of precut, labeled materials and was shipped for assembly on-site by the U.S. Lighthouse Board. The residence was abandoned when the lighthouse was automated in 1939 and keepers were no longer needed on-site (though they still visited once a week to change batteries and perform maintenance). The residence, on the National Register of Historic Places, fell into serious disrepair but was restored by a group known as Outer Banks Conservationists starting in 1980. It is not open for tours, except by appointment during the first two weeks in November.

Today, the keeper's main duties, among many others, are keeping the lighthouse open for tourists, overseeing preservation work, and hiring volunteers and staff. In 2005 the Currituck Beach Lighthouse celebrated its 130th anniversary as a working lighthouse. Be sure to visit the on-site Museum Shop.

Visitors climb the lighthouse for a fee of $6.00. Children younger than age eight climb for free. School groups and other large groups are offered a discounted rate. The lighthouse is open daily from Easter through Thanksgiving. Climbing hours are 10:00 A.M. to 6:00 P.M. during Eastern Standard Time (generally early April to late October) and to 5:00 P.M. during daylight saving time. If you're climbing, you must go up at least 15 minutes before closing time. During periods of lightning or high winds, the lighthouse tower may be closed to climbers.

In 2003 the U.S. Coast Guard awarded the Currituck Beach Lighthouse to the nonprofit Outer Banks Conservationists. The OBC group spent more than 20 years raising private dollars to restore, maintain, and operate the lighthouse.

Corolla Chapel
Old Corolla Village Road, Corolla
(252) 453-4224

The Corolla Chapel, built in 1885, is one of Corolla's most-treasured historic structures. Snuggled into the soundside village, two and a half blocks behind the lighthouse, the chapel served generations of native Corollans in its small sanctuary.

In its early years, the church was used primarily by Missionary Baptists, although originally it was supposed to be interdenominational. Catholic Masses were first said at the church in 1917 and continued on a sporadic basis through the world wars for Coast Guard personnel stationed nearby. In 1938, the Baptists dropped Corolla from their circuit, saying it was too remote, and the church became interdenominational. In the 1960s, Corolla's population reached its all-time low, and the church was no longer used. It laid idle for 25 years.

The last living trustee of the chapel was John Austin, and when he died, the church passed to the hands of his son, Norris Austin, who still lives in the village. In 1987, as Corolla began to grow again, Austin invited Pastor John Strauss to be the minister of the chapel. Strauss led a restoration, adding a vestibule, bathroom, and storage area in 1992. With regular interdenominational services, he also began to develop a following.

The church outgrew its small chapel. In the summer months, the village chapel that seats only 100 would have at least that many (or more) people standing outside. On Easter of 2001, Pastor Strauss offered communion to 2,000 people during four services. This led to construction of a new church building across the road from the original chapel. The old Corolla Chapel was then moved across the street and melded into the new sanctuary to form the shape of a cross. The new sanctuary has the same tongue-and-groove beaded-board paneling and details as the old one, so that the two blend seamlessly together, inside and out. The new facility was planned to hold 200 to 250 worshipers.

The best way to see the Corolla Chapel is to attend a service there. Interdenominational services are held year-round on Sunday morning at 10:00 A.M. From Memorial Day through October, an additional Sunday service is held at 8:30 A.M. A local priest holds Catholic services at the chapel on Wednesday night at 6:00 P.M., every week in the summer and the second and fourth weeks in the off-season. Four interdenominational services are held on Easter, one on the beach.

Pine Island Audubon Sanctuary
NC 12, between Duck and Corolla

Set between remote villages of sprawling vacation rental cottages, Pine Island Audubon Sanctuary is a secluded outdoor enthusiast's paradise and a major resting area for birds along the great Atlantic flyway. Ducks, geese, rabbits, deer, fox, and dozens of other animals make their home in this 5,400-acre wildlife refuge on the northern Outer Banks. Hundreds of other species fly through during spring and fall migrations.

Live oaks, bayberry, inkberry, pine, yaupon, holly, and several species of marsh grass grow naturally in this wild, remote wetland habitat. The Pine Island

CLOSE-UP

The Wild Horses of Corolla

Corolla's wild horses are part of the mystique of the Outer Banks: a symbol of the roots, endurance, and resilience of an isolated land and its tough inhabitants. They are also the symbol of the toll taken by breathtaking growth in Corolla.

Visitors to the northernmost stretches of barrier beach no longer see pastoral views of horses grazing on golf courses or newly planted lawns. They no longer see the majestic beasts loping on oceanside sands. They won't even see close-ups of the few that were once corralled at the Currituck Beach Lighthouse.

There are no horses left in Corolla. They are now fenced in the Currituck National Wildlife Refuge.

Believed by many to be descendants of Spanish mustangs, the wild horses have the compact, stocky confirmation and, according to one scientist, the genetic markers of the Barb horses that were brought to the Outer Banks as early as 1523 by Spanish explorers. One native Outer Banker who has studied the "Banker ponies" said they may be the oldest breed of horse in North America. Though the horses have Span-

ish origins, they are of a breed all their own, due to nearly 400 years as an isolated species. The horses are recognized as a significant cultural and historical resource by the state of North Carolina.

Before development in Corolla intensified in the mid- and late 1980s, wild horses ranged freely among the sea grasses and dunes of the northern barrier islands. A late discovery for developers, the area didn't have electricity until 1968, telephone service until 1974, or a public paved road until 1984. Tourists driving on the new road were charmed that undomesticated horses milled freely in plain view. Less than 10 years later, horses were lounging in shade under rental cottage decks, nosing through garbage cans, and strolling nonchalantly through the grocery store's automatic door. Tourists took to feeding and petting them—or attempting to. Close calls with horse bites and kicks became part of the local lore.

But as the area grew, the interaction between horses and humans became more dangerous. After the road between Duck and Corolla was made

Clubhouse and grounds are privately owned, but if you're a member of the Audubon Society, tours are available.

Hikers, bikers, and strollers can park at Sanderling Inn to access a 2.5-mile clay trail through a portion of the sanctuary. The maintained path is open year-round.

DUCK

**U.S. Army Corps of Engineers
Field Research Facility
NC 12, Duck
(252) 261-6840, ext. 401
www.frf.usace.army.mil**
Set on a former Navy weapons test site,

public in 1984, 17 horses were killed in vehicle accidents in just four years.

A group of local citizens established the Corolla Wild Horse Fund in 1989 to protect the animals after three pregnant mares were killed. The group rallied public support, managing to have the county pass an ordinance to help protect the horses from harm. The wild horses, in fact, became the area's most popular attraction.

Still, horse-fund volunteers and staffers were unable to protect their charges. After a poll revealed that most people wanted to preserve the horses in their own environment instead of relocating them, the fund erected a mile-and-a-half-long fence, stretching from sound to sea near where the pavement ends in Corolla. The idea was not to enclose the wild animals but to allow them to roam freely—but safely—in the more than 1,600 acres of public and private land north of the fence. On March 24, 1995, the horses were herded behind the fence. But the Corolla wild-horse story was not yet over.

Like clever children, some of the herd, which numbered 100 by then, strayed around the fence up to Virginia, where they were not welcome. Other horses, led by a particularly stubborn stallion, began sneaking back into Corolla Village. They were always herded back home, but the few recalcitrant horses always found a way out. In 1999 the Corolla Wild Horse Fund took the wandering horses to the private Dews Island in Currituck Sound, where they had 400 acres to graze. Today there are no horses on Dews Island, but 65 horses stay behind the fence and roam the vast area between the off-road ramp and Carova.

The horses are better protected than ever. The staff at the Corolla Wild Horse Fund is responsible for overseeing the health and safety of the herd. Volunteers are needed to help with activities such as a census, marking the horses, and taking health samples. The Corolla Wild Horse Fund Office is at the Currituck County Satellite Building at 1123 Ocean Trail in Corolla proper. The office phone number is (252) 453-8002. The mailing address is P.O. Box 361, Corolla, NC 27927, or you can visit www.corollawildhorses.com.

the Waterways Experiment Station of the U.S. Army Corps of Engineers has helped scientists study ocean processes since 1977. This 173-acre federally owned scientific mecca has gained a reputation as one of the premier coastal field research facilities in the world. Just north of Duck Village, the site includes state-of-the-art equipment to monitor sand movement, wave forces, water currents, temperatures, and sedimentation. Its 12 full-time employees regularly host dozens of scientists from around the globe to conduct experiments on sand movement, beach erosion, and coastal dynamics. In 1997, during the world's largest near-shore research experiment, 250 coastal engineers gathered at the research facility to study the near-shore zone of breaking waves to determine the dynamics of beach erosion.

The public is invited to tour the research facility from mid-June through mid-August. One free tour is held each day, Monday through Friday, at 10:00 A.M. Reservations are not necessary, and the tour is held rain or shine, except in lightning. The tours last about an hour and a half, sometimes longer, and include an eco-lecture about how the sound and ocean waters coexist, barrier island environments, and ocean currents. Researchers lead the tours onto the beach, into the observation tower, and into the research facility. The public is not allowed on the pier because of the great amount of research equipment there. Since part of the tour is outside on a sandy trail and on the beach, participants should be prepared for a strenuous walk.

Besides the 1,840-foot pier, the U.S. Army Corps of Engineers' experiment station owns a 125-foot observation tower and a 35-foot-tall Coastal Research Amphibious Buggy, the CRAB, which carries people and equipment from the shore into the sea. The Corps works in cooperation with the U.S. Army and Navy and the National Oceanic and Atmospheric Administration, using the latest technically advanced equipment to improve the design of coastal navigation projects. Research conducted at the station could eventually alter the way engineers design bridges, help people pick sites for beach nourishment projects, improve projections about where the shoreline might erode, determine how and why sandbars move, and predict what effect rock jetties might have on Oregon Inlet.

KITTY HAWK

Kitty Hawk Public Beach & Bathhouse
NC 12, MP 4, Kitty Hawk
Across the road from the ocean, a bathhouse and a small, free parking area offer visitors access to the beach as they arrive on the Outer Banks at Kitty Hawk. If you arrive too early for check-in, you can change into bathing suits here and enjoy a few hours at the ocean until it's time to head to your hotel or beach cottage. Public showers also are available to rinse off after one last stop in the sand on the way home. Another parking lot is available close by, right off Byrd Street.

Kitty Hawk Village
Along Kitty Hawk Road, west of US 158
Kitty Hawk
If you want to check out one of the islands' oldest neighborhoods and see where the Wright brothers stayed when they first visited the Outer Banks, head west on Kitty Hawk Road, turning just north of the 7-Eleven in Kitty Hawk. This winding, two-lane street dead-ends after about 3 miles at Kitty Hawk Bay. Drivers pass through at least two centuries in the process.

The old post office for this isolated village still stands on the north side of the road and was restored to become the town's police station. Several two-story farmhouses still stand along the shady streets and shallow canals. Boats on blocks and fishing nets tied to trees are strewn along backyards. On warm weekend afternoons, families ride horses down lanes lined with live oaks, waving to neighbors sitting on their covered porches. You can forget you're at the beach in this quaint, quiet community on the western shores of the Outer Banks.

Monument to a Century of Flight
Off US 158 Bypass, behind the Aycock
Brown Welcome Center, Kitty Hawk
(252) 441-6584
www.icarusinternational.com
This sculptural garden was conceived by local artist Glenn Eure and brought to

fruition by the nonprofit group Icarus International. It features stainless-steel pylons placed in ascending order by height, symbolizing the steps humans have taken to reach the heavens. Adorning the pylons are black granite slabs that name 100 of the most important moments in the history of flight. The courtyard contains 5,000 bricks, each engraved with a sponsor's message. (At the time of printing, about 600 bricks, three pylons, a flagpole, and numerous pavers and benches were still available for sponsorship.)

Outer Banks Music Showcase
Kitty Hawk Plaza, US 158, MP 4½
Kitty Hawk
(252) 261-7505
www.outerbanksmusicshowcase.com
Outer Banks Music Showcase, billed as "where Branson meets the Outer Banks," features America's favorite music. Local performers entertain an audience of all ages, weaving comedy and music from a variety of genres— country, show tunes, 1950s and 1960s pop, gospel, and patriotic songs—into family-friendly shows. There are two performances nightly in season. In 2005 tickets were $20.95 for adults and $11.95 for children age 12 and younger.

KILL DEVIL HILLS

Wright Brothers National Memorial
US 158, MP 8, Kill Devil Hills
(252) 441-7430
www.nps.gov/wrbr
Set atop a steep, grassy sand hill in the center of Kill Devil Hills, the trapezoidal granite monument to Orville and Wilbur Wright is within easy walking distance of the site of the world's first powered airplane flight. Below where this lighthouse-style tower now stands, on the blustery afternoon of December 17, 1903, the two bicycle-building brothers from Dayton, Ohio, soared over a distance of more than 852 feet, staying airborne for an unheard-of 59 seconds in their homemade flying machine.

The monument was erected to honor Orville and Wilbur Wright in 1932. In the low, domed building on the right side of the main drive off U.S. Highway 158, the National Park Service operates a visitor center, gift shop, and museum. Here, you can view interpretive exhibits of humankind's first flight and see displays on later aviation advancements. Exhibits about the Wright brothers' struggles to fly include parts of their planes, engines, and research notes. Reproductions of their gliders are displayed in the flight room, and rangers offer free guided historical tours year-round.

The visitor center is itself an attraction. Opened in the early 1960s, it is recognized as a significant example of modernist architecture. It's one of only a handful of examples of modernist architecture built in eastern North Carolina during the 20th century, mainly because the National Park Service was one of a few groups in the region that had the financial resources to hire architects from outside the region.

The Philadelphia architectural firm of Ehrman Mitchell and Romaldo Giurgola designed the building to reflect the natural environment of the Outer Banks and symbolically portray flight in static form. The horizontal roof with a shallow concrete dome reflects the surrounding landscape of beach and dunes, while the overhang of the dome represents the soaring possibilities of flight. The National Historic Register–listed structure is considered a key work in the Philadelphia School of expressive modernist architects.

The 100th anniversary celebration of the first flight was held in December 2003. An olive-shaped, domed Centennial Pavilion was added for the celebration and will remain on the grounds. It holds an exhibit hall and an auditorium. The Centennial Pavilion houses an expanded U.S. Air Force exhibit and an expanded NASA exhibit as well as new exhibits from the Cirrus Corporation and the Wright Experience. The Wright Experience details the story of replicating the original Wright flyer. In a nearby temporary facility, one of the two Wright Flyer replications is stored. The facility is open occasionally for viewing, but not at regularly scheduled times. Harry Combs, deceased Wright Brothers historian and aviator, donated more than $1 million to build and replicate the flyer housed here.

Outside the exhibit center, four markers set along a sandy runway commemorate the takeoff and landing sites of each of Orville and Wilbur's December 17 flights. Reconstructed wooden sheds replicating those used at the Wrights' 1903 camp and hangar also are on the grounds and open to visitors. These sheds are furnished with tools, equipment, and food canisters similar to those the brothers used.

A short hike takes you from the visitor center to the monument hill, but if you'd rather drive or ride, parking is available closer to the base of the hill. Paved walkways make access easy. The grass is filled with cacti and sand spurs, so you're advised to stay on the paths. Also, be aware that the walk up the monument hill is longer and more strenuous than it looks. On a hot summer day, consider visiting the site in the morning or late afternoon, when the sun is not as strong.

At the bottom of the south side of the monument hill, a sculpture added for the 100th anniversary celebration of flight is displayed. It re-creates Orville flying the plane, with Wilbur running alongside and local John Daniels taking the historic photo of the event.

Besides tours, the Exhibit Center at the Wright Brothers National Memorial offers a variety of summer programs. Grounds and buildings are open to vehicles from 9:00 A.M. until 5:00 P.M. Labor Day through Memorial Day. Hours are from 9:00 A.M. to 6:00 P.M. in the summer. Thirty-minute flight-room talks are given by rangers every hour on the hour, year-round. Expect the entire tour to take about one to two hours. Add an additional 30 minutes if you'd like to attend a program.

Cost for entry at the guard gate is $3.00 for adults ages 16 and older, and admission is good for seven days. Persons age 15 and younger get in free, as do seniors with Golden Age Passports and other passports, which are available at the gate.

Outer Banks Opry
First Flight High School
Veterans Drive off Colington Road
Kill Devil Hills
(252) 256-2081
www.outerbanksopry.com
The Outer Banks Opry entertains with a family-oriented evening of music and fun for all ages. Weekly guest performers join regular headliners Coyote and Molasses Creek. The Opry is held at First Flight High School late June through mid-August on Friday at 8:00 P.M. Tickets are $15.00 for adults and $5.00 for children younger than age 12.

Nags Head Woods Ecological Preserve
Ocean Acres Drive, Kill Devil Hills
(252) 441-2525
www.nature.org
If you've had a little too much sun, or if you'd like to spend time in a secluded forest on a part of the Outer Banks few people get to see, allocate an afternoon for The Nature Conservancy's Nags Head Woods Preserve, west of US 158. The maritime forest itself is well hidden, and many rare plant and animal species live within this protected landscape. It's one of the most tranquil settings on the Outer Banks.

The Nature Conservancy, an international, nonprofit conservation organization, oversees this maritime forest. Nags Head Woods is not a park—it is an example of a successful private-public partnership between The Nature Conservancy, the towns of Nags Head and Kill Devil Hills, and private landowners.

More than 5 miles of trails and footbridges wind through forest, dune, swamp, and pond habitats as well as graveyards and farm sites from the 19th and 20th centuries. Trails are open to visitors on weekdays from 10:00 A.M. to 3:00 P.M., while members of The Nature

Conservancy are welcome during any daylight hours. No camping, firearms, picnicking, or alcoholic beverages are allowed in the preserve. Bicycling, pets on leashes, and other activities that might damage the trails are restricted to the Old Nags Head Woods Road, which winds from north to south through the woods.

For more information, write to The Nature Conservancy at 701 West Ocean Acres Drive, Kill Devil Hills, NC 27948. All donations are welcome, and memberships start at $25. Monies support the preserve's environmental education and research programs.

NAGS HEAD

Jockey's Ridge State Park
US 158, MP 12, Nags Head
(252) 441-7132
www.jockeysridgestatepark.com
The East Coast's tallest sand dune and one of the Outer Banks's most phenomenal natural attractions, Jockey's Ridge has long been a favorite stop for tourists. In the early 1970s, bulldozers began flattening the surrounding dunes to make way for a housing subdivision. A Nags Head woman, Carolista Baum, single-handedly stopped the destruction and formed a committee that saved Jockey's Ridge.

State officials made the sand hill a protected park in 1975, but the dunes are unruly. Since then, the steepest side of the hill has shifted more than 1,500 feet to the southwest. Jockey's Ridge is also getting shorter. At the turn of the 20th century, the highest mound was estimated at 140 feet. In 1971, it was about 110 feet tall.

Today, the 1.5-mile-long, 420-acre-plus dune—which varies from 90 feet to 110 feet in height—is open to the public year-round until sunset. It's a popular spot for hang gliders, summer hikers, small children who like to roll down the steep slopes, and teenagers who delight in sand-boarding or flinging and flipping themselves down the sandy hills. Sand-

boarding is allowed only from October 31 through March 31. More than one million people visit Jockey's Ridge each year.

Park headquarters is near the northern end of a parking lot off the west side of US 158. You'll notice an entrance sign at MP 12, Carolista Drive, in Nags Head.

A visitor center, museum, and gift shop are near park headquarters. The free museum features photo displays of the history and recreation at the dune and a diorama of the animals that inhabit the area. Information panels of plants and animals and an auditorium where slide shows and videos are shown are also at the facility. Maps available from the park ranger indicate walking areas. Two trails—the Soundside Nature Trail, a very easy 45-minute walk, and Tracks in the Sand, a 1.5-mile trek—are open to hikers looking for a change of scenery. Jockey's Ridge State Park offers natural history programs throughout the summer, including star-gazing and wildlife discovery evening hikes and early-morning bird-watching and natural history discovery adventures. Fantastic educational programs for kids are also offered, but rangers warn that they fill up fast, and many require advance registration. Call for program schedules. Sheltered picnic areas are available for lunches.

It's a long hike to the top of the ridge. Bring shoes or boots. Don't try it barefoot in summer; you'll burn your feet. Also, some lower areas around the dune are covered with broken glass. At the top of Jockey's Ridge, you can see both ocean and sound. Cottages along the beach look like tiny huts from a miniature train set. Kite-flying and hang-gliding enthusiasts catch the breezes that flow around the steep summit, shifting the sand in all directions. (See our Recreation chapter for information on hang gliding.)

If your mobility is impaired, a 360-foot boardwalk affords wheelchairs and baby strollers a slightly sloping incline onto a wooden platform overlooking the center of the dune. For the visually impaired, audio guides are available at the park office. Park rangers can also provide a ride on a four-wheeler to the top of the dune if you call in advance.

The park opens at 8:00 A.M. every day except Christmas. Closing time depends on the season: November through February, 6:00 P.M.; March and October, 7:00 P.M.; April, May, and September, 8:00 P.M.; and June through August, 9:00 P.M.

This is sunset-watching central, especially in the summer months, when hundreds of people may climb the dunes to watch the sun sink into Roanoke Sound. A soundside access is on the southwest side of Jockey's Ridge. This also provides access to a great beach on the gentle sound waters.

Nags Head Beach Cottage Row Historic District
NC 12, MP 12–13, Nags Head

The long row of rustic, weather-worn cottages on the ocean in Nags Head around mileposts 12 and 13 is famously known as the "Unpainted Aristocracy." The homes have been on the National Register of Historic Places since 1977. They feature the "Nags Head style" cedar siding grayed in the wind and salt, wraparound porches, propped-open shutters, dormers, and gabled roofs. Although Nags Head was a vacation destination earlier, it wasn't until 1855 that an Elizabeth City doctor built the first house on the oceanfront. He was lonely, so he sold the land around him to other people who vacationed in the wooded area by the sound. By 1885 13 homes sat at the ocean's edge.

Many of the cottages are still in the original families. Nine of the original 13 are still standing. Two were replaced with similar structures, one was destroyed by fire, and one was razed. Several of the other cottages in the mile-long row between mileposts 12 and 13, though not of the original 13 homes, are historic in their own rights, having survived since the early 1900s. The land around these homes is private, and the homes are occupied. Feel free to drive by or walk by and admire, but please respect the owners' privacy and don't trespass on their property.

Jennette's Pier
MP 16½, Nags Head
(252) 441-6421
www.jennettespier.net

Jennette's Pier is a local historic landmark that lost most of its pier during Hurricane Isabelle in 2003. Just before the hurricane, the North Carolina Aquarium Society had purchased the site. In 2006, the remaining pier house will be taken down and rebuilt, and a 1,000-foot concrete pier will be constructed. Plans are for the pier to have wooden rails and decking to create a traditional feel, yet the concrete pylons will make the site much more substantial. Look for the pier to reopen in 2007.

ROANOKE ISLAND

Roanoke Island brims with attractions. Anyone visiting the Outer Banks should definitely come over for the day, although with many new bed-and-breakfasts, restaurants, and shops in town, it's becoming more of an overnight destination in its own right.

If you're planning to visit many of the attractions on Roanoke Island, a Roanoke Island Attractions Pass or Queen's Pass will save you up to 25 percent of the admission fees. The Attractions Pass combines admission to the North Carolina Aquarium, The Elizabethan Gardens, and Roanoke Island Festival Park for $17.00 for adults and $8.25 for children ages five and older. The Queen's Pass allows admission to the same three attractions, plus *The Lost Colony,* for $31.00 for adults and $16.25 for ages five and older. Children younger than age five can visit all of these attractions except *The Lost Colony* for free. The passes are good for one calendar year and are available at the local attractions and the Outer Banks Visitors Bureau.

The Elizabethan Gardens
Off US 64, Roanoke Island
(252) 473-3234
www.elizabethangardens.org

Created by the Garden Club of North Carolina Inc. in 1960 to commemorate the efforts of Sir Walter Raleigh's colonists at establishing an English settlement, these magnificent botanical gardens offer an exquisite, aromatic environment year-round. They include 10.5 acres of the state's most colorful, dazzling flora. The flower-filled walkways contrast the wind-blown, barren Outer Banks beaches.

Six full-time gardeners tend more than 1,000 varieties of trees, shrubs, and flowers in the Elizabethan Gardens. The tree-lined landscape is divided into a dozen gardens, where translucent emerald grass fringes marble fountains, and beauty blooms from every crevice.

Visitors enter at the Gate House into formal gardens along curving walkways carefully crafted from brick and sand. The bricks were handmade at the Silas Lucas Kiln, in operation during the late 1800s in Wilson, North Carolina.

Although this botanical refuge is breathtakingly beautiful all year, vibrant with seasonal colors and fragrances, it is perhaps the most striking in spring. Azaleas, dogwood, pansies, wisteria, and tulips bloom around every bend. Rhododendron, roses, lacecap, and other hydrangea appear in May. Summer brings fragrant gardenias, colorful annuals and perennials, magnolia, crape myrtle, Oriental lilies, and herbs. Chrysanthemums and the changing colors of leaves signal the beginning of fall, and camellias bloom from fall all the way through the winter.

In the center of the paths, six marble steps down from the rest of the greenery, sits the crown jewel of the Elizabethan Gardens: a sunken garden, complete with Roman statuary, tiered fountains, and low shrubs pruned into geometric flower frames. The famous Virginia Dare statue nearby is based on an Indian legend that says Virginia, the first English child born in America, grew up among Native Americans (see the Roanoke Island section of our Area Overview chapter).

A wonderful treat is to see an outdoor (weather permitting) performance of *Elizabeth R*. This one-woman, hour-long show

Virginia Dare, the first child born to the colonists on Roanoke Island, was born on August 18. Each year on that day a wonderful celebration is held at the Elizabethan Gardens. Madrigal singers fill the air with their beautiful songs, and a 45-minute play is performed at this free event. The play changes each year.

features Queen Elizabeth I in her full regalia and is held on summer Tuesdays at 2:30 P.M. (See more about *Elizabeth R* later in this chapter.)

The gardens are closed Thanksgiving Day, Christmas Eve, Christmas Day, and New Year's Day. From March through November, the gardens open at 9:00 A.M., and closing time varies depending on the season (between 5:00 and 7:00 P.M.). The gardens are open daily from 10:00 A.M. to 4:00 P.M. in December, January, and February. When *The Lost Colony* is running, the gardens stay open until 8:00 P.M. so that visitors can tour the gardens then head next door to see the outdoor drama. Garden admission is $6.00 for adults, $4.00 for youths ages 6 through 18, $5.00 for adults age 62 and older, and free for children younger than age 5 when accompanied by an adult. Season passes are available.

Wheelchairs are provided. Most paths are wheelchair accessible. Some plants are for sale in the garden gift shop. A meeting room is available for a fee to community groups up to 100 people. The gardens also are a favorite wedding locale (see our Weddings chapter).

Fort Raleigh National Historic Site
Off US 64, Roanoke Island
(252) 473-5772
www.nps.gov/fora

When you visit Fort Raleigh, don't expect to see a fort. What exists on the site is a small earthworks fortification. It is not a daunting barricade, but a lovely spot drenched in American history. On the north end of Roanoke Island, near the

Roanoke Sound's shores, Fort Raleigh marks the beginning of English settlement in North America. Since this attraction is next to the Elizabethan Gardens and *The Lost Colony*'s Waterside Theatre, many people combine a trip to all three.

Designated as a National Historic Site in 1941, this more than 500-acre expanse of woods includes the "outerwork"—an area built intentionally away from living space—along with a soundside beach, the National Park Service's Cape Hatteras National Seashore headquarters, the Fort Raleigh Visitor Center, and nature trails.

The Fort Raleigh Visitor Center offers interpretive exhibits in a small museum. The museum is not particularly interesting to children, though adults will be fascinated by the story of the colonists who attempted the first English settlements in the New World. A 17-minute video provides an introduction to the historic site. Also, a 400-year-old Elizabethan room from Heronden Hall in Kent, England, is on display. It was removed from an authentic 16th-century home. The room gives visitors a feel for the type of living accommodations the aristocratic English were used to at the time of the attempted settlements. A gallery inside displays artifacts excavated from the site and copies of watercolors by John White, governor of the Roanoke colony.

Outside, Fort Raleigh has a variety of options for experiencing the history of Roanoke Island. Behind the visitor center is the earthworks, which is not very impressive, but gives you an idea of the original. The Thomas Hariot Nature Trail, named for the scientist who accompanied one of the voyages, winds through the woods behind the visitor center. Hariot's descriptions of the New World are quoted on interpretive signs along the trail. The pine-needle path leads to the sandy shores of Roanoke Sound.

Self-guided tours and tours led by Park Service personnel are available at this archaeologically significant site. Interpretive programs on African-American history, European colonial history, Native American history, and Civil War history are offered in the summer. Fort Raleigh National Historic Site is open year-round from 9:00 A.M. to 5:00 P.M. seven days a week. Hours are extended in the summer. The grounds of Fort Raleigh provide a place for a picnic, especially under the huge live oaks on the grass median of the parking lot. Restrooms are on-site.

Freedmen's Colony Site, Weirs Point, and Fort Huger
Roanoke Island
(252) 473-5772

At the northernmost end of Roanoke Island, on the east side of the Manns Harbor bridge, are several historic landmarks that are part of the Fort Raleigh National Historic Site. You can access these sites by the Freedmen's Trail, a 2-mile, self-guided trail that starts near the Elizabethan Gardens entrance. You can get there by car and park in the sizable lot or ride a bike along the Manteo Bike Path, which ends at this site. Weirs Point is an attractive public beach on Croatan Sound. The beach is wide enough to allow for a picnic or game of Frisbee, and the sound water is warm and shallow. Picnic benches, a Dare County information kiosk, and restrooms are provided at Weirs Point. Watch for stumps and broken stakes in the water. The tide creeps up quickly, so keep blankets out of its encroaching flow.

Next to the beach is an exhibit about the Freedmen's Colony, a community for runaway slaves between 1862 and 1867. During the Civil War, Roanoke Island was seized by Union soldiers in 1862. After that, runaway slaves were welcomed on the island, given food, and allowed to settle in the Union camp. Slaves from all over northeastern North Carolina flocked to the safe haven. Male freed slaves worked for the Union forces for $10 a month plus rations and clothing. Women and children were paid $4.00 a month. In 1863 the colony was officially established, and the freed slaves were given land and agricultural tools. Many of the freed slaves joined the Union effort, but the ones who remained behind were given health and education services. By 1866, however, most of the freedmen were forced to leave. Exhibits at the site explain the story.

In 1901, from a hut on Weirs Point beach, one of the unsung geniuses of the electronic age began investigating what was then called "wireless telegraphy." Reginald Fessenden held hundreds of patents on radiotelepathy and electronics, but he died without any credit for many of them. In a letter dated "April 3, 1902, Manteo," Fessenden tells his patent attorney that "I can now telephone as far as I can telegraph . . . I have sent varying musical notes from Hatteras and received them here with but 3 watts of energy." Thus, the world's first musical radio broadcasts were completed on this soundside sand of the Outer Banks.

About 300 yards north of Weirs Point, under 6 feet of water, lay the remains of Fort Huger. This was the largest Confederate fort on the island when Union troops advanced in 1862. The island migrated quite a bit in the last 140 years; the fort formerly sat securely on solid land.

The Lost Colony
Off US 64, Waterside Theatre
Roanoke Island
(252) 473-3414, (800) 488-5012
www.thelostcolony.org

The nation's longest-running outdoor drama, this historical account of the first English settlement in North America is a must-see for Outer Banks visitors. It's almost as legendary as the story it depicts. Pulitzer Prize–winning author Paul Green brought the history of English colonization to life through an impressive combination of Elizabethan music, Native American dances, colorful costumes, and vivid drama on a soundside stage in 1937. His play continues to enchant audiences today at Waterside Theatre, near Fort Raleigh, on Roanoke Island.

The Lost Colony is a theatrical account of Sir Walter Raleigh's early explorers, who first settled on the shores near the present-day theater in 1585. (Andy Griffith got his start playing Sir Walter Raleigh for several seasons.) Children and adults are equally captivated by the performers, staging, and music; many locals see the show every year and always find it spellbinding. If you have youngsters, come early and have them sit in the front row by the stage. The closer you sit to the stage, the more you'll enjoy the show.

In 2001 The Lost Colony got a boon when Tony Award–nominated Broadway actor Terrance Mann agreed to direct the show. Mann, who has held principal roles in Cats, Les Miserables, Beauty and the Beast, and The Scarlet Pimpernel, performed in The Lost Colony as a dancer and in the role of Old Tom before making it big on Broadway. Mann made many changes to the play, returning many of the nostalgic nuances of the glory days of the show. Another famous name associated with the show is William Ivey Long, who won a second Tony Award in 2001 for his costume design work on The Producers. Long has been the costume designer for The Lost Colony for more than 15 years and has been associated with the show since he was a young boy, when his parents worked on The Lost Colony.

It can get chilly in the evenings when the wind blows off the sound, so we recommend sweaters, even in July and August. Mosquitoes at this outdoor drama can be vicious, especially after a rain, so bring plenty of bug repellent. The theater is wheelchair accessible and the staff is glad to accommodate special customers.

Once you arrive, settle back and enjoy a thoroughly professional, well-rehearsed,

---

Backstage tours at **The Lost Colony** *are offered within the season for only $3.00 per person. Get an up-close look at the theater, costume shop, and prop rooms. The tours are held Monday through Saturday from 6:30 to 7:30 P.M. and take a maximum of 50 people. Call (252) 473-3414, ext. 225 to reserve a spot.*

technically outstanding show. The leads are played by professional actors. Most of the backstage personnel are pros—and it shows. Supporting actors are often locals, with some island residents passing from part to part as they grow up. On August 18, four local infants are chosen to participate in the play in honor of Virginia Dare's birthday.

The drama has changed its pricing structure and is now charging slightly more for the best seats in the house (though the theater is so well designed that they're all pretty good). All seats in The Producer's Circle, Rows O through T, which offer the most panoramic view of the show, are $20. General Admission seats are $16.00 for adults, $15.00 for seniors age 62 and older, and $8.00 for children age 11 and younger. Family nights are Friday and Saturday, when children are admitted at half price ($4.00). Groups of 20 or more may reserve seats for $14 each. Group reservations must be made in advance.

The show begins at 8:30 P.M. and runs six nights a week (closed Sunday) from the end of May through late August.

This is probably the most popular summertime event on the Outer Banks, so we recommend that you make reservations, though you can try your luck at the door if you wish. Make paid mail reservations by writing The Lost Colony, 1409 U.S. Highway 64/264, Manteo, NC 27954; or reserve tickets by phone. Tickets can also be purchased at 70 outlets across the Outer Banks. Call for locations. If a production is rained out, ticket holders can exchange their passes for another night or get a refund.

North Carolina Aquarium on Roanoke Island
374 Airport Road, Roanoke Island
(252) 473-3494
www.ncaquariums.com

The North Carolina Aquarium on Roanoke Island is an outstanding facility. Its 68,000 square feet of space includes a $16 million expansion that was completed in May 2000. The theme of the aquarium is Waters of the Outer Banks, and visitors get to see a variety of marine communities: coastal freshwaters, wetlands, estuaries, roadside ditches, the Gulf Stream, and the Graveyard of the Atlantic on the ocean floor.

A major attraction is the Graveyard of the Atlantic tank, holding 285,000 gallons of salt water, or about 2.35 million pounds. It takes 209 pilings sunk about 35 feet into the ground to support the weight of this enormous tank. The tank's highlight is a 53-foot-long replica of a Civil War ironclad, the USS *Monitor*. Expert scuba divers who have seen the real *Monitor* wreck say the replica is extremely accurate. Scuba divers give educational presentations from the tank and answer spectators' questions while inside. Also in the tank are sea turtles and nearly 1,000 other sea creatures, including sharks, cobia, tarpon, jack crevalle, bluefish, and black and red drum.

Wetlands on the Edge is another favorite exhibit. In this tree-filled atrium, river otters swim and play in a clear pool of river water, while visitors watch through a glass screen. Also here are several American alligators, who bask in the sunlight near their pond. You'll also see turtles.

The Coastal Freshwaters exhibit explores freshwater marine animals and habitats. From ponds and lakes to the Albemarle Sound, this exhibit displays turtles, sunfish, gars, and bowfins. The Croatan Sound tank showcases the fish that local anglers catch. Marine Communities features nine tanks representing environments from grass flats to the Gulf Stream, displaying blue crabs, summer flounder, puppy drum, lobster, a porcupine puffer, and much more. Close Encounters is the touch tank area, where kids can touch horseshoe crabs and other creatures. Staff members are on hand to answer questions.

Walk outside, behind the aquarium, and you're right on the banks of Roanoke Sound. Rest on a bench or walk along a path through the trees. Bleached-white whale bones form a natural sculpture garden. Along the short path, interactive exhibits tell the story of the area's birds and plant life.

The aquarium offers educational films, lectures, and classes year-round. Field trips to nearby salt marshes and fishing areas are available for a fee. For information about daily programs or special activities, such as crabbing classes, call (252) 473-3494, ext. 242. The gift shop is a real treasure, with a multitude of toys that teach children to think and become environmentally aware. Posters, stuffed animals, gifts, souvenirs, puzzles, games, T-shirts, and more are top-quality and based on a natural theme.

The North Carolina Aquarium on Roanoke Island is open year-round from 9:00 A.M. to 5:00 P.M. daily, except Christmas and New Year's Days. Prices are $7.00 for adults, $6.00 for seniors and active military personnel, and $5.00 for children age 6 to 17. Kids age five and younger are admitted free. Preregistered school groups are granted free admission.

Old Swimming Hole
Airport Road, Roanoke Island
(252) 473-1101, ext. 313
Go for a swim after a visit to the aquarium. Right next door, the county facility maintains a beach, picnic tables, grills, picnic shelter, kids' playground, sand volleyball court, and restrooms. The beach is lifeguarded from 10:00 A.M. to 6:00 P.M. from Memorial Day to Labor Day. Families with small kids love the sound waters.

Kitty Hawk Aero Tours
Main Terminal, Airport Road
Manteo Airport, Manteo
(252) 441-TOUR, (877) 274-2461
For a bird's-eye view of the Outer Banks and a shocking perspective on how fragile the barrier islands really are, take a 30-minute air tour over the land and ocean in a small plane.

Pilots will gear tours to passengers' wishes but usually head south to Bodie Island Lighthouse and back. Bring your camera for this high-flying cruise. Rates

Rainy summer days are by far the most crowded days at the North Carolina Aquarium on Roanoke Island. To avoid the crowds, go on a sunny day when everyone else is at the beach.

are $39 per person for parties of three to six and $48 per person for parties of two.

Biplane flights in an open-air-cockpit authentic 1941 Waco are also available from the same site starting at $88 per person for two passengers. These 15-minute trips take you back in time, complete with goggled leather helmets. Pilots fly south to Bodie Island Lighthouse and back to the Manteo Airport.

Air tours are offered year-round, weather permitting. Advance reservations are accepted.

Elizabeth R/Bloody Mary and the Virgin Queen
The Elizabethan Gardens and the Pioneer Theatre
Roanoke Island Festival Park
(252) 473-1061
Adding to the cultural delights of Roanoke Island are the finely crafted short plays *Elizabeth R* and *Bloody Mary and the Virgin Queen.* Performed by the acclaimed Barbara Hird, these two dramatic performances give insight into the life of Queen Elizabeth I. *Elizabeth R* is an internationally acclaimed one-woman show that examines the private life of Elizabeth Tudor, or Queen Elizabeth I. During the hour-long performance, the queen, dressed in her full regalia, reveals the private details of her life, including her likes and dislikes, the reasoning behind her decisions, and information about the people around her. Performances are held once a week.

Bloody Mary and the Virgin Queen is a humorous musical farce based on the relationship between Queen Elizabeth I and her half sister, Mary Tudor. The two absolutely loathed one another, yet they're buried in the same tomb in London's Westminster Abbey. Through fast-paced dialogue of bantering, arguing, cajoling, singing, crying, and laughing, the two actors teach a history lesson in a most entertaining way. Barbara Hird plays Elizabeth, and Marsha Warren plays Mary. *Bloody Mary* is performed one day each week during July and August. The performance is about an hour long. Neither of these plays is suitable for young children. While the dialogue is witty and interesting for adults, there really isn't enough action for young attention spans. *Elizabeth R* is suitable for ages 14 and over; *Bloody Mary and the Virgin Queen* is recommended for ages 10 and up.

Mother Vineyard
Off Mother Vineyard Road
Roanoke Island

The oldest-known grapevine in the United States grows on Roanoke Island. When the first settlers arrived here, the Outer Banks were covered with wild grapes. Arthur Barlowe wrote to Sir Walter Raleigh in 1584:

". . . Being where we first landed very sandy and low toward the water side, but so full of grapes as the very beating and surge of the sea overflowed them, of which we found such plenty, as well there as in all places else, both on the sand and on the green soil, on the hills as in the plains, as well on every little shrub, as also climbing toward the tops of high cedars, that I think in all the world the like abundance is not to be found."

The Mother Vine is one of those grapevines, so old that it may have been planted even before Europeans arrived in the New World. Certainly it was already old in the 1750s, as records attest, and scuppernong grapevines do not grow swiftly. Another story is that this vine was transplanted to Roanoke Island by some of the Fort Raleigh settlers. Whichever story is true, the Mother Vine is more than 400 years old, and it's still producing fine, fat, tasty grapes. In fact, for many years, a small winery owned by the Etheridge family cultivated the vine on Baum's Point,

making the original Mother Vineyard wine until the late 1950s.

Mother Vineyard Scuppernong, the Original American Wine, is still produced by a company in Petersburg, Virginia. It is a pink wine, quite sweet, similar to a white port.

The Mother Vine is on private property and a bit out of the way. To find it, drive north from Manteo on U.S. Highway 64. About 0.75 mile past the city limits, turn right onto Mother Vineyard Road. Go less than a half-mile, where the road makes a sharp turn to the right at the sound. About 300 feet past the turn, on the left, the patient old vine endures beneath a canopy of leaves, twisted and gnarled, ancient and enduring. Please stay on the road if you're sneaking a peek.

Downtown Manteo
Off US 64; Queen Elizabeth Avenue and Budleigh and Sir Walter Raleigh Streets
Manteo

Named for a Roanoke Island Native American who accompanied English explorers back to Great Britain in the 16th century, Manteo is one of the oldest Outer Banks communities and has long been a commercial and governmental hub for the area.

When Dare County was formed in 1870, this area along Shallowbag Bay became the county seat. Roanoke Island provided a central location that everyone could reach by boat. It wasn't until 1873, when a post office was established here, that the county seat became known as Manteo. In 1899 Manteo incorporated and became the Town of Manteo. Today hundreds of permanent residents make this Roanoke Island town their home, and many more county residents commute from other towns to work. On Budleigh Street, many of the county and town offices are scattered in older office buildings. Manteo's restaurants, shops, and bed-and-breakfast inns beckon tourists, and thousands of visitors arrive each summer to explore this historic waterfront village. (See the Roanoke Island section of our Area Overview chapter.)

On the docks of Manteo's waterfront, 53 modern dockside slips with 110- and 220-volt electrical hookups offer boaters overnight or long-term anchorage. A comfort station with restrooms, showers, washers, and dryers also serves vessel crews and captains. Shop and dine within walking distance in Manteo—or better yet, bike. This is a town to enjoy on two wheels.

Across the street from the waterfront, in the center of the downtown area, independently owned shops, eateries, and businesses offer everything from handmade pottery to books to clothing, all in a 4-square-block area.

Around the southeast point of the waterfront, the town's American Bicentennial Park is wedged between the courthouse and a four-story brick building housing shops and condominiums. Picnic benches afford a comfortable place to rest and enjoy the view across the bay to Roanoke Island Festival Park, where the state's replica 16th-century sailing ship *Elizabeth II* rocks gently on small sound waves. A wood-plank boardwalk leads along the town's waterfront. One end bustles with kayak and boat tours coming and going, boaters docking in the harbor, and tourists strolling along the docks or exploring shops and restaurants. Around the corner is a gazebo for resting and a long pier for fishing or crabbing. A children's playground with equipment is on the corner, as are picnic tables. At the far end of the docks, you'll find a bit of serenity, where the activity diminishes and the only company you'll have is a few cattails.

If, as most visitors do, you reach the Banks via US 158, you can get to Manteo by traveling south until you reach Whalebone Junction. Bear right onto US 64 at the traffic light near RV's restaurant. Continue across the causeway and high-rise bridge past Pirate's Cove, then bear right at the intersection, turning onto U.S. Highway 264 Business. Turn right at either of the town's first two stoplights to go downtown.

Roanoke Island Festival Park and the *Elizabeth II*
1 Festival Park, Manteo
(252) 475–1500
(252) 475–1506 24-hour events line
www.roanokeisland.com

An expansion of the *Elizabeth II* Historic Site, Roanoke Island Festival Park is one of the largest attractions on the Outer Banks. This vibrant history, educational, and cultural arts complex opened in 1998, with top-quality facilities that add a tremendous variety to the year-round interests on Roanoke Island. Visitors explore the evolution of Roanoke Island and the Outer Banks from the late 16th century to the early 1900s through living-history interpretation, exhibits, film, and visual and performing arts programs.

The site includes the 8,500-square-foot Roanoke Adventure Museum, where interactive displays allow you to touch, see, and hear the history of the Outer Banks. In the Film Theater, *The Legend of Two Path,* a 45-minute film developed especially for the site by the North Carolina School of the Arts, tells the story of the first English landing on Roanoke Island from the Native American point of view. There's an outdoor performance pavilion that offers classical and popular concerts on lush pastoral lawns; a gallery, with art shows that change monthly; a small theater where special films and plays are held in an intimate setting; and a museum store bursting with treasures.

Porches, lawns, and boardwalks add charm, and you're just as likely to encounter an Elizabethan settler there as you are inside. The Children's Performances, held daily in the summer months in the Film Theater, are excellent. Many special events are held at Festival Park year-round, such as a fishing rodeo, beach music festivals, and a Civil War encampment. See the Web site or call for details, and also see our Annual Events chapter.

The *Elizabeth II,* designed as the centerpiece for the 400th anniversary of the first English settlement in America, is a representative sailing ship similar to the one that carried Sir Walter Raleigh's colonists across the Atlantic in 1585. Interpreters clad in Elizabethan costumes conduct tours of the colorful 69-foot ship.

Although it was built in 1983, the *Elizabeth II*'s story really began four centuries earlier, when Thomas Cavendish mortgaged his estates to build the *Elizabeth* for England's second expedition to Roanoke Island. With six other vessels, the original *Elizabeth* made the first colonization voyage to the New World in 1585 and landed on the Outer Banks.

There wasn't enough information available about the original vessels to reconstruct an exact replica, so shipbuilders used the designs of vessels from 1585 to build the *Elizabeth II*. Constructed entirely in a wooden structure on the Manteo waterfront, the completed ship slid down hand-greased rails into Shallowbag Bay in front of a crowd of enthusiastic dignitaries and locals in 1983.

Stretching 69 feet long and 17 feet wide and drawing 8 feet of water, *Elizabeth II* was funded entirely through private donations. Her decks are hand-hewn from juniper timbers. Her frames, keel, planking, and decks are fastened with 7,000 locust wood pegs.

Every baulk, spar, block, and lift of the ship is as close to authentic as possible, with only three exceptions: a wider upperdeck hatch for easier visitor access; a vertical hatch in the afterdeck to make steering easier for the helmsman; and a controversial pair of diesel engines that were installed in the *Elizabeth II* in 1993. The 115-horsepower motors help the grand sailing ship move under its own power, instead of relying on expensive tug boats.

Now, the vessel can cruise up to 8 knots per hour with no wind and travel for up to 40 hours without refueling its two 150-gallon tanks. The state ship stays on the Outer Banks most of the year, but during the off-seasons, it sometimes travels to other North Carolina ports, serving as the state's only moving historic site.

Roanoke Island Festival Park is open year-round. Hours vary according to season. Admission is $8.00 for adults, $5.00 for students, and free for children younger than age five. Group rates are available. Call ahead for a schedule of events.

Illuminations Summer Arts Festival
Roanoke Island Festival Park Pavilion
1 Festival Park, Manteo
(252) 475-1500
www.roanokeisland.com
The outdoor pavilion at Roanoke Island Festival Park provides an idyllic setting for the cultural arts performances of the North Carolina School of the Arts. Visitors are invited to spread out blankets or set up folding chairs on the expansive, lush lawn facing the pavilion. Performances include dance, classical music, drama, film, and jazz. Picnics are welcome. The pavilion has an open back, so you often can see the waters of the Roanoke Sound flowing behind the performers, making an especially tranquil setting. Performances are held Tuesday through Saturday evenings at 8:00 P.M. from June 25 through August 10. A $5.00 donation is requested.

Outer Banks History Center
Roanoke Island Festival Park
1 Festival Park, Manteo
(252) 473-2655
Adjacent to the visitor center at Roanoke Island Festival Park, the Outer Banks History Center is a remarkable repository of North Carolina state and regional history. The North Carolina State Archives, Division of Archives and History, Department of Cultural Resources, administers this Outer Banks treasure.

Opened in 1988, the history center col-

First Friday on Roanoke Island is held from 6:00 P.M. until 8:00 P.M. on the first Friday of each month, beginning in April. Discover the magic of historic downtown Manteo. Locals and visitors mingle at this special night, which offers music, shopping, and dining. For more information call (252) 473-5121.

---

lection includes 100,000 manuscript items, 35,000 books, 35,000 photographs, 1,500 periodical titles, a large collection of important maps, hundreds of audio and video recordings, microfilm, and ephemera. Some of the more than 700 maps in the collection are more than 400 years old. The collection also includes items relating to lighthouses and other Outer Banks architecture, local history about towns, shipwrecks, the U.S. Lifesaving Service, Civil War artwork, and *The Lost Colony* outdoor drama records and memorabilia.

Materials are housed in closed stacks to ensure security and the climate control needed for preservation. However, staffers at the history center are knowledgeable and happy to help anyone access the facility's vast resources. Journalists, authors, history buffs, students, scientists, genealogists, and casual tourists find the stop worthwhile.

A special gallery features archived materials and photographs, and traveling exhibits are displayed from time to time. The reading room and gallery are open year-round from 9:00 A.M. to 5:00 P.M. Monday through Friday and 10:00 A.M. to 3:00 P.M. on Saturday. The Outer Banks History Center is a public facility and is free of charge.

Pioneer Theatre
113 Budleigh Street, Manteo
(252) 473-2216

This nostalgic movie house is the best place to see movies on the Outer Banks and the oldest theater continuously operated by one family in the United States. The original Pioneer Theatre, opened in 1918 by George Washington Creef, was located a block over and showed silent films accompanied by a local pianist. The current Pioneer Theatre opened in 1934 and is now run by Creef's grandson, H. A. Creef.

This movie house is a family gathering place for Manteo locals. All of the movies are first-run and usually family oriented (G, PG, or PG-13), and people come regardless of whether they're interested in

the show. Friday night the place is overrun with school kids, so it's best to avoid that night unless you're one of them. This place is definitely old-fashioned in its prices: $5.00 per ticket. You won't get gouged at the candy counter either. One movie is shown every night at 8:00 P.M. as long as there are at least three people in the theater. Listings change weekly, without fail, on Friday. Check the billboard on the highway in Manteo, or call the theater for the current listing and a brief synopsis of the movie.

North Carolina Maritime Museum on Roanoke Island
104 Fernando Street, Manteo
(252) 475-1750

In 1998 the vintage George Washington Creef Boathouse in downtown Manteo was revitalized as an outpost of the North Carolina Maritime Museum in Beaufort. This effort breathed new life into the old boathouse that has stood on the Manteo waterfront since 1940.

The museum is dedicated to North Carolina's place in boatbuilding history. The crew at the museum, many of them volunteers, stay busy refurbishing and rebuilding wooden boats. Inside, a number of crafts represent the region's maritime history. There's an 1883 original Creef shadboat, a variety of sailing skiffs, a Davis Runabout speedboat, and a multimedia presentation on the construction of the *Elizabeth II*, which was built on this site. This is also a working boat shop, where visitors observe staff and volunteers working on a variety of repair and building projects. If you're interested in becoming a volunteer, talk to the curator.

Before the boathouse, this site was home to much of Manteo's extensive boatbuilding history. A boatyard and repair railway were here from the 1880s until 1939, when nearly everything on the Manteo waterfront burned in a devastating fire. George Washington Creef Jr. constructed this boathouse in 1940 to build shallow-draft freight boats and repair the shadboats invented and built by his father,

George Washington Creef Sr. The shad-boat is now the North Carolina state boat. The boathouse was later used to build rescue craft for the military and world-record-holding speedboats.

The museum is worth the trip to Manteo for those interested in boats and boatbuilding of the past and present. It is open Tuesday through Saturday. Hours are 10:00 A.M. to 6:00 P.M. during summer months and 9:00 A.M. to 5:00 P.M. during the fall, winter, and spring.

Weeping Radish Brewery
US 64, Manteo
(252) 473-1157
www.weepingradish.com
Historians say the first beer made in America was brewed on Roanoke Island. In 1585, they write, English colonists made a batch to befriend the Native Americans—or maybe to calm their own nerves. Roanoke Island today boasts its own brewery at a Bavarian-style eatery called The Weeping Radish, 1 mile south of downtown Manteo.

On the shaded grounds, a full-time brewmaster makes both light and dark lager beer, available at the restaurant or to go in one-liter refillable bottles and six-packs of their Fest brew. Weeping Radish beer in 22-ounce bottles is sold at area retailers.

Half-hour brewery tours are given in June, July, and August at 1:00 and 6:00 P.M. The rest of the year, call for the schedule. Free samples are given on the tour for tasting in the pub or at outdoor patio tables.

An annual Oktoberfest is held the weekend after Labor Day. Events and activities include oompah bands and German folk dancers (see our Annual Events chapter for details). Locals find this a favorite evening spot in the off-season. Visitors feel at home, too. There's even a colorful playground for the kids.

Historically Speaking's Customized Evening Entertainments
(252) 473-5783
Nicholas Hodsdon and Douglas L. Barger, both seasoned actors and performers, offer made-to-order programs for tour groups, conferences, or conventions. They'll either come to the group or have the group meet them at a local venue. Programs can be adapted to meet any situation and are delightful alternatives to pub-hopping. The entertainment is available year-round on an as-requested basis.

Call for additional information. Two popular presentations offered by Historically Speaking are "A Sea Song Sing-Along," featuring Outer Banks folk music with entertaining commentary on 400 years of coastal Carolina history, and *The Troubadour,* a staged and costumed "living history" visit with a gentleman representing Queen Elizabeth's court. Meet a 400-year-old standup comic who leads songs and weaves in the history of Roanoke Island's colonization while playing seven Renaissance instruments. Historically Speaking also offers step-on guides and receptive services for motor coach groups. See our Getting Here, Getting Around chapter for more information.

Mill Landing
NC 345, Wanchese
Near the end of a winding 5-mile road, past a long expanse of wide, waving marshlands overflowing with waterfowl, Wanchese is well off the beaten path of most visitors (see the section on Roanoke Island in our Area Overview chapter) and remains one of the most unspoiled areas on the barrier islands. At the very end of North Carolina Highway 345, one of the most picturesque and unchanged areas of the Outer Banks is often overlooked: Mill Landing, which embodies the heritage of the Outer Banks. Here, active fishing trawlers anchor at the docks, their mesh still dripping seaweed from the wide roller wheels. Watermen in yellow chest waders and white rubber boots (known locally as Wanchese wing-tips) sling shark, tuna, and dolphin onto cutting-room carts. Pieces of the island's past float silently in the harbor, mingling with remade boats that are still afloat and sunken ships that have long since disappeared.

The fish houses at Mill Landing include Wanchese Fish Company, Etheridge's, Jaws Seafood, Quality Seafood, and Moon Tillett's. These houses ship seafood to restaurants in Hampton Roads, Baltimore, New York, Boston, and Tokyo. Scallops, shrimp, fish, and crabs are available here in season.

Wanchese Seafood Industrial Park
615 Harbor Road, Wanchese
(252) 473-5867
A 69-acre industrial park on a deep harbor at Wanchese, this state-supported facility was built in 1980 with $8.1 million in state and federal funds. It was designed to attract large-scale seafood-processing companies to set up shop on the secluded Roanoke Island waterfront. After federal promises about stabilizing Oregon Inlet failed to materialize, few deep-draw fishing trawlers could keep risking the trip through the East Coast's most dangerous inlet.

Oregon Inlet continued to shoal terribly through the 1980s, and the seafood park remained largely vacant until 1994, when some smaller area businesses and fish-processing plants began establishing themselves there. Unpredictable weather patterns still affect the channel's navigability.

Today the 30-lot industrial area is almost 100 percent full with marine-related industries. Outer Banks Marine Maintenance, Harbor Welding, Wanchese Trawl and Supply, Bay Country Industrial Supply (fish-box manufacturer), Davis Boatworks, Wanchese Boat Builders, O'Neal's Sea Harvest, Gregory Poole Power Systems, and the Division of Marine Fisheries are just a few of the companies here. The industrial park is an educational attraction for anyone interested in the maritime world of boatbuilding and sea harvesting. Visitors are welcome to drive or walk through and visit the boat docks. Stop by the office if you have questions.

Pirate's Cove Yacht Club
Nags Head–Manteo Causeway, Manteo
(252) 473-3906, (800) 367-4728
www.piratescove.com
If you're interested in what the boats are catching in the Gulf Stream someday, head over to Pirate's Cove Yacht Club between 4:00 and 5:00 P.M. When the charter boats return to their slips, the catches of the day are thrown out on the docks to be picked up by the fish cleaners. Visitors are welcome to stroll along the boardwalk and watch. You might see tuna, wahoo, dolphin (the fish, not the mammal), cobia, or any of a number of fish. This is especially exciting for kids, who may not have seen such big fish before. If you would rather see the fish on the end of your own line, charter opportunities are available at Pirate's Cove. See our Fishing chapter for more information.

DARE COUNTY MAINLAND

Wolf Howls
Alligator River National Wildlife Refuge
Dare County Mainland
(252) 473-1131, ext. 243
http://alligatorriver.fws.gov
Go to the Alligator River National Wildlife Refuge to hear the red wolves howl. After sunset, you meet a refuge staff person at Creef Cut Wildlife Trail at the intersection of US 64 and Milltail Road on the Dare County mainland. After a brief talk about the red wolves, you are led (in vehicles) about 6 miles back into the dark refuge. On the way, you might even see some bears. In the dark woods, you get out of your car and listen as the staffperson howls to elicit howls from the wolves. The wolves' response will give you goosebumps. You can't see the wolves, which makes them seem even more mysterious and adds to the allure of this experience. The two-hour howl tours are held every Wednesday night at 8:00 P.M. from late June through mid-August. Howls are also held on Earth Day, April 22, at 7:00 P.M., on the Friday of Memorial Day weekend at 7:30 P.M., in mid-October for National Wolf Awareness Week, and on Halloween. Call to double-check the starting times

and alternate dates. This experience is free—and unforgettable.

A threatened species, red wolves have made a comeback in northeastern North Carolina due to careful management since the early 1980s. There are 10 wolves in captivity at the Alligator River National Wildlife Refuge and nearly 100 roaming free over about one million acres in northeastern North Carolina, including the refuge. For more information, see our Natural Wonders chapter.

BODIE ISLAND

Cape Hatteras National Seashore
Bodie, Hatteras, and Ocracoke Islands
(252) 473-3111
www.nps.gov/caha

Cape Hatteras National Seashore is a tremendous treasure for the residents and visitors of the Outer Banks. Here you will find the Outer Banks's most captivating open spaces, where long reaches of rugged dunes, windblown brush, wide beaches, and soundside wetlands are protected from development. Established in 1953 by the National Park Service and dedicated in 1958, the National Seashore includes part of Bodie Island and most of Hatteras and Ocracoke Islands, except for the village centers and Pea Island National Wildlife Refuge. The northern boundary begins south of Whalebone Junction in Nags Head, and the southern boundary is on Ocracoke Island. This was the very first National Seashore in the nation. It consists of some of the narrowest land inhabitable by humans—skinny stretches of sand often less than a half-mile wide. The National Seashore provides miles-long stretches where there is not one simple structure obscuring the view. Wildlife, waterfowl, and seabirds are abundant in the National Seashore, including the American oystercatcher and the threatened piping plover. Sea turtles survive here, too, as they often come ashore to lay eggs on the beaches in summer. Designated shorebird and sea turtle sanctuar-ies are well marked for protection on the beaches.

The Cape Hatteras National Seashore beaches are some of the cleanest and least crowded on the East Coast. If you're looking for solitary recreational space or simple peace and quiet, you'll find it here. Most of the beaches do not have life-guards, however, so make sure you know swimming safety precautions before going in. Lifeguards are stationed in summer at Coquina Beach on Bodie Island, at the beach near the Cape Hatteras Light-house, and at the Ocracoke Guarded Beach. Numerous access points are offered all along NC 12, the highway that threads through the Seashore. Three of the Outer Banks's four lighthouses are located within the Cape Hatteras National Seashore, and there are four camp-grounds in the Cape Hatteras National Seashore (see our Camping chapter). Camping is prohibited on the beach.

Three visitor centers are established in the National Seashore. The Bodie Island Visitor Center (252-441-5711) is on NC 12, in Nags Head heading south. The Cape Hatteras Visitor Center (252-995-4474) is in Buxton next to the Cape Hatteras Lighthouse. The Ocracoke Island Visitor Center (252-928-4531) is near the Cedar Island ferry dock. All provide extensive information on camping and activities in the National Seashore.

The Cape Hatteras National Seashore is dedicated to community outreach and has a variety of summer programs to help visitors learn more about the natural sur-roundings. The National Parks Service pro-vides guided beach walks, bird walks, campfires, fishing trips, history tours, dozens of kids programs, snorkeling trips, turtle talks, and many more. The sched-ules are lengthy, so the best way to find out about programs is to pick up the information at one of the visitor centers, or call ahead and have it mailed to you.

Driving on the beach is allowed in the Cape Hatteras National Seashore at cer-tain access points only. Four-wheel-drive vehicles may enter only at designated ramps. Soundside off-road travel is permitted on established roads or trails. Off-road access ramps are available at the visitor centers. Beach bonfires require a permit. Several day-use areas are available throughout the area, and nature trails provide visitors with an up close look at the seashore environments. Personal watercraft like JetSkis and Wave Runners are prohibited in Cape Hatteras National Seashore.

Bodie Island Lighthouse and Keepers' Quarters
West of NC 12, Bodie Island
(252) 441-5711

This black-and-white beacon with horizontal bands is one of four lighthouses standing along the Outer Banks. It sits more than a half-mile from the sea, in a field of green grass, closer to the sound than the ocean. This site, 6 miles south of Whalebone Junction, is one of the most picturesque on the Outer Banks. Photographers are drawn to the immaculately kept, spacious lawns, the charming double keepers' quarters and oil house, and the proud tower.

The lighthouse itself is not open for climbing, but the setting is worth the trip. The keepers' quarters has exhibits about the lighthouse and a small bookshop. The grounds are perfect for a picnic, and nature trails lead into the wide expanses of marshland behind the tower, through cattails, yaupon, and wax myrtle. The trails end up at Roanoke Sound, offering a view of the private camp on Off Island. The slough that rushes through the water between Bodie and Off Islands is a popular fishing hole, and anglers often line the banks.

The current Bodie Island Lighthouse is the third to stand near Oregon Inlet, which opened during a hurricane in 1846. The first lighthouse was built south of Oregon Inlet in 1847 and 1848 and was the only one in the 140 miles between Cape Hatteras and Cape Henry, Virginia. The lighthouse developed cracks and structural damage within 10 years and had to be removed and rebuilt. The second light

was also built south of Oregon Inlet. It was complete and lighted in 1859. Confederate forces destroyed the second tower during the Civil War so that it wouldn't fall into Union hands. The 170-foot lighthouse that stands today was built in 1872, this time north of Oregon Inlet because the inlet was moving south at a steady pace. Wanchese resident Vernon Gaskill served as the last civilian lightkeeper of the Bodie Island Lighthouse. The U.S. Coast Guard operated the light for many years, and it was transferred to the National Park Service in 2000. The National Park Service hopes to restore the lighthouse so that it will one day be open to the public, but the price tag on the restoration work is $1 million. The First-Order Fresnel lens will be of particular interest to visitors. The visitor center is open from 9:00 A.M. until 5:00 P.M. every day except Christmas. The grounds are always open.

Coquina Beach
NC 12, Bodie Island

Though not as broad as it once was due to storms, Coquina Beach is still one of the widest beaches on the Outer Banks and a favorite getaway. Just 6 miles south of Whalebone Junction, this beach has half the crowd but all the amenities you need: a lifeguard in the summer, a bathhouse, restrooms, outdoor showers, and lots of parking. Part of the allure of this remote area is that it's miles away from any business or rental cottage, making it a superb spot to sunbathe, swim, fish, and surf. The sand is almost white, and the beach is relatively flat.

Drawing its name from the tiny butterfly-shaped coquina clams that burrow into the beach, at times almost every inch of this portion of the federally protected Cape Hatteras National Seashore harbors hundreds of recently washed-up shells and several species of rare shorebirds. Coquinas are edible and can be collected and cleaned from their shells to make a chowder. Local brick makers also have used the shells as temper in buildings.

The *Laura A. Barnes*
Coquina Beach, NC 12, Bodie Island

One of the last coastal schooners built in America, the *Laura A. Barnes* was completed in Camden, Maine, in 1918. This 120-foot ship was under sail on the Atlantic during a trip from New York to South Carolina when a nor'easter drove it onto the Outer Banks in 1921. The *Laura A. Barnes* ran aground just north of where it now rests at Coquina Beach. The entire crew survived. In 1973 the National Park Service moved the shipwreck to its present location, where visitors view the remains of the ship behind a roped-off area that includes placards with information about the *Laura A. Barnes* and the history of lifesaving.

Oregon Inlet Fishing Center
NC 12, Bodie Island
(252) 441–6301, (800) 272–5199
www.oregon-inlet.com

Sportfishing enthusiasts, or anyone remotely interested in offshore angling, must stop by this bustling charter-boat harbor on the north shore of Oregon Inlet. Set beside the U.S. Coast Guard station on land leased from the National Park Service, Oregon Inlet Fishing Center is owned by a group of 18 stockholders, most of them local fishermen. All vessels charge the same rate. A day on the Atlantic with one of these captains may give rise to a marlin, sailfish, wahoo, tuna, or dolphin on the end of the line. (See our Fishing chapter for details.) An exciting afternoon activity is to head to the boat docks at Oregon Inlet Fishing Center between 4:00 and 5:00 P.M. When the charter boats return to the docks, you'll have an opportunity to see a variety of Gulf Stream creatures as the mates unload the boats and hurl the huge fish on the docks. In summer, the docks are crowded with spectators. Next to the fishing center store is a display case housing a 1,152-pound blue marlin, caught in 1973 and brought back to this fishing center. The store stocks bait and tackle, supplies, hot dogs and snacks, T-shirts and hats galore, and more. The fishing center has an air-fill tank for putting air back into your tires after driving on the beach (there's a four-wheel-drive access across the street). The boat ramp at the fishing center provides easy access to some of the best fishing grounds on the East Coast. There is plenty of parking, and restrooms are on-site.

Oregon Inlet Coast Guard Station
NC 12, Bodie Island

In the 19th and early 20th centuries, the federal government operated two lifesaving stations at Oregon Inlet. The Bodie Island station was on the north side of the inlet. The Oregon Inlet station was on the south. Both of these original facilities are now closed. The Oregon Inlet station sits perilously close to the migrating inlet, the victim of hurricanes and decades of neglect. It is weatherworn and bedraggled, a testament to the ravages of salty winds and storms. Yet this building is a picturesque reminder of the history of the Outer Banks and how quickly changes occur. There is plenty of parking next to the station, and you can walk around the grounds and out to the jetties, but you can't go inside the building. This is also a popular and lucrative fishing spot. You can fish from the rock jetties, wade out into the deep cove, or walk the catwalk on the south end of the Bonner Bridge.

The Bodie Island station has been replaced by the Oregon Inlet Coast Guard station, which includes a 10,000–square-foot building, a state-of-the-art communications center, maintenance shops, an administrative center, and accommodations for the staff. Coast Guard crews have rescued dozens of watermen off the Outer Banks. They also aid sea turtles and stranded seals by helping the animals get back safely to warmer parts of the ocean.

Oregon Inlet and the Bonner Bridge
NC 12, Oregon Inlet

The view from the crest of the Herbert C. Bonner Bridge has to be the most beautiful vista on the Outer Banks. If only there was a place to pull over and enjoy it more fully! As you drive over, you get a sweeping glimpse of this infamous inlet and all its surrounding shoals, sandbars, and spoil islands. Sea captains call this the most dangerous inlet on the East Coast—and with good reason. Since 1960 at least 30 lives and an equal number of boats have been lost at Oregon Inlet. The current through the inlet is dangerously swift and reckless, and shoals form alarmingly fast, causing boats to run aground.

The only outlet to the sea in the 140 miles between Cape Henry, in Virginia Beach, and Hatteras Inlet south of Hatteras Island, Oregon Inlet lies between Bodie Island and Pea Island National Wildlife Refuge. It is the primary passage for commercial and recreational fishing boats based along the northern Outer Banks. Even though it's often dredged, the inlet is sometimes impassable by deep-draft vessels.

Although a safe inlet is crucial to the commercial and recreational fishing industries, federal officials have refused to authorize or fund construction of jetties, rock walls that some scientists say would stabilize the ever-shallowing inlet.

Oregon Inlet was created during a hurricane in September 1846, the same storm that opened Hatteras Inlet between Hatteras Village and Ocracoke Island. It was named for the side-wheeler *Oregon,* the first ship to pass through the inlet.

In 1964 the Herbert C. Bonner Bridge was built across the inlet. This two-lane span finally connected Hatteras Island and the Cape Hatteras National Seashore with the northern Outer Banks beaches. Before the bridge was built, travelers relied on ferry boats to carry them across Oregon Inlet.

Hurricane-force winds blew a dredge barge into the bridge in 1990, knocking out a center section of the span. No one was hurt, but the more than 5,000 permanent residents of Hatteras Island were cut off from the rest of the world for four months before workers could completely repair the bridge.

Four-wheel-drive vehicles can exit NC 12 on the northeast side of the inlet and drive along the beach, even beneath the Bonner Bridge, around the inlet. Fishing is permitted along the catwalks of the bridge and on the beach. Free parking and restrooms are available at the Oregon Inlet Fishing Center. There are also parking and portable toilets on the southern end of the bridge. This trip is especially beautiful at sunset or sunrise.

HATTERAS ISLAND

Pea Island National Wildlife Refuge
NC 12, Pea Island
(252) 987-2394

Pea Island National Wildlife Refuge begins at the southern base of the Herbert C. Bonner Bridge and is the first place you come to entering Hatteras Island from the north. The beach along this undeveloped stretch of sand is popular with anglers, surfers, sunbathers, and shell seekers. On the right side of the road, heading south, salt marshes surround Pamlico Sound, and birds seem to flutter from every grove of cattails.

Founded on April 12, 1938, the Pea Island refuge was federally funded as a winter preserve for snow geese. President Franklin D. Roosevelt put his Civilian Conservation Corps to work stabilizing the slightly sloping dunes, building them up with bulldozers, erecting long expanses of sand fencing, and securing the sand with sea oats and grasses. Workers built dikes near the sound to form ponds and freshwater marshes. They planted fields to provide food for the waterfowl.

With 5,915 acres that attract nearly 400 observed species of birds, Pea Island is an outdoor aviary. Few tourists visited this refuge when Hatteras Island was accessible only by ferry. After the Bonner Bridge opened in 1964, motorists began driving through this once isolated outpost.

Today, Pea Island is one of the barrier islands' most popular havens for birdwatchers, naturalists, and sea-turtle savers. Endangered species, from the loggerhead sea turtle to the tiny piping plover shorebirds, inhabit this area. Pea Island's name comes from the "dune peas" that grow all along the now grassy sand dunes. The tiny plant with pink and lavender flowers is a favorite food of migrating geese.

Four miles south of the Bonner Bridge's southern base, the Pea Island Visitor Center offers free parking and easy access to the beach. If you walk directly across the highway to the top of the dunes, you'll see the remains of the federal transport *Oriental*. Its steel boiler is all that remains of the ship, which sank in May 1862.

On the sound side of the highway, in the marshes, ponds, and endless wetlands, whistling swans, snow geese, Canada geese, and 25 species of ducks make winter sojourns in the refuge. Savannah sparrows, migrant warblers, gulls, terns, herons, and egrets also alight in this area from fall through early spring. In summer, American avocets, willets, black-necked stilts, and several species of ducks nest here.

Bug repellent is a must on Pea Island from March through October. Besides insects, ticks also cause problems. Check your clothing before getting in the car, and shower as soon as possible if you hike through any underbrush.

North Pond Trail
NC 12, Pea Island

A bird-watcher's favorite, this wheelchair-accessible nature trail begins at the visitor center parking area and is about a mile long. The trail runs along the top of a dike between two man-made ponds that were begun in the late 19th century and completed by the Civilian Conservation Corps in the 1930s. The walkway includes three viewing platforms, marshland overlooks, and mounted binoculars.

Wax myrtles and live oaks stabilize the dike and provide shelter for scores of songbirds. Warblers, yellowthroats, cardinals, and seaside sparrows land during biannual migrations. The quarter-mile Salt Flats Trail starts at the north end of the North Pond Trail.

The U.S. Fish & Wildlife Service manages Pea Island refuge's ecosystem.

Workers plant fields with fescue and rye grass to keep the waterfowl coming back. Pheasants, muskrats, and nutria live along these ponds year-round.

Pea Island Visitor Center
NC 12, Pea Island
(252) 987-2394

A paved parking area, free public restrooms, and the Pea Island Refuge Headquarters are 4 miles south of the Oregon Inlet bridge on the sound side of NC 12. Refuge volunteers staff this small welcome station year-round and are available to answer questions. Visitors see exhibits on wildlife, waterfowl, and bird life and browse the small gift shop. In summer, the facility is open seven days a week from 9:00 A.M. to 4:00 P.M. In the off-season, the center is open Thursday through Sunday from 9:00 A.M. to 4:00 P.M. It's closed Christmas Day. Free nature trail maps are available, and in summer months, special nature programs are offered, such as bird walks, turtle talks, and guided canoe tours.

Hunting, camping, and driving are not allowed in the refuge. Open fires are also prohibited. Dogs must be kept on leashes on the east side of the highway. Firearms are not allowed in the refuge; shotguns and rifles must be stowed out of sight even if you're just driving straight through Hatteras Island. Fishing, crabbing, boating, and other activities are allowed in the ocean and sound but are prohibited in refuge ponds.

About 3 miles farther south on NC 12, a kiosk just beyond the refuge headquarters marks the site of the remains of the nation's only African-American lifesaving station. Pea Island was established with the rest of the U.S. Lifesaving outposts in 1879 and was originally manned by mostly white crews. Black men were confined to tasks like caring for the horses that dragged surfboats through the sand.

The year after the station was set up, however, federal officials fired Pea Island's white crew members for mishandling the *Henderson* shipwreck disaster. Black personnel from other stations were placed under the charge of Richard Etheridge, who was of Native American and African-American descent. The new crew carried out its duties honorably.

Pea Island's surfmen rescued countless crews and passengers of ships that washed ashore in storms or sank in the seething seas. Etheridge became known as one of the best-prepared, most professional, and most daring leaders in the service. One of the crew's most famous rescues was in 1896 when the captain of the E. S. *Newman* sounded an SOS off Hatteras Island's treacherous shores, an area known as The Graveyard of the Atlantic.

In 1992 the U.S. Coast Guard Service, a latter-day version of the Lifesaving Service, dedicated a cutter to the Pea Island crew. About a dozen of the African-American surfmen's descendants witnessed the moving ceremony. A plaque onboard the big ship commemorates the lifesaving crew's heroism.

Chicamacomico Lifesaving Station
NC 12, Rodanthe
(252) 987-1552
www.chicamacomico.net

With volunteer labor and long years of dedication, this once-decrepit lifesaving station is beautifully restored and open for tours. Its weathered, silvery-shingled buildings sparkle on the sandy lawn, surrounded by a perfect picket fence. Even the outbuildings have been brought back to their former uses.

Chicamacomico was one of the Outer Banks's original seven lifesaving stations, opening in 1874 at its current site. The present boathouse building was the original station but was retained as a storage shed when the bigger facility was built in 1911. Under three keepers with the last name of Midgett, Chicamacomico crews guarded the sea along Hatteras Island's northern coast for 70 years. Between 1876 and the time the station closed in 1954, seven Midgetts were awarded the Gold Life Saving Award; three won the silver; and six others worked or lived at Chicamacomico. Perhaps the station's most

The shipwreck site of the USS Monitor *was the first site in the United States to be designated a National Underwater Marine Sanctuary. The* Monitor, *a Civil War ironclad, sank in 240 feet of water about 16 miles off Cape Hatteras in a storm on New Year's Eve of 1862. The sanctuary is federally protected, and divers can visit only if they have a federal permit.*

famous rescue was when surfmen pulled crew members from the British tanker *Mirlo* off their burning ship and into safety.

Today the nonprofit Chicamacomico Historical Association oversees and operates the lifesaving station. Volunteers set up a museum of area lifesaving awards and artifacts in the main building and have recovered some of the lifesaving equipment for the boathouse. Volunteers take school groups on tours of the station, showing how the britches buoy helped rescue shipwreck victims and explaining the precise maneuvers surfmen had to follow on shore (see our History chapter for more about the britches buoy).

The station is open from Easter weekend through the Saturday after Thanksgiving, Tuesday through Saturday from 9:00 A.M. to 5:00 P.M. Various programs have been added to the roster and are offered every open day in the summer and on Wednesday, Thursday, and Friday in the off-season. At 2:00 P.M., programs might include a guided tour, a knot-tying class, or a storytelling hour. Bonfires are held one evening a week in the summer at 8:00 P.M. All programs are suitable for all ages. The guided tour gives more details on the site, the lifesaving service, and the equipment used. Group tours can be accommodated with advance notice. Admission is free, although donations are welcome and are greatly needed to further the restoration and expand the programs at this site. Call for additional program information.

Salvo Post Office
NC 12, Salvo

If you're heading south on NC 12 through Hatteras Island, slow down as you leave Salvo to spot a tiny whitewashed building with blue and red trim on the right side of the road. That's the old Salvo Post Office, which was the country's smallest post office until an arsonist burned about half of it down in 1992. It sat atop low rails in the postmaster's front yard. Over the years, villagers moved it to the front yard of each new postmaster's house.

The wooden structure had beautiful gilt post boxes surrounding the small glass service window, but it didn't have a bathroom, air-conditioning, or a wheelchair-accessible ramp. Although community volunteers rallied and rebuilt their little post office quickly, the federal government refused to reopen the outpost, which was originally erected in 1901. Today, Salvo residents drive to Rodanthe to pick up their mail, and this tiny charmer sits empty by the road.

Canadian Hole
NC 12, Avon

If a breeze is blowing, pull off the west side of the road between Avon and Buxton (1.5 miles south of Avon) into the big parking lot on the sound. Known as Canadian Hole, this is one of America's hottest windsurfing spots—and a magnet for visitors from Canada. Whether you ride a sailboard or not, this sight is not to be missed. On windy afternoons, more than 100 windsurfers and kiteboarders spread out along the shallow sound, their brightly colored butterfly sails gently skimming into the sunset. There's a nice bathing beach here, so bring chairs and coolers and plan to watch the silent wave riders, some of whom are famous in windsurfing circles. The state recently expanded the parking area here. See our Water Sports chapter for more details.

Cape Hatteras Lighthouse
Off NC 12, Buxton
(252) 995-4474
www.nps.gov/caha

The Cape Hatteras Lighthouse is one of the most beloved and famous lighthouses in the nation, especially after it survived a move of more than 1,600 feet in 1999. The nation's tallest brick lighthouse at 208 feet, this black-and-white striped beacon was shown the world over as it was precariously jacked up and moved along roll beams to its new location, away from the encroaching sea. The monumental relocation project was named the 2000 Outstanding Civil Engineering Achievement by the American Society of Civil Engineers. The lighthouse now stands the same distance from the Atlantic Ocean as it did when it was first built in 1870.

The original Cape Hatteras Lighthouse was built in 1803. The tower sat near Cape Point and was only 90 feet tall. Lit with whale oil, it was barely bright enough to be seen offshore. Erosion weakened the structure, and in 1861 Confederate soldiers removed the light's lens. The current Cape Hatteras Lighthouse was erected in 1870 with more than one million bricks and 257 steps. A special Fresnel lens that refracts light increased its visibility. The lighthouse was 1,600 feet from the ocean when it was built, but by 1987, it was only 120 feet from the crashing waves. After years of study, the National Park Service came to the conclusion that it had to "move it or lose it." The lighthouse was moved 1,600 feet back from the shore in just a few weeks, from June 17 to July 9, 1999. About 20,000 visitors a day watched. It reopened to the public on May 26, 2000. Its 800,000-candlepower beacon, rotating every seven-and-a-half seconds, can be seen 18 miles out to sea.

The view from the top of the Cape Hatteras Lighthouse is surreal and unforgettable. Try to make the climb while visiting the historical site.

The visitor center, called the Museum of the Sea, and the bookstore, both housed in the historic former keepers' quarters, were moved to this location before the lighthouse was moved. Restrooms are located here. If you continue past the parking area, you'll pass the picnic area and the Buxton

Woods Nature Trail. If you continue on, you'll come to the Cape Point Campground and off-road vehicle ramps. The beach here is famous for swimming, sunbathing, surfing, and fishing, and you can take four-wheel-drive vehicles along many sections of the beach year-round. Park rangers and volunteers willingly answer questions and can be found in the visitor center and on the historic district grounds. Visitor center and bookstore hours are 9:00 A.M. to 5:00 P.M. daily, except for Christmas Day.

In Buxton, signs along NC 12 lead you to the lighthouse. To the left, you can visit the original lighthouse location, marked by a circle of granite stones that are etched with the names of 83 former lighthouse keepers. To the right is a parking area and the lighthouse's new location.

The *Altoona* Wreck
Cape Point, Buxton

Four-wheel-drive motorists may enter the beach at the end of Cape Point Way on Ramp 44. Here, the Outer Banks juts out into the Atlantic in a wide elbow-shaped curve near the Cape Hatteras Lighthouse. The beaches in this area offer some of the barrier islands' best surf fishing. Two rules of the beach: Do not try to drive on the beach in anything but a four-wheel-drive vehicle, and be sure to let the proper amount of air out of your tires before traversing sand (see our Getting Here, Getting Around chapter for more information).

For those not driving on the beach, park on solid ground near the road and walk over the ramp to a foot trail. The path begins at the base of the dune. At the edge of a seawater pond, you'll catch a glimpse of the remains of the shipwreck *Altoona*. Built in Maine in 1869, the *Altoona* was a two-masted, 100-foot-long cargo schooner based in Boston. It left Haiti in 1878 with a load of dyewood bound for New York. On October 22, a storm drove it ashore near Cape Point. Lifesavers rescued its seven crew members and salvaged some of the cargo, but the ship was buried beneath the sand until uncovered by a storm in 1962. The sea has

broken the big boat apart since then, but you can still see part of the bow and hull beneath the waves.

Diamond Shoals Light
In the Atlantic Ocean, off Cape Point
Buxton

You can only visit this attraction in private boats, but you can see this unusual light tower from the eastern shore of Cape Point and from the top of the Cape Hatteras Lighthouse. Its bright beacon blinks every two seconds from a steel structure set 12 miles out in the sea.

Diamond Shoals once held a lighthouse, but waves beat the offshore rocks that held the structure so badly that federal officials gave up the project. Three lightships have been stationed on the shoals since 1824. The first sank in an 1827 gale. The second held its ground from 1897 until German submarines sank it in 1918. The third beamed until 1967, when it was replaced by the current light tower.

Diamond Shoals, the rocks around the tower, are the southern end of the treacherous near-shore sandbars off Hatteras Island.

Buxton Woods Nature Trail
Cape Point, Buxton

Leading from the Cape Point Campground road about 0.75 mile through the woods, the Buxton nature trail takes walkers through thick vine jungles, across tall sand dunes, and into freshwater marshes (see also our Natural Wonders chapter). Small plaques along the fairly level walkway describe the area's fragile ecosystems. People who hike this trail learn about the Outer Banks's water table, the role of beach grass and sea oats in stabilizing sand dunes, and the effects salt, storms, and visitors have on the ever-changing environment.

Cottonmouths seem to like this trail, too, so beware of these unmistakable snakes. They are fat, rough-scaled, and stubby-looking in brown, yellow, gray, or almost black. If you see a cottonmouth, let it get away—don't chase it. If it stands its ground, retreat.

This hike is not recommended for disabled visitors or young children, but picnic tables and charcoal grills just south of the nature trail provide a welcome respite for everyone. The walk is fine for hardy nature lovers who don't mind mingling with the outdoor elements.

Frisco Native American Museum
NC 12, Frisco
(252) 995-4440
www.nativeamericanmuseum.org
This enchanting museum on the sound side of NC 12 in Frisco is stocked with unusual collections of Native American artifacts gathered since the 1930s, plus numerous other fascinating collections. The museum boasts one of the most significant collections of artifacts from the Chiricahua Apache people and has displays of other Native American tribes' works from across the country, ranging from the days of early humans to modern time. Hopi drums, pottery, kachina dolls, baskets, weapons, and jewelry are displayed in homemade cases.

A souvenir gift shop offers Native American art, crafts, jewelry, educational materials, toys, and books. Native craft items made by about 40 artisans from across the country are also available for sale. With advance notice, guided tours are available, as are lectures for school and youth groups. Call for prices. The museum property also includes outdoor nature trails through three acres of woods, with a screened-in pavilion, a large pond, and three bridges on the land. Hours are 11:00 A.M. to 5:00 P.M. Tuesday through Sunday, year-round. Admission is $2.00 per person or $5.00 per family. Seniors are charged $1.50. Group rates are available. The museum and trails are also designed to accommodate the vision impaired.

Hatteras–Ocracoke Ferry
NC 12, Hatteras Village
NC 12, Ocracoke Island
(252) 986-2353, (800) BY FERRY
The only link between Hatteras and Ocracoke Islands, this free state-run ferry carries passengers and vehicles across Hatteras Inlet daily, year-round, with trips from 5:00 A.M. to midnight. A fleet of 10 ferry boats, some 150 feet long, carry up to 30 cars and trucks each on the 40-minute ride. (See our Getting Here, Getting Around chapter for the full schedule.)

You can get out of your vehicle and walk around the open decks or stay inside the car. A passenger lounge a short flight of steps above the deck offers cushioned seats and wide windows. On the lower deck, telescopes give people a chance to see seagulls and passing shorelines up close for a quarter. Free restrooms also are on the deck; however, there's no food or drink to be found on this 5-mile crossing, so pack your own picnic. Beware if you decide to break bread with the dozens of birds that fly overhead. After they eat, they, too, look for free bathrooms. And they'll follow—overhead—all the way to Ocracoke. The experience is exciting but can be messy.

A souvenir shop is located at the Hatteras ferry docks; it sells everything from coloring books and Frisbees to sweatshirts and coffee mugs. Drink and snack machines also are on-site.

A day trip to Ocracoke is a must for every Outer Banks visitor, whether you're staying in Corolla or on Hatteras Island. (See the Ocracoke section of our Area Overview chapter for more about Ocracoke.) The free ferry is the only way to get there besides by private boat or airplane. On summer days, more than 1,000 passengers ride the flat ferries.

A 12-mile stretch through open marshlands and pine forests lies between the ferry and Ocracoke Village. NC 12 picks up at the ferry docks and continues to the southern end of the island. On the left, wide-open beaches await avid four-wheelers and those who like to have a piece of the seaside to themselves.

A National Park Service oceanfront campground is to the left before you get to the village. Ocracoke is a quaint fishing village that has recently grown into a popular tourist destination. About 750 people live on Ocracoke Island year-round. Boutiques, seafood restaurants, craft shops, and other retailers line the quiet, twisting lanes, but most are open only in the summer. We recommend that you park your car somewhere near the waterfront and rent a bicycle to tour this picturesque, isolated island.

Graveyard of the Atlantic Museum
NC 12, Hatteras Village
(252) 986-2995
www.graveyardoftheatlantic.com

The Graveyard of the Atlantic Museum showcases the maritime history and heritage of the Outer Banks and its people, from the earliest exploration and colonization to the present day. Particularly emphasized are the years from 1524 to 1945. The museum is still being completed, but the lobby, community room, and museum store are open to the public. Exhibits include artifacts from historical shipwrecks, unique "beach finds," and locally carved ships' models; there is a special exhibit on Billy Mitchell in Hatteras.

OCRACOKE ISLAND

Ocracoke Pony Pens
NC 12, Ocracoke Island

The Ocracoke Pony Pens are one of the most popular attractions on Ocracoke Island. The National Park Service maintains a herd of about 30 horses in a 180-acre pasture located off NC 12, about 6 miles south of the Hatteras–Ocracoke ferry docks. Visitors can walk up to the pens to view these once-wild horses. An observation platform allows a good view of the ponies.

Ocracoke ponies have played a large role in the history of the island. At times the herd's population ranged from 200 to 500, all of the animals roaming free on the island.

No one is really certain how the horses arrived at the island, but legend says they swam ashore from Spanish shipwrecks off the coast. The horses adapted well to a

diet of marsh grasses and rainwater. The locals used this natural resource for work and recreation, and even the Coast Guard and U.S. Lifesaving Service employed the ponies. In the 1950s the local Boy Scout troop practiced lassoing them.

When NC 12 was paved along the island in 1957, horse-car accidents became a problem. The herd was also causing extensive damage to dune vegetation, contributing to beach erosion. The National Park Service wanted to get rid of the entire herd, but islanders protested so strongly that the Park Service agreed to keep some of the ponies contained on the island. They were penned in 1960, where they still are today. Their shelters, food, and veterinary care are funded partly by donations. The pen is free to visit, but donations are certainly welcome. Though not running wild, the ponies are not tame, and they may try to kick or bite if you try to climb into the pen or feed or pet them.

Ocracoke ponies have distinctive physical characteristics: 5 lumbar vertebrae instead of the 6 found in other horses, 17 ribs instead of the 18 found in other horses, and a unique shape, posture, color, size, and weight. For more information see the Ocracoke Island section of our Area Overview chapter.

Hammock Hills Nature Trail
NC 12, Ocracoke Island

A 0.75-mile nature trail north of Ocracoke Village, Hammock Hills covers a cross-section of the island. The 30-minute walk begins near the sand dunes, traverses a maritime forest, and winds through a salt marsh. Hikers learn how plants adapt to Ocracoke's unusual elements and the harsh barrier island weather.

Bring your camera on this scenic stroll. We highly recommend bug repellent in spring and summer months. Watch out for snakes in the underbrush. The well-marked trailhead is on NC 12 just across the road from the National Park Service campground.

Ocracoke Island Visitor Center
NC 12, Ocracoke Village
(252) 928-4531

The National Park Service's Ocracoke Island Visitor Center, at the southern end of NC 12, is full of information about the island. It's in a small building with a large lawn next to the Cedar Island ferry docks. If you're arriving on the island from the Hatteras ferry, stay on the main road, turn right at Silver Lake, and continue around the lake counterclockwise until you see the low brown building on your right. Free parking is available at the visitor center.

Inside, there's an information desk, helpful staff, a small bookshop, and exhibits about Ocracoke. You can arrange to use the Park Service's docks here and pick up maps of the winding back roads that make great bicycle paths.

The visitor center is open March through December from 9:00 A.M. to 5:00 P.M. Hours are extended in the summer. Rangers offer a variety of free summer programs, including a beach walk, a walk through the village, turtle talks, a pirate play, snorkeling, an evening campfire, kids programs, and more. Programs last from 30 to 90 minutes and offer a fun way to learn more about the history and ecology of the island. Check at the front desk for changing weekly schedules. Restrooms are open to the public in season.

Ocracoke Island Museum and Preservation Society
Silver Lake, Ocracoke Village
(252) 928-7375

A visit to the Ocracoke Island Museum provides a wonderful peek into Ocracoke as it once was. The home of Coast Guard Capt. David Williams, the historic, two-story house was moved to this location in 1989 and restored to its former early 19th-century glory by the Ocracoke Preservation Society. The original wainscoting, floors, staircases, and wood-burning stove are still intact. Inside, a bedroom, living room, and kitchen are set up with period furnishings donated by local families. Origi-

nal photographs of island natives are throughout. Exhibits about fishing and seafaring are especially interesting, as is the exhibit on the island's traditional brogue.

Upstairs, the museum has a small research library that the public can use with the museum personnel's permission. Admission is free, and the museum is open from Easter through the end of November. In summer, hours are 10:00 A.M. to 5:00 P.M. Monday through Friday and 11:00 A.M. to 4:00 P.M. Saturday and Sunday. Off-season hours are 11:00 A.M. to 4:00 P.M. Monday through Saturday.

Ocracoke Village Walking Tour
West end of NC 12, around Ocracoke Village

The easiest ways to explore Ocracoke are by bicycle and on foot. The narrow, winding back lanes weren't meant for cars. And you miss little landmarks and interesting areas of the island if you drive through. People on Ocracoke are generally friendly, and you'll get a chance to chat with more locals if you slow down your touring pace through this picturesque fishing village.

No matter where you are in Ocracoke Village, just start walking and you'll find something interesting. One nice tour of the northeast side of the village starts at the Ocracoke Island Visitor Center. Park in the lot opposite the visitor center. Turn left out of the lot and walk down NC 12 around the shores of Silver Lake, past the sleepy village waterfront. You'll pass many small shops, boutiques, and some large hotels. Keep walking until you see a small brick post office on your right.

Opposite the post office, a sandy, narrow street angles to the left. This is Howard Street. It winds through one of the oldest and least-changed parts of the village. Note the humble old homes, the attached cisterns for collecting rainwater, and the detached kitchens behind these historic structures.

Continue walking past or stop in Village Craftsman, a gallery. After about 400 yards, Howard Street empties onto School

Street. Turn left, and you'll see the Methodist Church and K–12 public school that serves all the children on Ocracoke. With graduating classes of fewer than a dozen students, this is the state's smallest public school.

The church is usually open for visitors, but use discretion if services are in progress. And please wipe your feet as you go in. On entering, note the cross displayed behind the altar. It was carved from the wooden spar of an American freighter, the *Caribsea,* sunk offshore by German U-boats in the early months of 1942. By strange coincidence, the *Caribsea*'s engineer was Ocracoke native James Baugham Gaskill, who was killed when the boat sank. Local residents say that several days later a display case holding Gaskill's mate license, among other things, washed ashore not far from his family home.

Ocracoke has had a Methodist church since 1828. The current one was built in 1943 with lumber and pews salvaged from older buildings. A historical-sketch pamphlet is available in the vestibule for visitors.

On leaving the church, walk around the north corner of the school, past the playground, onto a narrow boardwalk. This wooden path leads to a paved road beyond it. Turn left. This was the first paved road on the island and was constructed by Seabees during World War II.

After walking less than a mile down this road, turn right at the first stop sign. A few minutes' walk along this narrow, tree-shaded street brings you to the British Cemetery, where victims of World War II are buried far away from their native soil. (See the subsequent listing in this section.) It's on your right, set back a bit from the road and shaded by live oak and yaupon. The big British flag makes it easy to spot.

To return to the visitor center, walk west until you reach Silver Lake, then turn right. You'll pass craft shops and several boutiques along the way. (See our Shopping chapter for details.) If the weather's nice, we suggest a stop for an outdoor drink at the waterfront Jolly Roger, the

Creekside Cafe upstairs above the bicycle stand, or Howard's Pub on the highway before heading back to the ferry docks. (See the Ocracoke Island section of our Area Overview chapter for additional information.)

Ocracoke Lighthouse
Southwest corner of Ocracoke Village

The southernmost of the Outer Banks's four lighthouses, this whitewashed tower is the oldest and shortest. It is the second-oldest lighthouse in the nation. It stands 77.5 feet tall and has an askew iron-railed tower set on the top. The lighthouse is not open for tours or climbing, but volunteers occasionally staff its broad base, offering historical talks and answering visitors' questions. Inquire about possible staffing times at the visitor center or National Park Service offices.

Ocracoke's lighthouse still operates, emitting one long flash every few seconds from a half-hour before sunset to a half-hour after sunrise. It was built in 1823 to replace Shell Castle Rock Lighthouse, which was set offshore closer to the dangerous shoals in Ocracoke Inlet. Shell Castle Light was abandoned in 1798 when the inlet shifted south.

The beam from Ocracoke's beacon rotates 360 degrees and can be seen 14 miles out to sea. The tower itself is brick, covered by hand-spread, textured white mortar. The walls are 5 feet thick at the base.

On the right side of the wooden boardwalk leading to the lighthouse, a two-story white cottage once served as quarters for the tower's keeper. The National Park Service renovated this structure in the 1980s. It now serves as the home of Ocracoke's rangers and the structure's maintenance supervisor.

To reach the light, turn left off NC 12 at the Island Inn and go about 800 yards down the two-lane street. You can park near a white picketed turnoff on the right. Visitors must walk the last few yards down the boardwalk to the lighthouse.

British Cemetery
British Cemetery Road, Ocracoke Village

Beneath a stand of trees, on the edge of a community cemetery, four granite gravestones commemorate the crew of the British vessel HMS *Bedfordshire*. This 170-foot trawler was one of a fleet of 24 anti-submarine ships that Prime Minister Winston Churchill loaned the United States in April 1942 to stave off German U-boats. On May 11 of that year, a German submarine torpedoed and sank the British ship about 40 miles south of Ocracoke.

All four officers and 33 enlisted men aboard the *Bedfordshire* drowned. U.S. Coast Guard officers stationed on Ocracoke found four of the bodies washed ashore three days later. They were able to identify two of the sailors. Townspeople gave Britain a 12-by-14-foot plot of land and buried the seamen in a site adjacent to the island's cemetery.

Since then, Coast Guard officers have maintained the grassy area within a white picket fence. They fly a British flag above the graves, and each year, on the anniversary of the sailors' deaths, the local military establishment sponsors a ceremony honoring the men who died so far from their own shores.

Deepwater Theater
School Road, Ocracoke
www.molassescreek.com

Deepwater Theater is the home of Ocracoke's most famous band, Molasses Creek. This high-energy acoustic folk-fusion band plays bluegrass and ballads and rolls everything together with a wacky sense of humor. Gary Mitchell, Kitty Mitchell, and fiddler Dave Tweedie compose the band, which has a loyal following in the United States and abroad. Based on the island, they play here all summer and at other times of the year. Molasses Creek also performs all over the nation, and it was featured on National Public Radio's *A Prairie Home Companion* with Garrison Keillor. Molasses Creek plays at Deepwater Theater on Tuesday and Thursday in summer. The screened-in-porch-style Deepwater Theater hosts other musicians as well, including singer-songwriter Noah Paley. Ocrafolk Opry is held on Wednesday night. There's no phone number, so when you get to the island ask around.

Portsmouth Village
South of Ocracoke Island, by private boat access, Portsmouth Island
(252) 728-2250
www.nps.gov/calo

The only ghost town on the Eastern Seaboard, Portsmouth Village is about a 20-minute boat ride south of Ocracoke Island and was once the biggest town on the Outer Banks. Today, the 23-mile-long, 1.5-mile-wide island is owned and managed by the National Park Service as part of Cape Lookout National Seashore. Wilderness camping, hiking, shelling, fishing, and other activities are available on the wide beach. Free, self-guided walking tours of the village are a fascinating way to see how islanders lived in the 19th century.

Visiting Portsmouth Village is utterly surreal. Many of the former homes and village buildings are intact and restored, but they sit hollow, yet hopeful, as if waiting to come to life. Peeking into the windows of some of the unrestored buildings, you'll see remnants of the families who once lived there—curtains, unmade beds, upturned old chairs, broken frames—as if they left in a hurry and never came back.

Portsmouth Village was established in 1753. Situated along the banks of a major trade route, Ocracoke Inlet, Portsmouth became known as a "lightering" village.

On Tuesday night at 7:30 P.M. (7:00 P.M. in the off-season), meet at the Village Craftsmen on Howard Street in Ocracoke Village. Local storyteller Philip Howard will take you on a 90-minute tour of the area complete with ghost stories and historical information. Space is limited, so call ahead: (252) 928-5541. The cost is $12.00 for adults and $6.00 for children ages 6 to 12.

Large ships could not pass through the inlet with a full load of cargo, so the Portsmouth villagers unloaded the cargo onto small flatboats while the ships passed through the inlet. On the other side, they put all the cargo back onboard and sent the big ships off to the mainland. When the more navigable Hatteras Inlet opened in 1846, lightering at Portsmouth was no longer needed. The Civil War and hurricanes drove Portsmouth residents inland over the next century, until only three residents remained on the island in 1970, two women and one man. When the man died in 1971, the two aging women reluctantly left the island. The National Park Service began restoring the village in 1976. It is listed on the National Register of Historic Places.

There is a visitor center on-site, staffed by volunteers who commit to living on the island for extended periods of time. You can see the old post office, the church, the old Coast Guard station, and other buildings. Some of the homes are private, their owners granted extended leases in exchange for restoration work. Portsmouth Island is a rugged adventure, and there are few conveniences. Restrooms are provided in the visitor center,

The Outer Banks is not entirely deserted during the winter months. In certain areas more museums, galleries, restaurants, shops, and other sites are remaining open year-round. If businesses do close for the winter, they usually stay open at least through the holidays because many visitors come for Thanksgiving and Christmas.

and there's a comfort station (toilets only) on the other side of the village. You must bring your own water, food, insect repellent, and sunscreen. Mosquitoes are notorious in the summer and fall.

You can get to the island by private boat or with a charter service. Capt. Rudy Austin runs round-trip boat trips to the island, daily in summer and by appointment in the off-season. Call at least one day in advance for reservations, (252) 928–4361 or (252) 928–5431. Portsmouth Island ATV Excursions, (252) 928–4484, leads guided tours of the village and island on ATVs from April through November. Call for reservations and information.

KIDSTUFF 👥

The beach is always a popular lure for children. They can play tag with the waves, build whimsical sandcastles, fly a kite, play volleyball, or dig for treasure they just know has been left. The Outer Banks is a large sandy playground, with opportunities for exploration that are only limited by your imagination. For kids, this means the possibilities are infinite, especially on sunny days at the beach. Be sure to check out our Waves and Weather chapter so your children have a safe vacation at the beach. If the skies are overcast or the temperature too cold to play by the shore, they'll need a little more help from you (and us!) to entertain themselves.

Read the chapters on Recreation, Attractions, and Water Sports for a more complete listing of activities children will enjoy. Kidstuff takes a look at the not-so-obvious as well as some favorites.

In compiling this chapter, we asked the experts themselves—kids from 5 to 15, both "locals" and veteran visitors—to recommend their favorite sunny- and rainy-day activities. Here's what they told us when we asked, "What are your favorite things to do on the Outer Banks?"

KIDS' FAVORITE THINGS TO DO

The Beach

They dig for coquinas, those tiny crablike creatures that burrow frantically into the wet sand when the surf pulls away from the beach. They chase sand crabs and

If skimboarders are playing in the surf, don't let your tot get too near the action. Skimboards travel fast and are very sturdy. An out-of-control board can cause onlookers a painful ankle injury.

sandpipers and poke at jellyfish with sticks. They draw in the sand, construct structures both simple and intricate, and cover themselves and others with sand, making you grateful that so many Outer Banks accommodations have outdoor showers so you can wash off at the end of the day. (As a convenience to visitors, some townships and villages offer public restrooms and shower facilities at one or more beach access areas.)

Little kids who aren't old enough or confident enough to immerse themselves in the ocean still find endless ways to enjoy the beach. They need adults to keep them safe (more on that shortly), keep them fed and watered, and then get out of the way of their creativity unless they make you the object of it.

An inflatable baby pool makes a day shoreside more pleasant for infants and toddlers. Set it up under a big umbrella and toss in some floating toys. Buckets and shovels and boogie boards are essential equipment for slightly older kids. Even if they're not old enough to ride the waves, little kids like to sit or lie on boogie boards at the very edge of the water. Older kids tend to gravitate to more expensive props such as body boards and surfboards.

At the risk of stating the obvious, here are a few things to remember about kids on the beach: Keep your young ones slathered in sunscreen, reapplying it frequently. Never take your eyes off of them at the ocean or the sound, and stay within close range. The surf, even where it is most shallow, is rough; undertows and currents are insidious. There are sudden drop-offs and deep holes in the ocean and the sound. Keep kids away from the water when the red warning flags are flying.

Please read carefully about beach safety, and choose a section of the beach that is served by lifeguards. A list of guarded beaches is provided in the Waves and Weather chapter.

If you have very young children, a soundside beach is a more tranquil alternative to the ocean. The gentle waters are perfect for children, enabling them to build their confidence and their swimming skills.

Fishing or Crabbing

SOUNDSIDE BEACHES, DOCKS, AND PIERS

Many a grown-up's most cherished childhood memories involve fishing at the Outer Banks. It's a wonderful way for you and your kids to share special time together.

You can rent or buy equipment at a tackle shop (see our Fishing chapter) or at a pier. Along with your equipment, get some advice on what's biting, what to use to catch it, and where to find it. Stake out a spot at the surf or head to one of the piers.

For a unique experience, treat the family to an excursion on a headboat, which offers per-person rates for half-day charters. Rookie anglers get plenty of help with their rods and reels, which are supplied, from experienced mates. Many passengers go along for the ride and spectacular scenery. Either way, it's a comfortable and affordable way to experience the Outer Banks from the water, which Insiders consider an essential part of the Outer Banks experience. Check the Fishing chapter for more information on the headboats that operate in the area. Also refer to our Recreation chapter for information on sunset and moonlight cruises.

Crabbing can be particularly memorable. If you dig in the early morning or late afternoon, you'll probably have more crabs to steam at the end of the day. Head west to the sounds. Try the soundside beaches or the soundside piers in Kitty Hawk on Kitty Hawk Bay (off West Tateway and Windgrass Circle) and in Kill Devil Hills (on Orville Beach between

Durham and Avalon Streets). In Corolla, there are some good crabbing spots near the Whalehead Club. One of the most popular locations is on Big Colington Island, below the second bridge on Colington Road near the firehouse. On Hatteras Island, crab in the sound at any quiet soundside location in the National Seashore.

Part of the fun of crabbing is rigging the simple equipment. You don't need to invest in crab traps or special bait. Fishing line, chicken necks, a net, and a deep bucket or cooler will do just fine. Tie a chicken neck to the end of your string, dangle it in the water, and wait for the crabs to come. Then scoop them up (quickly) with the net. It'll take a few tries, but you'll get the hang of it. Grown-ups or older kids can wield the net for the little ones. To free the crab from the net, don't use your hands; dangle the net over the cooler and wiggle it free. Tell the kids to keep their fingers out of the bucket!

If your catch measures 5 inches or less at the widest part of the shell, you have to throw it back. (Not only is this the law, but it will help ensure another batch of crabs for next year's visit.) Keep only "keepers," the ones that measure more than 6 inches.

The best part of crabbing, like fishing, is feasting on what you've caught. Steam the crabs with your favorite spice, pile the steamed crabs on a picnic table spread with newspaper, and serve with melted butter and lemon.

Hunt for Buried Treasure

ANYWHERE

What could be more exciting than finding a pirate's map leading to a treasure chest full of gold and silver and jewels? After all, some of history's most famous and feared pirates, including the notorious Blackbeard, frequented these shores.

This adventure doesn't leave it to chance. Create the treasure and map for the little kids to find. Recruit older kids to help set up the treasure hunt—but make sure they can keep a secret. This adventure requires some advance planning and preparation, but it's well worth it. For maximum excitement, talk about pirates and tell pirate stories—or, better yet, schedule a trip to Teach's Hole (see subsequent entry)—a day or two before.

What you'll need:

- A book about pirates (geared to the appropriate age for your children: *Blackbeard the Pirate,* by Robert E. Lee, is packed with information, or buy one of the many coloring books on the subject, which you'll find at drugstores, gift shops, and bookstores)
- A bag full of bright and colorful baubles (fake gold coins, plastic jewelry)
- Silver and gold spray paint
- A lot of small rocks and pebbles
- A wooden box to serve as a treasure chest
- Parchment paper
- Pretty shells

Turn the rocks and pebbles into precious metals by spraying them with the gold and silver paint. When they're dry, heap them into the treasure chest along with the baubles, leaving a few handfuls to scatter around the burial site. Stake out a likely spot to bury your treasure. Don't make it too difficult to find, but don't make it too easy, either! Somewhere close to your cottage will do. Draw the treasure map. Be creative with your route and clues. You can crumple the paper, smudge it, rub it in the dirt, and char the edges to make it look old. Remember "X" marks the spot. Now somehow you've got to have the good fortune to "accidentally" stumble upon this authentic pirate treasure map with the kids. Help them find their way to the buried treasure, and enjoy their excitement.

Take in a Show

Summer Children's Series
Roanoke Island Festival Park, Manteo
(252) 475-1506
www.roanokeisland.com
Roanoke Island Festival Park offers excellent children's programming with its Summer Children's Series. From late June through early August, programs are held Tuesday through Friday at 10:30 A.M. and change weekly. Past performances have included puppet and marionette shows, storytellers, and plays. Christmas programs, such as *The Littlest Angel,* are also held. The usual fee is waived if you have paid for park admission. Programs are held in the Film Theater, which seats about 200 people.

Professional Theater Workshop
(252) 473-2127
Performers and technicians with *The Lost Colony* stage at least one show for children every summer. These talented folk put on hilarious and imaginative interpretations of popular fairy tales, fables, and legends. The show usually plays once or twice a week from mid-July to early August. A small admission fee is charged. Locations vary, so call ahead for details.

Race a Hermit Crab

Scotch Bonnet Candies and Gifts
NC 12, Frisco
(252) 995-4242
www.scotchbonnetcandies.com
And they're off! Every Friday in season, hermit crabs race to the finish line at Scotch Bonnet Candies and Gifts. For lots of family fun, bring your crab or rent one at the store and get set to race. Crabs take off in separate contests to win prizes for their sponsors. Join the Scotch Bonnet crowd under the tent on Friday afternoon for free soft drinks and prizes.

Curl Up with a Good Book

Manteo Booksellers
105 Sir Walter Raleigh Street, Manteo
(252) 473-1221
www.manteobooksellers.com
Rediscover the pleasures of a bookstore that exists because its proprietor loves books.

Kids are welcome here. Little readers can plant themselves in little chairs in the children's section and browse an extensive selection of the very best books for kids. If you haven't already discovered the Crabby and Nabby series by author Suzanne Tate and artist/illustrator James Melvin, do yourself and your child a favor and start collecting. They introduce children to a variety of friendly indigenous creatures whose adventures afford a perfect opportunity to learn something about the Outer Banks.

The place stays lively throughout the year with author signings, readings, children's storytelling, and other special events. Check calendar listings in local newspapers or call for more information.

Summer Stories for Kids
Corolla Library, 1123 Ocean Trail, Corolla
(252) 453-0496
The storytelling hour is every Wednesday at 10:30 A.M. from late June through early August on the grounds of the Whalehead Club, at the picnic area.

If you need to check out a book, the library is open year-round, Monday through Wednesday from 10:00 A.M. to 5:00 P.M. and Thursday from 3:00 to 7:00 P.M. You need a picture ID to check out books.

StoryTime at the Dare County Library
Manteo (252) 473-2372
Kill Devil Hills (252) 441-4331
Hatteras (252) 986-2385
Preschool story hours are held at the libraries to aquaint young kids with the library and help them enjoy books at an early age. Story hours include games, songs, puppets, stories, and plays, sometimes with guest storytellers. Programs last 30 minutes and are held once a week at each of the library locations: Tuesday in Hatteras, Wednesday in Manteo, and Thursday in Kill Devil Hills. Separate programs are held for two- to three-year-olds, and four- to five-year-olds.

KIDS' FAVORITE PLACES TO GO

Miniature golf, waterslides, "dollar stores," movie theaters, and more attractions and gifts from nature than you could explore in two weeks' time provide an abundance of places to delight the most discriminating kid visitor. Here are some favorites. See our Recreation and Attractions chapters for more ideas.

Island Revolution Skate Park
Corolla Light Town Center
(252) 453-2440
A brand new killer skate park opened in 2006. Two bowls with a mini-ramp-spine street course offer 5,000 feet of island fun. Open everyday from 10:00 A.M. until 8:00 P.M. in season and Monday through Friday from 2:00 p.m. until dark in the off-season. Private parties can be booked here.

Jockey's Ridge State Park
US 158, MP 12, Nags Head
(252) 441-7132
www.jockeysridgestatepark.com
Jockey's Ridge is the tallest sand dune on the East Coast, and there's no better location for kite flying. Kids have plenty of room to run without getting their lines crossed or caught in a tree. See the Kite Flying section of our Recreation chapter.

Scrabbling around in the sand is a joy unto itself. Clamber to the top of the dune and enjoy the expansive ocean-to-sound views. If you make arrangements in advance, a park ranger will drive a physically challenged visitor up the dune in a four-wheel-drive vehicle. From October

Creation Stations

Do your kids have creative energy to burn? For hands-on fun, try one of these stores.

That Stained Glass Place: Drop-in mosaic classes and more. U.S. Highway 158, MP 5½, Seagate North Mall, Kill Devil Hills; (252) 441-9323; www.stained glassvisions.com.

Island Art Supply: Classes in painting, drawing, sculpting, and more for kids age five and older. North Carolina Highway 12, MP 1, Ocean Centre, Kitty Hawk; (252) 255-5078.

Home Depot: On the first Saturday of each month from 10:00 A.M. to noon, kids can build a project using hammers and nails. US 158 MP ½, Wal-Mart shopping complex, Kitty Hawk; (252) 261-4115.

---

through May, you can pick up a free permit at the park's offices for sandboarding, but you don't need any equipment to enjoy a good old-fashioned roll down the huge sandy hill.

Check local newspapers and at the park office for a current schedule of programs offered by the state park rangers. These are wonderful opportunities to stimulate and satisfy curious young minds. What could be more enchanting to a child than to climb the ridge at night and gaze at constellations or learn about animal tracks in the sand or net fishing in the sound?

Rinse off at the soundside beach at the park's southwest corner, which also has picnic tables and parking. Be sure to wear shoes.

The park headquarters is north of the dune and west of U.S. Highway 158 on Carolista Drive.

The Promenade
US 158, MP 0, Kitty Hawk
(252) 261-4400

The Promenade is one huge family fun center, with an outdoor play park for kids, an indoor arcade with everybody's favorite games, an 18-hole miniature golf course, a chip and putt, an ice-cream parlor, and a driving range. The watersports division offers parasailing, sailing, boating, and personal watercraft. You could spend the whole day and eat at the restaurant,

snack bar, and picnic tables on-site. The Promenade is open every day in the summer and closes October through March.

Glazin' Go Nuts and Garden of Beadin'
US 158, MP 6, Kill Devil Hills
(252) 449-2134

Glazin' Go Nuts, a paint-your-own-pottery studio, is a favorite place for kids and adults to spend a creative afternoon. Studio time costs $7.00 per painter for the day. You buy the pieces you want to paint for an additional charge, from $4.00 to $40.00, with most pieces averaging around $15.00. After you've painted, leave your masterpiece to be fired. It takes about three or four days for the turnover. The studio will ship your works to you if you go home before then.

Next door is a sister shop called Garden of Beadin'. It is a full-line bead store with glass, semiprecious stones, and unique specialty beads. The Garden is open year-round, and classes are held in the summer months. Call for days and times.

Kitty Hawk Kites
US 158, MP 13½, Nags Head
(252) 441-4124
www.kittyhawk.com

Just across the street from Jockey's Ridge State Park, Kitty Hawk Kites is a fun store for kids to visit. It has all sorts of kites, a rock-climbing wall, and toys galore, and store personnel lead kayak tours that kids are welcome to join. Family Fun Day takes place every summer Wednesday from noon to 4:30 P.M., with activities for children and adults. Call to inquire about kite-making workshops, where kids make their own kites and fly them. Kitty Hawk Kites sponsors many family-friendly events on Jockey's Ridge and at other locations. See our Annual Events chapter or call for information.

Nags Head Bowling Center
US 158, MP 10, Nags Head
(252) 441-7077

Nags Head Bowling offers fun for kids, but parents bowl peacefully here while their children are totally enthralled. This facility sports kiddie bumpers running the length of the lane, so even barely walking tykes can knock down pins every time.

Games cost $4.25 each; shoes rent for $2.75. Nags Head Bowling is open from noon until midnight daily. If you're sensitive to smoke, bowl early in the afternoon. See our Recreation chapter for evening specials.

Select from many video games in the entrance, including Tekken 2, Ultimate Mortal Kombat, Ms. Pac-Man, Stargate pinball, and air hockey. You must be 21 to play pool in the on-site bar unless accompanied by an adult. Yes, there is a snack bar!

Teach's Hole
Back Road, Ocracoke
(252) 928-1718
www.teachshole.com

This Ocracoke stop fascinates the younger crowd. The pirate shop features a historical exhibit about Edward Teach (aka Blackbeard) that includes a short video, weapons, old bottles, Blackbeard in full battle-dress, and dioramas for the kids. There is a small fee to view the exhibit, but children younger than age six get in free. The gift shop, a must for all ages, is filled with everything imaginable related to pirates and piracy. Teach's Hole is open Easter through Thanksgiving.

Wolf Howls
Alligator River National Wildlife Refuge
Dare County Mainland
(252) 473-1131, ext. 243
http://alligatorriver.fws.gov

Kids love hearing the red wolves howl eerily in the refuge at night. The staff leads a guided trip deep into the refuge, and a leader can usually get the wolves to howl. Sometimes kids get to howl to see if the wolves respond. Howls are held once a week in the summer and at other times during the year. It's free! See our Attractions chapter for more information.

The Fishing Docks

At the end of the day, kids love to go to the fishing docks to see the fish caught on the charter boats that day. Take the kids to the docks between 3:00 and 5:00 P.M. to see tuna, dolphin, wahoo, and more. This is a spectator event only. Head to Pirate's Cove Yacht Club in Manteo, Oregon Inlet Fishing Center south of Nags Head, or Hatteras Harbor Yacht Club or Oden's Dock in Hatteras Village.

Playgrounds

If you're looking for a place to let the kids burn off some energy, head to one of these playgrounds.

Behind Outer Banks Style
Schoolhouse Lane, Corolla

Across the bridge, Currituck
Turn east just south of Grigg's
On the sound

David Paul Pruitt Park
(for young children)
Woods Road, Kitty Hawk
Just before the Wright Bros. Bridge

County Family Recreation Park
Mustian Street, Kill Devil Hills

Nags Head Park
West Barnes Street, Nags Head

Manteo Tot Lot
Waterfront, Manteo

Old Swimming Hole
Airport Road next to the Aquarium
Roanoke Island

Rodanthe/Waves/Salvo
Community Center
NC 12, Rodanthe

Fessenden Center
NC 12, Buxton

Kids' Camps

**North Carolina Aquarium
at Roanoke Island**
Roanoke Island
(252) 473-3493
www.aquariums.state.nc.us/ri
The aquarium leads the Aquatic Adventures Summer Camp for students who have completed the fourth and fifth grades. The camps last for five half-days, with children learning about the Outer Banks waters and habitats through many hands-on activities and field trips. Each weeklong camp concludes with a sleepover at the aquarium. Also, the aquarium can be rented for sleepover parties among the fishes and sharks.

Outer Banks Family YMCA
US 158, MP 11, Nags Head
(252) 449-8897
The YMCA has weeklong day camps for all ages. Half-day Kindercamps are for ages 3 to 6, and full-day camps are for ages 7 to 12. Each week has a special theme, and kids do activities related to the theme in addition to going to the pool and ocean and on field trips. The YMCA also hosts several sports camps in beach volleyball, girls field hockey, soccer, basketball, and junior ocean rescue. Day passes are available for the superb new skate park. Call for information.

Summer Art Camps
KDH Cooperative Gallery
502 US 158, MP 8½, Kill Devil Hills
(252) 441-9888
The KDH Cooperative Gallery offers arts camps for kids in the summer. Each session rewards kids with art and craft projects they take home at the end of the week. Painting, drawing, sculpting, and printmaking are some of the classes taught by professional artists. Camps are held from 10:00 to 11:00 A.M. for five days. The gallery also offers candle-making workshops for ages 6 to 12 and a pottery class for teens.

Dare County Parks and Recreation
(252) 473-1101, ext. 313
www.co.dare.nc.us/parks&rec
Parks and Rec offers sports camps in basketball, soccer, cheerleading, gymnastics, triathlon training, and fishing. These weeklong camps, held Monday through Friday, are usually about five hours per day. There's also an Adventure Camp, where participants go on a weeklong camping trip. Toddler Camps for ages three to five last about two hours. Call for information.

4-H Camps
Dare County Cooperative Extension
(252) 473-1101, ext. 442
In the summer, 4-H offers weeklong day camps for elementary school children at four sites in the county: Kitty Hawk Elementary, First Flight Elementary, Manteo Elementary, and Munchkin Academy in Buxton. Camps last from 7:30 A.M. to 5:30 P.M. and include educational and fun activities and a field trip based on a particular theme. The Support Our Students is for middle-school students and alternates between Manteo and First Flight Middle Schools. This is a day-tripper's program, with off-site educational field trips. One-week camps away from home, in which campers travel to one of five 4-H camps in the state, are also held. You must preregister for all these camps. Call for information.

Kitty Hawk Sports Kids Kayak Clinic
(252) 441-6800
www.kittyhawksports.com

Kitty Hawk Sports holds kayaking clinics for kids in the summer. For $45, kids get a two-and-a-half-hour lesson in kayaking safety and paddling; they also get to play lots of really fun games. Clinics are held in July and August at Pea Island. Call to register.

Ocean Atlantic Rentals Surf School
(800) 635-9559

Corolla Light Town Center, Corolla
(252) 453-2440

Duck Road, Soundfront, Duck
(252) 261-4346

NC 12, MP 10, Nags Head
(252) 441-7823

NC 12, Avon
(252) 995-5868
www.oceanatlanticrentals.com

Kids and adults can learn to catch waves in the Ocean Atlantic Rentals Surf School. Classes are taught by a professional out of each of the four Ocean Atlantic locations, and the instructors will teach students of all skill levels.

Club Hatteras Kids
NC 12, Avon
(252) 995-4600
www.hatterasrealty.com

Kids age 4 to 12 come to Hatteras Realty to participate in fee-based programs, giving their caretakers time on their own. Club Hatteras Kids takes young ones to the soundside beach to crab and play in the water. They also play basketball, volleyball, miniature golf, croquet, and tennis and go for hikes. In quieter moments, they enjoy crafts and storytelling. The morning session includes lunch, and the evening session includes dinner; each program is $25. Hatteras Realty runs Club Hatteras Kids during summer months.

WEDDINGS

The wedding industry thrives on North Carolina's Outer Banks. For decades, the area has been a haven for honeymooners, though in recent years, more couples have opted to have their ceremonies here as well. While many still hold traditional church ceremonies, a growing number of couples plan outdoor weddings, either on the beach or in such historic settings as an old hunt club or the Elizabethan Gardens. Wedding receptions are often far from traditional, and many are held in the palatial three-story ocean-front rental homes that line the beaches from Corolla to Ocracoke.

In this chapter, we guide you through the intricacies of planning a wedding on the Outer Banks, including applying for a license, choosing a magistrate or minister, and hiring a caterer and photographer. We also provide information on locations, rental companies, musicians, florists, formal wear, transportation, gifts, and lodging. And for those of you who would rather pay someone else to handle all the headaches, we'll let you know about wedding consultants.

TYING THE KNOT

When asked their idea of the perfect place for romance, most everyone will say the beach. Maybe it's the melodic rhythm of the waves upon the sand or the gentle breezes that caress a bare shoulder. Perhaps it's a gust of wind laced with salt on a clear autumn day that infuses you with energy and renewal. One thing's for sure: The Outer Banks is becoming more and more popular as a place for brides and grooms to pledge their love to each other for eternity. Service providers (caterers, photographers, musicians, ministers, etc.)

are having trouble keeping up with demand. Everyone recommends that you start planning your wedding at the very least a year in advance.

The main wedding season on the Outer Banks is April through October. May and October are the most popular wedding months thanks to nice weather, fewer visitors, and off-peak accommodations rates. Remember that hurricane season is July through early November, so be sure to inquire with all your service providers about their policy concerning hurricane evacuations or other causes for cancellation.

North Carolina law requires that a wedding ceremony be conducted by an ordained minister or a magistrate. A boat captain can't do the trick any more.

The state has replaced its former justice of the peace system with court-appointed magistrates. These officials perform wedding services but are often severely limited as to the times and places they can accommodate. A magistrate's fee for performing a ceremony is $10. Magistrates are, however, required to marry any people who show up with a marriage license and two witnesses.

Most major Christian denominations are represented on the Outer Banks. Many do require a special counseling period, and some have specific requirements regarding remarrying divorced persons. If you wish to be married in the Outer Banks Catholic parish, you must meet with the priest at least six months before the wedding. There is no Jewish congregation on the Outer Banks; the nearest temple is in Norfolk, Virginia. Most Jewish couples bring a rabbi from their home temple. For more information on local churches, see our Places to Worship chapter or visit www.outer banks.org/locations for a list of churches.

Marriage Licenses

You must obtain a marriage license to be wed in North Carolina. Licenses are issued by the register of deeds in any North Carolina county. Both applicants must bring a photo ID and a Social Security card or proof of Social Security number. If you have been divorced, you must bring your legal divorce papers. The license costs $50, is good for 60 days after it is issued, and can be used in any county in North Carolina. There is no waiting period. A blood test is not required in North Carolina.

Bring your marriage license to the wedding. After the wedding ceremony, whoever performs the ceremony is required to give the couple a marriage certificate. This certificate includes the couple's names and address, the date of the marriage, the county that issued the license, and the date of the license. The minister or magistrate must sign the license. The license must be returned to the register of deeds in the county in which the couple was married.

Dare County
Register of Deeds (252) 473-3438
Magistrate's Office (252) 473-2010

Currituck County (Corolla)
Register of Deeds (252) 232-3297
Magistrate's Office (252) 232-3404

Hyde County (Ocracoke)
Register of Deeds (252) 926-3011
Magistrate's Office (252) 926-4101

LOCATIONS

In addition to the numerous churches on the Outer Banks, you might consider an outdoor wedding, perhaps a barefoot affair on the beach. The trend in Outer Banks weddings is to rent a large ocean-front house, or several in a row, and house all the family and friends together for the weekend or a week. The wedding takes place on the beach in front of one of the houses, and the reception takes place either in one of the homes or at a nearby location. More and more vacation rental companies are equipped to handle this, and some allow an unlimited number of guests for a reception in a few of their rental properties. If this appeals to you, call several of the companies in our Weekly and Long-Term Rentals chapter to look for a suitable home or homes. If you have trouble finding something, ask your wedding planner or caterer to recommend a company, or contact the Outer Banks Wedding Association at (252) 473-4800.

Church Weddings

A traditional wedding often requires that you have some affiliation with the church if you are planning to use its facilities. The best thing to do is to contact the minister of the church you would like to use, and he or she can give you the specifics. You also may have the option of bringing a minister from home to perform the ceremony in a local church.

Prepare to pay a fee for the use of the church as well as to compensate the minister for his or her services. It is customary to pay the minister from $50 to $250 for services and to add something for travel and accommodations if the wedding is taking place away from the minister's usual church.

Beach Weddings

Getting married on the beach is romantic and special—if you're one of those people who won't be upset if everything isn't perfect. You can't predict or control the elements. Wind is a major factor, something that brides with fancy hairdos should consider. The width and condition of the beach will depend on the tides and the wind direction on your wedding day.

Lighting is also difficult on the beach. Talk with your photographer about having the wedding at the proper time of day. You don't want everyone squinting in the wedding photographs. While sunset is a romantic time to be married, remember that the light will be very low, making it difficult for the photographer and videographer to get vivid shots.

The National Park Service charges a fee of $100 for gatherings within its boundaries, including the beach. You cannot bring in chairs, arbors, flowers, balloons, ribbons, or anything else that is not natural to the area. For information, contact the National Park Service at (252) 473-2111.

Outdoor Weddings

Many people choose to have their ceremony on the Outer Banks because of the magnificent outdoor settings. With more than 100 miles of pristine beaches from Corolla to Ocracoke, weddings on the shore are quite appealing. The Outer Banks weather can change quickly, so have an indoor alternative available.

There is no guarantee as to what the weather will be like on any given day on the Outer Banks, but generally the summer is sunny, hot, and humid; spring can be a bit rainy and cool; winter is cold and raw, but warm days make an appearance; and autumn offers warm clear days and crisp cool nights, perfect for an outdoor wedding.

The Whalehead Club
NC 12, Corolla
(252) 457-0128
www.whaleheadclub.com
Corolla's historic Whalehead Club (see our Attractions chapter), situated on the Currituck Sound, is a popular choice for an outdoor wedding. Waterfowl abound in this location, and sunsets are spectacular. An old arched, wooden bridge spans a channel that leads to the club's marina and boathouse; instead of a walk down the aisle, many brides walk across the bridge. A long pier on the premises leads to a gazebo where some couples exchange vows over the water. For added ambience, the Currituck Lighthouse is visible over the tree line. Fees to use the grounds range from $750 to $2,500. Alcohol is allowed on the grounds only for receptions.

Currituck Beach Lighthouse
NC 12, Corolla
(252) 453-8152
www.currituckbeachlight.com
The Currituck Beach Lighthouse allows weddings and receptions on its charming, well-kept property. The keeper's quarters, lighthouse, and outbuildings make a beautiful setting. The cost for weddings is $500, and the cost for receptions is an additional $500. If you plan to have alcohol at your reception, add a $250 fee for the alcohol license. All weddings are held on the southwest corner of the grounds.

Jockey's Ridge State Park
US 158, MP 12, Nags Head
(252) 441-7132
www.jockeysridgestatepark.com
The East Coast's largest sand dune provides amazing views of the ocean and sound as the backdrop for a wedding ceremony. The park also has a soundside beach that makes a great site for a small ceremony, especially at sunset. This state park charges only $30 to use the site for wedding ceremonies. There are no accommodations for receptions.

The Elizabethan Gardens
Off US 64, Roanoke Island
(252) 473-3234
www.elizabethangardens.org
This is one of the most romantic spots to exchange vows on the Outer Banks, and it's also one of the most popular. On some Saturdays, there are as many as four weddings here. These gardens provide an outstanding location for weddings year-round. Besides the large, grassy lawns that are ideal for the ceremony, the setting offers

many backgrounds for picture poses after the wedding. For more intimate gatherings, you may wish to investigate the rose garden or thatch-roofed gazebo overlooking the sound. Pricing for a wedding in the gardens is dependent upon the number of guests. For an additional fee, receptions may be held in the Meeting Hall. Wine, beer, and champagne may be served in the Meeting Hall.

Hatteras Island Soundfront Recreation Center
Rodanthe
(252) 987-2777
www.camphatteras.com

Camp Hatteras, a premier camping resort in the historic village of Rodanthe, provides a reception site. The 3,000-square-foot building has a fully equipped kitchen and two restrooms, plus a window-lined reception hall with views of Pamlico Sound. There's a corner stage for the cake-cutting ceremonies. If your guests decide to stay at Camp Hatteras, they'll also enjoy one of the finest outdoor recreation facilities found anywhere.

National Park Service Lighthouses
Bodie Island, Buxton, Ocracoke
(252) 473-2111, ext. 121

The Bodie Island, Cape Hatteras, and Ocracoke Lighthouses make beautiful backdrops for a wedding ceremony. The National Park Service charges a $100 fee for gatherings. Weddings at these sites are very simple because the NPS does not allow chairs, altars, flowers, or any of the usual wedding items. Receptions are not allowed on-site because there are no facilities, but there are places nearby for receptions.

Boat Weddings

Downeast Rover
Manteo
(252) 473-4866, (866) SAIL-OBX
www.downeastrover.com

If you really want to do something unique,

get married on a boat. The *Downeast Rover* is a 55-foot topsail schooner based in Manteo. It accommodates up to 29 people for a two-and-a-half-hour sail in Roanoke Sound in the afternoon or at sunset. The cost to charter the boat ranges from $500 to $800, depending on the time of day and season. You can bring your own food and drinks and have a party on the boat, or just have your ceremony on the boat and then have your reception at one of several locations in downtown Manteo. Call Capt. Mark Kopp for information.

Crystal Dawn
Pirate's Cove Yacht Club, Manteo
(252) 473-5577
www.themefifty.com/crystaldawn

The *Crystal Dawn* is a huge headboat that accommodates up to 97 passengers. You can have your ceremony and reception on the boat, floating through the scenic waters of Roanoke Sound. Cost to rent the boat is $250 an hour, with a minimum of two hours. Alcohol is allowed. The boarding location is Pirate's Cove Yacht Club.

ACCOMMODATIONS

On the Outer Banks, you may discover that your accommodations are the perfect place to host your rehearsal dinner or wedding. We've included a few suggestions here. See our Accommodations chapter and Weekly and Long-Term Cottage Rentals chapter for more options.

Midgett Realty
P.O. Box 250, US 12, Hatteras, NC 27943
Offices also in Avon and Rodanthe
(252) 986-2841, (800) 527-2903
www.midgettrealty.com

Host your family for the big event or find the perfect honeymoon spot in one of Midgett Realty's 550 rental cottages and condos. You can choose from a soundfront hideaway to an oceanfront paradise. Accommodations are available from Rodanthe through Hatteras. Online secure bookings are available. Call the toll-free number to receive a free rental brochure or to find out more information.

Élan Vacations
Hunt Club Drive,
Currituck Club Center
Corolla
(866) 760-ELAN
www.elanvacations.com

Élan Vacations is a full-service travel company representing fine vacation homes along the Outer Banks. Élan Vacations offers a special event package for weddings offered in many of their homes. For a relaxing and fun-filled event, Élan will help you find the home of your dreams for your special day.

ResortQuest Outer Banks
1184 NC 12, Duck
(800) 433-8805
www.resortquestouterbanks.com

ResortQuest represents premium vacation rental homes situated along some of the most pristine beaches and sounds on the East Coast. Many selections are oceanfront or soundfront and feature private pools and romantic hot tubs and fireplaces—perfect for an Outer Banks wedding. ResortQuest has a number of spacious homes that welcome small wedding parties. Any of these is an ideal choice for an intimate, one-of-a-kind seaside event.

Cypress House Inn
NC 12, MP 8, Kill Devil Hills
(252) 441-6127, (800) 554-2764
www.cypresshouseinn.com

The Cypress House Inn is an ideal location for a wedding. A tent up to 30 feet x 70 feet can be assembled in the yard to accommodate a caterer, dance floor, bar, and DJ. The wraparound porch is a romantic spot to have the rehearsal dinner or small intimate receptions. The six-room inn can be booked for a minimum of two nights for an on-site wedding.

Stan White Realty & Construction Inc./Duck's Real Estate
US 158, MP 10½, Nags Head
(252) 441-1515, (800) 338-3233

Duck Road, Duck
(252) 261-4614, (800) 992-2976
www.outerbanksrentals.com

If you're looking for a rental house at which to host your wedding by the sea, Stan White Realty & Construction Inc./ Duck's Real Estate offers legacy vacation rental homes on the northern Outer Banks. They offer oceanfront and soundfront homes, some with private pools, hot tubs, and fireplaces.

The Inn at Corolla Light
1066 Ocean Trail, Corolla
(252) 453-3340, (800) 215-0772
www.corolla-inn.com

Quiet, undiscovered, and romantic best describe the Inn at Corolla Light, with its luxurious soundfront rooms, pool, and hot-tub deck overlooking Currituck Sound. The inn has an on-site consultant to assist with your wedding, catering, and limousine service. Honeymoon packages with special pricing that include dinner and champagne are available all seasons of the year. The inn also offers receptions or rehearsal dinners in its intimate dining room or ceremonies in the pier gazebo on the sound.

Surf Side Motel
NC 12, MP 16, Nags Head
(252) 441-2105, (800) 552-7873
www.surfsideobx.com

The Surf Side Motel in Nags Head is a great place to accommodate a large wedding party, especially when the wedding events are in Nags Head or on Roanoke Island. The motel is on the oceanfront, with rooms facing the ocean with private balconies. For the bride and groom, the honeymoon suites have king-size beds and Jacuzzis. The motel has an indoor pool and hot tub and an outdoor pool. The Surf Side is open year-round.

The White Doe Inn
319 Sir Walter Raleigh Street, Manteo
(252) 473-9851, (800) 473-6091
www.whitedoeinn.com
The White Doe Inn is a picturesque turn-of-the-20th-century inn located in historic Manteo. The inn provides special yet comfortable surroundings decorated with antiques and reproductions—perfect for gathering the members of your wedding party. Weddings of up to 50 people are handled in the inn and lovely outdoor garden. All-inclusive wedding packages with every last detail covered are available.

The Cameron House Inn
300 Budleigh Street, Manteo
(252) 473-6596, (800) 279-8178
www.cameronhouseinn.com
The Cameron House Inn is a restored 1919 Arts & Crafts bungalow in the heart of historic Manteo. The inn offers five guest rooms, a comfortable sitting area, and a cozy back porch, making a wonderful place for the special members of your wedding party to stay together. For small weddings, both ceremonies and receptions, Cameron House has a spacious lawn covered by trees. The yard accommodates a wedding tent easily.

The Tranquil House Inn
405 Queen Elizabeth Street, Manteo
(252) 473-1404
www.tranquilhouseinn.com
The Tranquil House, right on the waterfront in Manteo, offers 25 rooms, making it an excellent lodging choice for wedding parties. And the on-site 1587 Restaurant provides an exquisite waterfront reception location, including catering.

WEDDING PLANNERS

Any out-of-town wedding requires early preparations and an established budget. Since visits to the area and long-distance phone calls add up, you may wish to hire a local wedding planner. A local contact can save you time and money by making phone calls, setting up appointments, and booking blocks of discounted hotel rooms. Since a wedding planner is already familiar with area musicians, florists, caterers, and everyone else necessary to make your day successful, he or she can really ease your mind and may even suggest options that you haven't yet considered. To find more coordinators and planners, try the Outer Banks Wedding Association's Web site; it has an extensive listing at www.outerbanksweddingassoc.org.

Avery Little Detail
(252) 441-1880
www.averylittledetail.com
From your first phone call to the final "I do," Avery Hesford Harrison orchestrates personal and stress-free planning. Specializing in budget management, Avery alleviates the burden on your time and finances by helping you plan the wedding of your dreams. She will confirm arrangements with vendors, make deliveries, and handle your last-minute tasks, allowing you to arrive relaxed, so you can properly welcome your guests—and most important—savor your wedding weekend.

Wedding Bells
Ann Bell
121 Garden Drive, Manteo
(252) 473-2635
www.annsweddingbells.com
A successful wedding involves many details, and a reliable wedding consultant can smooth the way and avoid last-minute

If you're planning an Outer Banks wedding, seek help on the Web. The Outer Banks Wedding Association Web site, www.outerbanksweddingassoc.org, is the most comprehensive. You can also try www.outerbanksweddingguild.com. The Outer Banks Visitors Bureau, too, has wedding-planning information on its Web site, www.outerbanks.org.

complications. In more than 25 years of Outer Banks wedding planning, Ann has assisted hundreds of brides and grooms and knows the answers to almost any question that could arise. She is thoroughly familiar with the Outer Banks from Corolla to Ocracoke. If you desire a small, private affair, Ann offers the Chapel in the Woods in her lovely garden in Roanoke Island Gardens. Ann is a nondenominational minister and can perform your wedding ceremony with your own special vows.

ALL OF THE PIECES
Flowers

The Outer Banks has a fine collection of talented florists who can create and customize anything you dream of. There are florists in almost every town up and down the beach. Here are a few samplings of what is offered.

Every Blooming Thing
NC 12 Piney Ridge Road, Hatteras
(252) 995-5486, (800) 515-1510
Jenny McBride has been in business for more than 15 years and prides herself on going the extra mile for her customers. She is a full-service florist who serves all of Hatteras Island. Not only can she supply your wedding with beautiful flowers but she also has tuxedos available for rent. If you would like plants at your big event, you can rent or purchase them from Every Blooming Thing. Jenny can also supply your wedding with candelabras, kneeling benches, and jewelry. As an added bonus, Jenny acts as a bridal consultant at no additional charge.

Holiday House
Wanchese
(252) 441-5959, (800) 628-6553
www.holidayhouseobx.com
Holiday House offers daily deliveries from Manteo to Corolla, and the staff works in fresh, dried, or silk flowers. Weddings are a specialty for these award-winning designers, who tout themselves as the "Outer Banks Wedding Specialists." Holiday House also creates balloon bouquets and carries gourmet baskets, candles, and bath products.

Sea Breeze Florist and Gifts
The Marketplace in Southern Shores
US 158, MP 1, Kitty Hawk
(252) 261-4274, (800) 435-5881
Owners Brandy and Tori Ferebee offer flowers and gifts "from the heart and soul." Because of the personal touch given to each customer, Brandy and Tori have a large following of repeat customers. These designers create artistic floral sculptures using fresh flowers or silk. Besides wedding flowers, Sea Breeze has a line of gifts for the bride or bridal party. Mood-enhancing oil candles, called firelights, are so popular that customers keep coming back for more.

Music

Music sets the mood of a wedding, adding to the beauty of the ceremony and the enjoyment of the reception. The Outer Banks is home to many musicians. The following is a small sampling of the varied choices for your special day. Check www.outerbanksweddingassoc.org for more listings.

John Harper
(252) 473-4528
Disc jockey John Harper, known for his music column in the *Carolina Coast,* is available to spin tunes at receptions and other events.

Nick Hodsdon
(252) 473-5783, (704) 372-9372
Nick Hodsdon offers classical, acoustic, vocal, and instrumental music for weddings. Solo, duet, and trio performances are available. Instruments include psaltery, guitar, cello, bass, recorder, and the

mandolin. Hodsdon offers selections from the Middle Ages through contemporary times, including Elizabethan, baroque, Celtic, folk, and contemporary music. He will learn and perform your favorite piece of music. Hodson is also a minister and can officiate at weddings.

The Crowd
(252) 207-1070
www.crowdband.net
The Crowd (formerly 3's a Crowd) plays for weddings and social events on and off the beach. The band is extremely versatile and can play at everything from sophisticated weddings to high-energy dance parties.

Live Oak Trio
P.O. Box 902, Ocracoke Island, NC 27960
(252) 928-7143
The Live Oak Trio (Cheryl Roberts, violin; Leslie Gilbert, flute; Nancy Hartlaub, piano) is Ocracoke's premier classical music ensemble. They are available for weddings, receptions, anniversaries, or other special occasions.

Roy Murray Jr.
(252) 480-1532
Roy Murray is the music director for around 200 weddings on the Outer Banks each year. He knows the area well and is able to advise on a musical presentation for many styles, situations, and locations. Trumpets, violins, flutes, and many other instruments and musicians are used according to your specifications. Flute duos and trios, chamber music, brass ensembles, acoustic piano, and church organ are some of the selections he offers.

Outer Banks Chamber Players
(252) 480-2493
www.obxchamberplayers.com
For classical melodies before, during, and after the ceremony, contact the Outer Banks Chamber Players, a duet consisting of Leslie Erikson (violin) and Jane Brown (viola).

Formal Wear

Since Outer Banks locals are generally a casual lot, there are few options for dress wear on this strip of vacationland. For nontraditional bridal wear, anything goes. A number of boutiques offer lovely garb appropriate for an island wedding. If you're a traditionalist, read on.

Davis Bridal Formals and Tuxedos
US 158, MP 9, Kill Devil Hills
(252) 441-2604
For everything from the bride's and bridesmaids' gowns to rental tuxedos, call Roy Parker at Davis Bridal. You'll get big-city selections at hometown prices, and Roy can deliver the gown to the church steamed and ready for the big day. Davis's wedding consultants are available to help you select your gown, the bridesmaids' dresses, and tuxedoes for the groom and the groomsmen, and they will coordinate dresses for your mother and mother-in-law. The selection of accessories provides just the right touch.

Bridal Works
Food Lion Shopping Center, US 158
Grandy
(252) 457-0200
On the Currituck mainland in Grandy, Bridal Works is a full-service bridal shop. For the bride, Bridal Works sells and fits bridal gowns, along with jewelry, shoes, garters, and headpieces (even made-to-order headpieces). Bridal Works offers dresses for bridesmaids, mothers, and flower girls, and shoes are dyed in-house. For the men, Bridal Works rents tuxedoes. Rentals are available for such items as arches, candelabras, unity candles, catering equipment, and linens. Bridal accessories, like cake toppers, glasses, and guest books, are sold in the store. Other services include wedding invitations, silk floral arrangements, and party favors.

Black Tie Affair
Seagate North, US 158, MP 5½
Kill Devil Hills
(252) 449–4889
www.blacktie-affair.com
Black Tie Affair commits to only one affair per day so that the staff can give you their full attention. This one-stop shopping location offers wedding planning, formal wear rentals, gifts, invitations, and more.

Keeping Up Appearances

You're going to be under enough stress on your wedding day; let someone else do your hair for you. While you're at it, you can have your nails done, enjoy a massage, and get a facial as well. You may even want to give massages or manicures and pedicures as bridesmaids' gifts. Go ahead, indulge.

Eden Spa and Salon
Barrier Island Shoppes, NC 12, Duck
(252) 255-0711
For your wedding and prewedding day, the women at Eden Spa will make you feel like a new person. They offer a full spectrum of services to help you with all your beauty needs. Hair, makeup, facial, and nail services are provided, as are massages and a wide range of relaxing and beautifying spa services. Our suggestion is to make two days of it: On day one get a full-body massage, a manicure, and a pedicure with a foot massage; on day two, the wedding day, come for makeup and a hairstyle.

The Waterfront Salon
Manteo
(252) 473-5323
www.thewaterfrontsalonandspa.com
The salon and boutique provide cuts and color, facials, spa treatments, waxing, acid peels, manicures, and pedicures—everything to feel beautiful on your wedding day. They also offer massage, La Stone therapy, and other wonderful nurturing therapies to make you feel more relaxed than ever.

Hairoics
US 158, MP 7, The Dare Centre
Kill Devil Hills
(252) 441-7983
This large, contemporary salon offers complete wedding packages for the bride, groom, and attendants, including formal, modern, or classic hairstyles; waxing; manicures; acrylic nails; and pedicures. Hairoics' staff includes five wedding specialists trained to create beautiful looks; brides receive a free wedding consultation. They recommend a demonstration of your selected style prior to your wedding day to be sure that it perfectly fulfills your expectations.

Food for Thought

The reception is usually the most expensive and most fun part of a wedding. Your options include choosing a hotel or restaurant that provides all the necessary food and beverage services or engaging a caterer. Our Restaurants chapter lists a number of excellent places to host either a rehearsal dinner or a reception. Sanderling Inn in Duck and Penguin Isle in Nags Head are two of the larger facilities on the Outer Banks at which to host an extravagant fete. For more intimate gatherings, consider Blue Point Bar & Grill in Duck, Ocean Boulevard in Kitty Hawk, 1587 in Manteo, or Island Inn Restaurant on Ocracoke. The Sanderling Inn, Island Inn, and 1587 (at The Tranquil House Inn) provide accommodations as well.

If you have your reception at a beach house, a caterer takes complete charge while you enjoy the company of your guests. The caterer cleans up afterward. Expect to spend from $20 to $55 per guest, depending on your choice of menu and type of bar service.

Kelly's Outer Banks Restaurant & Tavern
US 158, MP 10½, Nags Head
(252) 441-4116
www.kellysrestaurant.com
Kelly's has self-contained trailers and a

trained staff to provide hot and cold food for groups of 10 to 1,000 throughout eastern North Carolina. Mike Kelly and his staff have a lot of experience serving everything from casual hors d'oeuvres to elegant buffets and banquets.

Duncan's Bar-B-Q
US 64, Manteo
(252) 473-6464
If you're looking for an informal, Southern-style pig-pickin', Duncan's has a pig cooker and will travel. This is authentic North Carolina barbecue, and these people sure know how to put on a spread. For more information, see our Restaurants chapter.

Katering by Kim
Kill Devil Hills
(252) 441-7010
www.kateringbykim.com
Katering by Kim offers everything from a casual beach clambake to an elegant sit-down meal. For buffets, a food station can be simply planned, with individual tables for seafood, hand-carved roasts, pastas, salads, and desserts. In addition to your meal, Katering by Kim can supply you with a cake that serves as a focal point of the day, whether it's one with fresh flowers, something exceptionally decadent, or an impressive, simply decorated white cake. Katering by Kim has self-contained kitchen trailers. This catering company also provides exquisite floral arrangements by Lynn James.

Seamark Foods
US 158, MP 1, Kitty Hawk
(252) 261-2220

US 158, MP 14½, Nags Head
(252) 441-4121
Seamark Foods offers deli treats, hot and cold foods, and wedding cakes for small and large groups at reasonable prices. Delivery is available.

Sonny's Creative Kitchen
Caratoke Highway, Harbinger
(252) 491-9969
www.sonnyskitchens.com

For traditional gatherings or elaborate sit-down dinners, Sonny's brings only the best. Every detail from equipment setup to cleanup will be managed by their talented staff. Each menu is exclusive to the event, and the staff at Sonny's likes to say they will cater to every need.

Let Them Eat Cake

No wedding is complete without a wedding cake. And since this is the South, it's customary to have a groom's cake as well. If you need to make separate arrangements for your wedding cake, call well in advance because decorated wedding cakes take a lot of preparation. Also, if you're planning an out-of-doors midsummer wedding, bear in mind that the heat and humidity can cause some icings to melt. Be sure to advise the caterer or cake baker where the cake will be kept.

Tullio's Pastry Shop
Scarborough Faire Shops, NC 12, Duck
(252) 261-7111
www.tulliospastry.com
Pastry chef Walter Tullio will bake you a beautiful wonder of a wedding cake, plus any other desserts, rolls, breads, or pastries you may desire. Walter learned his craft at the Culinary Institute of America in Hyde Park, New York; he'll provide you with a delicious and memorable addition to your day. (He also prepares cakes for any occasion.) Tullio's cinnamon buns make the morning of the wedding even more special.

Brides-to-be want to attend the bridal show held on the Outer Banks each January. You can plan your wedding from A to Z at this event—caterers, florists, musicians, ministers, and more will attend. Bridal fashions are modeled throughout the show. Call Deborah Sawyer at (252) 473-4800, or visit www.outerbanksweddingassoc.org for more information.

Just Desserts
Melinda Gregory
(252) 441–2931
www.justdessertsobx.com
Just Desserts can create an original wedding-cake design for you using an array of flavors, colors, and custom artwork unmatched on the Outer Banks. These delicious cakes are available in assorted shapes and sizes and can be ordered on relatively short notice. Unusual decorative options include white chocolate seashells, pearl strands, gum-paste ribbon, flowers, and satin ribbon—all edible. Just Desserts also makes grooms' cakes with an array of flowers, colors, and designs. Custom artwork is available, and any concept can be reproduced in edible form.

Photographers and Videographers

Deborah Sawyer Photography
107-A Budleigh Street, Manteo
(252) 473–4800
www.beachportraits.com
Deborah Sawyer Photography offers more than 25 years of experience in portraiture, specializing in weddings, beach portraits, engagement photos, and special portrait gifts. In addition to color photos, you can choose from black-and-whites or sepia-toned prints. Brides-to-be: A wonderful groom's gift is a special portrait of you. Deborah shines in the creativity department and suggests some truly wonderful options.

J. Aaron Trotman Photographs
US 158, MP 9½, Kill Devil Hills
(252) 480–1070, (877) 764–5378
www.jaarontrotman.com
J. Aaron Trotman refers to his style of photojournalistic wedding photography as "storybook." Paying particular attention to your own special touches and circle of family and friends, he takes minimally posed shots in a candid, unobtrusive man-

ner, offering guidance where needed. All wedding options include a finished full-size album and various extras.

Thomas Gartman, Photographer
(252) 491–8566, (866) 275–6679
www.gartmanbeachpix.com
Thomas Gartman specializes in weddings, family portraits, and special events. Using high-quality medium-format equipment, Thomas captures your special day with a combination of relaxed candid shots and formal posed portraits. Thomas prides himself on taking wedding photographs that exude warmth and individuality.

Walter V. Gresham III Photography
Kill Devil Hills
(252) 441–5091, (800) 887–1415
www.gresham-photography.com
When the dress has been folded and put away, the cake has been eaten, and the flowers have withered and died, only the photographs remain. Walter Gresham promises the highest quality photography available anywhere, with a series of portraits that tell the story of your wedding day.

Shooters at the Beach
Central Square Shopping Center, MP 11
Nags Head
(252) 480–2395
www.shootersphotos.com
Shooters' professional photo services promises fun photos that capture great memories. Owner Biff Jennings specializes in weddings, anniversaries, reunions, and birthdays and works with groups of all sizes.

KTM Productions
P.O. Box 1676, Nags Head, NC 27959
(252) 480–0543, (888) 538–5832
You can capture your day forever with a professional wedding video. KTM Productions is an affordable way to preserve your Outer Banks wedding in brilliant sound and color. KTM offers complete wedding and reception coverage by a professional, premier video photographer with state-of-the-art equipment and more than 15 years'

experience with video production. KTM has packages to fit all budgets.

Photography By Geri
NC 12, Buxton
(252) 995-6740, (866) MYFOTOS
www.photographybygeri.com
Geri specializes in wedding photography from the northern reaches of the Outer Banks to Hatteras Village and beach portraits on Hatteras Island. At the most beautiful beaches on the East Coast, she aims to keep your most beautiful memories alive. And what's better, you receive your package the day following the photography session. Most of her clients are vacationers making special moments in their lives. Geri photographs all year.

Rental Equipment

Metro Rental
US 158 and Colington Road
Kill Devil Hills
(252) 480-3535
Metro Rental is the rental source on the Outer Banks for wedding and party supplies. They have a complete line of tents, tables, chairs, linens, fountains, china, glassware, chafing dishes, wedding arches, flower stands, and guest-book stands. You can even rent a portable bar and dance floor. Metro Rental offers the services of a certified wedding consultant, too. Delivery is available, and quality and dependability are guaranteed.

Ocean Atlantic Rentals
(800) 635-9559

Corolla Light Town Center, Corolla
(252) 453-2440

Duck Road, Soundfront, Duck
(252) 261-4346

NC 12, MP 10, Nags Head
(252) 441-7823

NC 12, Avon
(252) 995-5868
www.oceanatlanticrentals.com

Ocean Atlantic Rentals offers party tents and both round and rectangular banquet tables for rent. Rental chairs range from white padded wedding chairs and plastic folding chairs to classic beach chairs. Setup and take-down are optional.

Transportation

If you can't borrow Cinderella's coach, what better way to arrive at a wedding than in a limousine? The following limousine services are just a phone call away.

Island Limousine
Kill Devil Hills
(252) 441-5466, (800) 828-5466
www.islandlimo.com
Island Limousine rolls out the red carpet for a new bride. It also offers shuttle connections to the Norfolk Airport.

Karat Limo Service
Manteo
(252) 473-9827
www.karatlimo.com
Karat Limo Service offers VIP service in a stretch limousine. The vehicle holds up to 10 people, and the company offers service to Norfolk Airport.

Outer Banks Suburban Limousine Service
(252) 305-LIMO, (877) 751-8617
Outer Banks Suburban Limousine offers wedding services anywhere from Corolla to Ocracoke. Available for rides in style are a 12-passenger super-stretch Suburban limo and a vintage Rolls Royce sedan.

GIFTS

Jewelry By Gail, Inc.
207 East Driftwood Street, Nags Head
(252) 441-5387
www.jewelrybygail.com
Jewelry By Gail features jewelry uniquely crafted in precious metals and high-quality gemstones. At this award-winning studio,

you can get advice on diamond selection and find extraordinary engagement and wedding rings and anniversary gifts, as well as gifts for the bride, groom, and members of the wedding party.

Diane's Lavish Linens
Scarborough Lane Shoppes, NC 12
Duck
(252) 255-0555
www.dianeslavishlinens.com
Diane's offers luxury linens, sheets, blankets, and towels, plus fabulous nightgowns of cotton and silk. You can register your choices of patterns with Diane Strehan so that friends and family can purchase matching items for your new home.

OUTER BANKS HONEYMOONS

The Outer Banks has traditionally been for honeymooners, especially off-season, when the crowds are scarce, the prices are low, and the island feels like a private paradise. Consult our Accommodations and Weekly and Long-Term Cottage Rentals chapters for information on lodging. Then, think about all the wonderful diversions the Outer Banks has to offer that will make your honeymoon even more memorable. Depending upon the time of year and the amount of physical activity you're up for, you can do everything from visiting art galleries to trying your hand at hang gliding. Outdoor activities include bicycling, swimming, diving, playing golf, fly-fishing, deep-sea fishing, kayaking, sailing, and lying on the beach. Together, you can take an aero or dolphin tour, walk through the Elizabethan Gardens, or adventure off-road. You may wish to have a beach portrait taken or spend the day at a full-service spa. Numerous fine restaurants, rustic eateries, and establishments that provide outdoor entertainment are scattered through this area. Leaf through this guide; you'll find suggestions for each of the aforementioned activities and then some. We're convinced that couples who decide to honeymoon on this stretch of barrier islands will enjoy it so much that they'll want to keep coming back for each anniversary.

ARTS AND CULTURE

The Outer Banks is the kind of place where many artists envision spending their days painting the beauty that surrounds them or sculpting forms wrought by visions brought forth by the ocean. For many, this dream has come to fruition, and the beach has become a haven for artists of all kinds. The powerful influence of the ocean and wetlands appears in many works of art, as do the abundant wildlife and spirit of the residents as they work and play. Our historic landmarks provide inspiration for an artistic appetite. The relative isolation of our barrier islands, though seen by some as a drawback to year-round living, is a real plus to the artist, especially in the off-season. This is the time to contemplate and study, then commune with the muse and put insights into a tangible piece of art. When a nor'easter blows on a gray February day, the muse may be an artist's only visitor! Take the time to visit our many galleries and talk with some of our local artists and writers. Through their eyes you are sure to gain more appreciation of this special area.

You can get a feel for this fascinating visual arts arena, which runs the gamut from conceptual art to classical painting, by attending several annual events. One of the longest running of these is the Dare County Arts Council's Frank Stick Memorial Art Show, which was started back in 1978. The show is held at the Ghost Fleet Gallery in Nags Head every February and features more than 150 artworks (see our Annual Events chapter for more information).

For some family fun of the artistic kind, set aside the first weekend in October for the arts council's annual Artrageous Art Extravaganza, which features hands-on creative booths with cookie decorating, hat creations, weaving, face painting, and much more. Fashion shows, food, live music, art collaborations, and local art and craft booths highlight the two-day event. During an elegant Sunday auction, fine art by adults and children is put on the block. Dedicated volunteers who coordinate the weekend event outdo themselves year after year. (See our Annual Events chapter for more information.)

Another must-see is the New World Festival of the Arts each August on downtown Manteo's waterfront, an ideal site for showcasing the talents of approximately 80 local and national artists and artisans. Look for painting, photography, jewelry, pottery, and an assortment of handcrafted items. If you would like to show your work or need more information about the festival, see our Annual Events chapter for contact information. The literature for this show usually comes out in January.

Private visual art studios are scattered from Corolla to Ocracoke for art seekers. Many local artists offer lessons, mostly in watercolor and other painting techniques. We do have a large concentration of landscape painters here, but our 50 or more commercial art/craft galleries are packed with expressions as individualistic as grains of sand.

The Outer Banks has become a bona fide art community. Artists living here and in the surrounding areas are a close-knit group, sharing tips and encouraging each other in their endeavors. Perhaps because of the lifestyle here, our artists are eager to meet visitors. The Town of Nags Head has certainly done its part in supporting local artists by setting aside up to $20,000 a year in surplus revenues to purchase artwork for its Town Hall. Since 1997, the town has purchased more than 90 pieces of art by local and regional artists. The collection, selected by the town's Artwork Selection committee, includes paintings, sculpture, photographs, wood carvings, etchings, mobiles, found-object art, and more. The public is invited to view this collection during Town Hall operating hours.

Local theater groups present plays, comedies, and dramas both seasonally and year-round. Music streams from some nightclubs, and standup comics perform summer stints. Symphonies, vocal groups, and individual classical, folk, and pop artists enliven our local auditoriums throughout the year. What we can't generate ourselves in the way of cultural experiences, we import with the help of volunteer-based nonprofit organizations. Thanks to the efforts of the Dare County Arts Council, Outer Banks Forum, the Theatre of Dare, the Roanoke Island Historical Association (producers of *The Lost Colony*), the North Carolina School of the Arts, and Roanoke Island Festival Park, Insiders on the Outer Banks enjoy exposure to local, regional, and national cultural opportunities.

We begin our pilgrimage with a description of the area's major arts organizations and follow with a north-to-south excursion through the Outer Banks's eclectic galleries and other creative venues. Please see our Annual Events chapter for arts events.

ORGANIZATIONS

Dare County Arts Council
104 Sir Walter Raleigh Street, Manteo
(252) 473-5558
www.darearts.org
Celebrating its 31st year in 2006, the Dare County Arts Council supplies the Outer Banks with a wide variety of creative opportunities with the help of countless volunteers, generous patrons and members, and some state and county support. This nonprofit group has a permanent office/gallery in downtown Manteo at the

address above. The gallery, called Sea and Sounds Gallery, hosts visual arts shows, and visitors are encouraged to stop by to view these shows or to gather information on arts and cultural events in the area. Office hours are 10:00 A.M. to 5:00 P.M. Monday through Friday and occasional weekends when volunteer staff is available.

The council is affiliated with the North Carolina Arts Council as the local distributing agency of the state's Grassroots funds. The DCAC also subsidizes other area arts organizations, such as Theatre of Dare, The Writers' Group, the Outer Banks Forum, and Icarus International, which hosts an art exhibition honoring humankind's first powered flight each December at two Nags Head galleries (see our Annual Events chapter).

DCAC sponsors several cultural programs in the community and local schools every year. In 2004, for example, DCAC brought nationally known poet Glenis Redmond into the community to read her poems and run private poetry workshops with students. It also brought illustrator Michael White to demonstrate his craft and inspire Dare County students to write and illustrate. In addition, DCAC put on its annual Frank Stick Memorial Art Show, a photography competition, a watercolor competition, the Mollie Fearing Memorial Art Show, *The Beach Book* Cover Competition, eight visual arts exhibitions in its gallery, and the annual Artrageous Art Extravaganza weekend for kids and families.

In addition, DCAC publishes its quarterly newsletter, *Art Throb*, full of events listings, feature articles, profiles of local artists, and poetry. The publication, distributed to members and at events, is a way for artists to voice concerns and share news as well as keep people up to date on the happenings in the arts community. DCAC's regularly updated Web site also offers a wealth of information on the arts.

DCAC operates on funds from grants, fund-raisers, and annual memberships. Memberships generally range from $20 for students to $35 for artists to $100 for patrons. This is a great way to support the arts in the community.

Elizabeth R & Company
(252) 473-1061

Elizabeth R & Company sponsors scholarly research projects centered on North Carolina history and professional films, audio presentations, and performances that interpret history. Two of its most popular interpretive performances are staged on Roanoke Island every summer—*Elizabeth R* and *Bloody Mary and the Virgin Queen. Elizabeth R* will celebrate its 15th anniversary in 2007. It stars Barbara Hird and portrays the life of Queen Elizabeth I. It is held in the Elizabethan Gardens on Tuesday at 2:30 P.M. from early June through mid-August. *Elizabeth R* tours internationally the rest of the year; it was part of the 1995 Edinburgh Festival and has been performed in London, New York City, and across the mid-Atlantic United States. *Bloody Mary,* also starring Barbara Hird and Marsha Warren, tells the story of Queen Elizabeth I and her half sister Mary Queen of Scots in a hilarious farce. It is performed mid-July through mid-August at the Pioneer Theatre in downtown Manteo on Wednesday at 3:30 P.M. For more information, see our Attractions chapter.

Outer Banks Forum for the Lively Arts
(252) 202-9732
www.outerbanksforum.org

The Outer Banks Forum organizes six lively arts performances a year, bringing world-class performers to this remote stretch of the world. Since 1983 the forum has scheduled these performances from October through April, making the off-season months brighter for many folks. The forum seasons are filled with interesting and varied selections, including bluegrass, opera, and folk tales. All performances are held in the First Flight High School auditorium. Starting times vary. Season subscriptions cost $85. If you arrive 45 minutes before each performance, you can attend an informative lec-

ture series to enhance your appreciation of the performance.

Roanoke Island Festival Park
1 Festival Park, Manteo
(252) 475-1500
(252) 475-1506 24-hour events line
www.roanokeisland.com

Roanoke Island Festival Park blends art, history, and education in celebration of Roanoke Island's role as birthplace of English-speaking America. The state park is on its own small island across from the Manteo waterfront, also the home berth of the *Elizabeth II.* Completed in 1998, the park features a variety of cultural opportunities year-round. The park's Art Gallery is a beautiful space that holds monthlong art shows. At receptions for these shows on Sunday afternoons, arts-minded folk meet. The Film Theater's house film is *The Legend of Two-Path,* a 45-minute film depicting the English landing on Roanoke Island from the Native Americans' point of view; other top-notch cultural arts performances and films are also staged in the theater year-round.

The outdoor pavilion, which seats up to 3,500 people on the lawn, is a marvelous place to watch cultural arts performances. North Carolina School of the Arts students perform here five nights a week at 8:00 P.M. in the "illuminations" Summer Performance Art Series in July. Visiting symphonies and musicians often perform here as well. Also on-site are an 8,500-square-foot Adventure Museum, which has 400 years of Outer Banks history, a museum store, and the Outer Banks History Center. For more information, see our Attractions chapter.

Roanoke Island Historical Association
1409 US 64/264, Manteo
(252) 473-2127
www.thelostcolony.org

The dramatic arts have a unique outlet on the Outer Banks in *The Lost Colony* outdoor drama, staged throughout the summer in a waterside theater on Roanoke Island (see our Attractions chapter). Each year, *The Lost Colony* entices 125 actors and crew across the nation to answer the casting call for the symphonic drama that chronicles the fate of the first English settlement in America.

Many of *The Lost Colony* thespians also try out for the Lost Colony's Children's Theater that wows junior audiences during the summer months with classics such as *The Princess and the Pea*. Others take on roles as time-warped sailors for hilarious and educational interpretive tours of the *Elizabeth II*.

A full day of special events, including free children's theater selections, interpretive park tours, and special performances, takes place on Virginia Dare's birthday, August 18. Call the Lindsey Warren Visitor Center at Fort Raleigh (252–473-5772) for a schedule.

If you're interested in joining the Roanoke Island Historical Association and supporting *The Lost Colony,* write to the address listed above (zip code 27954) or call. Contribution details vary. You may become a member and/or contribute to the annual fund or the endowment fund.

The Theatre of Dare
(252) 473-1825
www.theatreofdare.org
The Theatre of Dare was established in 1992 with a grant from the Outer Banks Forum. Its members bring quality live theater to the Outer Banks by taking part in all phases of production, such as directing, set design, and performing. The Theatre of Dare produces three main stage productions a year from fall to spring. TOD embodies the true spirit of community theater by welcoming amateur and professional thespians alike. The organization thus far has produced hits such as *Arsenic and Old Lace, Steel Magnolias, The Odd Couple,* and *South Pacific.*

The Theatre of Dare lacks a permanent rehearsal space, but most of its performances are held at Manteo Middle School. Season tickets cost $30. For more information about membership, volunteer-

ing, auditions, or production dates, call Mike Hunter at the number listed here.

Icarus International
(252) 441-6584
www.icarusinternational.com
Icarus International was founded in 1993, purposely a decade before the centennial of flight in 2003, with the goal of celebrating flight through the arts. The organization has been widely successful in its efforts to raise the awareness of the history of flight. Each year, Icarus International holds an international visual arts competition and a literary competition based on a flight-related theme. Literary entries are published annually. Icarus International also sponsors an annual portrait commission for inductees into the First Flight Shrine at the Wright Brothers National Memorial. In 2003 the group completed the $1 million Icarus Monument, celebrating 100 years of flight. The monument is located at MP 1 in Kitty Hawk behind the Aycock Brown Welcome Center. Icarus International has also created a book called *Pioneer Aviators of the World*. It tells the story of the first pilots from 100 countries.

GALLERIES
Corolla

Outer Banks Style
NC 12, Corolla
(252) 453-4388, (800) 261-0176
Outer Banks Style offers a taste of local art, crafts, furniture, and home accessories in its Corolla shop. Owner Gary Springer has stocked the gallery with works by popular Outer Banks painter James Melvin and photographer Ray Matthews. Check out Troy Spencer's reproduction signs. Outer Banks Style acquired StoryPeople by Brian Andreas. This line of fanciful art includes prints, sculptures, books, and furniture decorated with short prose. The shop is open year-round. Hours vary, so call ahead.

Dolphin Watch Gallery
TimBuck II Shopping Village
Ocean Trail, Corolla
(252) 453-2592
www.dolphinwatchgallery.com
Dolphin Watch Gallery features the works
of owner/artist Mary Kaye Umberger. This
artist creates hand-colored etchings on
handmade paper drawn from scenes
indigenous to the Corolla area, including
wildlife, ducks and other waterfowl,
seascapes, and lighthouses. Other art
pieces here include pottery, stoneware,
carvings of marine life, and wax sculptures
(candles shaped by hand, with flower
petals molded by the artist's fingertips).
The gallery is open year-round; call for
off-season hours.

Duck

Greenleaf Gallery
1169 NC 12, Duck
(252) 261-2009
www.outer-banks.com/greenleaf
Greenleaf Gallery offers a chance to experience exquisite fine crafts and paintings
from nationally, regionally, and locally
known American artists. Approximately
300 artists and artisans are represented at
Greenleaf. Featured are one-of-a-kind
handcrafted jewelry, ceramics, wood,
glass, and furnishings, plus sculpture,
acrylic and watercolor paintings, etchings,
lithographs, and mixed-media pieces.
Expect to find both the delightful and the
serious at Greenleaf, anything from a
huge, whimsical praying mantis to the
works of some of the nation's finest glass
artisans. One of the best things about visiting Greenleaf is seeing the sublime
paintings of Outer Banks artist Rick Tupper, who owns the gallery with his wife.

Call for a schedule of artists' exhibitions. The gallery is closed on Sunday and
from January through mid-March.

The Wooden Feather
Scarborough Lane, NC 12, Duck
(252) 261-2808
www.woodenfeather.com
The Wooden Feather presents award-
winning handcarved decoys and shorebirds as well as driftwood sculptures. The
gallery features an outstanding collection
of antique decoys. It's open seven days a
week from March through December, with
longer hours during the summer season.

Kill Devil Hills

Nostalgia Gallery
Seagate North Shopping Center
US 158, MP 5½, Kill Devil Hills
(252) 441-1881
Norm Martinus specializes in paper memorabilia that deserves mention in any art
chapter. He knows his stuff as the coauthor of *Warmon's Paper,* an encyclopedia
of antiques and collectibles. You'll find
oodles of advertising art at Nostalgia as
well as the original art of Martinus's
daughter, Lee. Revel in old prints of Max-
field Parrish and Norman Rockwell. Martinus offers full-service custom framing and
matting. Insiders know that he's one of
the Outer Banks's finest framers. The shop
is open year-round.

First Flight Shrine
Wright Brothers National Memorial
Visitor Center, US 158, MP 8
Kill Devil Hills
(252) 441-7430
www.nps.gov/wrbr
While the First Flight Shrine is not a commercial art gallery, it has a body of portraiture that deserves recognition in any
Arts and Culture chapter. Every year for
more than 30 years, the First Flight Society has inducted into the shrine one or
more individuals who have accomplished
an outstanding "first" that has enhanced
the development of aviation. Hanging in
the same room as a replica of Wilbur and
Orville Wright's first flyer are more than

55 faces of great aviators, such as Amelia Earhart, Adm. Richard E. Byrd, Neil Armstrong, and Col. Edwin Aldrin. The portraits, which are donated by Icarus International, are produced annually and exhibited through a partnership with the National Park Service at the Wright Brothers National Memorial Visitor Center (see our Attractions chapter for more about the Memorial).

KDH Cooperative Gallery and Studios
US 158, MP 8½, Kill Devil Hills
(252) 441-9888
This is an artist-operated cooperative, the dream and reality of artist and owner Julie Moye. It's a centralized place to see the work of 29 local artists. The juried members of this cooperative show their work and assist in running the gallery. Oil, acrylic, watercolor, pastels, pen and ink, ceramics, jewelry, fiber, furniture, candles, pottery, glass, and metal are featured in the three-room gallery. Each member serves on panels to hang and display art, jury, organize shows, and assist customers during daily business hours. Upstairs is the Artists Attic, a lively studio space and classrooms. Several artists have set up studios upstairs and often work during business hours. Visitors are welcome upstairs to talk with the artists and watch them work. The other half of the upstairs is classroom space, where a variety of classes are held year-round for children and adults. Pottery, drawing, photography, stained glass, mosaic, candle making, and basket making are some of the classes offered, or you can design your own class and pitch it to the staff. KDH Cooperative offers art classes for kids, including creative writing, drawing, and comic strip drawing, as well as summer art camps and classes on school holidays.

Nags Head

A treasure trove of art galleries is tucked into Nags Head's Gallery Row. Seven galleries and a consignment shop are within a block of one another, and three more galleries are in the vicinity. This little art mecca is a great place to spend an entire afternoon, poking in and out of each gallery and chatting with the owners. Gallery Row is around MP 10 at Gallery Row and Driftwood Streets. Park at any of the galleries and walk to the others. This is a low-traffic, laid-back area so don't feel rushed to get out of your parking space. Nearby on the Beach Road are Seaside Art Gallery, Anna Gartell's Gallery by the Sea, and The Yellowhouse Gallery.

Lighthouse Gallery and Gifts
Gallery Row, 301 East Driftwood Street
Nags Head
(252) 441-4232, (800) 579-2827
www.seabeacons.com
Carole and Russ Burnett are the owners of this shop dedicated to the "Keepers of the Light." The gallery is a replica of an original Victorian-style lighthouse representing the U.S. Lighthouse Service in its prime at the turn of the 20th century.

Open every day of the year except Christmas, this shop features lighthouse art and artifacts, including hundreds of lighthouse models, collectibles, brass nautical memorabilia (such as compasses, sextants, and octants, both authentic and reproduction), books, jewelry, prints, paintings from all over the United States, and local artwork. The special collection of lighthouse books with photography by Bruce Roberts displays unique and breathtaking views of these beloved sentinels.

Add your name to the Outer Banks Lighthouse Society newsletter mailing list at the gallery, or call for information about joining the society, which boasts 600 members.

Sally Huss Gallery
Gallery Row, 300 East Driftwood Street
Nags Head
(252) 441-8098
www.ceramicsbythesea.com
Sally Huss Gallery features the upbeat original art and prints of the California artist of the same name. Huss creates impressionis-

tic paintings in bold colors featuring child-like scenes. Her designs, coupled with cheerful sayings, are transferred onto mugs, gift wrap, T-shirts, cards, and key chains. Adults and kids alike get a kick out of her lighthearted creations that are dotted with toucans, mermaids, elephants, hearts, and sailboats. You'll also want to see the original ceramics created by Bob Martin. In addition to Huss's art, this gallery features unique home decor, gifts, and work from local potters. The gallery is open all year.

Ipso Facto Gallery
206 Gallery Row, Nags Head
(252) 480-2793

The merchandise at Ipso Facto—antiques, curios, and objects of art from all over the world—is eclectic, and reasonably priced. Look for furniture, ethnic trinkets such as Mexican holiday candleholders, and original paintings. Ipso is really more of an antiques shop than a gift shop. It's a great place to browse, ooh and aah, and, of course, find a treasure to take home. Ipso Facto Gallery is open year-round; it's closed Sunday.

Morales Art Gallery
207 East Gallery Row, Nags Head
(252) 441-6484, (800) 635-6035
www.prints-r-us.com

Mitchell and Christine Lively at the Morales Art Galleries have made financial success a personal reality for many struggling artists by showcasing their work and producing fine-art prints shown at their three gallery locations on the Outer Banks.

Morales Art Gallery is the oldest art venue on Gallery Row; the late Jesse Morales first opened the doors in 1971. Today, the Morales galleries and Fine Art Print Shop carry fine original local, regional, and nationally known art. Showcased here are the works of Larry Johnson, Pat Williams, Dennis Lighthart, Pat Troiani, Tony Feathers, and Anda Styler. Expect to find limited-edition prints by the Greenwich Workshop, Mill Pond Press, Hadley House, Somerset Publishing, and Wild Wings. If

you want to view a major collection of original seascapes, this is the place.

Mitchell has been framing and publishing art for more than two decades. The couple's dedication to the arts has been felt community-wide, especially in their generosity to the Dare County schools. A member of the Professional Picture Framers Association, Morales Gallery offers a wide variety of choices in custom framing.

The Morales Art Gallery is open year-round.

Glenn Eure's Ghost Fleet
Gallery of Fine Art
Gallery Row, 210 East Driftwood Street
Nags Head
(252) 441-6584
www.angelfire.com/on2/ghostfleet

Glenn and Pat Eure, owners of the Ghost Fleet Gallery, run an original art establishment that primarily features Glenn's work. A printmaker, Glenn creates in a variety of forms including etching, wood cutting, collagraphy, serigraphy, and relief carving in addition to drawing, wood carving, and oil, acrylic, and watercolor painting. His oeuvre includes a series of collagraphs (thin collages run through a printing press) honoring Wilbur and Orville Wright's first flight. The fine-art prints, each hand-pulled by the artist, contain flight imagery from da Vinci's time to the present. Glenn specializes in large canvases that bulge out from their frames—irregular shapes that are painted in a nonobjective style. He also produces lighthearted watercolors that feature boat scenes.

The Eures rotate other artists' work in the West Wing Gallery and the Second Dimension gallery located a flight up. In the off-season Eure hosts several community shows: the Icarus International Art Show in December, the Frank Stick Memorial Art Show in February, and a county public school art show. Poetry readings also are held year-round at the gallery (see our Annual Events chapter). The Ghost Fleet Gallery is open year-round. Hours are cut back some in January and February.

Jewelry by Gail
Gallery Row, 207 Driftwood Street
Nags Head
(252) 441-5387
www.jewelrybygail.com
Gail Kowalski is a designer-goldsmith who has won national recognition for her creations in precious metals and stones. Most of the jewelry designed and made here falls into the "wearable art" category. Check out Selections by Gail, a department of very high-quality but moderately priced handmade jewelry from all over the world. Kowalski personally selects each piece exhibited here. The "Charming Lights" sterling and gold lighthouse jewelry collection is a favorite. Images of the four local lighthouses are fashioned into earrings, pendants, and charms. The gallery is open Monday through Saturday and is closed in January.

Anna Gartrell's Art & Photography
By the Sea
NC 12, MP 10, Nags Head
(252) 480-0578
Gartrell's artistry is evident in her expressive watercolors and photography. A deeply spiritual woman, Gartrell said she revels in "God's explosive beauty frozen forever for you." Examine her series of jeweled and crystal wave photos and her depictions of wild storms, sunrises and sunsets, ducks, dunes, wild stallions, lighthouses, crystal flounders, and amazing sea angels. Take a bit of Outer Banks brightness home with you.

The gallery is open daily, but hours are flexible. The owner posts a note on the door every day with the day's operating hours.

Seaside Art Gallery
NC 12, MP 11, Nags Head
(252) 441-5418
www.seasideart.com
Original etchings and lithographs by Picasso, Whistler, Rembrandt, and Renoir are among the thousands of original works of art on display at Seaside Art Gallery. Sculptures, paintings, drawings, Indian pottery, fine porcelains, Mexican silver jewelry (including the work of William Spratling), seascapes, and animation art from Disney and Warner Brothers are spread throughout numerous rooms in this sprawling gallery. Seaside is a Gold Circle dealer for Disney Classic Figurines. Prints by David Hunter are meticulously rendered and range from biblical portraiture to peaceful coastal scenes.

The gallery hosts several competitions annually, including an International Miniature Art Show (see the May listings in our Annual Events chapter) and the Icarus International Art Show. Printmaking workshops are held here each year by David Hunter. The gallery is open year-round.

Yellowhouse Gallery and Annex
NC 12, MP 11, Nags Head
(252) 441-6928
www.yellowhousegallery.com
Yellowhouse Gallery houses one of North Carolina's largest collections of antique prints and maps. Thousands of original old etchings, lithographs, and engravings are organized for browsing in several rooms of one of Nags Head's older beach cottages. Established in 1969, the gallery features Civil War prints and maps; prints of botanicals, fish, shells, and birds; and old views and antique maps and charts of the Outer Banks. Yellowhouse Gallery also offers a huge selection of decorative and fine-art prints and posters as well as souvenir pictures and maps of the Outer Banks. If the picture you want is not in stock, Uncle Jack, the proprietor, will order it for you.

Roanoke Island

Silver Bonsai Gallery
905 US 64/264, Manteo
(252) 475-1413
www.silverbonsai.com
Silver Bonsai Gallery, nestled in one of the island's original homes, is a distinctive art gallery. Owners Ben and Kathryn Stewart, both metalsmiths and bonsai artists, sell their own creations here, as well as the

works of other artists, and can often be seen at work in the studio at the back of the gallery. The Stewarts create simple yet elegant silver and gold jewelry and sculpture and design special pieces upon request. The gallery sells a broad range of fine art by local artists, including paintings, wood, glass, sculpture, quilts, and more. Silver Bonsai is open seven days a week, but closes for the month of January.

Wanchese Pottery
107 Fernando Street, Manteo
(252) 473-2099
Customers can watch local potters Bonnie and Bob Morrill at work in their studio in downtown Manteo. This shop is known for its beautiful, useful art graced with delicate, lead-free glazes. One savvy Insider bought a handsome mug here that holds a generous amount of coffee, sits easily without wobbling, and has an exquisite glaze that turns a morning routine into an artistic awakening. Choose dinnerware, oil lamps, hummingbird feeders, mugs, bowls, and pitchers among other items. The shop also features some handmade baskets and fresh cooking herbs.

Wanchese Pottery is open all year. Winter hours are 1:00 to 5:00 P.M. Thursday, Friday, and Saturday.

Sea and Sounds Gallery
104 Sir Walter Raleigh Street, Manteo
(252) 473-5558
www.darearts.org
Sea and Sounds Gallery is the gallery space for the Dare County Arts Council. The council holds monthly shows in this space, including group shows, competitions, and individual shows. Receptions for each show, held on Sunday afternoon, offer a chance to meet the artists. The gallery has a bin of unframed works of art for sale. This is also the DCAC office, so stop by if you want any arts-related information.

Nancyware Pottery
402 Queen Elizabeth Street, Manteo
(252) 473-9400
www.nancywarepottery.com

Early Christmas shoppers love a summer outdoor art show. The New World Festival of the Arts in Manteo in August welcomes 80 artists from the Outer Banks and all along the East Coast. You'll find pottery, paintings, metalwork, photography, basketry, painted tiles, and so much more. This show is held midweek. For more information, see our Annual Events chapter.

This is the pottery studio of artist Nancy Hase. The potter's wheel is on display and you can see her work from time to time. She also offers classes on the wheel. In this year-round shop you'll find Nancy's pottery, jewelry, and tile work. The pottery is high-fire functional stoneware that is dishwasher, microwave, and oven safe. The variety of kitchen items, including deep-dish fluted pie plates, colanders, and three-piece child dining sets, can be personalized, as can the vases, dishes, and spoon rests.

Roanoke Island Festival Park Art Gallery
Manteo
(252) 475-1506
www.roanokeisland.com
Roanoke Island Festival Park's Art Gallery is the finest arts exhibition space on the Outer Banks. The gallery is vast and uncluttered, allowing much room for appreciating the works of art hanging in the exhibitions. Gallery shows change monthly, featuring the works of an individual artist or sometimes groups of artists. In June 2004 the North Carolina Penland School of Crafts had a show representing all of North Carolina with both crafts and arts. The Priceless Pieces Past & Present Quilt Extravaganza is a popular show, held every year in March with dozens of quilts made or owned by locals. The Dare County Arts Council's Mollie Fearing Art Show is another popular show held here. Each monthly show has an opening reception on a Sunday afternoon. Roanoke Island Festival Park is closed in January.

Hubby Bliven, Wildlife Art
543 Ananias Dare Street, Roanoke Island
(252) 473-2632

Bliven runs a full-service frame shop and wildlife art gallery featuring his own work. He also operates a museum on the premises that includes Civil War, World War I, World War II, and Native American artifacts. Bliven's shop is the place to go if you're looking for lighthouse photos that include all eight North Carolina sentinels framed together or as individual prints. This group includes the Prices's Creek lighthouse in Southport, a rare find. Bliven is very fortunate to have been given access to photograph this structure on private property. His shop is open year-round.

Nick-E Stained Glass
813 Old Wharf Road, Wanchese
(252) 473-5036

This is the stained-glass studio of Ellinor and Robert Nick. The Nicks create their works of art here and hold demonstrations and classes in stained glass. The Nicks also sell stained-glass supplies and tools. If you want to see how the work is done, commission a piece, or talk with the artists, stop by this location. If you want to buy their stained-glass creations, go to their gallery at the Dare Shops in Nags Head.

Hatteras Island

Gaskins Gallery
NC 12, Avon
(252) 995-6617
www.gaskinsgallery.com

The Gaskins Gallery focuses on original local art and custom framing. Artists and owners Denise and Elizabeth Gaskins feature exclusively original family art, including their own watercolors and those of their octogenarian grandmother, who began painting several years ago. The paintings generally are coastal scenes or florals. You'll also find pottery, decorator prints, and posters. The Gaskins Gallery is open year-round.

Browning Artworks
NC 12, Frisco
(252) 995-5538
www.browningartworks.com

This fine-art and craft gallery, which opened in 1984, is reputed for showcasing top-notch North Carolina crafters, including many local artists. Browning also carries the work of 12 to 15 out-of-state artists who are considered exceptional exceptions to its strongly stated "North Carolina–only" rule. The collection includes the creations of 200 artisans who make stained and blown glass, weavings, porcelains, pottery, copper work, forged wrought-iron work, and stoneware. Woodturners, many of whom use North Carolina woods, have a variety of crafts showcased here. Browning's jewelry selections are breathtaking, incorporating a variety of colorful semiprecious stones to form necklaces, rings, pins, bracelets, and earrings. Several dozen jewelry designers are displayed, including the innovative and colorful creations of Outer Banker Austin Cake.

The gallery also exhibits paintings and prints, including an exclusive collection of Linda Browning's watercolor skyscapes as well as the color photography of Ray Matthews and Michael Halminski. Both photographers have a passion for the coastal scene. Antique tribal weavings by Majid are a beautiful attraction. Featured artists hold demonstrations on the gallery deck. Call for a schedule.

Browning Artworks is open March through December.

Indian Town Gallery and Gifts
NC 12, Frisco
(252) 995-5181

Nestled in the woods in Frisco, Indian Town represents artists from local villages. Many of the paintings have an Outer Banks theme. The offshore-fishing theme paintings are stunning. The gallery also features pottery, jewelry, chimes, cards, gifts, lighthouses, and jewelry. Artist Wayne Fulcher is often at work in the store.

Red Drum Pottery
NC 12, Frisco
(252) 995-5757
Accomplished potters Rhonda Bates and Wes Lassiter work in this studio, and you can watch them as they turn their wonderful creations at the wheel. These are well-crafted pieces, whether they are intended for functional or decorative use. It's definitely worth a stop to see their bowls, pitchers, vases, vessels, platters, teakettles, miniatures, and fabulous fish- and crab-imprinted hanging wall tiles. Do you raku? Come try it in the early evening—call for an updated schedule. The gallery is open seven days a week year-round.

Sandy Bay Gallery
NC 12, Hatteras Village
(252) 986-1338
This gallery features original fine art and crafts with an emphasis on Outer Banks artists. Sandy Bay is filled with original watercolor and acrylic paintings and photography, as well as crafts by potters, jewelers, glass artisans, and paper, wood, stained-glass, and fiber artists. The hand-carved decorative waterfowl, including egrets, blue herons, sandpipers, and dowitchers, have grace and personality. Glass boxes with silver trim by Mary Anne feature a geometric collage of colored and clear glass reminiscent of Mondrian's paintings. You also can choose from a selection of prints. The gallery is open March through Christmas Eve.

Ocracoke Island

Deepwater Pottery
School Road, Ocracoke
(252) 928-7472
www.deepwaterpottery.com
Artistic and functional stoneware and raku pottery are made here. You can choose from functional dining and kitchenware and decorative raku pottery with copper glazes. The shop carries an assortment of gifts; see our Shopping chapter for more details. It's open seasonally, so call ahead.

Village Craftsmen
Howard Street, Ocracoke
(252) 928-5541, (800) 648-9743
The artwork in this well-known gallery includes North Carolina pottery, handmade wooden boxes, jewelry, and other original items. The focus is on excellent craftsmanship and variety. Owner Philip Howard also sells his pen-and-ink and watercolor prints here. See our Shopping chapter for more about this local landmark, open year-round except the month of January.

Island Artworks
British Cemetery Road, Ocracoke
(252) 928-3892
Owner-artist Kathleen O'Neal has lived on Ocracoke for more than 25 years. "Art jewelry" aptly describes most of the finds here. O'Neal does all the copper enameling and silver- and goldsmithing work herself. The gallery also features local and North Carolina artwork such as large, contemporary-style watercolors of island scenes by Debbie Wells and the fused glass work of Libby Hicks. Local photography, sculptural assemblages created by O'Neal, glass art, hand-carved wooden boxes, and mixed-media art are just some of the exciting discoveries at Island Artworks. It's a real fine-art experience. The shop is open from mid-March until Christmas.

Over the Moon
British Cemetery Road, Ocracoke
(252) 928-3555
Over the Moon features handmade contemporary crafts from 150 artists across the nation. Shop for jewelry, porcelain, and Brian Andreas's StoryPeople—books, prints, and sculptures adorned with insightful sayings. See our Shopping chapter for other items found here. Over the Moon is open from Easter through Thanksgiving.

Heart's Desire
Back Road, Ocracoke
(252) 928-4104
This shop features a variety of fine crafts,

including pottery, glass works, jewelry, folk art, copper works, and beach glass creations. Heart's Desire is open April through December.

STUDIOS

These are private studios that can be visited by appointment only.

Southern Shores and Kitty Hawk

Russell Yerkes
(252) 261-6947

One of the Outer Banks's most popular artists is Russell Yerkes, probably best known for his vibrant "fish" paintings, though his subject matter encompasses much more than fins. This nationally recognized watercolorist creates imaginative images of aquatic scenes and accepts commissions.

The Greenleaf Gallery in Duck (see the separate listing under Galleries) carries a nice selection of Yerkes's work. Yerkes also serves as president of the Watercolor Society of North Carolina.

A visit to Yerkes's studio to view his work is a real treat. Those wishing to contact the artist may do so at the above telephone number.

Pat Troiani
(252) 261-4659

Pat Troiani is one of the Outer Banks's top watercolorists. She teaches her craft at her Kitty Hawk studio and primarily works in a realistic style. She's produced some gorgeous renditions of the Whalehead Club in the winter, beautiful florals, and various coastal scenes. Her work is sold at Indian Town art gallery in Frisco (see separate listings under Galleries). Troiani's work appeared on the 2004 cover of *The Beach Book,* a local phonebook. She offers classes twice weekly. Class size is limited to seven students. Troiani emphasizes

color, composition, and drawing instruction. Call for an appointment.

W. E. (Ellie) Grumiaux, Jr.
120 South Dogwood Trail
Southern Shores
(252) 255-0402

One of the most recognized artists on the Outer Banks, Grumiaux, who works in watercolor, specializes in portraying the buildings, boats, and landscapes that typify this resort area, as well as the lesser-known places in the surrounding towns. Grumiaux is also the one to call for a portrait of your cottage or boat. His work is found in local churches, homes, and galleries such as Greenleaf Gallery in Duck, Seaside Gallery in Nags Head, and the John Silver Gallery in Manteo (see separate entries under Galleries).

Kill Devil Hills

Marsh Ridge Studio
115 Ridge Road, Kill Devil Hills
(252) 441-6581

Award-winning watercolorist Chris Haltigan offers lessons and original art for sale in her private studio. She describes her work as impressionism and contemporary realism featuring scenes from the Outer Banks and general locale. Her work is characterized by iridescent sound waters and atmospheric early-morning boat scenes. The passage of light gets special attention in her pieces.

Call for an appointment to see Haltigan's work. The studio is open year-round.

E. M. (Liz) Corsa
(252) 480-0303

Think Beatrix Potter. Throw in some sophistication and humor, and you have an idea of the depth and delight of E. M. Corsa's work. Referred to as a "watercolor wordsmith," her original watercolors and prints feature both wild and domestic animals with an attitude, presented in an anthropomorphic style. Corsa's inspiration comes from nature and family and is coupled with her unique sense of humor. She's a published writer of humorous magazine essays who combines images and titles in a thought-provoking and fresh manner. Her work can be viewed at Greenleaf Gallery in Duck and Browning Artworks in Frisco. To view her work or find out where her next showing is, call the artist.

Carol Trotman
(252) 441-3590
Painter Carol Trotman specializes in floral watercolors. Her complicated garden scenes as well as poetic profiles of single blossoms are exceptional. You can purchase reproductions on cards or original full-size work by calling the artist for an appointment or by visiting Greenleaf Gallery in Duck or Sandy Bay Gallery in Hatteras Village.

Susan Vaughan
(252) 480-3301
www.wellsvaughan.byregion.net
Vaughan paints in a folk-art style, producing town portraits in acrylics that are very popular on the Outer Banks. Available prints include her representations of Manteo, Kill Devil Hills, Duck, Elizabeth City, and Corolla. Vaughan also paints local scenes, and she welcomes commissions. Call for commission information.

Nags Head

Marsha Cline
(252) 441-5167
Marsha Cline, a longtime resident of the Outer Banks, is well known for her dedication and versatility. Her medium constantly changes and expands, yet her style remains distinctive. People have come to recognize the vivid color and warm spirit in Cline's work. A passion for painting and love of life is evident in her local Outer Banks scenes, travel-inspired works, and latest passion to be captured on the canvas. Her work is on display in many popular local restaurants, such as the Rundown Cafe, Southern Bean, Quagmires, and Tortuga's Lie. Her work is also on display at the John Silver Gallery, at the KDH Cooperative Gallery, in area businesses, and in homes from coast to coast. She also paints by commission and welcomes contact by appointment at her home studio in Nags Head.

Ray Matthews Photographer
(252) 441-7941
www.raymatthews.com
Ray Matthews has been living on the Outer Banks for more than 25 years, during which time he has developed a love for nature that is presented masterfully in his prints. Matthews is a consummate custom-slide printer as well as a commercial photographer. His work is shown at Browning Artworks in Frisco and Outer Banks Style in Corolla. Call for an appointment. He is available year-round. Look for his Outer Banks calendar in finer retail stores.

Roanoke Island

The Hat Lady
(252) 473-1850
At her working studio, Genna Miles creates fine-art wearable hats in one-of-a-kind designs. Miles employs spinning and crochet techniques with natural, hand-dyed fibers and trinkets to set off these artistic creations that will warm heads and hearts. Her baby bonnets crafted in 100 percent cotton are precious. The Hat Lady specializes in spinning animal hair into yarn. Bring in your dog or cat's shedded hair, and she'll make it into a hat for you. Miles accepts commissions. You can see her work in many of the annual Outer Banks art exhibitions where she has been known to break away from headwear and create fiber and mixed-media sculptures that reflect her love for nostalgic items and thrift-store treasures.

Nick Sapone
292 The Lane, Wanchese
(252) 473-3136
Local decoy carver Nick Sapone produces hand-carved, hunting-style decoys. He makes both wooden decoys and the traditional Outer Banks–canvas style. He welcomes visitors to his home studio by appointment.

Hatteras Island

Michael Halminski Studio
Midgett Way, Waves
(252) 987-2401
Outer Banks seascapes and landscapes dominate the photography collection displayed at this studio. The bird photos are inspiring, especially Halminski's egret pictures. His fine collection of cards is stunning. Call for an appointment.

JURIED ART EXHIBITIONS

The Outer Banks offers several juried art exhibitions each year. While the traditional definition of "juried" implies that work is selected for showing by judges, most shows here have an open-entry policy, and the work is judged for excellence and originality. Entry fees generally average $10 to $15.

Here we've listed the major shows in the area; for detailed information, call either the galleries mentioned or the Dare County Arts Council (252–473-5558). New shows are always cropping up, so keep in touch with the arts council. See also our Annual Events chapter for more art activities.

Nags Head

Frank Stick Memorial Art Show
Glenn Eure's Ghost Fleet
Gallery of Fine Art
Gallery Row, 210 East Driftwood Street
Nags Head
(252) 473-5558

This February show is open to Dare County residents and Dare County Arts Council members. All genres of art are welcome; some restrictions (including the size of the work) apply.

International Miniature Art Show
Seaside Art Gallery, NC 12, MP 11
Nags Head
(252) 441-5418
Any artist may enter this May show held at Seaside Art Gallery. Work entered cannot exceed 40 inches. The show features mini-paintings, drawings, sculpture, wood-turned bowls, collages, and more.

Mollie Fearing Memorial Art Show
Roanoke Island Festival Park, Manteo
(252) 473-5558
www.darearts.org
The Dare County Arts Council puts on this annual art show, held at the beautiful Festival Park Art Gallery. Dare County Arts Council members and Dare County residents are invited to enter this show, which is held in May. Call DCAC at the number above for information.

Icarus International Art Show
Nags Head
(252) 441-6584
Open to any artist, the Icarus International Art Show is held in December at Glenn Eure's Ghost Fleet Gallery and the Seaside Art Gallery (see listings under Galleries). The theme always revolves around flight, as the show was created to pay annual homage to the Wrights' first powered flight.

***The Beach Book* Cover Competition**
Sea and Sounds Gallery
104 Sir Walter Raleigh Street, Manteo
(252) 473-5558
www.darearts.org
Open to all artists, this annual competition selects one entry to be the cover of *The Beach Book,* the Outer Banks's telephone directory. The winning entry also appears on a billboard on U.S. Highway 158, welcoming visitors to the Outer Banks. This

show is held at the Dare County Arts Council gallery each October. Past winners include a beach scene of a young girl painting, the Cape Hatteras lighthouse, a sandcastle, and a fisherman on the beach. For additional information, call the DCAC or *The Beach Book* at (252) 480-2787.

DANCE STUDIOS

Atlantic Dance Studio
Dare Center, US 158, MP 7, Kill Devil Hills
(252) 441-9009

The Atlantic Dance Studio, run by Victoria Toms and Mila Nurney, is a fantastic element of the Outer Banks creative scene. Toms brings with her an outstanding history of professional experience. She studied at the Martha Graham School of Contemporary Dance and the Joffrey Ballet in New York City and ran a very large dance studio in Florida before coming to the Outer Banks. Atlantic Dance Studio offers lessons for adults and children in genres of tap, ballet, and jazz. Both locals and visitors are welcome—from the beginner to the professional.

The Studio's boutique carries garments, shoes, bags, and dance paraphernalia—items needed to keep dancers on their toes.

Island Dance Studio
3017 Virginia Dare Trail, Nags Head
(252) 480-9107

Sophia Sharp has been teaching dance on the Outer Banks for more than two decades. Sophia, Miriam Michael, and their talented staff offer classes in ballet, jazz, tap, and preschool movement. The studio closes during the summer, so it caters mostly to local folks. Children and adults are instructed in the atmospheric setting of an old Nags Head cottage just off the ocean.

Outer Banks Centre for Dance
Central Square Mall, MP 11, Nags Head
(252) 480-0506

This dance school offers preschool through adult classes—in classical ballet, jazz, tap, Irish riverdance, Spanish flamenco, and more—throughout the week. Marjorie Knapp is the artistic director. A dancewear boutique is housed here as well.

ANNUAL EVENTS

The beach isn't just for summer anymore. The Outer Banks has become a favorite destination for visitors year-round, providing those vacationing during less crowded times with a selection of activities to enjoy when life slows a bit.

Roanoke Island Festival Park provides a choice venue for large events, something the area sorely lacked in previous years. Very often, our public buildings double as cultural centers, hosting plays, concerts, and symphony performances. Most local organizations prefer to host fund-raising events in the off-season, when it's easier to get the attention of locals who are too busy during the summer. In fact, the quiet seasons bring out the real character of the area, with hometown parades, a pig pickin' or two, oyster roasts, fishing tournaments—you name it.

When it comes to annual events on the Outer Banks, the environment and history are on our side. We have our time-honored cornerstones that draw national audiences, including the festivities each December commemorating the anniversary of humankind's first powered flight and the annual celebrations that revolve around Virginia Dare's birthday. Our environment is the calling card for national surfing championships, windsurfing and kiteboarding competitions, hang-gliding events, and world-class fishing tournaments.

Our restaurants offer the annual Taste of the Beach, featuring talented chefs with awe-inspiring credentials. Our St. Patrick's Day Parade that promenades down the Beach Road in Nags Head each March is said to be among the largest in the state. Retail stores, art galleries, the Outer Banks Chamber of Commerce, and state sites also sponsor happenings such as dramatic vignettes, printmaking workshops, nature films, luncheons, lectures, and book signings.

Manteo Booksellers in downtown Manteo holds author signings every Wednesday from mid-June through Labor Day. These generally are held from 11:00 A.M. to 1:00 P.M. and 2:00 to 4:00 P.M. Authors of local and national repute have participated, including National Book Award winner Bob Shacochis and Pen/Hemingway Award winner Mark Richard. Book subjects include both serious and humorous nonfiction and fiction works. Occasionally Manteo Booksellers schedules an evening reading by an author; call (252) 473-1221 for more information on these free happenings.

Check out our Arts and Culture chapter for other options. The Outer Banks Forum (252-202-9732) offers a variety of musical performances, dramas, and comedies in the off-season. Look to the Theatre of Dare (252-473-1825) for comedy and drama performances in the off-season. The Dare County Arts Council (252-473-5558) sponsors a variety of performing and visual arts events throughout the year.

Check www.outerbanks.org/events for recently added activities.

JANUARY

Outer Banks Wedding Expo
First Flight High School, Kill Devil Hills
www.outerbanksweddingassoc.org
The largest wedding event on the Outer Banks takes place every year in early to mid-January. More than 700 brides and families attend the Sunday exhibit and meet with many of the businesses on the beach that cater to the local wedding industry. Foods can be sampled from caterers, photographers display their work, and musicians play samples of their music throughout the day. A fashion show tops off the event.

Dare County Schools Annual Art Show
Glenn Eure's Ghost Fleet
Gallery of Fine Art
210 East Driftwood Street, Gallery Row
Nags Head
(252) 441-6584

For one week in mid-January, the Dare County Schools put together an art show that showcases works by kids from seven public schools, grades K–12. If you like children's art, this is the show for you. The works range from delightful watercolors to wild chairs crafted after such artists as Georgia O'Keeffe and Picasso. This show is primarily for viewing—it's difficult to wrestle work away from parents. Don't expect to make any purchases, although some high-school students may be more inclined to sell for some pocket money. The show's reception is on a Sunday, generally at 2:00 P.M. Call for more information. Admission is free, and you can't beat the brownies and other goodies they serve.

FEBRUARY

Frank Stick Memorial Art Show
Glenn Eure's Ghost Fleet
Gallery of Fine Art
210 East Driftwood Street, Gallery Row
Nags Head
(252) 473-5558

This art show has been held in early February every year since 1978 and features the work of more than 160 artists. If you want to submit work, you must be at least 18 years old and a Dare County resident or a member of the Dare County Arts Council, which sponsors the show. The evening reception is eagerly anticipated, and local artists and patrons flock to the gallery to view the newest offerings from the art world. But don't be shy; the event welcomes visitors to partake of the sights, sounds, and tastes of the evening. If you can't make the reception, stop by during the month of February and view this always exciting and innovative exhibit.

This is the best venue to see what area artists have been producing of late.

Many artists go out on a limb, introducing new styles. It's a fun show, and the reception becomes an annual get-together for locals and visitors alike.

A Literary Evening
Glenn Eure's Ghost Fleet Gallery
210 East Driftwood Street, Gallery Row
Nags Head
(252) 441-6584

This free event is held in mid-February as part of the monthlong Frank Stick Memorial Art Show. Members of the Dare County Writers Group and other guests read original recent works. Poetry as well as humorous essays have a forum here. The group, sponsored by the Dare County Arts Council, meets monthly at the Kill Devil Hills branch of the Dare County Library. It's open to all writers, and meetings are informal.

Roanoke Island 1862—A Civil War
Living-History Weekend
Roanoke Island Festival Park, Manteo
(252) 475-1500

This two-day festival explores the Civil War era and its effects on the Outer Banks. Reenactors and living-history encampments bring the era to life as do crafters, demonstrations, presentations, kids activities, and more. It's held on President's Day weekend and is free.

Elizabethan Rendezvous
Penguin Isle
(252) 473-1061

This seven-course gourmet feast includes musical entertainment and dramatic interpretations. Tickets are about $75 per person and include food, wine, and beer.

MARCH

Priceless Pieces Past & Present Quilt
Extravaganza
Roanoke Island Festival Park Art Gallery
Manteo
(252) 475-1500

If you love quilts and the fabric arts, you'll

love this popular annual show. The show features old and new quilts made by or belonging to Dare County residents. There are also demonstrations. It's held throughout the month of March.

Polar Plunge
(252) 261-4346

The Polar Plunge raises money for the "We Build People" campaign to help impoverished people on the Outer Banks attend programs at the Outer Banks YMCA. Child care, the swimming pool, and summer camp programs are also supplemented by taking the plunge. Refreshments are served before and after the event, which takes place on the beach at the Ramada Inn in Kill Devil Hills.

St. Patrick's Day Parade
NC 12, Nags Head
(252) 441-4116

The St. Patrick's Day Parade is held the Sunday before St. Patrick's Day every year. The parade begins at the Nags Head Fishing Pier at MP 12 on the Beach Road and proceeds north to about MP 10. Reputed to be one of the largest parades of its kind in North Carolina, the event is fun for the whole family. Float participants throw candy, so wear something with pockets! Kelly's serves free hot dogs and sodas after the parade and celebrates with an evening of live entertainment. All events are free.

Pirate's Cove Inshore/Offshore Fishing School
Pirate's Cove Yacht Club
Manteo-Nags Head Causeway, Manteo
(252) 473-3906, (800) 762-0245

Going strong since 1993, this one-day, mid-March program features North Carolina fishing experts conducting hands-on round-table sessions at Pirate's Cove Yacht Club. The three-session program is held at the club's restaurant, clubhouse, and fitness center. Pick up an entry form at Pirate's Cove Yacht Club. The day is rounded out with a pig pickin' and beer social. The fee is $85 per person. Anglers

of all skill levels are welcome. Offshore fishing and bait-rigging are demonstrated.

APRIL

Kelly's Midnight Easter Egg Hunt
Kelly's Outer Banks Restaurant & Tavern
US 158, MP 10½, Nags Head
(252) 441-4116

Adults enjoy searching for treats by flashlight. It's free fun. Anyone 21 or older may participate in this late-night egg hunt on the restaurant premises. The event's exact date depends on when Easter falls. Participants find eggs that may be empty or contain prizes such as gift certificates, free drink coupons, or free T-shirt coupons.

Kitty Hawk Kites
Annual Easter Egg Hunt
US 158, MP 12, Nags Head
(252) 441-4124, (800) FLY-THIS

This event is held at Kitty Hawk Kites in Nags Head, with the specific date dependent on when Easter falls. Kids enjoy chalk coloring contests, a variety of games, and an Easter candy dig on the premises. Small fries get a kick out of meeting KHK's fuzzy brown mascot WilBear Wright. All activities are free.

Outer Banks Home Show
(252) 449-8232

The Outer Banks Home Show typically is held the weekend before Easter. Builders, products, lending agencies, and other services are exhibited to consumers. Expect about 75 exhibits of home improvement items from hot tubs to tiles. A nominal fee admits you, and the proceeds are donated to local charity. Call for location.

The Outer Banks Senior Games
Thomas A. Baum Senior Center
300 Mustian Street, Kill Devil Hills
(252) 441-1181

Dare County seniors age 55 and older are eligible to compete in the Outer Banks Senior Games, a competition involving shuffleboard, billiards, spin casting, golf, bowling, horseshoes, table tennis, and much more. All ages are welcome to watch and cheer for the competitors in this mid-April event, which has been happening every year since 1988.

A modified version of the games is offered for disabled seniors. Volunteers work with each individual needing assistance. Games for this group can include door basketball and rubber horseshoes.

The local group of seniors sends hundreds of competitors to state competitions every year. Some have gone on to the national contest. Festivities include dinner at a local restaurant. The registration fee is $10 to participate in four events including the arts competition (see next listing) and includes lunch on opening day and track and field day.

Tux and Topsiders Dance
North Carolina Maritime Museum on Roanoke Island
(252) 475-1750

Hors d'oeuvres, music, and a silent auction are some of the fun things happening at the Tux and Topsiders Dance in Manteo. Dress is "yacht-club casual," and proceeds benefit the North Carolina Maritime Museum. Tuxedoes are not required. The 2006 event will be held April 22 at 8:00 P.M. Tickets are $50 and a silent auction will be held.

The Outer Banks Silver Arts Competition
Thomas A. Baum Senior Center
300 Mustian Street, Kill Devil Hills
(252) 441-1181

This is the art component of the Outer Banks Senior Games, featuring an exhibition of talent and craftsmanship in the visual, literary, heritage, and performing arts. The events last for several days, culminating in a free evening performance at the Kitty Hawk Elementary School. The $10 games registration fee covers entry into the arts competition.

Inner-Tribal Powwow "Journey Home"
Cape Hatteras School, Buxton
(252) 995-4440
www.nativeamericanmuseum.org

For something truly special come to the Inner-Tribal Powwow put on by the folks at the Frisco Native American Museum and Natural History Center. The Inner-Tribal Powwow gathers 75 to 100 members of many different tribes for a weekend of celebration on the ancestral grounds of Hatteras Island. Tribal representatives come from all over North Carolina, the East Coast, and from as far away as Canada, Ohio, Washington State, and Arizona. It's a family event, with emphasis on the sharing of cultures. Many of the Native Americans dress in full regalia. Storytelling, drumming, and dancing are all part of the celebration. You'll get to sample Native American food, buy Native American wares, and watch Native craftspeople at work, as vendors often craft their wares. Demonstration dances and Friendship Dances (in which the public joins), make this an exciting cultural event as does the Saturday night bonfire. Small admission fees are charged either by the day or for the entire weekend, and children, seniors, and families are discounted. The public is invited to this event, held April 29 and 30.

Earth Day Celebration
North Carolina Aquarium
on Roanoke Island
(252) 473-5121

Admission to the aquarium is free on Earth Day (April 22). From 11:00 A.M. until 3:00 P.M., the Junkman plays a free concert.

Tour de Cure
Roanoke Island Festival Park, Manteo
(757) 455-6335, ext. 3281
(919) 743-5400, ext. 3254

When attending any Outer Banks outdoor event, protect yourself with sunscreen and sunglasses, and bring extra clothing and drinking water. The weather changes quickly, and much of the land is exposed to the elements.

If you're into serious cycling, consider putting your legs to work for the American Diabetes Association. This mid-April event has two cycling events, both of which end up at Roanoke Island Festival Park in Manteo. The Saturday event starts in Virginia Beach, Virginia. As if that weren't far enough, the Sunday event starts in Raleigh, North Carolina. All proceeds go to a good cause, and there are fun celebrations at Festival Park after the rides.

Windfest
Frisco Woods Campground
NC 12, Frisco
(252) 995-5208, (800) 948-3942

Wind lovers enjoy this three-day festival, which features free demos by windsurfing and kiteboarding reps, instructional clinics, a regatta, and evening cookouts. As part of the fun, Kitty Hawk Kites hosts a Kite Surfing Fun Ride from Frisco to Hatteras or Avon (depending on wind direction). Bring your own boards and sails. Bed down at the campground for a fee (see our Camping chapter for details) and enjoy the rest of the event, including meals, for a donation. All donations go to the Cape Hatteras Meals on Wheels program.

Relay for Life
Whalehead Club, Corolla
(252) 261-1023

Held in late April, Relay for Life is a 20-hour relay walk that benefits the American Cancer Society. Competitors form teams and raise money prior to the event, which is held on the beautiful grounds of the Whalehead Club in Corolla. During the relay, one person from each team is on the track at all times from 3:00 P.M. on Saturday until 10:00 A.M. on Sunday. All during the day there are events on the lawn, including food vendors and music. It's fun and benefits a great cause.

Outer Banks Walk America
Roanoke Island Festival Park, Manteo
(800) 732-7097

This fund-raising walk benefits the March of Dimes. The walk starts at Festival Park, winds through downtown Manteo, and ends at Festival Park. Music and refreshments are offered after the walk. The 2006 event will be held April 29.

MAY

Hatteras Village Offshore Open Billfish Tournament
Hatteras Harbor Marina, NC 12
Hatteras Village
(252) 986-2555, (888) 544-8115
www.hatterasoffshoreopen.com

Anglers contend for cash prizes as they fish to catch and release the biggest billfish. A meat fish category is included for the largest tuna, dolphin, and wahoo caught daily. The three-day fishing tournament is held May 11 through May 13 and sponsored by the Hatteras Village Civic Association. This is a Governor's Cup–sanctioned event, and it's the kickoff tournament in the Governor's Cup challenge. All competitors must enter Level 1 for $700; three additional levels—Level 2 at $800, Level 3 at $500, and Level 4 at $1,000—are not mandatory. Fishing begins at 8:00 A.M., and lines come out of the water promptly at 3:00 P.M. Festivities with food and drink are usually held each evening, and the event closes with an awards banquet. The tournament is open to the public.

Mollie Fearing Memorial Art Show
Roanoke Island Festival Park, Manteo
(252) 473-5558
www.darearts.org

This exhibition, sponsored by the Dare County Arts Council, is open to all artists, and cash awards are given. It is held throughout the month of May and is open for public viewing. Call for membership, reception, and entry information.

Hang Gliding Spectacular and Air Games
Jockey's Ridge State Park, US 158, MP 12
Nags Head
(252) 441-4124, (800) FLY-THIS

Currituck County Airport
US 158, Barco
www.kittyhawk.com
Spectators and participants cover the dunes at the park every year to attend the longest-running hang-gliding competition in the country. Pilots from all over the world compete in a variety of flying maneuvers, including an aerotow competition. Beginners hang-gliding lessons are given. The event is sponsored by Kitty Hawk Kites, and a complimentary street dance and an awards ceremony add icing to the cake. Annual inductions to the Rogallo Hall of Fame (Francis Rogallo is the father of the Flexible Wing Flyer—the prototype for the modern hang glider) close the ceremony. Hang-glider pilots who have achieved their Hang One are welcome to compete. The public is invited to view the event for free. Participants pay an entry fee. In 2006 the event will be held May 15 through 19.

British Cemetery Ceremony
British Cemetery Road, Ocracoke Island
(252) 928-3711
This ceremony commemorates the 1942 sinking of a British ship. On May 11 of that year, the HMS *Bedfordshire,* a trawler stationed off Ocracoke to protect our shores during World War II, was torpedoed and sunk by a German submarine. All on board perished, and only four bodies were recovered. Island residents buried these men, and every year on May 7 the U.S. Coast Guard holds a service to honor them. The service is free. (See our Attractions chapter for more information.)

Nags Head Woods 5K Run
and Post-Run Beach Party
Nags Head Woods Preserve
Ocean Acres Drive, Kill Devil Hills
(252) 441-2431
www.outerbankskiwanisclub.org
Folks from all walks of life run side by side through Nags Head Woods in this annual event, held on the second Saturday in May. The run is limited to the first 400 runners registered. The postrun party features music, food, and drinks. For entry fees and tickets, call the number above.

International Miniature Art Show
Seaside Art Gallery, NC 12, MP 11
Nags Head
(252) 441-5418, (800) 828-2444
Artists from all over the world compete for cash prizes in this exhibition of miniature art. Past shows have seen more than 450 works from 38 states and 12 countries. The work includes paintings, sculpture, and drawings of all styles. The art is on view for about two weeks. The reception occurs in late May.

OBX Jaycees Beach Music Festival
Roanoke Island Festival Park, Manteo
(252) 475-1500
www.darecountyjaycees.com
Ready for some fun in the sun? The Jaycees put on this annual festival celebrating beach music and the coming summer season. Big crowds gather on the spacious lawn of the pavilion. Beach-music bands and local bands play all day long. Kick off your shoes and dance on the lawn. Bring plenty of sunscreen and blankets or folding chairs. Food and beverages, including beer, are available. Tickets can be purchased in advance or the day of the event, held on the Saturday of Memorial Day Weekend. Proceeds benefit the Cystic Fibrosis Foundation and the Outer Banks YMCA.

If you want to enter an art show sponsored by the Dare County Arts Council but you aren't a Dare County resident, simply join the arts council and you'll qualify to enter. You'll have a chance to win a cash prize, show your work, and help support the arts with your entry fee.

Pirate's Cove Memorial Weekend Tournament
Pirate's Cove Yacht Club
Nags Head–Manteo Causeway, Manteo
(252) 473-3700, (800) 537-7245
www.fishpiratescove.com
This tournament is for pure fun only. No monetary prizes are awarded, but contenders can go home with a trophy. The team entry fee is $300. Anglers head offshore to fish for billfish, tuna, dolphin, and wahoo. All billfish are released, and a prize is awarded for the largest release and the combined weight of the three largest meat fish caught per team. Call for entry dates and more information.

JUNE

Dare Day Festival
Downtown Manteo
(252) 475-5629
This is the quintessential small-town family event. Dare Day, held the first Saturday of June, is a much-loved local tradition that celebrates the wonderful county of Dare. You'll find locals, visitors, politicians, children, and just about everybody you can think of coming out to enjoy the day in downtown Manteo. Dare Day features arts and crafts booths, lots of food (including in-season soft-shell crabs), national and local musical entertainment, kids activities, games, rides, and much more. A free concert is held at Roanoke Island Festival Park in the pavilion. All of Festival Park's sites, including the *Elizabeth II*, are free on this day. For a taste of real local culture, don't miss this event.

Rogallo Kite Festival
Jockey's Ridge State Park, US 158
MP 12, Nags Head
(800) 334-4777
www.kittyhawk.com
This two-day, free, family fun fly in early June celebrates the beauty of kite flying and honors the father of hang gliding, NASA scientist Francis Rogallo. It is open to kite enthusiasts of all ages and features stunt kites, home-builts, kids' kite-making and -flying competitions, and an auction where you can bid on display and demo stunt kites. Rogallo, the inventor of the flexible wing, generally makes an appearance.

"Illuminations" Summer Arts Festival and Children's Performances
Roanoke Island Festival Park, Manteo
(252) 475-1506
Starting in late June and running through mid-August, Roanoke Island Festival Park stages wonderful cultural activities almost every day of the week. "Illuminations" is the performance series of the North Carolina School of the Arts, and the students perform Tuesday through Saturday nights in the pavilion. You'll see dance, jazz, classical music, film, and drama. See our Attractions and Arts and Culture chapters for more about this series. The Children's Performances are held in July, Tuesday through Friday, in the Film Theater. Performances are geared to all ages of children and include storytelling, puppets, and singers. See our Kidstuff chapter for more information.

Hatteras Marlin Club Billfish Tournament
Hatteras Marlin Club, off NC 12
Hatteras Village
(252) 986-2454
The Hatteras Marlin Club Billfish Tournament, going strong since 1959, offers a week of competition fishing and entertainment to participants and their guests. Teams head for offshore waters looking to catch the biggest billfish or meat fish, including blue marlin, tuna, dolphin, and wahoo. Evenings are filled with socials that include entertainment, cocktails, appetizers, and dinner. The tournament is for members and anglers invited by the tournament committee. Write to the Hatteras Marlin Club for membership and tournament information: Box 218, Hatteras, NC 27943. Call for registration fee information.

Roanoke Island House and Garden Tour
Roanoke Island
(252) 473-3234
The Roanoke Island Garden Club partners with the Elizabethan Gardens to host this tour, which covers area homes, gardens, and historic sites. Call for exact day and time.

JULY

Sand Sculpture Contest
On the beach north of Ocracoke Village
(252) 928-7689
This artistic endeavor kicks off Fourth of July festivities on the island. Kids and adults are welcome to participate in the early-morning event. You can work alone or in groups. Past events have seen sand transformed into turtles, jumping dolphin, pirates, and ships. The contest is free. Call for times and location.

Independence Day Parade and
Fireworks Display
Ocracoke Village
(252) 928-7689
This festive parade featuring a half-dozen floats makes its way through the streets starting around 3:00 P.M. on July 4. Local shopkeepers and residents create floats for what's dubbed the village's biggest annual event. The parade moves down North Carolina Highway 12 from Capt. Ben's Restaurant through Ocracoke Village. The evening ends with a gala fireworks display at Lifeguard Beach. Ocracokers say it's the best Fourth of July celebration on the Outer Banks.

Manteo Independence Day Celebration
Manteo
(252) 473-1101
Activities run from 1:00 to 9:00 P.M. and include a Wacky Tacky Hat Contest, children's games, food and other concessions, musical entertainment, and a street dance from 6:00 to 9:00 P.M., when a fireworks display begins. The event is free.

Fireworks in Hatteras Village
Hatteras Village
(252) 986-2719
The fireworks sponsored by the Hatteras Village Civic Association and the Volunteer Fire Department start at 8:30 P.M. at ramp 55 in the village. There is no admission fee.

Fireworks Festival and Fair
Whalehead Club, NC 12, Corolla
(252) 453-9040
The historic hunt club is the backdrop for the fireworks and fair that begin at 6:00 and run to 11:00 P.M. The Currituck County Board of Commissioners and the Corolla Business Association host this event. Expect fun, food, live musical entertainment, and, of course, pyrotechnics galore. Admission is free.

Annual Wright Kite Festival
Wright Brothers National Memorial
US 158, MP 8, Kill Devil Hills
(252) 441-4124, (800) 334-4777
This mid-July family event involves kite flying for all ages and also includes free kite-making workshops, stunt kite demos, and children's games. The event, sponsored by Kitty Hawk Kites and the National Park Service, has been held every year since 1978. You can watch for free. Adults are invited to participate in kite contests. Call for fees.

AUGUST

Hatteras Island Arts and Crafts Guild
Crafts Show
Cape Hatteras High School
NC 12, Buxton
(252) 995-4551, (252) 441-1850
This craft show on August 3 and 4 features pottery, dolls, clockmaking, shellwork, and countless other goodies. Hours are 10:00 A.M. to 4:00 P.M. both days and admission is free.

Annual Herbert Hoover Birthday Celebration
Manteo Booksellers
Sir Walter Raleigh Street, Manteo
(252) 473-1221
On August 10, browse through this superb bookstore, taste three cakes (each one inscribed with "Happy," "Birthday," or "Herbie"), sip some famous "Herbert Sherbert" punch, and chat with Hoover fans at this tongue-in-cheek free event. The reason for the fun? It's purely for the sake of having a celebration. The day includes a book signing. Look for a special display of Hoover memorabilia. Come eat, drink, and think Herbert Hoover!

Annual Senior Adults Craft Fair
Thomas A. Baum Center
300 Mustian Street, Kill Devil Hills
(252) 441-9388
Local senior citizens provide the crafts for this community project sponsored by the Outer Banks Women's Club. It's been a tradition for more than 25 years. Admission is $1.00.

Alice Kelly Memorial Ladies Only Billfish Tournament
Pirate's Cove Yacht Club
Manteo-Nags Head Causeway, Manteo
(252) 473-6800, (800) 367-4728
www.fishpiratescove.com
The tournament, sponsored by Pirate's Cove since 1989, honors the memory of local fishing enthusiast Alice Kelly, who died in her 30s from Hodgkin's disease. Kelly was a high-spirited woman whose love for fishing inspired many local women to try (and fall in love with) the sport. Women form teams and arrange for charter boats to carry them out to sea. The tournament occurs in early August. The 2006 entry fee is $400.

Pirate's Cove Billfish Tournament
Pirate's Cove Yacht Club
Manteo-Nags Head Causeway, Manteo
(252) 473-6800, (800) 367-4728
www.fishpiratescove.com
Pirate's Cove Yacht Club has hosted a bill-fish release tournament every August since 1983. Contenders fish for several days to catch and release the largest billfish. A meat fish (tuna, dolphin, and wahoo) category, in which a prize is awarded for the largest catch, adds to the fun. The tournament is an official part of the N.C. Governor's Cup Billfish Series and occurs mid-month. Call for entry-fee information.

New World Festival of the Arts
Manteo
(252) 473-2838
This mid-August event brings downtown Manteo alive with art every year. The outdoor two-day show features more than 80 artists showcasing fine art and crafts, including pottery, jewelry, paintings, and more. Outdoor booths and tents line the historic waterfront, attracting visitors who return each year looking for their favorite artists, free of admission. It's held on August 16 and 17 in 2006.

Virginia Dare Birthday Celebration
Fort Raleigh National Historic Site
Visitor Center
US 64/264, Roanoke Island
(252) 473-2127
This event, held August 18, commemorates the birth of Virginia Dare, the first English child born in the New World. The celebration features a daylong series of special happenings. Past events featured performances by members of the cast of *The Lost Colony* and demonstrations of arms from that period in history. Call the National Park Service for details. This event is free. The Elizabethan Gardens, right next to Fort Raleigh, honors Virginia Dare's birthday by offering free admission to the gardens on this day and a free play about Queen Elizabeth and Sir Walter Raleigh.

Virginia Dare Night Performance of *The Lost Colony*
Waterside Theatre
US 64/264, Roanoke Island
(252) 473-3414, (800) 488-5012
www.thelostcolony.org
On August 18, *The Lost Colony* celebrates

Virginia Dare's 1587 birth by casting local infants in the role of baby Virginia. This makes for a special and spontaneous performance; usually baby Virginia is played by a doll. (For details on the famous outdoor drama, see our Attractions chapter.)

National Aviation Day
Wright Brothers National Memorial
US 158, MP 8, Kill Devil Hills
(252) 441-7430
www.nps.gov/wrbr/
Explore planes galore at this free mid-August event. Aviation enthusiasts enjoy viewing about 25 different types of single-engine aircraft ranging from the antique to modern-day models. The schedule is not firm until a few days before the event so weather conditions can be taken into consideration. Past events have included a flyover with Air Force and Navy planes, jets from Langley Field, and the Blue Angels. The day's festivities include free admission to the memorial.

SEPTEMBER

The Allison **White Marlin Release**
Tournament
Pirate's Cove Yacht Club
Manteo-Nags Head Causeway, Manteo
(252) 473-6800, (800) 537-7245
www.fishpiratescove.com
Since 1992, *The Allison* has raised funds for disabled kids. Travel offshore to the infamous Outer Banks fishing grounds and search for billfish and other pelagic species. All billfish caught are released. Bait and tackle are provided. The event takes place the first weekend in September. There are four categories; entry in Category 1 ($1,000) is mandatory. Costs for the other categories are $500 for Category 2, $500 for Category 3 (which is the pool for the daily prize), and $500 for Category 4 (the prize for the largest meat fish). Call for more information.

Weeping Radish Restaurant and
Brewery Oktoberfest
US 64/264, Manteo
(252) 473-1157
www.weepingradish.com
The Weeping Radish hosts Oktoberfest the second week of September. Expect a family-oriented outdoor celebration featuring Bavarian-style food, an oompah band, children's games, specially brewed German beer, and a chance to win a trip to Germany. There is no admission fee.

Outer Banks Triathlon
Roanoke Island
(252) 480-0500
www.darevolunteercenter.org
An Outer Banks tradition since 1984, triatheletes compete in early September. Entrants swim 0.6 mile, run 3.1 miles, and bike 15 miles. The swimming segment is held at the Old Swimming Hole at the north end of Roanoke Island. Individuals can participate in all three events, or a team of three can split up the events. The entry fee for individuals is about $50 for Triathlon USA members and $60 for nonmembers. Team entries are $135 for Triathlon USA members and $165 for nonmembers. The event is limited to 330 participants.

Kitty Hawk Kites Annual
Boomerang Competition
First Flight Middle School, Kill Devil Hills
(252) 441-2124, (877) FLY-THIS
www.kittyhawk.com
Boomers from across the nation flock to the Outer Banks for this competition of the U.S. Boomerang Association. Novice throwers are welcome to compete, as are observers. Boomerang workshops are held on Sunday.

Hatteras Village Civic Association Surf
Fishing Tournament
Hatteras Village Civic Center
NC 12, Hatteras Village
(252) 986-2579
Since 1982, surf-fishing fans have met the third week in September for this tournament. Anglers fish for a wide variety of

eligible species, including drum, bluefish, trout, and more. Call for registration fees and information.

ESA Eastern Surfing Championships
Location varies
(800) 937-4733
www.surfesa.org
Competition is open to Eastern Surfing Association members only, but it's an exciting and free spectator event. Watch as surfers grab their boards and head to the ocean to pit their skills against the waves and their fellow competitors. For more information, write to Box 400, Buxton, NC 27920.

Wildfest
Manteo Middle School
US 64/264, Manteo
(252) 441-8144
Wildfest is an exciting family event. Kids get to learn about wildlife and wildlands in a fun way. Kids build birdhouses, make kites, compete in a critter-calling contest, identify animal tracks, see a live alligator, study bird beaks, make leaf prints, and participate in an environmental scavenger hunt. There's also face painting, games, photos with Smokey Bear and other animals, and a chance to see live animals. There's no fee to enter, but some activities may have a small charge. It's held from 10:00 A.M. to 2:00 P.M.

Kitty Hawk Heritage Day Celebration
The Promenade
US 158, MP ¼, Kitty Hawk
(252) 261-3552
This daylong festival at the end of September is great fun for everyone. Numerous food vendors, 30 crafters, children's events and games, local entertainers and singers, and a heritage display about Kitty Hawk are just some of the fun festival fare you'll find here. All of The Promenade's activity facilities are open throughout the day. It's sponsored by the town of Kitty Hawk, so call the town office at the number above for dates, rain dates, and times. Since parking is limited, a shuttle bus runs from the Wal-Mart parking lot to The Promenade.

OBX Surf Sport Competition
Kitty Hawk Kites Surfing School
US 158, MP 15, Nags Head
(252) 441-0265, (252) 207-1639
www.kittyhawk.com
Kitty Hawk Kites sponsors this event, which includes multilevel kiteboard and surf kayak competitions. Both amateurs and professionals demonstrate their skills and celebrate with food and fun. Participants compete for products and cash prizes. The 2006 competition will be held September 23 and 24.

OCTOBER

North Carolina Big Sweep
Dare County beaches
(800) 27-SWEEP
www.ncbigsweep.org
This is a local waterway cleanup that's hooked into a statewide and national event. Trash picking runs from 9:00 A.M. to 1:00 P.M. on the first Saturday in October. Folks have cleaned the waterways since 1986, performing their civic duty. Obviously, it's free. Call the above number for more information.

Nags Head Surf Fishing Club Invitational Tournament
Nags Head
(252) 441-5464
The Nags Head Surf Fishing Club's tournament celebrated its 55th year in 2005. Team fishing, held on a Thursday and Friday in early October, is usually booked solid for years. But participants are welcome to fish the individual tournament on Saturday from 8:00 A.M. to noon.

Outer Banks Homebuilders Association's Parade of Homes
Homes from Corolla to South Nags Head and Manteo
(252) 449-8232
www.obhomebuilders.org

The OBHA opens new and remodeled homes to the public for this early October event. It costs $10 to tour about 20 participating homes. Proceeds are donated to local charities.

Artrageous Art Extravaganza Weekend
Dare County Arts Council
Dare County Recreation Park
Mustian Street, Kill Devil Hills
(252) 473-5558
www.darearts.org

Artrageous, started in 1990, is a community art festival and auction sponsored by the Dare County Arts Council the first weekend in October. Children and adults are invited to spend Saturday painting, weaving, and creating various arts and crafts. All art supplies are provided. Listen to local musicians young and old, eat tasty food, and witness art in the making by professionals. Artists sell their wares. Collaborative paintings by children are auctioned on Saturday; a more formal adult auction, complete with hors d'oeuvres and cocktails, takes place on Sunday. Saturday's events do not require an admission fee. Average price for booth activities is $1.00. The Sunday evening auction is held at varying locations; call for details.

The Beach Book Cover Art Competition
Sea and Sounds Gallery
104 Sir Walter Raleigh Street, Manteo
(252) 473-5558
www.darearts.org

The Dare County Arts Council and *The Beach Book* hold this annual art show and competition in order to select the cover art for the local phone directory. Local judges select the winning piece, but visitors vote on the People's Choice award. The winner gets his or her work of art on thousands of copies of the phone book plus on a billboard in Currituck. Call the Dare County Arts Council for entry information. Submissions hang in the gallery throughout the month of October.

Outer Banks Stunt Kite Competition
Jockey's Ridge State Park
US 58, MP 12, Nags Head
(252) 441-4124, (800) FLY-THIS
www.kittyhawk.com

Entrants compete on the Eastern League Circuit of the American Kiting Association. The program features novice, intermediate, and expert challenges, as well as workshops and demos. Kids enjoy making kites. Music, kite ballet competitions, and team train competitions highlight the sanctioned event. Registration and competition fees are charged to competitors.

Carolista Music Festival
Roanoke Island Festival Park, Manteo
(252) 473-5121
www.carolistamusicfestival.com

This annual event benefits the Outer Banks Hotline, a nonprofit organization that offers community support and crisis intervention. The festival honors the memory of Carolista Baum, a Nags Head woman who saved Jockey's Ridge from destruction in the 1970s. The festival is billed as a celebration of many strong and beautiful women and the men who love and respect them. Well-known musical acts headline the mid-October event, which also includes an artisans' marketplace, a red-tent healing pavilion, kids' activities, and food. Admission is $15; children younger than age 12 are admitted free with a paying adult. The gates open at 1:00 P.M.

Red Drum Tournament
Frank and Fran's Fisherman's Friend
NC 12, Avon
(252) 995-4171

Two hundred anglers fish the surf and try to catch the largest red drum during this late October event, sponsored by the popular Avon tackle shop. Fees are about $100 per person. Limited space is available for this three-day tournament.

Kelly's/Penguin Isle Charity Golf Tournament
US 158, MP 15, Nags Head
Currituck Club, Corolla
(252) 441-4116
Six-person teams play 18 holes for charity during late October. Proceeds benefit the Outer Banks Community Foundation. Fees per team generally run around $500.

Teach's Lair Shootout King Mackerel Tournament
Teach's Lair Marina, NC 12
Hatteras Village
(252) 986-2460
In this Hatteras Village tournament, anglers try their luck in capturing the largest king mackerel at the end of October or early November. Entry fees range from $300 to $350. The tournament is open to the public.

Octoberfest at Frisco Woods Campground
Frisco Woods Campground
NC 12, Frisco
(252) 995-5208
Here's a great way to enjoy autumn on the Outer Banks and contribute to the community's Meals On Wheels program. Octoberfest events include a pig pickin' with all the trimmings, live music, crafts, a bake sale, and a rummage sale. Admission is free to this late-October event. Donations to the charitable cause are welcome.

NOVEMBER

Wings Over Water Festival
Many Outer Banks locations
(252) 441-8144
www.northeast-nc.com/wings/
Wings Over Water is a celebration of the Outer Banks's wonderful wildlife and wildlands. It offers a number of activities for those who want to learn more about this enchanting natural area. You select the field trips, programs, and seminars that interest you the most and then get an inside look at the various ecological settings and wildlife of the Outer Banks. For

example, go on guided bird-watching trips at Pea Island National Wildlife Refuge, one of the most popular fall birding sites in the southeast. Check out shorebirds at Cape Hatteras Lighthouse, or visit Buxton Woods and Nags Head Woods with a naturalist. Kayak or canoe into a salt marsh, motor out to the waters of the Gulf Stream to look at pelagic birds, or travel to Mattamuskeet National Wildlife Refuge, where eagles and raptors and wintering birds are common. Explore the swamp of Alligator River National Wildlife Refuge looking for bears, or listen to red wolves howl. Climb Jockey's Ridge at night to look at the stars, or paddle Milltail Creek by moonlight. Take a photography seminar, learn about coastal geography, or hear about the plight of the snow goose. There is such an enormous list of activities that this is only the tip of the iceberg. All programs charge a moderate fee. For information or to register for the event, call the number above or visit the Web site, where there's an online registration form. This event is held in early November.

Mt. Olivet United Methodist Church Bazaar & Auction
300 Ananias Dare Street, Manteo
(252) 473-2089
For this event, the church is filled with all sorts of goodies, including books, kitchenware, antiques, and baked treats. Get there early—this is a very popular event. Browse table after table covered with exciting finds—something old, something new. The day features a late afternoon/early evening auction. There's no charge.

Manteo Rotary Rockfish Rodeo
Roanoke Island Festival Park, Manteo
(252) 473-4268
www.rockfishrodeo.com
Whether you call them rockfish, striped bass, or stripers, the fish can win you big money and help a good cause in this tournament. Participants fish in the sound or ocean from 6:00 A.M. to 3:00 P.M. and bring one fish back to the weigh station. Trophies are given to the top

four winners in the ocean and sound categories, and the top winner can win up to $5,000. All nonfishing events and the weigh-in are held at Roanoke Island Festival Park. Registration, a social hour, and an anglers' rule meeting are held Friday night. Saturday it's fishing, the weigh-in, and an awards dinner. Manteo Rotary, the sponsor of this event, uses the profits to give college scholarships to local youth, and they have granted over $90,000 to students because of this tournament.

North Carolina Storytelling Festival
Roanoke Island Festival Park
(252) 475-1500
www.roanokeisland.com

The North Carolina Storytelling Guild and Roanoke Island Festival Park join together to bring this festival. Be prepared to hear fantastic tales and legends from around the world, with sessions for children and for adults. Several professional storytellers will tell tales throughout the day. Held annually in early November, a nominal fee is charged to festivalgoers.

Cape Hatteras Anglers Club Individual Surf Fishing Tournament
Buxton
(252) 995-4253

The Cape Hatteras Anglers Club sponsors a one-day individual surf-fishing tournament in mid-November. Registration is held at the Cape Hatteras Anglers Club in Buxton, and fishing takes place from 8:00 A.M. to noon. Prizes are awarded.

Chowder Cookoff and Oyster Roast
Seagate North Shopping Center
US 158, MP 5½, Kill Devil Hills
(252) 441-6600

This annual event is all about eating. Local amateur cooks and professional chefs compete for prizes for best seafood chowder and best nonseafood chowder, but you get the rewards by tasting them all for just $10. Standard chowders are offered, but some cooks get pretty creative. There's also an oyster roast and hamburgers and hot dogs. Beer, wine,

soda, and water are available. This event is quite popular with hungry locals. It's always held in mid-November on a Sunday afternoon, usually the second or third weekend. To enter as a competitor you must register early, pay a $25 entry fee, and bring at least six gallons of chowder. All proceeds benefit local charities.

Kitty Hawk Fire Department Turkey Shoot & Pig Pickin'
The Promenade, US 158, MP 1
Kitty Hawk
(252) 261-2666

This Kitty Hawk Fire Department–sponsored event, first held in 1980, usually happens in mid-November but dates may vary, so call ahead. It's a major fund-raiser for the firefighters. The fee includes the turkey shoot, annual auction and dinner, and pig pickin'. Fire department personnel also have fun events for kids. Call closer to the event date for more information.

Hatteras Island Arts and Crafts Guild Holiday Show
Cape Hatteras High School
NC 12, Buxton
(252) 995-4551, (252) 441-1850

This craft show on November 25 and 26 includes pottery, dolls, shellwork, and woodworking. Hours are 10:00 A.M. to 4:00 P.M. each day. Admission is free.

Christmas Arts & Crafts Show
Kitty Hawk Elementary School
Kitty Hawk
(252) 261-3196

The two-day show, held in late November, is sponsored by the Outer Banks Women's Club. Expect to see a wide variety of crafts, including woodworking, pottery, dolls, and more. Admission is $1.00.

Advice 5K Annual
Turkey Trot Duck
(252) 255-1050
www.advice5.com

Pump up your Thanksgiving Day appetite with an early morning 5K run. This annual, nonsanctioned 3.1-mile run starts at

Advice 5¢ behind Scarborough Lane Shops in Duck and ends at the Red Sky Cafe/Village Wine Shop, where everyone gathers for a raffle and to see the winners. The top male and female runners win a pumpkin pie. This is a lively event, kicking off your holiday. Walkers and runners are welcome, and no one is expected to take it too seriously. Register early by calling the number above, or register in person at the Red Sky Cafe on the Wednesday before Thanksgiving Day. There is no race-day registration. The entry fee is $20.

Kites with Lights
Jockey's Ridge State Park, Nags Head
(252) 441–4124

Stunt kites are strung with lights, creating a magical, multicolored nighttime scene. The kites fly sky high, dancing to tradi-tional Christmas carols. Climbing up Jockey's Ridge at night is fun, especially when you're treated with a show like this at the top. Christmas carols, hot apple cider, and cookies make it more fun. This event is held in late November. It's free and begins at sunset.

Chicamacomico Lifesaving Station
Christmas Lighting
Rodanthe
(252) 987–1552

This classic lifesaving station looks absolutely stunning when decorated for the holidays with lights, greenery, and rib-bons. In late November when the building is decorated in its finery, the folks at Chi-camacomico have a daylong celebration and open house.

DECEMBER

Lighting of the Town Tree
and Christmas Parade
Manteo
(252) 475–5629

Manteo and Dare County get ready for the holidays over the first weekend in Decem-ber with events for the whole family. On Friday evening, the big town tree, right on

the waterfront next to the Tranquil House Inn, is lit about 6:30 P.M. The event is accompanied by carols, a yule log, cake, and hot chocolate. It's a good place to gather and get in the holiday spirit.

On Saturday morning a hometown parade rambles through the streets of downtown Manteo. Kids love watching the floats, bands, dancers, local organizations, and, of course, Santa. Afterward, celebrate with food, holiday crafts, entertainment, and a chance to visit with Santa at the water-front. We like to go to the parade then early Christmas shop in downtown Manteo.

Christmas at Roanoke Island Festival Park
Manteo
(252) 475–1506 (24-hour events line)

This beautiful cultural center is alive in December with plenty of good cheer. Expect concerts, sing-alongs, children's per-formances, and a sale in the Museum Store. Call the events line for holiday offerings.

Outer Banks Hotline's Festival of Trees
(252) 473–5121

Since 1988, this popular auction and fund-raiser has taken place in early December. Businesses and individuals donate fully decorated Christmas trees and other holi-day items to be auctioned and delivered to buyers. Proceeds benefit Hotline's crisis intervention program and needy families in the area. Past trees have been deco-rated with Beanie Babies, handwoven tap-estry wear and accessories, and CDs. The festive event includes several days of cele-brations. Call the Hotline office for loca-tion and ticket information.

Man Will Never Fly Memorial Society
International Annual Seminar
and Awards Program
Comfort Inn South
NC 12, MP 17, Nags Head
(800) 334–4777

This tongue-in-cheek organization tries to prove every year that man never really flew and abides by the motto "Birds Fly, Men Drink." The banquet is held annually the night before the anniversary of the first flight and is open to the public. The food is prepared buffet-style and features meat as well as seafood. Call for ticket and reservation information.

Wright Brothers Anniversary of First Flight
**Wright Brothers National Memorial
US 158, MP 8, Kill Devil Hills
(252) 441-7430, (800) 334-4777**
On December 17, 1903, Wilbur and Orville Wright made their first successful flights before a handful of local residents. This event is celebrated every year on December 17, in the exact same place where those flights occurred. Bands play and planes fly as the monumental events of the Wright brothers are recalled. Speakers generally include military personnel, local dignitaries, and individuals who have dedicated their lives to the advancement of flight technology. A portrait of the year's induction to the First Flight Society is unveiled. There is no charge.

Icarus International Art Show
**Glenn Eure's Ghost Fleet Gallery
210 East Driftwood Street, Gallery Row
Nags Head
(252) 441-6584**

**Seaside Art Gallery
NC 12, MP 11, Nags Head
(252) 441-5418**
This international art show, started in 1993, carries the theme of the mystery and beauty of flight. Each year a specific flight-related theme is chosen, and artists submit original art in all genres to compete for a multitude of top-dollar prizes. The art is displayed through the month of December at two Nags Head galleries. A children's component is included at another location. Call the listed numbers to get on the mailing list. Children enter for free. Adult entries run between $10 and $15. A commission is taken for sold work by Icarus International, a nonprofit group. A literary competition is held on the same theme as the visual arts competition every year. The chapbook of juried entries is published in December.

NATURAL WONDERS

To become a true Outer Banks Insider, you must develop a relaxed attitude and deep respect for nature, especially the weather. Outer Bankers' lives are ruled by nature's temperaments. From the calm, humid, and sunny days of early summer to the windy days of autumn and the raw days of winter nor'easters, you'll marvel at the variable weather conditions. And then, spring, both warm and cold, sunny and rainy, comes around again.

The interplay of sand, land, water, and wind is the primal force that drives life on these barrier islands. During your visit, even if you're not inclined toward contemplation, slow down and spend some time getting acquainted with your temporary habitat and with what makes it unique.

Bounded by the Atlantic Ocean on the east and a vast expanse of sound waters to the west, and connected in between by waterways and wetlands, the Outer Banks is among the most fascinating and complex habitats in North America. The Gulf Stream and the continental shelf's edge influence us from a mere 37 miles away. Cradled within our boundaries are several unusual maritime forests, and Cape Hatteras marks the dividing line for northern and southern animal and plant species.

Because of our geographic location and environmental offerings, animal lovers from the world over come to the Outer Banks to sight rare pelagic birds, breaching humpbacks, and nesting waterfowl. Even manatees and harbor seals have visited our shores. Anglers ply the waters for anything from the humble flounder to the majestic blue marlin. Botanists study our ancient live oaks. Writers hole up in wooden beach cottages and ponder how poetically the wind howls. Families return year after year, generation after generation, to splash among the waves, explore tidal zones for sealife, and canvass the shores for colorful shells.

While the old-timers rightfully argue that things have changed dramatically here since the 1970s, there's always been a constant: We are at the mercy of the forces of nature. Our dependency is clear: Nature feeds us, creates and crumbles livelihoods, offers unlimited free entertainment, is the artist's muse, and sends us scurrying for shelter at a whim.

In this chapter we'll introduce you to the land and its wonders, shaped by our bountiful waters and our crazy Outer Banks weather.

Our roles as environmental stewards are an essential part of Outer Banks life. This stewardship is manifested in efforts to protect our waters, marine life, and beaches by fighting efforts to drill for natural gas off the coast. You can join our cause (the Outer Banks is your vacationland, after all) by learning more about LegaSea, an environmental group that was instrumental in stopping Mobil Oil from drilling for natural gas off the coast years back. LegaSea and many Outer Banks residents wish to preserve this wonderland for their descendants and the many visitors who come to this pollution-free haven. Visit the group's Web site at www.LegaSea.org.

Insiders also have self-imposed, state, and national restrictions on game fishing. We support tag-and-release programs and escort infant loggerhead sea turtles off the sand and into the water. Young and old alike participate annually in a nationwide coastal cleanup. All we ask of our visitors is that you treat the area's fragile ecosystem with care. This vacation paradise is home not only for us, but also for our less vocal friends who thrive on the air, sea, and land.

THE LAND

It doesn't take long to realize that the Outer Banks's barrier island system—a narrow stretch of sand—contains vast variety in topography. Geologists refer to the Outer Banks and similar land forms as "barrier islands" because they block the high-energy ocean waves and storm surges, protecting the coastal mainland. Winds, weather, and waves create the personality of the slender strips of sand. Inlets from the sounds to the sea are ever shifting, opening new channels to the ocean one century or decade, and closing off primary passageways the next.

Sand forms a partnership with the sea to create a wonderland that sweeps from Carova down through the Cape Hatteras National Seashore onto Ocracoke Island. At Jockey's Ridge State Park in Nags Head, huge migrating dunes heralded as the largest sand hills on the East Coast create one of the most popular attractions on the Outer Banks (see our Attractions chapter). It is an amazing sight to see the sand moving ribbonlike as the wind whips across the dunes. Human forms dot the landscape, insignificant against the towering backdrop as they climb the dunes to fly kites, hang glide, or simply view the sound and ocean.

At sunset, the visual drama intensifies. The forms coming and going become stark silhouettes. Come nightfall, the dunes are silent, but wildlife exists. Foxes roam the area, as do deer and opossum, and vegetation thrives in the sand. Wild grapes and bayberry, along with black cherry and Virginia creeper, live along the park trail.

Sand is a challenge and a blessing. It thwarts seaside gardeners who replace their sandy land with mainland soil to grow vegetables. Outer Bankers have a long-standing love/hate relationship with the gritty stuff: We play in it, pour it out of our shoes daily, and constantly suck it into vacuums, but we know that this movable earth has played a vital role in the formation of our natural habitat.

The next time you stroll along the shore, notice vegetation such as sea oats and spartina climbing the sloping dunes. Windblown sand collects behind these pioneer plants, which often grow in otherwise barren soil. With the right combination of currents and breezes, a dune can grow large enough to protect areas that lie behind them, forming tall barriers against the salty sea spray, hence allowing the birth of maritime forests. Our habitat has generated several such phenomena that interest the naturalist and lay person alike.

Nags Head Woods

Lo and behold! A maritime forest that seemingly defies nature flourishes on the Outer Banks. Normally, vegetation that is constantly battered by salt and wind is stunted and minimal. In the Nags Head Woods Preserve, 1,400 acres of maritime forest contain a diversity of flora and fauna that's very unusual in a harsh barrier island climate. This forest has been able to thrive due to a ridge of ancient sand dunes, some 90 feet high, that has shielded the land from the effects of the sea. The woods also owe their diversity to the freshwater supplied by the high dunes that absorb and slowly release rainwater into the underlying aquifer, swamps, and dozens of year-round and seasonal ponds.

Botanists have identified more than 300 plant species in the forest with a mixture of northern and southern varieties. This combination is rare, existing in only four places in the world. In fact, Nags Head Woods is classified as globally rare. The oldest tree in the woods is thought to be a 500-year-old live oak, but woody plants have been growing in this area for thousands of years.

Plant lovers appreciate the woods throughout the year. The forest is lush with ferns, pines, oaks, red bay, blueberry, grasses, bamboo, sassafras, gums, and hundreds more species. Several species rare to

Beach Nourishment— An Ongoing Debate

The Outer Banks's most important resource by far is its beaches. With more and more scientific evidence pointing to an increasing rate of global warming, rising sea levels, and the possibility that warmer sea surface temperatures will lead to increased frequency and intensity of hurricanes, perhaps no topic here is as important, or controversial, as beach nourishment.

Simply put, beach nourishment is the importation of sand to an area of the beach threatened by increasing erosion. The idea seems simple enough: take sand from an area where it's not needed (a choking inlet for example) and pump it onto a shrinking beach. Navigation through the inlet is improved, beachfront properties are protected, and the beach itself is preserved for everyone, including the fragile ecosystems closest to the ocean. How could such a win-win scenario be controversial? The devil is in the details.

The barrier islands that make up the Outer Banks beaches are phenomenally complex systems, and the beaches themselves are in constant motion. The Outer Banks is slowly rolling over itself, gradually retreating toward the mainland. Left alone, the beach would continue its migration, and the complex processes that move sand up and down the beach, cut inlets, and rearrange geography would continue as well. The only problem with this natural migration process is people. When buildings were built close to the ocean, our modern erosion problems began.

There are perhaps only three solutions to the problem of beach erosion: stabilization, retreat, or to do nothing. Doing nothing was the strategy of choice for many years, even as recently as the 1980s. Structures were left to face the retreating beach and when they inevitably succumbed to the sea, they were declared hazardous and demolished. Retreating, or moving away from the shoreline, is also problematic as a long-term strategy. If we decide to move threatened structures away from the rising sea, where will we move them? As a result of these unpalatable options, most coastal communities are relying on beach nourishment as their strategy to combat the inevitable process of erosion.

Wide flat beaches protect oceanfront property by absorbing wave energy more effectively than short steep ones. Some areas along the East Coast have tried to stabilize their beaches with hardened structures, such as sea walls and jetties, with sometimes disastrous results. Jetties interrupt longshore currents that transport sand down the coast, and the beaches down the coast can suffer much higher erosion rates as a result. Sea walls tend to reflect the wave energy back onto the beach, again leading to higher-than-average erosion rates. Beach nourishment seems to be the best way to ensure a wide beach, but it is not without its own problems.

One common problem with beach-nourishment projects is the sand itself. Not only is an ample supply needed, not just any sand will do. In fact, the quality of the sand to be pumped onto a beach is one of the biggest factors in determining how long the nourishment will last. Without careful control, the sand can contain gravel, stones, or even crushed shell, leaving the beach not only more susceptible to continued erosion, but ill-suited for recreation. Even worse, a poorly nourished beach can be an ecological nightmare. One nourished beach in southern North Carolina, for example, contained so many large stones that sea turtles could no longer nest there. Where the sand is taken from has to be carefully considered as well. If inlets are dredged, the change in flow can create erosion problems for the inlets and the beaches in their immediate vicinity. If the continental shelf is harvested for sand, the wave action along the immediate coast may be altered, changing the flow of sand and leading to even more erosion.

Even when a nourishment plan is well thought through and an ample supply of the proper quality sand is located, who pays for all this? Beach nourishment is famously expensive—these long-term projects have price tags into the multiple hundreds of millions, and can go on for decades. Currently, the federal government pays about 65 percent of the costs with the remainder being paid for by state and local governments. How the state and local money is raised is an area of contentious debate. Some say that as public "land," the beaches should be paid for by everyone. Others will say that such expenditures benefit only the elite who own oceanfront property, and point to nourishment sites with little or no public access.

While most would agree that the beaches are priceless, in order to fund such a huge undertaking as beach nourishment, careful valuations are necessary. Not only are the beaches valuable from the standpoint of protection from the ocean during storms, but they are directly or indirectly responsible for a huge percentage of the local economy, from the property taxes of oceanfront lots (houses with wide beaches are simply worth more than those with short steep ones) to the jobs and revenue provided by the tourism industry. Exactly how the calculations are made that put a dollar value on the beaches is yet another area of contentious debate.

If beach nourishment is to be part of a long-term solution to the geologic reality of a retreating shoreline, open communication and cooperation among federal, state, and local governments is essential. Local populations have the responsibility to stay well informed about decisions affecting the beaches, and about who is making the decisions and why.

By all accounts beach nourishment is both temporary and expensive. Whenever human engineering attempts to manipulate complex natural processes, the outcome can be problematic. Only with local support and careful, long-term planning can an undertaking as expensive and complex as beach nourishment be successful.

North Carolina thrive in the forest, including the wooly beach heather, water violet, southern twayblade, and mosquito fern.

Arguably, the most diverse population of reptiles and amphibians on the Outer Banks has found a permanent home in Nags Head Woods. These include 5 species of salamanders, 14 species of frogs and toads, more than 20 species of snakes, and multiple species of lizards and turtles. This unusual forest provides nesting spots for more than 50 species of birds and is home to a wide variety of mammals, including raccoons, river otters, gray fox, white-tailed deer, and opossum.

Insiders like to visit the forest in the fall and spring. Cooler weather and fewer mosquitoes make the trek more appealing, and there are plenty of visiting birds and waterfowl. The great blue heron and green heron are common to the woods. Several species of songbirds may serenade you as you walk: Carolina chickadees, great crested flycatchers, many thrushes, and numerous warblers.

More than 5 miles of trails are available to hikers. **Center Trail** is a quarter-mile long and features scenic pond overlooks. The **Sweetgrass Swamp Trail** takes hikers through rolling hills of forests, dunes, and ponds. The **Blueberry Ridge Trail** connects to the **Sweetgum Swamp Trail** for a total length of 3.5 miles. To head toward the sound, take the **Roanoke Trail** past the farm site and cemetery of the Tillett clan—allow about an hour for the 1.5-mile round-trip. And the **Discovery Trail** provides a quick quarter-mile view of the ponds, swamps, and dune ridges found on the longer trails.

Dogs on leashes, four-wheel-drive vehicles, and bikes are allowed on the road that runs through Nags Head Woods, but they are not allowed in other parts of the preserve. Visitation hours are 10:00 A.M. to 3:00 P.M. Monday through Friday during the off-season and Monday through Saturday during the summer. Members of the Nature Conservancy may tour the preserve during any daylight hours. These limitations help preserve the natural habitats of this rare ecosystem. There is no fee to enter, but a donation is requested.

The Nags Head Woods Preserve (252–441–2525) is overseen by The Nature Conservancy, an international nonprofit conservation organization. If you wish to contribute to The Nature Conservancy, you can send a donation to 701 West Ocean Acres Drive, Kill Devil Hills, NC 27948 or call (252) 441-2525 for membership information.

Buxton Woods

Buxton Woods on Hatteras Island is the largest maritime forest in North Carolina. The 3,000-acre forest measures 3 miles wide and 50 feet high at the tallest ridge. This landmass has the capacity to act as a storage area for freshwater. Only 900 acres are owned by the National Park Service. The state of North Carolina bought an additional 800 acres to protect as the North Carolina Coastal Reserve. The county also designates Buxton Woods as a special environmental district.

Buxton Woods is a much simpler ecosystem than Nags Head Woods because it sticks out 30 miles farther into the ocean and doesn't have the protection that the Nags Head forest has; however, compared with surrounding land at the Cape Hatteras National Seashore, Buxton Woods holds incredible diversity. A bird's-eye view shows an overall ridge and lowlands throughout the area.

The woods lie at the meeting place for several northern and southern species and have a viable population of dwarf palmetto and laurel cherry. A mix of wetlands and forests combines both northern deciduous maritime forests and southern evergreen maritime forests. Nowhere else on Hatteras Island is the mammal population so diverse as in Buxton Woods. The woods are home to white-tailed deer, gray squirrels, eastern cottontail rabbits, raccoons, and opossum. In the woods is Jennette's

Sedge, one of the largest, most highly developed and diverse freshwater marsh systems found on a barrier island in North Carolina. See our Attractions chapter for more information on Buxton Woods.

Alligator River National Wildlife Refuge

On the mainland to the west of Roanoke Island is the Alligator National Wildlife Refuge, covering parts of Dare, Hyde, and Tyrrell Counties. The refuge encompasses 150,000 acres of wetlands, wooded fields, and pocosin habitat. Pocosin is the Native American word for "swamp on a hill." These swamps are characterized by high organic content soils with deep peat deposits that hold vast quantities of water. In dry weather, pocosins are highly susceptible to wildfire.

The refuge is home to black bears, white-tailed deer, gray fox, bobcats, raccoons, mink, beaver, squirrels, opossum, river otter, nutria, alligators, and its most-talked-about residents—red wolves.

Red wolves are a critically endangered species because of hybridization and public fear of large carnivores in most habitats. In the early 1970s the U.S. Fish and Wildlife Service declared the species extinct in the wild because they had been eradicated in nearly every segment of their southeastern United States range. Fish and Wildlife captured the remaining red wolves and bred them until a location was found to bring them back into the wild. The location they found was Alligator River National Wildlife Refuge, chosen because it is within the red wolf's historical range, the human population is of moderate size and density, prey species are abundant, the area is surrounded by water on three sides (which, it was hoped, would restrict some movement by the wolves). The area had very few coyotes, which would lessen the chance that the wolves would hybridize.

In 1986 a five-year experiment to rebuild a self-sustaining red wolf population in the wild began. During this experiment, red wolves proved that they could adapt to life in the wild, find food, and avoid people. Today, close to 100 red wolves roam free in the five-county area of northeastern North Carolina. There are also free-ranging wolves on three islands off the coasts of South Carolina and Florida. The refuge staff offers a unique program called a "Wolf Howling" during which you can go into the refuge at night with a ranger and listen to the wolves howl. See our Kidstuff chapter or call (252) 473-1131 for information.

Mackay Island National Wildlife Refuge

On Knotts Island in both North Carolina and Virginia, Mackay Island contains 8,646 acres of important wildlife habitat and wintering grounds for waterfowl. Mackay Island offers both walking and driving trails that provide wildlife observation opportunities. Hunting and fishing are allowed at Mackay Island Refuge. To get there, take the free, short ferry ride from the Currituck mainland to Knotts Island and follow the signs. You'll see signs for the ferry as you drive on U.S. Highway 158.

Currituck National Wildlife Refuge

Just north of Corolla on the Currituck Outer Banks, this refuge was established in 1984. It consists of 3,213 acres managed by the Mackay Island staff. The refuge lacks public facilities but is open to the public during daylight hours. Visitors mostly look for wildlife and take photographs. The wild horses that used to roam in Corolla now roam here, along with deer, wild boar, and a variety of wildlife.

Audubon Wildlife Sanctuary at Pine Island

Audubon is a 5,000-acre wildlife sanctuary at Pine Island and a protected habitat for deer, birds, rabbits, and a huge variety of plant life. There is an unmarked 2-mile trail you can walk, but the sanctuary is not really a park for people. The land is primarily soundside marshland with pine trees and waterfowl. The sanctuary runs 3 miles long north to south and is approximately 200 yards wide from east to west.

Cape Hatteras National Seashore

The Outer Banks should get a medal for firsts. Not only do we claim First Flight and the first English pioneers to colonize in the New World, but Cape Hatteras was the first seashore in the United States to become a national seashore (in 1953). The park covers 85 percent of Hatteras Island, which stretches south of the Bonner Bridge for 33 miles to Hatteras Inlet.

The beaches are clean and uncrowded. Subtle beauty abounds in the park. The swaying sea grasses, shifting sands, and tenacious vegetation appear monochromatic at first glance. A closer study reveals pleasant surprises. Lush purple flowers and delicate white-petaled flowers with scarlet centers grow entwined in the roadside brambles. In the marshes, sea lavender, morning glories, and marsh aster add color. In the early morning or late afternoon, you can usually see dozens of brown marsh rabbits nibbling grasses. All

If you smoke on the beach, please take your cigarette butts with you when you leave. Cigarette butts take seven years to disintegrate, and the dolphins and sea turtles can mistake them for food.

along the seashore, ghost crabs burrow in the sand and scurry about by day and night—a pure delight for children. One of the more spectacular sights is the occasional glow of phosphorous visible in the waves breaking on shore during a dark night. Sometimes the crabs glow eerily.

The park offers visitors a respite from the busyness of a resort community. It's a peaceful ride down North Carolina Highway 12 and always a welcome one except when the ocean washes away the dune and claims the road. There are several attractions within the park borders that appeal to the nature lover, including the **Pea Island National Wildlife Refuge,** with more than 5,000 acres of wildlife habitat. The refuge is both a year-round and seasonal home for nearly 400 species, including the snow goose, Canada goose, and whistling swan. During the fall you can watch large flocks of snow geese ascend from their watery resting places. This section of the park may be one of the most poetic spots on the Outer Banks. The waterfowl are just far enough away to appear untouched by the human element. You can get up-close views through binoculars and a camera's lens. Photographers also enjoy this stretch for the interesting tree lines and sunsets on the salt marsh. Plan to stop and bird-watch at the platform just off the road.

The **North Pond Trail,** on Pea Island, is another bird-watcher's destination. The **Ocracoke pony pens** and **Hammock Hills Nature Trail** across from the Ocracoke Campground are two more hot spots in the Cape Hatteras National Seashore. See our Hatteras Island section in the Attractions chapter for more information on these sites; our Waves and Weather chapter for lifeguard information within park boundaries; and our Getting Here, Getting Around chapter for more about off-road driving.

In Buxton, at a jutting tip of Cape Hatteras, is an area of beach accessible only by four-wheel-drive vehicles. Locals call this "The Point," and it serves as a well-used haven for surf casters. The sea is powerful at this spot, marked by strong currents, deep holes, shoals, and opposing waves crashing into each other. Wildlife writers and anglers alike call it heaven. The bottom topography—created by strong shoaling and The Point's proximity to the Gulf Stream and its spinoff eddies—justifies calling this wet and sandy area a real Outer Banks natural wonder. (See our Fishing chapter for more about The Point.)

Whale watching is an exciting activity for park visitors, though sightings are not restricted to the park boundaries. There are more species of whales passing by the coast of North Carolina than anywhere in eastern North America. Mostly groups of small- to medium-toothed whales make passage both far offshore and in sight of the beach. Deeper offshore is the migration path for killer and blue whales.

The three largest species are the sperm whale, humpback, and fin whale. Sperm whales make their way past our coast in the springtime. In the winter you can see both humpback and fin whales. Humpbacks are particularly visible from shore. They can be seen breaching and lunge feeding. In the latter action, the whale blows a bubble net to corral fish, then leaps through it openmouthed to gulp in everything.

Pilot whales can be seen offshore year-round. Even the most endangered species, the Northern right whale, was identified while scratching its head on an Outer Banks sandbar. We've also had rare washups of the dense beaked whale. Offshore sightings have been made of the Cuvier's beaked whale, and the first live sighting of the True's beaked whale was 33 nautical miles southeast of Hatteras Inlet.

Visitors to the park delight in filling all available pockets and pails with shells. Hatteras Island is one of the farthest points out on the Eastern Seaboard. Its steep beaches cause high-energy wave action, so unbroken shells rarely make it to the shore. But the sea tosses up lovely blue mussels, quahog, jackknife clams, slipper shells, baby's ears, jingle shells, and oysters. A good time to search for shells is

at changing tides, after high tide, or following a storm. If you are seeking whole shells, continue south to Ocracoke Island, where the beaches have gentle slopes.

THE WATER

Estuary, Sound, and Salt Marsh

Fly over the Outer Banks in a small plane, and it becomes clear that this string of islands is more an offspring of the sea than the land. With more than 2.2 million acres of sounds and bays between its barrier islands and mainland, North Carolina ranks behind only Alaska and Louisiana in estuarine acreage. With 2 million acres covered by the vast Currituck-Albemarle-Pamlico sound system, the Outer Banks region ranks second in size only to the Chesapeake Bay in terms of water surface area. Each day more than 15 billion gallons of water pass into the barrier islands' estuaries. The bulk of it flows into the Pamlico Sound and then to the Atlantic through four major Outer Banks inlets.

The Albemarle Sound, the mouth of which sits west of Kitty Hawk, is fed by seven major rivers and is the largest freshwater sound on the East Coast. The Currituck Sound, also freshwater, lies northeast of the Albemarle. Due south of these bodies of water are two brackish sounds, the Roanoke and the Croatan. Farther south is the saltwater Pamlico Sound. Nestled in the crook of this sound, where Cape Hatteras indents toward the sea, is the famous Canadian Hole, one of the nation's top windsurfing spots (see our Water Sports chapter).

The Outer Banks landscape is also defined by its salt marshes. The marshes shelter the barrier islands from the sounds, and cordgrass and other vegetation break much of the wave action and act as safe havens for marine life. The wetlands are nursery grounds for many of the fish we enjoy dining on. Ninety per-

The Glowing Ocean

If you are out on the beach after dark and the ocean seems to shimmer and glow, you may be seeing a natural occurrence known as bioluminescence. Tiny pinpoints of greenish light in the ocean occur occasionally on moonless nights. Most often they appear as waves break onto the shore, or in your footprints along the edge of the water. According to Pat Raves at the North Carolina Aquarium on Roanoke Island, this phenomenon can be credited to incredibly small plants, called *Noctiluca,* that produce light when disturbed. Mole crabs also can be seen glowing; the crabs feed on *Noctiluca,* which sometimes stick to their backs.

Predicting when the ocean will glimmer with *Noctiluca* is difficult; no one seems to know exactly when this phenomenon will happen. So stroll outside on a moonless night: You may be lucky enough to witness bioluminescence; if not, you will still enjoy a beautiful walk.

cent of all commercial seafood species must spend at least part of their life cycle in the salt marsh. They spawn offshore and release their eggs into the inlets, where currents carry them into the marsh. Oysters, crabs, shrimp, and flounder flourish in the calmer waters of the marsh, which offer places to hide and lots of food. The salt marsh is also attractive to waterfowl and other bird species, which find food here.

The Sea

Perhaps the sea in its entirety is too huge for the human mind to comprehend, but it is only through trying to understand her that you come to appreciate the Outer Banks fully. The ocean dominates the islands, influencing their weather, land, flora, fauna, and the lifestyle of the people. Scientists work daily at the U.S. Army Corps of Engineers Field Research Facility in Duck studying currents to understand erosion. Outer Banks history is steeped in harrowing accounts of lifesaving efforts, and the economy is heavily based in sea-oriented tourism, the commercial seafood industry, and recreational fishing.

The position of Cape Hatteras, jutting into the Atlantic, puts us near the continental shelf's edge, which is approximately 37 miles southeast of Oregon Inlet and near the junction of three ocean currents: the Deep Western Boundary Current, Gulf Stream, and Shelf Current. These physical combinations create a nutrient-rich habitat for sea life, resulting in world-renowned offshore fishing and a wonderland for pelagic birds.

The Gulf Stream

A forceful flow of water in the Atlantic Ocean passes off the Outer Banks's shores every day. The Gulf Stream is a swift ribbon of blue sea that has been flowing by since time immemorial. It is powered by forces arising from the earth's rotation and the influence of the winds, and the energy and warmth it emits has had a profound effect on humankind. While the stream's course is influenced somewhat by gales, barometric pressure, and seasonal changes, the general flow remains fairly constant, creating a dichotomy: While the stream is ever-present, its contents are ever-changing. Millions upon millions of tons of water per second are carried along this ancient path. Swept along are fish, microscopic plants and animals, and gulfweed that originates in the Sargasso Sea.

Gulfweed lines the edge of the stream, creating a habitat for baitfish. You can easily scoop a handful of vegetation and find it teeming with life. The weed offers protection to infant fish, turtles, crabs, sea horses, and the most peculiar sargassumfish. Endangered loggerhead sea turtles less than two weeks old, their egg beaks still intact, have been spotted in the weed.

Flying fish are always fun to watch, although what we see as antics is actually the fish's sprint for life as it glides about 200 to 300 yards to escape a predator. The offshore life cycle is fascinating, and nowhere is it more evident than at the Gulf Stream.

BIRD-WATCHING

With ocean beaches, sand dunes, scrub thickets, marsh, pocosins, black-water swamps, and maritime and inland forests, the Outer Banks and surrounding inland regions are rich in waterfowl and other birds. Nearly 400 species of birds have been sighted within Cape Hatteras National Seashore and its surrounding waters. Many birds choose the area because of the diverse habitats and because it's a convenient stop along the eastern flyway. But occasionally a vagrant will blow in with strong winds or storms. Accidental species spotted on the Outer Banks are numerous, including the pacific loon, western grebe, white-winged dove, snowy owl, western tanager, cerulean warbler, sandhill crane, and many others.

Though birding is always exciting on the Outer Banks, the greatest variety of species occurs during the spring and fall migrations. Good numbers of migratory shorebirds can be seen on inlet tidal flats, the ponds at Pea Island and Bodie Island, and the salt ponds at Cape Hatteras Point. Land-bird observations occur in the shrub thickets along the dikes at Pea Island and in the maritime woods. Herons, egrets, terns, skimmers, and other birds that breed locally are best seen in the warmer months. These birds frequent both salt- and freshwater areas. Winter ducks, geese, and swans usually concentrate on ponds at Pea Island and Bodie Island and on Lake Mattamuskeet.

In the marshes herons, egrets, ibises, waterfowl, rails, and shorebirds are visible. These birds can be seen in the marshes all over the Outer Banks, but an easy access point into the marsh is the trails behind the Bodie Island Lighthouse.

Pea Island National Wildlife Refuge is one of the top birding sites on the whole East Coast. Impoundments, salt flats, and ponds house snow geese, Canada geese, willets, tundra swan, and several species of ducks. The live oaks house songbirds during fall migration. On the beaches shorebirds, gulls, terns, and pelicans keep busy. Nesting birds may include piping plover, American oystercatcher, terns, and skimmers.

Other great birding areas to visit include Nags Head Woods, Buxton Woods, Alligator River National Wildlife Refuge, Currituck National Wildlife Refuge, Jockey's Ridge State Park, and Ocracoke Island.

Pelagic Bird-Watching

You don't have to be a bird lover to realize you have entered a unique bird-watching area as you tool down NC 12 through the National Seashore. Off in the distance, in the wetlands, a variety of species feed and sun. What is not so obvious is the gold-mine of pelagic species offshore, where bird-watchers witness both common and rare birds that never come to shore.

Local fishing headboats have been taking bird-watchers to the deep water for years. In fact, the sightings are so fruitful that a good part of Capt. Allan Foreman's charter boat business involves these trips. Foreman's *Country Girl* (252–473–5577), which fishes out of Pirate's Cove Yacht Club on Roanoke Island, is a 57-foot headboat built to carry large parties offshore. Down in Hatteras, Capt. Spurgeon Stowe runs bird-watching excursions aboard the 72-foot *Miss Hatteras* (252–986–2365) from Oden's Dock (see our Fishing chapter for more information on these boats). Bird enthusiasts spend the day searching for more than two dozen species that live on the water.

The petrel and shearwater families are the largest groups of birds visible here. Traveling from the Caribbean and the coast of Africa, these species summer off the Outer Banks.

Among the petrels, the black-capped petrel is probably one of the most common to North Carolina waters. Twenty-five years ago this species was believed to be on the verge of extinction, and still today several varieties are a conservation concern. No one knew where the birds were. Scientists now say that the world's population lives in the Gulf Stream off the Outer Banks area. For comparison's sake, Florida bird-watchers may see one or two black-capped petrels per trip, whereas trips departing from the Outer Banks can yield as many as 100 sightings on a good day.

What's exciting about these trips is the chance to view species that are rarely, if ever, seen on land. These birds are highly adapted for life on the sea. They could be mistaken for gulls or ducks, but as a group they are unique. Their tubular nostrils allow them to drink salt water then expel the salt.

A much rarer bird sighted off North Carolina is the white-faced storm petrel. In a good year, one or two sightings are recorded. This bird shows up in the late summer or early fall and is very difficult to spot anywhere else in the world.

While bird-watching off the Outer Banks, Mike Tove, a biologist from Cary, North Carolina, discovered two species of petrel that were rarely seen near North America. One of them, called the herald petrel, until recently was known from only a handful of recordings going back to the 1920s.

"In 1991 boats started venturing offshore farther than usual," Tove said. "We started finding them. It's now a bird we see a half-dozen times a year. People come great distances looking for them."

Tove officially presented to discovery another rare species in May 1991. "I had a bird that was identified as a Cape Verde petrel," he said. Prior to Tove's sighting, resurrected field notes revealed only three other recorded sightings of the bird.

This species was entirely unknown in the United States and is extraordinarily rare anywhere in the world. "And we're seeing them with almost predictable regularity in late spring in very deep offshore waters past the edge of the continental shelf," he said. Tove's sightings form the baseline data for research. All the birds have been well documented with photographs.

You don't have to have a doctorate, as Tove does, to enjoy bird-watching. If you want to glimpse these offshore species, here are a few tips:

- Bring fairly low-power, waterproof binoculars (Zeiss or Leitz 7X or 8X are excellent).
- Don't bother to bring your spotting scope; if you're a photographer, bring a telephoto lens to help document rarities.
- Constantly scan the horizon and wave tops for birdlife, and call out your sighting with the boat as reference; for example, six o'clock is directly off the stern.
- Don't wait to try to identify the bird before calling it out; your fellow watchers will aid in that. Identification is often very difficult, and to do it accurately you

must have a great deal of field experience and ability to interpret flight and molt patterns, which can be even more difficult during heavy seas.

- Expect long periods where no birds are seen, but be prepared for the appearance of a good number and variety. Always take good notes on any unusual species before consulting your field guide. Describe and sketch exactly what you saw without allowing outside influences to color your recollection.

- Offshore bird-watching can be an exciting new adventure. If you haven't spent any time on the water, don't allow your fears to get the best of you. Captains won't take you out if the weather is too risky, and you can follow our tips on preventing seasickness (see our Fishing chapter).

Happy bird-watching!

WEATHER

By the end of this guidebook, you may well be tired of the word "variety." It aptly describes not only the above-mentioned natural wonders but our weather as well. We find the weather to be changeable on the Outer Banks. Business owners who specialize in outdoor attractions are plagued by phone calls when the skies turn dark.

We tell our visitors that because the weather is so mercurial, wait 10 minutes and those dark clouds very possibly may be gone. There's variation from town to town. It may be pouring in Corolla, but Manteo has sunny skies. Torrential rains could send beachgoers scattering at noon, but 20 minutes later sunshine pours down from the heavens.

It seems to rain less in winter, while late summer evenings hold their share of window-rattling thundershowers. The good part is that the skies are usually clear during the day.

The Atlantic Ocean, which is slow to warm and cool and heats to a maximum of about 80 degrees in the summer,

affects air temperatures. Our nearness to the sea keeps summer air temperatures about 10 degrees cooler than our mainland counterparts. In the winter, disregarding the windchill factor, our air temperatures do just the opposite. Air flowing over the Gulf Stream toward us warms the winter air.

Nor'easters, occurring most often in the fall and winter, plague homeowners and fishermen alike. The high winds keep boats at the docks, sometimes knocking out three to seven workdays. These same winds wreak havoc on precariously perched oceanfront property. If the high winds coincide with the high tide and—heaven forbid—the full moon, powerful storm waves cover the land and cause beach erosion, structural damage, and both ocean and soundside flooding.

March has seen a few nasty storms, too, including the infamous Ash Wednesday Storm that struck on March 7, 1962, and the more recent March storm in 1993 when winds were clocked at 92 mph. The sound waters rose 8 to 10 feet, causing great damage. Year-round residents see all this nasty weather as a trade-off for living in such a paradise. While we tend to highlight the more extreme weather patterns here, there are far more absolutely gorgeous days occurring year-round.

The wind blows most of the time at an average of 8 to 10 mph. Occasional gale-force winds range from 30 to 35 mph. In summer the wind blows predominantly out of the southwest, often increasing in the late afternoon. Southwest winds are warm, and if you're on a beach facing east, they create a generally flat ocean but stir up the sound. The wind frequently comes out of the northeast, which is a colder wind. Old-timers say that the wind always blows out of the northeast for an odd number of days—one, three, or five—before switching around again. Northeast winds create a rough ocean on east-facing beaches and are more predominant in fall and winter. Northwest and southeast winds are less common, but of course they do occur, usually as the wind is about to switch to northeast or southwest.

The weather is endlessly fascinating on the Outer Banks, something that almost every resident watches with vigilance. Surfers and anglers and anyone else who works or plays outside watch The Weather Channel (channel 16) for informa- tion. Many restaurants and bars even keep a TV tuned into The Weather Channel. Hurricanes, of course, are a whole different ballgame. See our Waves and Weather: How to Stay Safe chapter for additional information on what to do in case a hurricane threatens.

WAVES AND WEATHER: HOW TO STAY SAFE

The Outer Banks is known for its sparkling, clean beaches. Sun worshipers from all parts of the world come to the Outer Banks to delight in the surf. But the ocean is fickle and can change its mood in the blink of an eye. Each beach is different, and to stay safe you need to follow a few rules. Store these tips along with your seashells to help make your stay a comfortable and safe one.

THE OCEAN

Most of the time, you don't even notice the bare flagpoles dotting the dunes up and down our coast. But when the ocean is too rough for swimming, there's no way you can miss the red flags hoisted all along the beach. *If red flags are flying, do not go into the water.* Not only is the ocean too dangerous for swimming or wading, it is also against the law to swim during a red-flag warning. You will be fined for going into the water.

The flags signify not only dangerous waves but also deadly rip currents. Churning water can easily knock you down, and reports of broken bones are not uncommon. Rough water also produces floating debris—such as ships' timbers—that seems to come from nowhere. We've seen adult men wading in knee-deep water knocked down by powerful waves and dragged by rip currents on red-flag days. In short, even if you see surfers in the water, stay out while the flags are flying, and caution children to keep well away from the tide line. Keep in mind, too, that if you go into the water while the flags are flying and need rescuing, you are jeopardizing not only your life but also the lifeguard's life when he or she has to come in after you.

Water Sense

- Never swim alone.
- Never swim at night.
- Observe the surf before going in the water, looking for potentially dangerous currents.
- Nonswimmers should stay out of the water and wear life jackets if they're going to be near the water.
- Swim in areas with on-duty lifeguards, or use extreme care.
- Keep nonswimming children well above the marks of the highest waves.
- Keep an eye on children at all times; teach them never to turn their backs on the waves while they play at water's edge.
- Don't swim near anglers or deployed fishing lines.
- Stay 300 feet away from fishing piers.
- Watch out for surfers and give them plenty of room.

Losing Control in the Waves

If a wave crashes on you while surfing or swimming, and you get tumbled in bubbles and sand like a sheet in a washing machine, don't try to struggle to the surface against it. Curl into a ball, or go limp and float. The wave will take you to the beach, or you can swim to the surface when it soon passes.

Currents

A **backwash current** on a steeply sloping beach can pull you toward deeper water, but its power is swiftly checked by

Wear sunscreen! Sand, water, and concrete surfaces can reflect 85 percent of the sun's rays. Don't be fooled by a cloudy day: 90 percent of the sun's rays penetrate the clouds. Dermatologists say that nearly half of the damage to skin occurs in childhood and early adolescence. Everyone should wear waterproof sunscreen of SPF 15 or higher.

incoming waves. To escape this current, swim straight toward shore if you're a strong swimmer. If you're not, don't panic; wait and float until the current stops, then swim in.

The **littoral current** is a "river of water" moving up or down the shoreline parallel to the beach. It is created by the angled approach of the waves. In stormy conditions, this current can be very powerful due to high wave energy.

Rip currents often occur where there's a break in a submerged sandbar. Water trapped between the sandbar and the beach rushes out through the breach, sometimes sweeping swimmers out with it. You can see a rip; it's choppy, turbulent, often discolored water that looks deeper than the water around it. If you are caught in a rip, don't try to swim against the current. Instead, swim across the current, parallel to the shore, and slowly work your way back to the beach at an angle. Try to remain calm. Panic will only sap the energy you need to swim out of the rip.

When a wave comes up on the beach and breaks, the water must run back down to the sea. This is **undertow.** It sucks at your ankles from small waves, but in heavy surf the undertow can knock you off your feet and carry you offshore. If you're carried out, don't resist. Let the undertow take you out until it subsides. It will only be a few yards. The next wave will help push you shoreward again.

Sharks

To reduce your risk of shark bites, take the following precautions:

- Do not swim alone; sharks are more likely to attack a solitary individual.
- Do not wander from shore.
- Avoid the water at dawn or during twilight hours when sharks are most active and have a competitive sensory advantage for hunting.
- Don't wear bright clothing or reflective jewelry that attracts the attention of sharks and other fish.
- Be especially wary if you're bleeding or menstruating, since shark's olfactory senses are acute.
- Avoid thrashing about wildly—excessive splash can appear to be shark prey. For this reason, it is advised that you not swim with pets.
- Do not swim near fishing action.
- Stay away from inlets, fishing piers, and if possible, steep drop-offs and the areas between sandbars—these are favorite hangouts for sharks.
- If you see a shark, calmly leave the water as quickly and quietly as possible.

Jellyfish

Watch for jellyfish floating on the surface or in the water. While some can give little more than an annoying stinging sensation, others can produce severe discomfort. The Portuguese man-of-war is sometimes blown onto Outer Banks beaches and can be recognized by its distinctive balloon-like air bladder, often exhibiting a bluish tint. Man-of-war stings can be serious. Anyone who is stung by the tentacles and develops breathing difficulties or generalized body swelling should be transported to the nearest emergency facility for treatment. In extreme cases, death can result from anaphylactic shock associated with man-of-war toxin exposure.

BEACH SERVICES
Emergency Assistance

Many areas of the Outer Banks don't have lifeguards or flag systems warning you when to stay out of the water. Keep in mind that help can be a long way off, and an emergency is not the time to learn about ocean safety. Water conditions here call for unusual vigilance. We are vigilant about hanging red warning flags, but sometimes they are stolen by souvenir-seeking scavengers. It's always best to listen to local radio stations or call municipal headquarters for daily water conditions anytime you plan to enter the ocean, despite the season. The Weather Channel also posts rip-current warnings. Accidents can and do occur. If you have an emergency and need the rescue squad, dial 911 for help. Please remember that this number is for emergencies only.

Lifeguards

Lifeguard services are at fixed sites throughout Dare and Currituck Counties.

Corolla Ocean Rescue (252–453–3242) provides guards from 9:30 A.M. to 5:30 P.M. from Memorial Day weekend through Labor Day at the following Corolla beaches: Ocean Hill, Corolla Light, Bonito Street (Whalehead), Ocean Sands at Buck Island and Sections P, O, F, and D, and Pine Island at the South County Beach Access. Lifeguards also patrol the beaches from Pine Island to the Penny's Hill area of the off-road area.

Kitty Hawk Ocean Rescue (252–261–2666, www.kittyhawkfd.com/ocean rescue.html) operates two stands, one at Byrd Street and one at the Kitty Hawk Bathhouse. The stands are staffed from Memorial Day to Labor Day, 10:00 A.M. to 6:00 P.M. Roving lifeguards also patrol the beaches of the town. From Labor Day through mid-October, a supervisor stays on the beach.

In **Kill Devil Hills** (252–480–4066) lifeguard stands are at the following beaches: Helga Street, Hayman Boulevard, Fifth Street, Fourth Street, Second Street, First Street, Asheville Street, Woodmere Street, Carlow Street, Ocean Bay Boulevard, Oregon Street, Clark Street, Martin Street, Atlantic Street, Calvin Street, Ocean Acres Beach Access, and Lake Drive. There are also patrolling guards. Guards are on duty from 9:30 A.M. to 5:30 P.M. in the summer.

Surf Rescue places guards on the beaches in Duck and on Roanoke Island from Memorial Day weekend through Labor Day weekend. Hours are 9:30 A.M. to 5:30 P.M. Duck lifeguard locations change according to where the greatest population of swimmers is in any given year. Duck has four fixed but movable stands and two roaming lifeguards. On Roanoke Island a guard is at the Old Swimming Hole on the sound between the airport and the aquarium.

Nags Head Ocean Rescue Services (252–441–5909) are provided by the town of Nags Head to its beaches. This service is also provided to Southern Shores through a contracted arrangement. Guarded beaches are available daily beginning Memorial Day weekend through Labor Day, 10:00 A.M. to 6:00 P.M. Nags Head Ocean Rescue stands are located at the following beaches:

- In Southern Shores: Hillcrest and Chicahauk, plus two roving vehicles.
- In Nags Head: Albatross Street, Bonnet Street, Enterprise Street, Espstein Street, Forrest Street, Gray Eagle Street, Hargrove Street, and Juncos Street. There are also seven roving vehicles and two trucks.

Check out the following Web sites for information on water safety: www.usla.org and www.kittyhawkfd.com/oceanrescue .html.

Within the **Cape Hatteras National Seashore,** lifeguards are on duty from Memorial Day through Labor Day at Coquina Beach on Bodie Island, at the Cape Hatteras Lighthouse Beach, and at the Ocracoke Lifeguard Beach (use the first access road past the airport).

ALCOHOL

The effects of alcohol are amplified by the heat and sun of a summer afternoon, so be aware. It's illegal to operate boats or motor vehicles if you've had too much to drink, and enforcement officers keep an eye out for violators, so practice moderation. Alcohol and swimming is a potentially deadly combination. Even small amounts of alcohol can give you a false sense of security.

SAFETY IN THE SUN

It's amazing how many red-bodied people we see lying on the beach, limping into restaurants or, worse yet, waiting in medical centers while visiting the Outer Banks. The sun feels so good. Combined with the sea air, it seems to have a rejuvenating effect. Actually any form of tan or burn is now considered damaged skin. While we can't stop visitors and Insiders alike from toasting themselves, these tips will help keep you comfortable.

- Start out with short periods of sun exposure when you first arrive. It seems as if most visitors initially overdo it and have to be careful for the rest of their stay. The summer sun is intense, and you'd be surprised how much of a burn your skin can get in 20 or 30 minutes on an afternoon in July.
- Use ample sunscreen (SPF 15 or higher) whenever you're in the sun for any length of time. Put an extra coat on nose, cheeks, lips, and any other high-exposure spots. For maximum benefit, apply sunscreen at least 20 minutes before going out, since it can take a while for it to become fully effective.
- Avoid the hottest parts of the day, from 10:00 A.M. until 2:00 P.M., when the sun's rays are the strongest. Explore some of the other fun things listed in this guide.
- Don't hesitate to cover up on the beach. Healthy, protected skin is a sign of good sense.

Pets

Dogs must be on a leash unless they are in the water. Park Service rangers and lifeguards patrol the beaches, and they will fine you if your dog is running free. Voice command control is not enough. Fines are around $50. Some communities do not allow pets on the beach at all from mid-May through mid-September. Heed local signs. Not only are unleashed pets a nuisance to non-pet owners, but also they can damage turtle and bird nests and the fragile dune systems.

Litter

We shouldn't even have to say it, but, believe it or not, there are people who leave trash behind at the beach. If you're getting ready to throw down a soda bottle or candy wrapper, remember that while you may only be visiting the Outer Banks, you are littering in a year-round community, not to mention destroying natural beauty. Inevitably what is tossed in

Hot summer days are physically stressful for dogs, who lack sweat glands to cool themselves down. Avoid having your dog on the beach in the hottest part of the day, and make sure your dog has plenty of fresh water to drink. If your dog shows signs of heat stroke or exhaustion, spray him with cool water, get him to a shaded area, and call a vet.

one backyard winds up littering the lawn of another due to the wind factor. Secure all trash and trash bags carefully and carry them to a trash receptacle. Feel free to pick up any stray trash. It's not uncommon to see locals doing just this.

HURRICANES

June through November marks hurricane season. Basically, the whole shoreline of the East Coast is threatened when a hurricane visits, but because of our low elevation, lack of shelter, and our situation in the ocean, these barrier islands are especially vulnerable to storms. Forecasters and almanac writers state that a significant hurricane strikes the Outer Banks approximately once every nine years.

After Hurricane Isabel of 2003, visitors and locals alike were reminded of the dangers these storms bring. It's wise to be prepared by packing a hurricane kit in advance. See the sidebar in this chapter for a list of items to include in such a kit.

When Dare County officials order an evacuation, everyone must leave the Outer Banks. This includes vacationers who have already paid for their week's stay and permanent residents who are sometimes hesitant to leave their homes. Newspapers and radio and television stations keep the public notified about evacuations as well as reentry information. Make plans early especially if you have pets or elderly people with you. The Weather Channel issues early warnings or signs of an approaching storm. By all means, stay off the beaches and out of the water. More information about our emergency procedures can be gleaned by calling Dare County at (252) 473-3355, Currituck County at (252) 232-2115, or Ocracoke at (252) 928-1071.

Tornadoes spawned by hurricanes are among the worst weather-related killers. When a hurricane approaches, listen for tornado watches and warnings. (A tornado watch means conditions are favorable for tornadoes to develop. A warning

means a tornado has been sighted.) When a warning is issued, seek shelter immediately, preferably in an inside room away from windows. If you are outside at the time and a tornado is headed your way, move away from its path at a right angle. If you feel you don't have time to escape, lie flat in a ditch or ravine.

Hurricane watches mean a hurricane could threaten the area within 24 hours, but evacuation is not necessary at this point. If a warning is issued, however, visitors should leave the islands and head inland using U.S. Highway 64/264 or U.S. Highway 158 and following the green and white Hurricane Evacuation Route signs.

Here are some guidelines to help you stay safe if a hurricane threatens.

- By late May, recheck your supply of boards, tools, batteries, nonperishable foods, and other items you may need during a hurricane.
- Listen regularly to the latest weather reports and official notices. This will give you advance notice, sometimes before watches and warnings are issued. Keep a battery-powered radio on hand in case the power goes out.
- If your area comes under a hurricane watch, continue normal activities but stay tuned to The Weather Channel or to a local radio station and ignore rumors.
- If your area receives a hurricane warning, stay calm. Leave low-lying areas that may be swept by high tides or storm waves. If there's time, secure mobile homes before leaving for more substantial shelter. Move automobiles to high ground as both sound and sea can flood even central spots on the Outer Banks.
- Moor boats securely or haul them out of the water to a safe place.
- Board up windows or protect them with storm shutters. (Though some people recommend using tape on windows, many experts and most locals will tell you tape isn't strong enough, and it's very difficult to remove.) Secure out-

Hurricane Kit

Be sure to include these items in your hurricane kit:

- AM/FM radio with extra batteries
- Baby supplies, if necessary
- Bar soap
- Can opener
- Cash
- Change of clothing for each member of the family
- Eating utensils
- First-aid kit
- Flashlights and extra batteries
- Food (nonperishable) and water, enough for three days for the entire family
- Hygiene items: toilet paper, toothpaste, etc.
- Ice chest or cooler
- Important documents: birth certificates, medical records, insurance papers, etc.
- Matches
- Plastic bags for waste
- Plywood for windows
- Prescription medications, glasses, etc.
- Sleeping bags and blankets
- Spare key for home and vehicles

And don't forget your pets during a storm. They need special attention since they can't take care of themselves. Animals are barred from public shelters for health reasons, so make plans for evacuating your pet before the storm strikes by finding out which hotels and motels in safe areas allow pets. Have an up-to-date identification tag on your pet's collar, a current photograph, and current medical/vaccination records with you. Make sure your pet is properly restrained with a carrier or leash, since even the calmest animals become frightened in a storm. Bring a week's worth of food as well as any medications your pet might need, and don't forget a litter pan and litter if you have a cat.

door objects that might blow away, such as garbage cans, outdoor furniture, tools, etc. that may become dangerous missiles in high winds. If the items can't be tied down, bring them inside.

- Store drinking water in clean bathtubs, jugs, or bottles because water supplies can become contaminated by hurricane floods.
- Be sure you have lots of flashlights, batteries, and emergency cooking facilities.
- Keep your car fueled since service stations may be inoperable for several days following a storm.
- Stay indoors during a storm, and keep your pets inside. Do not attempt to travel by foot or car. Monitor weather conditions and don't be fooled by the calm of the hurricane's eye—the storm isn't over yet!
- Stay out of disaster areas unless you are qualified to help. Your presence might hamper rescue work.
- If necessary, seek medical attention at the nearest Red Cross disaster station or health center.
- Do not travel except in an emergency, such as transporting someone who is injured. Be careful along debris-filled streets and highways. Roads may be undermined and could collapse under the weight of the car. Floodwater could hide dangerous holes in the road.

- Avoid loose and dangling wires. Report them to the power company or the police.
- Report broken sewer or water mains to the county or town water department.
- Be careful not to start fires. Lowered water pressure may make fire fighting difficult.
- Stay away from rivers and streams.
- Check roofs, windows, and outdoor storage areas for wind or water damage.
- Do not let young children or your pets outside immediately after a storm. There are numerous dangers like fallen power lines and wild animals that have been disoriented because of the storm.

The most important safety tool is common sense. Use it and stay aware and observant to have a safe and enjoyable vacation.

RECREATION 🚲

From early on, these barrier islands have lured sunbathers, swimmers, surfers, and outdoor enthusiasts in search of excellent sportfishing and waterfowl hunting. The appeal has since widened to include more outdoor activities: windsurfing, hang gliding, parasailing, scuba diving, biking, golf, tennis, and in-line skating, just to name a few. And for a respite from these more strenuous workouts, you can choose among sightseeing cruises, ATV excursions, and beach combing. We have entire chapters covering water sports, fishing, and golf. In this chapter, we list some other recreation options.

Not all activities involve a fee. You can spend an afternoon walking the wide beaches searching for shells and pieces of sea glass or buy a kite and send it soaring atop the wafting winds. Bird-watching opportunities abound in the wildlife refuges along the Outer Banks; see our Natural Wonders chapter. Nags Head Woods offers both a shady respite during the heat of summer and a great place to take secluded hikes through one of the most marvelous preserved maritime forests on the Atlantic Seaboard. Bike paths line roads along the sounds and the sea, through towns, and along the Wright Brothers National Monument. If you need to get to sea for a while and enjoy the Outer Banks from a different vantage point, ride the free state ferry to Ocracoke Island.

When you've had a little too much fun in the sun, there are indoor activities such as bowling alleys, movie theaters, roller rinks, and noisy, state-of-the-art video arcades. Don't forget to check out our Kidstuff chapter for additional activities geared toward children.

If you're looking for parks, the Dare County Parks and Recreation Department has several throughout the county, some with playgrounds, tennis courts, picnicking sites, and ball fields. Call (252) 473-1101,

ext. 313 to find the one nearest you. See the Playgrounds section of our Kidstuff chapter for the best playgrounds.

If bingo is your bag, several fire stations and civic clubs along the barrier islands host regularly scheduled sessions in the early evenings throughout the summer. Colington Island's Volunteer Fire Department off Colington Road (252-441-6234) and Nags Head's Fire Department on U.S. Highway 158 just south of the Outer Banks Mall (252-441-5909) are home to two of the area's more popular part-time bingo parlors. Outer Banks Beach Bingo on Colington Road in Kill Devil Hills (252-449-8332) has games year-round several nights a week until 2:00 A.M., and the First Flight Lions Club at MP 5½ on US 158 in Kill Devil Hills (252-441-8308) hosts bingo nightly at 7:00 P.M.

For home entertainment, video sales and rental stores are scattered from Corolla to Ocracoke. The stores accommodate our transient tourist population, so memberships are not required. Try Ocean Atlantic Rentals (252-261-4346) with locations from Corolla to Avon; Good Vibes Video (252-453-3503) in Corolla; Carolina Video (252-255-0821) in Southern Shores; Good Vibes (252-441-2244) in Kill Devil Hills; Video Andy (252-441-2666) in Nags Head; Village Video (252-995-5138) with several locations on Hatteras Island; and Eleven 11 Shades and Movies on Ocracoke (252-928-9000). Many stores also rent video game consoles. You'll find at least one videocassette recorder in every rental cottage on the Outer Banks, but if you're staying in a hotel or motel that doesn't have one in the room, most stores do rent VCRs and DVD players.

It's nearly impossible to experience all the recreational opportunities the Outer Banks has to offer. We're sure you'll have fun trying, though.

AIRPLANE TOURS

Even people who have lived on the Outer Banks for years are awestruck when they first view this stretch of islands from the air. Small planes offer tours daily most of the year from Corolla through Ocracoke. Pilots are always pleased to dip their passengers over a school of dolphins frolicking in the Atlantic, circle one of the four lighthouses beaming from these beaches, or cruise around the Wright Brothers National Monument, where Wilbur and Orville flew the world's first successful heavier-than-air craft. Bring your camera, for these adventures provide great photo opportunities of both sea and sound shores and otherwise inaccessible wetlands.

Reservations are strongly recommended at least a day in advance of takeoff. All flights depend on the wind and weather. For information on charter flights to Norfolk and other destinations off the Outer Banks, please refer to the air service section in our Getting Here, Getting Around chapter. Several services offer flight instruction to obtain a pilot's license and certification.

If you're up for more high-flying excitement, try a trip in a 1941 Waco biplane, with its open cockpit. Twenty-minute trips take two passengers around the central Outer Banks for $88 per person. Leather helmets and old-fashioned Red Baron–style goggles are included in the price. Biplane tours are offered May through September from 9:00 A.M. until sunset. Reservations are preferred for both types of flights.

Outer Banks Seaplanes
Wanchese Seafood Industrial Park
Wanchese
(252) 475-1007
This company offers air tours via seaplane, taking off and landing on Roanoke Sound. Board the Cessna seaplane at the dock at the Wanchese Seafood Industrial Park, then take a half-hour tour above Jockey's Ridge, the Wright Brothers Memorial, Roanoke Island, the beach, and Oregon Inlet. Two passengers can fly at a time. To get to the industrial park, take North Carolina Highway 345 off U.S. Highway 64/264 on the south end of Roanoke Island. Once you're in Wanchese, a brown state sign will direct you to the park.

Roanoke Island

Kitty Hawk Aero Tours
Main Terminal
Airport Road, Roanoke Island
(252) 441-4460, (877) 274-2461
Based at the Manteo Airport, these air tours fly half-hour trips in Cessna aircraft year-round. Flights take you soaring south over Oregon Inlet, flying above the waves to see shipwrecks, over Jockey's Ridge and Roanoke Island, and back to circle the Wright Brothers monument. It costs $48 per person for parties of two and $39 per person for three- or four-person parties. Tours are offered from 10:00 A.M. to 5:00 P.M. in the off-season, and from 9:00 A.M. to sunset during summer.

Hatteras Island

Burris Flying Service
Frisco Shopping Center, NC 12, Frisco
(252) 986-2679
Burris Flying Service offers sightseeing tours of Hatteras Island and the surrounding areas. The short tour, about 30 minutes, takes you around Cape Hatteras and the lighthouse, while the longer tour, about an hour, can go either north to Rodanthe or south to Ocracoke Island. Both short and long tours fly two or three passengers. Additional trips are available, including a summer sunset tour. This is unparalleled opportunity for aerial photography. Tours are offered daily from May 1 through October 31. Advance reservations are recommended.

Ocracoke Island

Pelican Airways
Ocracoke Airstrip, Ocracoke
(252) 928-1661
Half-hour trips above Ocracoke and Portsmouth Islands are available any time of year in this Aero-Commander plane. Trips can be tailored to suit individual interests or narrated to explain interesting aspects of the southern Outer Banks area. A trip carries two or three people. Flight instruction is offered by appointment. Charter service is also available—see our Getting Here, Getting Around chapter.

ALL-TERRAIN VEHICLE, 4WD, AND HORSE TOURS

Whether you're cruising along the beach or chasing a sunset up the marshy sounds on an all-terrain vehicle (ATV), you're limited to 15 mph, and you can't ride on the dunes. These tours are available only on the northern Outer Banks north of Corolla.

Corolla

Corolla Outback Adventures
Wee Winks Shopping Center
NC 12, Corolla
(252) 453-4484
www.corollaoutback.com
This outpost on the northernmost area of the Outer Banks has been operating for more than 20 years and conducts guided tours with ATVs. Customers are transported by truck north of where the pavement ends to the four-wheel-drive area, where a Corolla Outback guide takes you by ATV along the beaches and through protected wildlife refuges. Even though the area is becoming more populated, you can still catch a glimpse of wild horses, rare waterfowl, wild boars, and feral hogs.

During summer season, two-hour guided tours cost $125 a vehicle; the ATVs seat two people. Off-season rates are available.

Backcountry Outfitters and Guides
Corolla Light Town Center, Corolla
(252) 453-0877
www.outerbankstours.com
Backcountry Outfitters and Guides offers Wild Horse Safari Tours that head to Carova, near the North Carolina border, looking for the famous wild horses—and they find them. Two-hour tours are led in Chevy Suburbans that hold up to 10 people. After the 15-mile drive up the beach to the horses' stomping grounds, passengers unload from the vehicle and take a few photos, while the guide educates everyone about the horses. This tour costs $46 for adults and is half-price for kids ages 4 to 11. Children age 3 and younger lap-sit for free. Along the tour you'll see other wildlife, plus the elements of the Outer Banks ecosystem. These tours take place year-round. Corolla Outback Adventures also offers four-wheel-drive/kayak expeditions. All tours and rentals are weather-dependent.

Corolla Adventure Tours
NC 12, Corolla
(252) 453-6899
Corolla Adventure Tours offers ATV and four-wheel-drive truck tours on the beaches north of Corolla, plus ocean and sound kayak tours (see our Water Sports chapter for information). ATV tours cover about 20 miles of territory and last about two hours. Truck tours (in Chevy Suburbans) are about the same length, covering the entire stretch of beach north of Corolla up to the Virginia line, where there are no paved roads. You may glimpse the wild horses. Corolla Adventure Tours operates March through January.

Ocracoke Island

Portsmouth Island ATV Excursions
NC 12, Ocracoke Village
(252) 928-4484
www.portsmouthislandatvs.com
A Portsmouth Island ATV Excursion allows you to ride the shoreline of one of the

most beautiful and remote beaches in the world on an island famous for its shore-birds, sea turtles, and seashells. Excursions begin with a 20-minute boat ride from Silver Lake Harbor in Ocracoke Village. Once on the island, you will discover the historic deserted village of Portsmouth, a settlement that in 1860 was a thriving port town with more than 685 residents. Now owned by the National Park Service, Portsmouth Island is home to the only ghost town on the East Coast (see our Day Trips and Attractions chapters for more details). As part of the tour, you will be guided through the village's U.S. Lifesaving Station, the Methodist church, the post office and general store, and the village visitor center.

Two trips a day are offered, from 8:00 A.M. to noon, and from 2:00 to 6:00 P.M., weather permitting. The season runs from April 1 through November 30. The cost is $75 per person, with a six-person maximum. Reservations are required.

ATHLETIC CLUBS

Despite all the outdoor activities the Outer Banks has to offer, many locals and visitors still crave vigorous indoor workouts at traditional gyms and health clubs. During the heat of the summer and the cold winds of winter, they're a good choice for strenuous exercise. These fitness centers are open year-round and include locker room and shower facilities. They are open to the public for annual, monthly, weekly, and walk-in daily membership rates.

Sanderling

The Spa at The Sanderling Inn
NC 12, Sanderling
(252) 261-4111, ext. SPA (772)
www.thesanderling.com
The Spa is an integral part of The Sanderling Inn Resort and Conference Center, a 12-acre luxury resort located 5 miles north of Duck. The Spa includes a complete fit-

ness center with state-of-the-art exercise equipment and the latest in cardiovascular training machines. Steam rooms, sports showers, a whirlpool, a heated lap pool, and other hydrotherapy options are also offered. Walk-in charges are $15 a day and $60 a week.

Kitty Hawk

Barrier Island Fitness Center
US 158, MP 1, Kitty Hawk
(252) 261-0100
Barrier Island Fitness Center (located behind Wal-Mart) is a complete, full-service health club. It has a full line of free weights, circuit-training equipment, and an assortment of cardiovascular equipment, including elliptical trainers, treadmills, stair-steppers, recumbent cycles, and Airdynes. Certified aerobics classes, including aquafit, are offered.

The staff includes fitness instructors, two personal trainers, and two massage therapists. Other amenities at the center include tennis courts, saunas, steam rooms, tanning beds, and an indoor pool. Parents rejoice: There is on-site babysitting and a cybercade with computer games for the kids. The cybercade is complete with high-speed Internet and e-mail access.

The facility is open to the public (ages 18 and older) Monday through Friday from 6:00 A.M. to 9:00 P.M.; Saturday, 9:00 A.M. to 7:00 P.M., and Sunday, 9:00 A.M. to 5:00 P.M. The pool is open until 10:00 P.M. daily. Drop-in rates are $15 a day or $45 a week.

Nags Head

Outer Banks Family YMCA
US 158, MP 11, Nags Head
(252) 449-8897
www.obxymca.org
This facility, opened in December 2001, includes a fitness room with weight and cardiovascular equipment. A wood-floored exercise room is available for

activities like aerobics, yoga, Pilates, and karate. The 7,000-square-foot gymnasium is marked for both basketball and volleyball and can be used for indoor soccer. An 8,000-square-foot indoor pool, 25 meters long with six lanes, is one highlight of the YMCA. Swim lessons, water aerobics, and lap times are available. A hot tub can accommodate up to 10 people. Another highlight is the outdoor skate park that opened in the spring of 2003. With more than 14,000 square feet of quarter pipes, bank ramps, pyramids, and a "tot lot" for little tikes, this is a challenging state-of-the-art skate park. A concrete bowl section with a snake run completes the park. Day passes and week passes are available for the skate park. The Y also has an outdoor water park that features two swimming pools. The upper pool is known as the deep well pool, with a depth of 12 feet and a 1-meter platform diving board. An area in this 150-gallon pool is designated for water sports like water polo and volleyball. The lower pool is known as the family pool and has a zero-grade entry. Two 25-yard lap lanes are available for recreational swimming. There's also a hydrotherapy area, as well as a very fun 20-foot waterslide.

Wellness programs and family programs, such as Parents Night Out, are available, as is a nursery where children are actively stimulated while parents work out. Children and youth sports leagues include soccer, hockey, basketball, volleyball, and wrestling, and there are adult basketball and volleyball leagues. Call for membership rates. No day passes are issued for most of the facility, except to members of other YMCAs who have a membership card

Traveling on two wheels? Pick up a new Dare County bicycle trails map published by the North Carolina Department of Transportation. It's free at the Outer Banks Visitors Bureau.

with them. Other YMCA members are charged a fee, and access is limited in summer. The one area of the Y to which passes are sold to the general public is the skate park. A day pass is $15; a one-month pass is $103.

Roanoke Island

Nautics Hall Health & Fitness Complex
US 64, Manteo
(252) 473-1191

A competition-size, indoor heated pool is the centerpiece of this health club at the Elizabethan Inn, where water aerobics, swimming lessons, and lap times are offered throughout the year. There's also a workout room with Nautilus and Paramount equipment, free weights, Stairmasters, treadmills, and an aerobicycle. Low-impact and step aerobics instruction is available daily.

Other amenities include an outdoor pool, a hot tub, a racquetball court, sundecks, a sauna, and massage therapy on the premises. Nautics Hall is open from 6:30 A.M. to 9:00 P.M., Monday through Friday, and from 9:00 A.M. to 9:00 P.M. on summer weekends. On Sundays during the off-season, hours are 9:00 A.M. to 5:00 P.M. Monthly memberships cost $50 per person.

BIKING AND SKATING

The flat terrain on these barrier islands is quite a treat for cyclists. But be forewarned that North Carolina Highway 12 is well-trafficked with fast-moving vehicles. Cyclists need to be skilled enough to ride without swerving and to anticipate the actions of car drivers, who, as many bikers know, often don't even see bicycles on the road or yield any sort of right-of-way to cyclists. It is unwise to allow children to ride their bikes on NC 12 and especially on US 158, where drivers often swerve out of their lanes as they're scoping the sights or looking for a business. It's best to restrict children to side streets or to the designated bicycle paths. These side streets and paths are also the best places to in-line skate. All roadways are either dusted or covered with sand.

- Corolla: extended shoulder along NC 12 on the Currituck Outer Banks, some separate paths in private developments
- Duck: separate bike path along NC 12, from Martins Point to Sanderling
- Southern Shores: separate bike path along NC 12 from Town Hall to Duck
- Kitty Hawk: separate bike path starting at Kitty Hawk Elementary School on US 158 south to Kitty Hawk Road
- Kill Devil Hills: separate bike path from the end of West First Street, along Colington Road, ending at NC 12
- Nags Head: separate bike path along NC 12 from MP 11½ to MP 21
- Roanoke Island: separate bike path running the entire length of the island along US 64/264 from the base of the Washington Baum Bridge at Pirate's Cove to the Manns Harbor Bridge
- Hatteras Island: extended shoulder along NC 12
- Ocracoke Island: extended shoulder along NC 12

While there is little crime on the Outer Banks, bicycles do disappear. Lock up carefully, and never leave your bike parked overnight in a front yard or in an easily accessed spot. If your bike is stolen, call the local police. Sometimes bikes are taken on nocturnal "joy rides" and later found by police, so call them before you panic. It's also a good idea to record your bike's serial number for identification purposes.

Since vehicular traffic is very heavy during summer months, and many of the drivers are unaccustomed to the roads, arm yourself with the following safety tips. If you have children who will be biking, make sure that they understand the rules of the road before they leave the driveway.

- Use designated bike paths when available.
- Wear safety helmets.
- Ride on the right side of the road with the flow of traffic.
- Always maintain a single file.
- Obey all traffic rules.
- Cross US 158 at a stoplight whenever possible.
- Use hand signals for stops and turns.
- Don't double up unless the bike is designed for more than one rider.
- Keep your hands on the handlebars.
- Observe pedestrians' right-of-way on walks, paths, and streets.
- Be alert for off-road areas with tire-puncturing cacti and sandspurs.
- Look out for soft sand that can cause a wipeout.
- Use a front-lighted white lamp and a rear red reflector when riding at night.

Corolla and Duck

Ocean Atlantic Rentals
Corolla Light Town Center
NC 12, Corolla
(252) 453-2440

NC 12, Duck
(252) 261-4346

NC 12, MP 10, Nags Head
(252) 441-7823

NC 12, Avon
(252) 995-5868
www.oceanatlanticrentals.com
Bicycles, kiddie carts, and pull-behind bikes (for kids) can be rented by the day or week from each location of Ocean Atlantic Rentals. These rental outfits also lease kayaks, baby equipment, videos,

The narrow tires of racing bikes make these bikes the least safe choice for the sandy roads of the Outer Banks. Beach bikes and mountain bikes have thicker, heavier tires with better grip.

DVDs, and various recreational equipment. Surf lessons are available for surfers and wannabes of any level. Most Ocean Atlantic outposts are open seven days a week year-round, from 10:00 A.M. to 5:00 P.M. in the off-season (call ahead for the Avon location) and 9:00 A.M. to 9:00 P.M. throughout the summer. Delivery is available from Corolla through Hatteras Island.

Kitty Hawk

Moneysworth Beach Home Equipment Rentals
947 West Kitty Hawk Road, Kitty Hawk
(252) 261-6999, (800) 833-5233
www.mworth.com
Moneysworth offers free delivery and pickup of all types of beach and sports rental equipment, including adults' and children's bikes, baby seats, bicycle helmets, volleyball and horseshoe game sets, and beach utility carts. Delivery is from Corolla to Ocracoke.

Kill Devil Hills

The Bike Barn
1312 Wrightsville Boulevard, MP 9½
Kill Devil Hills
(252) 441-3786
The locally owned and operated Bike Barn sells top-of-the-line bikes and biking accessories and is trusted by locals for bicycle repairs on various makes and models. The shop rents bikes (hybrids and Beach Cruisers) for $40 a week or $15 a day, helmets and locks included. Kiddie carts and strollers are available as well. The Bike Barn gives free maps of the area to all renters, and the helpful staff assists with touring information. The Bike Barn is located directly behind Taco Bell.

KDH Cycle
203 NC 12, MP 8½, Kill Devil Hills
(252) 480-3399
Open year-round, this full-service bicycle shop rents excellent equipment at competitive prices. The rental fleet includes cruisers, hybrids, road bikes, and mountain bikes. A 24-speed Trek with suspension rents for $15 per day or $50 per week. Cruisers rent for $10 per day or $35 per week. All safety equipment is included in the rental cost. KDH Cycle offers full-service repair on all makes and models of bicycles and sells parts, clothing, and bicycles, including Trek, Cannondale, and Specialized. KDH Cycle is open daily from 8:00 A.M. to 8:00 P.M. in summer and 9:00 A.M. to 6:00 P.M. in the off-season.

Nags Head

Ocean Atlantic Rentals
NC 12, MP 10, Nags Head
(252) 441-7823
See the complete listing of items available from Ocean Atlantic Rentals in the Corolla and Duck section.

Hatteras Island

Island Cycles
NC 12, Avon
(252) 995-4336, (800) 229-7810
This all-encompassing bicycle shop is in the Food Lion Shopping Center between ACE Hardware and East Carolina Bank. Sales, repairs, advice, and bicycle rentals are offered. Mopeds and scooters are also available for sale or rent. Cyclists lease seven-speed beach cruisers, single-speed beach cruisers, mountain bikes, and road bikes or higher-end bikes, recumbent bicycles, and tandems. Group and off-season rates are available. Island Cycle is open year-round. Summer hours are 9:00 A.M. to 6:00 P.M. Off-season hours vary, so call ahead.

Hatteras Island Boardsports
NC 12, Avon
(252) 995-6160, (866) HIB-WAVE
www.hiboardsports.com

Opened in 2002 by two guys who worked in the recreational retail business on Hatteras Island for several years, this shop has beach bikes to rent in addition to kayaks and other equipment for the many water sports practiced here. Rent for part of the day, the whole day, even an entire week. HIB is open every day in season. Custom surfboards are a recent addition to all they offer.

Lee Robinson's General Store
NC 12, Hatteras Village
(252) 986-2381

This store rents beach cruisers, some with baby seats, seven days a week in season for cycling tours around the southern end of Hatteras Island. Lee Robinson's is open until 11:00 P.M. in the summer, with abbreviated hours during the off-season.

Ocracoke Island

Slushie Stand
NC 12, Ocracoke
(252) 928-1878

Take a breather and rock a spell in a chair on the wraparound porch before renting a two-wheeler. You can't miss the bike racks spread out in front of this juniper-sided building across from Silver Lake Harbor. Traditional coaster and kids' bikes rent by the hour, day, or week from April through November. Daily rates are $15, and weekly rates are $40. Special tandem bicycles and tricycles also can be leased. Call for rental rates. After a long ride through Ocracoke Island, be sure to sample a hand-dipped ice-cream cone or an old-fashioned slushy at the snack bar.

Island Rentals
Silver Lake Road, Ocracoke
(252) 928-5480

This Ocracoke Island outpost rents adult bicycles for $10 a day. It's next to the Ocracoke Harbor Inn and is open Easter through Thanksgiving.

Beach Outfitters
NC 12, Ocracoke
(252) 928-6261, (252) 928-7411

Beach Outfitters, in the Ocracoke Island Realty office, is open all year and accepts reservations. You can rent bikes for $15 a day or $40 a week. See our Weekly and Long-Term Cottage Rentals chapter for more information.

BOWLING

Sometimes even the most dedicated sun-worshippers need an afternoon or evening in air-conditioned comfort.

Nags Head Bowling Center
US 158, MP 10, Nags Head
(252) 441-7077

Open for year-round league and recreational play, this is the Outer Banks's only bowling center. Here, 24 lanes are available for unlimited members of a party as well as a billiards room, pro shop, video arcade, and a cafe serving light meals, sandwiches, wine, beer, and hamburgers. Laser light and glow-in-the-dark bowling is offered at 10:00 P.M. on Friday and Saturday nights. Bowling costs $4.50 per game, and shoes rent for $3.00. Nags Head Bowling is open from 10:00 A.M. to midnight Monday through Thursday and 10:00 A.M. to 1:00 A.M. Friday through Sunday. Call for league information.

CLIMBING

Rock-climbing walls are available for all ages at the following locations.

Kitty Hawk Kites/Carolina Outdoors
Monteray Plaza, NC 12, Corolla
(252) 453-3685, (800) FLY-THIS

The Outer Banks YMCA in Nags Head has the only public skateboard park on the Outer Banks. Call (252) 449-8897 for details.

Across from Jockey's Ridge, US 158, MP 13
Nags Head
(252) 441-4124

Hatteras Landing, NC 12, Hatteras Village
(252) 986-1446
www.kittyhawk.com
If you're itching to climb, try one of Kitty Hawk Kites/Carolina Outdoors's climbing walls. Two climbs and basic instruction cost $7.00 per person. Rappelling equipment, climbing shoes, and ropes are all part of the package.

In the Nags Head store, scale the 22-foot-high wall with four main routes and an overhang for extra challenges. At Monteray Plaza, there's a 25-foot climbing wall with four main routes and an overhang. The Nags Head location is open year-round, but only on weekends in winter. The climbing wall in the Nags Head location is indoors, while the walls at Corolla and Hatteras are outside. Consider the weather when choosing the wall to climb. Call for hours at other locations.

DOLPHIN TOURS, BOAT RIDES, AND PIRATE TRIPS

Most Outer Banks boat cruises are included in our Water Sports and Fishing chapters. However, a few unusual ventures are mentioned here as well. These trips, of course, are weather-dependent and available only during warmer spring and summer months. Reservations are recommended for each of these tours. Unlike sailing and more participatory water adventures, you don't have to be able to swim to enjoy these activities and you probably won't even get wet on board these boats as they ply through the shallow sounds.

Nags Head

Bodie Island Adventures
Nags Head–Manteo Causeway
Nags Head
(252) 441-6822

For an up-close glimpse of bottlenose dolphins playing in Roanoke Sound, this company has daily trips throughout the summer. Dolphin trips are led on a 40-foot pontoon boat that can accommodate up to 44 passengers. Along the way, you'll see the Bodie Island marshes, the Bodie Island Lighthouse, Pelican Island, osprey nests, and a variety of other wildlife, including dolphins. This company also offers thrill-a-minute airboat rides along the same area south of Nags Head. Airboats, which can accommodate 14 people, are noisy and fast, so think twice about bringing very young children. Both trips cost $20 for adults and $10 for kids.

Nags Head Dolphin Watch
Willett's Wetsports, Nags Head–Manteo Causeway, Nags Head
(252) 449-8999
www.dolphin-watch.com
If you're interested in bottlenose dolphins, this is the best way to get to know more about them. Nags Head Dolphin Watch is run by a team of independent dolphin researchers who conduct the trips to pay for their ongoing research. The team of expert naturalists leads dolphin watches through Roanoke Sound three times a day, six days a week beginning the week before Memorial Day through the end of September. Two-hour tours are given on a speedy pontoon boat holding 36 people. Along the way you'll see bottlenose dolphins and learn about their fascinating feeding and social behavior and also about local ecology, history, and wildlife. Cost is $20 for adults and $15 for kids age 12 and younger. The researchers take photos of the dolphins' dorsal fins on every trip, and they call dolphins they see by name.

Roanoke Island

The *Crystal Dawn*
Pirate's Cove Marina, Manteo
(252) 473-5577
www.themefifty.com/crystaldawn

Sunset cruises around Roanoke Island take place every evening except Sunday throughout the summer on this sturdy, two-story 65-foot vessel that accommodates 100 passengers. Trips include commentary about the Outer Banks, while the boat cruises past Andy Griffith's house, Roanoke Island Festival Park, and Jockey's Ridge. The boat departs at 6:30 P.M., returning about 90 minutes later. Adult admission is $8.00 per person, and children 10 and younger pay $6.00 each. This is also a fishing headboat; for additional information see our Fishing chapter.

Outer Banks Cruises
Queen Elizabeth Avenue, Manteo
(252) 473–1475
www.outerbankscruises.com
Outer Banks Cruises offers dolphin tours, sightseeing tours, and evening cruises aboard the 53-foot covered pontoon boat *Capt. Johnny,* which can accommodate 49 passengers. The dolphin-watch tours are offered in Roanoke Sound from June through October, and ninth-generation native Capt. Stuart Wescott has a knack for finding the playful mammals. He even recognizes many of them by their fins and knows the names given them by local researchers. Dolphin sightings are guaranteed: If you don't see any on your trip, you are given a rain check for a free ride another time. The two-hour cruises cost $25 for adults and $15 for children age 12 and younger. The shrimp and crab cruise is educational, fun, and very popular. A two-hour cruise is $265 for six passengers, who will sort through a shrimp net on board the *Capt. Johnny.* Evening cruises are available by charter; call for schedules and rates. The *Capt. Johnny* is docked on the Manteo waterfront next to the little bridge that heads to Roanoke Island Festival Park.

Downeast Rover
Manteo Waterfront Marina, Manteo
(252) 473–4866
www.downeastrover.com
A 55-foot topsail schooner, the *Downeast*

Rover tall ship is a modern reproduction of a 19th-century sailing vessel. Two-hour cruises onto the placid waters of Roanoke Sound delight passengers with views of dolphin, osprey, heron, and seabirds. A hands-on adventure is also possible on this lovely boat: Passengers may help trim the sails and take a turn at the wheel. Tickets can be purchased on the *Downeast Rover,* which also has a ship's store and restroom on board. Deck seating and a belowdecks lounge are available. Daytime cruises are $15 for children age 2 to 12 and $25 for adults; they depart at 11:00 A.M. and 2:00 P.M. daily. Sunset cruises are $30 per person; they depart at 6:30 P.M. in the summer, earlier in the spring and fall. Call for updates and off-season schedules. Reservations are recommended but not required. Private charters for weddings, parties, and other special occasions are available. The *Downeast Rover* sails from early spring to late fall.

Outer Banks Jet Boats
Manteo Waterfront Marina, Manteo
(252) 441–4124
www.outerbanksjetboats.com
Take an adventure-packed ride with a Coast Guard–licensed captain on Outer Banks Jet Boats. A 34-foot boat, named *The Yellow Bird,* holds up to 24 passengers and departs on 90-minute trips from Manteo's scenic waterfront. The first 30 minutes take you on a search in the sound for dolphins, which are usually pretty easy to find. Along your journey, you'll see osprey, pelicans, cormorants, gulls, ducks, and other wildlife. During the next 30 minutes, you tour Wanchese by water and explore a working fishing harbor and see old wrecks and large and small fishing boats. After viewing uninhabited islands and navigating natural waterways, you get a final 30-minute thrill under full jet-boat power. It's a fun ride for all ages. Trips depart between 9:00 A.M. and 5:30 P.M. and cost $29 for adults and $15 for children younger than age 12. Call for reservations or purchase tickets at Carolina Outdoors at Manteo Waterfront.

Hatteras Island

Captain Clam
Oden's Dock, NC 12, Hatteras Village
(252) 986-2365
The *Captain Clam* is a fishing headboat (see our Fishing chapter) that also offers family-style pirate cruises that are a hit with the kids. The pirate cruise is Wednesday, Thursday, and Friday in summer from 6:00 to 7:00 P.M. The crew dresses as pirates and tells tales about Blackbeard and the area's pirate history as you cruise around Pamlico Sound. Complimentary swords and eye patches are given to every passenger. Cruises cost $20 (passengers younger than age 3 cruise free) and are available June through September. The boat can hold 40 people.

Miss Hatteras
Oden's Dock, NC 12, Hatteras Village
(252) 986-2365
www.odensdock.com/misshatteras
The headboat *Miss Hatteras,* which ties up at Oden's Dock, offers dolphin tours on Wednesday, Thursday, and Friday evenings from 6:30 to 8:00 P.M. in summer. Bird-watching cruises are available.

Ocracoke

The Windfall
The Community Store Docks
NC 12, Ocracoke
(252) 928-7245
www.villagecraftsmen.com/windfall
Sail around Blackbeard's former haunts aboard this gaff-rigged schooner that seats up to 30 passengers. One-hour cruises depart from The Community Store docks several times daily during summer months and cost $20 per adult, $10 for kids. The longer sunset cruise is $25 per person. Call for the schedule.

GO-KARTS

If you're looking for a way to race around without getting a speeding ticket, several go-kart rental outlets offer riders a thrill a minute on exciting, curving tracks. Drivers have to be at least 12 years old to take the wheel at most of these places, but younger children are often allowed to strap themselves in beside adults to experience the fast-paced action.

Corolla

Corolla Raceway
TimBuck II Shopping Village
NC 12, Corolla
(252) 453-9100
Corolla Raceway is the sister track of Nags Head Raceway. In TimBuck II Shopping Village, it features one large track with 16 cars. The go-kart raceway is open Easter through November. Corolla Raceway also has free-standing, gas-powered bumper cars. For more entertainment, a family arcade is on-site. Summer hours are 10:00 A.M. until 11:00 P.M. daily.

Kill Devil Hills

Colington Speedway
1064 Colington Road, Kill Devil Hills
(252) 480-9144
Colington Speedway features three tracks and about 40 Indy-style two-seaters or NASCAR-style 5.5 horsepower cars. Riders choose a kiddie track, a family road course, or a slick track. The facility's gift shop features NASCAR items, Outer Banks souvenirs, and children's toys. Colington Speedway is open daily from Memorial Day through Labor Day until 10:00 P.M. The track is also open on weekends until 10:00 P.M. in the spring. Call for opening hours and more information.

Nags Head

Dowdy's Go-Karts
NC 12, MP 11, Nags Head
(252) 441-5122

This is one of the area's oldest go-kart tracks. All the cars are only a few years old and turn tightly around the oval track. Outdoor bleachers provide a perfect place for parents to watch this noisy sport. These motorized karts can be ridden daily throughout the summer starting mid-morning until 11:00 P.M.

Speed-n-Spray Action Park
US 158, MP 15½, Nags Head
(252) 480-2877

This racetrack treats drivers to wild rides around quick curves that twist back toward the blacktop just as you think you might slip off into the sound. It's open from early May through September daily. Call for prices.

Nags Head Raceway
US 158, MP 16, Nags Head
(252) 480-4639

Speed demons and thrill seekers revel in this chock-full-of-fun roadway, complete with two-seater karts and slick new racers. Drivers time themselves trying to beat the clock or sprinting against their friends in hurried heats. Nags Head Raceway is open April through Thanksgiving. Calmer pursuits can be had at the family arcade on the premises. Summer hours are from 10:00 A.M. until 11:00 P.M., seven days a week.

Hatteras Island

Waterfall Action Park
NC 12, Rodanthe
(252) 987-2213

This sound-to-sea amusement area offers the biggest selection of go-kart tracks on the Outer Banks—and more recreational opportunities in a single spot than anywhere else on Hatteras Island. Here, kids of all ages enjoy seven separate race car

tracks where drivers test their skills on a different style vehicle at each pit stop. Wet racers are great for hot afternoon sprints against the wind—and other boaters. Bumper boats, two minigolf courses, waterslides, and a snack bar also are open from 11:00 A.M. to 10:00 P.M. daily May through October.

HANG GLIDING

The closest any human being will ever get to feeling like a bird is by flying beneath the brightly colored wings of a hang glider, with arms outstretched and only the wind all around. Lessons are available for fliers of all ages. Just watching these winged creatures soaring atop Jockey's Ridge or catching air lifts above breakers along the Atlantic is enough to make bystanders want to test their wings.

Kitty Hawk Kites/Carolina Outdoors
US 158, MP 13, Nags Head
(252) 441-4124, (800) FLY-THIS
www.kittyhawk.com

Kitty Hawk Kites, the country's most popular hang-gliding school, offers various ways to learn how to fly. The company's headquarters, in Nags Head across from Jockey's Ridge State Park, faces the main training site on the largest sand dune in the East. Here learn to fly solo 5 to 15 feet over the soft, forgiving sand, or soar through the clouds at altitudes up to 2,000 feet with an instructor. Either method, offered at various locations along the Outer Banks, is an exhilarating experience you'll never forget and undoubtedly will return home to brag about.

If hang gliding has kindled your desire to fly, Kitty Hawk Kites can also help you train to become a certified pilot. A number of packages are designed to help you achieve your goal.

This school, the world's largest, has taught more than 250,000 students to fly since 1974. No experience is necessary, and there are no age limitations. As long as you weigh within the parameters, you can fly!

Tandem hang gliding instruction is offered at three locations along the Outer Banks. There are no age restrictions and no minimum weight requirement for tandem instruction, which is also accessible to the disabled. Kitty Hawk Kites offers two methods of instruction—by plane or boat. Rates for tandem lessons begin at around $115.

Reservations are required for most recreation, so be sure to call ahead. Discount packages are available. Ask about fun and exciting events for adventure enthusiasts of all ages throughout the season!

The oldest continuous hang-gliding competition in the country is held at Jockey's Ridge State Park. Kitty Hawk Kites sponsors the Annual Hang Gliding Spectacular and Air Games, which began in 1973. Visit www.hangglidingspectacular.com for more information.

KITE FLYING

Kite flying is not what it used to be. Thanks to modern technology, today it's an adventurous, interactive activity, even a competitive sport. And the Outer Banks is the perfect place to try your hand at it, since one of the top kite stores in the world, Kitty Hawk Kites, is here. There are plenty of open spaces to fly kites on the Outer Banks, though Jockey's Ridge State Park in Nags Head is the absolute best because it offers acres unobstructed by power lines and trees.

Kitty Hawk Kites/Carolina Outdoors
US 158, MP 13, Nags Head
(252) 441–4124
www.kittyhawk.com
This is the only dedicated kite store in the area, and it offers an enormous range of

kites, from the backyard variety to competition style, which come with an instructional video. The staff is knowledgeable about what they sell, and they can help you pick out just the right kite for your skill level. In addition to lessons and repairs, they offer kite-making workshops in summer. There are several locations of Kitty Hawk Kites on the Outer Banks, but the Nags Head location across from Jockey's Ridge has the largest selection. This company hosts several kite-flying events throughout the year, including the annual Outer Banks Stunt Kite Competition and Festival at Jockey's Ridge in October. See our Annual Events chapter for more kite events.

MINIATURE GOLF COURSES

No beach vacation is complete without the timeless activity of miniature golf. More than a dozen minigolf courses adorn the Outer Banks from Corolla through Hatteras Island. Themed fairways featuring African animals, circus clowns, and strange obstacles await even the most amateur club-swinging families. Small children enjoy the ease of some of these holes, and even skilled golfers can get into the par 3 grass courses that have been growing in numbers over recent years.

You can tee off at most places by 10:00 A.M. Many courses stay open past midnight for night owls to enjoy. Several of these attractions offer play-all-day packages for a single price. Almost all minigolf courses operate seasonally, and since they are all outside, their openings are weather dependent.

Corolla

The Grass Course
NC 12, Corolla
(252) 453–4198
Offering the Outer Banks's first natural-grass course, these soundside greens are

open seven days a week throughout the summer season from 10:00 A.M. to 11:00 P.M. The 18-hole course includes par 3s, 4s, and 5s. The undulating hills winding around natural dunes provide intriguing challenges for beginning and better golfers. The course is open from April to October and at Thanksgiving and Christmas. The Grass Course sells hot dogs and barbecue.

Kitty Hawk

The Promenade
US 158, MP 1/4, Kitty Hawk
(252) 261-4900
This family fun park includes Victorian-style buildings, turn-of-the-20th-century streetlights, waterside recreation, a children's playground, and an 18-hole themed minigolf course called Waterfall Greens. There's also a 9-hole, par 3, natural-grass putting course, complete with separate putting greens; a target driving range; a par 3 chip-and-putt 9-hole course; and an 18-hole course. A restaurant, snack bar, and picnic tables are on-site. The Promenade is open Easter weekend through early October. Summer hours are from 8:30 A.M. to midnight, seven days a week.

Paradise Golf
US 158, MP 5½, Kitty Hawk
(252) 441-7626
More challenging than the usual minigolf fairways, this natural-grass site includes two 18-hole, par 56 courses. Most holes are 110 feet from the tees. The courses are open from 10:00 A.M. until midnight daily during summer. For one price ($7.00 for adults, $5.00 for children) you can play all day.

Kill Devil Hills

Lost Treasure Golf
US 158, MP 7½, Kill Devil Hills
(252) 480-0142

One of the barrier islands' newer—and most attention-getting—minigolf parks, Lost Treasure Golf features two 18-hole courses situated among five waterfalls illuminated with different colors at night. Kids love the little train that carts them up to the first hole and through a series of caves and mines. Professor Hacker, a fictional adventurer, tells his story about gold and diamond expeditions that kids read about as they play. Lost Treasure Golf is open April through November. Hours are 9:00 A.M. to 11:00 P.M. daily in the summer and are decreased accordingly in the off-season.

Nags Head

Galaxy Golf
NC 12, MP 11, Nags Head
(252) 441-5875
Aliens, flying saucers, and outer space objects surround 36 lighted holes of minigolf at this popular Outer Banks course on the Beach Road. Galaxy golf is open on weekends in April, early May, September, and October and daily throughout the summer. In-season hours are 9:00 A.M. to midnight. Children younger than four with a paying adult play free. The price doesn't change after dark as it does on many minigolf courses.

Blackbeard's Golf and Arcade
US 158, MP 16, Nags Head
(252) 441-4541
The Outer Banks's most infamous pirate wields his 6-foot sword above these greens. Open daily, summers only, until at least 10:00 P.M., Blackbeard's includes a video arcade for alternate entertainment after putting around.

Jurassic Putt
US 158, MP 16, Nags Head
(252) 441-6841
Life-size models of dinosaurs from the Jurassic period hover over and among Jurassic Putt's greens, delighting kids and adults alike. Two 18-hole courses

wind through caves and streams and around the dinosaur models. Jurassic Putt is open daily from mid-March until November. Hours are 9:00 A.M. until midnight. Call or stop by for rates.

Hatteras Island

Avon Golf
NC 12, Avon
(252) 995-5480
Adjacent to the Avon Pier, this 18-hole, natural-grass course is open from 11:00 A.M. to 11:00 P.M., seven days a week all summer. You can play as many games as you can squeeze in from noon until 6:00 P.M. for $8.00. In the off-season, you can play all day for $8.00. Avon Golf is open from Easter through the week after Thanksgiving, depending on business.

Cool Wave Ice Cream Shop
and Miniature Golf
NC 12, Buxton
(252) 995-6366
Located in the neighborhood of the Cape Hatteras Lighthouse, this nine-hole course is open from Easter through Thanksgiving. Summer hours are noon to 10:00 P.M., seven days a week. Call for prices. If you play one round of nine holes, the second time around is free. Ice cream, milk shakes, and the best banana splits on Hatteras provide extra incentive to play a good game.

Frisco Mini Golf and Go-Karts
NC 12, Frisco
(252) 995-6325
This 18-hole championship miniature golf course is a little more challenging than the average minigolf game, though all levels of players will enjoy the experience. Waterfalls splash amid the well-manicured course, and children feed goldfish. In addition to the course, there are also two go-kart tracks, a concession stand, and an arcade on the premises.

MOVIE THEATERS

On some steamy summer afternoons or those rainy Saturday nights, there's no better place to be than inside a dark, air-conditioned movie theater, catching the latest flick with a companion. First-run movies are offered at most Outer Banks theaters. Popcorn, candy, and sodas are, of course, sold at all movie houses.

Corolla

RC Theatres Corolla Movies 4
Monteray Plaza, NC 12, Corolla
(252) 453-2999
This seasonal establishment in Monteray Plaza includes four wide screens and is open from May through Labor Day. The theater reopens for shows again from Thanksgiving through New Year's Day. Movies are shown seven days a week from 2:00 P.M. to midnight. Tickets are $8.00 for adults and $6.00 for children younger than age 11. Matinees cost $6.00 for children and adults.

Kill Devil Hills

RC Theatres Movies 10
US 158, MP 6½, Kill Devil Hills
(252) 441-5630
This multiplex cinema opened in 2004 and houses 10 screens. Films are shown seven days a week in season from 2:00 P.M. until midnight. On summer days when the weather is bad, the theater adds a rainy-day showing at 11:00 A.M.

Roanoke Island

Pioneer Theatre
113 Budleigh Street, Manteo
(252) 473-2216
The nation's oldest theater operated continuously by one family, the Pioneer is

filled with nostalgia and smells of just-buttered popcorn. And it's been showing flicks since 1934. For the $5.00 admission price—and the old-fashioned feel of the place—it can't be beat. Even the popcorn, sodas, and candy are a great deal. The Pioneer is open year-round, and all movies start at 8:00 P.M. daily. Listings change weekly on Friday; call for a synopsis of the current show. See our Attractions chapter for more information.

Hatteras Island

RC Theatres Hatteras Cineplex 4
Hatteras Island Plaza, NC 12, Avon
(252) 995-9060
With four screens and first-run movies year-round, this large movie house shows films all day on weekends and throughout the summer, and on evenings only in the off-season. Admission is $8.00 for adults and $6.00 for children. Matinee shows are $6.00 for everyone.

NATURE TRAIL HIKES

The Outer Banks is home to several diverse ecosystems that house a wide variety of wildlife. If you love nature, you'll love the many self-guided nature trails that allow you to see the diversity of the Outer Banks up close. You can hike in wildlife refuges, across sand dunes, and through maritime forests. The National Park Service offers some guided walks; call (252) 473-2111 or visit www.nps.gov/caha for more information.

Corolla

Audubon Wildlife Sanctuary
at Pine Island
An unmarked trail leads through this 5,000-acre wildlife sanctuary, a protected habitat for birds, deer, rabbits, and a variety of plants. Park at The Sanderling Inn

to access the 2.5-mile soundside path through a portion of the sanctuary.

Nags Head

Nags Head Woods Preserve
Part of The Nature Conservancy, Nags Head Woods is a preserved maritime forest with diverse flora and fauna. There are more than 5 miles of trails through forest, dunes, swamp, and pond habitats. You'll also see 19th-century cemeteries. For maps and start locations, go to the visitor center at 701 West Ocean Acres Drive in Kill Devil Hills or call (252) 441-2525.

Jockey's Ridge State Park
Climbing the tallest sand dune on the East Coast is a challenging hike, but two nature trails wind through the lower regions of the dune. The Soundside Nature Trail is an easy 45-minute walk, and the Tracks in the Sand Trail is a 1.5-mile walk. Start at the state park visitor center at MP 12 in Nags Head.

Roanoke Island

Thomas Hariot Nature Trail at Fort Raleigh
This trail winds through a heavily wooded area from the Fort Raleigh National Historic Site to Roanoke Sound. Along the way are several interpretive markers with Hariot's descriptions of Roanoke Island in the 16th century. Call the Fort Raleigh National Historic Site at (252) 473-5772 for information.

Freedmen's Trail
This 2-mile trail commemorates the history of the Freedmen's Colony, a Roanoke Island community that provided a safe haven for freed slaves during the Civil War. Access to the trail is near the Elizabethan Gardens entrance, and exhibits are at the end of the trail on Roanoke Sound. Call the National Park Service for information at (252) 473-5772.

Colorful Beach Glass

Beachcombing has always been a time-honored activity on the Outer Banks. The ocean can deliver treasures from the truly valuable to the absolutely absurd—once grapefruits littered the beaches from Corolla to Nags Head. Of all the "junk" that can turn up on the beach, beach glass remains a prized find for some collectors. One person's trash is often another's treasure, but in the case of beach glass, trash literally becomes treasure.

For those not in the know, "beach glass" is simply pieces of glass or pottery that have been worn by waves, wind, and sand to a frosted, soft-edged jewel. As the elements wear the broken bits, the glass develops tiny crystals on its surface, literally transforming it into a gem. Some pieces may be only 30 years old and come from a common source, such as a soda bottle, while others may be hundreds of years old and quite rare.

In his beautifully illustrated book *Pure Sea Glass,* Richard LaMotte explores the history of the glass itself, including how the glass acquires its frosted patina and the processes used in its original production. Most prized pieces are coveted for their color, and the coloring of the original glass itself can be an indication of its history and rarity. Most of the beach glass you'll find comes from the mass-produced bottles of the late 19th and early 20th century, with green and brown being the most common. Clear glass became popular a bit later, but some of the chemicals used to keep the glass clear actually change over time, coloring the once-translucent pieces a variety of hues, from purple to pale yellow. Other colors of beach glass include almost the

Mainland

Alligator River National Wildlife Refuge
Two trails lead through this refuge. Sandy Ridge Wildlife Trail starts at the south end of the dirt Buffalo City Road. The trail, a half-mile out and a half-mile back, has footpaths and a boardwalk. Creef Cut Wildlife Trail starts on US 64 at the intersection with Milltail Road. A kiosk with parking marks the trailhead. It's also a half-mile out and back. Additionally, it has a fishing dock, an overlook, and a boardwalk. Both trails are wheelchair accessible. Call (252) 473-1131 for information.

Bodie Island

Bodie Island Dike Trail and Pond Trail
Starting at the Bodie Island Lighthouse, two trails wind through marsh and wetlands to the sound. Call the light station at (252) 441-5711 for information.

Pea Island

Pea Island National Wildlife Refuge
North Pond Trail starts behind Pea Island Visitor Center and leads hikers on a half-mile, 30-minute walk around the refuge. The quarter-mile Salt Flats Trail starts at the

entire spectrum, from very rare reds and oranges (colored with gold or selenium) to deep purples and blues. LaMotte estimates the chances of finding a piece of truly orange beach glass to be about 1 in 10,000 pieces collected.

While beach glass can be found on almost any beach, some places can be better hunting grounds than others. Beaches near active waterfronts will tend to be more productive, since these areas would have introduced more waste glass into the water. Also of particular importance is the prevailing wind and weather patterns, since beach glass is frosted by both waves and wind. Though the Outer Banks was never a major waterfront, it has certainly been visited by its share of strong storms over the last few centuries, and the hundreds of shipwrecks that make up the "Graveyard of the Atlantic" provide the beachcomber with ample opportunities to find beach glass.

Once collected, beach glass can provide the enthusiast with material for an almost unlimited number of projects, from jewelry to mosaics to lamps. Some glass artisans have made entire lampshades from beach glass, using stained-glass techniques, while others simply fill a favorite old jar and place it on a windowsill. In 2004, the first Sea Glass Festival was held in Gloucester Massachusetts, and featured authors, speakers, and artisans showing their work, which included clay pots, candles, lamps, and even switch plates.

The magic of beach glass lies in its ability to transport us back to the beach. Its colorful frost reminds us of the timelessness of the ocean and the perpetual cycles of wind, waves, and tides. Beach glass easily evokes the smell of salt in the air, the feel of cold sand on bare feet, and the often turbulent history of the coast.

north end of North Pond Trail. These are favorite walks for bird-watchers year-round, but especially in late fall and winter when migrating swans, ducks, and geese winter here. Call (252) 987-2394 for information.

Buxton

Buxton Woods Nature Trail
Starting at Cape Point Campground, this 0.75-mile trail leads through maritime forest, across dunes, and into freshwater marshes. Small plaques along the way explain the fragile maritime forest ecosystem.

Ocracoke

Hammock Hills Trail
This 0.75-mile trail, about a 30-minute walk, leads through the salt marsh and forest. The trailhead is north of the village on NC 12; signs direct you to it. Call the Ocracoke Island Visitor Center at (252) 928-4531 for information.

Portsmouth Island
This ghost-town island is accessible only by boat, but once you get there you'll find numerous trails that lead you on a fascinating exploration of this island, past abandoned but restored buildings. A

2-mile-long trail leads from the village to the beach through the heart of the island. Call Cape Lookout National Seashore for information at (252) 728-2250.

PARASAILING

If you've always wanted to float high above the water beneath a colorful parachute, adventures await at various locations along the Outer Banks. Although a boat pulls from below, allowing the wind to lift you toward the clouds, you don't get wet on these outdoor trips over the sounds unless you want to. You take off and land on the back of the boat. Riders soar with the seagulls above whitecaps and beach cottages. People of any age, without any athletic ability at all, enjoy parasailing and find it one of their most memorable experiences. And it's safe, too; unbreakable ropes are standard.

Corolla

Kitty Hawk Watersports
TimBuck II Shopping Village
NC 12, Corolla
(252) 453-6900
www.kittyhawksports.com
Parasail flights are offered daily throughout the summer at this shop, owned by Kitty Hawk Sports. Rates are set according to the heights you choose; call for rates and schedules.

Duck

North Duck Watersports
NC 12, Duck
(252) 261-4200
This watersports center is 3 miles north of Duck, on the border of Duck and Sanderling. Parasailing trips are offered at heights from 400 to 1,400 feet above the Currituck Sound. Call ahead for reservations and rates. Parasailing is offered in the spring, summer, and fall.

Nor'Banks Sailing Center
NC 12, Duck
(252) 261-7100
www.norbanks.com
Specializing in single, tandem, and triple flights, this was one of the original parasailing locations on the Outer Banks. All vessels that give you your ride are Coast Guard–inspected and are able to take passengers up 400 to 1,400 feet. Parasailing is available from May through October.

Kitty Hawk

The Promenade Watersports
US 158, MP ¼, Kitty Hawk
(252) 261-4400
The Promenade offers parasailing with an experienced captain in Currituck Sound. Persons of any age can take off for a single, tandem, or triple ride up to 1,400 feet.

Nags Head

The Waterworks
US 158, MP 17, Nags Head
(252) 441-8875
www.waterworks.ws
Parasailing captains from The Waterworks can take you high. Uplifting experiences are offered daily from April through November. These 8- to 15-minute flights allow you to float at 400 to 1,400 feet; cost depends on how high you want to fly.

Hatteras Island

Hatteras Watersports
NC 12, Salvo
(252) 987-2306
Hatteras Watersports offers parasailing trips from June through September. Take single or tandem flights without ever getting wet. Flight height ranges from 700 to 1,300 feet. Reservations are required.

Island Parasail
NC 12, Avon
(252) 995-0177
All summer long, you can soar over the Pamlico Sound beneath a rainbow-colored parachute based at this Avon outpost. Ten-minute flights are offered from 9:30 A.M. to 6:30 P.M. daily at heights of 700 to 1,200 feet.

RACES

Nags Head Woods Annual 5K Run
Nags Head Woods Preserve
Kill Devil Hills
(252) 441-2431
The Nags Head Woods Run is a well-loved spring tradition on the Outer Banks. Close to 400 runners, from ages 6 to 60 and beyond, gather to run (or walk) the soft dirt road that winds through this rare maritime forest. Afterwards, an awards ceremony then a big party are held at a local restaurant. There is no race-day registration so you must register early.

Outer Banks Triathlon
Roanoke Island
(252) 480-0050
The Dare Voluntary Action Center (DVAC) sponsors this annual sanctioned sprint-distance triathlon each September. The 0.6-mile swim, 15-mile bicycle ride, and 3.1-mile run are held on Roanoke Island, starting at the Old Swimming Hole on Airport Road next to the North Carolina Aquarium. Contact DVAC at the number above or register at www.active.com.

Advice 5K Turkey Trot
Duck
(252) 255-1050
www.advice5.com
The annual Turkey Trot is a Thanksgiving Day tradition in Duck. The race starts at Advice 5¢, a bed-and-breakfast in the village, and ends at the Red Sky Cafe, for a post-race party. There is no race-day registration. You must register in advance at the Red Sky Cafe at 1197 Duck Road or by mail: Advice 5K, c/o Advice 5¢, P.O. Box 8278, Duck, NC 27949. Entry fee for walkers and runners is $20. The race is limited to 350 people.

ROLLER SKATING

Family Life Center
US 158, MP 11½, Nags Head
(252) 441-4941
A recreational facility for the Outer Banks Worship Center, this Christian-affiliated roller-skating rink behind the ark-shaped church is open to the public on Friday and Saturday evenings from 7:00 to 9:30 P.M. all year. Here, kids rent regular, old-fashioned roller skates for $5.00 and cruise around the slick floor. Table tennis and video games also are available, as are special event and birthday bookings.

TENNIS

Many cottage rental developments throughout the Outer Banks have private tennis courts for their guests. Outdoor public tennis courts include the following free courts:

- Kill Devil Hills—two hard-surface courts are located near the Kill Devil Hills Fire Department at MP 6 on US 158, and four hard-surface courts are beside the Kill Devil Hills Water Plant on Mustian Street.
- Nags Head—a public court is behind Kelly's Restaurant, off US 158 at MP 10½.
- Roanoke Island—courts are available at Manteo High School on Wingina Avenue and at Manteo Middle School on US 64/264 after school hours.
- Hatteras Island—courts are available at Cape Hatteras School on NC 12 in Buxton after school hours.

If you don't own a racquet or left yours back on the mainland, you can rent one by the day or week from Ocean Atlantic Rentals (see our Weekly and Long-Term Cottage Rentals chapter).

Corolla

Pine Island Racquet Club
NC 12, between Corolla and Duck
(252) 453-8525
Home to the Outer Banks's only indoor tennis courts, Pine Island is 2.5 miles north of the Sanderling Inn. It is open to the public year-round for recreational play, and several tournaments are held each season.

Three hard-surface courts are under a vaulted roof for air-conditioned or heated comfort, while two clay courts and two platform tennis courts are outdoors. Restroom, locker, and shower facilities are included.

Pine Island also has two ball machines, a radar gun for timing serves, and a videotape analysis machine to help improve your game. Tennis pro Rick Ostlund and his assistant Betty Wright teach clinics for adults and children and offer individualized instruction at any skill level. The pro shop sells racquets, clothes, and tennis accessories and provides stringing services.

Reservations are suggested for indoor and outdoor courts, which cost $28 an hour. Pine Island is open every day except Christmas from at least 9:00 A.M. in the off-season and from 8:00 A.M. in season.

WATERSLIDES, ARCADES, AND OTHER AMUSEMENTS

On hot afternoons when you're ready for a break from sand and salt water, slip on down to a water park, and splash into one of its big pools. Most of these parks are open daily during the summer—some well into the evening. Waterslides generally close on rainy days.

Among the recreational outposts, many include video arcades in their offerings, but the Outer Banks's amusement centers also offer brightly lit computerized games and other unusual activities.

We can't list everything the owners of these establishments include, so you'll have to experience these places for yourself to discover all the surprises in store.

Hatteras Island

Waterfall Action Park
NC 12, Rodanthe
(252) 987-2213
You can't miss this palm-tree-lined playground, geared for hours of fun for both adults and kids. An Outer Banks fixture for more than 20 years, this amusement park has more than 20 rides and the area's only bungee-jumping outlet for daredevils. Two waterslides, the Corkscrew and the Cyclone, give heart-thumping, thrill-filled rides.

But this wonderland has a multitude of other offerings: two minigolf courses, model Grand Prix race cars, Winston Cup stock cars, Outlaw sprint cars, NASCAR super trucks, and free-fall go-karts—not to mention speedboats and bumper cars. Children have to be at least 12 years old to ride the adult rides. Kiddie Land features rides for ages three to nine. There's no admission charge to get into the park; call for prices to ride. Your best deal can be had with one of the 40 combination tickets, which save you more money the more you ride. Waterfall Action Park is open daily 10:00 A.M. to 9:00 P.M. from Memorial Day through Labor Day.

Frisco Mini Golf and Go-Karts
NC 12, Frisco
(252) 995-6325
This miniature golf and go-kart establishment also has an 1,800-square-foot arcade that keeps kids entertained on a rainy day with pool tables, air hockey, video games, and other games. A concession booth sells ice cream, snow cones, cotton candy, hot dogs, and drinks.

WATER SPORTS

Water is the Outer Banks's biggest draw. Everywhere you look on the Outer Banks there's wet, wonderful H$_2$O—the deep, blue Atlantic Ocean; the wide, shallow Currituck, Croatan, Roanoke, and Pamlico Sounds; brackish bays and estuaries teeming with wildlife; thick, sopping marshes; and dark, man-made canals sluicing through the islands. And everywhere you look there are people on or in the water. Whether it's on a surfboard, a kiteboard, a windsurfer, a JetSki, a kayak, or just in a bathing suit, everyone eventually finds their way to the water. Numerous watersports establishments happily accommodate anyone's wish to get wet.

Surfing, windsurfing, and kiteboarding are among the area's most popular water sports, next to fishing, which we cover in a chapter of its own. Each year, thousands of novice to expert athletes flock to the Outer Banks to whet their appetites for these outdoor adventures. The Outer Banks is renowned as having the best surf breaks on the East Coast, and the constant wind and wide sounds make for perfect conditions. Be forewarned: You may become addicted and find yourself, like many other watersports enthusiasts, moving to these barrier islands to be closer to the waves and shallow sounds year-round. The gear you need is available at local surf shops and outfitters. Some Outer Banks surf shops lease body boards and skimboards to daredevils who like to skirt the shoreline breakers.

The use of personal watercraft, including JetSkis, Sea Doos, and Wave Runners, has exploded in popularity. Rental outposts are established on the sound shores all along the Outer Banks to satisfy people's need for speed. The less-invasive sports of kayaking, canoeing, and sailing also are readily available, with ecotours and sunset cruises becoming increasingly popular pastimes. For more unusual endeavors, the National Park Service offers occasional snorkeling expeditions for families, and local dive shops will take you out wreck-diving in the Graveyard of the Atlantic. Divers from the world over come to the Outer Banks to explore the numerous shipwrecks on the ocean floor. Several outfitters along the barrier islands rent powerboats for near-shore fishing and waterskiing.

Weather, of course, plays a big factor in whether a particular water sport is currently desirable or even advisable. Many area surf shops offer surfing hotlines and wave or wind updates so you can check conditions. The waters are generally warm enough to get in from May through late September. Even in the off-season months, waters can stay warm enough for bathers to enjoy a quick frolic. In the winter, real watersport devotees take the plunge with a wetsuit. Local boaters and paddlers get out on the water every month of the year and relish the smattering of warm days that we usually get in the dead of winter.

Some water workouts require special training and equipment, and shops and sports schools in almost every area of the Outer Banks rent and teach whatever you need to know. (See our Waves and Weather chapter for information about riptides and other hazards.)

Whether you're an athletic adventurer or a couch potato, you should be able to find exactly what you want in the way of water sports. Kayaking, for example, requires neither physical prowess nor extraordinary skill if you take a few minutes to learn to do it properly. On the flip side, scuba diving in these waters is dangerous without proper training and experience.

In this chapter we give you a rundown of water sports and a list of places to rent or buy equipment and take lessons. We list prices to give you a general idea of how much things cost, but be aware that prices are subject to change.

SURFING

Warmer than New England waters and wielding more consistent waves than most Florida beaches, the Outer Banks's surf is reputed to have the best breaks on the East Coast. Local surfing experts explain that since we are set out farther into the ocean in deeper waters than most other coastal regions, our beaches pick up more swells and wind patterns than any place around. Piers, shipwrecks, and offshore sandbars also create unusual wave patterns. Along with those swells, the Outer Banks has the added bonus of sharp drop-offs and troughs right offshore, which make the waves break with more power and force.

The beaches from Corolla through Ocracoke are some of the only spots left that don't have strict surfing regulations: As long as you keep yourself leashed to your board and stay at least 300 feet away from public piers, you won't get a surfing citation.

By the late 1960s, station wagons loaded with teenagers and their surfboards began arriving on the sparsely populated Outer Banks. Surfers skirted the soft sands each weekend, traveling from Virginia Beach, Virginia, and Ocean City, Maryland, to hang 10 in Outer Banks waves. Hatteras Island native Johnny Connor Jr. said boys sold their boards when they ran out of money. He bought several and rented those surfboards to local friends and newcomers who also wanted to ride the waves.

Though good surf breaks tend to form around fishing piers, it's illegal to surf within 300 feet of a pier—for the surfers' own protection, of course.

In the late 1970s, the East Coast Surfing Championships started here, and they're still held here. The U.S. Championships were held on the Outer Banks in 1978 and 1982. Each summer, and during winter storms, famous surfers can be seen riding the competition circuit along the Atlantic or catching waves for fun.

The Outer Banks surfing subculture, those surfers who live here year-round, is a far cry from the young, suntanned stereotype. Lawyers, engineers, middle-aged parents, waiters, doctors, construction workers, architects, and restaurateurs all have been known to rearrange busy schedules to catch waves. In this region, a "board meeting" may refer to a surf break from work. When the surf is up, almost all surfers, young and old alike, make the necessary excuses to get in the water. If a house-construction crew doesn't show up one day or the grocery store is short on bagboys, assume there are good waves.

Shapers along the barrier islands design, shape, and sell their own boards, with prices ranging from $100 for used models to $600 or more for custom styles. Some stores offer lessons for beginner surfers, and many rent boards for as little as $10 a day plus a deposit. Don't forget board wax, or you won't be riding very long.

The best surfing is from late August through November in hurricane season, when swells from storms are likely to roll toward shore. Midsummer is traditionally the worst time for surfing. On small summer waves it's more fun to surf a longboard.

Surfing is a strenuous sport that requires a good amount of upper-body strength to swim well in wicked waves and paddle on the board. But with a variety of board lengths—and more than 90 miles of oceanfront to choose from—there are usually breaks to suit almost every surfer's style and stamina.

Since the beaches are getting increasingly crowded with summer surfers, some folks understandably don't want to reveal their favorite wave-catching locales. Plus, breaks, which are affected by shifting sandbars, change every year. After fall hurricane season and winter nor'easters, no one really knows which breaks subsided or where they reappear. It takes some looking around in the spring to find new breaks and relinquish old ones.

Piers always make for good breaks because of the sandbars that form around them. In Corolla, there is a good break on the beach in front of the Corolla Light swimming pool. You can't park there unless you're staying in the resort, so park at the south ramp road next to the lighthouse and walk up the beach. Swan Beach in the four-wheel-drive area is also good. Kitty Hawk Pier in Kitty Hawk and Avalon Pier in Kill Devil Hills each boast ample parking and pretty good waves. Also check out the area around First and Second Streets in Kill Devil Hills. Nags Head Pier is a good spot, but also check out the beaches north and south of there, especially around milepost 13.

When swells come from the south, Hatteras Island beaches have the best waves. If you don't mind hiking across the dunes with a board under your arm, Pea Island and Coquina Beach both have waves worth the walk. Rodanthe has always been a popular destination, and its name sparks fond recognition with surfers all over the world. If there are waves, you'll have no trouble spotting the area because you'll see hundreds of surfers squeezing into wet suits along the roadside. The surf is just a short hop over the dunes from the road. The ramps north and south of Salvo are also worth a try. Ramp 34, just north of Avon, is another location, as are the turnout north of Buxton, ramp 49 in Frisco, Frisco Pier, and the public beach access area between Frisco and Hatteras Village.

The best and biggest waves by far roll in around the original site of Cape Hatteras Lighthouse. Here at Cape Point, the beaches jut closest to the Gulf Stream and face in two directions, doubling the chances for good conditions. Concrete and steel groins jut out into the Atlantic,

Is your teenager looking for a happening beach hangout? The Pit in Kill Devil Hills is popular Monday, Wednesday, and Friday evenings when a drug-free, alcohol-free dance party is held from 9:30 P.M. to 1:00 A.M. during the season. Here teens can find out which beach accesses everyone will head to in the daylight hours. As the surf breaks change, so do the gathering spots.

though, so beware of being tossed into these head-bashing barriers.

Surf jargon measures waves in reference to body parts. In the summer, waves along the Outer Banks average knee to waist high, meaning 2 to 3 feet. Fall and winter swells can be head high or double overhead (6 to 8 feet). Many areas along the barrier islands also have strong rip currents, strange sandbars, and shipwrecks—so always surf with a friend and stay alert of water, weather, and beach conditions. You need a wet suit for surfing in the spring, fall, and winter.

Surf Reports

Local radio station WVOD 99.1 offers a daily surf report at 8:45 A.M.

Most surf shops have an even more up-to-the-minute pulse on the surf, but not all provide a formal "surf line" service. Following is a list of numbers to call for the daily wave report. Most shops give the scoop only on the portion of the beach in their geographical area.

**Corolla Surf Shop, Corolla
(252) 453–WAVE**

**Wave Riding Vehicles, Kitty Hawk
(252) 261–3332**

**The Pit, Kill Devil Hills
(252) 480–3128**

Whalebone Surf Shop, Nags Head
(252) 441-6747

Rodanthe Surf Shop, Rodanthe
(252) 987-2435

Natural Art Surf Shop, Buxton
(252) 995-4646

Besides calling for a surf report, you may want to see the conditions for yourself. Thanks to the Internet, you don't even have to leave your house to check on waves. For an online surf report, visit www.surfchex.com or http://surfreport .corollasurfshop.com, or check out surf-cams for the following locations:

Hatteras Lighthouse:
www.eastcoastsurf.com

Avalon Pier: www.avalonpier.com

Surf Shops

Ranging from sublime to specialized to hip, the Outer Banks is inundated with surfshops—hot spots for wave riders of all ages and skill levels. Each summer, surf shop managers post competition schedules for beginners through surfing-circuit riders near the storefronts. Most shops stock gear, and many offer instruction dur-

ing the season. The following list highlights some favorites of Outer Banks surfers.

Corolla Surf Shop
Corolla Light Town Center
110-A Austin Drive, Corolla
(252) 453-WAVE

Monteray Plaza
NC 12, Corolla
(252) 453-9273

TimBuck II Shopping Village
NC 12, Corolla
(252) 453-9273
www.corollasurfshop.com
Corolla Surf Shop is a full-service shop with boards, lessons, sales, repairs, and rentals. Its second store—in the TimBuck II shopping center—has all the goodies of the first store, including a portion of the surfer's museum. The store also has a full line of new surfboards for sale (more than 100 boards are in stock). A good stock of used boards is available for purchase, along with new skateboards, skimboards, and body boards. The store also carries a full skateboard department, clothing, shoes, shades, and jewelry.

Surf lessons, including all equipment, are $60 per student for a two-hour lesson. Up to six people take lessons together. Rentals are available on a daily and weekly basis. Call for rates. The shop is the home

of the Nalu Kai Surf Museum, a free exhibit of 15 collectible surfboards and other surfer memorabilia. Corolla Surf Shop is open year-round. Winter hours vary.

Whalebone Surf Shop
TimBuck II Shopping Village
NC 12, Corolla
(252) 453-2667
www.whalebonesurfshop.com
Whalebone is one of the oldest surf shops on the Outer Banks; owner Jim Vaughn opened his first shop at Whalebone Junction in the 1960s. The Corolla location is right on the sound. The shop sells major brands of surfboards and the best of the smaller brands. The owners and staff are surfers themselves. The store rents surfboards and is well stocked with surfwear and bathing suits for all ages.

Duck Village Outfitters
1207 Duck Road, Duck
(252) 261-7222
www.duckvillageoutfitters.homestead.com
With surfboards and body boards, Duck Village Outfitters (DVO) is surf-shop central for Duck. Surfing lessons are offered daily during the summer season. The shop conducts kayak tours every day in the summer and has a large assortment of rentals and retail items, including bikes, wet suits, fishing equipment, kayaks, and ocean toys.

Wave Riding Vehicles (WRV)
US 158, MP 2, Kitty Hawk
(252) 261-7952
www.waveridingvehicles.com
Carrying top-of-the-line surfboards, apparel, and accessories since 1967, WRV puts its emphasis on what the owner calls "the godfather of water sports"—surfing. Although this year-round shop also sells skateboards and snowboards, it's one of the largest full-service surf shops on the barrier islands. WRV is also the biggest surfboard manufacturing company under one label on the East Coast. The company produces in-house, private-label surfwear, which is sold wholesale from Maine to

Florida and overseas. Surfboards rent for $20 a day in season.

The Pit Surf Shop, Bar and Grill
US 158, MP 9, Kill Devil Hills
(252) 480-3128
www.pitsurf.com
The Pit bills itself as a "surf hangout." The setup includes a 3,000-square-foot surf shop that covers all board sports—surfing, body boarding, skimming, and skateboarding. Owners Steve Pauls and Ben Sproul, both devout surfers, sell a large selection of new, used, and custom boards, including the locally made Gale Force boards, plus a selection of wet suits and related accessories. All boards are available for sale or rent. Surfboards rent for $15 a day or $60 a week, and skimboards rent for $10 a day. Surf lessons and camps are offered in the summer months for groups or individuals. Lessons run about two hours and include board rental and a T-shirt.

Whalebone Surf Shop
US 158, MP 10, Nags Head
(252) 441-6747
www.whalebonesurfshop.com
Surfer-owned and -operated, Whalebone boasts that it has been in business since the 1960s. Major brands of surfboards, and the best of the smaller brands, are available at this well-stocked store. Surfboard rentals are available for trials. The store is open year-round, but hours vary so call ahead.

Secret Spot Surf Shop
US 158, MP 11, Nags Head
(252) 441-4030
www.secretspotsurfshop.com
No secret to surf enthusiasts, Secret Spot is one of the old-timers of the barrier islands' surf scene and claims to have the most boards available. Packed with the best of contemporary and classic boards and favorite surfwear, the store prides itself in catering to both younger and older surfers. The business has manufactured its own surfboards since 1977; the

shop opened five years later. A full line of shortboards, longboards, and custom and used boards is available, along with a selection of wetsuits.

Surfboards rent for $15 daily. Lessons are available. Call the shop or visit the Web site for surf reports. Secret Spot also sells items for women and girls, including sundresses, Ts, bathing suits, shorts, shoes, and accessories. The skate store has a full selection of skateboard paraphernalia, including decks, trucks, wheels, and accessories.

Cavalier Surf Shop
NC 12, MP 13½, Nags Head
(252) 441-7349

This classic shop, the only one on the Beach Road, has been in business since the 1960s. The family-run operation is dedicated to the surfing lifestyle. Cavalier rents a variety of surfboards, boogie boards, and skimboards, plus gloves, booties, and wet suits. They also rent umbrellas, chairs, and rafts for long beach days. Surfboard rentals start at $15 a day. When you're not in the surf, rent a surf video for excitement. New and used boards are for sale, and Cavalier also sells boards by consignment. You'll also find a huge collection of stickers and sunglasses, watches, and clothing for men and women.

Rodanthe Surf Shop
NC 12, Rodanthe
(252) 987-2412

Rodanthe Surf Shop owners Randy Hall and Debbie Bell moved to the southern Outer Banks to surf, and the shop evolved naturally from their lifestyle. A hands-on,

When you're surfing or kayaking in the ocean waves, look out for your fellow surfers and for swimmers. Do not cut across the path of someone actively riding a wave. Courteously ask swimmers to move down the beach a bit if they're swimming in the best breaks.

no-frills operation, the shop sells only the boards it makes, Hatteras Glass Surfboards, along with surfing equipment and surfer lifestyle clothing. Get a true surfing experience by renting a real fiberglass board here. The shop is closed Thanksgiving through March.

Hatteras Island Surf Shop
NC 12, Waves
(252) 987-2296
www.HISS-waves.com

Veteran surfers Barton and Chris Decker have operated Hatteras Island Surf Shop since 1971. They expanded their ventures to include windsurfing. The surf shop offers new and used equipment, rentals, and lessons. It sells surfboards, balsa boards, longboards, body boards, ocean toys, kayaks, and in-line skates. Wet suits, surfwear, beach clothing, and bathing suits are also for sale in this no-nonsense surf shop. The shop closes in January and February.

Hatteras Island Boardsports
NC 12, Avon
(252) 995-6160, (866) HIB-WAVE
www.hiboardsports.com

Just like the name suggests, this surf shop has boards—pick from all styles of surfboards (including custom designs), skimboards, and body boards. Wet suits and surf clothing are sold as well.

Natural Art Surf Shop
NC 12, Buxton
(252) 995-5682

Natural Art specializes in both custommade surfboards and a full line of handmade surfwear for men, women, and kids. The shop also carries shoes, wet suits, skatewear, and videos. The surfboards are shaped by owner Scott Busbey in a separate shop in the backyard. Busbey has gained a national reputation for his beautiful craftsmanship and reasonably priced boards. Surfboards can be rented for $10.00 a day or $50.00 a week, boogie boards for $5.00 a day or $25.00 a week, and wet suits for $10.00 a day without a board or $5.00 a day with a board. Videos rent for $3.00 daily.

Ride the Wind Surf Shop
NC 12, Ocracoke
(252) 928-6311
www.surfocracoke.com
In business since 1985, Ride the Wind features two floors of merchandise, ranging from the latest contemporary surf gear to casual, comfortable clothing and footwear for men and women. Ride the Wind rents surfboards, body boards, wet suits, and practically all Outer Banks watersports equipment, except windsurfing items. Surfboards rent for $18 a day. The shop is open seven days a week from March through December and is closed for the winter. Ride the Wind also offers outfitting trips to Portsmouth Island and a surf and kayak day camp for kids. Beginner surf lessons are available for adults and kids.

WINDSURFING

Springtime on the Outer Banks brings a specific annual migration, mostly from Canada and the northern United States. From a distance, we know where these migrating flocks are from and why they're here, for their vehicles give them away. Their luggage racks are laden with windsurfing equipment, and some tow trailers stacked with boards and sails for every wind condition. In spring and fall, tourism officials estimate that as many as 500 windsurfers a week arrive at the Outer Banks. Dozens of other visitors try the sport for the first time while vacationing in Dare County.

Owing to our position in the Atlantic, plus the area's prevailing winds, shallow sounds, and temperate weather, Hatteras Island is a windsurfing mecca on the East Coast. When the wind whips just right, hundreds of sails soar along the sound and ocean shores, skimming over the salty water like bright butterflies flitting near the beach.

Windsurfing is not an easy sport, although once you get the hang of it, it is one of the most intoxicating experiences imaginable. It's clean and quiet and just as easily lends itself to solitary excursions as it does to group outings. With the proper equipment, sailboarders glide into a sunset or cruise more than 40 mph across choppy breaks. On the Outer Banks, sailboarders can usually find some wind to ride year-round. Windsurfing is permitted any place you can set your sails, except lifeguarded beaches. This sport truly allows the rider to feel a part of the natural surroundings—and it's an incredible rush to fly with the wind.

Canadian Hole and Other Places to Windsurf

Hatteras Island's Canadian Hole, so named for all of our visitors from the far north, has often been touted in international windsurfing circles as one of the continent's best sailboarding spots. Formed in the early 1960s, Canadian Hole was created after a storm cut an inlet across Hatteras Island, just north of Buxton, and workers dredged sand from the sound to rebuild the roadway. Dredging activities carved troughs just offshore in the Pamlico Sound. The deep depressions, which extend well beyond 5 feet, help create ideal conditions for sailboarders. Additionally, Canadian Hole flanks one of the barrier islands' narrowest landmasses. The walk from ocean to sound is less than five minutes, enabling sailboarders to easily switch between the two bodies of water.

Besides the sound and the Atlantic, Canadian Hole's amenities include a 100-space paved lot in which to park big vans and trailers, toilets and showers, a phone booth, and trash cans. The beach at Canadian Hole is much wider than other soundside stretches of sand—it's about 50 yards wide and accommodates sunbathers, coolers, and plenty of spectators.

Nags Head's soundside beaches also provide areas that are great for sailboarding. The sounds are shallower than at Canadian Hole, and thus safer for beginners. The town of Nags Head has a sound-

CLOSE-UP

Canadian Hole

Wide-open sky, unobstructed by trees and skyscrapers, hovers over a ridge of sand. The wind blows from every direction, sweeping sometimes gently, sometimes with excited fury, across the island from sea to sound or sound to sea. Welcome to Canadian Hole.

Long before windsurfers and kiteboarders arrived in droves at Canadian Hole, Hatteras Island's local fishermen toiled night into day, day into night, plying fish from the salt- and freshwater sound. Arriving upon the shore, they toted their boats and fishing equipment, crossing the island at one of its narrowest locations to the Atlantic's beach.

Some days their journey took them from the ocean to the sound at this place, dubbed "The Haulover." The crossing was frequently made at this place between Avon and Buxton, where the ocean has met the sound in past storm rages and will do so again one day.

For now, Canadian Hole is available for wind and water lovers to use. It is a privilege granted by the National Park Service, which holds jurisdiction over the land as part of Cape Hatteras National Seashore. Americans, Canadians, indeed, people of the world, come here to sail across the shining seas known as the prime windsurfing and kitesailing spot on the United States' East Coast.

The place has a smell of its own, dusted by wind, sun, and island brush, wetted with rain and salt spray. At times, windriders wait in a quiet hush, lazily aware, keen to every movement of the wind. When the wind picks up, the scurry begins. Dashing across the parking lot, board over head, squeezing between cars, trucks, and vans, windsurfers in wet suits head to the shallow sound while new arrivals find a parking space, scope the scene, assess the wind speed, and follow suit.

side access at Milepost 16 that's perfect for windsurfers with plenty of parking. Jockey's Ridge State Park's soundside access area also provides parking and a small beach for launching sailboards. In Duck, most people launch on the sound. There are dozens of launch areas on the soundside all along the Outer Banks.

KITESURFING

Kitesurfing, or kiteboarding, is a relatively new sport, only a few years old, and it's the latest craze among windsurfers, wake boarders, and surfers alike. The Outer

Banks is widely recognized as one of the top places in the world to kitesurf because of the ever-present wind and shallow sounds. Kitesurfers favor the Pamlico Sound off Hatteras Island because it is so wide and has few obstructions to the kite lines. Some daredevil types also kitesurf in the ocean.

Kitesurfing does offer significant advantages over windsurfing: The gear is much more portable, you can do it in a wider range of winds (even low winds), and most people say it's much easier to learn. However, windsurfing is safer. Kitesurfing is a dangerous sport, though it's hard to perceive that danger when you're

The spot attracts visitors from Canada seeking warm water and air often accompanied by steady wind. The drive is accomplished in a day or two, consuming 16 to 20 hours from eastern locales, with eager anticipation pushing the wind lovers south.

A few resident windsurfers remember when the sport was new and first brought to the island in the early 1970s. One or two wet-behind-the-ear windsurfing pioneers ventured into the shores meeting the Graveyard of the Atlantic, where shoals and unpredictable shifting conditions wrecked more than 1,000 ships.

Enthusiasts soon determined that windsurfing in the safer sound is fun, not only for beginners but for intermediate and advanced windsurfers as well. At times, hundreds of sails flit about, dancing upon the sparkles.

Some brave and skilled sailors carry their boards and sails across the highway, over the dune, and ride the waves into the Atlantic. The experience, if successful, is surreal, intoxicatingly beautiful. But many a daredevil has been smashed by the surf and "denied" entry or has been swept along in a wicked current or lost equipment and pride, which is renewed in the next great session. More and more dedicated enthusiasts become wave-sailors, enticed by the never-ending challenges and thrills.

Now, kiteboarding has found its perfect spot. Those with kites rather than sails park along the sound in the sand and sail where the water is definitely shallow, away from the crowd of windsurfers, at Kite Point. Kite Point is just south of The Hole but part of the same park.

Despite the rise of windsurfing, followed by the rise of kiteboarding, the water is the same, and so is the wind. It's beautiful and free. Whether holding a sail or a kite, sailors smile, tasting freedom, keeping the feeling forever and ever.

watching from the shore. The amount of wind power behind the kite is enormous.

For this reason, you cannot simply rent a kite and board at the local outfitters and go on your merry way. You must attain a basic level of certification before you are allowed to rent or buy kitesurfing equipment, and some outfitters don't rent the gear at all, saying the risks are just too great.

Two types of kites are used in kitesurfing: an inflatable kite and a foil kite. The inflatable kite is crescent-shaped, with an inflatable leading edge that allows it to float. This kite is easier to use, is more stable and predictable, and can be used in a broader wind range. The foil kite is flatter and it fills with wind for a more powerful, high-performance ride. The foil kites are a little more unpredictable and are subject to unexpected gusts.

Many sailing shops on the Outer Banks offer kitesurfing lessons, but you should definitely look for responsible retailers who encourage proper training. Windsurfing Hatteras does not rent equipment at all because they feel it is too dangerous for both ill-trained users and any innocent bystanders. They do offer lessons, from beginner to advanced, but after that they encourage kitesurfers to buy their own equipment.

Kitty Hawk Kites Kite Surfing School does rent equipment, but only to people who have completed their Professional Air Sports Association–certified training courses at Carolina Outdoors at MP 16 in Nags Head. It takes about four hours of training to become certified, and then you are able to rent gear. The amount of training time depends on your previous kiting skills. If you're not familiar with kite physics, trainers suggest that you practice with a trainer kite until kite-steering techniques become ingrained in you.

If you want to buy kitesurfing gear, the whole setup will cost you $1,500 or more. If you want to watch or compete in kitesurfing, check out Kitty Hawk Kites Kiteboarding Center at milepost 15½ in Nags Head.

Windsurfing and Kiteboarding Shops and Lessons

Whether you're looking for a lesson, need a sail or a fin of a different size, or want advice, more than a dozen shops stock windsurfing and kitesurfing supplies, and many provide instructors in season.

Kitty Hawk Watersports
US 158, MP 16, Nags Head
(252) 441-2756
www.kittyhawksports.com
Dealing in windsurfing on the Outer Banks for more than 20 years, Kitty Hawk Watersports was one of the first windsurfing operations on the barrier islands. At its site on Roanoke Sound, the center is open almost all year-round and offers windsurfing instruction in spring, summer, and fall. With a $55, three-hour lesson, instructors guarantee you'll be skimming the Roanoke Sound on your own. Call the number listed for rates. Kitesurfing lessons are available, but rentals are not. Wind- and kitesurfing equipment is also available for sale.

Kitty Hawk Kites Kite Surfing School
US 158, MP 15½, Nags Head
(252) 449-2210
www.kittyhawk.com
Kitty Hawk Kites Kite Surfing School at Carolina Outdoors offers kitesurfing lessons with highly qualified instructors at this location on the Roanoke Sound in Nags Head, right next to Windmill Point restaurant. Two-hour introductory lessons, in which you learn to properly control kites, cost $99. More advanced lessons cost $200 for three hours. This school offers Level I, II, and III certification that is recognized by the Professional Air Sports Association. Once you have achieved a certain level of certification, you can rent kitesurfing gear at this location. Call for rental prices.

Windsurfing Hatteras
NC 12, Avon
(252) 995-5000, (866) 995-6644
www.windsurfinghatteras.com
With private access to Pamlico Sound, this widely respected store was opened in 1988 by a group of dedicated local windsurfers. The operation offers windsurfing and kitesurfing lessons and clinics every year for both beginners and advanced students. The clinics are staffed by some of the best kite- and windsurfing talent around.

Lessons come with guaranteed success for beginners. Windsurfing lessons start at $59 for beginners, including all equipment and on-water instruction. Windsurfing boards and rigs can be rented at the site. Kitesurfing lessons, starting at $100 for a 90-minute beginner lesson, are offered by highly qualified instructors. Kitesurfing gear is not available for rent. Call for rates on renting surfboards, body boards, kayaks, Hobie Cats, and other fun-inspired items. Windsurfing Hatteras stocks everything you could possibly need for wind- or kitesurfing.

Hatteras Island Sail Shop
NC 12, Waves
(252) 987-2292
www.HISS-waves.com
On the soundfront, this windsurfing shop

was opened in 1996 by the owners of Hatteras Island Surf Shop, which is 250 yards south. They offer sales, rentals, and lessons. Owner Barton Decker says the sailing site is the largest grassy rigging area on the Outer Banks with a sandy beach launch. With about 150 new and used boards in stock, the store also has necessary accessories in its complete inventory. A beginner windsurfing lesson costs $55 for about three hours. Rentals are available for $15 an hour, $35 a half-day, and $55 a day. The Sail Shop sells kites and kiteboards and offers lessons. Kitesurfing lessons cost $89 an hour; no rentals are available. The store closes in January and February.

REAL Kiteboarding
Cape Hatteras
(252) 995–4740, (866) REAL–KITE
www.realkiteboarding.com
REAL Kiteboarding is a full-service kiteboarding center that offers gear and instruction. With home bases on Hatteras Island and Puerto Rico, they offer instruction in many areas of the East Coast. Three-day Kite Camps ($895) are offered on Hatteras Island in spring, summer, and fall, and after one of these intense camps, you'll certainly be ripping. Less expensive lessons require less time but still cover basic skills.

Hatteras Island Boardsports
NC 12, Avon
(252) 995–6160, (866) HIB–WAVE
www.hiboardsports.com
For windsurfing and kiteboarding equipment, new or used, for sale or to rent, visit Hatteras Island Boardsports. Instructors teach all levels, catering to your specific needs, particularly with private lessons. The shop stocks casual clothing for the beach and to wear at home. Kayaks, kayak tours, and other watersport needs are served here. The shop is open all year; call for hours.

KAYAKING AND CANOEING

The easiest, most adaptable, and most accessible water sports available on the Outer Banks—kayaking and canoeing—are activities people of any age can enjoy. These lightweight paddlecraft are maneuverable, glide almost anywhere along the seas or sounds, and afford adventurous activity as well as silent solitude. They're also relatively inexpensive ways to tour uncharted waterways and see sights not observable from shore.

In recent years, more than a dozen ecotour outlets have opened on the barrier islands. Stores offer everything from rent-your-own kayaks for less than $40 a day to guided, daylong, and even overnight tours around uninhabited islands. With no fuel to foul the estuaries, no noise to frighten wildlife, and no need for a demanding skill level, kayaks and canoes offer a sport as strenuous or as relaxing as you want it to be.

Unlike the closed-cockpit kayaks used in whitewater river runs, most kayaks on the Outer Banks are a sit-on-top style from 7 to 10 feet long. They're molded in brightly colored plastic, are light to carry to a launch site, and are manufactured in one- and two-seat models. A double-blade paddle and a life jacket are the only other pieces of equipment needed, and these are included with rentals and lessons.

Canoes are heavier and harder to get into the water but slightly more stable than kayaks. They seat two or three people and include a more sheltered hull to haul gear or picnic lunches inside. Single-blade paddles, usually two per boat, are needed to maneuver this traditional watercraft.

These sports lend themselves to solitary enjoyment just as easily as group fun. Thrill seekers can splash kayaks through frothy surf in the Atlantic or paddle past the breakers and float alongside schools of dolphin. For more tranquillity, kayakers and canoeists can slip slowly through mysterious, marshy creeks at the isolated Alligator River National Wildlife Refuge, explore narrow canals that bigger boats can't access, or slip alongside an uninhabited island in the middle of the shallow sound. There are historical tours around Roanoke Island, nature tours through maritime forests, and self-guided trails with markers winding through a former logging town called Buffalo City on the Dare County mainland.

Learning to Paddle

Unlike other water sports, little to no instruction is needed to paddle a kayak or canoe. It is best to know how to swim, in case you capsize, but since most of the sounds are only a few feet deep, you can walk your way back to shore if you stay in the estuaries—or, at least, jump back in your boat from a standing position. If you fall out of your boat and cannot touch bottom to stand, try to grab onto the canoe or kayak and float to where you can stand.

Different strokes are required for each type of craft. For single kayaks, double-blade paddles are designed to be used by one person. The blades are positioned at opposing angles so you can work across your body with a sweeping motion and minimal rotation and paddle on both sides of the boat. The trick is to get into a rhythm and not dig too deeply beneath the water's surface. Double kayaks are paddled by two people alternating rhythmic strokes on opposing sides of the kayak. Canoeing is done with one person paddling on each side of the boat, if there are two passengers, or a single operator alternating sides with paddle strokes.

Most kayak- and canoe-rental outfits also offer lessons. Even if you prefer to be on your own, rather than with a guided group trip, people renting these watercraft are happy to share advice and expertise. If you have any questions or need directions around the intricate waterways, ask.

The sounds around the Outer Banks are ideal for kayaking and canoeing because they are shallow, warm, and filled with flora and fauna. There are marked pathways at Alligator River National Wildlife Refuge; tours through Nags Head Woods; buoys around Wanchese, Manteo, and Colington; and plenty of uncharted areas to explore around Pine Island, Pea Island, Kitty Hawk,

Corolla, the Cape Hatteras National Seashore, and Portsmouth Island. Unlike other types of boats, canoes and kayaks don't require a special launching site.

Kayak and Canoe Rentals

Corolla Outback Adventures
Wee Winks Shopping Center
NC 12, Corolla
(252) 453-0877
www.corollaoutback.com
Started by the Bender family in the 1960s, this guide service is still in the family—now run by the second generation. This company offers ATV tours through two nature preserves and along the Corolla shoreline.

Corolla Adventure Tours
NC 12, Corolla
(252) 453-6899
www.obxwaterworks.com
For kayak ecotours on the north beaches, look to Corolla Adventure Tours. Guides lead two-hour tours through Currituck Sound and marsh, where you'll see a variety of birds and wildlife. For those interested in dolphin watching, this company leads two-hour ocean tours on calm days. Make reservations in advance. This company has two locations on North Carolina Highway 12, one next to the Inn at Corolla Light and the other north of the post office. Kayak tours are offered March through January.

Carolina Outdoors
Monteray Shores Plaza, NC 12, Corolla
(252) 453-3685
www.kittyhawk.com
Carolina Outdoors, a division of Kitty Hawk Kites, offers kayak rentals for paddlers who want to explore the sound.

Kitty Hawk Sports
NC 12, Corolla
(252) 453-6900
www.kittyhawksports.com

Kitty Hawk Sports, behind TimBuck II Shopping Village, offers kayak rentals and kayak ecotours in Currituck Sound. Call for details. The Corolla store is open Memorial Day to Labor Day.

Carolina Outdoors Watersports Center
NC 12, Duck
(252) 261-4450
www.kittyhawk.com
Next to Kitty Hawk Kites in Duck is the Carolina Outdoors Watersports Center, complete with a pier and canal. This location rents kayaks for the ocean and sound. The Carolina Outdoors retail store is across the street.

Nor'Banks Sailing Center
NC 12, Duck
(252) 261-7100
www.norbanks.com
Single as well as tandem kayaks are available for sale or rent here. Prices range from around $15 an hour for a single kayak to $100 a week for a tandem kayak. Open May through October.

Duck Village Outfitters (DVO)
1207 Duck Road, Duck
(252) 261-7222
DVO will take you wherever you want to go in a kayak. Their preplanned tours are ocean kayak dolphin tours and scenic tours through the estuaries of Kitty Hawk Nature Preserve, Kitty Hawk Bay, and Ginguite Creek. The two-hour soundside tours cost $33 for a single kayak or $59 for a tandem. Kayak rentals cost around $29 each day or $59 a week, more for tandem models. Tours are conducted daily in the warm seasons, but call in the off-season and one of the enthusiastic guides will take you out. The shop is open all year.

Carolina Outdoors
US 158, Nags Head
(252) 441-4124, (800) 334-4777
www.kittyhawk.com
Carolina Outdoors, Kitty Hawk Kites' watersports operation, offers a selection of sound tours from Corolla to Hatteras, in addition to sea and surf kayak lessons. No experience is necessary, and tours include all necessary equipment, including single and tandem kayaks, paddles, and life jackets. Tours are offered around Kitty Hawk Woods, Manteo and Roanoke Island, Alligator River, and Pea Island. Sunset tours, dolphin tours, lighthouse tours, and tours with historical narration are offered. Tours range from one hour to more than two hours. Long, specialty tours are available; see the Web site for more information. Sea, surf, and touring kayaks as well as a selection of personal sailboats are available for sale, including Escape boats and the Wind-Rider trimarans. Special programs for kids are available in summer months. Equipment can be rented by the hour, day, or week.

Kitty Hawk Watersports
US 158, MP 13, Nags Head
(252) 441-6800
www.kittyhawksports.com
A division of Kitty Hawk Sports, the kayak service offers tours ranging from two hours to extended expeditions and covers the soundside areas from Corolla to Portsmouth Island, including Pea Island and Alligator River. Launch sites are in Corolla, Kitty Hawk, Nags Head, and Avon. Sales and rentals are available. Lessons for any experience level, from beginner to advanced, are available. Two-hour tours start at $35 for adults, $25 for children. Alligator River tours cost $44 for adults and $25 per child. Kayak rentals start at $29 per day, depending on the craft.

The Waterworks
US 158, MP 17, Nags Head
(252) 441-8875
www.waterworks.ws
Right on the sound in Nags Head, The Waterworks offers kayak and canoe rentals for those who want to be alone. Rent a variety of kayaks for adventures in the sound behind the shop.

Wilderness Canoeing Inc.
P.O. Box 789, Manteo, NC 27954
(252) 473-1960

Outer Banks native Melvin T. Twiddy Jr. conducts wilderness adventure tours by canoe around Alligator River National Wildlife Refuge and through the former frontier town Buffalo City and Milltail Creek. All equipment is provided, and the tours last a leisurely three and a half to four hours. Tours depart from Manns Harbor, usually around 9:00 A.M., but the times vary according to the group. Bring water and lunch or snacks to eat on the tour. Wilderness Canoeing is one of the few tour operations open year-round, and its trip through the Alligator River area is the longest guided tour available. Along the way, Twiddy steers past blooming water lilies and talks about local history and folklore. Advance reservations are recommended. Call for rates and more information.

Carolina Outdoors
Queen Elizabeth Street, Manteo
(252) 473-2357, (800) 334-4777
www.kittyhawk.com

Carolina Outdoors rents kayaks from its location, which is right on Shallowbag Bay in downtown Manteo. Ecotours through Shallowbag Bay and surrounding canals are given throughout the day for around $29 per person. The tours last about one and a half hours. Sunset and moonlight tours are also available.

Hatteras Island Sail Shop
NC 12, Waves
(252) 987-2292
www.HISS-waves.com

Kayak rentals and sales are offered at this soundfront shop. The site includes a large, grassy area and a sandy beach launch. The shop also rents Hobie Cats and day sailers. Kayak rentals cost $20 or $30 a day, with discounts for half-day rentals.

Hatteras Watersports
NC 12, Salvo
(252) 987-2306

On the soundside across from the Salvo Volunteer Fire Department, Hatteras Watersports rents and sells canoes and flat-water and surf kayaks. Ninety-minute soundside kayak tours are offered for $30 per person. Call for rental prices.

Hatteras Island Boardsports
NC 12, Avon
(252) 995-6160, (866) HIB-WAVE
www.hiboardsports.com

Rent a kayak (single or double) for the sound or ocean. Choose from a variety of styles and makes. Rent for a half day, a whole day, three days, or a week. HIB delivers, or you can pick up the gear yourself. To see Hatteras Island from a different perspective, sign up for a kayak tour, starting at $35. The Family Paddle and the Sunset Tour last two hours; the Adventure Tour and Shipwreck Tour last three hours. Open daily year-round.

Carolina Outdoors
Island Shops, NC 12, Avon
(252) 995-6060, (800) 334-4777

Hatteras Landing
NC 12, Hatteras Village
(252) 986-1446, (800) 334-4777
www.kittyhawk.com

These locations of Carolina Outdoors offer kayak rentals for the sound as well as the ocean. They also perform kayak ecotours on the sound.

Ocracoke Adventures
NC 12 and Silver Lake Road, Ocracoke
(252) 928-7873
www.ocracoke-nc.com/ocracoke adventures

Kayak ecotours in Pamlico Sound and around Ocracoke Island give paddlers the opportunity to learn about the fragile plant and animal life that inhabits these remote islands. Clamming tours, snorkeling trips, and late-night tours are available, too. Tours are often guided by native Michael O'Neal and biologist Shirley Schoelkopf, owners of Ocracoke Adventures, and last two to two and a half hours. The owners also oversee several Ocracoke natives who take out paddlers.

Fees include kayak, paddle, backrest, life jacket, dry bag, and instructions. Any size group can be accommodated, and customized tours are available. Kayaks rent on an hourly, daily, or weekly basis, with free delivery on Ocracoke. Reservations are recommended in summer. Surfish sailboats are also available for rent. Kids age 10 and younger ride free, and daily programs for children are available.

Ocracoke Adventures hosts Wave Cave Summer Surf Camp, Ocracoke's first and finest surf camp for anyone who can swim. The camp operates during summer on Tuesday, Wednesday, and Thursday from 10:00 A.M. until noon and includes surfing, body boarding, skimboarding, and surf kayaking. Ocracoke Adventures also hosts school groups on educational walking and kayak tours around Ocracoke Island. The store closes in January and February, but the owners will return your call if you leave a message.

Ride the Wind Surf Shop
NC 12, Ocracoke
(252) 928–6311
www.surfocracoke.com
Ride the Wind offers four two-and-a-half-hour kayak tours (The Sunrise, The Midday, The Sunset, The Full Moon) of Pamlico Sound and the surrounding estuarine waters every day in spring, summer, and fall, weather permitting.

Any size group can be accommodated with advance notice. The fee includes kayak, life jackets, and a four-page plastic field guide to area fish, shellfish, and fauna. Call for prices. Reservations are strongly suggested during summer.

SCUBA DIVING

Although cloudier and cooler than waters off the Florida Keys and the Caribbean Islands, offshore areas along the Outer Banks offer unique scuba-diving experiences in "The Graveyard of the Atlantic."

The area owes its moniker to the more than 1,000 shipwrecks (at least 200 named and identified) whose remains rest on the ocean floor from Corolla to Ocracoke. Experienced divers enjoy the challenge of unpredictable currents while exploring beneath the ocean's surface. From 17th-century schooners to World War II submarines, wreckage lies at a variety of depths, in almost every imaginable condition.

Some underwater archaeological shipwreck sites are federally protected and can be visited but not touched. Others offer incredible souvenirs for deepwater divers: bits of china plates and teacups, old medicine and liquor bottles, brass-rimmed porthole covers, and thick, hand-blown glass that's been buried beneath the ocean for more than a century. If you prefer to leave history as you find it, waterproof cameras bring back memorable treasures from the mostly unexplored underwater world.

Sharks, whales, dolphins, and hundreds of varieties of colorful fish also frequent deep waters around these barrier islands. The northernmost coral reef in the world is off Avon. Submerged Civil War forts are scattered along the banks of Roanoke Island in much more shallow sound waters.

Dive-boat captains carry charter parties to places of their choosing. Some shipwrecks have become popular with scuba divers and are among the most frequently selected sites. The freighter *Metropolis,* also called the "Horsehead Wreck," lies about 3 miles south of the Currituck Beach Lighthouse off Whalehead Beach in Corolla, 100 yards offshore and in about 15 feet of water. This ship was carrying 500 tons of iron rails and 200 tons of stones when it sank in 1878, taking 85 crewmen to a watery grave. Formerly the federal gunboat *Stars and Stripes* that worked in the Civil War, this is a good wreck to explore in the off-season. If you have a four-wheel-drive vehicle, you can drive up the beach and swim out to this shipwreck site.

Before You Dive

If you're going scuba diving, you might want to jot down these important numbers.

EMERGENCY NUMBERS

U.S. Coast Guard
24-Hour Search and Rescue
and all boating/diving emergencies
(252) 995-6411

U.S. Coast Guard Aids to
Navigation Team
(252) 986-2177

Divers Alert Network (DAN)
(919) 684-2948, 8:30 A.M. to
5:00 P.M. daily
(919) 684-8111 after hours

Ocean Rescue Squad
(helicopter available)
911

U.S. COAST GUARD STATIONS

Oregon Inlet
(252) 441-1685

Hatteras Inlet
(252) 986-2175

Ocracoke Inlet
(252) 928-3711

Off the shores of Kill Devil Hills, an unidentified tugboat rests about 300 yards south of Avalon Pier, approximately 75 yards off the beach, in 20 feet of water. Two miles south, the Triangle Wrecks—*Josephine, Kyzickes,* and *Carl Gerhard*—sit about 100 yards offshore, about 200 yards south of the Sea Ranch Motel, in about 20 feet of water. These vessels sank in 1915, 1927, and 1929, respectively. You can access these wrecks by boat or swim from the beach.

Nags Head's most famous dive site is the USS *Huron,* a federal gunship that sank in 1877, taking 95 crewmen to the bottom. This wreck is about 200 yards off the beach at MP 11, resting in an estimated 26 feet of water with many salvageable artifacts. The tugboat *Explorer* is nearby.

Long known as the East Coast's most treacherous inlet, Oregon Inlet rages between Bodie Island and Hatteras Island. It's infamous for the hundreds of ships—and scores of lives—that it has claimed through the ages. The liberty ship *Zane Grey* lies about a mile south of this inlet in 80 feet of water. A German sub sank northeast of the inlet in 100 feet of water in 1942. The *Oriental* has been sitting about 4 miles south of Oregon Inlet since sinking in 1862; its boiler is visible above the surf. Most of these dive sites can be accessed only from boats.

About a mile north of Rodanthe Fishing Pier, 100 yards offshore, the *LST 471* lies in only 15 feet of water. This ship sank in 1949 and is accessible by swimming from shore. Nearby off Rodanthe, about 22 miles southeast of Oregon Inlet, the tanker *Marore* is approximately 12 miles offshore. It sank when torpedoed in 1942 and lies in about 100 feet of water.

Experienced deepwater divers enjoy the *Empire Gem,* a British carrier that sank in January 1942, torpedoed by a German U-boat. This shipwreck sits about 17 miles off Cape Hatteras in 140 feet of water and was one of the first vessels to go down in these waters in World War II. It, too, must be reached by boat.

Learning to Dive

Unlike other water sports, scuba diving isn't something you can learn on your own. You have to be certified to do deep dives. This takes special training by certified instructors—and practice in a pool. Average recreational dives are 80 to 100 feet deep, while extreme divers reach depths of more than 300 feet. There are dangers associated with such deep dives, however. Every seasoned diver knows the perils associated with the sport: the potential for death in underwater caves, shark attacks, and the hazards of surfacing too fast and being afflicted with "the bends." Divers universally agree, however, that the thrill and tranquility of deep-wreck diving justify the risks.

Several Outer Banks dive shops offer lessons, advanced instruction, and the equipment you'll need to get started. This is a relatively expensive sport. Divers say it takes at least $1,500 just to get the necessary tanks, hoses, wet suits, and other paraphernalia to take the first plunge. Dive boat charters, which all dive-shop workers help arrange, begin at about $550 per day, depending on how far offshore you want to go.

Some dive shops can also recommend shallow dive spots that you don't need a boat to get to, as well as nearby-shore or sound areas that you can explore with a face mask and snorkel. All Ocean Atlantic Rentals locations rent fins, masks, and snorkels (call 252-261-4346). The National Park Service has sporadic snorkeling adventures along the Cape Hatteras National Seashore in the summer. Call (252) 473-2111 for tour times and information.

Dive Shops

Outer Banks Dive Center
US 158, MP 12½, Nags Head
(252) 449-8349
www.obxdive.com
This center in Nags Head meets the needs of all divers onboard its 46-foot crew boat named the *Pelican*. Guided beach dives are offered at the wreck of the *Huron* in Nags Head. Dive trips are offered to the offshore wrecks of the *Advance,* the *Jackson, U-85,* and others. The shop supplies all levels of diving instruction, rentals, equipment, repairs, and tank fills. It's open all year. Visit the Web site for information about trips, dives, and equipment.

Outer Banks Diving and Charters
57540 NC 12, Hatteras Village
(252) 986-1056
www.outerbanksdiving.com
Offering daily dives on Gulf Stream wrecks for individuals and groups, Outer Banks Diving and Charters specializes in family and group outings. Dive trips are made on *Bayou Runner,* a 42-foot U.S. Coast Guard–certified vessel, which is docked at Teach's Lair Marina, 1 mile from the dive shop. This full-service facility is open year-round and has equipment sales, full rental gear, tank fills, and Nitrox.

Atlantic Wreck Diving
Teach's Lair Marina, Hatteras Village
(252) 986-2835
Capt. Art Kirchner takes scuba divers out on his 36-foot custom dive boat, the *Margie II*. The boat, which is certified to carry 20 passengers, leaves from Teach's Lair Marina May through the end of August. Sport and technical divers explore any of about 30 wrecks in depths ranging from 40 feet to 360 feet. Captain Art is an experienced diver and captain; he has been diving since 1971. Call for reservations.

SAILING

Sir Walter Raleigh's explorers first sailed along these shores more than four centuries ago. Private sailboat owners have long enjoyed the barrier islands as a stopover while en route along the Intracoastal Waterway. Many sailors have also dropped anchor beside Roanoke or Hatteras Islands—only to tie up at the docks permanently and make Dare County their home.

Until recently, you had to have your own sailboat to cruise the area waterways. Now, shops from Corolla through Ocracoke rent sailboats, Hobie Cats, and catamarans to weekend water enthusiasts. Others offer introductory and advanced sailing lessons. Some take people who have no desire to learn to sail on excursions across the sounds aboard multipassenger sailing ships. Ecotours, luncheon swim-and-sails, and sunset cruises have become increasingly popular with vacationers. From 40-passenger catamarans sailed by experienced captains to piratelike schooners carrying up to six passengers to single-person Sunfish sailboats, you can find almost any type of sailing vessel you desire on these barrier islands.

Unlike loud motorized craft, which pollute the water with gasoline, sailing is a clean, environmentally friendly sport that people of all ages enjoy. You can sail slowly by marshlands without disturbing the waterfowl or cruise at 15 mph clips in stiff breezes. It all depends on your whim—and the wind.

If you've never sailed before, don't rent a boat and try to wing it. Winds in this area are trickier than elsewhere and either increase in intensity or shift direction without a moment's notice. If you get caught in a gale, you could end up miles from land if you don't know how to maneuver the vessel. A two-hour introductory lesson is worth the minimal investment to learn basic sailing skills such as knot tying, sail rigging, and steering.

Sailors with basic on-water experience manage to navigate their way around the shallow sounds. All boat passengers should always wear a life jacket.

Sailboat Cruises, Courses, and Rentals

Prices for sailboat cruises depend on the amenities, length of voyage, and time of day. Midday trips sometimes include lunches or at least drinks for passengers. Some sunset tours offer wine, beer, and appetizers. Almost all of the excursions let people bring their own food and drink aboard, and some even accept dogs on leashes. Special arrangements can also be made for disabled passengers. Prices generally range from $30 to $60 per person. If you'd like to book a boat for a private charter for you and your friends, some captains also offer their services along with the sailboats, beginning at $50 per hour per vessel.

Lesson costs, too, span a range, depending on how in-depth the course is, what type of craft you're learning on, and whether you prefer group or individualized instruction. Costs start at $10 and go to $50 per person. Call ahead for group rates for more than four people in your party.

If you'd rather rent a craft and sail it yourself, Outer Banks outfitters lease sailboats by the hour, day, or week. Deposits generally are required. Costs range from $25 to $60 per hour and $50 to $110 per day. Most shops accept major credit cards.

Kitty Hawk Watersports
NC 12, Corolla
(252) 453-6900
www.kittyhawksports.com
On the sound behind TimBuck II Shopping Village, Kitty Hawk Watersports rents day sailors and catamarans. Call for rates.

Nor'Banks Sailing Center
NC 12, Duck
(252) 261-7100
www.norbanks.com
In recent years, Duck has become one of

the Outer Banks's busiest sailing hubs and is among the easiest places in the area to learn to sail or take a calm cruise. Nor'Banks rents day sailers and catamarans hourly, by the half day, or daily and is open May through October.

Carolina Outdoors
1215 Duck Road, Duck
(252) 261-4450, (800) 334-4777
www.kittyhawk.com
A division of Kitty Hawk Kites, Carolina Outdoors rents the WindRider trimaran, a stable sailing vessel, for hourly and daily rates. The lightweight Escape, a less destructible and more portable version of the Sunfish, is also available for rent or sale. The Escape is equipped with a Windicator, which sets the sail by measuring wind speed and direction. WindRider trimarans are also available to rent in Corolla. Call (252) 453-3685.

The Promenade Watersports
US 158, MP ¼, Kitty Hawk
(252) 261-4400
At the foot of the Wright Memorial Bridge, The Promenade is the only full-service watersports center in Kitty Hawk. Of its multitude of services, it offers sailboat lessons and rentals. Try out a Precision 13, an 18-foot day sailer, Hobie Cats, or a 20-foot trimaran in the sound behind The Promenade. Call for prices. Reservations are recommended.

The Waterworks
US 158, MP 17, Nags Head
(252) 441-8875
www.waterworks.ws
Sailboat rentals are offered at this complete watersports center March through November. Try out a 14- or 18-foot day sailer or a Sunfish. This area of the Roanoke Sound is safe for day sailing. Stop and explore the several small islands for a break.

Kitty Hawk Watersports
US 158, MP 16, Nags Head
(252) 441-2756
www.kittyhawksports.com
Kitty Hawk Watersports, a division of Kitty

Hawk Sports, rents day sailers and catamarans from its soundside Nags Head location. This is a great place to learn to sail on a not-too-windy day. The sound is wide with few hazards to look out for—except JetSkiers and other watersports enthusiasts. Personal watercraft and kayaks are also available here.

Hatteras Island Sail Shop
NC 12, Waves
(252) 987-2292
www.HISS-waves.com
Catamarans, day sailers, and Hobie Cats are available for rent by the hour at this extension of the Hatteras Island Surf Shop. Kayaks and other ocean vessels are also available to rent. Sound access is on-site. Lessons are also offered. Call for more information. The sail shop is closed in January and February.

Carolina Outdoors
Island Shops, NC 12, Avon
(252) 995-6060
www.kittyhawksports.com
The Avon location of Carolina Outdoors rents WindRider trimaran sailboats, probably the easiest boats to learn to sail on. Carolina Outdoors also offers kayak rentals.

BOATING

From small skiffs to luxurious pleasure boats, there is dock space for almost every type of boat on the Outer Banks. Most marinas require advance reservations. Space is extremely limited on summer weekends, so call as soon as you make plans to visit the area. Prices vary greatly, depending on the dock location, amenities, and type of vessel you're operating.

If you don't own your own boat, you can still access the sounds, inlets, and ocean around the Outer Banks by renting powerboats from area outfitters. Most store owners don't require previous boating experience. If you leave a deposit and driver's license, they'll include a brief boating lesson in the rental price. Whether you're looking to lease a craft to catch this evening's fish dinner or want to take an afternoon cruise, you can find a vessel to suit your needs at a variety of marinas. Slow-going pontoon boats are popular with vacationers because they're easy to handle and accommodate a crowd of boaters. Prices range from $15 an hour to more than $100 per day, depending on the type of boat. Some places require a two-hour or more minimum. Most accept major credit cards. See our Fishing chapter for charter information. If you're interested in a boat tour, see our Recreation chapter.

Public Boat Launch Ramps

Find free public launch ramps at these locations:

- Whalehead Club in Corolla
- Soundside end of Wampum Drive in Duck
- Bob Perry Road on Kitty Hawk Bay in Kitty Hawk
- Avalon Beach off Bay Drive in Kill Devil Hills (small boats only)
- Washington Baum Bridge on Nags Head–Manteo Causeway, opposite Pirate's Cove
- Thicket Lump Marina near Thicket Lump Lane in Wanchese
- Foot of the bridge leading to Roanoke Island Festival Park in Manteo
- Oregon Inlet Fishing Center
- Oceanside end of Lighthouse Road in Buxton
- Frisco Cove in Frisco
- Between Cedar Island/Swan Quarter ferry docks on Ocracoke Island

Marinas and Dock Space

The following Outer Banks marinas offer services to boaters, such as fuel, bait and tackle, ice, supplies, and weighing stations. If you're interested in dockage at a marina, see our Getting Here, Getting Around chapter. If you're interested in chartering a boat at one of these marinas, see our Fishing chapter.

Dock of the Bay
Bob Perry Road, Kitty Hawk
(252) 255-5578
This fuel dock and convenience shop is a welcome service to boaters on the northern beaches. Dock of the Bay is easily accessed by boat from Kitty Hawk Bay. It offers ice, gas and diesel fuel, snacks and drinks, fishing tackle, and bait. Fishing and crabbing are allowed on the docks as well. It's located at the end of Bob Perry Road, on the Loving Canal at Hog Island, past the Dare County boat landing.

Pirate's Cove Yacht Club
Nags Head–Manteo Causeway, Manteo
(252) 473-3906, (800) 367-4728
www.fishpiratescove.com
This full-service marina is known for its good service and many amenities. It offers a fuel dock with gas and diesel fuel, and diesel is now available at every slip. An on-site restaurant, Hurricane Mo's (see our Restaurants chapter), serves lunch and dinner. Professional fish-cleaning staff is on-hand at the dock, or do it yourself at the facilities. The dock master's office monitors marine radio channels 16 and 78. Pirate's Cove is open year-round. For boat-ramp access, head across the street to the site just under the west side of the Washington Baum Bridge. This site has concrete ramps and plenty of parking for vehicles with trailers.

Manteo Waterfront Marina
207 Queen Elizabeth Avenue, Manteo
(252) 473-3320
Located within walking distance of restaurants, a movie theater, a bookstore, and retail shops, this marina has 53 slips and accommodates boats up to 130 feet.

Air-conditioned heads and showers are available as well as laundry facilities, a picnic area with gas grills, e-mail access, and rental cars. Fuel is not available. Both 30-amp and 50-amp power is on-site. Block and cube ice are sold on-site.

Rates start at $1.00 per foot during the off-season and for long stays. In season rates start at $1.25 a foot. During special events like Fourth of July weekend, rates may be higher. Ask about weekend packages and sailing and fishing charters. Manteo Waterfront Marina is open all year.

Thicket Lump Marina
Thicket Lump Road, Wanchese
(252) 473-4500

This family-owned and -operated, 28-slip marina rents dock space to pleasure and fishing vessels up to 45 feet by the day, week, month, or year. Yearly dockage is $7.00 a foot, and monthly dockage is $8.00 per foot. A ship's store and tackle shop are at the marina, and both gas and diesel fuel are available. Thicket Lump offers inshore and offshore charters; call for information. The marina is open throughout the year.

Manns Harbor Marina
US 64, Manns Harbor
(252) 453-5150

The Manns Harbor Marina serves boaters with a boat ramp that's the perfect put-in spot for those fishing for striped bass on the Manns Harbor and Croatan Sound bridges. Gas and diesel fuel are available. A bar/lounge and a small motel are also on-site.

Oregon Inlet Fishing Center
NC 12, Bodie Island
(252) 441-6301
www.oregon-inlet.com

The closest marina and fuel dock to Oregon Inlet, Oregon Inlet Fishing Center is on the north side of the Herbert C. Bonner Bridge, about 10 miles from Nags Head. The fishing center accommodates anglers with gas and diesel fuel and a well-stocked bait and tackle shop that opens at 5:00 A.M. The tackle shop carries a complete line of surf, inshore, and deep-sea fishing

equipment, plus drinks, snacks, coffee, hot dogs, T-shirts, ice, sunscreen, sunglasses, and other items. The boat ramp at Oregon Inlet Fishing Center, with five concrete ramps, is one of the nicest in the area, with plenty of parking for vehicles and trailers. Restroom and trash facilities are on-site.

Frisco Cove Marina
NC 12, Frisco
(252) 995-3052

On Pamlico Sound, about 9 miles north of Hatteras Inlet, this full-service marina has 30 slips available to rent for boats up to 35 feet long for $15 a day, $85 a week, or $950 a year. The on-site boat ramp costs $10. The facility sells marine and fishing supplies. The marina also sells and services major brands of outboard motors, including Suzuki, Nissan, and Yamaha. Regular fuel and bait and tackle are available.

A bathhouse with sinks and men's and women's showers, a convenience store, a large gift shop, and a fuel island are also located at Frisco Cove. The marina is open year-round.

Hatteras Harbor Marina
NC 12 and Gulfstream Way, Hatteras
(252) 986-2166, (800) 676-4939
www.hatterasharbor.com

This marina accommodates boats up to 68 feet for a day, month, or year. Rates in 2005 were $1.25 per foot per day or $15.00 per foot per month. Call for annual charges. Hatteras Harbor also has five apartments available for customers to rent. A full-service deli and ship's store are located at the marina. Diesel fuel is available. Hatteras Harbor is open year-round, and its public laundry facilities are open 24 hours a day.

The extra-long parking spaces near boat ramps are for vehicles pulling boat trailers. These are the only spaces for them to park and unload or load their boat. Vehicles with no trailers should be parked in the normal-size spots.

Willis Boat Landing
NC 12, Hatteras Village
(252) 986-2208

This marina accepts small craft up to 25 feet for short-term stays. About 20 boats can be accommodated at a time. Boat and motor repairs can be done on-site. Bait and tackle are available. Willis Boat Landing is open year-round.

Hatteras Landing Marina
NC 12, Hatteras Village
(252) 986-2205, (800) 551-8478

Hatteras Landing offers a complete ship's store with tackle, fresh and frozen baits, lures, sportswear, and a market with beer, ice, and groceries. Gas and diesel fuel are available. Hatteras Landing has fully metered slips, laundry facilities, bathrooms, and a fish-cleaning service. It's open year-round.

Oden's Dock
NC 12, Hatteras Village
(252) 986-2555
www.odensdock.com

Oden's Dock has a deep draft that accommodates vessels up to 65 feet. Of the 27 slips at the marina, 20 are deep draft. Reservations are suggested during the peak season.

Besides a seafood market, Breakwater Restaurant is at Oden's Dock. Diesel fuel and gasoline are sold at the ship's store, along with bait, tackle, food, and beverages. Showers are available during business hours, and fish-cleaning facilities are also available for anglers. One headboat and a charter fishing fleet dock here. Oden's is open year-round. Hours vary during the off-season. Please call ahead for details.

Teach's Lair Marina
NC 12, Hatteras Village
(252) 986-2460
www.teachslair.com

This year-round, full-service marina has 95 slips accommodating boats up to 65 feet. Depending on the size of your boat, rates are $1.50 per day per foot, $6.00 per week per foot, and $15.00 per month per foot. Two launching ramps are also located at the marina. Teach's Lair has a bathhouse, dry storage, and a ship's store. Fuel (diesel and gasoline), oil, and tackle are all available at the store. A headboat, charter fishing fleet, and two dive boats dock here. Parasailing adventures leave from the marina.

The National Park Service Dock
Silver Lake, Ocracoke Village
(252) 928-4531

April through November, dockage costs 80 cents per foot plus $3.00 a day for 110-volt electricity hookups, or $5.00 a day for 220-volt connections. The rest of the year, the cost is 40 cents per foot, while the electric hookups stay the same price. There's a two-week limit on summer stays, and dock space is assigned on a first-come, first-served basis. No water is available in the winter season. If no ranger is on-site when you arrive, pay at the visitor center across the street.

Anchorage Marina/Ocracoke Fishing Center
NC 12, Ocracoke
(252) 928-6661
www.theanchorageinn.com

Right in the heart of Ocracoke on Silver Lake, Anchorage Marina has 35 slips accommodating boats up to 120 feet long. Diesel fuel and gas are available. The marina is open year-round with no limit on the length of stays. The dockside sMacNally's Raw Bar is next door, and Anchorage offers bike rentals and small-boat rentals. Boaters have swimming pool and shower privileges.

Boat Rentals

If you don't own a powerboat but want to explore the vast waters of this region, rent one. Lots of places, even marinas or rent-all services, rent boats. Following are some reliable sources for motorboats.

North Duck Watersports
NC 12, Duck
(252) 261-4200
North Duck Watersports is on the west side of Duck Road, directly on Currituck Sound. Sport boats, pontoon boats, kayaks, and bicycles are all available. North Duck is open spring through fall. Call for rates.

The Promenade Watersports
US 158, MP ¼, Kitty Hawk
(252) 261-4400
www.promenadewatersports.com
Right across from the Wright Memorial Bridge on the Currituck Sound, The Promenade bills itself as the only full-service watersports center in the Southern Shores, Kitty Hawk, and Kill Devil Hills area. If you want to rent a boat, you are quite likely to find what you want at this complete fun spot. Sailboats, kayaks, pontoon boats, and 16-foot fishing and crabbing skiffs are all available for rent. The Promenade is open spring through fall.

The Waterworks
US 158, MP 17, Nags Head
(252) 441-8875
www.waterworks.ws
Not only can you rent 19-foot powerboats, pontoons, and jet boats at The Waterworks, you can also get any kind of watercraft supplies, plus a complete line of bike, kayak, and beach equipment rentals. This watersports center is the only one in the area that sells and repairs Yamaha watercraft, boats, and Yamaha outboard motors. It is open daily year-round.

Anchorage Marina
NC 12, Ocracoke
(252) 928-6661
www.theanchorageinn.com
Anchorage Marina rents 16- to 24-foot skiffs for half days, whole days, and weekly. Call for rates. The Marina is on Silver Lake and is open year-round.

PERSONAL WATERCRAFT

If you feel a need for speed and enjoy the idea of riding a motor-powered vehicle across the water, Outer Banks businesses rent personal watercraft by the hour. Personal watercraft (PWC) are most known and referred to by their brand names—Sea Doo, JetSki, and Wave Runner. No experience is necessary to ride these powerful boat-like devices, although a training session is a must if you've never before piloted a PWC. Unlike landlocked go-karts and other speedy road rides, there are no lanes on the open sound or ocean. But that doesn't mean you should ride with reckless abandon. With more and more people riding PWCs, it is imperative that each person practice responsible and safe riding.

Several styles of PWCs have developed over the past decade. Wave Runners allow drivers to maneuver these crafts sitting down with a second passenger holding on, also sitting, from behind. Most JetSkis don't have seats and accommodate only one person at a time in a standing or kneeling position. Newer Runabouts, also known as blasters, give riders the choice of standing or sitting. Wave Runners are the easiest style craft to balance and control. JetSkis are, however, more suitable for tricks—and prone to spills. Almost all of these motorized vessels cruise for up to two hours on five gallons of fuel.

PWCs are akin to motorboats with inboard motors that power a water pump. Like other motorized boats, however, PWCs are loud and are dangerous if you are not extremely cautious and aware. Most rental places include brief instructions and sometimes even a video on how to handle Wave Runners, JetSkis, and Runabouts.

While most rental shops are on the sound side of the Outer Banks, where the water's surface is generally slicker and depths are much more shallow, a few PWC outlets let you take the vessels into the ocean. There, shore break and offshore waves challenge experienced JetSki drivers. Watch out for surfers, swimmers, dolphins, turtles, sharks, and birds—and other JetSki drivers who might not see you coming.

Those who own their own PWCs can launch their craft at public boat ramps. Be aware, however, that PWCs are banned in certain areas of the Outer Banks. The National Park Service does not allow the launching of PWCs anywhere in Cape Hatteras National Seashore. The town of Southern Shores requires PWC launchers to get a permit from the police department. To get this permit, you must show proof of insurance and that you have taken a boating-safety course. You must stay at least 400 yards offshore in Southern Shores. In Nags Head, PWCs must stay at least 600 yards offshore and away from piers. Ocracoke Island forbids the use of PWCs.

Renting Personal Watercraft

New PWCs sell for $5,000 to $10,000. Several Outer Banks rental shops sell used PWCs for cheaper prices at the end of the summer. You'll probably need a trailer to haul these vessels behind your vehicle.

Shops from Corolla to Hatteras Island rent PWCs beginning at $30 for a half

hour. Price wars occasionally result in very low prices. More powerful models are generally more expensive. Additional charges also sometimes apply for extra riders. PWCs also can be rented by the hour, day, or even week at some places.

When you're out riding through the waves, keep in mind these personal watercraft rules:

- Stay in designated buoyed areas at all times.
- Stay at least 50 yards away from other personal watercraft, swimmers, and boaters.
- Give sail craft, such as windsurfers and sailboats, the right-of-way.
- Do not excessively flip your vehicle.
- Wear a life jacket.
- Keep the lanyard attached to your wrist at all times.
- Be aware that PWCs are low profile and often difficult for others to see. Stay a safe distance away.
- Return to shore immediately if the gas gauge has turned to "reserve" or if any mechanical problems are apparent.
- Do not wake jump, splash, race, or interact in any way with other watercraft.
- Check local regulations before using a PWC in a new area. Some municipalities, such as Ocracoke Island, strictly forbid their use.

**Corolla Watersports
at the Inn at Corolla Light
1066 Ocean Trail, Corolla
(252) 453-8602**
This sister store to North Duck Watersports rents the Wave Runner III. Call for rates and more information. Corolla Watersports is open May through October.

**Kitty Hawk Watersports
NC 12, Corolla
(252) 453-6900
www.kittyhawksports.com**
Kitty Hawk Watersports, behind TimBuck II Shopping Village and affiliated with Kitty

Know the rules of the water before you operate a boat! Observe NO WAKE signs, and slow down for smaller craft so that your wake doesn't swash them. Sail craft always have the right-of-way. When you pass through a channel, the red markers should be on your left as you're moving out to sea and on your right as you're coming in. Use this mnemonic device— Red on Right Returning—to remember which side of the channel to stay on.

Hawk Sports, rents Waverunners by the half hour and hour. Call for prices and more information. Waterbikes, paddleboats, kayaks, and parasailing are also offered through this store. Kitty Hawk Watersports is open in Corolla from early spring through fall. The Nags Head location at Milepost 16 on US 158 stays open longer.

North Duck Watersports
NC 12, Duck
(252) 261-4200

Three miles north of the village on the Sanderling border, this center rents Wave Runners to ride across the nearby Currituck Sound. Call for rates. North Duck Watersports is open April through October.

Nor'Banks Sailing Center
NC 12, Duck
(252) 261-7100
www.norbanks.com

Nor'Banks Sailing Center rents Wave Runners and Sea Doo jet boats. It is open spring through fall.

The Promenade Watersports
US 158, Kitty Hawk
(252) 261-4400

Before arriving at the Outer Banks from the Wright Memorial Bridge, The Promenade is on the right. A watersports and kiddie recreational park, Promenade includes enough to keep everybody delighted on land as well as on Currituck Sound on a PWC. Wave Runners and Runabouts rent by the half hour, hour, half-day, or full day. Early-bird specials are offered on Wave Runners. Call for price information. The Promenade says it has the largest riding area of any other PWC rental business because its share of Currituck Sound is not restricted by municipal regulations. Promenade closes in winter.

The Waterworks
US 158, MP 17, Nags Head
(252) 441-8875
www.waterworks.ws

One of the many activities and services Waterworks offers is PWC rental. JetSkis, Sea Doos, and Wave Runners are available at half-hour and hourly rates. Call for prices. Waterworks also sells PWCs, including Yamaha and Sea-Doo. Rentals are available March through November.

Kitty Hawk Watersports
US 158, MP 16, Nags Head
(252) 441-2756
www.kittyhawksports.com

This complete store rents Wave Runners by the half hour and hour. The store is on the sound in Nags Head, so launching is easy. Waterbikes, paddleboats, and kayaks are available for purists. Call for prices. There are also Kitty Hawk Watersports locations in Corolla, Duck, and Avon. The Nags Head location is open well into the fall.

Rodanthe Watersports and Campground
NC 12, Rodanthe
(252) 987-1431

This soundfront campground and watersports operation rents Wave Runners as well as surfboards, bikes, kayaks, and sailboats.

Hatteras Watersports
NC 12, Salvo
(252) 987-2306

Hatteras Watersports rents Wave Runner personal watercraft. The store is on the sound side, across from the Salvo Volunteer Fire Department.

FISHING

If fishing is your passion, these barrier islands should be enough to send you reeling. Situated as we are in the Atlantic, not only do we have fabulous close-range ocean and inlet fishing, but we're so close to the Gulf Stream and its bounty that offshore trips are just as popular. Half-day and full-day charters are available year-round, or if you're a seasoned boater with an ocean-worthy vessel, you can make the trip yourself. If you're looking to spend only a couple of hours' worth of angling, you can surf fish along nearly 100 miles of wide sandy beaches, or you can wet a line at any one of a number of fishing piers. And that's just covering the ocean. Our sound waters are home to numerous finned species, and interior freshwater ponds are stocked with fish. Outer Banks angling is the stuff of which dreams are made. The following fish stories are for real.

The International Game Fish Association lists 92 world records for fish caught in Outer Banks waters, though some of those are now retired. These record holders include a 405-pound lemon shark caught off of Buxton, a 67-pound amberjack caught in Oregon Inlet, a 41-pound bluefish, and a 72-pound red drum landed off Hatteras. A 348-pound bluefin tuna was caught in Hatteras waters as well, along with record-size black sea bass, Spanish mackerel, oyster toadfish, bigeye tuna, kingfish, and sheepshead landed in waters from Kill Devil Hills to Ocracoke. Even if you don't tip the scales with a record-breaking catch, you're bound to fill your coolers with anything from albacore to wahoo. Depending upon the season, where you fish, and your choice of bait, you'll also find speckled trout, gray trout, flounder, striped bass (or rockfish), black drum, largemouth bass, tautog, cobia, a variety of pan fish, and the big attraction, billfish.

You might think that the variety here draws expert anglers, hence the great catches. Chances of a good catch are enhanced by physical conditions existing here that don't exist anywhere else. And that's no fish story! We outline these characteristics in the offshore section that follows.

Another factor that hugely influences the catch is our charter fleets. Many consider the local sportfishing boats, called Carolina boats, the most beautiful in the world, and these vessels house the complete package of brains, talent, and beauty. Our experienced captains are without peer, and their charter mates will awe you with their knowledge, skill, and the manner in which they work. Some mates move as if their actions are choreographed: simultaneously working lines, assisting members of the fishing party, keeping the captain apprised of catches-in-progress, arranging poles, gaffing fish, and encouraging you to keep reeling when it feels as if your arm just won't manage another revolution. A good mate is worth his or her weight in gold.

While anyone who's ever gone fishing knows you can't predict catches, the local charter boat captains know what species may be in the area, and they will guide you. Charters leave the docks for inshore and offshore fishing every day that the weather permits. When you call to book a boat (see our Marinas listings in this chapter), you may find it hard to decide what kind of trip to choose unless you've fished before. Booking agents at each marina will help you.

In the following sections, we describe offshore and inshore angling, backwater, surf, fly, and pier fishing. Offshore trips generally leave the docks at 5:30 A.M. and return no later than 6:00 P.M. Inshore trips are half-day excursions that leave twice daily, generally at 7:00 A.M. and again around noon. Intermediate trips can last all day but generally don't travel as far as the Gulf Stream.

If you decide to fish without a guide or charter captain, the North Carolina Division of Marine Fisheries (800–682–2632) is a wealth of information. It's your resource for all available licenses, including recreational, commercial gear, and standard commercial licenses. A license to land flounder is available only through this Morehead City office. The division publishes an annual recreational-fishing handbook, the *North Carolina Coastal Waters Guide for Sports Fishermen,* a comprehensive guide to licenses, limits, and sizes. The helpful staff will also direct you to the appropriate contacts for obtaining federal permits for tuna and other controlled species.

For information on freshwater fishing permits and regulations, you'll need to contact the North Carolina Wildlife Resources Commission in Raleigh. The number for hunting and fishing licenses is (919) 662-4370. A regulations digest is available at sporting goods stores and tackle shops. Call either Wildlife Resources or the North Carolina Division of Marine Fisheries for information on motorboat registration. Official weigh stations are listed toward the end of this chapter.

OFFSHORE FISHING

The Outer Banks is famed as the Billfish Capital of the World. Though other fishing destinations debate that point, the Outer Banks waters are home to an incredible number of billfish—white and blue marlin and sailfish. These fighting fish are caught from spring through early fall, with peak catches for blue marlin in June and peak catches for white marlin and sailfish in August and September. To protect the species, billfish are almost always caught and released. You still get bragging rights for your released fish, though; the mate flies one flag per released billfish on the outriggers of the boat so everyone at the dock sees how many your party reeled in that day.

Next to billfish, some of the most pursued Gulf Stream fish are the yellowfin tuna and bluefin tuna. Other fish you're likely to catch are bigeye tuna, blackfin tuna, dolphinfish (mahimahi), king mackerel, wahoo, and mako shark.

The majority of Outer Banks captains who lead the way to offshore fishing grounds have been working these waters for years. Many are second- and third-generation watermen. They generally choose the daily fishing spot depending on recent trends, seasons, and weather. Occasionally, when there's a slow spell, a captain moves away from the rest of the fleet to play out a hunch. If the maverick meets with success, it's common for him or her to share this find with the rest of the fleet. In other words, the area fleets have a brother- or sisterhood that visiting anglers say they've experienced nowhere else. This camaraderie enhances the fishing experience, plus, fishing together is safer.

Anglers fishing offshore for big game fish generally troll (drag bait behind the moving boat). If you run into a school of fish, such as mahimahi, the captain stops the boat so the party can cast into the water that's been primed with chum, or fish bits. Chumming also is used on bluefin tuna trips. All these techniques are explained the day of the trip. Expect to pay $800 to $1,400 for six people to charter a fishing excursion. Bluefin tuna trips cost a bit more. Gulf Stream charters leaving from Hatteras marinas tend to be less expensive than those near Oregon Inlet.

Beginning January 1, 2007, a fishing license will be required to fish anywhere on the Outer Banks, including up to 3 miles offshore. If you are younger than age 16, you are exempt. July 4th is a free fishing day in North Carolina. No license is required, but recreational size and possession limits are still enforced.

One offshore area frequented with great regularity is called The Point (not to be confused with Cape Hatteras Point). Approximately 37 miles off the Outer Banks, this primary fishing ground for local boats is rich in game fish such as tuna, dolphin, wahoo, billfish, and shark. Blue marlin, wahoo, and mahimahi show up at The Point in April and May. Yellowfin, bigeye, and blackfin tuna are the anglers' mainstay year-round. A significant population of yellowfin inhabits this area in the winter, providing a tremendous seasonal fishery. You have to be patient to fish in the winter because plenty of bad weather days make traveling offshore a waiting game.

The Point has unique characteristics that give it a reputation for attracting and harboring a great variety and quantity of fish, from tiny baitfish to massive billfish. Deep-swimming reef fish, such as grouper, snapper, and tilefish, also inhabit The Point. Because of the strong current, however, you must travel a little bit south of The Point to fish effectively.

What also helps set this spot apart is its proximity to the edge of the continental shelf. Where there's a drop-off, baitfish concentrate because of the nutrient-rich waters and the currents playing off the edge, stirring things up. Anglers don't have to travel far to get to The Point since the continental shelf is particularly narrow off Cape Hatteras. The Point is the last spot where the Gulf Stream appears near the shelf before it veers off in an east-northeasterly direction. Weather permitting, some days the Gulf Stream entirely covers The Point. Other days, prevailing winds push it farther offshore.

Always dress in layers for an Outer Banks fishing trip. Cold mornings have been known to transform into a warm afternoon on many fall and winter days. Of course, the opposite is also true, and gales and thunderstorms notoriously appear out of nowhere.

At about 50 miles wide and a half-mile deep, the Gulf Stream's temperatures rarely drop below 65 to 70 degrees, providing a comfortable habitat for a variety of sea life. The Gulf Steam flows at an average rate of 2.5 mph, at times quickening to 5 mph. This steady flow carries millions of tons of water per second, continually pushing along sea life in its path, including fish, microscopic plants and animals, and gulfweed. Gulfweed lines the edge of the Gulf Stream when winds are favorable, creating a habitat for baitfish. You can pull up a handful of vegetation and find it teeming with miniature shrimp and fish. Anglers fish these "grass lines" as well as the warm-water eddies that spin off from the Gulf Stream. These warm pockets, which vary in size from 20 to 100 miles long by a half-mile to a mile wide, are sometimes filled with schools of dolphin, tuna, and mako shark. The Gulf Stream is about 30 miles off the Outer Banks. It takes about two hours to get there from Oregon Inlet, and about an hour and a half from Hatteras Inlet, depending on the prevailing winds and the speed of your boat.

Catch-and-release fishing for bluefin tuna has anglers from across the globe traveling to Hatteras Island to partake in a bonanza that revived winter offshore charter fishing along the Outer Banks. In 1994, captains began noticing a massive congregation of bluefin tuna inhabiting the wrecks about 20 miles from Hatteras Inlet. The quantity of bluefin available and the frequency with which they bite are phenomenal. Bluefin fishing takes place on the southern Outer Banks, with trips leaving from Hatteras and Ocracoke marinas. Charter boats that ordinarily dock on the northern Outer Banks make their home base on Hatteras during the bluefin months. Many motels on Hatteras Island gladly stay open year-round to accommodate bluefin anglers.

Bluefin tuna weighing 200 to more than 800 pounds have been caught in these waters. These giants are a federally protected species, so anglers almost always must release them. Restrictions state that during bluefin tuna season anglers may keep one fish from 27 to 73 inches per boat per day. The length of the tuna season is determined annually by the National Marine Fisheries and is contingent on overall poundage caught.

Reeling in a bluefin of any magnitude makes the blood of an avid angler run hot! The bluefin seem to strike with less provocation on the choppy days—plus there are fewer boats present during rougher weather. On days when the fish are spooked by excessive boat traffic or simply aren't biting for whatever reason, mates chum the water to increase the chance of a strike. These giants often jump 4 feet out of the ocean to bite bloody bait.

Local anglers troll, chum, and use live or dead bait. Many anglers even catch bluefin tuna and other game fish on a fly. We've seen great success with 130-pound test line. Some folks like to use lighter tackle for the sport of it, but the heavier the line, the better the condition of the fish when it's released. Circle hooks are also recommended, for they tend to lodge in the mouth cartilage rather than in the fleshy gullet or gills.

Even though most of the fish are caught on heavy tackle, carefully handled, and subsequently released, recreational charter boat captains are contemplating a self-imposed quota for catch and release to protect the fish even further. When there are large groups of boats present day after day, it's likely the same fish will have to do battle over and over.

You can enjoy offshore fishing year-round, but for bluefin fishing off Hatteras, book a trip from January through March. Some fish may show up earlier, and there are bluefin available in early April, but by then, captains begin concentrating on yellowfin again. Bluefin boats leave the dock between 5:30 and 7:00 A.M.

Offshore fishing charters accommodate six people. If your party is shy of six, many times the booking agents or captain can hook you up with another small party.

Anglers are expected to bring their own food and drinks on the trips. Coolers for any fish you want to take home can be left in your car at the dock to save room on the boat. Fish-cleaning facilities are available at all docks, and fish-cleaning services (for a fee) are available at most. Bring sunscreen and seasickness remedies (see our sidebar on preventing seasickness). All bait, tackle, instruction, and advice are included in the price of your charter. Mates work for tips, so be sure to tip them at least 15 percent and up to 20 percent of the cost of your trip.

If you really love offshore fishing, consider entering one of the fishing tournaments listed in our Annual Events chapter. If you're not up for Gulf Stream fishing but want to see the fish, show up at these docks at about 4:00 P.M. to watch the boats unload their catches. You'll see mahimahi, tuna, wahoo, cobia, and others, but no billfish since those are catch-and-release species.

INSHORE AND SMALL-BOAT FISHING

A variety of inshore opportunities strike the fancy of the novice or expert angler. Inshore generally refers to inlet, sound, lake, river, and some close-range ocean fishing on a boat.

Inshore captains generally book half-day trips but also offer intermediate all-day trips to take you farther out. If you're interested in bluefish, Spanish mackerel, cobia, king mackerel, bonito, trout, flounder, croaker, or red drum, book trips from virtually any marina. Half-day trips are a little easier on the pocketbook.

Spanish mackerel are a mainstay of the area. Ocracoke Island captains begin looking for them in late April and typically enjoy catches through late October. Farther north on the Outer Banks, Spanish mackerel usually arrive the first or second week in May, depending on the water temperature. Casting is the most sporting way of catching them. We suggest that

Battling and Preventing Seasickness

Almost everyone who has ever been on the water has gotten seasick or at least battled that unmistakable queasy feeling. We've spent plenty of time on the water and know what it's like to want to throw yourself overboard. Here are some suggestions to help you avoid that feeling. Experiment to find what works best for you.

1. Take an over-the-counter remedy for motion sickness the night before your trip and again an hour before departure. This allows time for the medicine to get into your system. Ask your pharmacist about the specifics on these medications. Some will make you more sleepy than others. If you're bringing children along, find out whether the medication is safe for them, too.

2. Topical patches are also available over the counter. The patch fits behind your ear or on your wrist and administers medication through your skin.

3. Eat nongreasy food the night before the trip (and go easy on alcohol), and always eat a nongreasy breakfast. Pancakes and toast are good choices. Despite what you may think, a full stomach is much better than an empty one.

4. Pack a lunch that is neither spicy nor greasy. It also helps to nibble on saltines or ginger snap cookies through the day. Ginger is an Asian remedy for motion sickness. Some people take ginger capsules, but we like the cookies.

5. Some swear that you should drink a lot of fluids while offshore. This makes sense when it comes to dehydration, but we've seen plenty of people get even sicker by downing a soda hoping to ward off the oncoming surge. Always bring water. While some people refrain from drinking anything until the latter part of the trip, others replenish fluids all day. Again, this is a highly personal choice.

6. If you do get sick, the worst may be over if you follow this simple rule: Eat immediately after getting sick (so says Hatteras native Capt. Spurgeon Stowe of the *Miss Hatteras*).

7. If you're feeling queasy, stay out on deck in the fresh air. Don't hole up in the salon, and do not go into the head (bathroom). If you're going to throw up, do it overboard. This is common and acceptable. Concentrate on the horizon if possible. Orient yourself with a stable point, and you should feel better. Above all, don't be embarrassed.

---

you use eight-pound test on a medium to medium-light spinning rod with a pink and white Sting Silver. Other colors work well also; if the people next to you are catching fish and you aren't, see what lures they are using.

If it's flounder you're after, you can find these flat fish in both Hatteras and Oregon Inlets, in clear water. Anglers drift bottom rigs on medium-light spinning tackle.

Croakers are found in the sounds around deep holes, oyster rocks, and sloughs.

You can dine on almost all inshore species. Tarpon, a bony fish with little food value, cannot be overlooked. A release-category fish, the tarpon is probably one of the strongest fighting fish inshore. While the Outer Banks is not a destination spot for tarpon, a handful of locals fish for them around Ocracoke in Pamlico Sound and south to the mouth of the Neuse River. We recommend fresh-cut bait, such as spot or trout, and very sharp hooks to penetrate the tarpon's hard mouth. Remember, it's one thing to hook up and a whole other to bring a tarpon to the boat. Good luck!

Outer Banks anglers enjoy fishing for rockfish (also called striped bass or stripers) year-round. They are fun to catch and make a great-tasting dinner. Though stripers are a regulated species, they've steadily been making a comeback during the last decade or so. Each year stripers spawn inland, and the young live in estuaries for several years before joining the Atlantic migratory population.

The ocean season for stripers is open year-round, but limits vary according to season. Though stripers are present in our waters year-round, the sound inhabitants are protected by restrictions. Since the sound fishing season fluctuates, call a tackle shop for up-to-date regulations. If you want to catch and release, go at it anytime.

When a cold snap hits the Chesapeake Bay area, stripers migrate down past Corolla into Oregon Inlet. November is one of the best months to fish for them around the Manns Harbor Bridge that connects Roanoke Island to the East Lake community. Anglers also fish in the winter for stripers behind Roanoke Island in Fast and South Lakes.

Stripers tend to congregate around bridge pilings. They cluster near these nutrient-covered supports that entice smaller baitfish. You can troll, use spinning tackle with lures, fly-cast, or surf fish. Stripers are bottom feeders, so a planer can be used to catch them. Insiders suggest using a butter bean with a white bucktail on the end or Rat-L Traps. You can catch these fish on slick calm days and in rougher weather, but a little current seems to help.

Summertime finds Outer Bankers fishing the sounds from Manteo to Ocracoke for speckled trout. Insiders suggest you move to the surf or a pier to catch them in fall. The speckled trout fishing is excellent in early fall around Oregon and Hatteras Inlets. They are best caught on light

tackle with artificial lures or on a fly rod. Light spinning tackle is another good choice. Artificial lures are the norm. Insiders suggest using a lead head jig with a soft plastic twister tail for sound, bridge, and inlet fishing. For the beach, try Mirrolures. Currently a keeper must be a 12-inch total length minimum. Call your local tackle shop for more information.

OFFSHORE AND INSHORE CHARTERS

To book offshore and inshore charters, contact one of the marinas listed here. You can request a certain boat and captain or let them offer you one. All of these marinas represent reputable, licensed captains. Call at least a month ahead, but earlier if you know your schedule. Fishing trips continue year-round. If everything is booked, ask to be put on a waiting list; somebody might cancel. You should know that it is the captain's call on whether to go out in inclement weather. Always defer to the captain's judgment. Prices are for full-day trips, unless specified otherwise.

Pirate's Cove Yacht Club
Nags Head–Manteo Causeway, Manteo
(252) 473-3906, (800) 367-4728
www.fishpiratescove.com
Pirate's Cove is a world-class fishing center known for its boats, captains, and large-purse tournaments. By far the most modern marina on the Outer Banks, its prices reflect its high quality. Seventeen sportfishing boats operate out of this marina, each at a price of $1,375 cash, plus mate's tip, for a full day of Gulf Stream fishing. Booking is centralized through the marina. Pirate's Cove Yacht Club is about a 15- to 20-minute boat ride from Oregon Inlet, the northernmost ocean-sound inlet on the Outer Banks. The Gulf Stream is about a two-hour ride from the inlet. Pirate's Cove is the central booking agent for four inshore boats. Half-day trips cost $425 cash, with a maximum of six people per boat. Trips run year-round. Pirate's Cove

sponsors several fishing tournaments each year; see our Annual Events chapter.

Custom Sound Charters
152 Dogwood Trail, Manteo
(252) 216-6765, (252) 473-8432
www.customsoundcharters.com
Captain Rick Caton has long been fishing the Outer Banks waters, both inshore and offshore, and offers a wide variety of trips. Year-round, you can charter sound-fishing trips with Caton, who specializes in catching striped bass. He'll take you fly fishing or light-tackle fishing for trout, puppy drum, flounder, striped bass, and bluefish. Everything you need is furnished.

Caton's inshore trips are offered on the 42-foot *Free Agent,* and he charges $425 for a half day and $850 for a full day. Caton also conducts shrimping and crabbing trips, inshore Spanish mackerel trolling trips, and light-tackle bottom fishing over wrecks for triggerfish and black sea bass. Or, you can choose to anchor and chum for sharks, cobia, and king mackerel. Call for more information.

Inlet Charters
(252) 441-2174, (252) 202-2174
Captain Billy Griggs offers inshore full or half-day inlet trips for red drum, large stripers, bluefish, Spanish mackerel, king mackerel, and cobia onboard his 24-foot custom Carolina-style boat. Trips range from $350 to $700. Griggs can fish with up to four anglers.

Tideline Charters
Thicket Lump Marina, Wanchese
(252) 261-1458
www.tidelinecharter.com
The 34-foot custom Carolina boat called the *Tideline* takes full- and half-day inshore and intermediate trips. Half-day inshore trips cost $400, and half-day intermediate trips cost $600. Full-day intermediate trips cost $800.

Nags Head Guide Service
(252) 475-1555
www.nagsheadfishing.com

Captain David Dudley offers light-tackle inshore trips for stripers, flounder, trout, bluefish, mackerel, cobia, drum, and large-mouth bass. Rates range from $200 to $475, depending on the number of people on board and the length of the trip.

Oregon Inlet Fishing Center
NC 12, Bodie Island
(252) 441-6301, (800) 272-5199
www.oregon-inlet.com
The Oregon Inlet charter fishing fleet is a historic landmark on the Outer Banks. Most of the 31 sportfishing boats in this marina were locally made and have the famous Carolina flared bow. Some of the Outer Banks's most seasoned captains fish from this marina and have done so since it opened in the 1960s. All offshore trips to the Gulf Stream from this marina cost $1,360 for a party of six. Five boats offer inshore and intermediate trips from Oregon Inlet Fishing Center. Intermediate trips of 5 to 10 miles cost $437 for a half-day and $565 for a full day with up to four people per boat.

Hatteras Harbor Marina
NC 12, Hatteras Village
(252) 986-2166, (800) 676-4939
www.hatterasharbor.com
This marina represents about 20 vessels that take anglers to the Gulf Stream via Hatteras Inlet. Trips cost from $840 to $1,150, depending on the size of the boat. The Gulf Stream is about a 90-minute boat ride from Hatteras Inlet. Inshore fishing trips are chartered year-round from this marina on one of two 24-foot boats. Half-day trips are available.

Hatteras Landing Marina
NC 12, Hatteras Village
(252) 986-2077, (800) 551-8478
www.hatteraslanding.com
Hatteras Landing Marina represents 12 off-shore fishing boats. Prices range from $700 to $1,350, depending on the size of the boat. If you don't have a full party, Hatteras Landing can put one together for you if you're willing to wait on standby for

a couple of days. Winter bluefin tuna trips run at about the same price range.

Oden's Dock Marina
NC 12, Hatteras Village
(252) 986-2555, (888) 544-8115
www.odensdock.com
Five or six offshore charter boats operate out of Oden's Dock. Prices range from $850 to $1,030, and winter bluefin tuna trips usually cost around $1,200. Oden's books inshore charters on a 22-foot boat and a 24-foot that each handle four people. These boats fish in the sound only. A larger 42-foot boat operates in the sound or ocean and accommodates six people.

Teach's Lair Marina
NC 12, Hatteras Village
(252) 986-2460
www.teachslair.com
Fourteen boats operate out of Teach's Lair. Full-day offshore trips cost between $750 and $1,250, and make-up charters are available for $190 per person. Bluefin trips are more expensive. Teach's Lair books inshore charters on morning or afternoon half-day trips. Morning trips run from 7:00 A.M. to noon, and afternoon trips run from 12:30 to 5:30 P.M. Prices range from $250 to $500, depending on the boat.

Albatross Fleet
Foster's Quay, Hatteras Village
(252) 986-2515
www.albatrossfleet.com
The Albatross Fleet of Hatteras, established by Capt. Ernal Foster in 1937, was the first charter fishing operation on the North Carolina coast. The original boat, the *Albatross*, still takes anglers to the Gulf Stream. The *Albatross* was designed by Foster to perfectly accommodate offshore fishing parties, and it was built across the sound in Harkers Island. The fleet now consists of three boats, all named *Albatross,* and is now operated by Foster's son, Ernal Foster Jr., who began working as a mate on his father's boat in 1958. The *Albatross I, II,* and *III,* all 44 feet,

dock at Foster's Quay. Offshore trips begin at $850 for a full day. Inshore half-day trips cost $350.

Ocracoke Fishing Center
and Anchorage Marina
NC 12, Ocracoke Village
(252) 928-6661
Three boats offer full-day offshore charters out of this marina. Full-day trips cost around $900 to $1,000. These boats use Ocracoke Inlet when heading to the Gulf Stream.

OFFSHORE AND INSHORE HEADBOAT FISHING

Headboat fishing can give you a great fishing experience without the expense of chartering a private boat. Several large boats take parties into the intermediate waters (in the ocean, though not as far as the Gulf Stream) all day, while others ply the inshore waters for half-days. Ocean trips typically track bottom species, such as black sea bass, triggerfish, tilefish, amberjack, snapper, tautog, grouper, and occasionally small sharks. The species vary slightly from north to south. Generally on these trips you're dropping a line down over artificial and natural reefs and wrecks, not trolling. Inshore trips ply the sounds and inlets and sometimes go several miles offshore to the wrecks on calm days. The trips usually yield croaker, trout, spot, flounder, sea mullet, blow toads, and pigfish. There is one headboat, the *Country Girl* out of Pirate's Cove, that takes trips to the Gulf Stream.

Headboats are built to accommodate a multitude of passengers, each person paying "by the head," hence the name. Open deck space from bow to stern holds anglers comfortably, and sometimes there is an enclosed cabin area. The boats are generally between 60 and 75 feet long and can hold up to 50 anglers. All gear and bait are supplied. All you have to bring is food, drinks, and sunscreen. Some boats provide snacks and drinks, so you should check when making reservations. You don't even need a fishing license. If you're new to fishing, the mates will help you with everything from baiting your hook to identifying your catch. Be sure to dress in layers if you're fishing any time other than summer. Mornings and evenings can be cool, even when days are warm.

Inshore headboat trips are the most suitable choice for families with young children, mainly because they're shorter. Deep-sea trips are full-day trips that can be as long as 8 to 10 hours, and the captain will not turn around except in a real emergency. Seasickness is not an emergency. Inshore trips are typically a half-day. Watch the kids carefully on the boats. The decks are often slippery, so you should enforce a no-running policy. Plus, these boats carry large crowds of people and fishing gear. Getting hooked can ruin a trip. That said, headboats are great places to teach children how to fish for a very small amount of money. Remain positive when fishing with kids. Everywhere in the world, there are days when the fishing is slow. If you're having one of those days, let the trip be a positive lesson in nature, patience, and people. A positive attitude will go far in hooking your kids on fishing for life. Besides, you often see dolphins, birds, turtles, and sometimes whales on these trips, so the day won't be a total loss.

Crystal Dawn
Pirate's Cove Yacht Club
Nags Head–Manteo Causeway, Manteo
(252) 473-5577
www.themefifty.com/crystaldawn
This 65-foot, two-story vessel offers inshore (inlet and sound) bottom-fishing trips from May through October. The boat holds up to 55 passengers. All bait and tackle are provided, but you have to bring your own snacks and drinks. Tickets cost $30 per person for everyone older than age 10, and $25 per child age 10 and younger. In peak season (Memorial Day to Labor Day), trips run from 7:00 A.M. to noon or 12:30 to 5:00 P.M. The rest of the time, the boat heads out from 8:00 A.M. to

1:00 P.M. The Crystal Dawn also takes sightseeing trips in the evenings (see our Recreation chapter).

Country Girl
Pirate's Cove Yacht Club
Nags Head–Manteo Causeway, Manteo
(252) 473-5577
The Country Girl heads offshore from 5 to 35 miles, depending on the weather and the fishing. The 57-foot boat holds 27 passengers, each paying $85. This is a full-day trip, lasting from 7:00 A.M. to 4:30 P.M. Older children and teenagers are welcome, but younger children are not. The Country Girl offers trips from May through October.

Miss Oregon Inlet
Oregon Inlet Fishing Center
NC 12, Bodie Island
(252) 441-6301
www.oregon-inlet.com
The Miss Oregon Inlet is a 65-foot headboat that offers half-day, inshore fishing trips for $31 per person or $21 for kids age six and younger. In early spring and fall, the boat makes one trip per day (except Sunday), leaving at 8:00 A.M. and returning at 12:30 P.M. From Memorial Day through Labor Day there are two trips: 7:00 to 11:30 A.M. and noon to 4:30 P.M. Buy tickets one day in advance, if possible, because the boat often fills up.

Miss Hatteras and Captain Clam
Oden's Dock, NC 12, Hatteras Village
(252) 986-2365
The Miss Hatteras headboat ties up at Oden's Dock in Hatteras Village and operates from February through November. She offers half-day fishing trips for $35 per person on Monday, Tuesday, and Thursday morning from 8:00 A.M. to noon and Tuesday and Thursday afternoons from 1:00 to 5:00 P.M. On Wednesday, Friday, Saturday, and Sunday, she offers full-day bottom-fishing trips from 6:30 A.M. to 4:30 P.M. for $90 per person. The boat accommodates 45 people. In late October and early November, she offers full-day

king mackerel fishing trips for $125 per person. All gear is included in the cost of the trip, and a snack bar is on board. In the summer, when the *Miss Hatteras* is booked, Oden's Dock also offers the *Captain Clam*, a 40-person-capacity headboat that conducts half-day, inshore sound, and inlet fishing trips for $36 a person. These trips run Monday through Saturday from 8:00 A.M. to noon and 1:00 to 5:00 P.M.

MARINAS

The Outer Banks is dotted with many marinas with slips, boat ramps, gas and diesel fuel, tackle, and supplies. Almost all offer fishing charters as well. We've listed the fishing opportunities available at marinas in our Offshore and Inshore Headboat Fishing category in this chapter. For information pertaining to slip rental, see our Getting Here, Getting Around chapter; and for information on amenities offered to boaters, such as boat ramps, gas, and supplies, see our Water Sports chapter.

BACKWATER FISHING

Fishing the backwaters means fishing the more-protected inland sounds, rivers, and lakes, either brackish or freshwater. The Croatan Sound, between Roanoke Island and the mainland, is a popular fishing spot for striped bass, also known as stripers or rockfish in these parts. Striper fishing is a year-round sport on the Outer Banks, though you can keep those caught in the sound only at certain times of the year. The Manns Harbor Bridge is renowned for its striper activity. Stripers congregate at the bridge, feeding around the pilings. They also feed over oyster bars located near the bridge. Be on the lookout for diving gulls and terns, which is a good identifying marker of the location of stripers. Both sides of the bridge have public parking and access for waders, but the western side has a marina with a boat-launch ramp. The Croatan Sound Bridge, just

If you're going fishing without a local captain or guide, check on current fishing regulations before embarking on your trip. Size and bag limits change frequently, and fines for illegal fish can be substantial.

beyond the Manns Harbor Bridge, has proven itself as a striper-attracting structure, so you should try both bridges. Many anglers fly fish for stripers. Others swear by live eel, jigging with a bucktail or grub, or casting a Rat-L-Trap.

Backwater fishing also includes the Alligator River and South and East Lakes. You can troll, spin-cast, bait-cast, or fly fish year-round in the backwaters. You'll find an interesting mix of freshwater and saltwater species, including crappie, striped bass, largemouth bass, flounder, bream, sheepshead, drum, perch, croaker, spot, catfish, and trout. It all depends on the season.

If you'd like a guide, there are a few that offer backwater services. The fishing is so laid-back that you might find the guide throwing in a line with you. Since these waters are more protected and less prone to harsh offshore winds, you can often fish here when you can't elsewhere. This is a nice alternative to ocean fishing, and it's a good choice for families. Bring your camera. You might spot birds, deer, and bears on land and alligators in the water.

You don't have to hire a guide, though. You can launch your own boat from any number of local ramps (see our Water Sports chapter) or contact a tackle shop or marina for information.

Phideaux Too
P.O. Box 343, Manns Harbor, NC 27953
(252) 473-3059
Captain V. P. Brinson uses a 150-hp Pathfinder to get you to the fish. Brinson offers spin-casting, fly rod, bait-casting, and trolling charters in lakes, sounds, and

rivers. Fish for rockfish, trout, red drum, flounder, bass, bream, crappie, and perch. Call for prices.

Custom Sound Charters
152 Dogwood Trail, Manteo
(252) 473-1209
www.customsoundcharters.com
Light-tackle backwater trips are taken on the *Iron Will,* an 18-foot center-console. Captain Rick Caton books trips on this boat in the spring and fall. Call for prices.

FLY FISHING

The Outer Banks has been a top fishing destination for decades, but fly fishing only recently caught on here. The fly-fishing bug on the Banks started in the 1960s and 1970s, when a few well-known fly anglers and locals cast flies into the surf for bluefish and were quite successful. In 1979 Chico Fernandez fly fished the Outer Banks, catching a white marlin. In 1981 he set an International Game Fish Association Fly Rod record with a 42-pound, 5-ounce red drum on a 12-pound tippet. Since then, anglers have slowly discovered the Outer Banks's varied fly-fishing opportunities. Fly-fishing magazines and television shows now regularly feature the Outer Banks and its fly-fishing guides.

Fly anglers fish in the same places conventional anglers do. Fly anglers catch dolphin, tuna, and marlin in the Gulf Stream. They catch amberjack, mackerel, albacore, and cobia on inshore wrecks. They reap pompano and bluefish in the surf and stripers in the sounds. The most successful and accessible fly fishing is in the sounds, where you'll find speckled trout, stripers, red drum, bluefish, and Spanish mackerel.

It can be difficult to learn to fly fish the Outer Banks, especially the vast Pamlico and Roanoke Sounds. Hiring a guide is the quickest way to learn the area. If you prefer to go on your own, ask for advice at local tackle shops.

Flat Out Fly-Fishing & Light-Tackle Charters
(252) 449-0562
www.outerbanksflyfishing.com
Captain Brian Horsley and Capt. Sarah Gardner are true Insiders when it comes to Outer Banks fly fishing. Both halves of this fly-fishing duo are guides and well-known fishing writers.

Horsley's *Flat Out* and Gardner's *Fly Girl* dock at Oregon Inlet Fishing Center. They run near-shore fly-fishing/light-tackle charters from April through November, though they move both boats to Harkers Island on the southernmost Outer Banks during October and November for false albacore fishing. They fish the Pamlico, Roanoke, and Croatan Sounds for speckled trout, bluefish, puppy drum, little tunny, flounder, and cobia. Half-day trips cost $300; full-day trips cost $525.

Fish Trap Charters
(252) 473-2657
www.outerbanksguideservice.com
Captain Tom Wagner of Fish Trap Charters offers light-tackle and fly-fishing charters in the sounds and near-shore waters. Expect to catch drum, trout, stripers, cobia, albacore, and more. Fish Trap offers full- and half-day trips, plus a special two-hour trip that is great for families with children. All anglers are welcome, so don't be shy if you're not experienced. All equipment, bait, tackle, and ice are provided. His 24-foot boat accommodates up to four people. You can take four-, six-, or eight-hour trips for prices ranging from $300 to $575. Call to arrange a meeting place. Captain Wagner has appeared on ESPN2 and OLN.

Riomar Fly-Fishing and Light Tackle
(252) 480-6416
www.fish-riomar.com
Captain David Rohde offers inshore, near-shore, and soundside charters onboard his 18-foot Parker boat, the *Riomar.* He offers fly and light-tackle trips for speckled

trout, bluefish, stripers, and drum. Rohde operates the *Riomar* in Harkers Island in the fall for albacore fishing. Half-day trips cost $300, and full-day trips cost $500. Call to arrange a meeting place.

Captain Bryan De Hart's
Coastal Adventures Guide Service
507 Barlowe Street, Manteo
(252) 473-1575
www.coastaladv.com

Captain De Hart books light-tackle fly-fishing charters inshore, in brackish and saltwater, and in coastal rivers and sounds. Prices start at $225 for two people to fish a half-day, and $400 for two people fishing all day. On the backwaters, De Hart uses an 18-foot War Eagle, and in the open sound, he fishes from a 22-foot Javelin. De Hart has been featured on ESPN's *Fly-Fishing America* program and is a regular on *The Carolina Outdoor Journal*.

Outer Banks Waterfowl
67 East Dogwood Trail, Kitty Hawk
(252) 441-3732
www.outerbankswaterfowl.com

Captain Vic Berg runs sound and inlet fly- or spinning-tackle fishing trips. Everything you need is included, or if you like, you can bring your favorite tackle. Berg also offers instruction on fly or surf fishing. Family and group rates are available for lessons. For full-day fishing for two people, he charges $450; add $25 for a third member. Half-day trips for the same number of anglers run $250. Berg is U.S. Coast Guard–licensed.

Berg is also an experienced hunting guide who leads hunting trips that can yield many species of waterfowl. A typical bag of 10 ducks can contain seven different species. Berg's blinds are located between Oregon Inlet and Pea Island and have proven their success for more than 25 years. He also offers swan-hunting trips. A rate of $150 per person covers the blind, guide, decoys, and retriever for one day.

SURF FISHING

Surf fishing is a popular Outer Banks pastime for the competitor or amateur alike. While there are miles of beach from which to cast a line, experienced local anglers say a surf caster's success will vary depending on sloughs, temperature, currents, and season. One of the hottest surfcasting spots on the Outer Banks is Cape Point, a sand spit at the tip of Cape Hatteras. Anglers often stand waist-deep in the churning waters, dutifully waiting for red drum to strike.

About nine months out of the year, anglers can fish for red drum on the Outer Banks. The best time to catch big drum is mid-October through mid-November. During this period large schools of drum are feeding on baitfish called menhaden that migrate down the coastline. Cape Point is the hot spot for drum, but it tends to be a very crowded place to fish. A good second choice is the beach between Salvo and Buxton. But in the fall, you can catch them from Rodanthe down to Hatteras Inlet. From mid-April through about the third week in May, red drum show up around Ocracoke Inlet, both in the ocean and shallow shoal waters at the inlet's mouth and also in the Pamlico Sound.

Serious drum anglers fish after dark for the nocturnal feeders. Insiders prefer a southwesterly wind with an incoming tide and water temperatures in the low 60s. Big drum are known to come close to the surf during rough weather. Puppy drum (or juvenile drum) are easier to catch than the adult fish. They show up in the surf after a northeast blow in late summer or early fall. Anglers use finger mullet with success as well as fresh shrimp (and we do mean fresh). Red drum are a regulated fish, both in size and limit. Call your local tackle shop for more information. If you're interested in learning more about red drum tag and release programs, call the Division of Marine Fisheries at (252) 473-5734 or (252) 264-3911.

There's a lengthy list of fish regularly caught at Cape Point. Common species include dogfish, bluefish, pompano, striped bass, and Spanish mackerel as well as bottom feeders such as croaker, flounder, spot, sea mullet, and both gray and speckled trout. More uncommon are tarpon, cobia, amberjack, jack crevalles, and shark weighing several hundred pounds.

Shoaling that takes place off Cape Hatteras makes Cape Point a haven for baitfish, and the influence of the nearby Gulf Stream and its warm-water jetties also contribute to excellent fishing. The beach accommodates many four-wheel-drive vehicles, and during peak season (spring and fall) it's packed with anglers. If you want to try fishing Cape Point, take North Carolina Highway 12 to Buxton and look for signs to vehicle access ramp 43. (For more information about driving on the beach, please see our Getting Here, Getting Around chapter.)

A section on surf fishing would not be complete without discussing bluefish. For years, anglers enjoyed the arrival and subsequent blitzes of big bluefish during the Easter season and again around Thanksgiving. During a blitz, big blues chase baitfish up onto the beach in a feeding frenzy. This puts the blues in striking distance of ready surf casters. It's a phenomenal sight to watch anglers reel in these fat and ferocious fish one after the other. Anglers line up along the shore like soldiers, and many a rod is bent in that telltale C-shape, fighting a bluefish. Some days you can see a skyfull of birds hovering, waiting to feast on the baitfish that the bluefish run toward the shore for.

The last few years, the blues have not blitzed like they used to. As with most species, population figures (or at least landings) tend to rise and fall in cycles; perhaps they're tending toward a low point in the pattern. Maybe the big bluefin tuna, which feed on bluefish, are taking over these days, but blitz or not, you can usually catch some bluefish in the surf or in greater numbers offshore.

Joe Malat's Outer Banks Surf Fishing School
415 Bridge Lane, Nags Head
(252) 441-4767
www.joemalat.com

For some pointers from an angler who has certainly put his time into the sport, pick up a copy of Joe Malat's *Surf Fishing*. This easy-to-read, illustrated book outlines methods of catching species common to our area. Malat shares tips on the lures, rigs, baits, and knots favored by local surf anglers. You can also read about catch-and-release techniques and how to locate and land fish. This comprehensive book also includes useful information about tides, currents, wind, and other factors that affect surf fishing. Malat's *Pier Fishing* (Wellspring, 1999) includes all you should want to know about pier fishing plus information on 15 species of fish. For even more information, read "Joe Malat's Fishing Notebook," which appears weekly in the *Outer Banks Sentinel*.

Malat's Outer Banks Surf Fishing School offers a two-and-a-half-day course that includes one day of classroom instruction, one-and-a-half days of on-the-beach instruction (bait included), classroom materials, and a copy of Malat's book. Malat and instructor Mac Currin offer personal instruction in an enjoyable, relaxed atmosphere, teaching students about such things as "reading the beach," fish identification, tackle, bait and lures, knot tying, casting, and beach driving. Cost is $275 per person, and there is a 25-person maximum per school. Two schools are held in the fall, and one is held in spring. There is also a two-day Surf Fishing School for Ladies Only. Malat and his wife, Nell, are the instructors during this weekend that includes one day of classroom instruction and one of fishing. This school is held once a year, in June, at $175 per person.

PIER FISHING

Pier fishing is a true Outer Banks institution and has delighted anglers young and old for decades. The appeal is obvious: low cost and a chance to fish deeper waters without a boat. The variety of fish available also lures anglers. Depending on the time of year, you can catch croakers, spot, sea mullet, red drum, cobia, and occasionally a tarpon, king mackerel, sheepshead, or amberjack.

Bait and tackle are sold at each pier, or you can rent whatever gear you need. Avid anglers usually come prepared, but newcomers to the sport are always welcome on the pier, and staff are more than willing to outfit you and offer some fishing tips. Pier fishing is a good way to introduce kids to the sport. Many Outer Banks locals spent their youth on the pier soaking in know-how and area fishing lore. For instance, Garry Oliver, who owns the Outer Banks Pier in South Nags Head, spent many a summer day at the Nags Head Fishing Pier when he was a lad. Today, Garry is a member of an award-winning surf-casters team.

The Outer Banks has no oceanfront boardwalks, but the piers more than make up for it. The smells of salt air and creosote-treated lumber greet you as you walk the wide planks over the ocean water. Looking down between the cracks, you see the waves crashing beneath you. You don't have to fish to appreciate the piers. For a small fee, you can just walk out on the piers to enjoy the vantage points.

Avalon Fishing Pier
NC 12, MP 6, Kill Devil Hills
(252) 441–7494
www.avalonpier.com

Avalon Pier, in the heart of Kill Devil Hills, was built in the mid 1950s and is 705 feet long. The pier has lights for night fishing, a snack bar, a bait and tackle shop, ice, video games, and rental fishing gear. A busy place in-season, the pier is open 24 hours a day. The pier house is open from 6:00 A M until midnight. The pier is closed December through mid-March. Admission prices are $8.50 for adults and $4.00 for

children younger than age 12. A weekly pass is $40. A three-day weekend pass is $20; ask about season passes. People with disabilities are admitted free.

Nags Head Fishing Pier
NC 12, MP 12, Nags Head
(252) 441–5141
www.nagsheadpier.com

This is one of the most popular fishing piers on the Outer Banks. It is 750 feet long and has its own bait and tackle shop. Enjoy night fishing, game tables for the kids, and a restaurant. The Pier House Restaurant features fresh seafood and wonderful views of the ocean. The restaurant serves breakfast, lunch, and dinner. (See our Restaurants chapter for more information.) The pier closes in December and reopens in March or April, depending upon whether the fish are biting. It is open 24 hours during the season. Admission is $8.00 per day for adults and $4.00 per day for kids age 11 and younger. Passes for three or more days cost $21. Season rates are $150 for singles and $240 for couples. Sightseeing costs $1.50 for adults and 75 cents for children.

Outer Banks Pier and Fishing Center
NC 12, MP 18½, South Nags Head
(252) 441–5740

This 650-foot ocean pier was originally built in 1959 and rebuilt in 1962 after the Ash Wednesday storm. Owner Garry Oliver has all you need in the bait and tackle shop for a day of fishing along this stretch of beach. A 300-foot sound fishing and crabbing pier is also available on the Nags Head-Manteo Causeway. The piers are open 24 hours a day from Memorial Day until mid-October and close from Thanksgiving through Easter. Rates in 2005 were $7.00 per day, $18.00 for three days, $35.00 per week, $135.00 per season for one person, and $250.00 per season for a couple. Tackle rental was $5.00. Senior citizen discounts and group rates are available. Snack at the pier's on-site oceanside deli.

Hatteras Island Resort Fishing Pier
NC 12, Rodanthe
(252) 987-2323, (800) 331-6541
www.obxfishingpier.com

After massive poundings by Hurricanes Dennis and Floyd, this pier collapsed in the fall of 1999. Even the land on which the pier house stood disappeared due to storm erosion. The land was refilled and in fall 2000 the pier reopened, a little farther back from its original location. The pier house sells drinks, snacks, sandwiches, tackle, and bait. The pier and pier house are open every day in the summer, 7:00 A.M. to 11:00 P.M. from Memorial Day to Labor Day and 7:00 A.M. to 10:00 P.M. the rest of the season. The Rodanthe Pier is closed December 1 through April 1. Prices are $8.00 per day to fish and $1.00 to walk on. Weekly and seasonal passes are available.

Avon Golf & Fishing Pier
NC 12, Avon
(252) 995-5480
www.avonpier.com

Avon Golf & Fishing Pier has a reputation for being a hot spot for red drum. The all-tackle world-record red drum, weighing in at 94 pounds, 2 ounces, was caught about 200 yards from the pier in 1984, and the record holds to this day. The pier opens at the beginning of April and remains open through Thanksgiving. Purchase or rent your fishing supplies here, buy sandwiches and drinks, and pick up nautical gifts, including T-shirts and sand mirrors. They also offer an 18-hole natural-grass putting green on the premises. Play is unlimited, and you can come and go as you please

When buying waders or boots, always buy them one-and-a-half sizes larger than your shoe size. The larger size will enable you to slip them off in the event that you step in a slough or fall overboard.

for $8.00. After Memorial Day, the pier remains open 24 hours a day until it closes for the season. Rates are $8.00 per day for adults, $5.00 per day for kids, and $1.00 to sightsee.

CITATION FISH

Citation fish are caught in the waters off the Outer Banks every year. The North Carolina Division of Marine Fisheries manages the North Carolina Saltwater Fishing Tournament, which recognizes outstanding angling achievement. The tournament runs yearlong. Other than charter boat captains and crews for hire, everyone is eligible for a citation fish award. Eligible waters include North Carolina sounds, surf, estuaries, and the ocean. This tournament is for the hook-and-line angler; use of electric or hydraulic equipment is not allowed. There is one award per species, and all fish must be weighed in at an official weigh station. Anglers receive a certificate after the close of the tournament. There is no registration fee. Following is a list of the area's weigh stations, where you can pick up a species list and receive rules for the tournament. Citations are also awarded for the catch and release of some species.

OFFICIAL WEIGH STATIONS

Corolla

TW's Bait & Tackle
NC 12, (252) 453-3339

Duck

Bob's Bait & Tackle
NC 12, (252) 261-8589

Kitty Hawk

Kitty Hawk Bait & Tackle
US 158, MP 4½
(252) 261-2955

TW's Bait & Tackle Shop
US 158, MP 4, (252) 261-7848

Whitney's Bait and Tackle
US 158, MP 4½
(252) 261-5551

Kill Devil Hills

Avalon Fishing Pier
NC 12, MP 6, (252) 441-7494

Stop 'N' Shop Convenience and Deli
NC 12, MP 8½, (252) 441-6105

Nags Head

Nags Head Fishing Pier
NC 12, MP 12, (252) 441-5141

Outer Banks Pier and Fishing Center
NC 12, MP 18½, (252) 441-5740

Outer Banks Fishing Unlimited
Nags Head-Manteo Causeway
(252) 441-5028

TW's Bait & Tackle Shop
US 158, MP 10½, (252) 441-4807

Whalebone Tackle
Nags Head-Manteo Causeway
(252) 441-7413

Manteo

Pirate's Cove
Nags Head–Manteo Causeway
(252) 473-3906

Oregon Inlet

Oregon Inlet Fishing Center
NC 12, 8 miles south of Whalebone
Junction, (252) 441-6301

Rodanthe

Hatteras Jack
NC 12, (252) 987-2428

Mac's Tackle & Island Convenience
NC 12, (252) 987-2239

Salvo

The Fishin' Hole
NC 12, (252) 987-2351

Avon

Frank and Fran's Fisherman's Friend
NC 12, (252) 995-4171

Buxton

Dillon's Corner
NC 12, (252) 995-5083

Red Drum Tackle Shop
NC 12, (252) 995-5414

Frisco

Frisco Rod & Gun
NC 12, (252) 995-5366

Frisco Tackle
NC 12, (252) 995-4361

Hatteras Village

Hatteras Harbor Marina
NC 12, (252) 986-2166

Oden's Dock
NC 12, (252) 986-2555

Pelican's Roost
NC 12, (252) 986-2213

Teach's Lair Marina
NC 12, (252) 986-2460

Willis Boat Landing
57209 Willis Lane, (252) 986-2208

Ocracoke

Ocracoke Fishing Center
NC 12, (252) 928-6661

O'Neal's Dockside Tackle Shop
NC 12, (252) 928-1111

Tradewinds
NC 12, (252) 928-5491

BAIT AND TACKLE SHOPS

Full-service tackle shops are scattered from Corolla to Ocracoke. They are good sources for not only rods, reels, bait, and other fishing equipment and accessories, but also for tips on what's biting and where. You'll find bait and tackle at all Outer Banks fishing piers and most marinas, too. Just about every department store and general store on the barrier islands carries some sort of fishing gear, and many shops also offer tackle rental. You can ask for guide information at any one of the following shops.

Duck

Bob's Bait & Tackle
NC 12, Duck
(252) 261-8589
Stop in Bob's if you're looking for advice on where to catch the really big one. The old building is left over from Duck's early days, when a soundside dock out back was the distribution point for shiploads of fresh ocean fish. The shop carries a good supply of rods, reels, bait, and tackle. Bob's also books offshore charters and provides a hunting and fishing guide service.

Kitty Hawk

TW's Bait & Tackle
US 158, MP 4, Kitty Hawk
(252) 261-7848
TW's Bait & Tackle, next to the 7-Eleven in Kitty Hawk, is a great place to find the right stuff for your fishing adventure. Owner Terry "T. W." Stewart has been in business since 1981 and can sell you what you need, including ice and live bait.

TW's also books inshore and offshore charter fishing trips. There is another location in Corolla (252–453–3339) at the Food Lion Shopping Center, but it's closed during January and February. The Kitty Hawk location stays open year-round. TW's has a Nags Head store at milepost 10½; call (252) 441–4807. The Nags Head location is open all year also.

Whitney's Bait & Tackle
US 158, MP 4½, Kitty Hawk
(252) 261-5551
Whitney's specializes in custom rods made by Whitney Jones, plus offshore and inshore bait and tackle. The shop also offers rod and reel repairs. The walls at Whitney's are lined with Jones's impressive freshwater and saltwater citations and trophies. Call for Whitney's fishing report.

Kill Devil Hills

Stop 'N' Shop Convenience and Deli
NC 12, MP 8½, Kill Devil Hills
(252) 441-6105
Located on the Beach Road across from the Kill Devil Hills beach access, Stop 'N' Shop has about anything you might need for a day of fishing or a day at the beach. This is a full-service tackle shop, with fishing and beach items that include bait, tackle, local information, beer, ice, gas, and rental equipment. Owners Tom and Vickie Byers stock a surprising amount of goods for anglers. Stop 'N' Shop is open seven days a week year-round.

T.I.'s Bait & Tackle
US 158, MP 9, Kill Devil Hills
(252) 441-3166
T.I.'s is a member of the North Carolina Beach Buggy Association. The shop offers quality tackle and fresh bait and is an authorized Penn parts distributor and repair station. T.I.'s is also a factory-authorized Daiwa service warranty center. The shop is open year-round. Check out their other location across from Cahoon's grocery on NC 12, milepost 16½, in Nags Head; call (252) 441–5242.

Nags Head

Whalebone Tackle
Nags Head-Manteo Causeway
Nags Head
(252) 441-7413
Whalebone is a full-service tackle shop offering ice, fresh bait, tackle, and rod and Penn reel repairs. As they say at the store, "All roads lead to Whalebone Tackle, the center of the universe." The store is open year-round.

Fishing Unlimited
Nags Head-Manteo Causeway
Nags Head
(252) 441-5028

Fishing Unlimited specializes in fresh bait and is a full-service tackle shop. You can purchase live bait, custom rigs, and lures here as well as crabbing supplies, snacks, and drinks. Services include 16-foot outboard and 20-foot pontoon boat rentals. Fish or crab from their 300-foot sound pier for a fee of $2.00. You can rent rods and reels for $5.00 a day. The shop is open from Easter until early December.

Salvo

The Fishin' Hole
NC 12, Salvo
(252) 987-2351

Operating on the Outer Banks since 1976, The Fishin' Hole is a full-service tackle shop that sells live bait, tackle, beach supplies, groceries, and T-shirts. Rod and reel repairs for Daiwa, Penn, and other brands are available here. It's an official weigh station for the North Carolina Beach Buggy Association. The shop is open from the end of March through mid-December.

Avon

Frank and Fran's Fisherman's Friend
NC 12, Avon
(252) 995-4171

A full-service tackle shop, official weigh station, and headquarters for the local Red Drum Tournament held every October, Frank and Fran's is an emporium of fishing gear. This is another official weigh station for the state and the North Carolina Beach Buggy Association.

Buxton

Dillon's Corner
NC 12, Buxton
(252) 995-5083

Stop here for an assortment of tackle, including custom rods and bait. The shop also carries a wide selection of gifts, T-shirts, and lighthouse replicas (see our Shopping chapter). The shop also offers rod repairs and has gas pumps. Dillon's Corner is open all year but has shorter hours in winter.

Red Drum Tackle Shop
NC 12, Buxton
(252) 995-5414

Get the latest in fishing information and select gear at Red Drum Tackle Shop. It offers everything you need in the way of custom rods, bait, and tackle, plus reel repairs. They're a Penn warranty center and official weigh station for the state, the North Carolina Beach Buggy Association, and the Cape Hatteras Anglers Club.

Frisco

Frisco Rod and Gun
NC 12, Frisco
(252) 995-5366
www.friscorodgun.com

Frisco Rod and Gun is a one-stop shop for everything you need for a hunting or fishing trip. The owner calls it his "hobby gone wild." You'll find inshore and offshore fishing equipment, fly-fishing gear, custom rods, guns, ice, bait, tackle, and one of the biggest and best selections of knives you'll ever see. They also offer rod and reel repairs and can help you find a hunting or fishing guide. Taxidermy services can be arranged. Camping supplies, name-brand outdoor apparel, Sperry footwear, T-shirts, groceries, gas, and convenience items round out the offerings.

Ocracoke

Tradewinds
NC 12, Ocracoke
(252) 928-5491

Tradewinds is a one-stop tackle shop that

FISHING REPORTS

For the latest word on what's biting, check with the following sources:

Nags Head Fishing Pier, (252) 441-5141

Pirate's Cove Yacht Club
(252) 473-3906

Oregon Inlet Fishing Center
(252) 441-6301

Red Drum Tackle Shop
(252) 995-5414

Frisco Pier, (252) 986-2533

O'Neal's Dockside, (252) 928-1111

can supply all your fishing needs, including fresh and frozen bait, tackle, clothing items, and plenty of good advice about fishing. The shop also offers tackle rentals and rod and reel repair. Tradewinds is an official North Carolina weigh station and is open seven days a week from March through December.

O'Neal's Dockside Tackle Shop
NC 12, Ocracoke
(252) 928-1111

O'Neal's offers fresh and frozen bait as well as fishing, marine, and hunting supplies and can furnish you with any license you need. They are a full-service tackle shop and offer tackle rentals. These folks have been in business for more than 20 years and are official North Carolina Wildlife and Marine Fisheries agents. If you have any questions on official regulations, stop here.

Also read the *Virginian-Pilot* daily North Carolina section and the *Carolina Coast* for Damon Tatem's report. Check out Joe Malat's informative weekly column in the *Outer Banks Sentinel.* The *ReelFisher News* is a free quarterly tabloid available at retail outlets throughout the Outer Banks; it has folksy fishing editorials plus a directory to area piers, ramps, marinas, and weigh stations. For more Insiders' information, you can pick up a copy of the *Sportfishing Report,* the Outer Banks's first saltwater fishing magazine, which has expanded to cover the entire East Coast. This bimonthly magazine is available on newsstands. A subscription is $25 for one year or $50 for three years. For information, call (252) 473-1553, or visit the Web site at www.sportfishing-report.com. Inside every issue of the *Hatteras Monitor Newsmagazine,* distributed throughout Hatteras Island, authors tell tales of recent fishing adventures and give the latest reports and predictions. Call the *Hatteras Monitor* office at (252) 995-5378.

GOLF

Whether you're a scratch golfer or a duffer, you'll find play to suit your game and style on or near the Outer Banks, where the number and variety of golf courses have increased dramatically in the past few years. Part of the pleasure of golf almost everywhere is in the lushness of the environment, but few locations outside of this area offer the astounding ocean-to-sound views you'll find at many courses along these barrier islands. Such distraction might not be good for your game, but it'll do wonders for the soul!

In this section, you'll find golf courses from Corolla to Hatteras Island, plus courses on the Currituck mainland, just north of the Wright Memorial Bridge. We've also included an excellent course in Hertford that's only an hour's drive from the heart of the Outer Banks.

Golfers have it made during the off-season and shoulder seasons. Accommodations are a bargain from the fall through the spring, and many hotels, motels, and cottage rental companies package special golf vacations. Depending on the season, you can usually plan a visit on the spur of the moment if you want to play at off-peak times. The temperatures on the Outer Banks remain fairly moderate throughout the year. A day in January might bring temperatures of 60 degrees or higher, so keep an eye on the weather and your clubs close at hand. To avoid disappointment, call for tee times at your course of choice before your visit; more and more golfers are discovering the Outer Banks in the off-season.

All the regulation courses in the following section are semiprivate, meaning the public can pay to play, and all welcome beginners and newcomers. Yardage and par figures are based on men's/white tees.

REGULATION AND EXECUTIVE COURSES

The Carolina Club
US 158, Grandy
(252) 453-3588
www.thecarolinaclub.com

More and more Outer Banks golfers are discovering the courses on the Currituck mainland, and The Carolina Club, designed by Russell Breeden, is one of the nicest of the bunch. Located in Grandy, the course is just 13.5 miles past the Wright Memorial Bridge, about a 20-minute drive from Kitty Hawk. The 7,000-yard, par 72 course has, according to the Southeastern director of the U.S. Golf Association (U.S.G.A.), "among the finest putting surfaces in the eastern U.S." Indeed, The Carolina Club management prides itself on its high level of course conditioning, slick bent-grass greens, and plush Tifway Bermuda fairways. Five sets of tees allow you to match your game to an appropriate level of challenge. On this course, you will encounter wetlands, woodlands, water, and bunkers galore. Hole 7, a par 3, has an island green that will challenge your club-selection skills. The par 5 hole 18 offers the ultimate in risk versus reward. Water and wind direction factor in on this hole, where the tee shot must be right on the mark.

There's a snack bar on the premises, plus a pro shop. Rental clubs and carts are available. Individual and group lessons are offered by PGA head professional Doug Kinser. Greens fees, including cart, are a good value, ranging from $79 in June to $39 in January, but they change monthly so call for accurate prices. Youth rates are available. Tee times are booked up to three months in advance. The course is open all year.

The Currituck Club
NC 12, Corolla
(252) 453-9400, (888) 453-9400
www.thecurrituckclub.com

When The Currituck Club opened in 1997, *Golf Magazine* named it one of the "Top 10 You Can Play." In 1999, *Golf Digest* ranked it as one of the Top 25 courses in North Carolina, a great compliment for a young course in a renowned golfing state. The Currituck Club was rated in 2004 *Golf Digest*'s best places to play. This 6,885-yard, par 72 course is situated on 600 acres of pristine wetlands along Currituck Sound, surrounded by luxurious homes in The Currituck Club resort community. The natural beauty of this course makes it one of the most peaceful golfing spots around. Prominent golf architect Rees Jones designed the stunningly scenic links-style course with respect to the wildlife and waterfowl that populate the area. While protecting their habitats, he also offers golfers a course set amid dunes, wetlands, and marsh fringes. From the rolling dunes, golfers enjoy views of the Atlantic Ocean and Currituck Sound. Within the property lie 15 acres set aside for the historic and private Currituck Shooting Club, whose lineage dates from 1857. The back nine has several holes with some of the most beautiful views you'll ever see. The view from the elevated 13th tee offers a panorama of the ocean, sound, and the Currituck Beach Lighthouse.

The course features a full driving range. Lessons are offered year-round, along with weekly clinics by PGA professionals. Golf schools take place from June through August on Tuesday, Wednesday, and Thursday from 9:00 to 11:00 A.M. Junior golf school is offered on Thursday from 5:00 to 7:00 P.M. Rates include golf cart rental and vary according to the season. The clubhouse includes a restaurant, a bar and lounge with full ABC permits, a pro shop, locker rooms, bag storage, and a private members' lounge.

Duck Woods Country Club
50 Dogwood Trail, Kitty Hawk
(252) 261-2609

Duck Woods is the club to play on windy days, since it provides more shelter than the soundside clubs. This 18-hole, 6,161-yard, par 72 course was built in 1968. Designed by Ellis Maples, Duck Woods features a traditional layout with tree-lined fairways. Shots must be placed with care, especially on the par 5 14th hole, where water dissects the fairway. Water comes into play on 14 holes. You might want to warm up before your round; the course begins with a 481-yard par 5 and ends with a 506-yard par 5.

While the club accommodates 900 members, it accepts public play year-round. Nonmembers can take advantage of the driving range and putting green on the day of play only. Target greens and a practice bunker are available. Duck Woods' pro shop is complemented by the presence of golf pro David Donovan, and club rentals. Members enjoy clubhouse and locker room privileges and the bar and restaurant. Beer and wine are sold to nonmembers, but no other alcoholic beverages are available, as the club does not hold a liquor license.

Riding is mandatory for nonmembers. Booking is accepted a week in advance for members and two days in advance for nonmembers. Call for more information. Greens fees vary.

Goose Creek Golf and Country Club
US 158, Grandy
(252) 453-4008, (800) 443-4008
www.outerbanksgolfgoosecreek.com

Goose Creek, a 5,943-yard par 72 public course on the mainland, offers an easygoing track complete with a hospitable atmosphere and some of the most affordable greens fees in the area. The greens and fairways on this flat course are blanketed with bermuda grass. Greens are relatively small. Trees line the course, with tighter fairways on the first nine but more undulating and open terrain on the back.

Designed by Jerry Turner and built by Jernigan Enterprises, Goose Creek is a player-friendly golf course. Goose Creek's Class A PGA golf professional is Tim Burkhart. Water comes into play on five holes. Hole 13 is considered the signature. The hole plays differently according to the wind (it's generally to your back during the summer and in your face in fall and winter).

The clubhouse is a former hunting lodge that the owners converted into private locker rooms. Take some time to relax in the pine-paneled lounge for a cool drink. The clubhouse menu includes all sorts of sandwiches, plus everything from buffalo wings to crab cakes.

A driving range and practice green are available. Walking is allowed for members only. This is a great course for the entire family, and children are both welcome and encouraged; however, it's recommended that young golfers check in after noon.

Holly Ridge Golf Course
US 158, Harbinger
(252) 491-2893

Holly Ridge Golf Course is 1.5 miles north of the Wright Memorial Bridge in Harbinger. Holly Ridge is under the management of Wright Flight Golf.

The front nine wind through a peaceful forest of native trees and picturesque ponds, while the more open back nine are affected by winds. Holly Ridge has a full-length, fully lighted grass practice area and putting green. PGA Pro Danny Miller has more than 20 years of experience in teaching golfers of all levels. Private lessons and group clinics are available, as are private lessons with video analysis. The pro shop carries a great selection of apparel, accessories, and equipment, and the staff help with selecting the right clubs. Walking is allowed on this course. Pull carts, golf clubs, and, of course, golf carts are available to rent. Greens fees are a good value here, and they vary throughout the year, so call ahead. Juniors may play for half-price but must have a valid driver's license to operate a cart.

Mill Run Golf and Country Club
US 168, Currituck
(252) 435-MILL

If you're willing to drive a ways, Mill Run Golf and Country Club offers a great bargain for Outer Banks golfers. The course, opened in 1999, is just south of Moyock on U.S. Highway 168, about 50 miles from the Outer Banks on the mainland and about 5 miles south of the Virginia state line. The course is fun and enjoyable, not overly difficult; so if you're looking for a good-time game, come here.

Mill Run is a great course for beginners. Course architect James Overton Sr. designed the 6,651-yard course to take advantage of the natural terrain and to provide challenging play for golfers of all levels. Mill Run is relatively flat and plays somewhat like a links-style course, though it's nowhere near the ocean or sound. It does offer some challenges with wind, ponds, and woods. Bunkers are still being added to the course. The signature hole is number 17, a par 3 with the carry over water. Greens are in tip-top shape. A driving range, practice putting green, and chipping green are available, and golf professional Kevin McCord offers lessons. Walking is allowed here. The pro shop is well equipped, and the on-site Hackers Grill serves breakfast and lunch.

Nags Head Golf Links
5615 South Seachase Drive, Nags Head
(252) 441-8073, (800) 851-9404
www.nagsheadgolflinks.com

This soundside 18-hole Scottish links-style course is in the Village at Nags Head off U.S. Highway 158 at milepost 15½. Architect Bob Moore left most of the natural setting intact, and the 6,100-yard, par 71 course is a real beach beauty. Golfers enjoy idyllic views of Roanoke Sound from nearly every hole. With the sound to the west and the ocean to the east, wind plays a significant role here.

It doesn't take but one quick gust of wind to blow your ball off course on the 221-yard 15th hole, a lengthy par 3. The green is fronted by a pond. All but four holes are affected by water here.

Nags Head Golf Links pro Gary Otto invites you to try this mercurial course. The environment is so refreshing that we think it's worth a round regardless of what's controlling the shots. Golf school is held mornings three days a week during summer.

Golf Digest called the holes along the sound "among the most beautiful in the eastern U.S.," and went on to say that "Nags Head Golf Links is the longest 6,100 yards you'll ever play."

Cart and greens fees vary, and starting times may be reserved up to one year in advance. Seniors pay special off-season rates. A nine-hole scramble is played June through August late Sunday afternoons. Please call to sign up.

Enjoy good food and excellent views of Roanoke Sound from the Links Grill, which is open for lunch only. Nags Head Golf Links also has a bar, golf shop, driving range, putting green, and rental clubs. The course is open every day, except Christmas, from sunrise to sunset. Call for more information.

Ocean Edge Golf Course
NC 12, Frisco
(252) 995-4100

Ocean Edge is a public, nine-hole executive course that also permits 18-hole play. Look out for the big pond—the first, second, fifth, and eighth holes play over the water.

Ocean Edge is open all year. This 1,400-yard, par 30 Hatteras Island course covers 23 acres of dunes. Tee times are required. Golf carts and club rentals are available. Walking is permitted.

The Pointe Golf Club
US 158 East, Powells Point
(252) 491-8388
www.thepointegolfclub.com

Golfer's heaven well describes this 5,911-yard, par 71, 18-hole championship golf course on the mainland. Both the recreational golfer and the professional will find a challenge on this verdant course created by Russell Breeden. Breeden's unique design features soundfront views from wooded and links-style holes with gentle mounds and slopes. This was the first course in the country to feature A1 bentgrass greens, a new disease-resistant dense grass. It's no surprise because the folks at Pointe are grass experts. Pointe owner Keith Hall is the president of United Turf.

The course sports a traditional design, with water hazards coming into play laterally on 15 holes. The signature hole is number 6, a 457-yard par 4 with a carry over wetlands, a blind shot to the fairway, water, bunkers, and slopes to the right.

You can fine-tune your game on the driving range, in the practice bunker, or on the full-size putting green. The Pointe offers a full-service pro shop headed by resident golf pro Doug Kinser. Other amenities include a clubhouse, carts, lessons, sales, and rentals. The Pointe Restaurant, which serves breakfast and lunch, has views of the 9th green and the 10th tee.

Walking is allowed after noon for greens-fee pass holders, October 1 through May 24. Greens fees vary, so it's a good idea to call for timely information. Annual golf packages are offered through Outer Banks Golf Getaways (800–916–6244) and Outer Banks Golf Packages (800–946–5383); accommodations packages are available through area rental companies.

The Pointe Golf Course is 3.5 miles north of the Wright Memorial Bridge. Call for tee times up to a month in advance.

Sea Scape Golf Links
300 Eckner Street, Kitty Hawk
(252) 261-2158
www.seascapegolf.com

Keep your eye on the ball and not the view on this 18-hole, links-style championship course. You get a real taste of Outer Banks beauty with water vistas from almost every hole, especially from the elevated ninth tee. Sea Scape is cut into Kitty Hawk's maritime forest, just off US 158 East at milepost 2½. Designed by Art Wall, the 6,052-yard, par 72 course features bent-grass greens and fairways, which are fairly wide. Sea Scape was host of the 2000 North Carolina Open.

Opened in 1965, the links-style course has been modernized, and now you can expect cart paths on all holes. Wind is a factor here, and you may find yourself puttering around in the sand and brush looking for your ball. Expect a challenge on number 11: Look to play against the wind on this 410-yard, par 4 hole. Sea Scape will test your ability as well as your patience, with five par 3s and five par 5s.

A scheduled golf clinic is offered for all ages from June through August. Sea Scape offers club fitting, rental clubs, and a driving range, bar, restaurant, and fully stocked pro shop. Sea Scape pro Chris Busbee is available to discuss your game or the course. Sea Scape's clubhouse features a fully stocked pro shop and Sully's Restaurant, serving breakfast and lunch.

Walking is not allowed. Greens fees range from $55 to $100, including the cart. Call ahead for tee times, especially if you plan to play during the summer (there's no established rule, but we were informed that eight months in advance isn't too soon). The course is open every day except Christmas from 7:30 A.M. until dark.

The Sound Golf Links
101 Clubhouse Drive, Hertford
(252) 426-5555, (800) 535-0704
Tucked within Albemarle Plantation, The Sound is a 6,504-yard, par 72, 18-hole course. It's also a world-class golfing and

boating community at the tip of the Albemarle Sound near Hertford. The beautiful 12,000-square-foot clubhouse overlooks the water. Owner and designer Dan Maples stamped his signature here. As with all Maples-designed courses, you get a break on the par 4s and 5s, but the par 3s are extremely difficult. It's a target golf course with a few similarities to a links course.

Fairways are narrow, and marsh must be carried frequently. It's a fair course overall but a tough one from the back tees. On the 7th and 13th holes, the landing areas are extremely small. Both are par 4s.

The golf pro is Jim Nodurft. The clubhouse includes a golf shop and restaurant, The Soundside Grille, which serves lunch and dinner. A driving range and putting green are also available. The marina, available to the public, is the largest in the area.

Walking is restricted, so call for details. Tee times may be booked up to nine months in advance. The course is a little over an hour's drive from Kitty Hawk. Call for greens fees.

PRACTICE RANGES

The Promenade
US 158 East, MP ½, Kitty Hawk
(252) 261-4900
www.promenadewatersports.com
Along Currituck Sound at the eastern terminus of the Wright Memorial Bridge, this 30-acre adventure spot features a nine-hole chip-and-putt course on natural grass. Separate putting green and target driving range facilities are available.

Snakes! Tiny slivers of snakes and much bigger ones slither through the tall grasses and marsh. Look out for them and proceed carefully, especially when retrieving a ball from the brush or near rocks, where they often hide. Snakes want to avoid you, but if trapped or surprised, they may strike in defense.

GOLF EQUIPMENT AND SUPPLIES

Smash Hit Tennis & Golf
NC 12, Duck
(252) 261-1138
www.smashhittennisandgolf.com
Smash Hit Tennis & Golf, in Duck's Scar-

borough Faire shopping center, offers a variety of top sports fashions. Loyal customers claim that Smash Hit has the finest selection anywhere for ladies' clothing. You'll also find men's and children's clothing, gifts, accessories, and some equipment. Visit the Web site and shop online. A great service is Smash Hit's mail-order goodie boxes. They send a selection of clothing from which you can keep what you like and return the rest. The store is open year-round; please call for hours.

DAY TRIPS 🚗

I n your eagerness to reach the beach, you may have kept your eyes straight ahead and not noticed the numerous attractions in the surrounding areas. The Outer Banks can serve as a "base camp," enabling you to easily explore all that is offered nearby, from historic sites to nature sanctuaries to autumn festivals that offer a glimpse into the lives of a small Southern town. Following are some exciting adventures you may wish to take while visiting the Outer Banks, each within a few hours' drive.

NATURE ADVENTURES

North Carolina Estuarium
223 East Water Street, Washington
(252) 948–0000
www.partnershipforthesounds.org
Less than two hours from Roanoke Island, this environmental education center offers more than 200 hands-on displays and interactive exhibits about estuarine ecosystems in creative ways kids enjoy. Estuaries—bodies of water with a mixture of fresh and salt water—are vital marine life breeding grounds. The region's Albemarle-Pamlico system, the second largest in the country after Chesapeake Bay, incorporates seven sounds that several river basins drain into. It totals more than 300,000 square miles.

The first of several major facilities completed by the nonprofit Partnership for the Sounds, the estuarium teaches kids and grown-ups about the threat of pollution and why marine species couldn't survive without clean estuaries. In addition to the two 130-gallon terrariums and five 130-gallon to 650-gallon aquarium tanks, there are a number of educational exhibits, including a salinity drip where you can actually sample the saltiness of different types of water bodies; a model of animal skulls that asks

you to guess which animals are represented; a working model of wind and tide, where fans are manipulated to move a miniature waterway; and a movie about estuaries that gives an emotional sense of the importance of the system to the coast.

The estuarium also features a nursery area with minnows, shrimp, and flounder, plus exhibits with snakes, turtles, lizards, and other creatures that live in estuarine areas. A glass-enclosed front room overlooking the Pamlico River is available for special educational workshops. Pontoon boat rides on the Pamlico River are available seasonally.

The North Carolina Estuarium is open year-round Tuesday through Saturday from 10:00 A.M. to 4:00 P.M. Hours may be extended in the summer months. Admission is $3.00 for adults, $2.00 for school-age children, and free for preschool children.

Merchants Millpond State Park
Access from US 158, NC 32,
and NC 37, Gatesville
(252) 357–1191
www.ncsparks.net
Less than a two-hour drive from the Outer Banks, Merchants Millpond is an isolated, undisturbed wonderland like no other place in the world. This scenic backwater swamp boasts family and wilderness campsites, miles of well-marked hiking trails and canoe runs, and some of the best largemouth bass fishing in eastern North Carolina.

Picnic tables, ranger programs, fishing, and at least 201 species of birds inspire people to flock into these boggy lowlands from early spring through late fall. More than 85,000 visitors tour the site each year. Poisonous snakes, mosquitoes, and ticks also inhabit the area—so beware.

Campers are welcome on a first-come, first-served basis at 20 drive-in campsites with drinking water and grills. Three-quarters of a mile from the boat-launching ramp are seven rustic canoe-in sites, and 3.5 miles into the woods are five primitive backpack sites. These sites offer more secluded camping and steel fire rings. The park also has three walk-in and three canoe-in sites 1.25 miles from the launching site for organized groups of up to 50 members. Primitive camping permits are sold at the ranger station for $9.00 per family. The tent and trailer area, which has hot showers, costs $15 per night. Campsites are closed December 1 through March 15, but primitive camping is available year-round. North Carolina requires anglers to have freshwater fishing licenses, and these are sold at nearby bait shops.

Even inexperienced boaters can manage to maneuver canoes around these serene, scenic waters. Canoes rent for $5.00 for the first hour and $3.00 for each additional hour. Canoes can also be rented overnight at canoe campsites for $20 for 24 hours. Both Merchants Millpond and the adjoining Lassiter Swamp, about a two-hour paddle away, have miles of water trails well-marked by brightly colored buoys. The park is best observed by boat, but it's easy to get lost in this eerie area after dark.

There's plenty of free parking at the canoe launching and picnic areas. The rangers supply paddles, life jackets, and trail maps. You must bring your own food and drinks into the park, although there is a snack and beverage machine on-site if you run out. Don't forget your camera—the strange sights in this secluded swampland speak thousands of unwhispered words.

Merchants Millpond State Park's new entrance includes a picnic area with a shelter, tables, and a bathroom. Large groups can reserve the area for $50. The park is open from 8:00 A.M. to 7:00 P.M. in March and October. Evening hours extend to 8:00 P.M. in April, May, and September and to 9:00 P.M. June through August. It closes at 6:00 P.M. November through February and is closed Christmas Day.

Alligator River National Wildlife Refuge
US 64, near East Lake
(252) 473-1131
http://alligatorriver.fws.gov

Stands of 6-foot-wide juniper stumps sparkle with the gray-green tentacles of sphagnum moss. Bobcats, wolves, bears, bald eagles, and alligators thrive amid these tangled thickets. Remnants of a century-old railroad track wind 100 miles through the thick forest, and rotting ties lead to a 19th-century logging town long since swallowed by the swamp.

On the Dare County mainland off U.S. Highway 64 between East Lake, Manns Harbor, and Stumpy Point, about a half-hour drive west of Manteo, Alligator River National Wildlife Refuge stretches across the Hyde County line into Alligator River. The U.S. Air Force owns a 46,000-acre Dare County Bombing Range in the center of the refuge, but the rest of this sprawling preserve is federally protected.

Endangered species—including the peregrine falcon, red-cockaded woodpecker, and the American alligator—roam freely through the preserve. Dozens of red wolves, extinct in the wild less than two decades ago, have been reintroduced into this region (see our Natural Wonders chapter). The refuge also is reputed to have one of the biggest black bear populations in the mid-Atlantic region.

The U.S. Fish and Wildlife Service has called the Alligator River Refuge one of the largest and wildest sections of land left on the East Coast. The entire 151,000-acre refuge is accessible to four-wheel-drive vehicles, and jeep trails traverse much of the flat, sandy marshlands. Two half-mile hiking trails and 15 miles of well-marked canoe and kayak trails also are open.

Activities are free and available year-round throughout daylight hours. Parking is available at the well-marked Milltail Road paved lot or at the end of the dirt Buffalo City Road off US 64. Two houses still stand alongside this dusty path leading to Milltail Creek, but only remnants of human existence remain. Once the Albemarle's largest logging town, Buffalo City had two hotels, a school, general store, scores of moonshiners, a tavern, and more than 3,000 people.

Today, there are a variety of ways for visitors to see the refuge. About 4 miles west of the US 64/U.S. Highway 264 split, travelers can stop at a wooden kiosk and pick up brochures about trails, wildlife, and flora. Behind the kiosk there's a paved 15-space parking lot, where the old, dirt Milltail Road ends. Here, a half-mile paved walkway with a boardwalk overlooking the water begins. This Creef Cut Wildlife Trail and Fishing Area is wheelchair accessible. It opens at a public fishing dock and culminates in a 50-foot boardwalk atop a freshwater marsh.

Interpretive plaques depicting the area's unusual flora and fauna are nailed along freshly plowed pathways. Beaver cuttings, wood duck boxes, rare sundew flowers, and warbler nesting areas are among the hidden attractions.

Refuge workers estimate that there are about 100 alligators in this preserve, which marks the northernmost boundary of the American alligators' habitat. On Milltail Creek Road, there's a platform winding around the creek. The waters surrounding that platform are supposed to be among the gators' favorite haunts. If you wait quietly, you might catch a glimpse of a scaly, dark green snout.

Sandy Ridge Wildlife Trail is a little more rugged. It starts where Buffalo City Road dead-ends off US 64 about 2 miles south of East Lake. Rough wooden pallets help hikers traverse swampy spots, but if rain has fallen during the past week, walkers are bound to get wet. Sweet gum, maple, and pine trees reach 30 feet high around this path.

Canoe and kayak trails through Sawyer Lake and connecting canals include four main routes marked by colored PVC pipe. Trails range from 1.5 to 5.5 miles, all along a wide waterway that is smooth with no rapids. You can bring your own boat in and paddle for free. On the Outer Banks, several rental outlets lease canoes and kayaks by the day (see our Water Sports chapter). Guided canoe tours are also offered at the refuge. Call Pea Island Visitor Center at (252) 987-2394 for schedule and prices. Several times a year and regularly in the summer, the refuge staff holds Wolf Howls, leading visitors deep into the refuge at night to hear the red wolves howl (see our Attractions chapter for more details).

Lake Mattamuskeet National Wildlife Refuge
**Hyde County mainland
(252) 926-4021
http://mattamuskeet.fws.gov**

About a 90-minute drive southwest of Manteo down lonely US 264 is the 50,000-acre Lake Mattamuskeet National Wildlife Refuge, home to sprawling marshland and the state's largest natural lake, which spans 40,000 acres and is very shallow. In addition to the lake, the refuge includes freshwater marsh, forested wetlands, managed impoundments, croplands, and forested uplands, providing a safe habitat for migratory waterfowl and other birds, including endangered species of bald eagles and peregrine falcons. This is also a refuge for endangered American alligators.

Nearly half of the nation's tundra swans swoop into this rare wilderness refuge to feed, nest, and wait out the winter. From November through March, Lake Mattamuskeet is filled with thousands of the regal white birds. Watch them and you'll be amazed. Each fall, an estimated 100,000 tundra swans make a cross-continent trek from the wilds of western Canada and Alaska to the warmer waters of North Carolina and the Chesapeake Bay. Lake Mattamuskeet, a world of isolated flatlands surrounded by 400 acres of wheat farms, is North Carolina's most popular roosting area. Between 20,000 and 40,000 swans winter here every year.

Photographers, bird-watchers, and people with only a casual curiosity can drive through the refuge, across the lake on a two-lane causeway, to get a good glimpse of the birds. Swans usually swarm around the water at sunrise and sunset.

They spend their days eating in the nearby fields. Besides these big birds, which can live 20 years or longer, you'll also see a huge variety of ducks, Canada geese, and snow geese.

If you can't get here in the winter, come anyway. The refuge is beautiful year-round, and you will always see a variety of birds, including wading birds, shorebirds, raptors, and bald eagles, depending on the season. You can walk the roads along the lake or on the designated trail or stand atop two observation towers for a sweeping view of the flatlands.

The lake is also famous for its blue crabs. The crustaceans creeping around this waterway in the summer can grow twice as big as the Outer Banks variety. Some say that's because the crabs feed off the unusually rich lake bottom, which was cultivated farm land at one time. If you make the trek to the refuge in the summer, be sure to buy some crabs at an area seafood shop and sample them for yourself. The lake and nearby canals have significant fishery resources, including largemouth bass, bream, white perch, crappie, and herring. The lake is open to public fishing from March through November, and three boat ramps give anglers access to the lake.

The old pumping station near the center of the refuge was built between 1915 and 1918. The pumping station was used to drain the lake so that people could farm the lake bed. The lake was drained and farmed on three occasions, but each company that did this went bankrupt. The pumping station was then sold to the U.S. Government, and the lake was converted into the Lake Mattamuskeet National Wildlife Refuge, a division of U.S. Fish and Wildlife, in 1934. The Civilian Conservation Corps renovated the building, adding rooms, bathrooms, and balconies and turning it into a hunting and fishing lodge. It was closed in 1974.

Public hunting opportunities are available in fall and winter for deer (October) and waterfowl (December and January). The refuge has 16 blinds that are assigned by a drawing for two-day hunts. Call the refuge office for details.

A popular event at Lake Mattamuskeet is Swan Days, held the first weekend in December. The Swan Quarter Service Group, in cooperation with the U.S. Fish and Wildlife Service and the staff of the Lake Mattamuskeet National Wildlife Refuge, puts on the celebration to welcome the thousands of tundra swan and other waterfowl. The event, which began in 1994, offers a variety of activities for the whole family, including guided tours of the refuge, workshops and lectures on a variety of wildlife and history topics, local arts and crafts, kids' activities, and delicious food. Many of the guided tours and workshops require reservations, so make plans early by visiting the Web site or calling the refuge and asking for a brochure.

Edenton National Fish Hatchery
1104 West Queen Street
(exit 224 off US 17), Edenton
(252) 482-4118
http://edenton.fws.gov

Run by the U.S. Fish and Wildlife Service on the grassy banks of the Chowan River, the Edenton National Fish Hatchery includes an expanse of outdoor ponds and a small aquarium. This fascinating hatchery is only about 90 minutes from the Outer Banks.

A waterfront walkway and pier at the facility provide access to Pembroke Creek for people with disabilities. The 15-acre area also gives nature lovers a look at some of the native wildlife and waterfowl indigenous to the surrounding wetlands.

The Hatchery expanded in 2001. Inside, groups of aquariums house fish native to local waters. Kids love seeing three alligators in one tank. A question-and-answer computer touch screen teaches about the fish and environment.

The most popular attraction, "Pathway to Fishing," a 12-station, one-hour tour, teaches youngsters the basics of fishing. Included are brief talks on angler ethics and safety, live bait and lures, ecology, rods and reels, knot-tying, casting, and local fish species.

The fish hatchery is open from 7:00 A.M. to 3:30 P.M. Monday through Friday in the off-season, and Monday through Sunday from 8:00 A.M. to 5:00 P.M. April through August, free of charge.

Cape Lookout National Seashore
Southern Barrier Islands
(252) 728-2250
www.nps.gov/calo

Low, unpopulated, and much less visited than the Outer Banks, the southern stretches of North Carolina's barrier islands extend 55 miles southwest from Ocracoke Inlet and include Portsmouth Island, Core Banks, Cape Lookout, and Shackleford Banks.

These remote sand islands are untouched by development and linked to the mainland and other barrier island beaches only by private ferries or private boats. (Call the listed number for ferry schedules and reservations.) In 1976 they came under the control of the National Park Service when a separate national seashore was established south of the Cape Hatteras holdings. Each year, more than 300,000 nature lovers visit these sparse strips of beach.

If you have your own boat, you can get to Cape Lookout by launching from ramps at marinas throughout Carteret County or from Silver Lake on Ocracoke. The easiest access to Cape Lookout is from Harkers Island. Concession ferries and private boats for hire also are available from Harkers Island to the Cape Lookout Light area, from Davis to Shingle Point, from Atlantic to an area north of Drum Inlet, and from Ocracoke to Portsmouth Village. Boats are also available from Beaufort.

There are no roads on these islands, but four-wheel-drive vehicles can cruise on the Core Banks or Portsmouth Island. There are few facilities along this sparse stretch of sand; however, the islands are perfect for primitive camping year-round, four-wheel driving, fishing, bird-watching,

and photography. Stay alert for sudden storms, because there is little shelter. To help foreshadow bad squalls, call the National Weather Service, (252) 223-5327, before you set out on an excursion. Visitors must supply their own water and food, and pets are not allowed.

Deer ticks, chiggers, deer flies, mosquitoes, gnats, and other annoying insects are abundant around the islands, so bring repellent and wear long sleeves even in the summer months. Water is available from pitcher pumps around Cape Lookout, but campers are encouraged to bring their own supplies. Primitive camping is allowed throughout the park, but there are no designated sites.

The Cape Lookout grounds include a lighthouse that was first illuminated in 1859, a lighthouse keeper's quarters that has been converted to a visitor center, and a Coast Guard station that is no longer active. Cape Lookout is closed Christmas and New Year's Day.

Portsmouth Island, site of the only ghost town on the Eastern Seaboard, is just a 20-minute boat ride south of Ocracoke Island. What was the biggest, most bustling town on the Outer Banks for more than a century is now uninhabited, except for two volunteer rangers. Owned by the National Park Service since 1976, the 23-mile-long, 1.5-mile-wide isolated outpost attracts about 10,000 visitors a year. Most come to camp, watch birds, scan for seashells on miles of wide empty beaches, or just hike through the remnants of the historic village and reenter a long-deserted world. Two dozen cottages, a weather-beaten post office, and an old church still remain of the former shipping community that was populated by more than 700 people in its prime before the Civil War.

Rudy Austin ferries visitors to Portsmouth Island most of the spring, summer, and fall. For reservations and further information, call (252) 928-4361 or (252) 928-5431. Whichever way you visit this remote land, bring plenty of bug spray, snacks, and drinks.

For more information about Portsmouth Island and Cape Lookout National Seashore, call or write the National Park Service, Cape Lookout National Seashore, 131 Charles Street, Harkers Island, NC 28531. Also, pick up a copy of the *Insiders' Guide to North Carolina's Central Coast* from any area bookstore or order one online at www.InsidersGuide.com.

HISTORIC ATTRACTIONS

Museum of the Albemarle
1116 US 17 South, Elizabeth City
(252) 335-1453
www.northeast-nc.com/moa

About 50 miles inland from the Outer Banks, on the west side of Elizabeth City, this state-owned museum preserves the Albemarle area's past with exhibits, photographs, and maps.

The Museum of the Albemarle includes permanent interpretive displays depicting Native American tribes and their tools and exhibits on the food, folk tales, crafts, and hunting artifacts of early English-speaking colonists. A 19th-century hearth exhibit allows visitors to contrast Colonial living with modern American amenities. Other offerings trace the development of boating, logging, and the U.S. Coast Guard in surrounding sites.

With two weeks' notice, the museum can provide guided tours, lectures, and audiovisual programs for groups and individuals. A small gift shop sells memorabilia. Admission to the museum is free, and the building is wheelchair accessible with assistance at the front door.

The museum is open Tuesday through Saturday from 9:00 A.M. until 5:00 P.M. and Sunday from 2:00 until 5:00 P.M. It is closed Monday and holidays. Please call the number listed for program schedules and reservations.

Historic Hertford
Intersection of US 17 and NC 1336
Hertford
(252) 426-5657
www.visitperquimans.com

One of the oldest towns in North Carolina, Hertford was incorporated in 1758 to serve as the Perquimans county seat and commercial center of the surrounding Albemarle area.

About 50 buildings dating from the early 1800s stand as stalwart sentries along the tree-lined lanes of the downtown. These magnificent mansions and well-kept gardens serve as reminders of the early inhabitants who spent their lives fishing, farming, and felling trees for lumber. Later, cloth was manufactured in nearby factories.

This tiny town is toured easily by car. We also advise walking around the shady streets to get a closer perspective. Hertford is about an hour's drive from the Outer Banks.

The Newbold-White House
110 Newbold-White Road
off US 17 South, Hertford
(252) 426-7567
www.albemarle-nc.com/newbold-white

About 60 miles from the Outer Banks in historic Perquimans County, North Carolina's oldest house was built in 1730 and is still open for tours today.

The Newbold-White House is an outstanding example of early American domestic architecture. It's set about a mile off the road across from an immense cotton field. The former plantation home is built entirely of handmade brick molded from the clay that can be found 12 inches below the soil on the grounds surrounding the house.

Joseph Scott, the original landowner, was a magistrate, legislator, and Quaker. The original owner of the home was Abraham Sanders, who built this elegant brick abode on a 600-acre tract along the Perquimans River and surrounded it with tobacco fields. Tobacco was frequently used as currency during the 18th century. Later, peanuts and other products also were farmed in these fields.

Numerous other families occupied the house, and Thomas Elbert White bought it in 1903. In 1943, his heirs sold the property to John Henry Newbold, whose heirs in turn sold it to the Perquimans County Restoration Association in 1973. Since then, the house has been beautifully restored to its original condition.

When visiting the house, stop at the Perquimans County Restoration Association headquarters on the way. This visitor center of sorts offers an informative audiovisual journey into the house's heyday and inhabitants. Hours at the Newbold-White House are 10:00 A.M. to 4:30 P.M. Tuesday through Saturday and 2:00 to 5:00 P.M. on Sunday. The museum is closed on Monday and December through February, but special tours can be arranged in advance during winter months. Admission is $2.00 for adults, and children and students pay 50 cents each.

Albemarle Plantation
1 Plantation Lane, Hertford
(252) 337–8029, (800) 535–0704
www.albemarleplantation.com

Albemarle Plantation, a golfing and boating community, is off U.S. Highway 17. Visit this sprawling complex of recreational and dining facilities along the waters of the Albemarle Sound for a great day trip. Albemarle Plantation is part of an upscale residential development that also includes a swimming pool, tennis courts, and a fitness center. Sound Golf Links, an 18-hole golf course open to the public, is one of the most popular venues in the region for dedicated golfers (see our Golf chapter for more information). Call the number listed for tee times. After a couple of rounds, you may be ready for lunch or

Check the gas tank before you drive off into the wild blue yonder of eastern North Carolina. This is sparsely populated farm country, unlike more urban areas where gas stations are around every corner.

dinner at the Soundside Grille, which overlooks the water.

The 200-slip marina, also open to the public, offers amenities and hookups to boaters. The 1,600-acre secured community is designed for 1,000 single-family homes with a few townhomes and condominiums as well. If you're interested in staying for several days, call about the Albemarle Plantation's getaway packages. Follow US 17 from Elizabeth City to Hertford. Drive time from Kitty Hawk is just over an hour.

Historic Edenton
US 17, Edenton
(252) 482–2637
www.edenton.com

Edenton is the oldest town in North Carolina and one of the oldest towns in America. It was settled in 1690 along the shores of the Albemarle Sound and Edenton Bay. It was incorporated in 1722 and established as the colonial capital of North Carolina in 1782.

Edenton is a charming historic town, perfect for a day trip or an overnight stay. It's an easy day trip from the Outer Banks by boat or automobile. It's a town with a colonial past, similar to Williamsburg, Virginia, in its historic significance but much less commercial and "touristy." Historic homes are the main attractions of this waterfront town. Twenty-five homes and public buildings encompass this North Carolina State Historic Site, though there are hundreds of magnificent historic homes in the town. Along with the homes, antiques stores inhabit iron-gate–sheltered alleys, grand bed-and-breakfasts offer extraordinary escapes, and a walk along the waterfront beckons. Everything in this quaint town is readily accessible by walking.

The Historic Edenton Visitor Center, an East Lake–style Victorian built in 1892, is at 108 West Broad Street, across the street from St. Paul's Episcopal Church. A short audiovisual presentation on the history of Edenton is offered throughout the day at the visitor center, plus there is a gift shop. The visitor center offers self-guided walking-tour maps. Or you can choose to take a guided walking or trolley tour, both of which begin and end at the visitor center. Trolley tours last 45 minutes and are led by an experienced interpreter. Trolley tours are offered year-round, Tuesday through Saturday at 10:00 A.M., 11:00 A.M., 3:00 P.M., and 4:00 P.M. They cost $10.00 for adults and $2.00 for K–12 students. Guided walking tours are offered at 10:30 A.M. Monday through Saturday and 2:00 P.M. every day, year-round. Walking tours also cost $10.00 and $2.00.

Historic Columbia
US 64, Columbia
(252) 796–0723
www.albemarle-nc.com/columbia

Visitors traveling to the Outer Banks on US 64 through eastern North Carolina used to completely overlook the isolated outpost of Columbia, whizzing through the town, rushing to the beach. In years past there wasn't really a reason to stop. But that's all changed today. Many visitors now stop in this burgeoning waterfront town to stretch their legs and soak up a healthy dose of ecotourism. More and more Outer Bankers make special trips to Columbia for the day; it's about a 30-minute drive from Manteo on US 64.

The beautiful, $1.1 million Tyrrell County Visitor Center, right on the Scuppernong River and visible from the road, opened in 1995. A combination rest area, welcome center, and environmental education center, it is dedicated to the preservation and understanding of North Carolina's coastal wetlands, which are abundant in this area. A 0.75-mile raised boardwalk winds along the river behind the visitor center, providing breathtaking views of coastal wetlands and the Scuppernong River as it slides slowly into Bull Bay. For thousands of feet along the river's edge, tiny electric lights twinkle across the dark water, illuminating the walkway that creeps through unspoiled timber wetlands. Interpretive signs tell you what you're looking at.

A fountain, gazebo, and wide turnouts accommodating wheelchair passengers are among the other attractions along this zigzagging boardwalk that twists around towering forest giants and flowering bushes that would have soon disappeared in more chainsaw-oriented communities. If you want to see the wetlands closer than this, rent a kayak at the visitor center.

Columbia has many other attractions. At the visitor center, pick up a brochure of the Columbia on the Scuppernong Walking Tour, which leads through town past 20 houses and churches built around the turn of the 20th century.

One of the most surprising residents of Columbia is the Pocosin Arts Gallery, an art museum, gift shop, gallery, and arts education center on the corner of Main and Water Streets. Pocosin is a highly evolved cultural center and holds a variety of classes and special events. Call (252) 796–2787 for information, or stop by to see what they have going on.

Another attraction is the Columbia Theater Cultural Resources Center on Main Street. Housed in the town's renovated movie theater, it's an environmental and cultural history museum that highlights the general way of life in Tyrrell County, including fishing, farming, and forestry. The museum has a gift shop and welcomes group tours. Admission is $2.00 for adults, $1.00 for students, and free for kids age five and younger. It's open Tuesday through Saturday from 10:00 A.M. to 4:00 P.M. Call (252) 766–0200.

The Columbia Marina is a charming marina that houses mostly permanent boats and has one slip for transient sailors. If you're walking around town, walk by the marina and have a look at the beautiful boats docked there. If you're hungry, there are a couple of restaurants and the Columbia Pharmacy for snacks. If you're having so much fun you want to stay the night, Columbia has a couple of great bed-and-breakfast inns.

If you happen to be here on the second weekend of October, the Scuppernong River Festival is a delight, featuring water tours, boat rides, kids' activities, arts and crafts vendors, and yummy food.

Somerset Place
Off US 64, Creswell
(252) 797-4560
www.ah.dcr.state.nc.us/sections/hs/ somerset/somerset.htm

On the swampy stretch of marshland surrounding Phelps Lake, bordered by hand-dug canals and majestic stands of sycamore, Somerset Place is a historic plantation in Washington County where visitors learn about antebellum lifestyles of wealthy plantation owners and their slaves.

This state-funded site is 5 miles outside Creswell, near Pettigrew State Park, about an hour's drive from areas of the Outer Banks. Guides offer free tours and special arrangements for school groups. Grounds include isolated walking trails and wooden boardwalks to the water, where nearby fishing is excellent. About 25,000 people visit the site annually.

Once one of North Carolina's four biggest plantations, Somerset Place used more than 300 slaves to grow corn and rice and work in the expansive wetlands. An incredible collection of the plantation's slave records is open at the house for genealogical research. In August 1986 more than 2,000 descendants of Somerset's slaves gathered for their first anniversary homecoming reunion.

Somerset Place is open April through October 8:00 A.M. to 5:00 P.M. Monday through Saturday and 1:00 to 5:00 P.M. on Sunday. From November through March, it's open Tuesday through Saturday 10:00 A.M. to 4:00 P.M., Sunday 1:00 to 4:00 P.M., and closed Monday. To make reservations for large groups, write to 2572 Lake Shore Road, Creswell, NC 27928. Admission is free.

Hope Plantation
NC 308, Windsor
(252) 794-3140
www.hopeplantation.org

In the 1720s, the Lord Proprietors of the Carolina Colony granted abundant Albemarle-area acreage to the Hobson family. David Stone, a delegate to the North Carolina Constitutional Convention of 1789, began building an impressive plantation home on the site around 1800. About a two-hour drive west of the Outer Banks, this mansion, included on the National Register of Historic Places, is open to the public for guided tours.

A well-preserved Federal residence furnished with period furniture, Hope Plantation reminds some visitors of Jefferson's Monticello estate and reminds others of Scarlett O'Hara's beloved Tara. The Historic Hope Foundation purchased the home and 18 acres around it in 1966. Now restored, the property includes two smaller structures, the King-Bazemore and Samuel Cox houses. Lovely 18th-century-style gardens surround the homesites, and the 16,600-square-foot J. J. Harrington Building nearby includes a museum-like center that promotes the area's history and culture.

To get to Hope Plantation, take US 64 out of Roanoke Island west to its intersection with U.S. Highway 13; go north on US 13 and you'll find the house 4 miles west of the US 13 Bypass. From Roanoke Island, it is about a 90-minute drive. Summer hours are Monday through Saturday from 10:00 A.M. to 5:00 P.M. and Sunday from 2:00 to 5:00 P.M. Winter hours are the same, except that it closes at 4:00 P.M. Monday through Saturday. Admission is $8.00 for adults and $3.00 for students.

SOMETHING DIFFERENT

Currituck County's Produce Stands Along US 158
on the Currituck County mainland

If you're looking for a little lushness near the barren barrier-island beaches—or if you're hungering for something sweet to eat on the long, last leg of your drive to the Outer Banks—Currituck County's mainland has the stuff to make your mouth water.

Visitors arriving from Hampton Roads areas travel through fertile farmlands on the last hour of their trip. Like an oasis in a desert of desolation, wooden produce stands pop out of the flatlands. Hand-painted signs hawk the homegrown wares: melons, cucumbers, corn, blueberries, tomatoes, butter beans, and peaches so juicy they should be sold with bibs.

More than 10 markets are strewn in sporadic fashion from the Virginia border in Chesapeake to just west of the Wright Memorial Bridge. Each has a personality—and produce—all its own. Many are run by local families who began selling vegetables from the backs of pickup trucks parked along the roadside. Some stands include frozen yogurt, dried flowers, and seafood stalls, and almost all sell produce grown within a few miles of the open-air markets.

Decor includes the hospitable deep-green awnings of Grandy Greenhouse and Farm Market, the baby-blue exterior of Tarheel Produce, and the pink-and-purple polka dots of S & N Farm Market. Margaret and Alton Newbern have been running the Hilltop Market for almost 50 years. Morris Farm Market is one of the larger outposts along the Currituck stretch. Rufus Jones Farm Market features colorful fruits stacked in tilted wooden troughs and large-wheeled carts. And Soundside Orchard specializes in peach sales beneath a pointy-roofed wooden gazebo.

Whether you know produce or not, local farmers and their families are always glad to give free advice. They can thump a watermelon, peruse a peanut display, or feel a pumpkin and know how long ago it was picked. And they'll load you up with bursting berries, jarred apricot preserves, and local lore if you stick around long enough.

The produce of Currituck County is so good, you just might want to come back for more—the markets are only a half-hour jaunt from the beaches.

For some people, nothing compares to a day of poking through treasures from long ago, bringing back memories and, with any luck, discovering a fantastic bargain. If you're one of these, a world of antiques and "junque" stores is waiting for you along U.S. Highway 158 on the Currituck mainland. This road teems with shops selling antiques and collectibles. If rain keeps you off the beach, a very enjoyable day can be spent exploring in Currituck County.

Hampton Roads and Williamsburg, Virginia

If you're in the mood for more citified fun after days at the beach, head to Hampton Roads, Virginia, home to the urban cities of Norfolk, Virginia Beach, Chesapeake, Portsmouth, Hampton, and nearby Williamsburg. Outer Bankers are constantly making the 90- to 120-minute drive to this area to stock up at the superstores, fly somewhere, or attend a cultural or entertainment event. Norfolk is home to the Chrysler Museum of Art, the Harrison Opera House, and other performing arts centers that bring in top-name performers. MacArthur Center is Norfolk's premier shopping mall, and it's near the city's waterfront, which also has many attractions, museums, historic buildings, restaurants, and accommodations. Virginia Beach is a busy tourist resort, but it also has a wealth of cultural offerings, an outdoor amphitheater that features national acts, and many shopping opportunities. Williamsburg, Virginia, is about 45 minutes from Virginia Beach. It's famous for its historic attractions and for Busch Gardens, Water Country USA, and its endless shopping opportunities.

Elizabeth City, North Carolina

Our nearby neighbor to the northwest, Elizabeth City, North Carolina, offers more than enough beautiful scenery; historic, architectural, and natural attractions; and cultural and culinary options to make for a great day trip—and it's all just about an hour from the Outer Banks. The area chamber of commerce is your best source for more information.

**Elizabeth City Area
Chamber of Commerce
502 Ehringhaus Street, Elizabeth City
(252) 335–4365, (888) 258–4832
www.elizcity.com**
The chamber offices are jam-packed with information on all there is to see and do in this Pasquotank County jewel of a city, and a friendly staff is on hand to provide assistance. Elizabeth City is steeped in history. The first Grand Assembly of North Carolina met in this county in 1665, the state's first public school opened its doors here 40 years later, and the nation's oldest operational canal—the one snaking through the Dismal Swamp—opened in the early 1800s.

The chamber can get you started on your explorations of these fascinating facts and has also developed a self-guided walking tour through the city's historic districts. Elizabeth City has five designated districts listed with the National Register of Historic Places. Chamber personnel can also point you toward the Museum of the Albemarle (see previous listing in this chapter), with its collections, exhibits, and artifacts that document the history of northeastern North Carolina.

Other great ideas to include on your day trip or weekend getaway (there are at least a dozen great places to stay in the city; again, ask at the chamber for more information) include the dynamite dirt-track excitement of the Dixieland Motorsports complex; the Elizabeth City State University Planetarium, art galleries, and professional theater; and dining from fast food to four-star finery. And remember, the Pasquotank River rolls right through town, so there are a number of water-related activities available as well.

If you prefer to write for more information, send correspondence to Elizabeth City Area Chamber of Commerce, P.O. Box 426, Elizabeth City, NC 27907.

REAL ESTATE

There's a certain feeling that many of us get when we cross a bridge to the Outer Banks. It's excitement mixed with awe, blended with the spirit that something wonderful might happen at any moment. It's also a feeling of coming home. Any visitor to these shores who has that feeling should know one thing: It only gets stronger, and it makes leaving increasingly difficult. When you get that feeling, you know that it's time to look at Outer Banks real estate.

It's the desire to belong here, as much as the desire to own here, that puts the ink on all those real estate contracts. Before you take up a pen, however, realize that no matter how much experience you have buying and selling real estate in other areas, you need a deep understanding of the Outer Banks and its unique real estate market in order to make a sound decision. There's a lot to learn about seasonal versus residential neighborhoods, coastal and wetlands regulations, investing in an income-producing property versus buying a second home, buying an existing home versus building—you get the picture. It's not unusual for real estate agents to work with prospective buyers for two or three years before it all comes together. Then again, you may find exactly what you want your first day out looking.

So if you're serious about buying on the Outer Banks, begin by reading this chapter, and when you're done, consider that you've learned just enough to be dangerous. Do two things: (1) Start interviewing real estate professionals, and (2) begin collecting and reading everything you can get your hands on that will help you decipher the real estate market. Subscribe to the local newspapers (see our chapter on Media), and get to know the areas, the issues, and the prices. Read the weekly column in the *Virginian-Pilot* by Shirley Mozingo, who has been writing about Outer Banks real estate for years and who imparts substantive information helpful to both buyers and sellers. Surf the Internet and pick up the free real estate magazines. Smart buyers begin performing this due diligence well before they're ready to make a purchase.

UNDERSTANDING THE LOCAL MARKET

The last several years have seen a strong, healthy real estate market all over these barrier islands. Some recent hot spots have been Currituck's northern beaches, soundside in Duck, South Nags Head, and, of course, anything oceanfront. With the declining availability of raw oceanfront land, we're seeing a trend toward buying older existing homes and either remodeling the outdated structures or moving them off altogether and starting anew. Each year, prices continue to appreciate, and those who put off buying in the past have usually regretted their delay. If you want to buy, buy now, for the same piece of real estate will probably not be available next year and prices are guaranteed to be higher. In a nutshell, a purchase of Outer Banks real estate has never been a bad investment.

As you learn about the Outer Banks, you'll come to understand that the market varies quite a bit by township and by proximity to water. Nowhere is the old adage about location, location, location more important than here on the Outer Banks. The rules of supply and demand apply, period. The closer to the ocean, the greater the demand—and nothing is more precious than an oceanfront lot. Bear in mind that all oceanfront lots aren't created equal. The shoreline along the entire East Coast is in a constant state of flux. With such a dynamic scenario, some areas of the beach will experience erosion, some will experience accretion, and it's all subject to change. There's always an element of risk in owning property in a coastal environment.

The priciest real estate on the Outer Banks is in Corolla, where the newer oceanfront homes sell for up to $6 million. Still, there are many excellent, established neighborhoods in other areas of the Outer Banks where you can buy a cottage for around $220,000 and still walk to the ocean. This chapter touches upon the flavor of the various sections of the beach; for more information on townships, see our Area Overviews chapter.

WORKING WITH A REAL ESTATE AGENT

Whether you decide to buy an existing home or build your own, a good real estate agent can supply you with the information you need to make a smart decision and can save you a great deal of time and, very often, money. You are wise to enlist the services of a knowledgeable agent when you buy real estate on the Outer Banks given the uniqueness of the market economics and the local environment.

Interview a few agents before you decide with whom you'd like to work. Ask around for referrals. It's important for you to know that any real estate agent or broker can represent your interests, but be careful to select an agent with expertise in the communities in which you're most interested. Generally, you're better off to work with an agent whose office is located near your preferred areas. An agent who understands the market in Corolla probably won't be quite as knowledgeable of markets in Hatteras or Manteo.

Real estate agents and brokers are licensed by the State of North Carolina and are subject to its laws and regulations. A Realtor is an agent or broker who also belongs to the Board of Realtors, represented in our area by the Outer Banks Association of Realtors. What sets a Real-

tor apart from any licensee is the Realtor Code of Ethics, a set of stricter rules of conduct to which members subscribe, and access to the Multiple Listing Service, the most comprehensive database of properties for sale. For a listing of local Realtors, contact the Outer Banks Association of Realtors, P.O. Box 1070, Kill Devil Hills, NC 27948, (252) 441-4036; www.outer banksrealtors.com. This organization represents more than 700 Realtors on the Outer Banks.

When you choose an agent or broker, technically you're entering into an agreement not only with that agent but also with the agent's firm. You'll need to decide whether you want exclusive representation from a buyer's agent, whether you're content to work with the seller's agent, or whether under certain circumstances you'll allow your buyer's agent to represent both you and the other party to the transaction, which makes your agent a "dual" agent. There are specific rules governing these relationships, and all agents and brokers are required to explain these rules at the first substantive contact with a prospective client or customer. You will be asked to sign an agency agreement; make sure you understand your options and your obligations to your agent as well as her or his obligations to you. Most agents collect their fees from the proceeds of the sale, but this is not always the case. Make sure you understand the compensation arrangement before you commit to an agent. According to North Carolina statute, even if an agent does not represent you, the agent must still be fair and honest and disclose to you all material facts that the agent knows or reasonably should know.

A conscientious, hardworking agent or broker will supply you with extensive information on the market—including comps (comparable properties currently listed and recently sold), neighborhood amenities and covenants, and financing options—and will be conversant in the pros and cons of building your own versus buying an existing home. She or he can also help you estimate the costs of ownership and what you might expect to realize in terms of income if you decide, as many owners do, to rent your home to others.

At the end of this chapter are listings of real estate companies and the areas they specialize in. Along with some community listings, we've supplied contact information for the developer, but do be aware that you don't have to work with the developer or the developer's agent directly; you should feel free to use your own buyer's agent if that's your preference.

BUILDING YOUR OWN

If you decide to build, your agent can help you choose a building contractor, or you can ask for a list of members from the Outer Banks Homebuilders Association, 105 West Airstrip Road, Kill Devil Hills, NC 27948, (252) 449–8232.

If you decide to build your own home, first be clear about its intended use: Do you want a second home, rental property, or year-round residence? Your answer to that question will determine where you build and the style of home. If you're designing for the rental market, you'll have to keep in mind not only your preferences, but those of others as well. Talk with your builder and property managers to learn the features that will make your home a popular rental. You'll be wise to listen to their advice.

Ask your builder to not only show you floor plans but also take you through other houses he or she has built. (If you do this in the off-season, you'll have a better chance of viewing homes, for they will probably be vacant. Understandably, property managers try not to interrupt their guests' summer vacations.) If your goal is to achieve the maximum income, ask a property manager whose firm represents a lot of homes in your area to show you the most popular rentals in their inventory, but be careful to focus on homes similarly located to the lot you've selected. You can't compare income on an oceanfront to income on a house four rows back from the ocean.

You'll want to familiarize yourself with the building codes and regulations unique to our area, including regulations relating to environmental protection set by the North Carolina Coastal Management Authority (CAMA). Throughout the process, keep in mind that your intended use of the property will dictate its design and construction. A home intended for weekly rental is usually substantially different in design than a home intended for year-round residential use. Wandering through open houses and model homes is a fun and informative way to refine your ideas before you begin to set them down on paper.

TUNE IN TO REALITY

Many prospective buyers wander into real estate offices insisting they be shown properties that will "pay for themselves." Trust this Insider: If that many properties paid for themselves, there would be precious few for sale. Even if you're planning to rent out your new home at the beach, know that in 99 percent of cases you'll have to shell out more money than you'll take in for the privilege of owning it. Just how much you'll have to pay is highly variable. It depends on how much you paid for the property, the financing terms you've arranged, and how much rental income it generates.

When you buy a beach cottage with the intention of realizing rental income, what you're really doing is operating a business, so learn about it. As an owner, you have a great deal of influence over how much income your property generates. Participate in setting your rates. Keep your home in good repair, and be realistic about the funds you'll need to designate for annual maintenance and periodic replacement of housewares and furnishings. Discuss your goals with your agent and speak with property managers at a few carefully selected real estate firms (see our chapter on Weekly and Long-Term Cottage Rentals). You'll also want to consult your tax adviser, since the IRS has specific rules you must follow depending on how you use your property.

Once you place your property in service, review its performance at least annually with your property manager and pay close attention to any complaints or comments from renters. Keep a guest book in the cottage for renters' comments and think of it as a quality-control device.

Nearly all owners realize that by renting out their cottages, they are letting others subsidize their dream of owning a home by the sea. Over time, as property values and rental rates creep up and other costs stabilize, many cottages will operate at break-even or better. Your best bet is to be conservative in your expectations and be pleasantly surprised when they're exceeded.

What follows is a brief overview listing the main residential resort communities, as well as information on time-share properties and a listing of real estate companies. Please also refer to the Area Overview chapter for more information.

RESIDENTIAL RESORT COMMUNITIES

We've listed a combination of newer and more established oceanside and sound-side residential communities to give you an idea of what's here on the Outer Banks. We start our journey in the four-wheel-drive beaches north of Corolla and then move south through the Outer Banks, ending on Ocracoke Island. These communities include resorts and developments that offer recreational amenities and easy access to the ocean and sound, those that provide a mixture of both seasonal and year-round living, and neighborhoods with more of a year-round lifestyle.

Most developments have strict architectural guidelines, or covenants, to ensure quality development. It should also be noted that there are many one-road

(cul-de-sac) subdivisions scattered throughout the Outer Banks. Some of these subdivisions offer private roads and private ocean or sound accesses. These neighborhoods offer great rental opportunities but fewer amenities. Call your local real estate professional for more information about sales or rentals (see the Real Estate Sales Firms section at the end of this chapter).

The Four-Wheel-Drive Beaches

**Carova, North Swan Beach, Swan Beach, Seagull, and Penny's Hill subdivisions
Off the paved road north of NC 12**

Access to these subdivisions is by four-wheel-drive vehicle only. Depending upon how far north you're heading, you'll drive 5 to 20 minutes once you cross the beach access ramp just north of The Villages at Ocean Hill. (Read the rules of the road.) Although there's no paved road linking these communities to the asphalt in Corolla, once you drive up the beach, you'll discover a network of dirt roads throughout the four-wheel-drive area. Many of these have standing water after heavy rains, so watch for puddles and deep holes. Even though these are some of the widest beaches anywhere, we recommend that you drive at low tide. Some parts of the beach are home to the remains of a petrified forest—an indication of how much this barrier island has migrated throughout the centuries. The black stumps are mysteriously beautiful but can easily puncture a tire. Use extra caution in these areas, especially at night. At one time, the beaches were open to vehicular travel clear past the northernmost town of Carova up to Virginia. Driving into Virginia is no longer permitted from here, and a fence and a gate prevent crossing the border. Watch for the wild horses!

Virginia's False Cape State Park borders Carova on the north, and North Swan

Beach borders Carova on the south. As you continue southward, you come to Swan Beach, Seagull, and Penny's Hill subdivisions. Development began in Carova Beach in 1967, followed by development in North Swan Beach and Swan Beach. Carova Beach is the largest subdivision off the paved road.

Carova consists of approximately 2,000 lots. Resales are available in most areas. There are approximately 400 improved lots from Ocean Hill to the Virginia line and 2,500 property owners, of which a small number are year-round residents. The Seagull and Penny's Hill subdivisions are much smaller than Carova, which offers lots fronting canals, sandy trails, and open water between Currituck Sound and the Atlantic Ocean. Swan Beach and North Swan Beach are ocean-to-sound developments. Ocean Beach and Penny's Hill do not include sound frontage. Basic amenities are offered, including electricity and telephone service and water/sewer by individual well and septic system. Cable television is not available, but we've been told that television reception from the Hampton Roads network affiliates is excellent. There is no garbage pickup; you must take your trash to a nearby dump. Some mail delivery is available to a bank of locked boxes.

Real estate agents working in Corolla tend to be the most knowledgeable about this area. Find one that specializes. The quality of lots varies widely, and some areas are more prone to erosion than others.

Corolla

Ocean Hill and The Villages at Ocean Hill
NC 12, Corolla
Ocean Hill and The Villages at Ocean Hill lie at the northernmost end of the paved road in Corolla. The Villages at Ocean Hill is a unique resort community covering 153 acres, including lakefront, oceanfront, and soundside lots. This development of primarily rental homes is still very much available to the buying public. Amenities include oceanfront and lakefront pools, tennis courts, and a freshwater lake. Wide, white, sandy beaches are also part of the package. Strict architectural guidelines ensure quality development. The adjacent Ocean Hill has no amenities to speak of, although lot sizes are larger.

Corolla Light Resort Village
NC 12, Corolla
More than 200 acres compose this northern Outer Banks resort. Construction began in 1985, and some very large luxury homes were built here as well as elegant three-bedroom condos and four-bedroom villas. Home sizes range from 1,300 square feet to 3,600 square feet. This beautiful ocean-to-sound resort boasts an oceanfront pool complex, tennis courts scattered throughout the resort, a soundside pool, and an indoor sports center that houses a competition-size indoor pool, tennis courts, racquetball courts, and exercise rooms.

Whalehead Beach
NC 12, Corolla
Whalehead Beach is the most established beach neighborhood in Corolla. Its wide beaches stretch for more than 3 miles along the ocean and have a dozen public beachfront walkways. Public parking lots are scattered throughout. Though Whalehead doesn't have a central water system (properties have individual wells) and there are few other amenities, its 20,000-square-foot lots are a remarkable draw.

Monteray Shores
NC 12, Corolla
While Whalehead Beach occupies only the east side of North Carolina Highway 12, Monteray Shores is situated on the soundside (or west side) of this northern Outer Banks area. Its Caribbean-style homes have red tile roofs, arched verandas, spacious decks, and an abundance of windows, contrasting with the wooden structures found in most Outer Banks residential communities. But if you prefer

Outer Banks–style homes, they also are available here. The community features single-family residences and offers sound or ocean views from every homesite. While there are no oceanfront lots, the full gymnasium, soundside clubhouse, junior Olympic swimming pool, hot tub, four tennis courts, jogging trails, stocked fishing ponds, boat ramps, and other recreational amenities provide a dash of sophistication.

Buck Island
NC 12, Corolla

In a small section of the northern Outer Banks lies the exclusive community of Buck Island. This oceanfront and oceanside development is across from the Tim-Buck II Shopping Village on Ocean Trail.

Buck Island is reminiscent of the nautical seaside villages of Kiawah and Nantucket and boasts timeless Charlestonian architecture along a promenade of hardwood trees and turn-of-the-20th-century streetlights. Amenities include a guarded entrance, pristine ocean beach, beach cabana, spa, pool, and tennis courts.

Crown Point
NC 12, Corolla

Crown Point is 1 mile north of Ocean Sands and 10 miles north of Duck. This is a single-family subdivision with oceanfront and oceanside properties. It is completely separate from the Ocean Sands subdivision. There are approximately 90 homes here. Amenities include a swimming pool, tennis courts, and private beach-access walkways.

Ocean Sands
NC 12, Corolla

Ocean Sands is an oceanside and oceanfront planned unit development, or PUD, considered to be a model of coastal development by land-use planners, government officials, and environmentalists alike. The Ocean Sands concept is centered around clusters of homes that form small colonies buffered by open space. This design eliminates drive-through traffic while increasing privacy and open vistas. Clusters are devoted to single-family dwellings, multi-family dwellings, and appropriate commercial usage. Many of the approximately 600 residences at Ocean Sands are placed in rental programs. Amenities include tennis courts, nature trails, and a fishing lake stocked with bass. The development has guarded private roads. Tucked within Ocean Sands is Ocean Lake, a little neighborhood with a three-acre lake, tennis courts, and a large swimming pool.

Ocean Sands is a family-oriented community buffered on the east by the Atlantic Ocean and on the west by the exclusive Currituck Club community. Lots are 6,000 square feet.

Spindrift
Ocean Trail, near the Currituck Club
Corolla

Spindrift is a small gated community with about 30 40,000-square-foot lots—large in comparison to neighboring developments. The single-family residential development offers few amenities, but the privacy here can't be beat. You can build a dream home and be assured you will not be within an arm's length of your neighbor.

The Currituck Club
NC 12, Corolla
(252) 453–9445
www.thecurrituckclub.com

This 600-acre world-class golfing community is bordered by the Currituck Sound and sports an 18-hole championship golf course (see our Golf chapter). Single-family homes, villas, and patio homes are available. The upscale, gated community features tennis, basketball, and volleyball courts; swimming pools; lighted bike and jogging paths; and a full fitness center. Private ocean access is available with a trolley system, and there's even a beach valet service. Overall density is just more than one family per acre. Located in a maritime forest environment, on the grounds of the historic Currituck Shooting Club, the scenery can't be beat. Don't miss touring the development's Mainstreet Corolla model homes.

Pine Island
NC 12, Corolla

Pine Island resort is on 385 acres, with 300 single-family homesites and 3 miles of oceanfront. This planned oceanfront and oceanside community is bordered on the west by 1,500 acres of perpetually preserved marsh, islands, and uplands that compose the National Audubon Society Pine Island Sanctuary. Homesites are generous with strict architectural guidelines. Central water and sewer and underground utilities are available.

Residents have access to a tennis court, two community swimming pools, beach club, jogging paths, and more. Property owners also have access to a private landing strip.

Duck

Palmer's Island
NC 12, Duck

Located between Pine Island and Sanderling, the exclusive Palmer's Island is an ocean-to-sound community with fewer than 15 homesites. Beach frontage ranges from 120 feet to 225 feet per lot, and the enormous homes are magnificent. This is the narrowest stretch of land on the Outer Banks, so residents have breathtaking views of both the ocean and Currituck Sound. Although no property is available in Palmer's Island, home values begin at several million dollars.

Sanderling
Duck Road (NC 12), Duck

This ocean-to-sound community several miles north of Duck consists of nearly 300 homes and lots and is one of the most desirable residential communities on the Outer Banks. The heavy vegetation, winding lanes, and abundant wildlife offer the most seclusion of any resort community on the beach. Developers have taken care to leave as much natural growth as possible, and strict building covenants ensure privacy and value. The Sanderling Inn Resort is just north of the residential area.

Homeowners have their own recreational amenities, including miles of nature trails, the Soundside Racquet and Swimming Club, and sailing and canoeing opportunities.

Port Trinitie
Duck Road (NC 12), Duck

Port Trinitie, situated on 23 acres of ocean-to-sound property, stretches across Duck Road and offers gorgeous soundfront views. Located 2 miles north of Duck, amenities include two swimming pools, two tennis courts, a soundside pier and gazebo, and an oceanfront sitting area. This development began with condominiums, which are co-ownership properties, but Port Trinitie now offers an even mixture of whole ownership single-family dwellings (cottages and townhomes) and co-owned condos.

Sea Ridge and Osprey
Duck Road (NC 12), Duck

This area, 1.5 miles north of the village of Duck, claims to have the best views on the Outer Banks and has lots and three- and four-bedroom single-family homes available. Natural beauty is this development's calling card.

NorthPoint
Duck Road (NC 12), Duck

Fractional ownership is popular at North-Point, though some lots remain for individual ownership and development. Residents enjoy an enclosed swimming pool, tennis and basketball courts, and a long soundfront pier for fishing, crabbing, and small boat dockage. One of the first fractional ownership developments on the

---

A number of real estate developers have on-site model homes open to the public. For an up-close and personal glimpse of some stunning design and architecture, look for the OPEN HOUSE signs. The Outer Banks Home Builders Association also has an annual Parade of Homes. For more information, call (252) 449–8232.

northern Outer Banks, NorthPoint has enjoyed good values on resales.

Ships Watch
1251 Duck Road (NC 12), Duck
(252) 261–2231, (800) 261–7924
www.shipswatch.com

Mid-Atlantic Country magazine portrayed this community as "the Palm Beach of the Outer Banks." Ships Watch is a community of luxurious seaside homes on the northernmost end of the village of Duck. Complete service, home maintenance, and attention to details are characteristics of this resort. Carefully placed on high rolling dunes, the homes offer spectacular views of the ocean, Currituck Sound, or both. An Olympic-size pool, tennis courts, jogging trail, soundside pier and boat ramp, and weekly socials offer entertainment options for the whole family. Full concierge service includes arranging tee times, dinner reservations, and babysitting. The resort provides rentals, along with fractional and whole ownership. Fractional, one-tenth deeded ownerships are available. Developer Buck Thornton and his associates have experienced great success with this high-end resort. Contact Ships Watch for sales and rental information.

Sea Pines
Duck Road (NC 12), Duck

SeaPines is a 61-lot development tucked away in the heart of Duck. Lot sizes for this oceanside village range from 15,000 to 20,000 square feet. There still are lots to choose, including some with ocean views from upper-level living areas. Amenities include a swimming pool and tennis court.

Schooner Ridge Beach Club
Duck Road (NC 12), Duck

Schooner Ridge is in the heart of Duck, but its oceanfront/oceanside homes are well hidden from the hustle and bustle. The high, sandy hills fronting the Atlantic Ocean are perfect for these large single-family homes with ample windows and decks. All lots are sold, but resales are available. The community offers indoor and outdoor recreational amenities. Bike paths wind through the area, and the shops in the village are within walking distance.

Nantucket Village
Duck Road (NC 12), Duck

Nantucket is an upscale private resort consisting of 35 large condominiums with garages and spacious decking. Situated on a high hill overlooking Currituck Sound, these units have panoramic views and magnificent sunsets. The year-round development offers an indoor pool and tennis court as well as sandy soundfront beaches, a pier with gazebo, and boat launch facilities. The sound beach is ideal for wading, children's activities, crabbing, fishing, windsurfing, and other watercraft sports.

Units in two luxury duplex condominium buildings have about 1,750 square feet of living space, two-car garages, three bedrooms, two-and-a-half baths, gas fireplaces, and panoramic water views.

Ocean Crest
Duck Road (NC 12), Duck

Near Nantucket Village, Ocean Crest is an ocean-to-sound resort consisting of 54 lots that hit the market in August 1992. Lots are 15,000 square feet or larger and are zoned for single-family dwellings. This is an upscale neighborhood with strict architectural guidelines. Homes must be 2,000 square feet or larger. Amenities include a swimming pool, tennis courts, private ocean access, and good water views.

Kitty Hawk

Martin's Point
US 158, MP 0, Kitty Hawk

Martin's Point is an exclusive waterfront community of custom homes and homesites with stringent building requirements, a guarded entry, and some of the most beautiful maritime forests found anywhere. Homes range from 1,200 square feet to 13,000 square feet. This primarily year-round neighborhood features a marina, dock, and pier on the Currituck Sound. Owners have easy access to the local elementary school, shopping, and golf.

When you arrive on the Outer Banks at the eastern terminus of the Wright Memorial Bridge, the entrance to Martin's Point is on your immediate left. The community is closed to drive-through inspections, but if you're considering a permanent move to the Outer Banks, it's an upscale area you should look at.

Southern Shores
US 158 and NC 12, Kitty Hawk
Southern Shores is a unique 2,600-acre incorporated town with its own government and police force. Although there are two shopping centers on its western boundary, commercial zoning/development is not allowed elsewhere. The town has dense maritime forests along the soundside fringe, wide-open sand hills in the middle, and beachfront property. The substantial year-round population attests to the popularity of Southern Shores. Kitty Hawk Land Company has carefully paced development through the years, and there are still many vacant lots. One of the newest developments within Southern Shores is Ginguite Woods, a neighborhood just south of Martin's Point. Southern Shores is considered one of the most desirable places to live on the Outer Banks.

Kitty Hawk Landing
W. Kitty Hawk Road, Kitty Hawk
This is a residential community with mostly year-round homeowners. It's on the far western edges of Kitty Hawk. To get there, turn west off U.S. Highway 158 at MP 4 onto West Kitty Hawk Road and just keep driving until you see the signs. The community borders Currituck Sound. It has deep canals, tall pines, and gorgeous sunsets.

Sandpiper Cay Condominiums
Sand Dune Drive, Kitty Hawk
(252) 261-2188
This resort community consists of 280

condominium units and is near Sea Scape Golf Course. About 155 of the units are second homes; some 40 percent of the units are either long-term rentals or primary residences, making this a year-round resort. Some units are available for short-term or weekly leases. All the original inventory has been sold, though some resales are available. Amenities include a large outdoor pool, clubhouse, and tennis court. Homeowner fees apply. Contact Sandpiper Cay for more information.

Kill Devil Hills

First Flight Village
First Street, Kill Devil Hills
This is one of the Outer Banks's most popular year-round neighborhoods in the central area of the beach. The entrance to First Flight Village is on the west side of US 158 at MP 7½. This is a family-oriented neighborhood, so if you're considering a permanent move to the Outer Banks with kids in tow, you should investigate this community. First Flight Village real estate is considered moderately priced.

Colington Island

Colington Harbour
Colington Road, Colington Island
Development on Colington Island began more than 25 years ago. To get there, turn off US 158 at the stoplight just south of the Wright Brothers Memorial onto Colington Road. Colington Harbour is about 4 miles down the winding road.

The community has some 12 miles of bulkheaded deepwater canals and soundfront lots, all easily accessing Albemarle Sound. Oregon Inlet, the closest ocean inlet, is approximately 25 miles by boat south of Colington Island. Choices range from extremely affordable "starter" homes to upscale soundfront or canalfront homes with private boat docks. This community combines a year-round population of more than 2,000 with seasonal and weekly renters. The picnic area, playground, sandy beach on Kitty Hawk Bay, boat ramp, boat slips for rent, and fuel dock are available to all residents, including year-round renters. Clubhouse activities, an Olympic-size swimming pool, a children's pool, and a tennis court are available to club members. What makes Colington Harbour popular is its private entry and the many canals that offer waterfront living to many residents. Colington Harbour is one of the best places to keep a deep-draft boat.

Colington Heights
Colington Island

This is the last developable subdivision within Colington Harbour. There are 23 lots on approximately 35 acres. The inventory includes wooded interior lots, waterview lots, and waterfront properties. Essentially, this is a maritime forest development. Large three-acre lot sizes contribute to the area's privacy. Roads are private, and there is private beach access on Albemarle Sound. Architectural controls are in effect, and the developer has paid all of the water-impact fees, making the real estate even more attractive.

WatersEdge
Off Colington Road, Colington Island
(252) 261-2131, (800) 488-0738
www.khlc.com

WatersEdge is a gated, year-round residential neighborhood on Colington Island. The community has a swimming pool, marina, and boat ramp with access to Roanoke Sound and its own owners' association. Sales are handled exclusively by Kitty Hawk Land Company.

Nags Head

South Ridge
Off US 158, MP 13, Nags Head
(252) 441-2800

This 42-acre parcel is a no-frills community with 140 homesites on the hill behind the Nags Head Post Office. The development features quarter-acre ocean- and soundview lots but no soundfront property. Three models are available for viewing. Square footage for new houses runs between 1,600 and 1,900 for three- and four-bedroom homes. Construction features cathedral or vaulted ceilings, lots of open space, and light, bright interiors.

The Village at Nags Head
US 158, MP 15, Nags Head
(252) 441-8533, sales
www.villagerealtyobx.com

The Ammons Corporation began developing this ocean-to-sound community, which has become one of the best sellers on the Outer Banks, about a decade ago. The golf course (with a beautiful clubhouse and popular restaurant) and the oceanfront recreational complex with tennis courts and an outdoor pool make this attractive residential community most desirable. Single-family homes and townhomes provide something for everyone. The oceanfront homes are some of the largest and most luxurious anywhere. There's plenty to do here. It's an excellent choice for beach living, vacation rentals, or investment.

Roanoke Island

Pirate's Cove
Manteo–Nags Head Causeway, Manteo
(252) 473-1451, (800) 762-0245

Pirate's Cove is a distinctive residential marina resort community. Hundreds of acres of protected wildlife marshlands border Pirate's Cove on one side, while the peaceful waters of Roanoke Sound are on the other. Deepwater canals provide each owner with a dock at the door, and the centrally located marina is home to many large yachts and fishing boats.

Pirate's Cove offers homesites, homes, condominiums, and "dockominiums" fronting deepwater canals. Activities abound. Fishing tournaments seem as important as sleeping to many of the residents, with locals and visitors getting in on the fun. Other recreational amenities include a hot tub, sauna, fitness center, restaurant, and beautifully appointed clubhouse, plus swimming pools and lighted tennis courts. Scheduled recreational activities for all ages are available. One of the prettiest Outer Banks settings enhances the Victorian nautical design of these homes.

Shallowbag Bay Club
US 64/264, Manteo
(252) 261–5500, (800) 395–2525
www.manteocondos.com

Manteo's newest development, this luxury condominium complex and marina has breathtaking views. There are 60 luxury three-bedroom condos in The Harbor and 17 condo suites in The Point. Amenities include 91 private boat slips, a full-service marina, a waterfront restaurant, fitness center, pool and hot tub, meeting room, water taxi to downtown Manteo, and clubhouse. Association fees are charged to owners. The entrance to Shallowbag Bay Club is on U.S. Highway 64/264, right behind McDonald's.

Roanoak Village
Manteo

Roanoak Village offers options for building a variety of homes ranging in size from 860 to 2,100 square feet. The development is being built in three phases and encompasses nearly eight acres with a potential of 57 homesites. Interiors range from two-bedroom, one-bath styles to four-bedroom, two-and-a-half-bath homes. Some models feature hardwood floors.

For the new neighborhood, local architect John Wilson IV designed approximately 10 house plans in keeping with the older building styles still evident in downtown Manteo, giving the project a homey feel with a historic thrust.

The neighborhood is within walking distance of Roanoke Island's bike trails, the public library, local churches, town, and the Manteo waterfront.

Heritage Point
Pearce Road, Northern Roanoke Island
(252) 473–1450

This year-round resort community is sub-divided into 111 lots off US 64/264 next to Fort Raleigh National Historic Site. Restrictive covenants are in place. Interior, soundview, and soundfront lots overlooking the Croatan and Albemarle Sounds are available. Lot sizes range from a half-acre to more than three-and-a-half acres. Each lot has a boat slip, and there is a fishing pier for homeowners. The community sports two tennis courts, and a parking area and common beach are provided. Homeowner association fees apply.

The Peninsula
Russell Twiford Road, Manteo
(252) 453–3600

This exclusive boating community includes 34 private waterfront homesites with a lighted dock in excess of 2,000 feet, a boat ramp, a pump-out station, deepwater canals, and three gazebos over the water. These homes on the Manteo sewage system feature looped water lines to prevent sediment buildup. Homes have direct access to the sound. Some covenant restrictions apply.

Hatteras Island

Resort Rodanthe
Resort Rodanthe Drive off NC 12
Rodanthe

This resort consists of one building with 12 two-bed and 8 one-bed condominium units. Views of the ocean and sound vary by unit. Lower floor units have sound views. The condos are for sale, but owners also rent them. Amenities include a swimming pool and private ocean access.

Hatteras High Condominiums
Resort Rodanthe Drive, off NC 12
Rodanthe

Hatteras High features four oceanfront condominium buildings with 12 units in each. These two-bed, two-bath condos connect to the beach by boarded walkway. A swimming pool is behind the buildings.

Mirlo Beach
NC 12, Rodanthe
This sound-to-oceanfront resort community is 12 miles south of the Oregon Inlet Bridge, adjacent to Pea Island National Wildlife Refuge. There are approximately 10 large oceanfront cottages in Mirlo Beach, each of which comfortably sleeps an average of 12. Amenities include tennis courts and private beach and sound accesses. This resort has a solid rental history.

St. Waves
NC 12, Waves
This subdivision, developed during the 1980s, consists of approximately 55 lots and 20 houses. Homes and homesites are available for sale. Properties offer ocean, sound, and lake views. The homes are upscale, and architectural controls are in effect. Amenities include a swimming pool, a tennis court, and a centrally located lake. St. Waves maintains an excellent rental history.

Kinnakeet Shores
NC 12, Avon
Once a desolate stretch of narrow land between the Atlantic Ocean and Pamlico Sound, Kinnakeet Shores is a residential community being quickly developed. It consists of 500 acres next to beautiful marshlands and one of the best windsurfing areas in the world. Recreational amenities include swimming pools and tennis courts. This is the largest development on Hatteras Island, and the homes tend to be big, reminding us of the ones on the northern beaches. This is primarily a second-home development, offering one of the most popular rental programs on the island.

Hatteras Pines
NC 12, Buxton
This 150-acre subdivision nestles in a maritime forest in the heart of Buxton. It consists of 114 wooded lots rolling along the dunes and ridges. The roads for this development are intact, along with protective covenants. A pool and tennis court are part of the package.

Sunset Village
Sunset Strip, Frisco
(252) 995-3313
www.landsendinc.com
Only a few homesites are currently available in this new soundside community, but the area is beginning to develop. Lots come with a deeded boat slip.

Hatteras Landing
NC 12, Hatteras Village
This development features 41 homesites, a restaurant, gift shop, bookstore, deli, convenience store, coffee shop, clothing stores, and other retail opportunities. Homeowners have access to the on-site Holiday Inn Express pool. Oceanfront and soundfront lots are available. Homeowners build the homes of their choice.

Hatteras By The Sea
NC 12, Hatteras Village
This rather small community of 36 lots on 25 acres is one of the last oceanfront areas available for residential living. The southern end of the Outer Banks has little land, and a good portion is preserved by the National Seashore designation. A large pool and some carefully designed nature paths are included. Sunrise and sunset views are unobstructed here.

Ocracoke Island

Ocracoke Horizon Condominiums
Silver Lake Road, Ocracoke
(252) 928-5711
These five soundfront condominiums were developed by Midgett Realty in Hatteras but are handled by Sandy Shores Realty on Ocracoke Island. Features include two two-bedroom and three three-bedroom units with either two or two-and-a-half baths and whirlpool tubs. The units overlook Pamlico Sound and Portsmouth Island. Sales and rentals are available.

TIME-SHARING

Time-sharing is a deeded transaction under the jurisdiction of the North Carolina Real Estate Commission. A deeded share is 1/52 of the unit property being purchased (one week of a year). This deed grants the right to use the property in perpetuity. Always ask if the property you're inspecting is a deeded time-share because there is such a thing as undeeded time-shares—these give the right to use a property, but the property reverts to the developer in the end.

What you buy in a time-share is the right to use a specific piece of real estate for a week per year. The weeks are either fixed at the time of sale or rotate yearly. Members trade their weeks for different time slots at a variety of locations around the world. Qualifying for the purchase of a time-share unit can be no more difficult than qualifying for a credit card, but be aware of financing charges that are higher than regular mortgages.

Most time-share resorts on the Outer Banks are multifamily constructions with recreational amenities varying from minimal to luxurious and sometimes include the services of a recreational director. Time-share units usually come furnished and carry a monthly maintenance fee. Tax advantages for ownership and financing are not available to the purchaser of a time-share.

Many time-share ventures offer "free weekends"—you agree to a sales pitch and tour of the facilities in exchange for accommodations. Listen, ask questions, and stay in control of your money and your particular situation. If you get swept away, you'll only have five days to change your mind, according to the North Carolina Time Share Act that governs the sale of time-shares.

It is best to keep the purchase of time-shares in proper perspective; your deeded share only enables you to vacation in that property during a designated time period each year for as long as you own that share. This makes time-share very different from other potential investments.

All real estate investment decisions require thorough research and planning, and time-share is no exception. Time-share salespeople are licensed (to everyone's advantage) and earn commissions. Some great arrangements are out there, while others are not so good. Check thoroughly before buying. Several Outer Banks companies specialize in time-sharing. The following list includes some of these.

Barrier Island Ocean Pines
NC 12, Duck
(252) 261-3525
Ocean Pines offers time-sharing opportunities featuring oceanfront one- and two-bedroom condominiums. Amenities include an indoor pool, tennis courts, whirlpool tubs, and, of course, the beach.

Barrier Island Station
NC 12, Duck
(252) 261-3525
Barrier Island, one of the largest time-share resorts on the Outer Banks, is on a high dune area of ocean-to-sound property. These are multifamily units of wood construction. There is an attractive, full-service restaurant and bar with a soundside sailing center, in addition to the beach. A full-time recreation director is on board for a variety of planned activities and events. Indoor swimming, tennis courts, and other recreational facilities round out a full amenities package. This is a popular resort in a just-as-popular seaside village.

Barrier Island Station at Kitty Hawk
1 Cypress Knee Trail, Kitty Hawk
(252) 261-4610
www.bistation.com
Barrier Island Station at Kitty Hawk is a multifamily vacation ownership resort set in a maritime forest. The 100 acres of private land sport a million-dollar sports complex featuring an indoor pool, free weights, circuit training, and aerobic and massage facilities. Shoot pool or play table tennis in the game room. Condominiums have one, two, or three bedrooms. The community is near two shopping centers.

Sea Scape Beach and Golf Villas
US 158, MP 2½, Kitty Hawk
(252) 261–3837

There are plenty of recreational opportunities here: tennis courts, three swimming pools, an indoor recreation facility, an exercise room, and a game room. The Villas are next to the Sea Scape golf course. The two-bed, two-bath units are of wood construction, and they are on the west side of US 158. Sea Scape offers a unique opportunity for time-share ownership and an active rental program.

Outer Banks Beach Club
NC 12, MP 9, Kill Devil Hills
(252) 441–6321

The round, wooden buildings of the Outer Banks Beach Club were the first time-sharing opportunities built and sold on the Outer Banks. The 160 units include oceanfront and oceanside units, plus club-house units across the Beach Road, near the clubhouse and its indoor pool. There are two outdoor pools in great oceanfront locations. One-, two-, and three-bedroom units have access to whirlpools, tennis courts, and a playground. There is a full-time recreation director offering a variety of activities and games.

Outer Banks Resort Rentals
Croatan Centre, MP 13½, Nags Head
(252) 441–2134

This company deals exclusively with time-shares, handling rentals and resales at all the time-share complexes on the Outer Banks. All the units this company represents are furnished and self-contained, and all have swimming pools.

Dunes South Beach and Racquet Club
NC 12, MP 18, Nags Head
(252) 441–4090

Townhome time-sharing at this resort features two- and three-bedroom units with fireplaces, washers and dryers, and whirlpool tubs. The 20 units are mostly oceanfront; the remainder of the units are oceanside. A pool, tennis court, putting green, and playground make up the recreational amenities.

REAL ESTATE SALES FIRMS

Following are some Outer Banks real estate sales companies, their locations, and contact information. While this list is not all-inclusive, it is representative of reputable real estate sales companies on the Outer Banks. Most, if not all, of these companies are members of the Outer Banks Association of Realtors.

Riggs Realty
Austin Building, 1152 Ocean Trail
NC 12, Corolla
(252) 453–3111
www.riggsrealtycorp.com

Riggs specializes in northern beach land and home properties, especially in the four-wheel-drive areas like Swan, North Swan, and Carova Beach. Riggs Realty has more than 28 years of real estate experience.

Brindley & Brindley Real Estate
A ResortQuest Company
Brindley Building, NC 12, Corolla Light
(252) 453–3000
www.brindleyandbrindley.com

Brindley & Brindley represents property from Carova to Southern Shores.

Twiddy & Company Realtors
NC 12, Duck
(252) 261–8311, (800) 342–1609

NC 12 and Second Street, Corolla
(252) 453–3325, (800) 579–6130
www.twiddy.com

Twiddy represents properties from Carova through Kitty Hawk.

Stan White Realty & Construction
812 Ocean Trail, Corolla
(252) 453–3161, (800) 753–6200

US 158, MP 10½, Nags Head
(252) 441–1515, (800) 753–9699
www.builderouterbanks.com

Stan White represents properties from Corolla to Hatteras Village.

**Beach Realty & Construction/
Kitty Hawk Rentals**
790-B NC 12, Corolla
(252) 453-3131

1450 NC 12, Duck
(252) 261-6600

US 158, MP 2, Kitty Hawk
(252) 261-3815, (800) 849-9888

US 158, Kill Devil Hills
(252) 441-1106
www.beachrealtync.com
Steve Blaisdell is one of the expert consultants at Beach Realty, which handles real estate sales, rentals, and construction. The firm represents property from Carova to South Nags Head.

Coastland Realty
NC 12, Corolla
(252) 453-2105, (888) 207-4209
Coastland offers real estate sales only, representing the northern Outer Banks—specifically, Ocean Sands and Crown Point.

Karichele Realty
66 Sunset Boulevard
TimBuck II, NC 12, Corolla
(252) 453-4400, (800) 453-2377
www.karichele.com

Karichele covers properties from the Virginia line to Nags Head.

Duck's Real Estate
NC 12, Duck
(252) 261-2224, (800) 992-2976
www.ducksrealestate.com
Duck's Real Estate represents property from Corolla to Nags Head.

Southern Shores Realty
NC 12, Southern Shores
(252) 261-2000, (800) 334-1000
www.southernshores.com
Southern Shores Realty represents properties from Corolla to Nags Head.

Joe Lamb Jr. & Associates, Realtors
US 158, MP 2, Kitty Hawk
(252) 261-4444, (800) 552 6257
www.joelambjr.com
Joe Lamb represents properties from northern Duck to South Nags Head.

Kitty Hawk Land Company
US 158, Kitty Hawk
(252) 261-2131, (800) 488-0738
www.khlc.com
Kitty Hawk Land Company has been in the real estate business for more than 50

years. KHL is credited with developing Southern Shores, Spindrift on the Currituck Outer Banks, WatersEdge on Colington Island, Sea Pines and Oceancrest in Duck, and The Currituck Club in Corolla. They offer properties within these developments as well as select listings of outside properties on the Outer Banks.

Outer Banks Vacation Realty
US 158, MP 4½, Kitty Hawk
(252) 449-9034, (888) 685-9581
www.vacationouterbanks.com
Properties from Kitty Hawk to South Nags Head are offered through Outer Banks Vacation Realty.

Properties at the Beach
The Dunes Shops, US 158, MP 4½
Kitty Hawk
(252) 261-2855, (800) 245-0021
Properties at the Beach represents property from Carova Beach to South Nags Head.

Kitty Dunes Realty
US 158, MP 5, Kitty Hawk
(252) 261-2173

Corolla Light Town Center
Unit 1110, Corolla
(252) 453-DUNE
www.kittydunes.com
Kitty Dunes represents Corolla to South Nags Head. This company also owns Colington Realty. Residents of Canada can contact the Canadian representative at (514) 252-9566.

Jim Perry & Company
Executive Center, US 158, MP 5½
Kill Devil Hills
(252) 441-3051, (800) 222-6135
www.jimperry.com
Jim Perry represents properties in all areas of the Outer Banks.

RE/MAX Ocean Realty
US 158, MP 6, Kill Devil Hills
(252) 441-2450
www.obxrealtor.com
RE/MAX represents properties from Corolla to Hatteras Village.

Sea Oats Realty
P.O. Box 3399, Kill Devil Hills, NC 27948
(252) 480-2325
www.seaoatsrealty.com
Sea Oats handles real estate sales from Duck to South Nags Head.

Bodie Island Realty
NC 12, MP 7, Kill Devil Hills
(252) 441-9443, (800) 839-5116

NC 12, MP 17, Nags Head
(252) 441-2558, (800) 862-1785
www.bodieislandrealty.com
Bodie Island Realty offers general real estate covering Corolla to north Hatteras.

Harrell and Associates
US 158, MP 7, Kill Devil Hills
(252) 441-7887
www.harrellandassociates.com
This company specializes in property throughout Dare County, including commercial and residential listings, plus many condominiums.

Colington Realty
2141 Colington Road, Colington Island
(252) 441-3863
www.colingtonrealty.com
Colington Realty specializes in Colington Harbour properties.

Sun Realty
US 158, MP 9, Kill Devil Hills
(252) 441-8011

NC 12, Corolla
(252) 453-8811

NC 12, Duck
(252) 261-4183

US 158, Kitty Hawk
(252) 261-3892

NC 12, Salvo
(252) 967-2755

NC 12, Avon
(252) 995-5821
www.sunrealty.com
This realty represents properties throughout the Outer Banks.

Outer Banks Ltd.
US 158, MP 10, Nags Head
(252) 441-7156
www.outerbanksltd.com
Outer Banks Ltd. represents property
from Kitty Hawk to South Nags Head.

Frank Mangum Realty
US 158, MP 10⅓, Nags Head
(252) 441-3600, (800) 279-5552
www.mangumrealty.com
Frank Mangum handles sales covering the
entire Outer Banks.

Conner Resorts
US 158, MP 10½, Nags Head
(252) 261-8861, (800) 624-7432
www.connerresorts.com
Conner Resorts sells and rents a select
group of homes throughout the Outer
Banks.

Gateway Realty
2808 North Croatan Highway, Nags Head
(252) 480-0093, (800) 633-4491
www.gatewayobx.com
Gateway specializes in sales, long-term
rentals, and property management from
North Currituck beaches to South Nags
Head.

Nags Head Realty
US 158, MP 10½, Nags Head
(252) 441-4311, (800) 222-1531
www.nagsheadrealty.com
Nags Head Realty represents property
from Corolla to Oregon Inlet.

Outer Banks Resort Rentals
Croatan Centre, MP 13½, Nags Head
(252) 441-2134
www.outerbanksresorts.com
Ronda Williams represents the sales and
rentals of time-shares only. The company
offers time-share options from Duck to
South Nags Head as well as a few in Hatteras. (See our Weekly and Long-Term Cottage Rentals chapter for further details.)

Cove Realty
Between NC 12 and US 158
MP 14, Nags Head
(252) 441-6391, (800) 635-7007
www.coverealty.com
Cove represents Nags Head and South
Nags Head and specializes in Old Nags
Head Cove.

Village Realty
US 158, MP 14½, Nags Head
(252) 480-2224, (800) 548-9688
www.villagerealtyobx.com
Village Realty represents properties from
Corolla through South Nags Head.

Pirate's Cove
Manteo–Nags Head Causeway, Manteo
(252) 473-1451, (800) 762-0245
www.pirates-cove.com
The realty arm of Pirate's Cove Yacht
Club represents properties in this boating
paradise.

20/20 Realty Ltd.
516 US 64, Manteo
(252) 473-2020
Roanoke Island properties are the focus
for 20/20 Realty.

Midgett Realty
NC 12, Rodanthe
(252) 987-2350

NC 12, Avon
(252) 995-5333

NC 12, Hatteras Village
(252) 986-2841, (800) 527-2903
www.midgettrealty.com
Midgett Realty represents properties on
the southern end of the Outer Banks.

Surf or Sound Realty
NC 12, Rodanthe
(252) 987-1444, (800) 237-1138

NC 12, Avon
(252) 995-6052
www.surforsound.com
Surf or Sound represents properties from
Rodanthe to Hatteras Village.

Mercedes Tabano Realty
NC 12, Rodanthe
(252) 987-2711
Mercedes Tabano represents properties on Hatteras Island

Cape Escape
NC 12, Salvo
(252) 987-2336, (800) 996-2336
www.capeescaperealty.com
Cape Escape, across from the local post office, handles sales in Rodanthe, Waves, and Salvo.

Outer Beaches Realty
NC 12, Waves
(252) 987-1102, (800) 627-3750

NC 12, Avon
(252) 995-6041, (800) 627-3150

NC 12, Hatteras
(252) 986-1105, (888) 627-3650
www.outerbeaches.com
Outer Beaches Realty specializes in properties throughout Hatteras Island.

Hatteras Realty
NC 12, Avon
(252) 995-5466, (800) HATTERA
www.hatterasrealty.com
Hatteras Realty covers residential and commercial lots and homes on Hatteras Island.

Dolphin Realty
NC 12, Hatteras Village
(252) 986-2562, (800) 338-4775
www.dolphin-realty.com
This company provides real estate properties in the villages of Avon, Buxton, Frisco, and Hatteras for buyers and sellers on Hatteras Island.

Ocracoke Island Realty
NC 12, Ocracoke
(252) 928-6261, (252) 928-7411
www.ocracokeislandrealty.com
Ocracoke Island Realty represents Ocracoke Island properties.

Sandy Shores Realty
NC 12, Ocracoke
(252) 928-5711
www.sandyshoresocracoke.com
Formerly Sharon Miller Realty, Sandy Shores represents Ocracoke Island properties.

RETIREMENT 🌴

When some people dream of retirement, they might picture themselves strolling along stretches of deserted beaches on a mild winter afternoon. Perhaps later, they would enjoy a round of golf with friends on an award-winning course to be followed by a good meal at one of many area restaurants. Sound too good to be true? It's possible right here on the Outer Banks. But beware, this isn't your normal retirement community! The retirees here eagerly pursue an active lifestyle, participating in the many activities the beach has to offer. Many seniors also enjoy working with the public, filling a spot in the workplace through retail sales or other tourist-oriented jobs. As for fun activities, the senior centers offer all kinds of group trips and classes. And with the hospital that opened in 2002 (see our Health Care and Wellness chapter), the Outer Banks now offers all the benefits of places on the mainland.

If you're thinking of retiring to the Outer Banks, you're in good company. Each year, it seems that more retirees are lured to these barrier islands by some sort of siren call. Moderate winters (remarkably quiet due to the small year-round population) provide for a tranquil environment, and 90-plus miles of broad, soft-sand beaches might figure into the equation as well. North Carolina is now the third most attractive state to retirees, after Florida and Arizona.

In 1998 the *Wall Street Journal* published an article called "Your Next Address," in which five atypical retirement communities were highlighted. "This ain't your father's Florida," the introduction reads. No, these are retirement locations that tend to attract early-retiring baby boomers who are seeking out relatively remote areas on the water where outdoor recreation is an integral part of life. Not surprising to anyone who has retired to the Outer Banks, Corolla was one of the five communities showcased in the article. Corolla tends to draw the retirees and second-home owners who are looking for upscale housing, although options for any type of dwelling abound all along the Outer Banks. If you're looking for a seaside mansion in a gated community, you'll find it. And if your tastes lean more toward a bungalow in the woods or to a traditional three-bedroom home with a yard, you'll find those, too.

If you're looking for property, check out our Real Estate and Area Overview chapters before you start shopping. For information on our community's senior services, read on.

Seniors are encouraged to participate in the Outer Banks Senior Games sponsored by Dare County Older Adult Services. But be warned, these senior athletes are a dedicated and talented bunch, capable of putting much younger athletes to shame. This is a year-round program to promote health and fitness for Dare County residents age 55 and older. Competition events include track and field, bicycle racing, swimming, tennis, bowling, golf, softball and football throwing, basketball shooting, archery, shuffleboard, billiards, horseshoes, and croquet. Medal winners automatically qualify to compete at the North Carolina Senior Games in September. Besides athletics, there is a Silver Competition for the visual and performing arts. See our listings in the Annual Events chapter under April, or call the Thomas A. Baum Center, (252) 441-1811, for more information.

SENIOR CENTERS

Thomas A. Baum Center
300 Mustian Street, Kill Devil Hills
(252) 441-1181

The Thomas A. Baum Center is as bright and full of life as the many seniors who cross its threshold each and every day. The center is named after a Dare County native who was a pioneer in ferry transportation. His daughter, Diane Baum St. Clair, arranged for the town of Kill Devil Hills to purchase the land, known locally as the Baum Tract, on very generous terms. Dare County bought a section of the land, which today is home to the senior center, water plant, library, two public schools, the local chamber of commerce, and the town's administration and water departments. .

The senior center was dedicated on December 7, 1987. The 10,000-square-foot-plus building houses the senior center and the county's older adult services. A handful of paid staff and countless senior volunteers operate the center, which is the hub for senior activity north of Hatteras Island. Dare County residents or property owners who are age 55 or older may use the center for free; if you are younger than age 55 but your spouse meets the age requirement, you also may use the center.

The facility includes a multipurpose room with a stage where the center's drama group, Center Front, performs various productions annually. The Outer Banks Senior Chorus, which performs two con-certs per year, also uses this room for practice sessions. The Baum Center is home to the Wright Tappers, a seniors tap-dancing group, and the Dare Devils, the official cheerleaders for the Outer Banks Senior Games. Line- and square-dance groups round out the foot-tapping activities. And going hand in hand with its name, the multipurpose room does double-duty for aerobic classes three days a week.

A full-service kitchen is used for social functions and fund-raisers such as the popular annual eat-in or take-out spaghetti supper. The center does not offer daily lunches on the premises.

Head to the lounge to chat, relax, or read a book borrowed from the center's honor-system library filled with a variety of paperbacks. Adjacent to the lounge is the game room, where you can play bridge weekly, work puzzles, play cribbage or canasta, or sit in on seminars in history, tax aid, or health education, to name a few. The center also hosts support-group meetings for such organizations as the Outer Banks Cancer Support Group and the Amputee Coalition of Coastal Carolina. Twice a month, seniors gather at the center for an afternoon movie with popcorn.

If you're an outdoor lover, eat lunch on the deck or watch for resident deer and foxes. Five picnic tables and various chairs encourage relaxation or conversation. The nearby yard is host to a football target that tests throwing accuracy, horseshoe pits, and spin-casting targets. Outer Banks Senior Games contenders practice discus and shot put as well as archery using bales of hay for targets.

The recreation room comes alive as competitors play a leisurely game of billiards, table tennis, or shuffleboard. There's plenty of elbow room in this spacious area complete with three pool tables, two Ping-Pong tables, and several huge, floor-painted shuffleboard games. Coffee is available in the kitchenette just off the recreation room, and cups are in the cabinet. Donations are welcome. Bring your lunch and store it in the refrigerator or heat it in the microwave.

> ℹ️ *You don't have to limit yourself to the senior centers to socialize. Dare Voluntary Action Center is always looking for community volunteers, (252) 480-0500. Cultural arts nonprofit groups such as the Theatre of Dare, Dare County Arts Council, and Outer Banks Forum offer plenty of opportunities for you to volunteer your time and offer your expertise. See our Arts and Culture chapter for more information.*

Off the rec room is a craft room complete with two sinks, a projector, storage space, seven tables with four chairs each, and a sewing machine. Check the center's newsletter, *Senior Soundings,* for craft courses and special activities that take place in this room. The newsletter comes out by the 15th of the month and is available at both county senior centers and the three public libraries.

The center has an information and referral room where you can sign up for programs on preparing healthful food, bird-watching, growing perennials, and acrylic painting. Some activities have a small supplies fee; scholarships are available. A wall of pamphlets cover topics such as taxes, health, and fire safety. Countywide information is available via the computerized Senior Connection information and referral system. Questions on Alzheimer's disease, in-home services, marriage licenses, and the like can be answered by using this program staffed by trained volunteers.

A small computer room is set up with a Packard Bell unit. An exercise suite features a treadmill, a rowing machine, and four stationary bicycles, and a staff exercise specialist offers regular exercise programs.

Seniors also can take advantage of the center's 20-seat conference room complete with a telephone and white marker board. Community groups also use this space from time to time.

The senior center plays a vital role in providing transportation for elderly and disabled Dare County residents. A paid staff member is on hand at the center to schedule free rides to doctor appointments and hospitals in Chesapeake and Norfolk, Virginia, as well as Greenville, North Carolina. The transportation volunteer needs 24 hours' notice.

Rides also are available for shopping trips and getting to and from the center and to the nutrition site at Mount Olivet United Methodist Church in Manteo, where lunch is served Monday through Friday. Seniors are asked to make a $1.00 donation, but it's not mandatory. Menu selec-

tions may include herb-baked chicken with mixed vegetables and rice pilaf or spaghetti with a tossed salad. Two-percent milk and dessert top off the meal. The meals are prepared off the premises by the Columbia 4-H center. A day's notice is all they need to make sure the food count is correct. If you can't make it to the luncheon, home delivery is available.

The Baum Center is open Monday through Friday from 8:30 A.M. until 5:00 P.M. and for special functions.

Fessenden Center
NC 12, Buxton
(252) 995-3888

The Fessenden Center offers services and programs for county residents and property owners of all ages, although you must be age 55 or older to participate in the older adult activities for free. However, the center schedules activities, such as aerobic classes, for adults of all ages for various fees.

The building has a gym with a basketball court. The center operates as a senior center and a site for youth athletic activities. Open gym is from 3:00 to 5:00 P.M. Monday through Friday. You can enjoy basketball and volleyball as well as fishing, believe it or not. Throw a line in the creek off the back deck—chances are you'll snag a puppy drum (juvenile channel bass).

The full-service kitchen/conference room is available for preparing meals. Every second and fourth Thursday of the month, seniors attend a luncheon. The second Thursday lunch is prepared at the center by seniors; the fourth Thursday lunch is a covered-dish affair. Funds for the lunches are provided by Fesstivities, a volunteer senior group that raises money by running the center's concession stand at athletic functions. Seniors contribute a $1.00 donation if they are able. The kitchen/conference room does double-duty as a county meeting facility.

The center also sports an activity room, a sitting room, and a library. Seniors are invited to hone their skills at the outdoor tennis courts or play with grandchildren at the on-site playground. The soccer

Put Harmony in Your Life with the Sea Notes

A barbershop quartet on the beach? Absolutely! Who doesn't like four-part harmony?

When four distinct voices of the Sea Notes (an offshoot of the Chorus of the Outer Banks) combine with four different personalities, usually in perfect harmony, their expertise in the art of musical sound turns to magic, infecting everyone around them.

The Sea Notes' melodies are led by Mike Buchko and anchored by Ron Snell, singing bass. At the other end from Ron is Bob Watson, tenor. Singing the leftover notes is Bill Brobst, baritone. Each Sea Note has been performing for several years, many of those spent in four-part harmony. The group has performed at civic functions, contests, and social gatherings. Their bright spirit and musical talent have brought them a local reputation for adding high-quality a cappella music to many occasions. In 2001, this talented foursome won the Senior Performing Arts Championship, and they were invited to sing the National Anthem at the opening of the North Carolina Senate in April 2002.

The term "barbershop" denotes a chromatic four-part harmony sung by four unaccompanied voices. The melody is sung by the lead, while the tenor part is sung above the lead. The bass sings in a range an octave below the lead, and the baritone provides in-between notes, completing the chords. Most traditional barbershop music focuses on relationships—love, lost love, friendship, and the girl next door. Recently, modern songs have been arranged in the barbershop style to appeal to younger listeners.

The Sea Notes' repertoire includes songs from the past century, from barroom ballads to ragtime, along with some songs that have been sung since the 1800s. One of the group's personal favorites is the national anthem, which they have performed at sporting events as well as special occasions and celebrations. Songs from the Beatles, Rodgers and Hammerstein, Cole Porter, and even Elvis are some of their most requested. The Sea Notes also sing a variety of Valentine selections, Mother's Day greetings, marching songs, novelty songs, and inspirational music. So for a special way to celebrate a birthday, anniversary, wedding, or any other event, just call the Sea Notes: (252) 261-3068.

and baseball fields give them plenty of room to stretch or jog.

Adults can participate in organized step aerobics, toning and stretching, abdominal exercise, tae kwon do, tai chi, walking, basketball, and dance. Take Spanish or sign language classes; attend seminars, workshops, and classes on fire safety, cardiac rehabilitation, credit fraud, nutrition, home decorating, quilting, and painting; or take cultural arts trips to shows and parks outside the area. Minimal fees are attached for supplies ($5.00 to $10.00).

Transportation is available through the center's coordinator by calling the center's main number. Shopping trips are scheduled for seniors and disabled adults with transportation problems. Rides are available to medical appointments and out-of-town hospitals and doctors' offices in Norfolk and Chesapeake, Virginia, as well as Elizabeth City, Nags Head, and Greenville, North Carolina.

The Fessenden Center is open Monday through Friday from 8:30 A.M. to 5:00 P.M. and weekends for youth and special activities.

SENIOR SERVICES

Helping Hand
Manteo Police Department
410 Ananias Dare Street, Manteo
(252) 473-2069
Working from a list of voluntary participants, Manteo officers check on more than 70 elderly or disabled citizens twice a week in person or by phone to make sure they are healthy and their needs are being met. The town list is divided among the officers, who prefer to go in person but telephone from time to time. Participants include seniors, disabled individuals, and persons who live alone. This program is particularly useful in a community like the Outer Banks, where storms occasionally threaten the coast and require residents to evacuate. Officers are in such close contact with the community that they are able to alert homebound individuals in the event of a weather emergency. If you're interested in being on the Helping Hands list, call the police department. Anyone there will give you more information on this free service.

Hatteras Island Adult Care
(252) 995-5208, (252) 995-4890
This meals-on-wheels program offers lunch to needy seniors and disabled individuals on Hatteras Island. The year-round program serves meals Monday through Friday, including holidays. Meals are prepared by several local restaurants and markets.

Little Grove United Methodist Church
Monthly Luncheon
NC 12, Frisco
(252) 986-2149
Little Grove usually has a luncheon the third Thursday of the month for anyone interested in food and fellowship. The luncheon includes singing and storytelling that begins at 11:30 A.M. Call the above number on the Monday before the third Thursday of the month to reserve your space. Donations are appreciated.

The local chapter of SCORE (Service Corps Of Retired Executives) provides free counseling on business matters such as putting together a marketing plan, starting a business, compiling financial statements, computerizing an office, obtaining small business loans, and expanding business plans. Weekly sessions are held on Tuesday at the Outer Banks Chamber of Commerce in Kill Devil Hills. For more information, call the chamber of commerce: (252) 441-8144.

HEALTH CARE Ⓗ
AND WELLNESS

Ah, paradise. Beach umbrellas instead of bus shelters, shingled cottages instead of skyscrapers, communing with nature instead of commuting to work. Yes, it is idyllic—until an accident or illness disrupts your life. Don't worry. In the event of an emergency, the Outer Banks has a multitude of trained medical personnel, both staff members and volunteers, who can be on-site in a remarkably short time after they receive a call from the 911 dispatcher. Local EMTs, firefighters, and ocean rescue workers can all provide immediate medical assistance and continued care while patients are transported to a local medical facility.

The Outer Banks hospital, the first and only such facility in our region, opened in 2002. It is centrally located in Nags Head. This is really exciting for locals and visitors because one of the biggest complaints about this area for years was the lack of medical facilities. Pregnant women had to travel to Elizabeth City or Virginia to have their babies, and many babies were born en route to the hospital. Many retirees hesitated to move here because of the lack of medical facilities. Anyone who experienced a major emergency or illness in the past had to be flown by helicopter or transported by ambulance to a hospital at least 50 to 100 miles away. The hospital may still be a long distance from Corolla or Ocracoke, but it's a heck of a lot closer than Virginia.

In addition to the new hospital, there are a number of medical centers and clinics on the Outer Banks, along with an ever-increasing roster of alternative medical service providers.

HOSPITAL

The Outer Banks Hospital
4800 US 158, MP 14, Nags Head
(252) 449-4500, (877) 359-9179
www.theouterbankshospital.com
This 73,500-square-foot facility is the Outer Banks's first and only hospital, a welcome addition to the community. The hospital is a partnership between Chesapeake Health of Chesapeake, Virginia, and University Health Systems of Eastern Carolina. The two entities collaborated on Outer Banks emergency and primary health care in the past with HealthEast Medical Centers in Nags Head, Avon, and Hatteras Village.

The Outer Banks Hospital is a 24-hour facility with 19 acute-care beds and emergency services. Rooms include emergency observation rooms for monitoring patients, two labor/delivery rooms, and two operating rooms. A helipad is on-site. Patients with serious emergencies or major trauma are stabilized, then flown to a hospital in North Carolina or Virginia for further medical care. The hospital employs 55 physicians and 125 other staff members. Services include cardiology, dermatology, urology, endrocrinology, ophthalmology, obstetrics and gynecology, pulmonology, ENT (ear, nose, and throat), and senior services.

The hospital provides services for which in the past people had to travel off the Outer Banks. Sophisticated lab tests are performed here. Two operating rooms accommodate general surgery (in- and outpatient), orthopedic surgery, oral surgery, cesarean sections, and vascular surgery, among others, with pre- and post-operative recovery rooms serving the patients. Diagnostic services include anesthesia, pharmacy, lab and pathology, and physical and respiratory therapy. Oncology services and support groups are available, as well as radiology, including CT scans, ultrasound, and mammography. Wellness and preventive medicine programs are another service provided by this community-minded hospital.

For more information about the Outer Banks Hospital, visit the Web site or call the numbers above.

MEDICAL CENTERS AND CLINICS

Tarheel Internal Medicine Associates
1123 Ocean Trail, Corolla
(252) 453-8616
Tarheel Internal Medicine Associates offers year-round family health care on the northern beaches. Walk-ins are welcome. Summer hours are Monday through Friday 9:00 A.M. to 4:45 P.M. Call for winter hours.

Tarheel Internal Medicine Associates
Juniper Trail, North Beach Medical
Center, Kitty Hawk
(252) 255-5933
Tarheel Internal Medicine's second location also offers year-round family health care. The Kitty Hawk location is open Wednesday and Friday from 9:00 A.M. to 3:00 P.M.

Chesapeake Health
Medical Offices
The Marketplace, US 158, MP 1
Southern Shores
(252) 261-5800
Physician specialists form the framework for this affiliate of Virginia's Chesapeake General Hospital. Services include oncology, urology, endocrinology, audiology, nutrition counseling, diabetes education, rheumatology, dermatology, allergy care, and ear, nose, and throat care. Minor office surgery is performed on the premises, and surgeons specializing in colon/rectal and plastic surgery see patients at this complex. This is not an emergency-care facility. Call for insurance information. The facility serves patients by

appointment Monday through Friday from 9:00 A.M. to 5:00 P.M. all year.

Regional Medical Center
US 158, MP 1½, Kitty Hawk
(252) 261-9000
The communities of the Outer Banks rely on this medical center for convenient, high-quality health care. The facility offers a wide range of services and strives to provide quick and easy access to the appropriate diagnostic and health care departments for those in need. Preventive and educational programs are also offered here.

Family Medicine and Urgent Care (seeing patients 9:00 A.M. to 7:45 P.M.) are located in the Regional Medical Center along with a rotation of more than 50 medical specialists, who include gastroenterologists, allergists, OB/GYNs, a rheumatologist, a neurosurgeon, and cardiologists. A directory of physicians and specialties can be obtained by calling (252) 261-9000. In addition to outpatient surgery, a diagnostic laboratory is on-site, and blood tests are handled quickly for in-house diagnosis. Outer Banks Radiology (252-261-4311) provides routine as well as diagnostic services such as mammograms, ultrasounds, fluoroscopy, CT, and MRI. Regional Medical Center is an affiliate of Albemarle Hospital in Elizabeth City.

The Surgery Center
Regional Medical Center, US 158
MP 1½, Kitty Hawk
(252) 261-9009
This is an outpatient surgery center. Procedures such as breast biopsy, hernia repair, laparoscopy, tonsillectomy, adenoidectomy, oral surgery, cataract surgery,

---

When you check into your rental cottage, write down the street address (which will differ from your rental company's house identification number) and phone number and keep them next to the phone. That way you'll have the info handy in case of an emergency.

ℹ️ *Since most of the medical offices on the Outer Banks are urgent-care facilities, we advise you to call ahead for nonemergency visits to inquire how long the wait might be. The receptionist will suggest the least hectic time to come in.*

colonoscopy, and tendon repair, among many others, are performed here.

Virginia Dare Women's Center
US 158, MP 10½, Nags Head
(252) 441-2144

Appointments are available for female-related medical needs. Patty Johnson is the center's certified nurse-midwife and family nurse practitioner. Baby and youth care and pap smears are offered along with generalized care. Call for an appointment.

HealthEast Family Care/Nags Head
US 158, MP 14, Nags Head
(252) 441-7111 (urgent care)
(252) 441-3177 (primary care)

The Nags Head office of HealthEast Family Care (located behind the Outer Banks Hospital) has five physicians on staff offering pediatric and internal medicine care. Same-day appointments are accepted and patients are seen from 8:00 A.M. until 5:00 P.M. Monday through Friday. HealthEast is affiliated with University Health Systems of Eastern Carolina.

Outer Banks Center for Women
4917 US 158, MP 14, Nags Head
(252) 449-2100

Outer Banks Center for Women is across the street from The Outer Banks Hospital in Nags Head. The center is affiliated with Chesapeake General Hospital of Chesapeake, Virginia. It offers a broad spectrum of women's care, including obstetrics and gynecology, midwifery, women's health maintenance, menopausal care, hormone replacement, pelvic ultrasounds, and infertility issues. Minor surgical procedures are performed here.

Island Medical Center
715 US 64, Manteo
(252) 473-2500

Dr. Johnny Farrow and nurse practitioner Janice Jenkins provide complete family medical care at this office. X-ray services are available, and some lab work is done on the premises. Call for an appointment. The center's hours are 8:00 A.M. to 5:00 P.M. Monday, Tuesday, Thursday, and Friday and 8:00 A.M. to 11:30 A.M. on Wednesday. Island Medical Center is across the street from the Elizabethan Inn in Manteo.

Dare Medical Associates
US 64, Manteo
(252) 473-3478

Dr. Walter Holton provides family service and acute care from this office. X-ray services are available. Hours are 8:00 A.M. to 5:00 P.M. Monday through Thursday, and Friday from 8:00 A.M. until noon.

Dare County Health Department Clinic
109 Exeter Street, Manteo
(252) 475-1089

NC 12, Buxton
(252) 995-4404

The Dare County Health Department Health Care Services Clinic has a maternal health program, a family-planning program, and outreach for pregnant women and new mothers. It also has a full-time nurse who deals with communicable and sexually transmitted diseases. Flu-shot clinics are held every fall. For diabetics, an education program, support group, and dietitian are available. Fees are paid on a sliding-scale basis according to income.

HealthEast Family Care/
Avon and Hatteras
NC 12, Avon
(252) 995-3073

NC 12, Hatteras Village
(252) 986-2756

The two Hatteras Island HealthEast Family Care offices offer comprehensive family medical care and urgent care from board-certified physicians. X-ray and lab services

Helpful Phone Numbers

AIDS Hotline
(800) 342-AIDS
(800) 344-7432 (Spanish)
(800) 243-7889 (TTY Hearing Impaired)

Al/Anon
(252) 480-3896

Albemarle Hospital Referral Services
(252) 384-4610

Alcoholics Anonymous
(252) 261-1681, Kitty Hawk
(252) 261-4818 (if no answer at above number)
(252) 441-2769 (if no answer at above number)
(252) 995-4240, Hatteras Island

Albemarle Mental Health Center
(252) 473-1135, Manteo
(252) 441-9400, Nags Head
(252) 995-4951, Avon
After hours and holidays:
(252) 261-1490 (north of Oregon Inlet)
(252) 995-4010 (south of Oregon Inlet)

Dare County Emergency Medical Facilities
(252) 441-1551 (north of Oregon Inlet)
(252) 473-3444 (south of Oregon Inlet)

Dare County Health Department
(252) 473-1101, ext. 220
(252) 995-4404, Buxton

Dare County Home Health Services
(252) 473-1101

Dare County Older Adult Services
(252) 441-1181

Dare County Social Services
(252) 473-1471

Dare Home Health and Hospice
(252) 473-5828

HIV Support Group
(252) 473-6151

Hotline Crisis Intervention
(252) 473-3366
(252) 473-9814, Main Office

Narcotics Anonymous
(252) 480-4931

N.C. Community Child Abuse Educator
(800) 982-4041

Outer Banks Crisis Pregnancy Center
(252) 480-4646 (pro-life counseling)

Poison Control Center
(800) 848-6946

Senior Connection Information and Referral Service
(252) 480-1100

Veterans Services Office
(252) 473-1101

are available. Walk-ins are accepted, but appointments are preferred. Hours for both offices are weekdays from 8:30 A.M. to 5:00 P.M. and Saturday from 9:00 A.M. to 3:00 P.M. On Saturday and Thursday, only one office is open. HealthEast maintains 24-hour emergency call coverage at one of the two locations.

Ocracoke Health Center
Back Road, adjacent to the
school playground, Ocracoke
(252) 928-1511
A physician's assistant and nurse practitioner provide general medical care for all ages at this small island clinic, which is overseen by Dr. Seaborn Blair of HealthEast

Family Care on Hatteras Island. Walk-ins are accepted, but appointments are preferred. Hours are Monday, Wednesday, and Friday from 8:30 A.M. to 5:00 P.M. (closed at lunch hour), Tuesday from 4:00 to 9:00 P.M., and Thursday from 1:00 to 5:00 P.M. Hours are subject to change, so call ahead. For emergencies after hours, call the office number and you will be given a pager number to call. This is a Blue Cross Blue Shield of North Carolina provider.

EMERGENCY HELICOPTER TRANSPORT

Dare Medflight
Dial 911
The Dare County Emergency Medical Service operates this advanced life support air-ambulance service, which flies major trauma and emergency cases to Albemarle Hospital in Elizabeth City; Chesapeake General Hospital in Chesapeake, Virginia; Norfolk General Hospital in Norfolk; and Virginia Beach General Hospital in Virginia Beach. The helicopter flies from Outer Banks clinics or from the trauma scene.

ALTERNATIVE HEALTH CARE

Chiropractic Care

Wellness Center of the Outer Banks
The Marketplace, US 158, MP 1
Southern Shores
(252) 261-5424
Daniel Goldberg, DC, offers a full range of chiropractic services and nutrition management, including family chiropractic care and sports injury treatment. The Wellness Center of the Outer Banks is the exclusive participant in this area for many health care plans. The office is in The Marketplace shopping center. Hours are Monday and Wednesday 8:30 A.M. to noon and 3:00 to 5:30 P.M., Tuesday 2:00 to 6:00 P.M., Thursday 3:00 to 6:00 P.M. and Friday 8:30 A.M. to 1:00 P.M. Massage therapy is also offered here. Please call for an appointment.

Family Chiropractic Center
Overseas Building, 2400 US 158, Suite I
MP 6, Kill Devil Hills
(252) 261-8885
www.obxchiro.com
Dr. Eugene Flynn offers affordable chiropractic care for the entire family with extensive specialized training in sports and fitness injuries, work-related injuries, and auto injuries. He stresses regular chiropractic care as a means to overall well-being and health. Office hours are Monday, Tuesday, Wednesday, and Friday 10:00 A.M. to 1:00 P.M. and 3:00 to 7:00 P.M., Thursday 3:00 to 7:00 P.M., and Saturday 10:00 A.M. to 1:00 P.M. No appointment is necessary.

Outer Banks Chiropractic Clinic
US 158, MP 10, Nags Head
(252) 441-1585
David Hargraves, DC, offers chiropractic services with office hours Monday through Friday 8:00 A.M. to 5:30 P.M. Massage therapy is also available.

Massage Therapy

Massage therapy is available in a variety of forms, including Swedish massage, shiatsu, and reflexology. Since each therapist's techniques differ, it helps to have a conference to clarify your needs and to determine if the individual's area of specialization will suit you. Massage therapy can be invaluable in helping to recover from physical trauma or simply to relax. We've listed a smattering of services available. Check the local phone book for a complete list. Fitness centers, salons, and resort facilities often have massage therapists on staff. Check with them.

Dianna Carter and Associates, CMT
208 West Ocean Acres Drive
Nags Head
(252) 441-0698
Dianna Carter specializes in Swedish as well as therapeutic massage, craniosacral therapy, and neuromuscular trigger point

therapy. She also performs prenatal and infant massage. Dianna Carter and Associates also has locations in Kitty Hawk and Corolla; you can arrange for home or office visits. Call the Nags Head number for information on services at all sites or to schedule an appointment with any of the certified therapists.

In Touch Massage and Wellness Center
NC 12, Frisco
(252) 995-4067

Dhanyo Merillat-Bowers's massage techniques center around neuromuscular work, deep tissue massage, relief from pain and injury, relaxation, and stress reduction. Merillat-Bowers is nationally certified in therapeutic massage and body work and is a member of the American Massage Therapy Association. Call for an appointment.

Island Acupuncture
Nags Head, (252) 449-8122
Frisco, (252) 995-4481

Nationally board certified Cheryl Blankenship practices traditional Chinese medicine through Chinese herbs, food therapy, and acupuncture. Cheryl offers options other than traditional Western medicine for physical treatments of ills and ails. Her methods derive from the Eight Principle Theory and the Five Element Theory, both based on yin and yang. According to this principle of balance, illnesses and injuries are caused by imbalance; balance is health. For more information, or to make an appointment, call one of the above-listed numbers.

HEALTH-RELATED SERVICES

Dare Home Health and Hospice (DHHH)
106 Sir Walter Raleigh Street, Manteo
(252) 473-5828

DHHH offers skilled nursing, speech therapy, physical and occupational therapy, and home health aid. This group is Medicare-certified and accredited by the Accreditation Commission for Home Care. The services are available for homebound Dare County citizens. DHHH will bill Medicare, Medicaid, and other insurance companies, or fees can be set on a sliding scale, depending on income.

Outer Banks Hotline
US 64, Manteo
(252) 473-3366

Hotline is a 24-hour crisis counseling service that also provides shelter to victims of abuse. To generate funds, Hotline operates thrift shops in Manteo, Kill Devil Hills, Kitty Hawk, and Hatteras Island. Hotline conducts regular public-awareness seminars and training. For crisis counseling, please call.

EDUCATION AND CHILD CARE

Education has evolved a lot since the days when some Outer Banks kids paddled their skiffs to the one-room schoolhouse. Today there are more than 4,700 students attending 11 schools on the Outer Banks, 10 in Dare County and one on Ocracoke Island.

Higher education opportunities on the Outer Banks include a community college campus, College of the Albemarle, in Manteo. COA provides associates degrees, certificates, and diplomas, and many of the hours are transferable to other colleges. Some students make a 45-minute commute to Elizabeth City to attend that city's College of the Albemarle campus or Elizabeth City State University. Other students commute over an hour and a half to attend Old Dominion University in Norfolk, Virginia, or over two-and-a-half hours to attend East Carolina University in Greenville, North Carolina.

For children who are not school-age or who need care after school, Outer Banks parents depend on a patchwork of day-care providers: grandparents, teenagers, and the neighborhood retiree who cares for one or several children in the home; licensed home providers who care for a number of children in their homes; after-school care services at local schools; or day-care centers that watch dozens of children in a more controlled and regulated setting. We cannot provide listings for grandparents, teenagers, and neighborhood retirees here, but we have provided information about area preschools, day-care facilities, and babysitting services.

EDUCATION

Public Schools

Dare County Schools
(252) 473-1151
www.dare.k12.nc.us
More than 4,700 elementary and secondary students from Corolla to Hatteras Island attend one of the 10 Dare County schools—four elementary schools, two middle schools, one combination middle and high school, two high schools, and one alternative high school.

As the population of year-round residents grows, the Dare County Board of Education is constantly besieged with finding new ways to meet the demands of more students. With almost every one of the current schools at, near, or over capacity, the biggest goal is more space. A high school opened in fall 2004 in Kill Devil Hills, and two new schools (elementary and middle) opened in January 2006 in Nags Head and Manteo.

But for all the concerns over raising enough funds and providing better classrooms, Dare County offers children a quality education. It is one of the top-scoring districts statewide. Despite the area's remoteness and distance from cultural and educational hubs, schools here have measured up exceedingly well. Dare County schools have consistently ranked in the top five on student achievement among school systems statewide. The district, one of the first to connect to the state's Information Highway in 1994, provides computers in every classroom, Internet access for students, and a commitment to technological advancement. Each school has an interactive room with audio and visual equipment.

Dare County schools open before Labor Day and close early in June. All elementary schools have after-school day care available until 6:00 P.M. (See the Child Care section of this chapter for information.)

For more information about the Dare County schools, contact the Dare County Board of Education at (252) 473-1151.

Kitty Hawk Elementary (K-5)
US 158, MP ½, Kitty Hawk
(252) 261-2313

First Flight Elementary School (K-5)
Run Hill Road, off Colington Road
Kill Devil Hills
(252) 441-1111

First Flight Middle School (6-8)
Run Hill Road, off Colington Road
Kill Devil Hills
(252) 441-8888

First Flight High School (9-12)
Veteran Drive, off Colington Road
Kill Devil Hills
(252) 449-7000

Nags Head Elementary School
3100 Wrightsville Avenue, Nags Head
(252) 480-8880

Manteo Elementary School (K-5)
NC 64/264, Manteo
(252) 473-2742

Manteo Middle School (6-8)
NC 64/264, Manteo
(252) 473-5549

Manteo High School (9-12)
Wingina Avenue, Manteo
(252) 473-5841

Dare County Alternative School (9-12)
NC 64/264, Manteo
(252) 473-3141

Cape Hatteras Elementary School (K-5)
NC 12, Buxton
(252) 995-5730

Cape Hatteras Secondary School (6-12)
NC 12, Buxton
(252) 995-5730

The Ocracoke School
1 Schoolhouse Road, Ocracoke Island
(252) 928-3251

Part of the Hyde County school system, The Ocracoke School is one of the smallest public schools in the United States, serving an island where the entire year-round population is only 750. It is a K-12 school and in 2005 had about 100 students, with only seven graduating seniors. The Ocracoke School was built in 1931. For the last several years it has been designated a School of Excellence, a state honor awarded to schools where more than 90 percent of students are performing at or above their grade level. The Ocracoke School is also repeatedly honored as an Exemplary School, which means that academic growth has exceeded expectations by more than 10 percent. Though small, The Ocracoke School is sophisticated. Every classroom is equipped with computers that are linked to the rest of the state via the Information Highway. Student clubs, a student newspaper, and a basketball team provide extracurricular activities. The basketball team is not in a league but plays numerous independent games throughout the season.

Private Schools

The Wanchese Christian Academy
39 The Lane, Wanchese
(252) 473-5797
www.wcacademy.org
The oldest private school on the Outer Banks, this K-12 facility was founded in 1978 by members of the Wanchese Assembly of God Church, who wanted to teach their children moral values and Bible

studies. This Christian school is open to members of any religion. About 110 students from Currituck to Avon attend. (Transportation is not provided.) The Wanchese Christian Academy meets North Carolina private-school requirements.

Higher Education

**College of the Albemarle
Dare Campus
132 Russell Twiford Road, Manteo
(252) 473-2264
www.albermarle.cc.nc.us**
The Manteo campus of the College of the Albemarle (COA) was established in 1984 as a second branch of the main campus in Elizabeth City. A third branch is in Edenton. The College of the Albemarle is part of the state's 59-member North Carolina System of Community Colleges. This is the only institution of higher learning on the Outer Banks and is a great asset to the citizens of these remote islands. The campus overlooks the marsh on the east end of Roanoke Island near the junction of U.S. Highway 64/264 and North Carolina Highway 345. The campus includes classrooms, laboratories, offices, a library, a student lounge, a new technology building, and a new auditorium and conference facility.

Certificate, diploma, and associate degrees are offered in numerous areas. For example, associate degrees are offered in arts, fine arts, and general edu-

cation; associate of applied science degrees are offered in business administration, office systems technology, information systems, early childhood education, criminal justice, electronics, and computer engineering; diplomas are offered in heating and air-conditioning; and certificates are offered in nursing assistance, real estate, and medical transcription. This, of course, does not cover all areas of study. A Cisco Systems Academy prepares students to work with Cisco Systems network. The campus is connected to the North Carolina Information Highway so that students may take classes or seminars from remote locations. The school has an active Student Government Association. Students at the Dare branch can apply credits earned at COA toward degrees at other state colleges and universities. Day, evening, and weekend classes are scheduled during the school year and summer. Federal financial aid and other student assistance is available.

Continuing-education programs are wide-ranging at COA. Certifications, trainings, and just-for-fun classes are offered in nursing assistance, notary, effective teacher training, computers, Spanish, science, English as a second language, yoga, cooking, photography, art, and more. The college's Small Business Center, based in Elizabeth City, loans videos, books, audio tapes, and CD-ROMs. A list of publications is available by calling (252) 335-0821, ext. 223.

The North Carolina Sea Grant Extension Program, the aquatic equivalent of Cooperative Extension, offers classes on a broad range of water-related skills, especially for anglers. Most seminars are free and include instruction on crab shedding, shrimping, and net making. The Nags Head office at Caribbean Corners is also a resource for environmental information about water. Call (252) 441-3663 for more information.

CHILD CARE

North Carolina law mandates child/staff ratios at licensed day-care centers and home providers that are different for each age group and type of facility. The state also requires that all teachers meet certain criteria for health and continuing education. Anyone who watches more than two children (who are not relations) for more than four hours a day must be licensed. Home-care providers can care for a maximum of eight children with no more than five preschoolers in the group, including the provider's own kids (if the provider has school-age children, they are not counted toward the eight children). Regulators inspect facilities and teacher records on an annual basis. For information on ratios and license requirements, call the state Division of Child Development at (800) 859-0829.

Recently some centers have stretched their hours to accommodate parents who work nights in one of the restaurants across the barrier islands. Others have put out the welcome mat for tourists who need child-free time during vacations. A list of registered and licensed providers is available from the Dare County Department of Social Services. Contact the office at (252) 473-5857.

Dare County schools offer the After School Enrichment Program to serve working parents of K–5 students. Children are cared for in the same building where they attend school, but their after-hours time is spent in free play inside or on the playground. Crafts and games are available for kids to play with one another and the staff. Help with homework is also available, and an optional homework period is set aside every day. Call the Dare County Board of Education, (252) 473-1151, for scheduling and information.

The North Carolina Cooperative Extension 4-H provides summer camp programs for elementary and middle school youth, rolling child care and supervised fun activities into one service. And 4-H also offers day care at the schools during spring and winter breaks. Contact the Cooperative Extension office in Manteo at (252) 473-1101, ext. 243. Also see our Kidstuff chapter for a list of summer camps.

Additional day-care options are also available through a Head Start program run by the Economic Improvement Council, (252) 473-5246.

Preschool/Day-Care Facilities

First Assembly of God Preschool and Daycare
812 Wingina Avenue, Manteo
(252) 473-2664

At this "Christ-centered" facility, children are given Bible lessons daily. Attendees do not have to be Christian. Children age three through kindergarten age are taught preschool three times a week, including phonics and numbers. The kids are also taken on regular field trips to educational attractions, such as the aquarium or the Norfolk Zoo. The school invites members of the community, such as firefighters or police officers, to give on-site presentations.

The school is conducted Tuesday, Wednesday, and Thursday from 8:30 A.M. to noon. Full-time day care, which includes preschool, is available. Sessions include lunch and two snacks daily. A transitional class for children not quite ready for kindergarten is also offered. The day care is state certified. Hours are 7:30 A.M. to 6:00 P.M. Monday through Friday. Drop-off service is not available.

Heron Pond Montessori School
3910 Poor Ridge Road, Kitty Hawk
(252) 261-6077

831 Herbert Perry Road, Kitty Hawk
(252) 261-5358

Based on the philosophies of Italian physician/educator Maria Montessori, Heron Pond offers half-day and full-day licensed day-care programs, kindergarten programs, and junior elementary programs through the sixth grade. Both locations of the school are in historic Kitty Hawk Village, one of them in the Unitarian Universalist Church building. The staff of nine well-trained teachers has extensive child-care and educational experience and is trained in the Montessori method.

The Montessori spirit of education is rooted in the belief that children are naturally eager to learn, and all the teaching tools at Heron Pond are centered on encouragement of the child's ability to teach him- or herself. The school has a summer program.

Munchkin Academy
NC 12, across from Cape Hatteras School, Buxton
(252) 995–6118
This state-certified facility offers preschool, prekindergarten, after-school care, and full-time, and drop-in child-care service. The only A-licensed child-care facility on Hatteras Island, Munchkin Academy also offers 4-H summer camp programs for school-age youth. A homey center with an unusually large playground, the academy provides care for children ages birth through 12 years. All teachers are certified in first aid and CPR and have state child-care credentials. According to director Kyle Williams, the facility far exceeds state standards for teacher/child ratio. A registered nurse is also on-site. Preschool and pre-K are held Monday through Friday from 7:45 A.M. to 5:15 P.M. Two-, three-, and four-day schedules are also available. Call ahead to reserve a drop-in space. Munchkin Academy is open Monday through Friday year-round from 7:45 A.M. to 5:15 P.M.

Child-Care Centers and Services

At Your Service
(252) 261–5286
www.atyourserviceobx.com
The oldest babysitting service on the Outer Banks, At Your Service offers bonded adult babysitters who drive themselves to your home. Sitters are screened thoroughly, and all references are checked. Owner Barbara Hall attracts most of her business from referrals and repeat business from happy clients. At Your Service is the only business of its kind recommended by the Outer Banks Chamber of Commerce. Rates are based on the number of children and number of hours (there is a four-hour minimum). Parents must also pay the travel expenses of the sitter. The service also provides linen, maid, housekeeping, delivery, personal chef, and grocery services. At Your Service is available year-round. Call for rates and off-season information. (See also the listing in the Weekly and Long-Term Cottage Rentals chapter.)

Better Beginnings, Inc.
108 West Sibbern Drive, off US 158
Kitty Hawk
(252) 261–2833
State-licensed, Better Beginnings provides full-time or after-school care in a safe, educational environment for children ages six weeks to 12 years. The daily schedule is geared to provide structure but allows for flexibility, establishing a rhythm of active play between quiet periods. In addition to the regular curriculum, the center also has a music program, an after-school program, a preschool class, and a full-time summer program for school-age children. Nutritional snacks and meals are provided. Call for a complete rate schedule. Better Beginnings is open 8:00 A.M. to 6:00 P.M. Monday through Friday year-round.

Ferris Wheel Day Care and Preschool
109 East First Street, off US 158
Kill Devil Hills
(252) 441–3808
Ferris Wheel takes pride in providing a warm, stable environment that encourages learning. Licensed by North Carolina, the center offers full-day child care for infants, toddlers, and preschoolers. An early-education program is held for toddlers and preschoolers. Field trips are also part of the curriculum here. Healthy snacks and lunches are provided, and drop-in rates are available. Ferris Wheel is open from 7:30 A.M. to 6:00 P.M. year-round.

Ocracoke Child Care, Inc.
45 Old Beach Road, Ocracoke
(252) 928-4131

What's unique about Ocracoke Child Care, the only licensed center on Ocracoke Island, is that it is owned by its members. For an annual fee, participants are entitled to attend membership meetings and receive the quarterly newsletter. The center, which has a capacity of 40 children, is overseen by a six-member Board of Directors, which sets rules and policies. Fully trained staff who prefer to think of themselves as teachers rather than babysitters care for children ages 6 weeks to 12 years. The facility has a special infant-toddler room and an age-three-and-older pre-school room. Based on the motto "Peace begins in the playground," Ocracoke Child Care has structured playtime as well as indoor and outdoor play areas and revolves activities around a different theme each week. Visitors to the area are asked to come in a day in advance to fill out forms. Immunization records are not necessary for out-of-towners. Ocracoke Child Care is open 7:45 A.M. to 5:15 P.M. Monday through Friday all year.

MEDIA 📺

If you happen upon two contractors leaning out of their truck windows while stopped on North Carolina Highway 12, one facing north and the other facing south, you'll witness how most information is passed on in this part of the world. Insiders generally disseminate information by talking to each other—either on the roads, at the post office, in stores, or by telephone. More options are available, including newspapers, magazines, radio stations, telephone information lines, Internet sites, and, of course, the TV. This chapter highlights those sources.

Before we turn you on to what's available, we'd like to share a little bit of radio history. Despite being an Atlantic Ocean outpost of sorts, the Outer Banks is the site from which the first wireless telegraph signal was sent by Reginald Fessenden in 1902 (see our History chapter). While Guglielmo Marconi has been credited with developing wireless telegraphy, Fessenden successfully experimented on the Outer Banks during the same time period with transmitting sound using an entirely different system that's credited as the true basis for radio broadcasting. Read our section in this chapter on radio stations to see how it's progressed on the Outer Banks since Fessenden's day.

NEWSPAPERS

We have a variety of newspapers that range from a daily Virginia paper with a North Carolina section to weekly, tri-weekly, monthly, quarterly, and biannual periodicals with Outer Banks–focused coverage. Writing styles vary in these publications—some are highly editorialized; some take a more laid-back approach; and others adhere to a tighter, stricter journalistic structure.

Even though a couple of the smaller papers frequently disregard *The Associated Press Stylebook* rules, these publications offer a wealth of local information. The pages are loaded with community news—educational, political, environmental, and civic happenings.

The *Virginian-Pilot*
Nags Head Bureau, US 158, MP 10
Nags Head
(252) 441-1620
www.pilotonline.com
This Norfolk, Virginia–based daily broadsheet combines "big-city paper" experience with local knowledge to cover national news and regional news from northeastern and coastal North Carolina and, predominantly, Hampton Roads, Virginia. The *Pilot*'s total circulation is about 230,000, with close to 18,600 of that number going to the Outer Banks and northeastern North Carolina.

A separate North Carolina section is published daily, with articles and photographs composed by an Outer Banks–based news staff, but this section also includes lots of coastal Virginia news due to our proximity to the state line and the small amount of hard news the Outer Banks generates. (If you're looking for community news such as wedding coverage, civic club updates, job promotions, and social stuff, pick up one of the weekly or tri-weekly publications listed in this chapter.)

The *Virginian-Pilot* is available at area newsstands and convenience stores for 50 cents Monday through Saturday and $1.25 for Sunday's edition. Home delivery is available by subscription.

The *Coast,* a free, weekly entertainment and news publication produced by the *Virginian-Pilot,* is available each weekend at grocery and general stores and other locations throughout the Outer Banks from

March through December. It is published monthly in January and February. Winter circulation is 20,000, while height-of-summer circulation reaches 45,000. The *Coast* is delivered as part of the Sunday edition of the *Virginian-Pilot* to North Carolina newsstands and subscribers.

The *Coastland Times*
501 Budleigh Street, Manteo
(252) 473-2105

US 158, MP 7½, Kill Devil Hills
(252) 441-2223
Touting itself as the "Journal of the Walter Raleigh Coastland of North Carolina," the *Coastland Times* has been published since 1935. This local paper is published on Sunday, Tuesday, and Thursday, and is available at area newsstands and convenience stores for 50 cents; mail delivery is available by calling the above numbers.

Reporters cover Currituck, Dare, Hyde, and Tyrrell Counties. You'll find the most extensive local classifieds here, including yard sale ads (mostly in Thursday's issue). Pick up this paper for wedding, birth, obituary, reunion, community, and civic club information.

The *Outer Banks Sentinel*
Central Square, US 158, MP 11, Nags Head
(252) 480-2234
www.obsentinel.com
The *Outer Banks Sentinel* is a broadsheet newspaper owned by Sentinel Publishing, operating since March 1996. With a circulation of 9,000, it covers news from Corolla to Ocracoke, on Roanoke Island, and on the Dare County mainland.

The *Sentinel* provides news and features on area personalities, editorials, and columns about the Outer Banks. Insiders laugh themselves silly while reading local humorist Jack Sandberg's satiric column "Uncle Jack." Calendars and listings include information on weather, fishing, tides, surf conditions, entertainment, and community events.

The *Sentinel,* published every Thursday and Sunday, is sold for 50 cents at

For free National Park Service news and information, pick up a copy of In The Park, *published once a year and available at National Park Service visitor centers.*

area newsstands and bookstores. Mail delivery is available to subscribers.

Ocracoke Observer
P.O. Box 427, Ocracoke, NC 27960
(252) 928-7152
Ocracoke Observer is a tabloid newspaper published once a month for distribution to Ocracoke and connecting points. This free publication is a handy resource for tide charts, cable TV listings, library hours, ferry schedules, and almanac reports. It also includes interesting editorials regarding Ocracoke Island and is available free at Ocracoke retail and grocery stores.

The *Island Breeze*
NC 12 and Dunes Drive, Hatteras Village
(252) 986-2421
The *Island Breeze,* a small-town tabloid published by the *Virginian-Pilot,* comes out monthly January through December. This publication features a variety of folksy, local articles on personalities, businesses, and community-related news. Free, it is available at area shops and restaurants.

ReelFisher News
P.O. Box 1146, Kitty Hawk, NC 27949
(252) 261-8210
The *ReelFisher News* is published four times a year by Gulfstream Graphic Arts & Publishing. It's a free tabloid available at retail outlets throughout the Outer Banks. The paper prints fishing editorials while acting as a directory to area piers, ramps, marinas, and weigh stations.

The *North Beach Sun*
1106 NC 12, Kill Devil Hills
(252) 449-2222
Covering the northern beaches—predomi-

nantly, but not limited to, Southern Shores to Corolla—the *North Beach Sun* is a free quarterly publication. It is available in racks at retail outlets in the beach communities. The tabloid-style paper features recaps and announcements of local events, feature stories, arts articles, a wine column, a spiritual column, tennis tips, and more.

MAGAZINES AND MISCELLANEOUS PUBLICATIONS

There are quite a few specialty magazines published on the Outer Banks, though only two qualify as regional publications. They focus on either the specific—fishing, golf, dining—or the general—Outer Banks living. We have included several free guides in this section that contain restaurant and shopping information and coupons to help you stretch your vacation dollars, as well as a fun newsletter from one of our favorite bookstores.

The *Edge Outer Banks*
Outer Banks Press
P.O. Box 2829, Kitty Hawk, NC 27949
(252) 261-0612, (888) 261-4411
www.outerbankspress.com
The *Edge Outer Banks* is a slick, four-color annual magazine focusing on the entire Outer Banks with brief forays into surrounding geographical areas. This regional magazine is distinctive for its quality, both in appearance and in lively editorial content. Readers of this publication will find informative, entertaining articles on aviation, food and wine, architectural design, golf, high-energy recreation, and area destinations. Everything about the *Edge* is cutting-edge: design, photography, art, and editorial. It's available at area retail outlets and grocery stores for $4.00, or by subscription by calling or e-mailing Outer Banks Press.

Sportfishing Report
P.O. Box 3806, Kill Devil Hills, NC 27948
(252) 473-1553
www.sportfishing-report.com
Sportfishing Report was first published in the winter of 1991 and has gradually expanded from an Outer Banks–only magazine to include the coastal areas from Virginia Beach to Georgia. Readers of this bimonthly publication find informative saltwater fishing tips; profiles and history of surf, sound, and sea venues; plus product reviews and information on shows and tournaments. Gorgeous color photography brings the fishing experience into your living room. The magazine is available at most local news and magazine stands, or by subscription. For information, call or visit the Web site.

The *Hatteras Monitor*
P.O. Box 364, Frisco, NC 27936
(252) 995-5378
The *Hatteras Monitor,* a news magazine, is published 10 times a year, March through December, and is filled with historical stories and photographs, real estate planning, fishing reports, poetry, environmental news, a telephone guide, a visitors' guide and map, community news, and want ads for Hatteras and Ocracoke islands. Copies are distributed, free of charge, throughout Hatteras Island.

The *Beach Book*
Central Square, US 158, MP 11, Nags Head
(252) 480-2787, (800) 844-3128
www.beachbook.com
Our first "local" phone book is full of local information. Owners Jeff Graham and Tom Chisholm host an art contest each year to determine the next year's cover design and highlight artwork by local children throughout the book. The phone book includes a vacation guide and restaurant menu section; articles on history, nature, and flight; information on first aid, governing officials, and hurricane preparedness; maps; and a calendar of events. Business as well as residential phone numbers are listed for Coinjock, Mamie, Corolla, Duck,

Kitty Hawk, Southern Shores, Kill Devil Hills, Nags Head, Manteo, Hatteras Island, and Ocracoke Island. Free copies of the *Beach Book* are available at either the Outer Banks Chamber of Commerce or at the *Beach Book* offices.

Big Game Tournaments Magazine
Pirate's Cove Yacht Club
Nags Head–Manteo Causeway, Manteo
(252) 473-3906, (800) 537-7245
This free magazine covers offshore Gulf Stream fishing from a tournament angle. It features Pirate's Cove Yacht Club–sponsored and North Carolina Governor's Cup tournament schedules, rules, and guidelines and their histories. The tournaments are nonprofit, charitable functions. You can pick up a copy of *Big Game* at the Pirate's Cove Yacht Club's Ship's Store.

TELEVISION

WITN
P.O. Box 775, Manteo NC 27954
(252) 473-4705
WITN is an NBC affiliate based in Washington, North Carolina, and it's the only TV station that has made the commitment to place a full-time news bureau on the Outer Banks. WITN's local reporter and bureau chief, Aaron Tuell, is always on the go, tracking stories. Monday through Friday you can see his local reports on the CNN Headline News station every half-hour, at 24 and 54 minutes past each hour. Tuell's reports are also aired on WITN, broadcast throughout eastern North Carolina. NBC national news picks up Tuell's reports when something nationally newsworthy occurs on the Outer Banks.

Charter Cable Television
NC 12, MP 10½, Kill Devil Hills
(800) 955-7766
This company supplies cable TV service for most of the Outer Banks, except Ocracoke Island. Most motels, hotels, and cottages have cable connections. Some add special features such as HBO, Showtime,

The Currituck Chamber of Commerce (252–453–9497) and the Outer Banks Chamber of Commerce (252–441–8144) provide area information booklets for the asking. Call to request vacation or relocation materials.

Cinemax, or Disney Channel. Charter also offers pay-per-view movies, sporting events, and concerts with proper equipment obtained from the company. Charter service includes The Weather Channel, one of the most-watched stations on the Outer Banks; Beach Channel 12, with information on restaurants, real estate, and recreational opportunities; and Government Access Channel 20, with programming by the local townships. Digital cable access is available; call for details.

RADIO STATIONS

Radio began on the Outer Banks when Reginald Fessenden sent the first transmissions between two 50-foot towers, one near Cape Hatteras and the other on Roanoke Island, in the early 1900s. He continued his mission, sending waves across the Atlantic Ocean to Europe. Sixty-eight years later, the first Outer Banks radio station, WOBR-1530 AM, went on the air, joined three years later by WOBR-95.3 FM. We now have nine local stations featuring country, gospel, album and alternative rock, adult contemporary, and oldies formats. One company owns four of these stations. Since the FCC opened new frequencies in the mid-1980s, radio stations have multiplied, creating a highly competitive field when it comes to maintaining listeners and obtaining advertising dollars.

Several local stations have informative talk shows once a week that share information on community events such as upcoming symphonies, art shows, entertainment, plays, and more. We have one Christian station on the AM frequency and two stations that unfailingly cover live local high-school basketball. Formats often shift annually as stations try to capture listeners and as the music world evolves on a national level, but the primary listening target is the adult population ranging from age 25 to 54.

National Public Radio is broadcast to transmitters in Manteo and Hatteras from Chapel Hill.

WOBR-95.3 FM
US 158, MP 10½, Nags Head
(252) 449-8331
This station features album-oriented rock. The music is speckled with frequent weather reports, public service announcements, and morning surf reports. WOBR is owned by East Carolina Radio, Incorporated. The contest and request line is (252) 473-2444.

WOBX-98.1 FM
US 158, MP 10½, Nags Head
(252) 441-1024
OBX 98.1 plays adult contemporary hit radio. Mornings kick off with Rick Dees from 5:00 to 10:00 A.M. Local and national news segments are aired throughout the day.

WZPR-92.3 FM, WYND-97.1 FM, WFMZ-104.9 FM
637 Harbor Road, Wanchese
(252) 475-1888
WZPR plays the Top 40, while sister station WYND pleases the easy-listening crowd and WFMZ spins classic hits.

WRSF-105.7 FM
US 158, MP 10½, Nags Head
(252) 441-1024, (800) 553-DIXI
Dixie 105.7 plays "today's hottest country" and airs local and world news and weather broadcasts. The contest and request line numbers are (252) 441-4566 and (800) 422-3494.

WVOD-99.1 FM
637 Harbor Road, Wanchese
(252) 475-1888, (252) 473-9863
(request line)
This station, known as The Sound, broadcasts from a studio on the Manteo waterfront. Announcers play a varied format centering around alternative music.

The Sound features a Coastal Calendar airing area events, reports on fishing, surf conditions, weather, and hourly national news. Local news is broadcast several times a day. The Sound is a source for information on local school closings, lost pets, and road conditions.

WCXL-104.1 FM
104 Radio Road, Powells Point
(252) 491-9295
This 100,000-watt boomer of a station, Beach 104, covers the Outer Banks and Hampton Roads with adult contemporary music. Every morning on this station Best Buys on the Beach auctions local goods and services for a fraction of their regular prices. WCXL also offers regional and national news and fishing and farm reports.

WERX-102.5 FM
US 158, MP 10½, Nags Head
(252) 441-1025, (888) 75-SHARK
If you like oldies, The Shark supplies plenty of hits from the 1950s, '60s, '70s, and '80s to accompany you on your trip down memory lane. Couple this with their *Charlie Byrd Beach Blast* on Sunday from 5:00 until 8:00 P.M., and you'll never want to come back. Killer classics air right after Byrd's segment until midnight. CNN, regional, and local news air daily. Traffic updates and seasonal fishing reports round out their Good Times–Killer Oldies format. The Shark is owned by East Carolina Radio, Incorporated.

WUNC 90.5 and 91.9 FM
(919) 966-5454, (800) 962-9862
WUNC is a National Public Radio station based in Chapel Hill, North Carolina. The station has two transmitters on the Outer Banks, one in Manteo and one in Buxton. Most local announcements are for the Triangle area, but Outer Banks weather and public service announcements get cover-

age. Two music shows air on the weekends: *Back Porch Music* (bluegrass) and *Thistle and Shamrock* (Celtic music). The news and talk lineup includes, among others, *BBC World News, Morning Edition* from 5:00 to 9:00 A.M., *The Connection, Fresh Air, Talk of the Nation, All Things Considered, Marketplace,* and *The State of Things,* a show covering issues in the state of North Carolina. On the weekends look for special shows like *Car Talk, The People's Pharmacy,* and *A Prairie Home Companion.*

ONLINE MEDIA AND INTERNET SERVICE PROVIDERS

Beach Access
(252) 441-1521 (voice line)
(252) 480-0817 (modem line
for users only)
www.beachaccess.com
Beach Access is a 56K and ISDN Internet provider that also offers Web design services, hosting, and domain name hosting. Call for rates and information.

Aginet
Second Floor, La Isla Bakery
Ocean Plaza, US 158, MP 4½
Kitty Hawk
(252) 255-5557
www.aginet.com
Aginet provides Internet service ranging from T-1 lines to 56K dial-up service, including ISDN service. Weekly accounts are available. They also operate three Cybercades on the Outer Banks at the locations listed above. The Cybercades are set up so that anyone can come in, establish an account, and use the Internet. Cost is $10.00 an hour or $6.00 for a half hour. Locals set up an account for $30 a month.

Beachlink
3915 Welch Street, Kitty Hawk
(252) 261-0744, (800) EAT-SPAM
www.beachlink.com
Beachlink provides 56K and broadband connections, technical support, and vacation accounts. Soundwaves, a division of the company, provides custom design programs.

PLACES OF WORSHIP

The freedom to worship as we please is a right and privilege many people take for granted. But for those early settlers to the Outer Banks, this freedom was worth risking everything for, worth a dangerous trip across a vast ocean to unexplored lands filled with unknown perils. It wasn't important that there were no churches to worship in when they arrived. After all, God had gotten them safely across the ocean and deposited them in this wild and beautiful land He had created. What better way to thank Him for their blessings than under a canopy of leaves or a star-studded sky?

The first recorded religious event in the area was the baptism of Manteo, an Algonkian Native American for whom the town of Manteo is named. The event happened on August 13, 1587, on Roanoke Island. However, it wasn't until approximately 200 years later that formal buildings were erected where people could gather together to worship in the way they saw fit. These early churches were mostly Baptist, Methodist, and Pentecostal.

The Outer Banks now can boast numerous churches ranging from simple wooden structures to modern buildings that have kitchens, day-care rooms, and meeting rooms. Some of the older churches are undergoing renovations to keep pace with the continued development that brings more people to services. The interdenominational Corolla Chapel experienced such rapid growth that it was forced to expand its tiny 100-seat setting. On summer Sundays, more people would be standing outside than in. Pastor John Strauss led an expansion effort that included building a new facility across the street and moving the old, historic chapel over to it and combining the two. The new church facility seats 250. It also allows the addition of a ministry to teens as well as a senior citizens group along with other outreach programs.

The Holy Redeemer Church in Kill Devil Hills, which burned down in 1998, was rebuilt at a new site in Kitty Hawk on Kitty Hawk Road. The new church is much larger and more modern than the old one was. For up-to-date information on service times, call the church information line, (252) 261-1168.

If you're a fan of stained glass, be sure to see the exquisite windows of Mount Olivet United Methodist Church in Manteo. Late-afternoon light provides the best viewing time. If you're into the natural beauty of the Outer Banks, stop by the Duck United Methodist Church, designed by architect Greg Frucci. As the story goes, Frucci had a difficult time convincing the powers that be to forgo conventional stained glass for a natural view. Why not have a perpetually changing scene fashioned by the Maker Himself, Frucci argued. The church eventually agreed, enabling worshipers to admire a wooded soundside landscape through a huge bay window behind the altar. The view obviously inspired the late Reverend Bill Ruth, for one Sunday he invited the entire congregation up to the altar to see a red-tailed hawk perched on a tree limb.

Our varied array of religious congregations includes Baptist, Southern Baptist, Catholic, Charismatic, Christian Scientist, Assembly of God, Methodist, United Methodist, Jehovah's Witnesses, Lutheran, United Church of Christ, Mormon, Episcopal, Full Gospel, Seventh-Day Adventist, Presbyterian, Unitarian Universalist, and Interdenominational. Still, there are some missing (spiritual) links. If you wish to attend services other than those mentioned above (Jewish, Greek Orthodox, etc.), you must drive to Virginia Beach or Norfolk.

Most of our Outer Banks churches have full-time year-round pastors who are assisted by visiting clergy during the peak season, when attendance increases several-fold. It's not uncommon for a summertime congregation to spill out of a church and into the parking lot. Hatteras Island has a host of United Methodist parishes, and often one minister will travel to two or more communities to conduct Sunday services.

As in the islands' early days of worship, nature provides some special alternatives to indoor church services. It's not unusual to find oceanfront services, and, on occasion, *The Lost Colony*'s outdoor amphitheater serves as a venue. If you're here on Easter Sunday, you're in for an early-morning treat: Scores of people flock to the ocean for nondenominational sunrise services in many communities along the Outer Banks. Favorite locales include Kitty Hawk Pier, Jockey's Ridge,

and the Corolla Light Homeowners Association oceanfront swimming pool, where the Corolla Chapel Sunrise Service is held. When attending one of these services, allow yourself plenty of time to vie for parking and be sure to bring a coat or a blanket, as the early hours can be on the chilly side.

Some religious groups are branching out beyond traditional Sunday services, offering Christian counseling, athletic opportunities, thrift-store shopping, and even entertainment. The Dream Center in Nags Head (252–441-1155) has mostly Christian-oriented theater and musical performances during the summer season as well as a coffeehouse, a small Christian gift shop, and a bookstore. The environment is nonsmoking and no alcoholic beverages are served on the premises.

Worship schedules vary seasonally for the many churches on the island. Pick up the most recent Sunday edition of the *Coastland Times* for comprehensive information on worship services and locations.

INDEX OF ADVERTISERS

INDEX

ABOUT THE AUTHOR

Karen Bachman moved to the Outer Banks in 1985. She lives there with her husband and two daughters.